THIRD EDITION

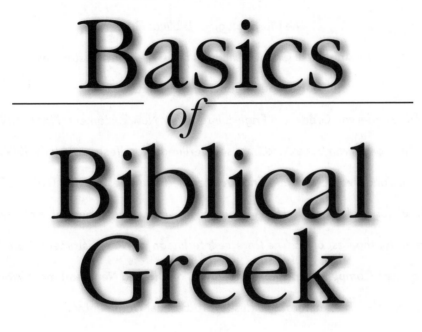

Basics
of
Biblical
Greek

GRAMMAR

Also by William D. Mounce

Basics of Biblical Greek Workbook

Basics of Biblical Greek Vocabulary Cards

Basics of Biblical Greek Audio CD

The Morphology of Biblical Greek

The Analytical Greek Lexicon to the Greek New Testament

A Graded Reader of Biblical Greek

The Zondervan Greek and English Interlinear New Testament (NASB/NIV)

The Zondervan Greek and English Interlinear New Testament (NIV/KJV)

The Zondervan Greek and English Interlinear New Testament (TNIV/NLT)

Greek for the Rest of Us: Using Greek Tools without Mastering Biblical Greek

Interlinear for the Rest of Us: The Reverse Interlinear for New Testament Word Studies

Mounce's Complete Expository Dictionary of Old and New Testament Words

The Pastoral Epistles (Word Biblical Commentary)

The Crossway Comprehensive Concordance of the Holy Bible: English Standard Version

THIRD EDITION

Basics
of
Biblical
Greek

GRAMMAR

William D.
MOUNCE

ZONDERVAN®

ZONDERVAN.com/
AUTHOR**TRACKER**
follow your favorite authors

ZONDERVAN

Basics of Biblical Greek Grammar: Third Edition
Copyright © 2009 by William D. Mounce

This title is also available as a Zondervan ebook. Visit www.zondervan.com/ebooks.

Requests for information should be addressed to:

Zondervan, *Grand Rapids, Michigan 49530*

Library of Congress Cataloging-in-Publication Data
    Mounce, William D.
      Basics of biblical Greek grammar / William D. Mounce. — 3rd ed.
        p. cm.
      Includes bibliographical references and index.
      ISBN 978-0-310-28768-1 (hardcover)
      1. Greek language, Biblical—Grammar. 2. Bible. N.T.—Language, style. I. Title.
PA817.M63 2009
487'.4—dc22
                                         2009023109

Edited by Verlyn D. Verbrugge

Typeset by Teknia Software

Printed in China

09 10 11 12 13 14 15 16 17 18 19 20 • 20 19 18 17 16 15 14 13 12 11 10 9 8 7 6 5 4 3 2 1

This text is affectionately dedicated to my parents,

Bob and Jean Mounce.

It is my wish that a study of biblical Greek will help to produce in you
the same qualities that have always been exhibited in both their lives:
a love for their Lord and His Word;
an informed ministry based on His Word;
a sense of urgency to share the good news of Jesus Christ
with those they meet.

ὁ νόμος τοῦ κυρίου ἄμωμος,
ἐπιστρέφων ψυχάς·

ἡ μαρτυρία κυρίου πιστή,
σοφίζουσα νήπια·

τὰ δικαιώματα κυρίου εὐθεῖα,
εὐφραίνοντα καρδίαν·

ἡ ἐντολὴ κυρίου τηλαυγής,
φωτίζουσα ὀφθαλμούς·

ὁ φόβος κυρίου ἁγνός,
διαμένων εἰς αἰῶνα αἰῶνος·

τὰ κρίματα κυρίου ἀληθινά,
δεδικαιωμένα ἐπὶ τὸ αὐτό.

καὶ ἔσονται εἰς εὐδοκίαν τὰ λόγια
τοῦ στόματός μου καὶ ἡ μελέτη
τῆς καρδίας μου ἐνώπιόν σου
διὰ παντός, κύριε βοηθέ μου καὶ
λυτρωτά μου.

ΨΑΛΜΟΙ ΙΗ 8–10, 15

Table of Contents

Preface

A publisher once told me that the ratio of Greek grammars to Greek professors is ten to nine. It is reasonable to ask, therefore, why this one should be written. There are several good reasons. Most existing grammars fall into one of two camps, deductive or inductive. Deductive grammars emphasize charts and rote memorization, while inductive grammars get the student into the text as soon as possible and try to imitate the natural learning process. Both methods have advantages and disadvantages. The deductive method helps the student organize the material better, but is totally unlike the natural learning process. The inductive method suffers from a lack of structure that for many is confusing. My method attempts to teach Greek using the best of both approaches. It is deductive in how it initially teaches the material, and inductive in how it fine-tunes the learning process. (See the following "Rationale Statement" for more details.)

Most grammars approach learning Greek primarily as an academic discipline; I make every effort to view learning Greek as a tool for ministry. My assumption is that you are learning biblical Greek so you can better understand the Word of God and share that understanding with those around you. If some aspect of language study does not serve this purpose, it is ignored.

I try to include anything that will encourage students. This may not be the normal way textbooks are written, but my purpose is not to write another normal textbook. Learning languages can be enjoyable as well as meaningful. There is much more encouragement on the website (see page xviiiff.).

Probably the greatest obstacle to learning, and continuing to use, biblical Greek is the problem of rote memorization, both vocabulary and charts. When I was first learning Greek, I used to ask my father what a certain form meant. He would tell me, and when I asked how he knew he would respond, "I'm not sure, but that's what it is." What was frustrating for me then is true of me now. How many people who have worked in Greek for years are able to recite obscure paradigms, or perhaps all the tense forms of the sixty main verbs? Very few I suspect. Rather, we have learned what indicators to look for when we parse. Wouldn't it be nice if beginning students of the language could get to this point of understanding the forms of the language without going through the excruciating process of memorizing chart after chart? This is the primary distinctive of this textbook. Reduce the essentials to a minimum so the language can be learned and retained as easily as possible, so that the Word of God can be preached in all its power and conviction.

The writing style of *BBG* is somewhat different from what you might expect. It is not overly concerned with brevity. Rather, I discuss the concepts in some depth and in a "friendly" tone. The goal is to help students enjoy the text and come to class knowing the information. While brevity has its advantages, I felt that it hinders the self-motivated student who wants to learn outside the classroom. For teachers who prefer a more succinct style, I have included overview and summary sections, and have placed some instruction in the footnotes and the Advanced Information sections. The section numbers also make it easy for teachers to remove information they feel is unnecessary. For example: "Don't read 13.4–5 and 13.7."

It is possible to ignore all the footnotes in this text and still learn Koine Greek. The information in the footnotes is interesting tidbits for both the teacher and the exceptional student. They will most likely confuse the struggling student.

I follow standard pronunciation of Koine Greek (also called "Erasmian"). There is increasing interest in modern Greek pronunciation, and some are making the argument that this is closer to the true pronunciation of Koine. I have included some modern Greek pronunciation on the website. But the majority of students learn the standard pronunciation, and those who learn modern often have difficulty communicating with students from other schools.

There are many people I wish to thank. Without my students' constant questioning and their unfailing patience with all my experiments in teaching methods, this grammar could never have been written. I would like to thank especially Brad Rigney, Ian and Kathy Lopez, Mike De Vries, Bob Ramsey, Jenny (Davis) Riley, Handjarawatano, Dan Newman, Tim Pack, Jason Zahariades, Tim and Jennifer Brown, Lynnette Whitworth, Chori Seraiah, Miles Van Pelt, and the unnamed student who failed the class twice until I totally separated the nouns (chapters 1–14) from the verbs (chapters 15–36), and then received a "B." Thanks also to my students at Gordon-Conwell Theological Seminary and my T.A.'s, Matthew Smith, Jim Critchlow, Jason DeRouchie, Rich Herbster, Juan Hernández, Ryan Jackson, Steven Kirk, David Palmer, Andy Williams, and especially my colleagues and friends, Edward M. Keazirian II, George H. Guthrie, and Paul "Mr." Jackson.

I want to thank those professors who were willing to try out the grammar in its earlier stages, and for those upon whom I have relied for help: Robert H. Mounce, William S. LaSor, Daniel B. Wallace, Thomas Schreiner, Jon Hunt, Nancy Vyhmeister, Keith Reeves, Ron Rushing, George Gunn, Chip Hard, Verlyn Verbrugge, and Craig Keener. A very special thank you must go to Walter W. Wessel, who used the text beginning with its earliest form and who was constant and loving in his corrections, criticisms, and praise. When I thought the text was basically done, my excellent editor, Verlyn Verbrugge, continued to fine-tune my work, not just by finding typos and grammatical errors, but by adding substantially to the content and flow of the chapters. (As always, any errors are my fault, and I would appreciate notification of any errors or suggestions. Correspondence may be sent through www.Teknia.com, where a list of the corrections made between printings is maintained.) If it were not for the diligent efforts of Ed van der Maas and Jack Kragt, this grammar may never have been published and marketed as well as it has been. I must also mention my marvelous Greek teachers who first planted the seed of love for this language and nurtured it to growth: E. Margaret Howe, Walter W. Wessel, Robert H. Mounce, William Sanford LaSor, and George E. Ladd.

Much of the work, especially in the exercises, could not have been done without the aid of the software programs *Gramcord* and *Accordance*. Thanks.

As this is the third edition of the textbook, I would also like to thank those who have used *BBG* over the past nearly two decades, and Rick Bennett, Randall Buth, Christine Palmer, and Ed Taylor for their help. BBG's acceptance has been gratifying; I trust that you will find the fine-tuning in this edition helpful.

A special thank you to my wife Robin, for her unfailing patience and encouragement through the past twenty-five years, and for believing in the goals we both set for this grammar. And finally I wish to thank the scholars who agreed to write the exegetical insights for each chapter. As you see how a knowledge of the biblical languages has aided them in their studies, I trust you will be encouraged in your own pursuit of learning and using Greek. Thank you. Bill Mounce

Abbreviations

Accordance	Roy Brown, Oaktree Software, (www.Accordancebible.com)
BBG	*Basics of Biblical Greek*, William D. Mounce (Zondervan, 2003)
BDAG	*A Greek-English Lexicon of the New Testament and Other Early Christian Literature*, eds. W. Bauer, F. E. Danker, W. F. Arndt, F. W. Gingrich, third edition (University of Chicago Press, 2000)
Bl-D	*A Greek Grammar of the New Testament and Other Early Christian Literature*, eds. F. Blass, A. Debrunner, trans. R. Funk (University of Chicago Press, 1961)
Fanning	*Verbal Aspect in New Testament Greek*, Buist M. Fanning (Clarendon Press, 1990)
Gramcord	Paul Miller, *The Gramcord Institute*, (www.Gramcord.org)
Klein	*A Comprehensive Etymological Dictionary of the English Language*, Ernest Klein (Elsevier Publishing Co., NY, 1971), from which I drew heavily for cognates in the vocabulary sections
LaSor	*Handbook of New Testament Greek*, William Sanford LaSor (Eerdmans, 1973)
Machen	*New Testament Greek for Beginners* (Macmillan, 1951)
MBG	*The Morphology of Biblical Greek*, William D. Mounce (Zondervan, 1994)
Metzger	*Lexical Aids for Students of New Testament Greek*, Bruce M. Metzger (BakerBooks, 1997)
Smyth	*Greek Grammar*, Herbert Weir Smyth (Harvard University Press, 1980)
Wallace	*Greek Grammar Beyond the Basics: An Exegetical Syntax of the New Testament*, Daniel B. Wallace (Zondervan, 1995)
Wenham	*The Elements of New Testament Greek*, J. W. Wenham (Cambridge University Press, 1965)

The Professor

I will give you an overview of every chapter, a review half way through, and the final summary.

In the third edition I am introducing the Professor. This is the cartoon character who appears in the margins. Everything he says is optional, but they can be helpful tidbits. I will be adding more of the Professor between printings as I discover additional things that are fun to learn.

There's no telling what I have to say!

At the end of every chapter I will give you the chance to write down what you learned in the Workbook. Pay special attention to the Summary section.

I'm the funnest of all! I am going to teach you some conversational Greek, like how to count to ten, ask where the bathroom is, and stuff like that.

I may the most relationally challenged—some say I am boring—but I think my little tidbits of information are interesting to know, even if they are not necessary.

Rationale Statement

With so many introductory Greek grammars available, it is appropriate to begin with a rationale for yet another. *BBG* is not just new to be different, but approaches the instruction of the language from a different perspective that I hope makes learning Greek as easy as possible, as rewarding as possible, and, yes, even enjoyable.

The following explains my approach, why it is different, and why I think it is better. The widespread acceptance of the first two editions has been encouraging.

Goals

1. To approach learning Greek not as an intellectual exercise but as a tool for ministry.

2. To provide constant encouragement for students, showing them not only what they should learn but why.

3. To teach only what is necessary at the moment, deferring the more complicated concepts until later.

4. To reduce rote memorization to a minimum.

5. To utilize current advances in linguistics, not for the purpose of teaching linguistics but to make learning Greek easier.

6. To be able to read most of the books in the New Testament with help from a lexicon.

1. A Tool for Ministry

Biblical Greek should not be taught simply for the sake of learning Greek. Although there is nothing necessarily wrong with that approach, it is inappropriate for a great number of students in colleges and seminaries. Too often they are taught Greek and told that eventually they will see why it is important to know the material. In my opinion, they should be shown, in the process of learning, why they are learning Greek and why a working knowledge of Greek is essential for their ministry.

2. Encouragement

Most students come to Greek with varying degrees of apprehension. Their enthusiasm often wears down as the semester progresses. *BBG*, therefore, has built into it different ways of encouraging them.

a. Most of the exercises are from the Bible, mostly the New Testament, but some from the Septuagint. From day one, the students are translating the biblical text. If a passage has a word that is taught in a later chapter, it is translated. This gives students the satisfaction of actually having translated a portion of the Bible. Whenever the Greek in the exercises clarifies an exegetical or theological point, I have also tried to point it out.

The disadvantage of using the biblical text is that the student may already know the verse in English. But with a little discipline on the student's part, this disadvantage is far outweighed by the advantages. There are also made-up sentences in the exercises.

b. The frequency is given for every vocabulary word. It is one thing to learn that καί means "and," but to see that it occurs 9,161 times in the New Testament will motivate students to memorize it.

c. There are some 5,423 different words in the New Testament that occur a total of 138,167 times. After every vocabulary section, students are told what percentage of the total word count they now know. By the eighth chapter the student will recognize more than one out of every two word occurrences.

d. Many chapters end with an Exegesis section. This section expands on the basic grammar of the chapter and enables students to see that grammar makes a difference in exegesis. For example, after they learn the present active indicative, I show them examples of the punctiliar, progressive, customary, gnomic, historic, and futurist use of the present tense. If this is more information than a student needs, it can be skipped.

e. The website (www.teknia.com) is full of additional helps that will encourage students, such as relevant blogs, YouTube videos, and additional exercises.

3. Teaching Only What is Necessary

Students only learn what is necessary in order to begin reading the biblical text. After they have mastered the basics and have gained some experience in reading, they are taught more of the details. In order to encourage the better student and make the text more usable for more teachers, additional detailed material is put in footnotes or in two sections at the end of the chapter called "Advanced Information" and "Exegesis."

For example, some of the rules for accents are included in the Advanced Information, so it is up to the student or teacher as to whether or not they should be learned. The adverbial participle provides another example. Students are taught to use the "-ing" form of the verb, prefaced by either a temporal adverb ("while," "after") or "because." In the Advanced Information, students can also read that they may include a personal pronoun identifying the doer of the participle, and that the time of the finite verb used to translate the participle is relative to the main verb.

4. Memorization

Rote memorization for most people is difficult. It makes language learning a chore, and often results in students forgetting the language. I will do everything I can to keep the amount of memorization to a minimum. For example, in the noun system you will learn only one paradigm and eight rules instead of memorizing dozens of charts. As I often say in the website lectures: "You're welcome."

5. Modern Linguistics

Modern studies in linguistics have much to offer language learning. *BBG* does not teach linguistics for linguistics' sake, but the basic principles can be taught and applied generally.

For example, the "Square of Stops" is mastered since it explains many of the morphological changes of the verb. Also, a basic set of case endings are learned, and then students are shown how they are modified, only so slightly, in the different declensions. Once it is seen that the same basic endings are used in all three declensions, memorization is simplified. In the lexicon, all words are keyed to my *The Morphology of Biblical Greek* (see bibliography on page xii). As the students' knowledge and interest progresses, they will be able to pursue in-depth morphological work in this text.

6. Innovative

BBG approaches the joyful task of learning Greek from new and innovative angles, not merely for the sake of newness but from the desire to make learning Greek as rewarding as possible. The easier it is to learn the language, the more the language will be used by pastors and others involved in ministry.

a. All definitions are derived from Prof. Bruce Metzger's *Lexical Aids for Students of New Testament Greek* and Warren Trenchard's *The Student's Complete Guide to the Greek New Testament*. This way, when students move into second-year Greek and use one of these two excellent study aids for increasing their vocabulary, they will not have to relearn the definitions.

b. A lexicon is provided that lists all words occurring ten times or more in the Greek Testament along with the tense forms for all simple verbs. (Any word in the exercises that occurs less than ten times will be identified in the exercise itself.) This will be needed for the additional and review exercises. There also is a full set of noun and verbal charts.

c. Instead of switching students back and forth between nouns and verbs, *BBG* teaches nouns first and then verbs. Because verbs are so important, some have questioned the wisdom of not starting them until chapter 15. Here are my reasons.[1]

    • Over the years I found that excessive switching between nouns and verbs was one of the most confusing aspects to teaching Greek.

    • Nouns are learned so quickly that you get to chapter 15 sooner than you might expect.

    • If you listen to a child learn to speak, you can see that it is more natural to learn nouns first and later move on to the verbal system.

    While this approach has proven itself over the years, I wanted to be sensitive to other teachers' preferences. Therefore, in the second edition I added a "Track Two" of exercises. It is an alternate set of exercises that allows you to move from chapter 9 up to chapter 15 and learn about verbs, and after several chapters on verbs come back and finish nouns. This involves switching back and forth between nouns and verbs only once, and in my experience it has shown itself to be effective. If you utilize Teknia.com, it is especially easy to follow Track 2.

d. At the beginning of every chapter is an Exegetical Insight based on a biblical passage. These are written by New Testament scholars and demonstrate the significance of the grammar in the chapter.

e. Next comes a discussion of English grammar, and in the summary of Greek grammar that follows as many comparisons as possible are made between English and Greek, with emphasis on the similarities between the two languages.

---

[1] I have since learned that the US Diplomatic Service uses the same approach in teaching modern languages.

f. Greek grammar is initially taught with English illustrations. When illustrations for new grammatical constructions are given in Greek, students spend much of their concentration on identifying the Greek forms, and often do not fully understand the grammar itself. In *BBG* the grammar is made explicit in English, and only when it is grasped is it illustrated in Greek. For example,

> A participle has verbal characteristics. "*After eating*, my Greek teacher gave us the final." In this example, *eating* is a participle that tells us something about the verb *gave*. The teacher gave us the final after he was done eating. (*After* is an adverb that specifies when the action of the participle occurred.)

> A participle also has adjectival aspects. "The woman, *sitting by the window*, is my Greek teacher." In this example, *sitting* is a participle telling us something about the noun "woman."

g. There are many free resources available at Teknia's website. Go to www. Teknia.com, click on "Basics of Biblical Greek" under QuickLinks, and go to the bottom of the page. There you will find many tools to help you learn Greek, such as free flash card software.

Most importantly, you have free access to three Greek classes that will help walk you through the textbook (see below).

It is my hope that Teknia.com will become a centralized rallying point for learning Greek, where we can all share our insights and help one another.

www.Teknia.com

The summary lectures on the website are 8-10 minute lectures over the main points of the chapter.

There also are full length lectures available for sale at Teknia.com. These lectures cover everything in the chapter.

Teachers: I don't take class time lecturing over the textbook any more; I use these full lectures. This way I am saving valuable class time for the most important thing I can do: work with the exercises. It really works doing it this way.

We also have an *Everything You Need to Learn Greek* package for sale at a discount price at Teknia.com; it includes the grammar and workbook, lectures, answer sheets, paper flashcards, and the Get an A+ summary sheet.

As we move into the digital age, there are so many ways that I can help you learn Greek beyond just writing the grammar and workbook. One way is to be able to share my teaching with you.

This is especially for those who are tired or need a little extra help. I have recorded my two-semester course in which I go through each chapter in detail. These lectures can be purchased at my website:

I am more excited about the possibilities of this website than I have been since the creation of the CD-ROM. The possibilities are endless as to how we can create a community to teach and learn biblical Greek. This site is constantly changing, so what follows is where I am right now and where we are going in the foreseeable future.

For the textbook

- Walks you chapter by chapter through the textbook
- Section lectures. Before each new major section, there is a video lecture giving the grand overview.
- Video devotionals for encouragement (see also Bill and Bob's Blog at BillMounce.com, which centers on translation issues)
- Study Guide for the summary lecture
- Summary lecture (iPod and QuickTime formats)
- Mnemonic devices for learning vocabulary; students can even add their own (see page xxi)
- Color-coded hints for every parsing and translation exercise (see page xx)
- Quizzes (and keys) for testing yourself on each chapter

For the workbook

- Answers for the entire workbook
- Audio helps for the workbook. These are my discussions of the difficult parsing and sentence exercises. It's like me being in class with you.

For the class

- Sample syllabi
- Overheads for each chapter
- Workbook exercises in PowerPoint and Keynote formats
- Teacher forums, so we can work together
- Student forums for each chapter, so students can interact with each other
- Greek Bingo game
- Fun songs rewritten in Greek
- Latest version of FlashWorks (vocabulary learning software)
- Free Greek and Hebrew fonts
- Biblical passages to read when you are done with the textbook

Color-coded hints

- Every parsing word and every translation exercise is color-coded. Notice what I am doing (except that you cannot see the color).

- Sentences are broken into phrases.
- Subjects are given a gray background and a blue dotted border.
- Objects are given a gray background and a red dotted border.
- The words that we are learning in the current chapter are also color-coded into their morphemes (e.g., βλέπ ο υσι is in three colors).

This is the best way I know to help students without actually giving them the answer.

Community-built mnemonics

I am especially excited about this resource available at the website class. At the top of the screen is the basic information on the word, and you can hear how it is pronounced in standard and modern pronunciation.

Below it are all the silly helps I have developed, and a place for you to add your own. Just click Add mnemonic and share.

εὑρίσκω

Related forms: [εὑρισκον], εὑρήσω, εὑρον and εὑρα, εὑρηκα, –, εὑρέθην

Root: εὑρ

Definition: I find

Frequency: 176

Notes: An η is inserted after the tense stem in the future active, just as in γίνομαι.

Cognate(s): *Heuristic* is an adjective that describes a person who learns by discovery.

Eureka, meaning "I found it," is an interjection used by Archimedes when he discovered how to measure the purity of the king's gold crown.

Song: Lord now indeed *I find*
thy power and thine alone.

Etymology:

Mnemonics:

✎ ✗

by Bill Mounce - Wednesday, 20 August 2008, 06:42 PM

Eureka, I found it!

Edit | Delete

Add mnemonic

FlashWorks

FlashWorks is a vocabulary drilling program for Macintosh and Windows computers. It is available as a free download at Teknia.com.

FlashWorks tags each vocabulary word as to its chapter, category (noun, verb, adjective, preposition, other), and its degree of difficulty (1-5). Then, for example, you can call up all the verbs in chapters 15-20 with a degree of difficulty 3 through 4. The words are then randomly mixed and the fun begins. As you learn the words, you can change the difficulty rating to a lower number, or *FlashWorks* can watch how you are doing and change the rating automatically.

FlashWorks has help information built in. Start the program and from the Help menu select Help; it defaults to the QuickHelp screen. There is more exhaustive help in the help system, and there is a tutorial at Teknia.com.

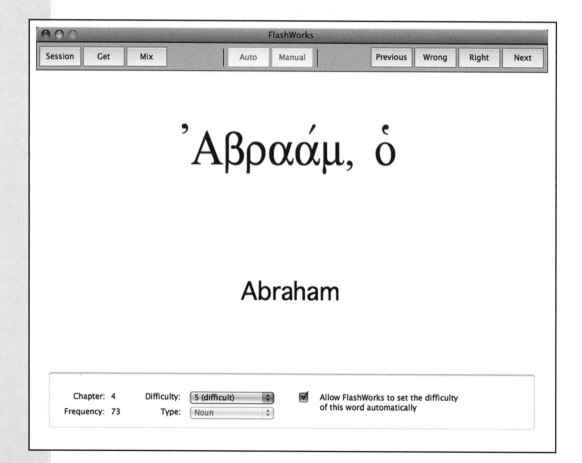

Chapter 1

The Greek Language

The Greek language has a long and rich history stretching all the way from the thirteenth century B.C. to the present. The earliest form of the language is called "Linear B" (13th century B.C.). The form of Greek used by writers from Homer (8th century B.C.) through Plato (4th century B.C.) is called "Classical Greek." It was a marvelous form of the language, capable of exact expression and subtle nuances. Its alphabet was derived from the Phoenician's as was that of Hebrew. Classical Greek existed in many dialects of which three were primary: Doric, Aeolic, and Ionic (of which Attic was a branch).

Athens was conquered in the fourth century B.C. by King Philip of Macedonia. Alexander the Great, Philip's son, was tutored by the Greek philosopher Aristotle. Alexander set out to conquer the world and spread Greek culture and language. Because he spoke Attic Greek, it was this dialect that was spread. It was also the dialect spoken by the famous Athenian writers. This was the beginning of the Hellenistic Age.

As the Greek language spread across the world and met other languages, it was altered (which is true of any language). The dialects also interacted with each other. Eventually this adaptation resulted in what today we call Koine Greek. "Koine" (κοινή) means "common" and describes the common, everyday form of the language, used by everyday people. It was not considered a polished literary form of the language, and in fact some writers of this era purposefully imitated the older style of Greek (which is like someone today writing in King James English). Koine was a simplified form of Classical Greek and unfortunately many of the subtleties of Classical Greek were lost. For example, in Classical Greek ἄλλος meant "other" of the same kind while ἕτερος meant "other" of a different kind. If you had an apple and you asked for ἄλλος, you would receive another apple. But if you asked for ἕτερος, you would be given perhaps an orange. It is this common Koine Greek that is used in the Septuagint, the New Testament, and the writings of the Apostolic Fathers.

For a long time Koine Greek confused scholars because it was significantly different from Classical Greek. Some hypothesized that it was a combination of Greek, Hebrew, and Aramaic. Others attempted to explain it as a "Holy Ghost language," meaning that God created a special language just for the Bible. But studies of Greek papyri found in Egypt over the past one hundred years have shown that this language was the language of the everyday people used in the writings of wills, private letters, receipts, shopping lists, etc.

There are two lessons we can learn from this. As Paul says, "In the fullness of time God sent his son" (Gal 4:4), and part of that fullness was a universal language. No matter where Paul traveled he could be understood.

But there is another lesson here that is perhaps a little closer to the pastor's heart. God used the common language to communicate the gospel. The gospel does not belong to the erudite alone; it belongs to all people. It now becomes our task to learn this marvelous language so that we can more effectively make known the grace of God to all people.

This is a lectionary from the thirteenth to fourteenth century containing parts of Matthew and John. Photo provided by the Center for the Study of New Testament manuscripts (Dr. Daniel B. Wallace, director) and used by permission of Institut für neu-testamentliche Textforschung.

Chapter 2

Learning Greek

Before we start learning Greek, let's talk about how to learn. If you have developed any bad study habits, they are going to be magnified as you set out to learn Greek.

Goal

The main purpose of writing this book is to help you to understand better and to communicate more clearly the Word of God. This must be kept in mind at all times. It should motivate you, encourage you when you are frustrated, and give you perspective when you think you are going to crack. Remember the goal: a clearer, more exact, and more persuasive presentation of God's saving message.

But is knowing Greek essential in reaching this goal? If you are not fully convinced that this is so, you will have difficulty reaching the goal. In other words, is knowing Greek worth the effort? We have been blessed with a wealth of good translations. A careful use of these goes a long way in helping the preacher understand the Word of God. It would be unfair to claim that the only way to be a good preacher is to know Greek.

However, allow me a little parable and the point will become clear. You need to overhaul your car engine. What tools will you select? I would surmise that with a screw driver, hammer, a pair of pliers, and perhaps a crow bar, you could make some progress. But look at the chances you are taking. Without a socket wrench you could ruin many of the bolts. Without a torque wrench you cannot get the head seated properly. The point is, without the proper tools you run the risk of doing a minimal job, and perhaps actually hurting the engine.

The same is true with preaching, teaching, and preparing Bible studies. Without the proper tools you are limited in your ability to deal with the text. When Jesus says of communion, "Drink ye all of it" (Matt 26:27; KJV), what does the "all" refer to? All the drink, or all the people?[1] When Paul writes to the Ephesians that it is "by grace you have been saved through faith, and this is not of yourselves; it is a gift from God" (Eph 2:8), what does "it" refer to?[2] When Paul asks, "Do all speak in tongues?" (1 Cor 12:30), is he implying that the answer is "Yes"?[3]

But there is more. Almost all the best commentaries and biblical studies require a knowledge of Greek. Without it, you will not have access to the lifelong labors of scholars who should be heard. I have seen a rather interesting pattern develop.

---

[1]   The people.

[2]   The whole process of salvation, which includes our faith.

[3]   He is stating that the answer is "No."

The only people I have heard say that Greek is not important are those who do not themselves know Greek. Strange. Can you imagine someone who knows nothing about tennis say that it is unnecessary ever to take tennis lessons? Sounds ridiculous, doesn't it?

The point of all this is to emphasize that you must think through why you want to learn Greek, and then you must keep your goal in sight at all times. John Wesley, perhaps one of the most effective ministers ever to mount a horse, was able to quote Scripture in Greek better than in English. How far do you want your ministry to go? The tools you collect, Greek being one of them, will to a significant degree determine your success from a human point of view. Set your goals high and keep them in sight.

Memorization

In order to learn any language, memorization is vital. For Greek you will have to memorize vocabulary words, endings, and various other things. In Greek the only way to determine, for example, whether a noun is singular or plural, or if a word is the subject or object of the verb, is by the ending of the word. So if you have not memorized the endings, you will be in big trouble.

Along with grammar is the importance of memorizing vocabulary. There is little joy in translating if you have to look up every other word in the lexicon. Rote memory is more difficult for some than others, so here are some suggestions.

1. Make flash cards for vocabulary words and word endings. You can put them in your pocket and take them anywhere. Use them while waiting in lines, during work breaks, before classes, etc. They will become your life saver. 3 x 5 index cards cut in thirds are a nice size. You can also purchase my pre-made cards, *Basics of Biblical Greek Vocabulary Cards* (Zondervan).

2. Use FlashWorks, my computer flash card software that can be downloaded for free (see page xxii). You can tell it which words you have difficulty remembering, and it can quiz you just on those.

3. When memorizing words use mnemonic devices. For example, the Greek word for "face" is transliterated as *prosōpon*, so it could be remembered by the phrase, "pour soap on my face." It seems that the sillier these devices are the better, so don't be ashamed. At Teknia.com you can see all my mnemonic devices and contribute yours. I encourage you to become involved in this community.

4. You must pronounce Greek consistently and write it neatly. If your pronunciation varies, it is difficult to remember the words.

5. Say the words and endings out loud. The more senses involved in the learning process the better. So pronounce the words, listen to them, and write them out so you can see them.

Exercises

The greatest motivation for learning Greek comes during the homework assignments. Because most of the exercises are drawn from the New Testament, you are constantly reminded why you are learning the language. I have tried to point out in the footnotes whenever a knowledge of Greek helps you exegetically or devotionally to better understand the verse's meaning.

I will also be introducing you to intermediate grammar through the footnotes to the exercises. Whereas the footnotes in the grammar are not essential, they are very important in the exercises.

Be sure to treat the exercises as tests. Learn the chapter, do as many of the exercises as you can, then work back through the chapter and do the exercises again. The more you treat the exercises as a test, the better you will learn the material and the better you will do on actual tests. There are many sample quizzes available on the website.

Time and Consistency

Very few people can "pick up" a language. For most of us it takes time, lots of it. Plan for that; remind yourself what you are trying to do, and spend the necessary time. But along with the amount of time is the matter of consistency. You cannot cram for tests; Greek will not stick, and in the long run you will forget it. Spend time every day; getting to know the language of the New Testament deserves at least that. Remember, "Those who cram, perish."

Partners

Few people can learn a language on their own. For sake of illustration, let me quote the story of John Brown as told by the great Greek grammarian A. T. Robertson.

> At the age of sixteen John Brown, of Haddington, startled a bookseller by asking for a copy of the Greek Testament. He was barefooted and clad in ragged homespun clothes. He was a shepherd boy from the hills of Scotland. "What would *you* do with that book?" a professor scornfully asked. "I'll try to read it," the lad replied, and proceeded to read off a passage in the Gospel of John. He went off in triumph with the coveted prize, but the story spread that he was a wizard and had learned Greek by the black art. He was actually arraigned for witchcraft, but in 1746 the elders and deacons at Abernethy gave him a vote of acquittal, although the minister would not sign it. His letter of defence, Sir W. Robertson Nicoll says (*The British Weekly*, Oct. 3, 1918), "deserves to be reckoned among the memorable letters of the world." John Brown became a divinity student and finally professor of divinity. In the chapel at Mansfield College, Oxford, Brown's figure ranks with those of Doddridge, Fry, Chalmers, Vinet, Schleiermacher. He had taught himself Greek while herding his sheep, and he did it without a grammar. Surely young John Brown of Haddington should forever put to shame those theological students and busy pastors who neglect the Greek Testament, though teacher, grammar, lexicon are at their disposal.[4]

This story points out how unusual it is for someone to learn Greek without the communal help of the class. Find a partner, someone who will test and quiz you, encourage and support you, and vice versa. Make use of the social network at Teknia.com; the forums are especially good places to help and be helped.

---

[4] *A Grammar of the Greek New Testament in the Light of Historical Research* (Broadman, 1934) 4th edition, xix.

Discipline

Discipline is the bottom line. There are no magical solutions to learning Greek. It is achievable if you want it. It comes at a cost, but the rewards are tremendous. So get ready for the journey of your life as we travel through the pages of the Greek Testament. Enjoy the excitement of discovery and look forward to the day when it will all bloom into fruition.

Hi. I am the Professor. I live over there to the left in the margin. The things I have to teach you aren't necessary for learning Greek, but I can make your studies a lot more fun. I will show you my different faces depending on what I am teaching you. Check out page xiii for more specifics.

Here is a great Greek coin. After the next chapter you will be able to read the name of the back of the coin.
© Georgios Kollidas / www.istockphoto.com

Chapter 3

The Alphabet and Pronunciation

Overview

I start each chapter with an overview of what you will be learning. This will give you a feel for what is to come, and should also be an encouragement when you see that there is not too much information in each chapter.

In this chapter you will learn:

■ to write and pronounce the alphabet (consonants, vowels, diphthongs);

■ that "breathing marks" are on every word beginning with a vowel.

Footnotes in the Grammar are not necessary to learn, although they are often interesting. The footnotes in the Workbook, however, are important.

The Greek Alphabet

3.1 The Greek alphabet has twenty-four letters.[1] At first it is only important to learn the English name, small letters, and pronunciation. The transliterations[2] will help. In our texts today, capitals are used only for proper names, the first word in a quotation, and the first word in the paragraph.[3] There is some disagreement as to the correct pronunciation of a few of the letters; these are marked in the footnotes. I have chosen the standard pronunciations that will help you learn the language the easiest.

---

[1] There were several more, but they dropped out of use before the Classical period. In some cases their influence can still be felt, especially in verbs.

[2] A transliteration is the equivalent of a letter in another language. For example, the Greek "beta" (β) is transliterated with the English "b." This does not mean that a similar combination of letters in one language has the same meaning as the same combination in another. κατ does not mean "cat." But the Greek "β" and the English "b" have the same sounds and often similar functions, and therefore it is said that the English "b" is the transliteration of the Greek "beta."

[3] Originally the Bible was written in all capital letters without punctuation, accent marks, or spaces between the words. John 1:1 began, ΕΝΑΡΧΗΗΝΟΛΟΓΟΣ. Capital letters, or "majuscules," were used until the sixth century A.D. ("Uncials" are a form of capital letters.) "Cursive" script is like our handwriting where the letters are joined together. Cursive script started being used in the third century A.D. In Greek texts today, John 1:1 begins, Ἐν ἀρχῇ ἦν ὁ λόγος.

Notice the many similarities among the Greek and English letters, not only in shape and sound but also in their respective order in the alphabet. The Greek alphabet can be broken down into sections. It will parallel the English for a while, differ, and then begin to parallel again. Try to find these natural divisions.

The following chart shows the name of the letter (in English and Greek), the English transliteration (in italics), the letter written as a capital and as a small letter, and its pronunciation.

Alpha	ἄλφα	*a*	A	α	a as in father[4]
Beta	βῆτα	*b*	B	β	b as in Bible
Gamma	γάμμα	*g*	Γ	γ	g as in gone
Delta	δέλτα	*d*	Δ	δ	d as in dog
Epsilon	ἒ ψιλόν	*e*	E	ε	e as in met
Zeta	ζῆτα	*z*	Z	ζ	z as in daze
Eta	ἦτα	*ē*	H	η	e as in obey
Theta	θῆτα	*th*	Θ	θ	th as in thing
Iota	ἰῶτα	*i*	I	ι	i as in intrigue[5]
Kappa	κάππα	*k*	K	κ	k as in kitchen
Lambda	λάμβδα	*l*	Λ	λ	l as in law
Mu	μῦ	*m*	M	μ	m as in mother
Nu	νῦ	*n*	N	ν	n as in new
Xi	ξῖ	*x*	Ξ	ξ	x as in axiom
Omicron	ὂ μικρόν	*o*	O	o	o as in not[6]
Pi	πῖ	*p*	Π	π	p as in peach
Rho	ῥῶ	*r*	P	ρ	r as in rod
Sigma	σίγμα	*s*	Σ	σ/ς	s as in study
Tau	ταῦ	*t*	T	τ	t as in talk
Upsilon	ὒ ψιλόν	*u/y*[7]	Υ	υ	u as the German ü[8]
Phi	φῖ	*ph*	Φ	φ	ph as in phone

To see how modern pronunciation is different, get the download from the class website on Chapter 3. Here is where they are different.

- β as "v" in "vase
- γ as "y" in "yes" (when followed by ε, η, ι, or υ) or "ch" in "loch" (when followed by α, o, or ω)
- δ as "th" in "the"
- η as "ee" in "feet"
- ι as the long "i" in "intrigue"
- o as "o" in "note"
- ρ has a slight trilled sound
- υ as short "i" in "intrigue"

---

[4] Technically, the alpha can be long or short, but the difference in time required to distinguish the two is so miniscule that for now just concentrate on saying the alpha as the "a" in "father."

In standard pronunciation, the sound of the short alpha was not different from the sound of the long alpha; the short alpha does not go to the sound of the "a" in "hat." There is much discussion on this type of issue among scholars.

[5] The iota can be either long ("intrigue") or short ("intrigue"). Listen to how your teacher pronounces the words and you will pick up the differences.

[6] The omicron is pronounced by some with a long "o" sound as in the word "obey." It is pronounced by others with a short "o" sound as in the word "not." In modern Greek it is long as is omega. Standard pronunciation uses a short *o* sound in order to differentiate the omicron from the omega.

[7] When upsilon occurs as a single vowel (i.e., not preceded by a vowel), it is transliterated as a "y." ὑπέρ becomes *hyper*. αὐτός becomes *autos*.

[8] Other suggestions are the u in "universe" and the oo in "book."

Basics of Biblical Greek

Chi	χῖ	*ch*	X	χ	ch as in Loch[9]
Psi	ψῖ	*ps*	Ψ	ψ	ps as in lips
Omega	ὦ μέγα	ō	Ω	ω	o as in tone

3.2 Writing the Letters

1. Notice how α β δ ε ι κ ο ϛ τ and υ look like their English counterparts.

2. In Greek there are four letters that are transliterated by two letters.

   ■ θ is th

   ■ φ is ph

   ■ χ is ch

   ■ ψ is ps

3. It is important that you do not confuse the following.

   ■ η (eta) with the English "n"

   ■ ν (nu) with the "v"

   ■ ρ (rho) with the "p"

   ■ χ (chi) with the "x" or

   ■ ω (omega) with the "w"

4. There are two sigmas in Greek. ς occurs only at the end of the word and σ occurs elsewhere: ἀπόστολος.

5. The vowels in Greek are α, ε, η, ι, ο, υ ω.

3.3 Pronouncing the Letters

1. You will learn the alphabet best by pronouncing the letters out loud as you write them, over and over. Be sure to listen to the summary lecture on Teknia.com for practice.

2. The name of a consonant is formed with the help of a vowel, but the sound of the consonant does not include that vowel. For example, μ is the letter "mu," but when mu appears in the word, there is no "u" sound.

3. The following letters sound just like their English counterparts: α β γ δ ε ι κ λ μ ν ο π ρ σ/ς τ.

4. Gamma (γ) usually has a hard "g" sound, as in "get." However, when it is immediately followed by γ, κ, χ or ξ, it is pronounced as a "n."

   For example, the word ἄγγελος is pronounced "angelos" (from which we get our word "angel"). The gamma pronounced like a "n" is called a **gamma nasal**.[10]

5. Alpha and iota can be either long or short. Epsilon and omicron are always short while eta and omega are always long.

   "Long" and "short" refer to the relative length of time it requires to pronounce the vowel. In the case of iota, the sound of the vowel actually changes as well.

It is fun to use the Greek alphabet to write out English words. Of course, they aren't really Greek words, but they do help you get familiar with the alphabet. What English words do the following refer to? When done, write out a few of your own.

βεδ, κατ, βιλλ, βαλλ, σιτ, στανδ, φλυφε (someone's dog), ρεδ βυλλ, φησβουκ, τεξ.

---

9 Pronounced with a decided Scottish accent.

10 Most gamma nasals are formed from the γγ combination.

3.4   Breathing marks

Greek has two breathing marks. Every word beginning with a vowel or rho has a breathing mark.

- The **rough** breathing is a ʽ placed over the first vowel and adds an "h" sound to the word. ὑπέρ is pronounced "huper." Every word that begins with a rho or upsilon takes a rough breathing.

- The **smooth** breathing is a ʼ placed over the first vowel and is not pronounced. ἀπόστολος is pronounced "apostolos."

If a word begins with a capital single vowel, the breathing is placed before the vowel (e.g., Ἰσαάκ).

3.5   Pronouncing diphthongs

1. A **diphthong** is two vowels that produce one sound. The second vowel is always an ι or an υ. They are pronounced as follows.[11]

αι	as in aisle	αἴρω
ει	as in eight	εἰ
οι	as in oil	οἰκία
αυ	as in sauerkraut	αὐτός
ου	as in soup	οὐδέ
υι	as in suite	υἱός
ευ, ηυ	as in feud[12]	εὐθύς / ηὔξανεν

υι and ηυ are less common than the others.

2. An **improper diphthong** is made up of a vowel and an **iota subscript**. An iota subscript is a small iota written under the vowels α, η, or ω (ᾳ, ῃ, ῳ) and normally is the last letter in a word. This iota has no effect on the pronunciation but is essential for translation, so pay close attention to it.

ᾳ	ὥρᾳ
ῃ	γραφῇ
ῳ	λόγῳ

3. If a word begins with a diphthong, the breathing mark is placed over the second vowel of the diphthong (αἰτέω, Αἴγυπτος).

4. In some words you will find two vowels that normally form a diphthong, but in the case of this word do not. To show that these two vowels are pronounced as two separate sounds, a **diaeresis** (¨) is placed over the second vowel.

αι normally forms a diphthong, but in the case of Ἠσαΐας, the diaeresis indicates that αι forms two separate sounds: Ἠ σα ΐ ας. Cf. naïve in English.

Here is how the diphthongs are different in modern Greek.

- αι as "e" in "hen"
- ει as "ee" in "meet"
- οι as "ee" in "meet"
- αυ as "af" or "av"
- ευ as "eff" or "ev"
- υι as the short "i" in "intrigue"

---

[11] ωυ is used in Classical Greek, but occurs in the New Testament only in the name Μωϋσῆς where there is always a diaeresis, indicating that it is not a diphthong.

[12] Some suggest that the pronunciation of ηυ is the same as saying "hey you" if you run the words together.

Summary

1. It is essential that you learn the Greek alphabet right away. You cannot learn anything else until you do.

2. Learn the English name, how to write the small letter, and how to pronounce the letter.

3. The vowels in Greek are α, ε, η, ι, ο, υ, and ω.

4. Every word beginning with a vowel must have either a rough or smooth breathing mark. If the word begins with a diphthong, the breathing mark is over the second vowel. If the word begins with a single vowel and is capitalized, the breathing goes before the first vowel.

5. A diphthong consists of two vowels pronounced as a single sound. The second vowel is always an iota or upsilon.

6. An improper diphthong is a diphthong with an iota subscript under the first vowel. The iota subscript does not affect pronunciation but is important in translation.

Advanced Information

In most of the chapters there is information that some teachers consider essential, but others do not. I have included that kind of information in the Advanced Information section of each chapter.

3.6   **Capital letters**. If you want to learn capitals, notice that there are very few unexpected forms. The unusual ones are in blue. Notice which ones might be confusing (Ξ Θ, Σ Ε, Ρ and the English P).

capital	small		capital	small
Α	α		Ν	ν
Β	β		Ξ	ξ
Γ	γ		Ο	ο
Δ	δ		Π	π
Ε	ε		Ρ	ρ
Ζ	ζ		Σ	σ/ς
Η	η		Τ	τ
Θ	θ		Υ	υ
Ι	ι		Φ	φ
Κ	κ		Χ	χ
Λ	λ		Ψ	ψ
Μ	μ		Ω	ω

Now write these English words with Greek letters:

computer, Skype, Bible (write as "Bibel"), program, thud, monster drink (with gamma nasal).

What are some more English words you could practice on?

Chapter 4

Punctuation and Syllabification

Exegetical Insight

When the New Testament was first written there were no punctuation marks. In fact, the words were run together one after another without any separation. Punctuation and versification entered the text of manuscripts at a much later period.

Obviously this has created some difficulties for contemporary scholars since the way a verse is punctuated can have a significant effect on the interpretation of the verse. One outstanding example is Romans 9:5. If a major stop is placed after κατὰ σάρκα ("according to the flesh"), then the final section of the verse is a statement about God the Father (the *NEB* has "May God,

supreme above all, be blessed for ever! Amen"). However, if a minor stop is placed at that point, the final words of the sentence speak of Christ (the *NIV* has "Christ, who is God over all, forever praised! Amen").

Does it make any difference? Most scholars believe it does. If the latter punctuation brings out what Paul intended, then we have in this verse a clear-cut statement affirming the deity of Jesus Christ. He is, in fact, God. The way a translation handles an ambiguous verse such as this reveals the theological leanings of the translator.

Robert H. Mounce

Overview

In this chapter you will learn:

■ four Greek punctuation marks and three accents;

■ how to break a Greek word into parts so you can pronounce it ("syllabification").

Greek Punctuation

4.1 Punctuation

Character	Looks like the English	Greek meaning
θεός,	comma	comma
θεός.	period	period
θεός·	period above the line	semicolon
θεός;	semicolon	question mark[1]

4.2 Diacritical Marks

1. **Diaeresis**. This has already been explained in 3.5.

2. **Apostrophe**. When certain prepositions[2] and conjunctions end with a vowel and the next word begins with a vowel, the final vowel of the first word drops out. This is called **elision**. It is marked by an apostrophe, which is placed where the vowel was dropped.

   ἀπὸ ἐμοῦ ▸ ἀπ᾽ ἐμοῦ

   This is similar to the English contraction (e.g., "can't").

3. **Accents**. Almost every Greek word has an accent mark. It is placed over a vowel and shows which syllable receives the stress.

   Originally the accent was a pitch accent: the voice rose, dropped, or rose and dropped on the accented syllable. Eventually it became a stress accent as we have in English.[3] Most teachers are satisfied with students simply placing stress on the accented syllable.

   The **acute** accent shows that the pitch originally went up a little on the accented syllable (αἰτέω).

   The **grave** accent shows that the voice originally dropped a little on the accented syllable (καὶ θεὸς ἦν ὁ λόγος).

   The **circumflex** accent shows that the voice rose and then dropped a little on the accented syllable (ἀγνῶς).

> Some words appear to have two accents. There are certain words that lose their accent to the following word ("proclitic") or the preceding word ("enclitic"), and you end up with one word not having an accent, and another word possibly having two accents.
>
> - εἰς is a proclitic, and so we find εἰς τὴν οἰκίαν.
> - ἐστιν is an enclitic, and so we find, οὗτός ἐστιν.

---

[1] The form of a Greek question is not necessarily different from a statement; the punctuation and context are your main clues.

[2] Prepositions will be discussed in Chapter 8. They are little words such as "in" and "over" that describe the relationship between two items.

[3] In English we use "stress" accents. This means that when we come to the syllable that receives the accent, we put a little more stress on the pronunciation of that syllable. But in Classical Greek, the accent originally was pitch, not stress. The voice rose or fell a little when the accented syllable was pronounced. By the time of Koine Greek, the accent may have been stress. However, in modern Greek the accent is pitch; some scholars argue that the accent has always been pitch.

There is an interesting story about a cannibal tribe that killed the first two missionary couples who came to them. The missionaries had tried to learn their language, but could not. The third brave couple started experiencing the same problems with the language as had the two previous couples until the wife, who had been a music major in college, recognized that the tribe had a developed set of pitch accents that were essential in understanding the language. When they recognized that the accents were pitch and not stress, they were able to learn the language and finally translate the Bible into that musically-minded language. Luckily for us, while Greek accents were originally pitch, they are not that important in learning the language and we will not be killed if we make a mistake.

Most people teach Greek as a dead language; you only learn to write it. But the more senses you employ, the better you learn; so let's start learning to speak a little Greek. If you like doing this, check out KidsGreek.com for a lot more fun. I will also be adding more of these kinds of exercises to the website class. Check there often. I will start on page 16.

Notice how the shape of the accent gives a clue as to the direction of the pitch.

The question then becomes, when do you use which accent? Opinions vary from viewing the rules of accent placement as essential to being unnecessary. Since the original biblical manuscripts did not have them, and since in my opinion they unnecessarily burden the beginning student, I skip the rules of accent placement. If your teacher thinks you need to learn them, they are listed in the Advanced Information section of this chapter.

However, this does not mean that accents are worthless and should be ignored. Far from it. Accents serve us very well in three areas.

✓ **Pronunciation**. If all the students in the class accent any syllable they wish, it will be difficult to talk to each other. Consistently placing stress on the accented syllable creates a desirable and necessary uniformity.

✓ **Memorization**. If you do not force yourself to say a word the same way every time, vocabulary memorization becomes difficult. Imagine trying to memorize the word κοινωνία if you could not decide which syllable to accent. Try pronouncing *"koi no ni a"* four times, each time accenting a different syllable. See why consistency is desirable?

✓ **Identification**. There are a few words that are identical except for their accents. τίς can mean "who?" and τις can mean "someone." There are also a few verbal forms where knowing the accent is helpful. I will point out these words and forms as you meet them. However, just remember that accents were not part of the original text and are open to interpretation.

Syllabification

4.3 **How to Divide Words**

In order to pronounce a Greek word, you must break it down into syllables. This is called "syllabification," and there are two ways you can learn it.

The first is to recognize that Greek words syllabify in basically the same manner as English words do. Therefore, if you "go with your feelings" (and you are a native English speaker), you will syllabify Greek words almost automatically. If you practice reading 1 John 1 in the exercises of this chapter, syllabification should not be a problem. I have read it for you on the website class.

It is essential that you master the process of syllabification, otherwise you will never be able to pronounce the words consistently, and you will have trouble memorizing them and communicating with your classmates.

4.4 **Rules**. The second way is to learn the basic syllabification rules. Here they are.

1. *There is one vowel (or diphthong) per syllable.*

   ἀ κη κό α μεν   μαρ τυ ροῦ μεν

   Therefore, there are as many syllables as there are vowels/diphthongs.

2. *A single consonant by itself (not a cluster⁴) goes with the following vowel.*

   ἑ ω ρά κα μεν   ἐ θε α σά με θα

   If the consonant is the final letter in the word, it goes with the preceding vowel.

3. *Two consecutive vowels that do **not** form a diphthong are divided.*

   ἐ θε α σά με θα   Ἠ σα ΐ ας

4. *A consonant cluster that can **not** be pronounced together⁵ is divided, and the first consonant goes with the preceding vowel.*

   ἔμ προ σθεν   ἀρ χῆς

5. *A consonant cluster that can be pronounced together goes with the following vowel.*

   Χρι στός   γρα φή

   This includes a consonant cluster formed with μ or ν as the second letter.

   ἐ πί γνω σις   ἔ θνε σιν

6. *Double consonants⁶ are divided.*

   ἀ παγ γέλ λο μεν   παρ ρη σί α

7. *Compound words⁷ are divided where joined.*

   ἀντι χριστός   ἐκ βάλλω

Summary

1. A period above the line is a Greek semicolon, and an English semicolon is a Greek question mark.

2. There are three accents. You do not have to know why they occur where they do, but pay attention to them as you pronounce the word.

3. English syllabification basically follows Greek syllabification. Listen to your teacher pronounce the words and it should become automatic.

---

⁴ A consonant cluster is two or more consonants in a row.

⁵ One way to check whether a consonant cluster can be pronounced together is to see whether those consonants ever begin a word. For example, you know that the cluster στ can be pronounced together because there is a word σταυρόω. Although the lexicon may not show all the possible clusters, it will show you many of them.

⁶ A "double consonant" is when the same consonant occurs twice in a row.

⁷ Compound words are words made up of two distinct words. Of course, right now you cannot tell what is a compound word because you do not know any of the words.

Vocabulary

One of the frustrating parts of learning a language is memorization, especially memorizing vocabulary. And yet, memorizing vocabulary is one of the essential elements if you are going to enjoy the language. If you have to look up every other word, the language loses its charm. Because you are learning biblical Greek, there are a set number of words, and statistically there are a few significant facts.

There are 5,423 different words in the New Testament. They occur a total of 138,167 times.[8] But there are only 313 words (5.8% of the total number) that occur 50 times or more. For special reasons I will also ask you to learn six more words that occur less than fifty times. These 319 words account for 110,425 word occurrences, or 79.92% of the total word count, almost four out of five.[9] For example, καί (the word for "and") occurs 9,161 times. Learn that one word and you know 6.6% of the total word count.

The point is that if you learn these 319 words well, you can read the bulk of the New Testament. I think it is counterproductive at this point to learn more, unless you really like doing things like that. Your time is better spent reading the Bible or learning grammar. And 319 words are not very many. Most introductory textbooks for other languages have about 2,000 words.

For encouragement, I have included in parentheses how many times each vocabulary word occurs, and at the end of every chapter I will tell you what percent of the 138,167 word occurrences you now know.

In this chapter I have listed some Greek words that have come directly into English ("cognates").[10] Seeing the similarities between languages can be helpful. Some of the cognates are not part of many peoples' vocabulary, but I have found that it is still helpful to know that the cognates exist. Most of the cognates and their definitions are drawn from Ernest Klein's masterful study, *Etymological Dictionary*, with good suggestions from Bruce Metzger's *Lexical Aids*.

But remember: never define a Greek word on the basis of its English cognate! English was not a language until much later, so it had no impact on the meaning of Greek. Think of as many cognates as you can for the following words. I list cognates in the footnotes.

Notice that I list more information for each word than just the word and its meaning. For example, for ἄγγελος I have ἄγγελος, -ου, ὁ. For now, ignore the additional information; you will learn what it means in subsequent chapters.

The definitions I give (called "glosses") are, at best, rough approximations of the meaning of the Greek word. In any two languages, there are rarely, if ever, equivalent words. The multiple glosses are an attempt to replicate the semantic range of the Greek word.

ἄγγελος, -ου, ὁ	angel, messenger (175)
ἀμήν	verily, truly, amen, so let it be (129)

Let's learn to identify our teacher and ourselves. Here is how you say "He is my teacher." αὐτός ἐστιν διδάσκαλος μου.

- αὐτός means "he."
- ἐστιν means "he is."
- διδάσκαλος means "teacher."
- μου means "my."

In Greek we put words like "my" after the word they modify. Say each word together as a class; and then put them all together, point at your teacher and say out loud, in Greek, "He is my teacher." Be sure to say it out loud; you need to use all your senses. Who is the loudest student in the room?

---

[8] All frequency numbers come from the software program Accordance.

[9] There are also a few special forms of words you are given in the vocabulary. If a vocabulary word does not have its frequency listed after it, that word is not included in this frequency counting.

[10] As you will see, kappa came over into English as a "c." Remember also that when upsilon is not in a diphthong, it is transliterated as "y."

ἄνθρωπος, -ου, ὁ	man, mankind, person, people, humankind, human being (550)[11]
ἀπόστολος, -ου, ὁ	apostle, envoy, messenger (80)
Γαλιλαία, -ας, ἡ	Galilee (61)
γραφή, -ῆς, ἡ	writing, Scripture (50)[12]
δόξα, -ης, ἡ *dao se*	glory, majesty, fame (166)[13]
ἐγώ	I (1,718)[14]
ἔσχατος, -η, -ον	last (52)[15]
ζωή, -ῆς, ἡ	life (135)[16]
θεός, -οῦ, ὁ	God, god (1,317)[17]
καί	and, even, also, namely (9,018)[18]
καρδία, -ας, ἡ	heart, inner self (156)[19]
κόσμος, -ου, ὁ	world, universe, humankind (186)[20]
λόγος, -ου, ὁ	word, Word, statement, message (330)[21]
πνεῦμα, -ατος, τό	spirit, Spirit, wind, breath, inner life (379)[22]
	By "Spirit" I mean the Holy Spirit. Remember, in Greek there are no silent consonants, so the pi is pronounced; unlike in English where, for example, the "p" is not pronounced in the word "pneumatic."
προφήτης, -ου, ὁ	prophet (144)
σάββατον, -ου, τό	Sabbath, week (68)
	σάββατον often occurs in the plural, but can be translated as a singular.
φωνή, -ῆς, ἡ	sound, noise, voice (139)[23]

---

[11] *Anthropology*, the study of humans.

[12] An *autograph* is a writing of one's own (αὐτός) name.

[13] The *doxology* is a "word" (λόγος, see below) of "praise."

[14] *Ego*, the "I" or "self" of a person.

[15] *Eschatology* is the study of last things.

[16] *Zoology* is the study of animal life.

[17] *Theology* is the study of God.

[18] *Triskaidekaphobia* is the fear (φόβος) of the number 13. 3 is τρεῖς, and (καί) 10 is δέκα.

[19] *Cardiology* is the study of the heart. The kappa came over into English as a "c."

[20] *Cosmology* is the philosophical study of the universe.

[21] This word has a wide range of meaning, both in Greek and in English. It can refer to what is spoken, or it can be used philosophically / theologically for the "Word" (John 1:1-18). As you can see from examples above, λόγος (or the feminine λογία) is often used in compounds to denote the "study" of something.

[22] *Pneumatology* is the study of spiritual beings.

[23] The double meaning of φωνή as "sound" and "voice," along with the double meaning of πνεῦμα as "wind" and "spirit," creates the pun in John 3:8. "The wind (πνεῦμα) blows where it wishes, and you hear its sound (φωνή), but you do not know where it comes from or where it goes. So it is with everyone who is born of the Spirit (πνεῦμα)."

A *phonograph* is a "writer of sounds."

What if your teacher is a lady? The Greek word for "she" is αὐτή. It looks like αὐτός, doesn't it? Just the last two letters have changed. If your teacher is a lady, point at her as say, "She is my teacher."

Χριστός, -οῦ, ὁ	Christ, Messiah, Anointed One (529)

In the Old Testament and the earlier parts of the New Testament, "χριστός" is a title; but as you move through Acts, it becomes so closely associated with Jesus that it is a personal name and should be capitalized (Χριστός).

Proper names are easy to learn.

Ἀβραάμ, ὁ	Abraham (73)
Δαυίδ, ὁ	David (59)
Παῦλος, -ου, ὁ	Paul (158)
Πέτρος, -ου, ὁ	Peter (156)
Πιλᾶτος, -ου, ὁ	Pilate (55)
Σίμων, -ωνος, ὁ	Simon (75)

Total word count in the New Testament:	138,167
Number of words learned to date:	26
Number of word occurrences in this chapter:	15,958
Number of word occurrences to date:	15,958
Percent of total word count in the New Testament:	11.55%

Remember that 11.55% translates into knowing more than one out of every ten word occurrences. One out of ten! Encouraged?

Advanced Information

4.5   **Basic rules for accents**. If you want to know the basic rules of accents, here they are.[24]

1. The **acute** (´) can occur on any of the last three syllables.

    ■ ἀκηκόαμεν

    ■ λόγου

    ■ αὐτός

2. The **circumflex** (ˆ) can occur only on one of the last two syllables and will always be over a long vowel. η and ω are long vowels. ᾳ is always long. α , ι, and υ can be either long or short.

    ■ πλανῶμεν

    ■ ἀρχῆς

3. The **grave** (`) is formed when a word is normally accented with an acute on the final syllable. When the word is not followed by a punctuation mark, then the acute becomes a grave.

    ■ καὶ

    In other words, if the word is accented on the final syllable, the Greeks always dropped their voices at the end of a word, but raised it when the word was at the end of a clause or sentence.

---

[24]   If you want to learn all the rules, check out my *Morphology of Biblical Greek.*

4. Accents on nouns try to stay on the same syllable. This is called *consistent accent*. Accents on verbs try to move as far back toward the beginning of the verb as possible. This is called *recessive accent*.

4.6 Here are some more Greek words. What are some of their English cognates? You do not need to memorize the Greek words now.

word	definition
ἀγάπη	love
ἀδελφός	brother
ἅγιος	holy
αἷμα	blood
ἁμαρτία	sin
γλῶσσα	tongue, language
ἐκκλησία	church, Church, assembly, congregation
ἔργον	work
εὐαγγέλιον	good news, Gospel
θάνατος	death
θρόνος	throne
Ἰησοῦς	Jesus
Ἰσραήλ	Israel
λίθος	stone
μέγας	large, great
μήτηρ	mother
Μωϋσῆς	Moses
νόμος	law
παραβολή	parable
πατήρ	father
πρεσβύτερος	elder, older
πῦρ	fire
ὕδωρ	water
Φαρισαῖος	Pharisee
ψυχή	soul, life, self

If he or she is your teacher, who are you? You are the student.
- ἐγώ is "I."
- εἰμί is "I am."
- μαθητής is "a (male) student."
- μαθήτρια is "a (female) student."

So tell your teacher you are a student.
ἐγώ εἰμι μαθητής.

Or you could be a little more personal.
- αὐτοῦ is "his."
- αὐτῆς is "her."

"His" and "her" go after μαθητής, just like μου did.

So now you can say, "I am his student," or "I am her student."

Overview 1

Chapters 5 – 9

Before every major section of the grammar I will give you an overview of what is to come. A more detailed multimedia overview is given on the website. If you do not understand everything I say here, don't worry about it. It will all come clear in time.

Chapter 5

In chapters 5–9 I introduce you to the noun system. Chapter 5 is an overview of English noun grammar, and we get into cases in Chapter 6.

Chapter 6

English uses word order to determine the meaning of a sentence. Consider this sentence.

> "The student ate dinner."

Who ate what? Did the student eat the dinner or did the dinner eat the student? How do you know? You know the student did the eating because "student" comes *before* "ate" in word order. What was eaten? The dinner. How do you know? "Dinner" comes *after* the verb in word order.

The word that does the action of the verb (in this case, "ate") is the subject ("student") and is in the subjective case. The word that receives the action of the verb is the direct object ("dinner") and is in the objective case.

Greek does not rely on word order. Rather, it appends different suffixes onto the word. The suffixes are called "case endings." Consider this sentence.

> ὁ θεὸς ἀγαπᾷ τὸν κόσμον.

ὁ θεός means "God," and the ς shows that it is the subject of the verb ἀγαπᾷ (which means "love"). In Greek this is the nominative case. κόσμος means "world," and the ν shows it is the direct object of the verb. In Greek this is the accusative case.

You can even change the order around and have the same basic meaning.

> ἀγαπᾷ τὸν κόσμον ὁ θεός.

This still means, "God loves the world."

The ὁ before θεός and the τόν before κόσμον are different forms of the definite article, usually translated "the," as in "the world." But Greek uses ὁ where English does not, such as with proper names, ὁ θεός. In translation we can just ignore the ὁ in this case.

Chapter 7

English shows possession by adding " 's" onto the end of a word: "God's word." We can also use the "of" construction: "the word of God."

Greek shows possession by putting genitive case endings onto the word. ὁ λόγος τοῦ θεοῦ means, "God's word." The υ on θεοῦ shows it is in the genitive case. (τοῦ is another form of ὁ.)

The indirect object is the word that is indirectly involved in the action of the verb. Consider this sentence.

"Karen threw Brad the ball."

The direct object is "ball"; she threw the ball. But she threw the ball to Brad. Brad is the indirect object. (If "Brad" were the direct object, he would get hurt.) In Greek, we put the indirect object in the dative case by putting dative case endings on the word. The dative carries other meanings as well, such as "by," "in," and "for" along with "to."

Chapter 8

Now we meet prepositions, those little words that describe the relationship between things, such as "in," "under," "around," and "through." The peculiarity of Greek prepositions is that the word that follows it (its object) is controlled by the preposition. ἐν means "in," and the case of its object will always be dative. ἐν τῷ θεῷ means "in God." Other prepositions take objects in other cases, and many prepositions take objects in more than one case. In the case of the latter, the meaning of the preposition changes. μετὰ τοῦ θεοῦ (object in the genitive) means "with God." μετὰ τὸν θεόν (object in the accusative) means "after God."

The verb "to be," which occurs in many forms like "I am," "you are," "they were," is not followed by an object in the accusative. It takes a predicate nominative. ὁ θεός ἐστιν ἀγαθός means "God is good." ἐστιν is a form of the verb "to be." ἀγαθός is in the nominative case.

Chapter 9

In this chapter we learn about adjectives, words that modify a noun or pronoun. Consider this sentence.

"The angel sent the good apostle."

"Good" (ἀγαθός) tells you something about the noun "apostle."

In Greek, all nouns have not only case but also number (singular or plural) and gender (masculine, feminine, or neuter). An adjective has to be the same case, number, and gender as the word it modifies.

In the case of this example, "apostle" is accusative (because it is the direct object), singular (because there is only one), and masculine. It would be ἀπόστολον. For "good" to modify it, ἀγαθός would also have to be accusative singular masculine: ἀγαθόν.

A great way to get the alphabet into your head is to sing it. If you go to the website class, you can download the sheet music and hear my friend sing it.

Chapter 5

Introduction to English Nouns

Overview

In this chapter you will learn the following:

- terms used in English grammar (inflection, case, number, gender, lexical form);
- other terms such as definite article, predicate nominative, and declension;
- parts of speech (noun, adjective, preposition, subject/predicate);
- a brief introduction to verbs.

Introduction

5.1   As strange as it may seem, the first major obstacle many of you must overcome is your lack of knowledge of English grammar. For whatever reasons, many do not know enough English grammar to learn Greek grammar. I cannot teach about the Greek nominative case until you know what a case is. You must learn to crawl before walking.

For this reason I begin our discussion of Greek nouns (chapters 6–14) with a short introduction to the English grammar relevant for studying nouns. Also, at the beginning of every chapter I will introduce some of the finer points of English grammar that are relevant for that chapter.

There is a lot of information in this chapter. The purpose is not to overwhelm you, but to introduce you to nouns and provide a central location for reference. As you have questions in the later chapters, refer back to this chapter.

Inflection

5.2   Sometimes a word changes its form. This is called "inflection."

■ A word might change its form when it performs different functions in a sentence. For example, the personal pronoun is "she" when it is the subject of the sentence (e.g., "She is my wife."), but changes to "her" when it is the direct object (e.g., "The teacher flunked her.").

■ A word might also change its form when its meaning changes. For example, the personal pronoun is "he" if it refers to a male, and "she" if it refers to a female. If the king and queen have one son, he is the "prince," but if they have two they are "princes." If their child is a girl she is called a "princess."

All these changes are examples of inflection. Compared with most languages, English is not highly inflected. Greek, on the other hand, is highly inflected. Almost every word is altered depending upon its use in the sentence and its meaning.

The following grammatical concepts can affect the form of a word in both languages.

5.3   **Case**. Words perform different functions in a sentence. These different functions are called "cases." In English there are three cases: subjective, objective, and possessive. Some English words change their form when they switch functions, while other words stay basically the same. (In the following examples, the personal pronoun "he" will change depending upon its case.)

Subjective case

If a word is the **subject** of the sentence, it is in the **subjective** case. ("*He* is my brother.") The subject is that which does the action of the active verb.

■ The subject is usually the first noun (or pronoun) before the verb in a sentence. For example: "*Bill* ran to the store." "The *ball* broke the window." Word order shows that both *Bill* and *ball* are the subjects of their verbs.

■ However, sometimes it is hard to determine which word is the subject. You can usually find out by asking the question "who?" or "what?" For example, "Who ran to the store?" "Bill." "What broke the window?" "The ball."

Possessive case

If a word shows possession, it is in the **possessive** case. ("*His* Greek Bible is always by *his* bed.")

Objective case

If a word is the **direct object**, it is in the **objective** case. The direct object is the person or thing that is directly affected by the action of the verb. This means that whatever the verb does, it does so to the direct object. ("The teacher will flunk *him* if he does not take Greek seriously.")

- The direct object usually follows the verb in word order. For example: "Robin passed her *test*." "The waiter insulted *Brian*." *Test* and *Brian* are the direct objects.

- You can usually determine the direct object by asking yourself the question "what?" or "whom?" Robin passed what? Her test. The waiter insulted whom? Brian.

case	function	example
Subjective	subject	"*He* borrowed my computer."
Possessive	possession	"He borrowed *my* computer."
Objective	direct object	"He borrowed my *computer*."

I chose the pronoun "he" for some of the illustrations above because it changes its form quite readily. Most words will not, except for the possessive case. For example, the word "teacher" stays the same whether it is the subject ("The *teacher* likes you.") or the direct object ("You like the *teacher*."). However, to form the possessive it will change by the addition of an apostrophe s. ("She is the *teacher's* pet.")

5.4   **Number**. Words can be either **singular** or **plural**, depending upon whether they refer to one, or more than one. For example, "*Students* (plural) should learn to study like this *student*" (singular).

5.5   **Gender**. Some words, mostly pronouns, change their form depending upon whether they are referring to a **masculine, feminine**, or **neuter** object. For example, "*He* (masculine) gave *it* (neuter) to *her* (feminine)." (*He, it*, and *her* are all forms of the same pronoun, the third person singular personal pronoun.)

Another example is the word "prince." If the heir to the throne is male, then he is the "prince." But if the child is female, she is the "princess." Most English words do not change to indicate gender. "Teacher" refers to either a woman or a man.

If a word refers to neither a masculine nor feminine thing, then it is neuter.

5.6   **Natural gender** means that a word takes on the gender of the object it represents. We refer to a rock as an "it" because we do not regard the rock as male or female. But we refer to a man as "he" and a woman as "she."

In Greek, pronouns follow natural gender but nouns for the most part do not. ἁμαρτία is a feminine noun meaning "sin," although "sin" is not a female concept; ἁμαρτωλός can be a masculine noun meaning "sinner," although "sinner" is not a masculine concept.

5.7   **Declension**. In English, there are different ways to form the plural. For example, to form the plural of most words you add an "s" ("books"). However, other words form their plurals by changing a vowel in the word ("man" becomes "men"). Although these two words form their plurals differently, both plurals perform the same function. They indicate more than one item.

Notice that it does not matter how a word forms its plural as far as meaning is concerned. "Children" and "childs," if the latter were a word, would mean the same thing.

A declension is a pattern of inflection. English does not really have declensions any more,[1] but it does have patterns. Words forming their plural by adding "s" are one pattern. A sub-pattern would be words adding "es." Another pattern is words that change their stem vowel, such as "goose" to "geese."

Greek has three declension patterns, three basic patterns of inflection to indicate things like case and number.

Parts of Speech

5.8   **Noun.** A noun is a word that stands for someone or something. In the sentence, "Bill threw his big black book at the strange teacher," the words "Bill," "book," and "teacher" are nouns.

5.9   **Adjective.** An adjective is a word that modifies a noun (or another adjective). In the sentence above, "big," "black," and "strange" are adjectives that modify nouns. In the sentence, "The dark brown Bible costs too much," "dark" is an adjective modifying another adjective "brown."

5.10   **Preposition.** A preposition is a word that shows the relationship between two other words. For example, the relationship can be spatial ("The Greek text is *under* the bed.") or temporal ("The student always studies *after* the ball game.").

       The word or phrase following the preposition is the **object** of the preposition ("bed" in the first example, "the ball game" in the second).

5.11   **Subject and predicate.** A sentence can be broken down into two parts. The term **subject** describes the subject of the verb and what modifies the subject. **Predicate** describes the rest of the sentence, including the verb, direct object, etc.

5.12   **Definite article.** In English, the definite article is the word "the." In the sentence, "The student is going to pass," the definite article is identifying one student in particular (even though context is required to know which one it is).

5.13   **Indefinite article.** In English, the indefinite article is the word "a." In the sentence, "A good student works every day on her Greek," the article is indefinite because it does not identify any one particular student. It is indefinite about the person of whom it is speaking.

       If the word following the indefinite article begins with a vowel, the indefinite article will be "an."

---

[1]   English retains vestiges of its old declension system, visible mostly in pronouns ("who" changing to "whom"), but the system of cases largely dropped out during Middle English.

Greek Subject and Verbs

5.14   The formal study of verbs has been deferred until Chapter 15. For now, you are to concentrate on nouns and learn them well.

However, there is an important grammatical note you need to learn in order to make sense of the exercises. *The ending of the Greek verb indicates person and number.*

"I" and "we" are considered first person, "you" is second person, and everything else (including "he," "she," "it," and all nouns) are third person.

■   The εις ending on γράφεις tells you that the subject is "you." γράφεις means "you write."

■   The ει ending on γράφει tells you that the subject is "he," "she," or "it." γράφει means "he writes," "she writes," or "it writes."

You will see how this works out in the exercises.

5.15   An important consequence of this is that a Greek sentence does not need to have an expressed subject; the subject can be contained in the verb. So, σὺ γράφεις and γράφεις both mean, "You write." The "you" comes from both the pronoun σύ as well as the ending on the verb.

In the exercises, I will always include the pronoun (e.g., "he," "they," "we") in the translation of the verb. If there is an expressed subject, you would not use the pronoun.

> ἄνθρωπος γράφει (he/she/it writes) τὸ βιβλίον.
> A man writes the book.

In this sentence, you would not translate, "A man he writes the book." You would simply say, "A man writes the book." However, if the subject were not expressed (i.e., if ἄνθρωπος were not present), then you would translate, "He writes the book."

5.16   One more point. γράφει can mean "he writes," "she writes," or "it writes." The ει ending is used with all three genders. Only context will help you decide which gender is correct. I will always translate verbs in the exercises up to Chapter 15 with all three pronouns, and it is up to you to decide which is the more appropriate translation based on context.

> ὁ θεὸς ἀγαπᾷ (he/she/it loves) τὸν κόσμον.
> God loves the world.

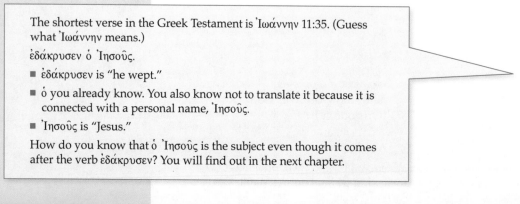

The shortest verse in the Greek Testament is Ἰωάννην 11:35. (Guess what Ἰωάννην means.)

ἐδάκρυσεν ὁ Ἰησοῦς.

■ ἐδάκρυσεν is "he wept."

■ ὁ you already know. You also know not to translate it because it is connected with a personal name, Ἰησοῦς.

■ Ἰησοῦς is "Jesus."

How do you know that ὁ Ἰησοῦς is the subject even though it comes after the verb ἐδάκρυσεν? You will find out in the next chapter.

Chapter 6

Nominative and Accusative; Definite Article

(First and Second Declension Nouns)

Exegetical Insight

The nominative case is the case that the subject is in. When the subject takes an equative verb like "is" (i.e., a verb that equates the subject with something else), then another noun also appears in the nominative case—the predicate nominative. In the sentence, "John is a man," "John" is the subject and "man" is the predicate nominative. In English the subject and predicate nominative are distinguished by word order (the subject comes first). Not so in Greek. Since word order in Greek is quite flexible and is used for emphasis rather than for strict grammatical function, other means are used to distinguish subject from predicate nominative. For example, if one of the two nouns has the definite article, it is the subject.

As we have said, word order is employed especially for the sake of emphasis. Generally speaking, when a word is thrown to the front of the clause it is done so for emphasis. When a predicate nominative is thrown in front of the verb, by virtue of word order it takes on emphasis. A good illustration of this is John 1:1c. The English versions typically have, "and the Word was God." But in Greek, the word order has been reversed. It reads,

καὶ	θεὸς	ἦν	ὁ	λόγος
and	God	was	the	Word.

We know that "the Word" is the subject because it has the definite article, and we translate it accordingly: "and the Word was God." Two questions, both of theological import, should come to mind: (1) why was θεός thrown forward? and (2) why does it lack the article?

In brief,[1] its emphatic position stresses its essence or quality: "What God was, the Word was" is how one translation brings out this force. Its lack of a definite article keeps us from identifying the *person* of the Word (Jesus Christ) with the *person* of "God" (the Father). That is to say, the word order tells us that Jesus Christ has all the divine attributes that the Father has; lack of the article tells us that Jesus Christ is not the Father. John's wording here is beautifully compact! It is, in fact, one of the most elegantly terse theological statements one could ever find. As Martin Luther said, the lack of an article is against Sabellianism; the word order is against Arianism.

To state this another way, look at how the different Greek constructions would be rendered:

καὶ ὁ λόγος ἦν ὁ θεός
"and the Word was the God"
(i.e., the Father; Sabellianism)

καὶ ὁ λόγος ἦν θεός
"and the Word was a god"
(Arianism)

καὶ θεὸς ἦν ὁ λόγος
"and the Word was God"
(Orthodoxy).

---

[1] This verse is dealt with in more detail by Wallace, GGBB, pages 266-269.

Jesus Christ is God and has all the attributes that the Father has. But he is not the first person of the Trinity. All this is concisely affirmed in καὶ θεὸς ἦν ὁ λόγος.

Daniel B. Wallace

Overview

In this chapter you will learn:

- ■ to identify whether a noun is first or second declension;

- ■ two cases and their endings: the nominative (used when the noun is the subject); the accusative (used when the noun is the direct object);

- ■ the forms of the word "the" and how they "agree" with the noun they are modifying;

- ■ two hints for effective translation;

- ■ the first three of eight noun rules.

Introduction

6.1   This is by far the longest chapter in this text. You are meeting some important ideas for the first time, and I want to cover them adequately. Most of it is grammar and not much is memory work, so take heart. There is a review part way through and a summary at the end.

The chapters in *BBG* are laid out consistently.

- ■ Each one starts with an exegetical insight designed to illustrate some point you will be learning in the chapter.

- ■ Overview of the material you will learn

- ■ A discussion of relevant English grammar

- ■ Greek grammar

- ■ A summary of the entire discussion

- ■ Vocabulary

- ■ Sometimes there is an Advanced Information section and an Exegesis section.

- ■ On many chapters there is a "Halftime Review."

> The website contains many blogs and other items that will encourage you on a chapter by chapter basis.

English

6.2   Everything you need to know about English grammar in this chapter has been covered in Chapter 5.

Greek

The Form of the Greek Noun

6.3   Do not memorize the endings in the following illustrations. All I want you to see is how inflection works.

Case endings. The case of a word in Greek is indicated by the "case ending." This is a suffix added to the end of the word. For example, the basic word for "apostle" is ἀποστολο.

■   If the word is functioning as the subject of the verb, it takes a case ending that is equivalent to the subjective case in English: ς (ἀπόστολος).

■   If it is functioning as the direct object of the verb, it takes a case ending that is equivalent to the objective case in English: ν (ἀπόστολον).

> ὁ ἀπόστολος πέμπει τὸν ἀπόστολον.
>
> The apostle sends the apostle.

In English, we normally use word order to determine the function of a word. If the word is the subject of the verb, it comes before the verb; if it is the direct object of the verb, it comes after the verb. But in Greek, it is the case ending, *not the word order*, that indicates the function of a word; therefore, it is extremely important to learn the case endings well.

The following issues affect which case ending is used in a specific instance.

6.4   **Stem**. If you take the case ending off a noun you are left with the stem. The stem of λόγος is λογο. It is the stem of a noun that carries the actual meaning of the word.

It is essential that you be able to identify the stem of a word. It is listed in the Vocbulary section marked with an asterisk (*λογο).

6.5   **Gender**. A noun is either masculine, feminine, or neuter. A noun has only one gender and it never varies.[1]

A word is not always the gender you might expect (cf. "natural gender," 5.6). ἁμαρτωλός means "sinner" and is masculine, but it does not mean that a sinner is male. ἁμαρτία means "sin" and is a feminine noun, but it does not mean that sin is a feminine trait. This is called "grammatical gender."

However, there are certain patterns that will help you remember the gender of a word. Words listed in the vocabulary section that end in ος are usually masculine, words ending with ον are usually neuter, and words ending in eta or alpha are mostly feminine.

6.6   **Number**. Instead of adding an "s" to a word, Greek indicates singular or plural by using different case endings.

■   ἀπόστολος means "apostle"
■   ἀπόστολοι means "apostles"

The difference between the singular and plural is indicated by the case endings ς and ι.

---

[1]   There are a few words that are both masculine and feminine, but you will not meet them for some time.

6.7 **Declensions**. I discussed in 5.7 how there are different inflectional patterns that English nouns follow in forming their plural. Some add "s," some add "es," and others change the vowel in the stem of the word (e.g., "men"). The pattern a word follows does not affect its meaning, only its form. "Children" and "childs" would mean the same thing, if the latter were actually a word.

In Greek there are basically three inflectional patterns. Each of these patterns is called a "declension." What declension a particular noun follows has no bearing on the meaning of the word. *The different declensions affect only the form of the case ending.*

■ Nouns that have a stem ending in an alpha or eta are **first declension**, take first declension endings, and are primarily feminine (e.g., γραφή).

■ Nouns that have a stem ending in an omicron are **second declension**, take second declension endings, and are mostly masculine or neuter (ἀπόστολος; ἔργον).

■ If the stem of a word ends in a consonant it is **third declension**. We will deal with the third declension in Chapter 10.

For example, a first declension case ending for the subject of the verb is nothing; the stem stands by itself (γραφή; ὥρα).

> ἡ ὥρα ἐστὶν νῦν.
>
> The hour is now.

A second declension case ending for the subject of the verb is ς (ἀπόστολος).[2]

> ὁ ἀπόστολος λέγει τὸν λόγον.
>
> The apostle speaks the word.

Remember: declension affects only the case ending used; it does not affect meaning.

Since the final letter of the noun stem determines its declension, *a noun can belong to only one declension.*

Indeclinable. Some words in Greek are indeclinable, such as personal names and words borrowed from other languages. Their form, therefore, does not change regardless of their meaning or function in the sentence. For example, the word for "Israel" is written as Ἰσραήλ whether it is the subject or the direct object.

First Two Cases

6.8 **Nominative**. In this chapter you will learn two of the five Greek cases. The first is the nominative case. The primary function of the nominative case is to indicate the **subject** of the sentence. In other words, if a word is the subject of the verb it will have a nominative case ending.

As you have seen above, one of the nominative singular case endings is sigma. In the following sentence, which word is the subject? (ἀγαπᾷ means "he loves" and τόν means "the.")

> ὁ θεὸς ἀγαπᾷ τὸν κόσμον.

---

[2]   If ἀπόστολος (masc) and ἀποστόλη (fem) were both words, they would have the same meaning (except ἀπόστολος would designate a man and ἀποστόλη a woman).

6.9 **Accusative.** If a word is the **direct object** of the verb it will be in the accusative case. This means that it will have an accusative case ending.

One of the accusative singular case endings is ν. In the following sentence, which word is the direct object?

Χριστὸν ἀγαπᾷ ὁ θεός.

Word Order and Lexicons

6.10 **Word order.** Notice in the example above that you do not determine whether a word is the subject or the object by its order in the sentence as you do in English. *The only way to determine the subject or direct object of a Greek verb is by the case endings.*

This cannot be stressed too much. Your natural inclination will be to ignore the case endings and assume that the word before the verb is the subject and the word after the verb is the direct object. Fight this tendency!

In Greek, the ending ς shows you that this word is in the nominative case and therefore is the subject. The ending ν shows you that this word is accusative and therefore is the direct object.[3] In the following examples, locate the subjects and direct objects. Note that although each example has the same meaning ("God loves the world"), the order of the words is different.

Θεὸς ἀγαπᾷ τὸν κόσμον.
ἀγαπᾷ τὸν κόσμον Θεός.
τὸν κόσμον Θεὸς ἀγαπᾷ.
ἀγαπᾷ Θεὸς τὸν κόσμον.

As a general rule, as you translate, try to maintain the same order as the Greek if possible. There is a rhythm to the order of words in Greek, although it is a different rhythm than in English. Try to keep the same English order as the Greek, for now, and this will keep you from making certain mistakes.

6.11 **Lexicons and lexical form.** Whereas most people call them "dictionaries," scholars call them **lexicons**.

The form of the word found in the lexicon is called the **lexical form**. The lexical form of a Greek noun is its form in the nominative singular. For example, the lexical form of κόσμον (accusative singular) is κόσμος.

Your vocabulary words are given in their lexical forms. Whenever you are asked to explain the form of an inflected Greek word, you must be able to indicate its lexical form; otherwise, you will not be able to look up the word in the lexicon and find its meaning.

> While word placement does not determine function, it does help in some situations to understand the author's intention. For example, Ephesians 2:8 starts, "For by grace you have been saved through faith." Paul wanted to emphasize, above all else, that salvation is due to God's grace, and therefore he places that fact first for emphasis. Your translation should retain that emphasis, as long as it is acceptable English.

---

[3] As you will see, these letters are also endings for other cases, but for the sake of this illustration I make the simplification.

Halftime Review

You are halfway through this lesson, so let's stop and review what you have learned. I will include these reviews in all the chapters unless they are short.

■ Greek uses different case endings to indicate the case (nominative; accusative), gender (masculine; feminine; neuter), and number (singular; plural).

■ The stem of the word is the basic form of the word that carries its meaning. It is discovered by removing the case ending.

■ Stems ending in an alpha or eta are in the first declension; stems ending in omicron are in the second declension.

■ If a word is the subject of a verb, it is in the nominative case and uses nominative case endings.

■ If a word is the direct object of a verb, it is in the accusative case and uses accusative case endings.

■ Word order does not determine the function of a word.

■ The lexical form of a noun is the nominative singular.

Case Endings

6.12 **Form**. The following chart is called a "paradigm." It is the paradigm of the case endings used by the first and second declensions, nominative and accusative.[4] A dash (-) means that no case ending is used and the stem of the noun stands by itself. The underline ($\underline{\alpha}$) means that the case ending joins with the final stem vowel.[5] These endings must be learned perfectly.

	2 masc	1 fem	2 neut
nom sg	ς	–	ν
acc sg	ν	ν	ν
nom pl	ι	ι	$\underline{\alpha}$
acc pl	υς[6]	ς	$\underline{\alpha}$

---

[4]   If you have studied Greek before, you will notice a few differences. Just about every grammar teaches that the final stem vowel is part of the case ending, ος and not ς. Not only is this incorrect, but in my opinion it makes learning Greek more difficult. If you learn the true case endings, you will find that memorization is kept to a minimum!

[5]   This is called "contraction," and I will discuss it in detail later. For example, the stem of the noun ἔργον is ἔργο. When it is in the neuter plural its form is ἔργα. The omicron and alpha have "contracted" to alpha. ἔργο + α ‣ ἔργα.

[6]   If you really want to be technical, the ending for the masculine accusative plural is νς. But because of the nature of the nu, it drops out. In order to compensate for the loss of the nu, the omicron of the stem lengthens to ου when followed by a sigma (*λογο + νς ‣ λογος ‣ λόγους). It is easier to memorize the ending as υς.

When attached to the final stem vowel, they look like this.

	2 *masc*	1 *fem*		2 *neut*
nom sg	ος	η	α	ον
acc sg	ον	ην	αν	ον
nom pl	οι	αι		α
acc pl	ους	ας		α

As you can see, we have to make allowance for the two stem vowels in the feminine.

The Structure of the Paradigms

- The singular forms are on top, and the plural below.

- The order left to right is masculine, feminine, neuter.

- The "2 - 1 - 2" along the top means that the masculine follows the second declension, the feminine follows the first declension, and the neuter follows the second.

Important

- Learn these endings! Without them, you will never be able to translate anything.

- Be sure to memorize the endings by themselves, not only what they look like when attached to a word. Otherwise you may not be able to identify the endings on other nouns.

- The key to learning these paradigms is to realize that *translation does not require you to repeat paradigms; it requires you to recognize the endings when you see them.*

- I suggest that you read the paradigms left to right, not top to bottom. When you are translating a verse, you will be looking for a word in the nominative, and at first you do not care about its number or gender.

- Use flash cards. Put each ending on a different card, carry them with you wherever you go, mix them up, and review them over and over again.

- Always say the endings out loud. The more senses you employ in memorization the better. Pronounce the ending out loud; listen to yourself speak; write the ending down; look at what you have written.

Older methods of learning Greek required you to memorize paradigm after paradigm, fifty-two in all. You can still do that if you wish, but that means that for the rest of your life you will have to review paradigm after paradigm. You get the picture. I offer you a different approach. Memorize the definite article, one other paradigm, and eight rules. That's all there is to it. Which way would you like to go?

6.13 **Hints**

- The masculine and feminine case endings are often similar or even identical. In the nominative and accusative, the neuter is usually distinct from the masculine.

- In the neuter, the nominative and accusative singular are always the same, and the nominative and accusative plural are always the same (see 6.18 below). Context will usually show you whether the neuter word is the subject or direct object.

Nouns

6.14 **Paradigm of the word and case endings**. Now let's add the case endings to the nouns. Be sure to differentiate between the stem and the case ending.

	2 *masc*	1 *fem*		2 *neut*
nom sg	λόγος	γραφή	ὥρα	ἔργον
acc sg	λόγον	γραφήν	ὥραν	ἔργον
nom pl	λόγοι	γραφαί	ὧραι	ἔργα
acc pl	λόγους	γραφάς	ὥρας	ἔργα

Notice which endings are going to give you trouble. The nu and alpha occur in several places.

6.15 **Feminine**. In the paradigm there are two feminine nouns, γραφή and ὥρα. The only difference between the forms of these two words is the final stem vowel. γραφή ends in eta, and ὥρα ends in alpha. If you think of the alpha and eta as being related vowels, then you will not have to learn two different patterns for feminine nouns. They are identical except for the final stem vowel.

Notice, however, that in the plural the stem of γραφή ends in an alpha and not an eta. All first declension nouns that have eta in the singular shift to alpha in the plural.

6.16 **Parse**. When asked to "parse" a noun, you should specify five things about the word.

1. Case   (nominative, accusative)
2. Number   (singular, plural)
3. Gender   (masculine, feminine, neuter)
4. Lexical form   (nominative singular)
5. Inflected meaning

For example, λόγους is accusative plural masculine, from λόγος, meaning "words."

This is only my suggestion. Teachers may vary on their preferred order of parsing.

6.17 **Parsing neuter nouns**. When parsing a neuter word that is either nominative or accusative, my suggestion is to list both possibilities.

For example, ἔργον is nominative or accusative singular neuter, from ἔργον, meaning "work."

When you are translating a sentence and come across one of these forms, it is important to see that the word can be either the subject or direct object. If you make an assumption that it is the subject when in fact it is the direct object, you may never be able to translate the sentence. But if you are accustomed to parsing it as "nominative/accusative," you will be less likely to make this mistake.

The First Three Noun Rules

6.18 These are the first three of the famous eight noun rules. Learn them exactly!

1. Stems ending in alpha or eta are in the first declension, stems ending in omicron are in the second, and consonantal stems are in the third.

2. Every neuter word has the same form in the nominative and accusative.

   ἔργον could be either nominative or accusative.

3. Almost all neuter words end in alpha in the nominative and accusative plural.

All of the eight noun rules are listed in the Appendix, page 346.

Definite Article

6.19 **Summary**. The definite article is the only article in Greek. There is no indefinite article ("a," cf. 6.25). For this reason you can refer to the Greek definite article simply as the "article."

6.20 **Agreement**. *The article agrees with the noun it modifies in case, number, and gender.* For this reason, unlike nouns, the article can occur in any gender.

In other words, if a noun is nominative, singular, masculine (ἄνθρωπος), the article that modifies it will be nominative, singular, masculine (ὁ).

The lexical form of the article is the nominative, singular, masculine (ὁ). As a general rule, the lexical form of any word that occurs in more than one gender is the masculine form.

6.21 **Form**. Here is the paradigm of the article. Compare the forms to the case endings to see all the similarities. The feminine follows the first declension, the masculine and neuter the second.

	2 *masc*	1 *fem*	2 *neut*
nom sg	ὁ	ἡ	τό
acc sg	τόν	τήν	τό
nom pl	οἱ	αἱ	τά
acc pl	τούς	τάς	τά

6.22 Hints

■ The article begins with either a rough breathing or a tau. Then you have the characteristic vowel of that declension and the case ending. The only exception is the neuter singular.[7]

■ The article does not care about the declension of the word it is modifying. ἡ will modify a feminine noun whether it is first or second declension.[8] This makes the article consistent, easy to learn, and important.

6.23 Here is the noun paradigm with the definite article.

	2 masc	1 fem		2 neut
nom sg	ὁ λόγος	ἡ γραφή	ἡ ὥρα	τὸ ἔργον
acc sg	τὸν λόγον	τὴν γραφήν	τὴν ὥραν	τὸ ἔργον
nom pl	οἱ λόγοι	αἱ γραφαί	αἱ ὧραι	τὰ ἔργα
acc pl	τοὺς λόγους	τὰς γραφάς	τὰς ὥρας	τὰ ἔργα

6.24 *Knowing the forms of the article is the key to recognizing the forms of nouns in Greek.* If you learn the forms of the Greek article well, you will not have much more to learn for nouns. Almost all nouns are preceded by the article. If you cannot decline a noun you can look at the article and will know what the noun is.

A second reason why the article is important is that most of the case endings found on nouns are similar to the definite article. Therefore, if you know the article, you know many of the case endings.

---

[7] Here are some more hints.

- The vowel in the feminine article is always eta in the singular, never alpha as can be the case with nouns.

- The nominative singular is easy to memorize. In the feminine and masculine there is no case ending and no tau. The vowel stands alone, and since you have already associated the eta with the first declension and omicron with the second you already know these forms. But note the breathing.

  The neuter could not follow suit, otherwise it would have been identical to the masculine. Therefore you have the characteristic tau followed by the omicron that you associate with the second declension.

- In both the masculine and feminine, the nominative plural endings are a vowel followed by an iota. Again you see the characteristic omicron and alpha. If you learn that the vowel-iota combination indicates nominative plural, then if it is οι the word is masculine, and if it is αι the word is feminine.

- τήν and τόν are exactly alike except that the feminine has an eta and the masculine has an omicron.

- In the accusative plural you have the characteristic omicron and alpha. You will discover that the vowel-sigma combination is typical for the accusative plural, and the alpha is common in neuter plural words (Noun Rule 3).

[8] You have not yet seen any second declension feminine nouns.

Translation Procedure

6.25 When students start learning Greek, one of their initial problems is that a Greek sentence looks like a collection of unrelated words. One of the keys to this problem is learning to split a sentence into its different parts. At this point, you can separate the subject and the direct object from the verb.

> θεὸς σώσει ψυχάς.
>
> God will save souls.

The subject is θεός and the direct object is ψυχάς. You would divide the sentence like this:

> θεὸς / σώσει / ψυχάς.

If there is an article, keep it with the noun.

> ὁ θεὸς / σώσει / ψυχάς.

As you get further into Greek and sentence structure becomes more complex, this practice becomes more significant.

6.26 **Article**. As in English, the Greek article is generally translated "the." The rule is to translate according to the presence or absence of the article. If an article is present, translate it. If there is no article, do not use "the."

If there is no article you may insert "a" before the noun if it makes better sense in English. For example, "ὁ ἄνθρωπος" means "the man" and "ἄνθρωπος" means "man" or "a man."

6.27 You will soon discover that the Greeks do not use the article the same way we do. They use it when we never would, and they omit it when English demands it. Languages are not codes, and there is not an exact word for word correspondence. Therefore, you should be a little flexible at this point. As you work through the following chapters, I will note some of the differences. You will meet these two differences in this chapter:[9]

Names. Greek often uses the definite article before a proper name. For example, you will often find ὁ Ἰησοῦς ("the Jesus"). You may omit the article in your translation of proper names.

Abstract nouns. Greek often includes the article with abstract nouns such as "the Truth" (ἡ ἀλήθεια). English does not normally use the article with abstract nouns and you may omit it in translation.

6.28 **Postpositive**. A postpositive is a word that cannot be the first word in a Greek sentence or clause, even though in your translation it is the first word. It usually is the second word and sometimes the third. There are only a few postpositives, but in this chapter you will learn δέ, meaning "but." ὁ δὲ εἶπεν ... is translated "But he said ...."[10]

> If you are saying "hi" to one friend, you say, χαῖρε (Luke 1:28). This is also the word the soldiers used to mock Jesus, often translated as "hail" (John 19:3).

---

[9] See Chapter 36 for more discussion on the article.

[10] In this example you can see another use of the Greek article. ὁ δέ often means, "but he," the article functioning as a personal pronoun. The Greek article is a lot of fun and full of variety and meaning. But more on this later.

Summary

1. **The fog**. You are now entering the fog. You will have read this chapter and think you understand it—and perhaps you do—but it will seem foggy. That's okay. If living in the fog becomes discouraging, look two chapters back and you should understand that chapter clearly. In two more chapters this chapter will be clear, assuming you keep studying.

2. Greek uses case endings to show the noun's function. Different case endings are used to designate case (nominative, accusative), number (singular, plural), and gender (masculine, feminine, neuter).

3. The stem of a noun is what is left after removing the case ending. It carries the basic meaning of the word.

4. The subject of a verb uses nominative case endings, and the direct object uses accusative case endings.

5. Memorize the paradigm of the case endings and the article.

6. The article agrees with the noun that it modifies in case, number, and gender.

7. Learn the endings by themselves. Then learn the full paradigm that lists the article, noun stem, and case endings.

	2 *masc*	1 *fem*	2 *neut*
nom sg	ς	–	ν
acc sg	ν	ν	ν
nom pl	ι	ι	<u>α</u>
acc pl	υς	ς	<u>α</u>

	2 *masc*	1 *fem*		2 *neut*
nom sg	ὁ λόγος	ἡ γραφή	ἡ ὥρα	τὸ ἔργον
acc sg	τὸν λόγον	τὴν γραφήν	τὴν ὥραν	τὸ ἔργον
nom pl	οἱ λόγοι	αἱ γραφαί	αἱ ὧραι	τὰ ἔργα
acc pl	τοὺς λόγους	τὰς γραφάς	τὰς ὥρας	τὰ ἔργα

8. The first three noun rules.

   1. Stems ending in alpha or eta are in the first declension, stems ending in omicron are in the second, and consonantal stems are in the third. The declension of a noun affects only its form, not its meaning.

   2. Every neuter word has the same form in the nominative and accusative.

   3. Almost all neuter words end in alpha in the nominative and accusative plural.

9. Divide the sentence you are translating into its parts: subject; verb; direct object. Keep the article with the noun it modifies.

Vocabulary

Nouns are listed with their article (e.g., ἀγάπη, ἡ). Be sure to memorize the article with the word so you can remember its gender. The stem of the word is listed with an asterisk (e.g., *ἀγαπη). The forms with a dash following the words (e.g., "-ης" with ἀγάπη, and "-η, -ο" with ἄλλος) will be explained in following chapters.

ἀγάπη, -ης, ἡ	love (116; *ἀγαπη)[11]
ἄλλος, -η, -ο	other, another (155; *αλλο)[12]
αὐτός, -ή, -ό	singular: he, she, it (him, her) (5,597; *αυτο)[13] plural: they (them)
	Although you do not yet know why, αὐτόν is only masculine, not neuter.
βασιλεία, -ας, ἡ	kingdom (162; *βασιλεια)[14]
δέ (δ᾿)	but, and (2,792)
	δέ is a postpositive. δέ is sometimes written as δ᾿ when it is followed by a word beginning with a vowel (e.g., δ᾿ ἄν...).
ἐν	in, on, among (2,752)
ἔργον, -ου, τό	work, deed, action (169; *ἐργο)[15]
καιρός, -οῦ, ὁ	(appointed) time, season (85; *καιρο)
	The parentheses mean that καιρός can mean "time" or "appointed time."
νῦν	adverb: now (147; adverb) noun: the present
ὁ, ἡ, τό	the (19,867)
ὅτι	that, since, because (1,296)
	ὅτι can also act as quotation marks. Modern Greek texts capitalize the first word in what the editors feel is a quotation; in these cases they are expecting you to view ὅτι as quotation marks.
οὐ (οὐκ, οὐχ)	not (1,623)
	οὐ is used when the following word begins with a consonant (οὐ δύναται). οὐκ is used when the next word begins with a vowel and smooth breathing (οὐκ ἦλθον), while οὐχ is used when the next word begins with a vowel and rough breathing (οὐχ ὑμεῖς). All forms mean "not." οὐ tends to precede the word it modifies.
ὥρα, -ας, ἡ	hour, occasion, moment (106; *ὡρα)[16]

> Alternate forms of the same word, like οὐ, οὐκ, and οὐχ, are called "allomorphs."

---

[11] The *agape* was the love feast of early Christians.

[12] An *allegory* is a description of one thing using the image of *another*.

[13] An *autocrat* (αὐτοκρατής) is a ruling by *oneself*. You will see in Chapter 12 that αὐτός can also mean "self" or "same," which is reflected in most English cognates and derivatives.

[14] A *basilica* (βασιλική) is a royal palace. Originally it meant "royal colonnade." In Latin its cognate meant "a public hall with double colonnades," and came to be used of early Christian and medieval churches of a certain architectural type.

[15] *Ergonomics* is the science that coordinates the design of machines to the requirements of the worker to aid in the work.

[16] An *hour* is a time period of the day.

Total word count in the New Testament:	138,162
Number of words learned to date:	39
Number of word occurrences in this chapter:	34,867
Number of word occurrences to date:	50,825
Percent of total word count in the New Testament:	36.79%

Previous Words

As you learn more grammar, it will be necessary from time to time to go back to words you have already learned and fine-tune our understanding of those words. When that happens, the words in question are listed in this section. This is when I explain the parts of your vocabulary words you did not understand.

Be sure to learn the article and stem of every vocabulary word.

Ἀβραάμ, ὁ	*Ἀβρααμ	κόσμος, ὁ	*κοσμο
ἄγγελος, ὁ	*ἀγγελο	λόγος, ὁ	*λογο
ἄνθρωπος, ὁ	*ἀνθρωπο	Παῦλος, ὁ	*Παυλο
ἀπόστολος, ὁ	*ἀποστολο	Πέτρος, ὁ	*Πετρο
Γαλιλαία, ἡ	*Γαλιλαια	Πιλᾶτος, ὁ	*Πιλατο
γραφή, ἡ	*γραφη	πνεῦμα, τό [17]	*πνευματ
Δαυίδ, ὁ	*Δαυίδ	προφήτης, ὁ [16]	*προφητη
δόξα, ἡ	*δοξα	σάββατον, τό	*σαββατο
ζωή, ἡ	*ζωη	Σίμων, ὁ [16]	*Σιμων
θεός, ὁ	*θεο	φωνή, ἡ	*φωνη
καρδία, ἡ	*καρδια	Χριστός, ὁ	*Χριστο

If you are saying "hi" to more than one friend, say χαίρετε. This form is also used to say "rejoice!" (1 Thess 5:16).

---

[17] This word does not follow the declension patterns you have learned so far. I will discuss it later.

Exegesis

It is often helpful for students to see how the grammar they have just learned is actually used in exegesis. That's what this section is for. If you are struggling as a student, this may be too much information for you, but it is here when you are ready. If you are in a class, your teacher will tell you if you are responsible for this information.

Nominative

The primary function of the nominative case is to indicate the subject of the verb. Another use will be introduced in Chapter 8.

Accusative

1. The primary use of the accusative is to indicate the direct object.

    > ἠγάπησεν ὁ θεὸς τὸν κόσμον *(John 3:16)*.
    > God loved *the world.*

2. Some verbs require two objects to complete their meaning (double accusative).

    > ἐκεῖνος ὑμᾶς διδάξει πάντα *(John 14:26)*.
    > He will teach *you all things.*

    Sometimes a translation will add a word like "as" before the second accusative to help you understand its meaning.

    > ἀπέστειλεν τὸν υἱὸν αὐτοῦ ἱλασμόν *(1 John 4:10)*.
    > He sent his Son *as* the propitiation.

3. The accusative can behave as an adverb, modifying the verb (adverbial accusative; accusative of manner or measure).

    > δωρεὰν ἐλάβετε, δωρεὰν δότε *(Matt 10:8)*.
    > *Freely* you received, *freely* give.

    > ζητεῖτε πρῶτον τὴν βασιλείαν τοῦ θεοῦ *(Matt 6:33)*.
    > Seek *first* the kingdom of God.

Many signs in modern Greece are written in both Greek and English.

Chapter 7

Genitive and Dative

First and Second Declension Nouns

Exegetical Insight

"Peace on earth, good will toward men" (Luke 2:14, KJV). You have probably all received Christmas cards containing this part of the angels' song to the shepherds on the fields of Bethlehem. But most modern translations read differently: "on earth peace to men on whom his [God's] favor rests" (NIV); "and on earth peace among those whom he [God] favors" (NRSV). The difference between the KJV and the others is the difference between the nominative and the genitive.

The Greek manuscripts used to translate the KJV contain εὐδοκία (nominative), whereas the older manuscripts used to translate the modern versions contain εὐδοκίας (genitive) —literally translated, "of good will" or "characterized by [God's] good pleasure." In other words, the peace that the angels sang that belonged to the earth as a result of the birth of Christ is not a generic, worldwide peace for all humankind, but a peace limited to those who obtain favor with God by believing in his Son Jesus (see Romans 5:1). What a difference a single letter can make in the meaning of the text!

Verlyn Verbrugge

Overview

In this chapter you will learn:

- the final two major cases, the genitive (when the noun is showing possession) and the dative (when the noun is used as the indirect object);

- the concept of key words;

- Noun Rules 4, 5, and 6.

English

7.1   The **possessive case** in English is used to indicate possession. You can either put "of" in front of the word ("The Word *of God* is true."), an "apostrophe s" after the word ("*God's* Word is true."), or just apostrophe if the word ends in "s" ("The *apostles'* word was ignored.").

7.2   The **indirect object**, technically, is the person/thing that is "indirectly" affected by the action of the verb. This means that the indirect object is somehow involved in the action described by the verb, but not directly.

For example, "Karin threw Brad a ball." The direct object is "ball," since it is directly related to the action of the verb. It is what was thrown. But "Brad" is also related to the action of the verb, since the ball was thrown to him. "Brad" is the indirect object. If Karin threw Brad, then "Brad" would be the direct object.

One way to find the indirect object is to put the word "to" in front of the word and see if it makes sense. "Karin threw Brad a ball." "Karin threw to Brad a ball." To whom did Karin throw the ball? To Brad. "Brad" is the indirect object.[1] The indirect object answers the question "to whom?" or "to what?"

English does not have a separate case for the indirect object. It uses the same form as the direct object (objective case). "Him" is used for both a direct and an indirect object.

Greek Genitive Case

7.3   The **genitive** case in Greek can be used when showing possession. Instead of adding an "apostrophe s" or using "of," the genitive case endings are added to the Greek word. For example, if the sentence "Everyone breaks the laws of God" were in Greek, "God" would be in the genitive case and have a genitive case ending.

υ is a genitive singular ending, and ων is the genitive plural ending.[2] If you were to see the word λόγου you would know it is singular and may be showing possession. If you were to see the word λόγων you would know it is plural and also may be showing possession.

In English the possessive case can be indicated by the apostrophe. "Everyone breaks God's laws." Greek, however, does not have this construction, and so all Greek constructions are in the form "of ...." "Laws of God" (νόμοι τοῦ θεοῦ) would never be τοῦ θεοῦ's νόμοι. Therefore, in translating you should think with the "of" construction.[3]

The word in the genitive usually follows the word it is modifying (νόμοι τοῦ θεοῦ). The word it modifies is called the **head noun**.

---

[1]   In English when the word "to" is used, it would go after the direct object. "Karin threw the ball to Brad."

[2]   The final stem vowel is absorbed by the omega, just like the alpha does in the nominative and accusative plural neuter (λογο + ων ▸ λόγων).

[3]   Follow this practice for now. Once you are comfortable with the genitive case, your teacher may allow you to shift to the " 's " construction in your translation.

7.4 You now meet an important technique that is helpful in learning Greek. It is the use of what I call **key words**. Key words are words that are associated with a particular case that you should put in front of the translation of the actual word. Doing this will help you understand the function of the case.

The key word for the genitive is "**of**."

> ἡ δόξα ἀνθρώπου
> The glory of mankind.

Greek Dative Case

7.5 The dative case in Greek has a wide range of usage, roughly equivalent to the ideas behind the English "to," "in," and "with." In the following examples, τῷ is the dative form of the definite article.

> ἄγγελος κυρίου κατ᾽ ὄναρ ἐφάνη αὐτῷ (*Matt 1:20*).
> An angel of the Lord appeared *to him* in a dream.

> Μακάριοι οἱ πτωχοὶ τῷ πνεύματι (*Matt 5:3*).
> Blessed are the poor *in spirit*.

> πᾶς ὁ ὀργιζόμενος τῷ ἀδελφῷ αὐτοῦ (*Matt 5:22*).
> everyone who is angry *with* his *brother*

These become three key words for the dative, with "to" being primary. Context will help you determine which is appropriate in a specific instance.

7.6 Under the category of "to" comes the **indirect object**. The indirect object functions the same in Greek as it does in English. In Greek, the indirect object is put in the dative case, which means it uses the dative case endings. For example, if the sentence "God gave the world his Son" were in Greek, "the world" would be in the dative case since it is the indirect object.

> ἔδωκεν ἄν σοι ὕδωρ ζῶν (*John 4:10*).
> He would give *you* living water.

For the time being it is best to use the key word "to" in your translation of the indirect object. As you become comfortable with the construction, your teacher may allow you a little more flexibility.

7.7 Iota is the dative singular case ending and ις is a dative plural. In the singular, the final stem vowel lengthens[4] and the iota subscripts. ("Subscript" means it is written under a letter.)

αι ► ᾳ	*βασιλεια + ι ► βασιλείᾳ
ηι ► ῃ	*ἀγαπη + ι ► ἀγάπῃ
οι ► ῳ	*λογο + ι ► λογοι ► λογωι ► λόγῳ

---

[4] Because alpha lengthens to long alpha, and eta is already long, you do not see the lengthening in the first declension; but it is visible in the second declension because omicron lengthens to omega.

If you were to see the word λόγῳ you would know it is singular and may be functioning as the indirect object. If you were to see the word λόγοις you would know it is plural and may be functioning as the indirect object.

Genitive and Dative Case Endings

7.8 Here is the full paradigm for the first and second declension. The genitive and dative are placed between the nominative and accusative.[5]

	2 *masc*	1 *fem*	2 *neut*
nom sg	ς	–	ν
gen sg	υ[6]	ς	υ[6]
dat sg[7]	ι	ι	ι
acc sg	ν	ν	ν
nom pl	ι	ι	α̱
gen pl	ων	ων	ων
dat pl	ις	ις	ις
acc pl	υς	ς	α̱

If you are going to say "hello," you should also be able to say "goodbye."

- If you are saying goodbye to one person, you say, ἔρρωσο.
- If you are saying goodbye to more than one person, say, ἔρρωσθε (Acts 15:29).

When attached to the final stem vowel they look like this.

	2 *masc*	1 *fem*		2 *neut*
nom sg	ος	η	α	ον
gen sg	ου	ης	ας	ου
dat sg	ῳ	ῃ	ᾳ	ῳ
acc sg	ον	ην	αν	ον
nom pl	οι	αι		α
gen pl	ων	ων		ων
dat pl	οις	αις		οις
acc pl	ους	ας		α

These forms are from the verb meaning, "to be strong." If your teacher lets you, take a break, walk around the room, and say "hello" and "goodbye" to one another.

---

[5] In my opinion, it would be preferable to order the cases as nominative, accusative, dative, and genitive. It seems smoother to move from subject to object to indirect object. In the neuter the nominative and accusative are the same, and this arrangement would keep them together. But I gave in to conventional usage and listed the cases in the standard format.

[6] As is the case with the masculine accusative plural case ending υς, the genitive singular ending actually is not upsilon. It is omicron which, when combined with final stem vowel contracts to ου. (This is a slight simplification. See Smyth, #230 D1 for details.) But I have found it easier to memorize the ending as υ.

[7] In the singular (first and second declensions), the iota will always subscript. This is the only place in the noun system where the iota subscripts.

When attached to words, they look like this.

	2 *masc*	1 *fem*		2 *neut*
nom sg	λόγος	γραφή	ὥρα	ἔργον
gen sg	λόγου	γραφῆς	ὥρας	ἔργου
dat sg	λόγῳ	γραφῇ	ὥρᾳ	ἔργῳ
acc sg	λόγον	γραφήν	ὥραν	ἔργον
nom pl	λόγοι	γραφαί		ἔργα
gen pl	λόγων	γραφῶν		ἔργων
dat pl	λόγοις	γραφαῖς		ἔργοις
acc pl	λόγους	γραφάς		ἔργα

7.9 Hints

a. Both the masculine and neuter have the same case endings in the genitive and dative. This is *always* true.

b. In the dative an iota is *always* present for all three genders. In the singular it is subscripted.

c. The dative plural is also an iota and a sigma. The dative plural is also a longer ending (two letters) than the singular (one letter); you can associate "longer" with the plural.

d. All three genders have the ending "ων" in the genitive plural. This is *always* true.

e. Many feminine nouns ending in ας can be either genitive singular or accusative plural. Look either at the definite article (τῆς/τάς) or the context to decide.

In modern Greek, we use the plural when being formal or polite, even when speaking to one person. So perhaps in speaking to your teacher you should say, ἔρρωσθε.

The Article

7.10
Because the article is the key to learning the noun system, you should commit it to memory. There are no more forms of the article, no more possibilities; this is all you need to know. Learn them well.

	2 *masc*	1 *fem*	2 *neut*
nom sg	ὁ	ἡ	τό
gen sg	τοῦ	τῆς	τοῦ
dat sg	τῷ	τῇ	τῷ
acc sg	τόν	τήν	τό
nom pl	οἱ	αἱ	τά
gen pl	τῶν	τῶν	τῶν
dat pl	τοῖς	ταῖς	τοῖς
acc pl	τούς	τάς	τά

The Full Paradigm

7.11   Here is the full paradigm of first and second declension nouns with the article.

	2 *masc*	1 *fem*		2 *neut*
nom sg	ὁ λόγος	ἡ γραφή	ἡ ὥρα	τὸ ἔργον
gen sg	τοῦ λόγου	τῆς γραφῆς	τῆς ὥρας	τοῦ ἔργου
dat sg	τῷ λόγῳ	τῇ γραφῇ	τῇ ὥρᾳ	τῷ ἔργῳ
acc sg	τὸν λόγον	τὴν γραφήν	τὴν ὥραν	τὸ ἔργον
nom pl	οἱ λόγοι	αἱ γραφαί		τὰ ἔργα
gen pl	τῶν λόγων	τῶν γραφῶν		τῶν ἔργων
dat pl	τοῖς λόγοις	ταῖς γραφαῖς		τοῖς ἔργοις
acc pl	τοὺς λόγους	τὰς γραφάς		τὰ ἔργα

Halftime Review

1.   The genitive case can indicate possession ("of"). The word it modifies is the head noun.

2.   The dative case can indicate the ideas of "to" (indirect object), "in," and "with."

3.   The most important paradigm to memorize is 7.11.

Noun Rules

7.12   You have already learned the first three of the eight noun rules. You now need to learn the next three. Be sure to memorize them exactly.

4.   In the dative singular, the iota subscripts if possible.

γραφη + ι ‣ γραφῇ. This rule explains what happens to the dative singular case endings in the first and second declension. An iota can subscript only under a long vowel.

5.   Vowels often change their length ("ablaut").

λογο + ι ‣ λογῷ. "Ablaut" is the technical term for this. By "change their length" I mean that they can shorten (omega to omicron), lengthen (omicron to omega) as in the dative singular, or disappear entirely.[8]

---

[8]   As I said earlier, the accusative plural case ending is actually νς. When the nu drops out the stem vowel omicron lengthens to ου to "compensate" for the loss. This is called "compensatory lengthening" and is common (λογο + νς ‣ λογος ‣ λόγους). This is a form of ablaut.

6. In the genitive and dative, the masculine and neuter will always be identical.[9]

There are only two more rules to learn, and you will see them in Chapter 10 on third declension nouns.

Other Declension Patterns

7.13 **Partially declined words**. Certain words are not fully declined, or else they follow rare patterns. This is especially true of proper nouns. Instead of listing all of these separate paradigms, you will be told about the differences as you meet the words.

In this chapter you will meet the name "Jesus." Proper names are usually preceded by the definite article. Here is its declension.

nom sg	ὁ Ἰησοῦς
gen sg	τοῦ Ἰησοῦ
dat sg	τῷ Ἰησοῦ
acc sg	τὸν Ἰησοῦν

How can you tell the difference between the dative and genitive? Correct! The definite article that precedes his name will tell you.

7.14 **Alternate first declension pattern**. There are 36 first declension words in the New Testament that shift their final stem vowel in the genitive and dative singular from alpha to eta. Only four of these words occur with any frequency (see *MBG*, n-1c; see *MBG* for an explanation of this coding).

nom sg	δόξα	*n/v pl*	δόξαι
gen sg	δόξης	*gen pl*	δοξῶν
dat sg	δόξῃ	*dat pl*	δόξαις
acc sg	δόξαν	*acc pl*	δόξας

Here is the rule for the alpha to eta shift. *If a first declension word has a stem ending in alpha where the preceding letter is epsilon, iota, or rho, it will form the genitive and dative singular with alpha. Otherwise, the alpha will shift to eta.* Ask your teacher if you need to memorize this rule.

All feminine plural stems end in alpha, regardless of their form in the singular.

> Alternate way to state the rule:
> - If stem ends in a vowel or ρ, it is formed like ὥρα, -ας
> - If stem ends in a sibilant (σ, ξ, ζ), it is formed like δόξα, -ης.
> - All other feminine words are formed like γραφή, -ῆς.

Detective Work

7.15 One way to approach parsing is to think of it as a detective game. Some case endings occur in only one location. For example, λόγους must be accusative plural. It can't be anything else. A subscripted iota must be dative singular. These are the easy endings.

But other endings can occur in two or more locations. These are the endings that may require more detective work, and it is important to know

---

[9] This may lead you to think that the masculine and neuter forms are more closely aligned than the masculine and feminine. As you will see in Chapter 10, the masculine and feminine are actually more similar.

which endings fit in which category. For example, ἔργα can be nominative or accusative plural. ὥρας can be genitive singular or accusative plural.

Translation

7.16 Hints for translating genitive and dative forms.

    a.   Be sure to use your key words when you translate a word in the genitive or dative.

    b.   Whenever you see a noun, do not stop but look further to see if there is a word in the genitive following it.

> ὁ λόγος τοῦ θεοῦ σώσει ψυχάς.
>
> The word of God will save souls.

    c.   As you divide the sentence, you already know to keep the article with the noun it modifies. Now you will also keep the genitive (and its article) with the noun it modifies.

> ὁ λόγος τοῦ θεοῦ / σώσει / ψυχάς.

Summary

1. There is a chart in the Appendix that covers all the Greek cases and their different uses (page 344). Use it for reference.

2. The genitive case may indicate possession. It uses genitive case endings, and its key word is "of."

3. The dative case is used to express the ideas of "in," "with," and especially "to."

4. The indirect object "indirectly" receives the action of the verb. If you can put the word "to" in front of it, it is the indirect object. It answers the question "to whom?" or "to what?" It uses the key word "to" and dative case endings.

5. Memorize all the case endings and the twenty-four forms of the definite article. When you study the full paradigm, be sure to identify the true case endings.

6. Rule 4: In the dative singular, the iota subscripts if possible.

7. Rule 5: Vowels often change their length ("ablaut").

8. Rule 6: In the genitive and dative, the masculine and neuter will always be identical.

9. If a first declension word has a stem ending in alpha where the preceding letter is epsilon, iota, or rho, it will form the genitive and dative with alpha. Otherwise, the alpha will shift to eta.

10. When dividing a sentence into its parts, be sure to keep the article and the word in the genitive with the words they modify.

You now know the four main cases and most of the case endings. Congratulations!

Vocabulary

Now that you know the genitive case, I can explain the full form of the vocabulary listing. A noun is listed followed by sufficient letters to show you its form in the genitive, and then by its article. ἁμαρτία, -ας, ἡ means ἁμαρτία is a feminine noun (ἡ) with the genitive ἁμαρτίας. Always memorize the genitive form with the nominative. This habit will become especially important later on.

ἁμαρτία, -ας, ἡ	sin (173; *ἁμαρτια)[10]
ἀρχή, -ῆς, ἡ	beginning, ruler (55; *ἀρχη)[11]
γάρ	for, then (1,041)
	γάρ is postpositive.
εἶπεν	he/she/it said (613)
	εἶπεν is third person singular. The frequency of this form is not included in the running totals because it is an inflected form. You will meet its lexical form later.
εἰς	into, in, among (1,767)[12]
ἐξουσία, -ας, ἡ	authority, power (102; *ἐξουσια)
εὐαγγέλιον, -ου, τό	good news, Gospel (76; *εὐαγγελιο)[13]
Ἰησοῦς, -οῦ, ὁ	Jesus, Joshua (917; *Ἰησου)
κύριος, -ου, ὁ	Lord, lord, master, sir (717; *κυριο)[14]
μή	not, lest (1,042)
	μή has the same basic meaning as οὐ but is used in different situations that I will discuss later. When οὐ μή occur together, they form an emphatic negation: "No!"
οὐρανός, -οῦ, ὁ	heaven, sky (273; *οὐρανο)[15]
	You will often find οὐρανός in the plural. This is the result of a Jewish way of speaking, and you can translate the plural as a singular if it fits the context.
οὗτος, αὕτη, τοῦτο	singular: this (one) (1,387; *τουτο)[16] plural: these
	As an adjective it means "this" (singular) and "these" (plural), and as a noun it means "this one."

---

[10] ἁμαρτία describes both a specific act of sin ("a sin") as well as the concept itself ("sin," "sinfulness"). *Hamartiology* is the study of sin.

[11] The *archbishop* is the *chief* bishop over the archbishopric. The chief angel is the *archangel*.

[12] In Classical Greek there was less overlap in meaning between εἰς ("into") and ἐν ("in"), but in Koine Greek there is more. *Eisegesis* is poor hermeneutical practice because it reads a meaning into the text instead of drawing it out of (*exegesis*) the text.

[13] An *evangelist* preaches the good news of the gospel.

[14] *Kyrie eleison* is a petitionary prayer used by some Eastern and Roman churches.

[15] *Uranus* is the Greek god of heaven.

[16] There is much more to this word than I am presenting here. Its form changes considerably in its different genders, and the initial tau of the root is sometimes replaced with a rough breathing. οὗτος is covered in detail in Chapter 13.

σύ	you (singular) (1,067)
	In English, "you" can be either singular or plural. σύ is always singular. Greek has a different form for the plural.
υἱός, -οῦ, ὁ	son, descendant; child (377; *υἱο)
ὥστε	therefore, so that (83)

Total word count in the New Testament:	138,162
Number of words learned to date:	53
Number of word occurrences in this chapter:	9,077
Number of word occurrences to date:	59,902
Percent of total word count in the New Testament:	43.35%

WORKBOOK SUMMARY

Previous Words

You need to learn the genitives for all the nouns in chapters 4 and 6. You will notice that several of the nouns have no expressed genitive form. This is because they are indeclinable. They can function in any of the cases but will not change their form.

Do not worry about the genitive of πνεῦμα and Σίμων until Chapter 10.

Ἀβραάμ, ὁ	θεός, -οῦ, ὁ
ἀγάπη, -ης, ἡ	καιρός, -οῦ, ὁ — *appointed Time*
ἄγγελος, -ου, ὁ	καρδία, -ας, ἡ
ἄνθρωπος, -ου, ὁ	κόσμος, ου, ὁ
ἀπόστολος, -ου, ὁ	λόγος, -ου, ὁ
αὐτός, -οῦ *-he/she/it pl: they*	Παῦλος, -ου, ὁ
βασιλεία, -ας, ἡ	Πέτρος, -ου, ὁ
Γαλιλαία, -ας, ἡ	Πιλᾶτος, -ου, ὁ
γραφή, -ῆς, ἡ	προφήτης, ου, ὁ[17]
Δαυίδ, ὁ	σάββατον, -ου, τό[18]
δόξα, -ης, ἡ — *glory*	φωνή, -ῆς, ἡ — *sound, noise*
ἔργον, -ου, τό — *work/deed*	Χριστός, -οῦ, ὁ
ζωή, -ῆς, ἡ[19] — *life*	ὥρα, -ας, ἡ — *hour*

---

[17] Did you notice that this word is different from what you are used to? The ης ending looks like a genitive singular but actually is nominative singular. Also, it is a first declension word but is masculine. Remember I said that most—not all—first declension nouns are feminine.

 The genitive singular of this word is προφήτου. In essence, it borrowed the second declension genitive singular case ending so it could be different from the nominative singular. The rest of the paradigm follows the regular first declension pattern. See paradigm n-1f in the *Appendix* for the full paradigm.

[18] The dative plural occurs as σάββασι(ν), as if it were a third declension word (Chapter 10).

[19] ζωή never occurs in the Bible in the genitive plural, but it would be ζωῶν. The two omegas would not simplify to a single omega.

Exegesis

Genitive

1. The most common use of the genitive is when the word in the genitive gives some description of the head noun (descriptive).

    > ἐνδυσώμεθα τὰ ὅπλα <u>τοῦ φωτός</u> *(Rom 13:12).*
    > Let us put on the armor *of light.*

2. The word in the genitive can be possessed by the head noun (possessive).

    > ὕπαγε πώλησόν <u>σου</u> τὰ ὑπάρχοντα *(Matt 19:21).*
    > Go, sell *your* possessions.

3. In a general sense, if you have a noun that in some way equals the meaning of another noun, the writer can put the noun in the genitive, and it is said to be in apposition to the head noun. It is as if you drew an equals sign between the two words. The translations will often add a word or punctuation to help make this clear.

    > λήμψεσθε τὴν δωρεὰν <u>τοῦ ἁγίου πνεύματος</u> *(Acts 2:38).*
    > You will receive the gift, *the Holy Spirit.*

4. The word in the genitive can indicate something that is separate from the head noun or verb. It will often use the helping word "from" (separation).

    > ἀπηλλοτριωμένοι <u>τῆς πολιτείας</u> τοῦ Ἰσραὴλ *(Eph 2:12)*
    > being alienated *from the commonwealth* of the Israel

5. This category and the next two are extremely important. They occur with a head noun that expresses a verbal idea (i.e., the cognate noun can also occur as a verb). These three categories often present the translator with significantly different interpretations.

    Sometimes the word in the genitive functions as if it were the subject of the verbal idea implicit in the head noun (subjective). You can use the helping word "produced" to help identify this usage. "The love produced by Christ."

    > τίς ἡμᾶς χωρίσει ἀπὸ τῆς ἀγάπης <u>τοῦ Χριστοῦ</u> *(Rom 8:35).*
    > Who will separate us from *Christ's* love?

6. The word in the genitive functions as the direct object of the verbal idea implicit in the head noun (objective). This is the opposite of the subjective genitive. You can use the key word "receives." "The blasphemy received by the Spirit."

    > ἡ <u>τοῦ πνεύματος</u> βλασφημία οὐκ ἀφεθήσεται *(Matt 12:31).*
    > The blasphemy *against the Spirit* will not be forgiven.

7. Sometimes it appears that the word in the genitive is a combination of both the objective and subjective genitive (plenary).

    > ἡ γὰρ ἀγάπη <u>τοῦ Χριστοῦ</u> συνέχει ἡμᾶς *(2 Cor 5:14).*
    > For the love *of Christ* compels us.

8. The genitive can indicate a familial relationship between a word and its head noun (relationship). Often the head noun is not expressed, so it is up to the translator's interpretive skills to determine the exact nature of the relationship.

> Σίμων Ἰωάννου *(John 21:15)*
> Simon, *son of John*

> Μαρία ἡ Ἰακώβου *(Luke 24:10)*
> Mary the *mother of James*

9. Sometimes the noun in the genitive is a larger unit, while its head noun represents a smaller portion of it (partitive).

> τινες τῶν κλάδων *(Rom 11:17)*
> some *of the branches*

Dative

It is common for grammars to break the dative into three sub-sections: dative proper; locative; instrumental.

Dative Proper ("to")

1. The indirect object functions the same in Greek as it does in English, with the indirect object placed in the dative case.

> ἐξουσίαν ἔδωκεν αὐτῷ κρίσιν ποιεῖν *(John 5:27)*.
> He has given *him* authority to execute judgment.

2. The dative can express the idea of "for" (dative of interest).

> ἡ γυνή σου Ἐλισάβετ γεννήσει υἱόν σοι *(Luke 1:13)*.
> Your wife Elizabeth will bear a son *for you*.

When the idea is for the person's advantage, as in Luke 1:13 above, we call it a "dative of advantage." When context tells us that it is not for the person's advantage, we can call it a "dative of disadvantage" and often use a different preposition based on the meaning of the phrase.

> μαρτυρεῖτε ἑαυτοῖς *(Matt 23:31)*.
> You testify *against yourselves*.

3. The dative can indicate what in English is awkwardly expressed by the phrase "with respect to," or here with "to" (reference, respect).

> λογίζεσθε ἑαυτοὺς εἶναι νεκροὺς τῇ ἁμαρτίᾳ *(Rom 6:11)*.
> Consider yourselves to be dead *to sin*.

Locative ("in," "with")

4. There is a little more nebulous use of the dative, indicating the sphere or realm in which something occurs (sphere).

> μακάριοι οἱ καθαροὶ τῇ καρδίᾳ *(Matt 5:8)*.
> Blessed are the pure *in heart*.

5. A time designation in the dative specifies when something occurs (time).

> τῇ τρίτῃ ἡμέρᾳ ἐγερθήσεται *(Matt 17:23)*.
> *On the third day* he will be raised.

6. The dative can indicate the idea of "with" (association).

> μὴ γίνεσθε ἑτεροζυγοῦντες ἀπίστοις *(2 Cor 6:14)*.
> Do not be unequally yoked *with unbelievers*.

Instrumental ("by")

7. The dative can indicate the manner in which something is done (manner).

> παρρησίᾳ λαλεῖ *(John 7:26)*.
> He speaks *boldly*.

8. The dative can also show the means (or the instrument) by which an action was accomplished (means, instrument).

> Τῇ γὰρ χάριτί ἐστε σεσῳσμένοι *(Eph 2:8)*.
> For it is *by grace* you have been saved.

Ever feel like your mind is as barren as Sinai? If God kept the Children of Israel fed in a place like this, he can help you to persevere in Greek. This picture was taken half way up Mt. Sinai.

Basics of Biblical Greek

Chapter 8

Prepositions and εἰμί

Exegetical Insight

"Hand this man over to Satan, so that the sinful nature may be destroyed and his spirit saved on the day of the Lord" (1 Cor 5:5, NIV). So reads Paul's command to the Christians about the man who was having an affair with his stepmother. The NIV margin notes that "sinful nature" (literally, "flesh") could also be translated "body." Commentators are divided as to whether Paul envisions simple excommunication or actual death here, though the former seems more probable. But either way, this command seems harsh by modern standards, particularly in the majority of our congregations that exercise little or no formal church discipline of any kind.

An understanding of the preposition εἰς can shed some light on this verse. The NIV reads as if there were two equally balanced purposes behind Paul's command: one punitive and one remedial. But the Greek prefaces the first with an εἰς and the second with the conjunction ἵνα. Εἰς can denote either result or purpose; ἵνα far more commonly denotes purpose. Paul's change of language is likely deliberate—to point out that his *purpose* in discipline is entirely rehabilitative, even if one of the *results* of his action is temporary exclusion and ostracism of

the persistently rebellious sinner. Or in Gordon Fee's words, "What the grammar suggests, then, is that the 'destruction of the flesh' is the anticipated result of the man's being put back out into Satan's domain, while the express purpose of the action is his redemption."

Not every scholar agrees with this interpretation. But being able to read only a translation like the NIV would never alert us to this as an option. Growing exposure to the Greek of the New Testament brings us into frequent contact with numerous prepositions and other connective words that are often left untranslated in English versions, for the sake of literary style and fluency. But in reading only the English, we may miss altogether the originally intended relationship between sentences and clauses, and we may import motives to writers they never held. Whatever the final solution to 1 Cor 5:5 turns out to be, it is certainly true that in every other New Testament instance of church discipline, the purpose was exclusively remedial or rehabilitative and never punitive or vengeful. "The Lord disciplines those he loves" (Heb 12:6), and so should we.

Craig L. Blomberg

In this chapter you will learn the following:

- prepositions are little words like "over," "under," and "through" that define the relationship between two words;

- the word following the preposition is called the *object* of the preposition;

- how the meaning of a preposition changes;

- dependent clauses;

- εἰμί and predicate nominatives.

English

8.1   **Prepositions**. A preposition is a word that indicates the relationship between two words. In the sentence, "The book is *under* the table," the preposition "under" describes the relationship between "book" and "table," which in this case is a spatial relationship. What are some other prepositions in English?

> Her feet are *on* the chair.
>
> The ball went *over* his head.
>
> John came *with* his disciples.
>
> John came *before* Jesus.

The word that follows the preposition is called the **object of the preposition**. In the first example above, the object of the preposition "under" is "table."

The object of the preposition is always in the objective case. You would not say, "The book is under he." You would say, "The book is under him." "He" is subjective and "him" is objective.

The preposition together with its object and modifiers is called a **prepositional phrase**.

8.2   **Predicate nominative**. The verb "to be" gives rise to a special situation. (The verb "to be" has many different forms: "am"; "are"; "was"; "were"; etc.) If you say, "The teacher is I," the pronoun "I" is not receiving the action of the verb. Rather, it is telling you something about the subject. In grammarians' terminology, the pronoun "I" is "predicating" something about the subject.

Because it is not receiving the action of the verb, the pronoun cannot be a direct object. Rather, it is called a "predicate nominative" and is put in the subjective case. It is incorrect English to say, "The teacher is me," regardless of current usage, because "me" is objective while "I" is subjective.

Greek

8.3 The function of a preposition in Greek is the same as English. There is one important fact, however, you need to understand about Greek prepositions. *In Greek, the meaning of a preposition depends upon the case of its object.* For example, the preposition διά means "through" if its object is in the genitive, but "on account of" if its object is in the accusative.[1] The object almost always immediately follows the preposition.

Some prepositions are always followed by the same case, so they only have one set of meanings. For example, the preposition ἐν always takes an object in the dative and has the basic meaning "in." But other prepositions can be followed by two cases, and a few can even be followed by three cases. The object will never be in the nominative (except under rare circumstances).

8.4 **Flash cards**. For the purpose of memorization, you should make a separate flash card for each case. In other words, one flash card should say, "διά with the genitive," while another should say, "διά with the accusative."

To address a man as "Sir" or "Mr," say, κύριε.

To say "Miss" or "Mrs.," say, κυρία.

Just like αὐτός, the difference between masculine (κύριε) and feminine (κυρία) is in the ending. These endings are technically in the vocative case, which we will learn in Chapter 13.

8.5 **Key words**. Earlier you learned to use the key word "of" with the genitive and "to" with the dative. *However, if a word is in the genitive or dative because it is the object of a preposition, do not use the key word.*

For example, ὁ λόγος τοῦ θεοῦ means, "the word *of* God." The key word "of" is used since θεοῦ is showing possession. However, the phrase ὁ λόγος ἀπὸ θεοῦ is translated "the word from God." (ἀπό is a preposition meaning "from" and takes its object in the genitive.) You would not say "the word from *of* God," since θεοῦ is genitive due to the preposition.

8.6 **Not inflected**. The form of a preposition does not vary depending on its usage; it is not inflected. παρά will be παρά whether its object is in the genitive, dative, or accusative.

The only time the preposition changes its form has nothing to do with inflection. When certain prepositions ending in a vowel are followed by a word beginning with a vowel, the final vowel of the preposition may be dropped and marked with an apostrophe. This is called "elision" (cf. 4.2).

> μετὰ αὐτόν ‣ μετ᾿ αὐτόν

When a preposition ends in a vowel and the following word begins with a vowel *and a rough breathing*, the consonant before the vowel in the preposition often changes as well. These changes were necessary in order to pronounce the combination of sounds more easily.

> μετὰ ἡμῶν ‣ μετ᾿ ἡμῶν ‣ μεθ᾿ ἡμῶν

You may want to make separate vocabulary cards for each of these altered forms. Each form will be listed in the vocabulary section.

---

[1] Technically, this is not accurate. The object does not govern the preposition, but the preposition governs the object. In other words, when a preposition has a specific meaning, it requires that the object be in a certain case. But from the translator's point of view, it is easier to look at the case of the object, and from that determine the meaning of the preposition.

8.7 When memorizing the definition of a preposition, I suggest you use this formula:

> _____ with the _____ means _____ .
> ἐν with the *dative* means *in*.

8.8 When asked to explain why the object of the preposition is in a given case, I suggest you respond with the complete formula:

> _____ is in the _____ because it is the object of the preposition _____ that takes the _____.
> αὐτῷ is in the *dative* because it is the object of the preposition ἐν that takes the *dative*.

Dependent Clauses

8.9 In this chapter you will learn the word ἵνα meaning "in order that." ἵνα is always the first word in what is called a "dependent clause." In Chapter 6 you learned the word ὅτι. It also introduces a dependent clause.

A dependent clause is a collection of words that cannot stand alone. It has meaning only when it is part of a complete sentence; it is dependent upon that sentence. For example, in English the clause "if I go home" is not a sentence. It is incomplete when standing on its own. It is therefore dependent on the main sentence. "If I go home, I will eat dinner."

Here is the important point: *as you are looking for the main subject and verb in a sentence, you will never find them in a dependent clause.* There will be a subject and verb in the dependent clause, but they will not be the main subject and verb of the sentence.

Halftime Review

- It has been said that a preposition is anything a rabbit can do with its home. He can go in it, around it, dig under it, etc.

- A prepositional phrase is the preposition and its object (with modifiers).

- Prepositions govern the case of their object, and so key words are not used.

- Prepositions are not inflected but the ending can change.

- A dependent clause will not contain the main subject and verb of the sentence.

εἰμί

8.10 The formal study of verbs has been deferred until Chapter 15. For now, you are to concentrate on nouns and learn them well. Later you will tackle verbs. However, there is one common verb worth learning right now, εἰμί.

You may want to review the verbal grammar discussed at 5.14-16.

8.11 **Basic verbal grammar**. The basic part of a verb is called the **stem**. The stem carries the basic meaning of the verb. **Personal endings** are added to the end of the stem to indicate person and number.

There are three **persons**, grammatically speaking. You have already seen them in pronouns. ἐγώ is first person, "I." σύ is second person, "you." αὐτός is third person, "he," "she," or "it." These are all singular pronouns; there are plural forms as well.

Likewise, personal endings on verbs indicate person. For example, the εις ending on γράφεις tells you that the subject is "you" (singular). The ει ending on γράφει tells you that the subject is "he," "she," or "it." γράφεις means "you write," and γράφει means "he writes."

A verb **agrees** with its subject, which means that its personal ending is the same person and number as its subject.

8.12 εἰμί is the most common verb in Greek and needs to be memorized. In the paradigm below, "1st" means "first person," etc. "Sg" means "singular," and "pl" means "plural." This is the present tense form of the verb.

1st sg	εἰμί	I am
2nd sg	εἶ	You are
3rd sg	ἐστίν	He/she/it is
1st pl	ἐσμέν	We are
2nd pl	ἐστέ	You² are
3rd pl	εἰσίν	They are

Except for εἶ, the forms of εἰμί are enclitics, which means they push their accent back on the previous word; they will normally not have an accent of their own.

8.13 **Movable nu**. A movable nu is a nu occurring at the end of a word that ends with a vowel when the following word begins with a vowel (e.g., εἰσὶν αὐτοί). The purpose of adding the nu was to avoid pronouncing two successive vowels. By adding a nu, a pause is created and the two vowel sounds can be distinguished. This is like changing the English "a" to "an" when the next word begins with a vowel.

The nu in the third singular ἐστίν is a movable nu, but ἐστί occurs only once in the New Testament (Acts 18:10). The nu in the third plural εἰσίν is also a movable nu, but εἰσί never occurs.

Often in Koine Greek the movable nu is used even when the following word begins with a consonant, especially in the dative plural; it also occurs when it is the last word in a clause. Since you are learning to read Greek and not to write it, this presents no problem.

8.14 The past tense form of ἐστί(ν) is ἦν, "he/she/it was." It occurs frequently and you should memorize it now.

---

² In English we use the same word ("you") for the second person pronoun, both singular and plural. Various ways have been suggested to distinguish them in your translation (e.g., "thou" and "ye," "you" and "y'all"). I will use "you" for both, but your teacher may prefer another method. In class I tend to use "y'all" for plural, but I lived in Kentucky for several years and like the word.

8.15 **Predicate nominative**. The second function of the nominative case is the predicate[3] nominative. Just as it is in English, a noun that follows εἰμί is not receiving the action from the verb but rather is telling you something about the subject.[4] Therefore the word is in the nominative case. (κύριος means "Lord.")

θεὸς ἐστιν κύριος.

Notice that in this sentence both the first and last words are in the nominative case. Context should make clear which is the subject and which is the predicate.[5]

Translation

8.16 When you are dividing your sentences into sections, make sure to separate the prepositional phrase (or any other dependent clause) as a distinct group and see what word the preposition modifies. It usually will be a verb.

ὁ λόγος / ἔρχεται / εἰς τὸν κόσμον.
The word / goes / into the world.

8.17 Greek regularly drops the article in a prepositional phrase. If it fits the context, you may put it back in.

ὁ λόγος ἔρχεται εἰς κόσμον.
The word goes into *the* world.

Summary

1. The word following the preposition is the object of the preposition, and the preposition and its object and modifiers form a prepositional phrase.

2. The meaning of a preposition is determined by the case of its object. Always memorize the prepositions with the case(s) of their objects.

3. Do not use the key words when translating the object of a preposition.

4. Prepositions are not inflected, but their endings can change depending on the following word.

5. A dependent clause cannot contain the main subject and verb in a sentence.

6. Memorize εἰμί. It is always followed by a predicate nominative.

7. The article is often omitted from Greek prepositional phrases. You can supply it if the context requires it.

---

[3] Grammatically, the "predicate" is the verb and everything that follows it. It is what is left when you remove the subject and its modifiers.

[4] The verb "to be" is called an "equative verb" in that it draws an equals sign between the subject and the predicate nominative.

[5] This sentence would actually be written, κύριός ἐστιν ὁ θεός, the article also indicating the subject.

Vocabulary

In this chapter you will learn seven prepositions, two-thirds of all major prepositions. Many students find a graphic representation easier than relying on rote memory. The following chart illustrates the spatial relationship of the prepositions learned in this chapter. Notice that only some of the meanings can be spatially mapped.

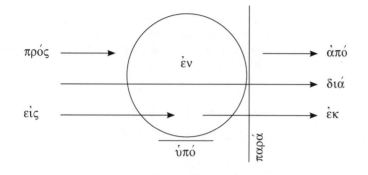

Learning the prepositions in pairs (e.g., πρός and ἀπό) may also help memorization.

ἀλλά (ἀλλ᾽)	but, yet, except (638)
	When the word following ἀλλά begins with a vowel, the final alpha elides (ἀλλὰ Ἰησοῦς › ἀλλ᾽ Ἰησοῦς).
ἀπό (ἀπ᾽, ἀφ᾽)	gen: (away) from (646)[6]
	When ἀπό is followed by a word beginning with a vowel, the omicron drops out (ἀπ᾽ αὐτῶν). If the following word begins with a vowel and rough breathing, it becomes ἀφ᾽ (ἀφ᾽ ὑμῶν).
διά (δι᾽)	gen: through (667)[7]
	acc: on account of
εἰμί	I am, exist, live, am present (2,462)
ἐκ (ἐξ)[8]	gen: from, out of (914)[9]
	When ἐκ is followed by a word beginning with a vowel, it is written ἐξ (ἐξ ὑμῶν).
ἡμέρα, -ας, ἡ	day (389; *ἡμερα)[10]
ἦν	he/she/it was (315)
θάλασσα, -ης, ἡ	sea, lake (91; *θαλασσα)[11]

There are places on the internet where you can look for more if you want. Google "Greek name" to find many options.

You can also get software modules for Josephus, Philo, or a Classical Greek lexicon for many Bible search programs like Accordance. Search away!

---

[6]   *Apostasy* (ἀποστασία) is when a person stands off from the truth.

[7]   The *diameter* (διάμετρος) measures through the middle of an object.

[8]   If you are really curious, the preposition proper is ἐξ. When it is followed by a word beginning with a consonant, the "sigma" in the xi drops out (think of ξ as "xs") because it is an "interconsonantal sigma," i.e., the sigma occurs between two consonants (exs + consonant › ex › ἐκ).

[9]   *Ecstasy* (ἔκστασις) is to stand outside of oneself.

[10]   *Ephemeral* (ἐφήμερος) means that it lasts only one day, is short-lived.

[11]   *Thalassian* (θαλάσσιος) means "pertaining to the sea."

θάνατος, -ου, ὁ	death (120; *θανατο)[12]
ἵνα	in order that, that (663)
Ἰωάννης, -ου, ὁ	John (135; * Ἰωαννη)
	This word follows the same pattern as προφήτης (n-1f, page 343).
λέγω	I say, speak (2,353)
μετά (μετ᾽, μεθ᾽)	gen: with (469)[13]
	acc: after
	When μετά is followed by a word beginning with a vowel, the alpha drops out (μετ᾽ αὐτοῦ). If the next word begins with a vowel and rough breathing, it becomes μεθ᾽ (μεθ᾽ ὑμᾶς).
οἰκία, -ας, ἡ	house, home (93; *οἰκια)
οἶκος, -ου, ὁ	house, home (114; *οἰκο)[14]
ὄχλος, -ου, ὁ	crowd, multitude (175; *ὀχλο)[15]
παρά (παρ᾽)	gen: from (194)[16]
	dat: beside, in the presence of
	acc: alongside of
παραβολή, -ῆς, ἡ	parable (50; *παραβολη)[17]
πρός	acc: to, towards, with (700)[18]
ὑπό (ὑπ᾽, ὑφ᾽)	gen: by (220)[19]
	acc: under
	When ὑπό is followed by a word beginning with a vowel, the omicron drops out (ὑπ᾽ αὐτοῦ). If the following word begins with a vowel and rough breathing, it becomes ὑφ᾽ (ὑφ᾽ ὑμᾶς).

---

[12] *Euthanasia* ("easy death") refers to a painless death, or allowing or putting to death by withholding medical treatment. *Thanatophobia* is an abnormal fear of death. *Thanatopsis* is a contemplation of death, and the name of a poem by William Cullen Bryant, a good poem but unorthodox in theology. "When thoughts of the last bitter hour come like a blight over thy spirit, and sad images of the stern agony, and shroud, and pall, and breathless darkness, and the narrow house, make thee to shudder, and grow sick at heart; — go forth, under the open sky, and list to nature's teachings...."

[13] The object of μετά with the genitive will usually be a person or a personal concept. Another preposition (σύν) is used when the object is impersonal. *Metaphysics* is the discussion in Aristotle that comes after his discussion of physics (τὰ μετὰ τὰ φυσικά).

[14] There is no real difference between οἰκία and οἶκος.

[15] *Ochlocracy* is mob rule.

[16] A *paragraph* (παράγραφος) was originally a line in the margin beside the writing that marked a division.

[17] A *parable* is a story "thrown beside" (παρά + βάλλω) life.

[18] A *proselyte* (προσήλυτος) is a person who has come over to another religion.

[19] The object of ὑπό will usually be a person or a personal concept. An *hypothesis* (ὑπόθεσις) is a foundational supposition, which is placed (*θε, forming the Greek word, "I place") under other arguments. A *hypodermic* needle is one that goes under the skin (δέρμα).

Total word count in the New Testament:	138,162
Number of words learned to date:	72
Number of word occurrences in this chapter:	11,093
Number of word occurrences to date:	70,995
Percent of total word count in the New Testament:	51.38%

You now know more than one out of every two word occurrences in the New Testament. Congratulations!

Previous Words

εἰς   acc: into, in, among[20]

ἐν   dat: in, on, among

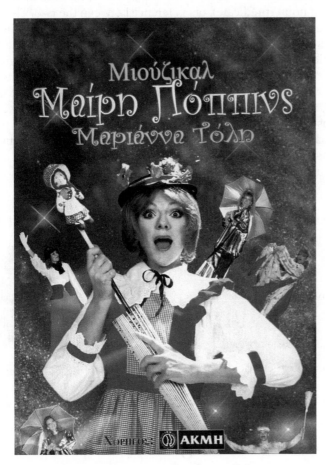

I'll let you figure out what this is all about.

---

[20] "Eisegesis" is poor hermeneutical practice because it reads a meaning into the text instead of drawing it out of ("exegesis") the text.

Chapter 9

Adjectives

Exegetical Insight

Adjectives have a theological importance that is hard to rival. They can modify a noun (attributive), assert something about a noun (predicate), or stand in the place of a noun (substantival). Sometimes it is difficult to tell exactly which role a particular adjective is in.

Take the adjective πονηροῦ ("evil") in Matthew 6:13, for example. The King James Version (as well as more than one modern translation) translates this as "but deliver us from *evil*." But the adjective has an article modifying it (τοῦ), indicating that it is to be taken substantivally: "the evil one."

And there is no little theological difference between the two. The Father does not always keep his children out of danger, disasters, or the ugliness of the world. In short, he does not always deliver us from evil. But he does deliver us from the evil *one*. The text is not teaching that God will make our life a rose garden, but that he will protect us from the evil one, the devil himself (cf. John 10:28-30; 17:15).

Daniel B. Wallace

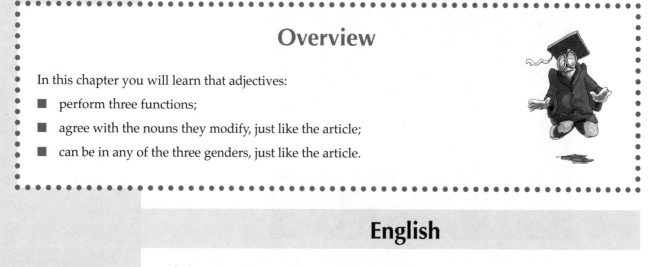

Overview

In this chapter you will learn that adjectives:

■ perform three functions;

■ agree with the nouns they modify, just like the article;

■ can be in any of the three genders, just like the article.

English

9.1 An **adjective** is a word that modifies a noun or pronoun. Adjectives can perform three functions.

9.2　An **attributive** adjective gives a quality—an attribute—to the word it is modifying. This is the normal use of the adjective.

> "She learned *modern* Greek."

The term it modifies is called the **head** term.

> "She learned modern *Greek*."

9.3　A **substantival** adjective functions as if it were a noun.

> "The *Good*, the *Bad*, and the *Ugly* are all welcome here."
> "Out with the *old* and in with the *new*."

In this case the adjective does not modify anything.[1]

9.4　A **predicate** adjective asserts something about the subject, and the verb "to be" is either stated or implied.

> "The students are *good*."
> "God is *true*."

So now that you have a name, let's say "Hi, my name is ...." and supply your Greek name.

ὄνομα μοι ＿＿＿ ἐστιν.

- ὄνομα is "name."
- μοι is "to me."
- ἐστιν you learned as "he is," but it can also mean "it is."

The order is different for us, but this is how a Greek person would make this statement.

Greek

9.5　Greek adjectives function much like their English counterparts.

9.6　**Form**. The adjectives in this chapter all use the same case endings you have learned for nouns. Notice that adjectives can occur in all three genders, like the article. ἀγαθός is an adjective meaning "good."

	2 *masc*	1 *fem*	2 *neut*
nom sg	ἀγαθός	ἀγαθή	ἀγαθόν
gen sg	ἀγαθοῦ	ἀγαθῆς	ἀγαθοῦ
dat sg	ἀγαθῷ	ἀγαθῇ	ἀγαθῷ
acc sg	ἀγαθόν	ἀγαθήν	ἀγαθόν
nom pl	ἀγαθοί	ἀγαθαί	ἀγαθά
gen pl	ἀγαθῶν	ἀγαθῶν	ἀγαθῶν
dat pl	ἀγαθοῖς	ἀγαθαῖς	ἀγαθοῖς
acc pl	ἀγαθούς	ἀγαθάς	ἀγαθά

Notice the many similarities among these endings and those already learned for nouns and the article.

9.7　**Lexical form**. The lexical form of any word that can appear in more than one gender is the nominative singular masculine (as you have already seen with the article). For example, the lexical form of the dative plural feminine ἀγαθαῖς is ἀγαθός, not ἀγαθή.

---

[1]　In a sense you could say the noun it modifies is assumed, and the substantival function is really a subset of the attributive.

Functions of the Adjective

9.8 **Attributive**. When an adjective functions as an attributive, it *agrees with the word it modifies in case, number, and gender*. This is the most common use of the adjective in Greek.

> ὁ ἀγαθὸς λόγος ἐστίν …
>
> The good word is …

■ Because nouns can be in three different genders, and because an attributive adjective must agree with the noun it modifies in gender (as well as case and number), an adjective must be able to be masculine, feminine, or neuter.[2]

■ It is essential to memorize the gender of all nouns. It will help you determine which noun the adjective is modifying. For example, the adjective ἀγαθή could not be modifying the noun ἄνθρωπος, because ἀγαθή is feminine and ἄνθρωπος is masculine.

9.9 **Substantival**. When an adjective functions as a substantive, its *case is determined by its function* as is true of any noun. For example, if the adjective is functioning as the subject of a verb, it will be in the nominative case.

> ὁ ἀγαθός ἐστιν …
>
> The good (person) is …

Its *gender and number are determined by what it stands for*. For example, if it stands for a single entity, and that entity is masculine, then the adjective would be masculine singular (as above).

Use your common sense to translate a substantival adjective. Ask these questions of the text in order to translate the adjective.

■ What case is it?

If, for example, the adjective is in the accusative case, it must be the direct object of the verb or the object of a preposition.

■ What gender and number is it?

You can often follow natural gender in deciding how to translate. You can add an extra word (e.g., "man," "woman," "thing," "person," "one") to make sense of the construction in English.

inflected	parsing	translation
ἀγαθός	masculine singular	a good man a good person
ἀγαθαί	feminine plural	good women
ἀγαθόν	neuter singular	a good thing
οἱ ἀγαθοί	masculine as generic	the good ones the good people

The other half of the conversation is to ask, "What is your name?"

τί σοι ὄνομά ἐστιν;

■ τί is "what?" It can also mean "why?"

■ σοι looks like μοι but means "to you," not "to me."

■ ὄνομα you know.

■ ἐστιν; you know, but notice the punctuation.

In modern Greek you indicate a question by raising your voice at the end of the question. Perhaps they did the same in Koine Greek.

---

[2]   Whether an adjective has a feminine stem ending in eta (ἀγαθή) or alpha (νεκρά) is determined not by the noun it modifies but by the adjective itself. All that an adjective must do is agree in case, number, and gender. How it does this, and what form it uses, is a function of the adjective. Thus the adjective may have an –ης in the genitive even though the noun that it modifies has –ας (e.g., τῆς ἀγαθῆς ὥρας).

Of course, ἀγαθός could be simply translated "good" if that meets the needs of the sentence.

9.10 **Predicate**. When an adjective functions as a predicate, it does not modify another word but rather asserts—predicates—something about the subject. If the verb εἰμί is implied (rather than explicitly stated), you may have to supply it in your translation.

> ὁ ἄνθρωπος ἀγαθός
> The man is good.

Halftime Review

- An attributive adjective gives an attribute to a noun, which is called the "head noun." The attributive adjective agrees with its head noun in case, number, and gender.

- A substantival adjective functions as a noun. Its case is determined by function, number and gender by what it stands for. They tend to follow natural gender.

- A predicate adjective asserts something about the subject and uses the verb "to be."

- The lexical form of any word that occurs in more than one gender is the nominative singular masculine.

Recognition of the Adjective

9.11 The question then becomes, how can you identify which function an adjective is performing? It all depends on whether the definite article is present or not.

"Anarthrous" means there is no article; "articular" means there is an article.

9.12 **Presence of the article**. If the article occurs immediately before the adjective, then you have either an attributive or substantival adjective.

- *Attributive*. If there is a noun to modify, then the adjective is attributive. The adjective can come before or after the noun; there is no significant difference in meaning. However, the adjective must be preceded by the article. Both examples mean, "the good man."

    First attributive position: ὁ ἀγαθὸς ἄνθρωπος
    Second attributive position: ὁ ἄνθρωπος ὁ ἀγαθός

    You will never find ὁ ἀγαθὸς ὁ ἄνθρωπος.[3]

---

[3]   There is a third attributive position. See Advanced Information.

- *Substantival*. However, if there is no noun for the adjective to modify, then it is probably functioning substantivally.

ὁ ἀγαθός	the good (man; person)
τὴν πιστήν	the faithful (woman)

- *Predicate*. If the noun is articular but the adjective is anarthrous (e.g., ὁ ἄνθρωπος ἀγαθός), then the adjective is functioning as a predicate adjective. In this case you will supply the verb "is" to show the predicating nature of the adjective.

ὁ ἄνθρωπος ἀγαθός	The man is good.
ἀγαθὸς ὁ ἄνθρωπος	The man is good.

9.13   **Absence of the article**. If there is no article before either the noun or the adjective, context becomes the guide to translation. You must decide whether the adjective is giving an attribute to a noun or is asserting something about the verb. If the verb εἰμί is not explicitly present, it may be implied and you can supply it in your translation if English requires it.

ἀγαθὸς ἄνθρωπος	"A good man" or "A man is good."
ἄνθρωπος ἀγαθός	"A good man" or "A man is good."

Be sure not to supply the article in your translation unless English demands it.

It is possible for an anarthrous adjective to function substantivally, but it is unusual.

ἀγαθός	a good (man; person)

Odds 'n Ends

9.14   **Article and a prepositional phrase**. You will often find the article followed by a prepositional phrase. You will generally translate these as relative clauses.

- Sometimes this occurs in an "article-noun-article-modifier" construction where the second article tells you the prepositional phrase is modifying the noun.

  τοὺς παῖδας τοὺς ἐν Βηθλέεμ *(Matt 2:16)*
  The children *who are in Bethlehem (Matt 2:16)*

- Other times the article is in effect turning the prepositional phrase into a substantive.

  ἐλάλησαν τὸν λόγον τοῦ κυρίου πᾶσιν τοῖς ἐν τῇ οἰκίᾳ.
  They spoke the word of the Lord to all *who were in the house.*

9.15   **2-2 Adjective**. You will meet an adjective in this chapter listed as αἰώνιος, -ον. This means αἰώνιος can be either masculine or feminine; αἰώνιον is neuter. Context will show if αἰώνιος is masculine or feminine.

It is a "2 - 2" pattern because the masculine and feminine follow the second declension, and the neuter also follows the second declension.[4]

---

4   In our nomenclature, these adjectives are classified as "a-3," specifically a-3b(1). See *MBG* for the full paradigm.

9.16 **Neuter plural subjects**. Greek normally uses a singular verb when the subject is neuter plural. It is an indication that the writer is viewing the plural subject not as a collection of different things but as one group. To keep proper English, you will use a plural verb.

> δοκιμάζετε τὰ πνεύματα εἰ ἐκ τοῦ θεοῦ <u>ἐστιν</u> *(1 John 4:1)*.
> Test the spirits (and see) if *they are* from God.

Translation Procedure

9.17 As you divide your sentences into the different parts, be sure to keep the adjective with the noun it is modifying. They form a unit of thought.

> ὁ ἀγαθὸς ἄνθρωπος / γράφει / τὸ βιβλίον.
> The good man writes the book.

Summary

1. Adjectives can function as an attributive, a substantive, or a predicate.

2. If the article precedes the adjective and the adjective modifies another word, then it is an attributive adjective. The adjective agrees with the noun it modifies in case, number, and gender.

3. If the article precedes the adjective and the adjective does not modify another word, then it is a substantival adjective. The case of this adjective is determined by its function, its gender and number by what it stands for.

4. If an anarthrous adjective occurs with an articular noun, the adjective is a predicate and you may need to supply the verb "is."

5. If there is no article before either the adjective or the word it is modifying, let context be your guide.

6. A prepositional phrase preceded by an article can be an attributive modifier or a substantive.

7. A 2-2 adjective has the same form in the masculine and feminine, and follows the second declension. The neuter likewise is second declension.

8. A singular verb can be used when the subject is neuter plural and viewed as a whole.

Are you getting frustrated with all there is to learn? Go back to chapters 6 and 7, reread them, and see how easy they are now. But remember how difficult they may have been when you first learned them? The fog has just moved from Chapter 6 to Chapter 9. Keep working, and the fog will continue to move. Ask your teacher to remind you again *why* you are learning biblical Greek. Check out the website for encouragement.

Vocabulary

The endings following the lexical form of an adjective (e.g., "-ή, -όν") show the feminine and neuter forms of the word. The feminine of ἀγαθός is ἀγαθή and its neuter is ἀγαθόν. The roots of adjectives are listed with the final stem vowel for the masculine (e.g., *ἀγαθο).

Good

ἀγαθός, -ή, -όν	good, useful (102; *ἀγαθο)[5]
ἀγαπητός, -ή, -όν	beloved (61; *ἀγαπητο)[6]
αἰώνιος, -ον	eternal (71; *αἰωνιο)[7]
ἀλλήλων	one another (100; *ἀλληλο)[8]

This is an unusual word because it never occurs in the nominative or in the singular. Its lexical form is therefore genitive plural.

ἀπεκρίθη — he/she/it answered

This is a common form of a common verb, occurring 82 times in the New Testament. It takes its direct object in the dative, and therefore you do not use the key word with its direct object. ἀπεκρίθη αὐτῷ means, "He answered him," not, "He answered to him."

δοῦλος, -ου, ὁ	slave, servant (126; *δουλο)
ἐάν	if, when (350)

Introduces a dependent clause. ἐάν is a crasis of εἰ and ἄν. "Crasis" occurs when two words are "pushed together" to make one. When ἐάν appears after a relative pronoun (ὅς), it has the effect of appending "-ever" to the end of the pronoun (just like ἄν). ὅς ἐάν ... means "whoever ...."

ἐμός, ἐμή, ἐμόν — my, mine (76; *ἐμο)

This adjective always means "my" regardless of its case. If it is used substantivally, it always means "mine."

ἐντολή, -ῆς, ἡ	commandment (67; *ἐντολη)
καθώς	as, even as (182)
κακός, -ή, -όν	bad, evil (50; *κακο)[9]
μου (ἐμοῦ)	my (564)

This is the genitive singular of ἐγώ. Unlike ἐμός, μου only means "my" when it is in the genitive case. It can also be written with an initial epsilon and an accent: ἐμοῦ. This word is discussed in detail in Chapter 11.

νεκρός, -ά, -όν — adjective: dead (128; *νεκρο)[10]
               noun: dead body, corpse

πιστός, -ή, -όν — faithful, believing (67; *πιστο)

---

[5] *Agatha* is a woman's name.

[6] This is the cognate adjective of the noun ἀγάπη.

[7] *Aeonian* means "eternal."

[8] *Parallel* lines (παράλληλος) are lines that are beside (παρά) one another (ἄλλος).

[9] "Caco" is a common combining form. A *cacophony* is a harsh or bad sound. *Cacoepy* is poor pronunciation. *Cacography* is poor writing skill.

[10] *Necrophobia* is an abnormal fear of death.

πονηρός, -ά, -όν   evil, bad (78; *πονηρο)[11]

πρῶτος, -η, -ον   first, earlier (155; *πρωτο)[12]

τρίτος, -η, -ον   third (56; *τριτο)[13]

Total word count in the New Testament: 138,162
Number of words learned to date: 87
Number of word occurrences in this chapter: 1,669
Number of word occurrences to date: 72,664
Percent of total word count in the New Testament: 52.59%

Previous Words

These are words you already know that can occur in more than one gender. You need to learn their feminine and neuter forms.

ἄλλος, -η, -ο   other, another

There are a few words such as ἄλλος, ὁ, αὐτός, and οὗτος that do not use a case ending for the nominative and accusative singular neuter, and therefore the bare stem stands alone. They are a-1a(2b) adjectives; their full paradigm is in the Appendix.

αὐτός, -ή, -ό   he/she/it, they

ἔσχατος, -η, -ον   last

οὗτος, αὕτη, τοῦτο[14]   this; these

Advanced Information

9.18   **Genitive or accusative?** If the next to the last letter in the stem of an adjective is a rho or a vowel, the feminine stem ends in alpha (e.g., νεκρά) and the ending ας can indicate either the genitive singular or accusative plural.

nom sg	ἁγία	nom pl	ἅγιαι
gen sg	ἁγίας	gen pl	ἁγιῶν
dat sg	ἁγίᾳ	dat pl	ἁγίαις
acc sg	ἁγίαν	acc pl	ἁγίας

If the next to the last letter in the stem is any letter other than a rho or a vowel (e.g., ἀγαθή), the feminine stem ends in eta and the ending ας can only be accusative plural.

The final stem vowel in the plural will always be alpha for all feminine nouns. Can νεκράς be genitive singular?

---

[11] *Ponera* is a genus of stinging ants.

[12] A *prototype* is the first of its kind, a model, a pattern.

[13] A *triangle* has three sides.

[14] The stem of this word changes quite significantly. It is fully explained in Chapter 13. It is an a-1a(2b) adjective; its full paradigm is in the Appendix.

9.19 **Third attributive position**. There is a third attributive position: ἄνθρωπος ὁ ἀγαθός. It is rare in the New Testament when the modifier is an adjective, but more common when the modifier is a phrase.

Exegesis

The Greek article is actually quite complex in how it is used, and as a result you will see it translated many different ways.

1. ὁ can function as the definite article.

> οἱ μαθηταὶ Ἰωάννου νηστεύουσιν πυκνά *(Luke 5:33)*.
> *The* disciples of John often fast.

2. ὁ can function as a grammatical marker, for example showing that the following word modifies the previous.

> μετὰ τῶν ἀγγέλων τῶν ἁγίων *(Mark 8:38)*
> with the holy angels

3. Greek uses ὁ when English does not, such as with proper names.

> ἀποκριθεὶς δὲ ὁ Ἰησοῦς εἶπεν πρὸς αὐτόν *(Matt 3:15)*
> But *Jesus* answering said to him

4. Sometimes ὁ functions with a participle (e.g., ἔχοντι) or an adjective to make it into a noun, even with words between them (τὴν ξηρὰν χεῖρα). These are often translated as a relative clause.

> λέγει τῷ ἀνθρώπῳ τῷ τὴν ξηρὰν χεῖρα ἔχοντι *(Mark 3:3)*
> He says to *the one who has* the withered hand

5. Other times Greek doesn't use ὁ when English requires it.

> Ἐν ἀρχῇ ἦν ὁ λόγος *(John 1:1)*.
> In *the* beginning was the Word.

6. ὁ can function as a personal or possessive pronoun.

> Οἱ δὲ εἶπαν πρὸς αὐτόν *(Luke 5:33)*
> And *they* said to Him
>
> Οἱ ἄνδρες, ἀγαπᾶτε τὰς γυναῖκας *(Eph 5:25)*.
> Husbands, love *your* wives.
>
> ὅμοιοί εἰσιν παιδίοις τοῖς ἐν ἀγορᾷ καθημένοις *(Luke 7:32)*.
> They are like children *who* sit in the market place.

7. When one ὁ governs two nouns, the two nouns are being viewed as a single unit. These are often theologically nuanced and significant.

> προσδεχόμενοι τὴν μακαρίαν ἐλπίδα καὶ ἐπιφάνειαν τῆς δόξης τοῦ μεγάλου θεοῦ καὶ σωτῆρος ἡμῶν Ἰησοῦ Χριστοῦ *(Titus 2:13)*.
> waiting for our blessed hope, the appearing of the glory of our great God and Savior Jesus Christ

Track One or Track Two?

"Two Roads Diverged in a Yellow Wood"

As in the words of the Robert Frost poem, we have come to a fork in the road in the life of Greek. What should you learn next? Which path you take determines which exercises you do for the next several chapters.

	Track One: Finish Noun System		Track Two: Get Into Verbs
9.	Adjectives	9.	Adjectives
	Review 2		Review 2
10.	Third Declension Nouns	15.	Introduction to Verbs
11.	First and Second Person Personal Pronouns	16.	Present Active Indicative
12.	αὐτός	17.	Contract Verbs
13.	Demonstratives	18.	Present Middle/Passive Indicative
14.	Relative Pronouns	21.	Imperfect Indicative
	Review 3 — Track 1		Review 3 — Track 2
15.	Introduction to Verbs	10.	Third Declension Nouns
16.	Present Active Indicative	11.	First and Second Person Personal Pronouns
17.	Contract Verbs	12.	αὐτός
18.	Present Middle/Passive Indicative	13.	Demonstratives
19.	Future Active/Middle Indicative	14.	Relative Pronouns
20.	Verbal Roots, and Other Forms of the Future	19.	Future Active/Middle Indicative
	Review 4 — Track 1	20.	Verbal Roots, and Other Forms of the Future
21.	Imperfect Indicative		Review 4 — Track 2
22.	Second Aorist Active/Middle Indicative	22.	Second Aorist Active/Middle Indicative

My preference is to finish the noun system (Track One) and then move on to verbs (see page xvi for my rationale). However, some teachers want their students to get into verbs earlier, and for them there is "Track Two." If you want to follow Track

Two, then follow the second ordering of chapters and use the exercises in the appendix to the Workbook.

If you follow Track Two, please recognize that the exercises will not include every vocabulary word given in that chapter. The vocabulary was chosen based on the exercises in Track One. Also, you will see three vocabulary words in Chapters 17 and 18 whose forms, especially their genitive forms, will look strange. For now, memorize the words. They are third declension and will be discussed in Chapter 10.

17. πλείων, πλεῖον

18. νύξ, νυκτός, ἡ

    ὅστις, ἥτις, ὅτι

This dual track system affects only the exercises. In other words, there is only one Chapter 10 in the textbook, and it is the same whether you are following Track One or Track Two.

The website makes it especially easy to follow Track Two.

ΗΡΩΔΗΣ ΜΟΝΙ-

ΜΟΥ ΚΑΙ ΙΟΥΣΤΟΣ

ΥΙΟΣ ΑΜΑ ΤΟΙΣ

ΤΕΚΝΟΙΣ ΕΚΤΙ-

ΣΑΝ

ΤΟΝ ΚΙΟΝΑ

This inscription is on a column in the synagogue in Capernaum. The synagogue was built on top of a first century synagogue. The inscription reads, Ἡρώδης Μονιμοῦ καὶ Ἰοῦστος υἱὸς ἅμα τοῖς τέκνοις ἔκτισαν τὸν κίονα, of course without the accents. It means, "Herod (the son) of Monimos and Justos (his) son together with their children erected this column."

Overview 2
Chapters 10 – 14

Chapter 10

Third declension words have stems ending in a consonant. There are three things you need to know.

■ It is common for the final letter of the stem to be altered by the case ending in the nominative singular and dative plural. The stem *σαρκ changes to σάρξ when the ς is added in the nominative singular, and to σαρξί in the dative plural by the case ending σι. It is the same case ending as in λόγος. Because the nominative singular form looks different from first and second declension forms, it is easy to think that third declension words are totally different. They are not.

■ The key is to memorize the genitive singular; it shows the true stem of the word. The genitive singular of *σαρκ is σάρκος. Drop off the ος case ending and you have the stem.

■ As you can see from the genitive σάρκος and the dative σαρξί, third declension words use a few alternate case endings.

Other things happen as well, especially in the nominative singular. For example, the stem *παντ becomes πᾶς because ντ drop out before the sigma (*παντ + ς ▸ πᾶς). The trick here is to realize that third declension words are not really that different from other words, and to memorize the stems.

Chapter 11

We finally meet the full paradigm of the first and second person personal pronouns, ἐγώ and σύ. You have already learned most of the grammar pertaining to pronouns, so there is not that much new in this chapter.

You will also learn a few more third delcension patterns, but nothing too earth-shaking.

Chapter 12

This chapter focuses on αὐτός. You have already learned it as the third person personal pronoun, and this is by far its predominant use. However, it can function two other ways as well.

■ αὐτός in the predicate position carries an intensive meaning. αὐτὸς ὁ ἀπόστολος means, "the apostle himself." When used this way, αὐτός normally modifies the subject.

■ αὐτός in the attributive position can mean "same." ὁ αὐτὸς λόγος means, "the same word."

Chapter 13

You now meet the demonstratives. You have already met one of them, οὗτος.

οὗτος means "this" ("these" in the plural), and ἐκεῖνος means "that" ("those" in the plural). The peculiarity of these words is that when used adjectivally, they are in the predicate position. οὗτος ὁ ἄνθρωπος means, "this person," not, "this is the person."

The demonstratives can also be used as pronouns. Sometimes you will have to provide an extra word or two to make sense. ἐκείνη could mean, "that woman." You may also translate them as personal pronouns, depending on the needs of the context. ἐκείνη could be, "she."

You will also learn a few odds 'n ends, such as the vocative case (used when directly addressing a person). For the most part, it looks like the nominative.

Chapter 14

The last major topic to learn in the noun system is the relative pronoun: "who/ whom" (not when asking a question), "that" (in one of its uses), and "which."

The relative pronoun introduces a relative clause that will have its own subject and verb. It is a dependent construction, either modifying something ("The book *that is open on the table* is too expensive.") or performing a function ("*Whoever is not for me* is against me.").

The case of the relative pronoun is determined by its function inside the relative clause. Its number and gender are determined by its antecedent, who or what it is referring to.

> There's already a lot to learn in the next chapter, so perhaps it is best to learn just a little fun stuff for now.
>
> As you meet people you will want to know where they are from.
>
> - "From?" is ἀπό.
> - "Where" is ποῦ.
> - If you think through the paradigm for εἰμί, you should be able to figure out the right form of the verb. If you are asking one person, you would say, εἶ; if more than one person it is ἐστέ.
>
> Put it all together and you ask,
>
> ἀπο ποῦ εἶ (or ἐστέ);

Basics of Biblical Greek

Chapter 10

Third Declension

Exegetical Insight

A casual first-century reader of the Fourth Gospel's prologue (John 1:1–18) would have little difficulty understanding John's description of the λόγος. As a concept it was simple enough. Λόγος was the intelligible law of things. Ὁ λόγος τοῦ θεοῦ was God's transcendent rationality that gave the universe order and purpose. A Hellenized Jew would quickly reach for a volume of wisdom literature explaining that God's wisdom, his word (or λόγος), provided the universe with its form and coherence. As such, ὁ λόγος τοῦ θεοῦ was foreign to human ways, above us and distant from us, guiding us from afar.

John 1:14, on the other hand, would make any such reader pause in stunned silence. "And the λόγος became flesh (σάρξ) and dwelt among us." Σάρξ is the earthly sphere, the arena of human decisions and emotions, human history, and human sinfulness (cf. John 1:13; 3:6;

17:2; etc.). John 1:14 contains the risk, the scandal, and the gospel of the Christian faith: ὁ λόγος became σάρξ. The center of God's life and thought entered the depths of our world and took up its form, its σάρξ, its flesh, in order to be known by us and to save us.

This affirmation about λόγος and σάρξ is the very heart of our faith. *God has not abandoned us.* No lowliness, no misery, no sinfulness is beyond God's comprehension and reach. He came among us, embraced our world of σάρξ in his incarnation, and loved us. It is easy enough to say that God loves the world (John 3:16). But to say that God loves me, in my frailty and my faithlessness—that he loves σάρξ—this is another matter. This is the mystery and the power of what God has done for us in Jesus Christ.

Gary M. Burge

Overview

In this chapter you will learn:

- the third (and final) declension (i.e., stems ending in a consonant);

- four hints for the third declension;

- the Master Case Ending Chart;

- Noun Rule 7, the "Square of stops," and the effect of a sigma on stops;

- Noun Rule 8.

Introduction

10.1 What is the difference between the first and second declension? Right. First declension words have stems ending in alpha or eta. Second declension nouns have stems ending in omicron. And what declension a noun falls into has no effect on its meaning. Regardless of whether ἀπόστολος is first or second declension, it still means "apostle."

10.2 **Function and meaning**. Remember that all Greek nouns, whether they are first, second, or third declension, function the same. Only their form may be somewhat different.

10.3 *Nouns with stems ending in a consonant follow the third declension pattern*. This is part of the first noun rule.

$$^*σαρκ\ +\ ων\ ▸\ σαρκῶν$$

10.4 **Final consonant and the case ending**. When you first look at a paradigm of a third declension noun, you may think that it is totally different from a first or second declension paradigm. It is not! Because the stem of a third declension noun ends in a consonant, that consonant sometimes reacts to the first letter of the case ending, especially if the case ending begins with a sigma.

For example, the stem of the second declension noun λόγος is *λογο. The omicron joins with the nominative masculine case ending sigma to form λόγος (*λογο + ς ▸ λόγος). No problem. But the stem of the third declension word σάρξ is *σαρκ. The kappa is united with the *same* nominative singular case ending, and the combination of κσ forms ξ (*σαρκ + ς ▸ σάρξ).

While the ending of σάρξ may look totally different from that of λόγος, it really isn't.

10.5 **Different case endings**. The third declension does use a few case endings that are different from those used in the first and second declensions, but not that many. If you have been memorizing the case ending with the final stem vowel (e.g., ος and not ς for nominative singular), you may want to go back and learn the true case endings.

10.6 **Hints**. If you can remember just four hints, these changes will not be a problem. As you will see, the basic issue is what happens when a sigma follows a consonant.

1. Because of the changes that take place in the nominative singular, it is often difficult to determine the stem of a third declension noun.

   The solution to this problem is always to memorize the genitive singular form with the lexical form. If you drop the genitive singular case ending (e.g., ος), you will normally have the word's stem.

   The lexical entry σάρξ, σαρκός, ἡ shows that the stem is *σαρκ.

2. Whatever happens in the nominative singular (ς) also happens in the dative plural. This is because the dative plural case ending (σι) also begins with a sigma.

   $$^*σαρκ\ +\ ς\ ▸\ σάρξ$$
   $$^*σαρκ\ +\ σι\ ▸\ σαρξί$$

To answer the question on page 76, you say,
εἰμὶ ἀπὸ _____ .
Depending on where you are from, there may not be a Greek word for your country (or state, province, or town).

For states and towns, the convention in Modern Greek is to use a Greek pronunciation, so Michigan is Μίτσιγκαν, California is Καλιφόρνια.

Here are some country names:
Greece: Ἑλλάς
Macedonia: Μακεδονία
Israel: Ἰσραήλ
Italy: Ἰταλία
Egypt: Αἴγυπτος
Asia: Ἀσία
America: Ἀμερική
Korea: Κορέα

3. A nu drops out when followed by a sigma.

    *τιν + ς ▸ τίς

    *τιν + σι ▸ τίσι

4. A tau drops out when followed by a sigma or if it is at the end of a word.

    *ὀνοματ + σι ▸ ὀνόμασι

    *ὀνοματ + – ▸ ὄνομα

In the case of ὄνομα, it is neuter and does not use a case ending in the nominative or accusative singular. That is why the tau is at the end of the word.

This is a slight simplification of the situation, but if you can remember these four hints, the rest of the third declension is easy to learn.

Since Greek has only three declensions, once you understand these you will be familiar with all the basic noun paradigms in the New Testament. So work on these and you are well on your way toward success. But remember, any declension can have several variations.

A Walk Through

10.7   Following is the paradigm of a third declension noun: σάρξ (*σαρκ). The case endings are in blue. Don't be frightened; σάρξ really has only three case endings you have not seen, and two other endings similar to those you already know. At this point, don't try to memorize the case endings; just see how they work. The paradigms of λόγος and γραφή are listed for comparison.

nom sg:	*σαρκς	▸	σάρξ	λόγος	γραφή
gen sg:	*σαρκος	▸	σαρκός	λόγου	γραφῆς
dat sg:	*σαρκι	▸	σαρκί	λόγῳ	γραφῇ
acc sg:	*σαρκα	▸	σάρκα	λόγον	γραφήν
nom pl:	*σαρκες	▸	σάρκες	λόγοι	γραφαί
gen pl:	*σαρκων	▸	σαρκῶν	λόγων	γραφῶν
dat pl:	*σαρκσι(ν)	▸	σαρξί(ν)	λόγοις	γραφαῖς
acc pl:	*σαρκας	▸	σάρκας	λόγους	γραφάς

Let's walk through this paradigm so you can see how easy it is.

σάρξ. The normal nominative singular case ending is ς. When you add it to this stem, the κσ combination is rewritten as a xi. σαρκ + ς ▸ σάρξ.

σαρκός. ος is a new ending, but it is easy to remember. The genitive singular case ending for first declension nouns is sigma (e.g., γραφῆς), and for second declension nouns it actually is omicron (which contracts with the final stem vowel to form ου, *λογο + ο ▸ λόγου). Put those two case endings together, and you have the case ending for the third declension: ος. σαρκ + ος ▸ σαρκός.[1]

---

[1]   How will you not become confused and think that σαρκός is a nominative singular masculine from a second declension word, σαρκός? Vocabulary memorization! The lexical form is σάρξ.

σαρκί. The dative singular case ending is the same as for the other declensions: ι. But because a third declension stem ends in a consonant and not a long vowel, the iota cannot subscript. σαρκ + ι ▸ σαρκί.

σάρκα. The accusative singular case ending is different for the third declension: α. σαρκ + α ▸ σάρκα.

σάρκες. The nominative plural case ending is different for the third declension: ες. σαρκ + ες ▸ σάρκες.

σαρκῶν. As always, the genitive plural case ending is beautifully consistent: ων. σαρκ + ων ▸ σαρκῶν.

σαρξί. The dative plural case ending for a third declension noun is the exact opposite of the first and second declension (ις) and sometimes includes the movable nu: σι(ν). Because it begins with a sigma, whatever change we see in the nominative singular also appears here. σαρκ + σι(ν) ▸ σαρξί(ν).

σάρκας. The accusative plural case ending is different for the third declension: ας. σαρκ + ας ▸ σάρκας. Do not confuse this with a first declension word where the alpha is part of the stem (γραφάς), although the similarity may help you remember the case ending.

10.8 There! That wasn't very difficult, was it? There are only three new endings (ος, α, ες), and two that are similar (σι(ν), ας). You now know all the major case endings. Congratulations! Let's work through the formal presentation of the third declension.

Forms

10.9 Third declension words are categorized according to the last consonant of the word's stem. Below you will find the σάρξ paradigm and then two more paradigms of third declension words: stems ending in ματ (149 words) and stems ending in ν (77 words). The case endings are in blue to emphasize the similarities with the first and second declensions. You will learn a few more third declension sub-patterns in Chapter 11.

My recommendation is not to memorize the paradigms. Read through the footnotes so you can see why the forms do what they do, and then be sure you can recognize the same endings and changes on other words. The time for memorizing will come in 10.14.

10.10

	κ stem *σαρκ	ματ stem *ονοματ	ν stem *τιν
nom sg:	σάρξ	ὄνομα²	τίς³
gen sg:	σαρκός	ὀνόματος	τίνος
dat sg:⁴	σαρκί	ὀνόματι	τίνι
acc sg:	σάρκα	ὄνομα⁵	τίνα
nom pl:	σάρκες	ὀνόματα⁶	τίνες
gen pl:	σαρκῶν	ὀνομάτων	τίνων
dat pl:⁷	σαρξί(ν)	ὀνόμασι(ν)	τίσι(ν)
acc pl:	σάρκας	ὀνόματα	τίνας

10.11 τίς is the interrogative pronoun (e.g., "who?"). τις (no accent) is the indefinite pronoun (e.g., "anyone"). Both are formed from the same root, *τιν. The masculine and feminine are identical in form, and all genders are third declension. The change in the nominative singular is explained by the fact that nu drops out when followed by a sigma. *τιν + ς ‣ τίς.

	masc & fem	neut	masc & fem	neut
nom sg	τίς	τί	τις	τι
gen sg	τίνος	τίνος	τινός	τινός
dat sg	τίνι	τίνι	τινί	τινί
acc sg	τίνα	τί	τινά	τι
nom pl	τίνες	τίνα	τινές	τινά
gen pl	τίνων	τίνων	τινῶν	τινῶν
dat pl	τίσι(ν)	τίσι(ν)	τισί(ν)	τισί(ν)
acc pl	τίνας	τίνα	τινάς	τινά

τίς is always accented on its first syllable. τις is either not accented or is accented on its last syllable (the "ultima").

---

² No ending is used and the final consonant of the stem, which is a tau, drops out because a tau cannot stand at the end of a word (10.21).

³ nu drops out before sigma. See the dative plural and 10.11 below.

⁴ Note that the iota does not subscript in the third declension as it does in the first and second. This is because iota can subscript only under a long vowel.

⁵ All nouns ending in -μα are neuter. This is one of the few consistent patterns in the third declension. And like all neuter nouns, the nominative and accusative forms are always the same.

⁶ The way to tell the difference between this form and the nominative singular is to see if the whole stem is present (e.g., *ονοματ). If it is (ὀνόματα), then you are in the plural; if not (ὄνομα), then you are in the singular.

⁷ Whatever change you see in the nominative singular is also present in the dative plural because both case endings begin with sigma. The case ending is σι, the reverse of the first and second declension ending. The nu in parentheses after every form is a "movable nu" (8.13).

Modern Greek uses the equivalent of εἷς as its indefinite article "a." The nominative forms today are ἕνας, μία, ἕνα.

10.12 εἷς is an adjective meaning "one." The stem of the masculine and neuter is *ἑν and the feminine is the first declension *μια. In the nominative singular the nu drops out before the sigma, and the stem vowel epsilon lengthens to ει (*ἑν + ς ▸ ες ▸ εἷς).

	masc	*fem*	*neut*
nom sg	εἷς	μία	ἕν
gen sg	ἑνός	μιᾶς	ἑνός
dat sg	ἑνί	μιᾷ	ἑνί
acc sg	ἕνα	μίαν	ἕν

Notice that this word has a rough breathing in the masculine and neuter. This will help differentiate it from the prepositions εἰς and ἐν. Why is there no plural to this word? Where is it different from τίς?

10.13 In the first and second declensions, the masculine and feminine are often different in form. In the third declension, however, they are usually similar. There is, in fact, more similarity between masculine and feminine than there is between masculine and neuter, since in the nominative and accusative, the masculine and neuter are usually different.

Halftime Review

- Third declension words have stems ending in a consonant. Always memorize the genitive singular so you can see the stem.

- When the final consonant is joined with the case endings, sometimes the consonant is changed. This generally affects nominative singular and dative plural.

- nu and tau drop out before a sigma.

- Third declension words use three different case endings: ος, α, ες.

Characteristics of Third Declension Nouns

10.14 **Master Case Ending Chart.** My recommendation is not to memorize the previous paradigms, but to memorize the case endings in this chart and see how the case endings appear when attached to a noun. Study them carefully, note what they have in common, and especially what they have in common with the first and second declensions. There are other patterns within the third declension, but if you know these, the rest are relatively easy to recognize. Try to list all the similarities.

The first chart shows the true case endings. The second shows what the endings look like when attached to the final stem vowel.

	first/second declension			third declension	
	masc	*fem*	*neut*	*masc/fem*	*neut*
nom sg	ς	–	ν	ς	–[a]
gen sg	υ[b]	ς	υ	ος	ος
dat sg	ι[c]	ι	ι	ι[d]	ι
acc sg	ν	ν	ν	α / ν[e]	–

	masc	*fem*	*neut*	*masc/fem*	*neut*
nom pl	ι	ι	α	ες	α[f]
gen pl	ων	ων	ων	ων	ων
dat pl	ις	ις	ις	σι(ν)[g]	σι(ν)
acc pl	υς[h]	ς	α	ας[i]	α

	masc	*fem*		*neut*	*masc/fem*	*neut*
nom sg	ος	α	η	ον	ς	– –
gen sg	ου	ας	ης	ου	ος	ος
dat sg	ῳ	ᾳ	ῃ	ῳ	ι	ι
acc sg	ον	αν	ην	ον	α / ν	–

	masc	*fem*	*neut*	*masc/fem*	*neut*
nom pl	οι	αι	α	ες	α
gen pl	ων	ων	ων	ων	ων
dat pl	οις	αις	οις	σι(ν)	σι(ν)
acc pl	ους	ας	α	ας	α

---

[a] Be prepared for the final stem letter to undergo changes (rule 8).

[b] The ending is actually omicron, which contracts with the final stem vowel and forms ου (rule 5).

[c] The vowel lengthens (rule 5) and the iota subscripts (rule 4).

[d] Because third declension stems end in a consonant, the iota cannot subscript as it does in the first and second declensions; so it remains on the line.

[e] On some words the case ending alternates between alpha and nu; see 11.12.

[f] As opposed to the first and second declensions, this alpha is an actual case ending and not a changed stem vowel. This is also true in the accusative plural.

[g] The nu is a movable nu. Notice that the ending σι is a flipped version of ις found in the first and second declensions.

[h] The actual case ending for the first and second declension is νς, but the nu drops out because of the following sigma. In the first declension the alpha simply joins with the sigma (*ωρα + νς ‣ ὥρας), but in the second declension the final stem omicron lengthens to ου (rule 5; λογονς ‣ λογος ‣ λόγους).

[i] As opposed to the first declension (e.g., ὥρα), the alpha here is part of the case ending.

10.15 **Gender.** The gender of third declension words can be difficult to determine because the inflectional patterns are not as distinct as those in the first and second declensions. You must memorize the gender of every word.

There are, however, a few patterns. In this chapter you will meet stems ending in ματ (e.g., ὄνομα, ματος, τό). All ματ stems are neuter.

10.16 **The article**. The article becomes especially important now. Even though a noun itself changes its form, the article always remains the same. τῷ will always be τῷ whether the noun it modifies is first, second, or third declension. Most nouns are modified by the article, which makes it easy to determine the noun's gender.

Square of Stops

10.17 A **stop** is a consonant whose sound is formed by slowing down or completely stopping the flow of air through the mouth.

10.18 "Stops" are broken down into three classifications.

- **Labial**. π, β, and φ are formed by using the lips to impede the air flow momentarily, which is essential in creating the sound. Try to say π without letting your lips touch.

- **Velar**. κ, γ, and χ are formed by pushing up the middle of the tongue against the soft part of the roof of the mouth.[8]

- **Dental**. τ, δ, and θ are formed by clicking the tongue against the back of the teeth.[9]

10.19 Rule 7: Square of Stops. The seventh of the eight noun rules is this chart. Be sure to memorize it exactly. Not only should you be able to repeat it left to right but also top to bottom.[10]

Labial	π	β	φ
Velar	κ	γ	χ
Dental	τ	δ	θ

The chart is important because the stops behave in a consistent manner. Whatever happens to a stem ending in tau also happens to a stem ending

---

[8] Some people use the term "palatals" to describe these three consonants because the soft part of the mouth's roof is the "palate."

[9] Actually, it is not the teeth but the "alveolar ridge" behind the teeth that is used, but the word "teeth" is easier for most to associate with "dental."

[10] The final column of stops, φ, χ, and θ, technically are not stops but "aspirates" because the air flow is not stopped but only slowed down. However, because they fit into the pattern so well, it is easier to view them as stops. The rough breathing is also an aspirate.

There are also titles for the columns. π, κ, and τ are "unvoiced" because the voice box is not used in their pronunciation. β, γ, and δ are "voiced" because the voice box is used. (Place your fingers on your voice box and pronounce these letters. You will feel it vibrate when you say the voiced stops.)

in delta, because tau and delta are both dentals. If you learn the chart, you will often be able to predict what is going to happen. This is much easier than memorizing different paradigms. This same Square of Stops will also be important when we study verbs, so a little time spent here saves hours of frustration later.

10.20 **Stops plus a "σ."** Whenever a stop and a sigma come into contact the results are predictable. Learn these changes well because you will encounter them often.

Labial	+	σ	‣	ψ
Velar	+	σ	‣	ξ
Dental	+	σ	‣	σ

*σκολοπ + σ ‣ σκόλοψ[11]

*σαρκ + σι ‣ σαρξί

*ὀνοματ + σι ‣ ὀνόμασι[12]

10.21 Rule 8: A tau cannot stand at the end of a word and will drop off. For example, the stem of the word for "name" is *ὄνοματ. No case ending is used in the nominative singular and the final tau drops off.

*ονοματ + – ‣ ὄνομα

This is the final rule for case endings. You know all eight. They are listed in the Appendix, page 346.

πᾶς

10.22 πᾶς is a 3-1-3[13] type adjective and is often used as the paradigmatic word for the third declension. The root of the word is *παντ, which in the feminine is altered to *πασα.[14] Armed with this knowledge and the rules in this chapter, you should be able to write out the entire paradigm for this word without looking below. Try it. If you can, you are doing well.

---

[11] There are only seven nouns in the New Testament whose stems end in a pi, but many stems end in a kappa or tau.

[12] Technically, the dental forms a sigma and the double sigma simplifies to a single sigma (*ὀνοματ + σι ‣ ὀνόμασσι ‣ ὀνόμασι).

[13] "3-1-3" means the masculine and neuter follow the third declension while the feminine follows the first declension. See 10.23.

[14] For you who are interested in advanced morphology, it is altered because a consonantal iota was added to form the feminine stem, and ντ + consonantal iota form σα (see *MBG* on πᾶς).

	3 masc	1 fem	3 neut
nom sg	πᾶς[15]	πᾶσα	πᾶν[16]
gen sg	παντός	πάσης[17]	παντός
dat sg	παντί	πάσῃ	παντί
acc sg	πάντα	πᾶσαν	πᾶν
nom pl	πάντες	πᾶσαι	πάντα
gen pl	πάντων	πασῶν	πάντων
dat pl	πᾶσι(ν)[18]	πάσαις	πᾶσι(ν)
acc pl	πάντας	πάσας	πάντα

If you like to memorize paradigms, this is the one! Not only does it show the first and third declension, but it is key for learning participles (Chapter 26).

Because πᾶς is an adjective, it can function substantivally. When it does, it may require the use of an additional word like "people" or "things." But unlike other adjectives, πᾶς usually is in the predicate position when modifying a noun.

πᾶς ὁ ἄνθρωπος means "every man."

Categories

10.23 Adjectives fall into four categories, depending on which declension they follow and whether the feminine and masculine forms are the same or different. The masculine and neuter always follow the same declension. You met the 2-1-2 and 2-2 patterns in Chapter 9.

category	masculine	feminine	neuter	example
2-1-2	2 declension	1 declension	2 declension	ἀγαθός, ή, όν
3-1-3	3 declension	1 declension	3 delcension	πᾶς, πᾶσα, πᾶν
2-2	2 declension	2 declension	2 declension	αἰώνιος
3-3	3 declension	3 declension	3 declension	τίς, τί

Article

10.24 There are two special situations concerning the translation of the article that you need to look at.

---

[15] The ντ drops out before sigma (11.11 and 10.21).

[16] No case ending is used, and a tau cannot stand at the end of a word, so it drops off (10.21).

[17] Do you remember the rule governing the final stem vowel in the gentive and dative singular? If a first declension word has a stem ending in alpha where the preceding letter is epsilon, iota, or rho, it will form the genitive and dative with alpha. Otherwise, the alpha shifts to eta.

[18] The ντ drops out before sigma (11.11 and 10.21); also in the dative plural neuter.

The article in Greek is much more than just the word "the." It is a "weak demonstrative," which means it can perform as a demonstrative ("that"), a relative ("who"), or even a personal pronoun ("he," "one"), depending upon the needs of the context. You will usually have to add a word into your translation to help, such as "who" or "which." Let the context determine which is appropriate.[19]

When you find the phrase ὁ δέ, the article is usually functioning as a personal pronoun, "but he."

> ὁ δὲ ὀπίσω μου ἐρχόμενος ἰσχυρότερός μού ἐστιν *(Matt 3:11)*.
> But *he* who is coming after me is mightier than I.

10.25 Sometimes you will find the article before a prepositional phrase. I mentioned this at 9.14.

> λαμπεῖ πᾶσιν τοῖς ἐν τῇ οἰκίᾳ *(Matt 5:15)*.
> It gives light to all *who are* in the house.

The article is showing you that the following prepositional phrase (ἐν τῇ οἰκίᾳ) is in an attributive relationship to πᾶσιν. It is the same type of relationship that we have seen with adjectives: "article-noun-article-modifier," only here the modifier is a prepositional phrase.

In order to translate this construction, you will normally turn the prepositional phrase into a relative clause and supply whatever words are necessary. The article will be in the same case, number, and gender as the noun. This way you can tell what word the prepositional phrase modifies.

Summary

1. Words whose stems end in a consonant use third declension case endings.

2. To find the stem of a third declension noun, locate the genitive singular and drop the case ending.

3. To remember the gender of a third declension noun, memorize its lexical form with the article. To remember the stem of a third declension noun, memorize its genitive form.

4. Memorize the *Master Case Ending Chart* perfectly.

5. Rule 7: The Square of Stops.

Labial	π	β	φ
Velar	κ	γ	χ
Dental	τ	δ	θ

6. Labial + σ forms ψ. Velar + σ forms ξ. Dental + σ forms σ.

7. Rule 8: A tau cannot stand at the end of a word and will drop off.

---

[19] This is more second year grammar than first year. Something to look forward to.

8. ὁ δέ can be translated "but he," and an article before a prepositional phrase is probably signaling that the prepositional phrase is an attributive construction.

9. πᾶς is a paradigmatic word for grammar yet to come (participles), so learn it well.

10. Know the four different categories of adjectives.

Be encouraged! You now know all three declensions and almost all noun forms.

Vocabulary

Be sure to memorize the nominative, genitive, and article for each third declension noun.

ἅγιος, -ία, -ιον	adjective: holy (233; *ἁγιο; 2-1-2)[20] plural noun: saints
εἰ	if (503) This is not the same as εἶ, which means "you are." Watch the accents carefully, because εἰ does not have its own accent. Like ἐάν, εἰ always introduces a dependent clause and therefore you will not find the main subject or verb of the sentence in the εἰ clause.
εἰ μή	except; if not (86) These two words together can form an "idiom" (see below) meaning "except." Other times they are best translated, "if not." It often introduces a dependent clause. An "idiom" is a phrase that does not have the same meaning as the sum of its parts. When looking at the meaning of each word in the idiom, you can seldom find the meaning of the idiomatic phrase.
εἷς, μία, ἕν	one (344; *ἑν/*μια; 3-1-3)[21]
ἤδη	now, already (61)
ὄνομα, -ατος, τό	name, reputation (231; *ονοματ)[22]
οὐδείς, οὐδεμία, οὐδέν	no one, none, nothing (234; οὐ[δε] + *ἑν/*μια) The second half of this word declines just like εἷς.
πᾶς, πᾶσα, πᾶν	singular: each, every (1,244; *παντ/*πασα; 3-1-3)[23] plural: all

---

[20] The *Hagiographa* (ἁγιόγραφα) are the holy writings, the third and final part of the Jewish canon. *Hagiolatry* is the worship of saints.

[21] A *hendiadys* is a figure of speech in which two nouns describe one thing. It is from the phrase ἓν διὰ δυοῖν, meaning "one thing by means of two." *Henotheism* is the belief in one God while allowing for the existence of other gods.

[22] *Onomatopoeia* (ὀνοματοποιία) is when the name of a word sounds like its meaning, such as "bang" and "whisper."

[23] *Pantheism* is the belief that God is in all things.

περί	gen: concerning, about (333)[24] acc: around
σάρξ, σαρκός, ἡ	flesh, body (147; *σαρκ)[25]
σύν	dat: with (128)[26]
σῶμα, -ατος, τό	body (142; *σωματ)[27]
τέκνον, -ου, τό	child, descendant (99; *τεκνο)[28]
τίς, τί	who? what? which? why? (556; *τιν; 3-3) When this word means "why?" it will usually be in the neuter (τί).
τις, τι	someone/thing (533; *τιν; 3-3) certain one/thing, anyone/thing

WORKBOOK SUMMARY

Total word count in the New Testament:	138,162
Number of words learned to date:	102
Number of word occurrences in this chapter:	5,151
Number of word occurrences to date:	77,815
Percent of total word count in the New Testament:	56.32%

10.26 Hint. It is common for students to stop memorizing vocabulary because there is so much grammar to learn. Even if you are struggling with grammar, be sure to stay up with your vocabulary, and be sure you are reviewing. How well you know the grammar serves little purpose (or has little value) if you do not know what the words mean. You will not be able to translate a passage. So hang in there; the remaining noun chapters are much easier than this chapter.

Previous Words

πνεῦμα, -ατος, τό	spirit, Spirit
Σίμων, -ωνος, ὁ	Simon

---

[24] The perimeter (περίμετρος) is the boundary around an object or area. The rule is that the final iota elides only when the following word begins with an iota, but there is no example of this in the New Testament.

[25] A *sarcophagus* (σαρκοφάγος) is a stone coffin. In Greece they were made of limestone, which was believed would consume, or "eat" (φαγέω), the flesh.

[26] "Syn" is a common prefix. A *synagogue* (συναγωγή) is a place where people come together. *Synaeresis* (συναίρεσις) is the contraction of two sounds into one.

[27] A *psychosomatic* disorder is a physical disorder caused by the psychic/emotional processes. *Somatology* is the study of the body.

[28] *Teknonymy* is the custom of naming the parent from the child. My software company is named *Teknia.com,* because it was my intention to get out of commercial database programming and help children learn, such as at KidsGreek.com.

Chapter 11

First and Second Person Personal Pronouns

Exegetical Insight

Small words sometimes carry a big punch, especially when combined with other features of the Greek language. Pronouns can be those kind of small words. They, like moving vans, can carry a big load. I am thinking of a particularly sinister example of this in Jesus' temptations in Luke 4:6. The devil has taken Jesus on a cosmic ride so he can see all the kingdoms of the world. Then he says to Jesus, "To you I will give all of this authority and their glory; for it has been delivered to me and I give it to whom I will. If you, then, will worship me, it shall be yours."

Here is a great (but deceitful) offer, and all the freight is carried in the various exchanges of personal pronouns throughout the passage. To read through the verse one must follow the bouncing ball through various pronoun changes. The devil (I, me) offers authority over all the earth (it), if Jesus (you, yours) will but worship the devil.

But there is one other touch to this verse. To sweeten the offer the pronoun "to you" (σοι) is put at the front of the Greek sentence for emphasis in verse 6. Though some translations suggest this emphasis (RSV), a knowledge of Greek reveals its significance. The devil makes the personal and unique nature of the offer clear. The devil is saying, "This offer is just for you!" He tries to present the offer in as attractive a way as possible to Jesus. It is a good thing the devil is not a used car salesman! Fortunately, loyalty to God was more important to Jesus than seizing power. He did not let the devil's use (and abuse) of pronouns trip him up.

Darrell L. Bock

Overview

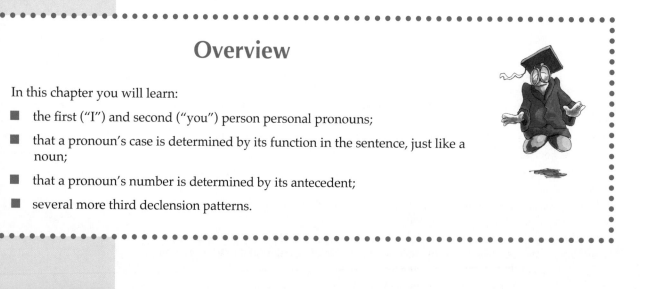

In this chapter you will learn:

- the first ("I") and second ("you") person personal pronouns;

- that a pronoun's case is determined by its function in the sentence, just like a noun;

- that a pronoun's number is determined by its antecedent;

- several more third declension patterns.

English

11.1 A **pronoun** is a word that replaces a noun. In the sentence, "It is red," "It" is a pronoun referring back to something.

A **personal pronoun** is a pronoun that replaces a personal noun.[1] In the sentence, "My name is Bill; I will learn Greek as well as possible," "I" is a personal pronoun referring to me, Bill.

The word that a pronoun refers back to, "Bill," is the **antecedent**.

11.2 **Person**. Pronouns can be first person, second person, or third person.

- First person refers to the person speaking ("I", "we").

- Second person refers to the person being spoken to ("you").

- Third person refers to the person being spoken about ("he," "she," "it," "they"). All nouns are considered third person.

Notice how highly inflected the English pronoun is. Pronouns are radically changed, depending upon their function.

There is no easy way to distinguish between second person singular and plural. Some grammars retain the old "thou" (singular) and "ye" (plural).[2]

11.3 **Case, Number, and Person**

The case of a pronoun is determined by its function in the sentence, its number and person by its antecedent. This is similar to adjectives that function substantivally.

1. The **case** of a pronoun is determined by its function in the sentence. For example, if the pronoun is the subject of the sentence, you would use "I" and not "me" since "I" is in the subjective case. You would not say, "Me would like to eat now," because "me" is objective.

   This is different from an attributive adjective, which determines its case by the word it is modifying. A pronoun (except in the genitive) does not modify a word.

2. The **number** of the pronoun is determined by the antecedent. Because "Bill" is singular, you would use "I" and not "we."

3. The **person** of the pronoun is determined by the antecedent. If the antecedent was the person speaking (first person), you use "I," not "you."

4. There is no **gender** in the first and second person. "I" or "you" can be either a woman or a man. The third person pronoun has gender, but you will meet it in the next chapter.

---

[1] A personal noun is a noun referring to a person.

[2]

	singular	*plural*
subjective	thou	ye
possessive	thy, thine	your, yours
objective	thee	you

Another option is to use "you" for the singular and "y'all" for the plural.

11.4 English forms

	first person	second person
subjective sg	I	you
possessive sg[3]	my	your
objective sg	me	you
subjective pl	we	you
possessive pl	our	your
objective pl	us	you

Greek

11.5 The Greek pronoun is similar to the English pronoun.

- ■ It replaces a noun.
- ■ Its case is determined by its function in the sentence.
- ■ Its number and person is determined by its antecedent.
- ■ First and second person pronouns do not have gender.

11.6 Greek forms

We have already learned some of these forms and have seen many of them in the exercises. They should be quite familiar and easy to learn. The alternate forms in parentheses are discussed in 11.8.

	first person			second person		
nom sg	ἐγώ		I	σύ		you
gen sg	μου	(ἐμοῦ)	my	σου	(σοῦ)	your
dat sg	μοι	(ἐμοί)	to me	σοι	(σοί)	to you
acc sg	με	(ἐμέ)	me	σε	(σέ)	you
nom pl	ἡμεῖς		we	ὑμεῖς		you
gen pl	ἡμῶν		our	ὑμῶν		your
dat pl	ἡμῖν		to us	ὑμῖν		to you
acc pl	ἡμᾶς		us	ὑμᾶς		you

Characteristics of 1st and 2nd Person Pronouns

11.7 Form. Notice the many similarities among the case endings of the pronouns and the case endings for the nouns you have already learned.

- ■ The nominative (singular and plural) and accusative (singular) are a little different, but the others should remind you of endings you already know.

---

3   If the possessive forms are used substantivally, they are translated "mine," "yours," and "ours."

- In the plural, the first and second person personal pronouns are identical except for the first letter.[4]

- Although there are many similarities among these forms and those you already know, some students prefer just to memorize this paradigm.

11.8 **Accents**. In the first person singular, the genitive, dative, and accusative cases will sometimes include an epsilon and an accent (ἐμοῦ, ἐμοί, ἐμέ). The second person pronoun will not add an epsilon but it can add an accent (σοῦ, σοί, σέ).[5] These accented forms are called the **emphatic** forms.

The emphatic and unemphatic forms basically have the same meaning. The emphatic form is used when the author wants to be especially emphatic, usually in contrasting one person with another.

> ἐγὼ ἐβάπτισα ὑμᾶς ὕδατι, αὐτὸς δὲ βαπτίσει ὑμᾶς ἐν πνεύματι ἁγίῳ.
>
> *I* baptized you in water but *he* will baptize you with the Holy Spirit.

The contrast is usually difficult to bring into English.

Emphatic forms also tend to be used after prepositions.

> ἔργον γὰρ καλὸν ἠργάσατο εἰς ἐμέ *(Mt 26:10).*
>
> For she has done a beautiful thing *to me.*

11.9 **Parsing**. When asked to decline a first or second person personal pronoun, I suggest that you list the case, number, person (not gender), lexical form, and inflected meaning.

> σοῦ is genitive singular second person, from σύ, meaning "of you" (or "your")

The lexical forms of the first and second person personal pronouns are the nominative. Some teachers view ἐγώ as the lexical form of ἡμεῖς while others see ἡμεῖς as a separate word. The same holds true for ὑμεῖς.

11.10 **Translation procedure**. If the pronoun is the subject or direct object, then treat it as you would any other subject or direct object. If it is in the genitive, treat it like any other possessive.

> ἐγώ / πιστεύω / λόγον σου.
>
> I believe your word.

The possessive forms of the pronouns (μου, σου) usually follow the word they modify.

> κύριός μου εἶπεν ....
>
> My Lord said ....

> Here are some other phrases that might help you get acquainted with one another.
>
> - πῶς ἔχεις is, "How are you?"
> - εὖ ἔχω or καλῶς ἔχω is, "I am well."
> - κακῶς ἔχω is, "I am not well."

---

[4] Since the upsilon with the rough breathing makes a "hoo" sound, you can remember the person of the plural form by associating "hoo" with "συ."

[5] The nominative singular σύ always occurs in our NT texts with an accent.

Halftime Review

- Pronouns are words that replace nouns.

- Pronouns are first (the person speaking), second (the person spoken to), or third (the person spoken about) person.

- First and second person pronouns agree with their antecedent in person and number. Their case is determined by their function in the sentence.

- The forms of the personal pronouns need to be memorized.

- Personal pronouns in oblique cases (i.e., not in the nominative) can have accents when they are used emphatically.

More on the Third Declension

11.11 **Stems in tau and delta**. In Chapter 10 you learned the basics of the third declension. There are a few more patterns you need to learn, although these patterns are still governed by the same rules.

Stems ending in tau or delta behave the same way, since both letters are dentals. Remember, dentals (τ, δ, θ) drop out before sigma.

	*χαριτ	*φωτ, τό	*ελπιδ	*σαρκ
nom sg:[6]	χάρις	φῶς	ἐλπίς	σάρξ
gen sg:	χάριτος	φωτός	ἐλπίδος	σαρκός
dat sg:[7]	χάριτι	φωτί	ἐλπίδι	σαρκί
acc sg:	χάριτα[8]	φῶς	ἐλπίδα	σάρκα
nom pl:	χάριτες	φῶτα	ἐλπίδες	σάρκες
gen pl:	χαρίτων	φώτων	ἐλπίδων	σαρκῶν
dat pl:[9]	χάρισι(ν)	φῶσι(ν)	ἐλπίσι(ν)	σαρξί(ν)
acc pl:	χάριτας	φῶτα	ἐλπίδας	σάρκας

A special note on χάριτα. The ending α is used in the accusative singular by all the New Testament words in this category except for χάρις. Of its 44 occurences, χάρις forms its accusative singular as χάριν 42 times, twice as χάριτα (Acts 24:27; Jude 4).

---

[6] A tau of the stem drops out when followed by a sigma (χαριτ + ς › χάρις). The same is true of the delta (ἐλπίς).

[7] The iota does not subscript in the third declension as it does in the first and second. This is because iota can subscript only under a long vowel (α, η, ω).

[8] α is used in the accusative singular by all the New Testament words in this category except for χάρις. Of its 44 occurences, χάρις forms its accusative singular as χάριν 42 times, twice as χάριτα (Acts 24:27; Jude 4).

[9] Whatever change is seen in the nominative singular is also present in the dative plural because both case endings begin with sigma. The case ending is σι, the reverse of the first and second declension ending. The nu in parentheses after every form is a "movable nu" (8.13).

11.12 **Consonantal iota stems**. πίστις appears to have a final stem vowel of iota.

nom sg:	πίστις
gen sg:	πίστεως[10]
dat sg:	πίστει
acc sg:	πίστιν[11]
nom pl:	πίστεις[12]
gen pl:	πίστεων[13]
dat pl:	πίστεσι(ν)
acc pl:	πίστεις[12]

11.13 Originally that iota was another letter called the "consonantal iota." This letter dropped out of the Greek alphabet long before Hellenistic Greek, but the fact that it used to be present helps explain a lot of apparently weird behavior in both nouns and verbs.[14]

The final iota in πίστις used to be a consonantal iota. When the consonantal iota dropped out of use, it was replaced with either an iota or epsilon. On the one hand, it may not be important to know when it will be what; just recognize that the stem of πίστις type words will end in either iota or epsilon. But if you really want to know, here is the rule.

- If the case ending begins with a vowel, the final stem vowel is an epsilon;

- if the case ending begins with a consonant, then the final stem vowel is an iota. But in the dative plural an epsilon precedes a sigma.

11.14 All nouns with stems that end in consonantal iota are feminine (e.g., πίστις, πίστεως, ἡ).

> ναί is "Yes."
> οὐ is "No."
> οὐχὶ is "No!" (emphatic)
> ὀρθῶς is "right"
> κακῶς is "wrong"
> ἴσως or τάχω is "maybe"
> ἀκριβῶς is "exactly"

---

[10] Think of the ως as a lengthened ος.

[11] This particular pattern of third declension nouns uses nu as the accusative singular case ending.

[12] The nominative case ending is the same as χάριτες (πιστε + ες › πίστεις, εε contracting to ει). The accusative plural uses the same case ending as the nominative plural, as if the word were neuter.

[13] Notice that the ων case ending does not swallow up the final stem vowel as it does in the first and second declensions. This is evidence that the epsilon has replaced the consonantal iota.

[14] It is called a consonantal iota because the old character shared the characteristics of both a vowel and a consonant. It is written in the grammars as "ι." It is discussed in more detail in 20.31.

11.15 Two final patterns. Here are the paradigms for πατήρ ("father") and ὕδωρ ("water"). ἀνήρ ("man") and μήτηρ ("mother") are formed like πατήρ.

nom sg:	πατήρ	ὕδωρ, τό
gen sg:	πατρός	ὕδατος
dat sg:	πατρί	ὕδατι
acc sg:	πατέρα	ὕδωρ
nom pl:	πατέρες	ὕδατα
gen pl:	πατέρων	ὑδάτων
dat pl:	πατράσι(ν)	ὕδασι(ν)
acc pl:	πατέρας	ὕδατα

πατήρ is formed from the root *πατερ. The second stem vowel fluctuates between an eta (πατήρ), epsilon (πατέρα), and nothing (πατρός). In the dative plural the stem vowel is lost and an alpha added (πατράσι) to aid pronunciation.

This stem of ὕδωρ appears to end in a tau, as can be seen in most of its forms. But when there is no case ending (nominative and accusative singular), the original final rho reappears.

Summary

1. A personal pronoun is a word replacing a personal noun.

2. The English personal pronouns are "I, my, me, we, our, us" (first person) and "you, your" (second person).

3. The case of a pronoun is determined by its function in the sentence, number and person by its antecedent.

4. Most of the forms of these two pronouns are similar to the case endings you already know. Concentrate on those similarities.

5. πίστις type words end in a consonantal iota, which now appears as ι or ε, and are all feminine.

Vocabulary

ἀδελφός, -οῦ, ὁ	brother (343; *ἀδελφο)[15]
ἄν	an untranslatable, uninflected particle, used to make a definite statement contingent upon something, e.g., changing "who" to "whoever" (166). You usually cannot translate it.

---

[15] *Philadelphia* is the city of brotherly love.

ἀνήρ, ἀνδρός, ὁ	man, male, husband (216; *ἀνδρ)[16]
	See the Appendix for the full paradigm of this word (n-3f[2c]). It is similar to the pattern of πατήρ.
ἐκκλησία, -ας, ἡ	a church, (the) Church, assembly, congregation (114; *ἐκκλησια)[17]
ἐλπίς, -ίδος, ἡ	hope, expectation (53; *ἐλπιδ)[18]
ἔξω	adverb: without (63)
	preposition (gen): outside
ἐπί (ἐπ᾽, ἐφ᾽)	gen: on, over, when (890)[19]
	dat: on the basis of, at
	acc: on, to, against
	When ἐπί is followed by a word beginning with a vowel and smooth breathing, the iota elides (ἐπ᾽ αὐτόν). If the following word begins with a rough breathing, the iota elides and the pi aspirates to a phi (ἐφ᾽ ὑμᾶς).
ἡμεῖς	we (864)[20]
θέλημα, θελήματος, τό	will, desire (62; *θελημᾳτ)[21]
ἴδε	See! Behold! (29; interjection)[22]
ἰδού	See! Behold! (200; interjection)[23]
καλός, -ή, -όν	beautiful, good (101; *καλο)[24]
μήτηρ, μητρός, ἡ	mother (83; *μητρ)[25]
	Follows the same declension pattern as πατήρ. See n-3f(2c) in the Appendix.
οὐδέ	and not, not even, neither, nor (143)
πατήρ, πατρός, ὁ	father (413; *πατρ)[26]
	See the declension pattern of this word in 11.15.

---

[16] *Androgynous* (ἀνδρόγυνη) is being both male and female (i.e., hermaphroditic).

[17] *Ecclesiology* is the study of the church. *Ecclesiastical* means "relating to the organization of the church."

[18] The Christian "hope" is not a wondering if something will happen, but the "confident anticipation" of what we know will surely come to pass. This is a great word for a word study. In a less serious vein we might mention that *Elvis* fans hope that he did not really die.

[19] The *epidermis* (ἐπιδερμίς) is the outer layer of skin, "that which is on the skin."

[20] The frequency includes all plural inflected forms.

[21] *Monothelitism* is a seventh century heresy that stated Jesus had only one nature and therefore only one will.

[22] Originally ἴδε was an aorist active imperative of εἶδον, but came to be used as a particle. It only occurs 29 times but because of its similarity with the following ἰδού, I thought it best that you learn it. It is used with the same basic meaning as the following ἰδού.

[23] This form of the verb occurs 200 times. It is actually the aorist middle imperative form of εἶδον, but it is used so many times in this particular form that I thought it best to view it as a separate word.

[24] *Calligraphy* (καλλιγραφία) is "beautiful handwriting." The frequency includes Acts 27:8 where it is used as a proper name.

[25] A *matriarchal* society is one in which the mother is the dominant figure.

[26] The *patriarch* (πατριάρχης) is the father and head of a family or tribe.

πίστις, πίστεως, ἡ	faith, belief (243; *πιστι)[27]
ὕδωρ, ὕδατος, τό	water (76; *ὑδατ)[28]
	See the declension pattern of this word in 11.15.
ὑμεῖς	you (plural) (1,840)[29]
φῶς, φωτός, τό	light (73; *φωτ)[30]
	Because φῶς is neuter, the accusatives are identical to the nominatives. See the declension pattern of this word in 11.11.
χάρις, χάριτος, ἡ	grace, favor, kindness (155; *χαριτ)
ὧδε	here (61)

Total word count in the New Testament:	138,162
Number of words learned to date:	123
Number of word occurrences in this chapter:	6,188
Number of word occurrences to date:	84,003
Percent of total word count in the New Testament:	60.80%

There is no word in Koine Greek for "please." It doesn't mean they were a rude people; they just had other ways to express the idea. In Modern Greek the word for "please" is παρακαλώ, which is also an old Koine word.

The Modern Greek word for "thanks" is ευχαριστώ. This is basically the same as in Koine. Jesus would have said, εὐχαριστῶ σοι, when he wanted to say "thank you."

---

27 *Pistology* is the study of faith.

28 *Hydrology* is the study of water. *Hydraulic* (ὕδραυλις) refers to something operated by water.

29 The frequency includes all plural inflected forms.

30 A *photograph* is a picture drawn by light.

Basics of Biblical Greek

Chapter 12
αὐτός

Exegetical Insight

Pronouns have many different uses in Greek. One of the most common pronouns is αὐτός. Its ordinary use is to "stand in" for a noun to avoid repetition. "James loved Mary, but Mary couldn't stand James" reduces to "James loved Mary, but she couldn't stand him." But sometimes the pronoun is used with a noun to add some kind of stress to it. This is a construction that Peter uses in 1 Peter 5:10, where he writes, "And the God of all grace, who called you to his eternal glory in Christ, after you have suffered a little while, will *himself* restore you and make you strong, firm and steadfast." Here Peter reinforces the subject of the sentence by adding the pronoun αὐτός, and the force of the addition is to indicate that God is personally involved in caring for his people.

In his comment on this verse P. H. Davids says, "Our author is emphatic, indicating that God is not removed from their situation, but personally involved." Such a verse would thus have come as all-the-more powerful comfort to Christians who faced hostility from the people round about them. They were being told to recognize in their activity the malevolent working of Satan and to resist him firmly, lest they succumb to the temptation to give up their faith because the going was too tough. In such a situation they needed to be convinced that, just as Satan was at work in their opponents, so God himself was not far away, leaving them to struggle on their own, but was personally concerned for each one of them, to strengthen and sustain them, and eventually to summon them to their eternal reward with him.

I. Howard Marshall

Overview

In this chapter you will learn:

- the three different ways αὐτός is used;
- that since αὐτός is a 2-1-2 adjective, we already know all its forms.

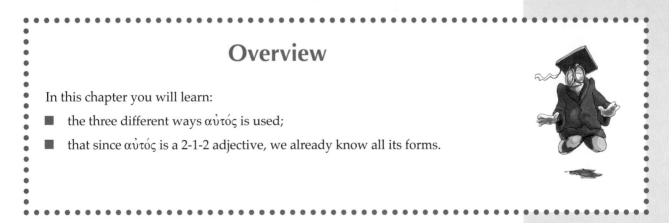

English

12.1 Here are the inflected forms of the third person personal pronoun.

	masc	fem	neut
subjective sg	he	she	it
possessive sg	his	her	its
objective sg	him	her	it
	all genders		
subjective pl	they		
possessive pl	their		
objective pl	them		

12.2 The only significant difference between the third person pronouns and the first and second is that third person singular pronouns have gender.

■ The case of a pronoun is determined by its function in the sentence.

■ The gender and number of a pronoun is determined by its antecedent.

For example, if "Robin" is the antecedent, you would say, "I would like to talk to her." You would not say, "I would like to talk to it," because Robin is not an "it." You would not say "them" because Robin is only one, and you would not say, "I would like to talk to she," since the pronoun is the object of the preposition, which takes the objective case ("her").

Greek

12.3 You have already met αὐτός functioning as the third person personal pronoun meaning "he" (αὐτός) and "him" (αὐτόν).[1] Unlike ἐγώ and σύ, αὐτός uses the normal case endings and has gender in the singular and plural.

	2 masc	1 fem	2 neut	translation		
nom sg	αὐτός	αὐτή	αὐτό	he	she	it
gen sg	αὐτοῦ	αὐτῆς	αὐτοῦ	his	her	its
dat sg	αὐτῷ	αὐτῇ	αὐτῷ	to him	to her	to it
acc sg	αὐτόν	αὐτήν	αὐτό	him	her	it
nom pl	αὐτοί	αὐταί	αὐτά	they		
gen pl	αὐτῶν	αὐτῶν	αὐτῶν	their		
dat pl	αὐτοῖς	αὐταῖς	αὐτοῖς	to them		
acc pl	αὐτούς	αὐτάς	αὐτά	them		

---

[1] We have also seen ὁ δέ meaning "but he" (10.24).

12.4 Form

■ αὐτός uses case endings just like adjectives (2-1-2).

■ The feminine follows the first declension (which has eta as the final stem vowel) and the masculine and neuter follow the second declension.

■ In the neuter nominative and accusative singular, αὐτός does not use a case ending, so the word ends with the final stem vowel (αὐτό). This is a normal subpattern for the neuter, and you have already seen it with the article: τό (see the a-1a[2b] paradigm in the Appendix, page 347).

■ αὐτός always has a smooth breathing.[2]

12.5 Declining. αὐτός is declined just like an adjective (i.e., case, number, gender, lexical form, and inflected meaning).

αὐτοῖς: dative plural masculine/neuter from αὐτός meaning "to them."

12.6 Gender. Do not be confused by the difference between Greek and English in the plural. Although in English we do not designate gender, they did in Greek.

The Three Uses of αὐτός

12.7 Summary. Do not think of αὐτός as the third person pronoun. Think of αὐτός as a word that performs three distinct functions.

12.8 Use 1: Personal pronoun. αὐτός can function as the third person personal pronoun. This is by far its most common use.[3] Translate it as you have become accustomed to.

αὐτός	he	αὐτοί	they
αὐτή	she	αὐταί	they
αὐτό	it	αὐτά	they

In this usage, the case of the pronoun is determined by its function.

Subject

αὐτοὶ τὸν θεὸν ὄψονται *(Matt 5:8).*

They will see God.

Direct object

παραλαμβάνει αὐτὸν ὁ διάβολος εἰς τὴν ἁγίαν πόλιν *(Matt 4:5).*

The devil took *him* to the holy city.

When showing possession (genitive), the pronoun usually follows the word it modifies.

καλέσεις τὸ ὄνομα αὐτοῦ Ἰησοῦν *(Matt 1:21).*

You shall call *his* name Jesus.

---

[2] This is important to remember. In Chapter 13 we will meet a word whose form is similar; the only consistent difference between the two is that αὐτός always has a smooth breathing.

[3] In the oblique cases (genitive, dative, accusative), αὐτός is used 5,322 times in the New Testament out of the total 5,597 times as a personal pronoun.

The pronoun's gender and number are determined by its antecedent.

■ If the antecedent is personal, αὐτός follows natural gender.

αὐτός ἐστιν Ἠλίας ὁ μέλλων ἔρχεσθαι *(Matt 11:14)*.
He is Elijah who is to come.

ὁ δὲ οὐκ ἀπεκρίθη αὐτῇ λόγον *(Matt 15:23)*.
But he did not answer *her* a word.

διὰ τί ἡμεῖς οὐκ ἠδυνήθημεν ἐκβαλεῖν αὐτό; *(Matt 17:19)*.
Why could we not cast *it* out?

■ But if the antecedent is not personal, αὐτός follows grammatical gender. So, for example, if the antecedent is "world" (κόσμος), Greek will use the masculine form of the pronoun (αὐτός). However, you would not translate αὐτός as "he" but as "it." We think of the world not as a "he" but as an "it."

ὀλίγοι εἰσὶν οἱ εὑρίσκοντες αὐτήν *(Matt 7:14)*.
Those who find *it* are few (referring to the narrow gate, πύλη).

12.9 **Use 2: Adjectival intensive.** αὐτός can also function intensively when it is used adjectivally.[4] In this case αὐτός normally modifies another word and is usually in the predicate position.[5] Translate αὐτός with the reflexive pronoun (himself, herself, itself, themselves, etc.).[6]

αὐτὸς ὁ ἀπόστολος	the apostle himself
αὐτὸ τὸ δῶρον	the gift itself

αὐτὸς γὰρ ὁ Ἡρῴδης ἀποστείλας ἐκράτησεν τὸν Ἰωάννην *(Mark 6:17)*.

For Herod *himself* sent and seized John.

αὐτός agrees with the noun it modifies in case, number, and gender. In English translation, choose the gender of the reflexive pronoun based on the natural gender of the word αὐτός modifies.

ἡ ἐκκλησία αὐτή	the church itself/herself
ἐγὼ αὐτός	I myself

---

[4] "Adjectival intensive" is non-standard terminology but it is helpful. It is the terminology used by *Accordance*.

   Accordance lists 143 occurrences in the New Testament of αὐτός as the adjectival intensive pronoun, but it includes the uses of αὐτός as the identical adjective (below). It lists fourteen occurrences as a strictly reflexive pronoun.

[5] Some beginning Greek grammars such as Machen (105) say that αὐτός must be in the predicate position to function as an intensive. As you will see from the exercises, this is not always the case. In fact, this chapter makes a significant departure from other grammars. They tend to translate αὐτός on the basis of its position, specifically, whether it is preceded by the article or not. Because there are so many exceptions to this way of looking at αὐτός, and because I feel it is theoretically preferable, I have classified αὐτός on the basis of function rather than position.

[6] The Greek reflexive pronoun ἐμαυτοῦ was formed through the combination of the personal pronoun ἐγώ and αὐτός. This illustrates the close relationship between αὐτός and the reflexive idea.

Do not confuse this with the predicate position of other adjectives. When an adjective is in the predicate position you must insert the verb "to be." When αὐτός is in the predicate position, it is modifying the noun adjectivally.

ὁ Ἰησοῦς ἀγαθός   Jesus is good

αὐτὸς ὁ Ἰησοῦς   Jesus himself

12.10 When functioning as an intensive, αὐτός is usually in the nominative case and modifies the subject.[7]

αὐτὸς Δαυὶδ εἶπεν ἐν τῷ πνεύματι τῷ ἁγίῳ *(Mark 12.36).*

David *himself* spoke by the Holy Spirit.

Ἰησοῦς αὐτὸς οὐκ ἐβάπτιζεν ἀλλ᾽ οἱ μαθηταὶ αὐτοῦ *(John 4:2).*

Jesus *himself* was not baptizing but his disciples.

This is the same use of the personal pronoun we saw with ἐγώ and σύ. Remember, because the verb indicates its own subject, the use of αὐτός is technically unnecessary, and therefore its presence can be emphatic.

Different suggestions are made on how to translate αὐτός when it occurs in this situation. Some suggest using a reflexive pronoun as in the illustrations above. It is David himself and not someone else who spoke by the Holy Spirit.

Others suggest ignoring the personal intensive use of αὐτός in the nominative because this translation does not sound proper to English ears. If you do ignore it, be sure to remember that it can add an intensifying force.

The subject of the verb does not have to be third person. When used with the first or second person, αὐτός still adds emphasis.

σὺ αὐτὸς λέγεις τοῖς ἀνθρώποις.

You *yourself* speak to the men.

12.11 **Use 3: Identical adjective.** αὐτός is sometimes used as the identical adjective meaning "same." This is its least frequent usage. It is normally in the attributive position when used this way, but not always.[8] Its case, number, and gender are determined by the word it modifies, as is the case with any adjective.

καὶ πάλιν ἀπελθὼν προσηύξατο τὸν αὐτὸν λόγον *(Mark 14:39).*

And again after going away he prayed *the same thing.*

Ἐν αὐτῇ[9] τῇ ὥρᾳ προσῆλθάν τινες Φαρισαῖοι *(Luke 13:31).*

In *the same hour* some Pharisees came.

---

[7] Some grammarians argue that αὐτός can be used in the nominative without any sense of emphasis, simply as the personal pronoun and not as an intensive pronoun.

Accordance separates this use from the adjectival intensive, calling it the "personal intensive." For didactic reasons I have put them together. αὐτός is used 243 times in the New Testament as a personal intensive, 239 times in the nominative.

[8] αὐτός is found in the attributive position 60 times in the New Testament.

[9] Notice that there is no article with αὐτός in this example. This shows that the anarthrous αὐτός can function as the identical adjective, despite what many grammars say.

Summary

1. αὐτός uses the normal case endings except for the nominative and accusative neuter singular, which drop the nu. This is a common variation.

2. When αὐτός functions as a pronoun, its case is determined by function, its number and gender by antecedent.

3. When αὐτός adds emphasis it is usually translated with the reflexive pronoun. It usually will be in the predicate position, in the nominative case.

4. αὐτός can function as the identical adjective and be translated "same." In this usage it normally is in the attributive position.

Vocabulary

αἰών, -ῶνος, ὁ *3rd dec.* *I - own*	age, eternity (122; *αἰων) The idioms εἰς τὸν αἰῶνα and εἰς τοὺς αἰῶνας τῶν αἰώνων both mean "forever."
διδάσκαλος, -ου, ὁ	teacher (59; *διδασκαλο)[10]
εὐθύς	immediately (58)[11] εὐθύς occurs 51x as an adverb and 7x as an adjective.
ἕως	conj: until (146) preposition (gen): as far as
Masculine μαθητής, -οῦ, ὁ	disciple (261; *μαθητη)[12] μαθητής is declined just like προφήτης.
μέν	on the one hand, indeed (179) Postpositive. Sometimes this word is untranslatable. It can occur as a correlative conjunction with δέ. In this case you can translate μέν ... δέ as "on the one hand ... but on the other." Usually in English you do not translate μέν and translate δέ as "but."
μηδείς, μηδεμία, μηδέν	no one / thing (90; μη(δε) + *ἑν / *μια) Declines just like οὐδείς.
μόνος, -η, -ον	alone, only (114; *μονο)[13] All adjectives can function adverbially. This word does so quite often, usually as an accusative neuter (μόνον).
ὅπως	how, that, in order that (53)

---

[10] Different teachers have different *didactic* (διδακτικός) methods.

[11] This adverb is different from the adjective εὐθύς, -εῖα, -ύ, meaning "straight," which occurs only nine times in the New Testament.

[12] A disciple is a "learner." *Math* is related to μάθημα, meaning "that which is learned." *Mathematics* is from μαθηματική.

[13] A *monogamous* marriage is a marriage in which a person has only one spouse.

ὅσος, -η, -ον	as great as, as many as (110; *ὁσο)

The initial ὁσ retains the same form, but the second half of the word declines like the relative pronoun. For example, the nominative plural masculine is ὅσοι. This word is idiomatic; rely on context to help with a precise definition.

οὖν	therefore, then, accordingly (499)

Postpositive.

ὀφθαλμός, -οῦ, ὁ	eye, sight (100; *ὀφθαλμο)[14]
πάλιν	again (141)[15]
πούς, ποδός, ὁ	foot (93; *ποδ)[16]

πούς is declined like ἐλπίς, ἐλπίδος, except that in the nominative singular the omicron of the root lengthens to ου (*ποδ + ς ▸ πος ▸ πούς). The dative plural is ποσί(ν).

ὑπέρ	gen: in behalf of (150)[17]
	acc: above

Total word count in the New Testament:	138,162
Number of words learned to date:	138
Number of word occurrences in this chapter:	2,176
Number of word occurrences to date:	86,179
Percent of total word count in the New Testament:	62.37%

I hope you have been singing Greek songs well before this chapter, but here is a familiar tune. You can download the sheet music and hear my friend sing it on the class website.

ὁ Ἰησοῦς με ἀγαπᾷ,	Jesus me he-loves
ὅτι γραφὴ κηρύσσει·	because Scripture proclaims;
παιδία εἰσὶν αὐτῷ,	Children are to-him,
ἀσθένουσι δύναται.	They-are-weak; he-is-strong
ναί, Ἰησοῦς ἀγαπᾷ	Yes, Jesus loves,
ναί, Ἰησοῦς ἀγαπᾷ	Yes, Jesus loves,
ναί, Ἰησοῦς ἀγαπᾷ	Yes, Jesus loves,
ἡ γραφὴ κηρύσσει.	The Scripture proclaims.

---

[14] *Ophthalmology* is the study of the eye.

[15] A *palimpsest* (παλίμψηστος, "scraped again") is a parchment that has had the original writing scraped off so it can be used again. *Palilogy* (παλιλογία) is the repetition of words for emphasis. The *palingenesia* (παλιγγενεσία) is the rebirth, both of the Christian (Titus 3:5) and of the world in Stoic thought.

[16] A *podiatrist* is a doctor dealing with foot disorders. Notice how the word's root came over into English with the "d," even though it is not visible in the nominative πούς. Most cognates are formed from the Greek root and not an inflected form such as the nominative.

[17] "Hyper" is a common prefix designating excess, abundance. An *hyperbole* is an exaggeration for effect.

Chapter 13

Demonstrative Pronouns/Adjectives

οὖτος, ἐκεῖνος

this/these   that/those

Exegetical Insight

δικαιοσύνη is one of the great words in Christian theology. Basically it means, "the character or quality of being right or just." It is a word used to describe God. He is in the ultimate sense the Just One (Rom 3:5, 25). It is also used to describe the righteous life of the believer, i.e., a life lived in obedience to the will of God (Rom 6:13, 16, 18, 19, 20; Eph 6:14, etc.).

But the most important use of δικαιοσύνη in the New Testament is to describe the gracious gift of God by which through faith in Jesus Christ one is brought into a right relationship to God. Such a relationship is apart from law, i.e., apart from the works of the law—we can do nothing to obtain it. However, the "Law and the Prophets," i.e., the Old Testament Scriptures, testify to it. It was all a part of God's redemptive plan that we should have been put into a right relationship with him through his Son.

Luther was right when he wrote: "For God does not want to save us by our own but by an extraneous righteousness, one that does not originate in ourselves but comes to us from beyond ourselves."

My hope is built on nothing less
Than Jesus' blood and δικαιοσύνη.

Walter W. Wessel

Overview

In this chapter you will learn:

- the demonstrative pronouns and adjectives "this" and "that";

- that they behave just like pronouns and adjectives except that when functioning as adjectives they are in the predicate position;

- the fifth and final case, the vocative, used when addressing a person directly.

English

13.1 Demonstratives in English are "this/these" and "that/those" (singular/plural). For example, "This book is the greatest Greek textbook." "Those students really work hard." The demonstratives are never inflected except to indicate singular and plural.[1]

13.2 The same word can be either a pronoun (*"That* is mine.") or an adjective (*"That* car is mine.").[2]

Greek

13.3 The demonstratives in Greek are οὗτος (this/these) and ἐκεῖνος (that/those). They function the same way as they do in English, both as pronouns and as adjectives. The difference between the English and Greek demonstratives is that the Greek demonstratives have case and gender.

- When a demonstrative functions as a pronoun, its case is determined by its function in the sentence. Its number and gender are determined by its antecedent, just like any pronoun.

- When a demonstrative functions as an adjective, its case, number, and gender are determined by the noun it is modifying, just like any adjective.

In the following paradigms, translate each form as an adjective and then as a pronoun.

13.4 The forms of οὗτος

	2 *masc*	1 *fem*	2 *neut*
nom sg	οὗτος	αὕτη	τοῦτο
gen sg	τούτου	ταύτης	τούτου
dat sg	τούτῳ	ταύτῃ	τούτῳ
acc sg	τοῦτον	ταύτην	τοῦτο
nom pl	οὗτοι	αὗται	ταῦτα
gen pl	τούτων	τούτων	τούτων
dat pl	τούτοις	ταύταις	τούτοις
acc pl	τούτους	ταύτας	ταῦτα

> Since you have been learning pronouns, let's practice them a bit conversationally.
>
> Tell someone that Jesus loves them. If you are speaking to one person you would say,
>
> ὁ Ἰησοῦς σε ἀγαπᾷ.

(handwritten margin notes)

This: οὗτος
These: οὗτοι

That: ἐκεῖνος
Those: ἐκεῖνα

(handwritten notes on table: How-Tay; πιο τ)

---

[1] A distinction some find helpful is between the "near" and "far" demonstratives. The near is "this/these" and the far is "that/those." The idea is that "this/these" refers to something in relative proximity, and "that/those" to something relatively far away.

[2] For the sake of simplicity I will call them the "demonstratives," not the "demonstrative pronoun" or "demonstrative adjective."

13.5 The forms of ἐκεῖνος

	2 *masc*	1 *fem*	2 *neut*
nom sg	ἐκεῖνος	ἐκείνη	ἐκεῖνο
gen sg	ἐκείνου	ἐκείνης	ἐκείνου
dat sg	ἐκείνῳ	ἐκείνῃ	ἐκείνῳ
acc sg	ἐκεῖνον	ἐκείνην	ἐκεῖνο
nom pl	ἐκεῖνοι	ἐκεῖναι	ἐκεῖνα
gen pl	ἐκείνων	ἐκείνων	ἐκείνων
dat pl	ἐκείνοις	ἐκείναις	ἐκείνοις
acc pl	ἐκείνους	ἐκείνας	ἐκεῖνα

Characteristics of Demonstrative Pronouns

13.6 **Form**. The demonstratives use the regular case endings. There are three peculiarities that need to be learned carefully.

1. The neuter singular nominative and accusative do not use a case ending, so the form ends in the stem omicron rather than ον. This is the same as αὐτός, ἄλλος, and ὁ.

2. οὗτος always begins with a rough breathing or tau. Think of the two as interchangeable. This is important in distinguishing the feminine demonstrative (αὗται) from αὐτός, which always has a smooth breathing (αὐταί).

3. The first stem vowel used in οὗτος depends upon the final stem vowel.

   ■ If the final vowel is alpha or eta, the demonstrative will have alpha in the stem (e.g., ταύταις, ταύτης).

   ■ If the final vowel is omicron, the stem will have omicron (e.g., τούτου).[3]

13.7 **Pronoun**. If a demonstrative is functioning as a pronoun, it will not modify a word (just like the substantival adjective).

οὗτος			ἐκεῖνος	
οὗτος	this (man/one)		ἐκεῖνος	that (man/one)
αὕτη	this (woman)		ἐκείνη	that (woman)
τοῦτο	this (thing)		ἐκεῖνο	that (thing)
οὗτοι	these (men/ones)		ἐκεῖνοι	those (men/ones)
αὗται	these (women)		ἐκεῖναι	those (women)
ταῦτα	these (things)		ἐκεῖνα	those (things)

As a pronoun, the translation of the demonstrative may require an additional word such as those in parentheses above. Pick whatever makes the

---

[3]   This point is not as significant as the first two since we are only learning to recognize the forms and not memorizing paradigms.

best sense, following natural gender. For example, ἐκείνη would not be translated "that man."

13.8 **Adjectives.** If a demonstrative is functioning as an adjective, it occurs in the **predicate** position although it functions as an attributive adjective.

> οὗτος ὁ ἄνθρωπος
>
> This man
>
> ὁ ἄνθρωπος οὗτος
>
> This man
>
> ἐκεῖνοι οἱ ἄνθρωποι
>
> Those men

This is the opposite of regular adjectives, so do not get them confused.[4] The noun it modifies will always have the article.

How would you tell a group of people that Jesus loves them?

ὁ Ἰησοῦς ὑμᾶς ἀγαπᾷ.

13.9 Sometimes the demonstrative pronoun weakens in its force and functions as a personal pronoun.

> οὗτος ἔσται μέγας καὶ υἱὸς ὑψίστου κληθήσεται *(Luke 1:32).*
>
> *He* will be great and will be called "Son of the Most High."

As you might have guessed, there is substantial overlap among the article, the personal pronoun, and the demonstrative pronoun.

Vocative

13.10 The fifth, and final, case is the vocative, the "case of direct address." A noun uses vocative case endings when it is being directly addressed. In the following example, the person is addressing the "Lord" directly.

> Οὐ πᾶς ὁ λέγων μοι, Κύριε κύριε, εἰσελεύσεται εἰς τὴν βασιλείαν τῶν οὐρανῶν *(Matt 7:21).*
>
> Not everyone saying to me, *"Lord, Lord,"* will enter into the kingdom of heaven.

The forms of the vocative, for the most part, are quite simple. It is usually obvious from context when the word is in the vocative.[5]

■ In the plural, the vocative is always identical to the nominative plural.

> ἄνδρες Γαλιλαῖοι, τί ἑστήκατε ἐμβλέποντες εἰς τὸν οὐρανόν; *(Acts 1:11).*
>
> *Men* of Galilee, why do you stand staring into heaven?

■ In the singular first declension, the vocative is the same as the nominative.

> ἐρῶ τῇ ψυχῇ μου· ψυχή, ἔχεις πολλὰ ἀγαθά *(Luke 12:19).*
>
> And I will say to my soul, *Soul,* you have ample goods.

---

[4]   We have already seen this grammar in connection with αὐτός used as an intensive and with πᾶς.

[5]   There are 607 vocatives in the New Testament. The most common are κύριε (121x), ἀδελφοί (106x), πάτερ (29x, or πατήρ, 6x as πατέρες), ἄνδρες (32x), and διδάσκαλε (31x).

- In the singular second declension, the vocative ending is usually epsilon.

  > ἄνθρωπε, ἀφέωνταί σοι αἱ ἁμαρτίαι σου *(Luke 5:20)*.
  > *Friend*, your sins are forgiven you.

- In the singular third declension, the vocative is usually the bare stem of the word, sometimes with the stem vowel being changed (ablaut).

  > Πάτερ ἡμῶν ὁ ἐν τοῖς οὐρανοῖς *(Matt 6:9)*
  > Our *Father* who is in heaven

There are a few other forms of the vocative, but this information is enough for now. Normally context will warn you when a form is in the vocative.[6]

Odds 'n Ends

13.11 **Degrees of an adjective**. An adjective can have three "degrees."

- The **positive** degree is the uncompared form of the adjective: "large" (μέγας).

- The **comparative** degree denotes the greater of two items: "larger" (μείζων).

- The **superlative** degree describes the greatest, or a comparison of three or more: "largest" (μέγιστος).

In Koine Greek the superlative was dying out and its function was being assumed by the comparative (see *BDF*, #60). For example, someone might use μείζων when context technically requires μέγιστος. As usual, context is the key in translation.

13.12 **Crasis** is when a word is formed by combining two words. In this chapter you will meet κἀγώ, which is a crasis of καί and ἐγώ. See the Appendix for a list of all forms of crasis in the New Testament, page 342.

13.13 **Πολύς**. You also meet the word πολύς, meaning "much" or "many." It looks like a cross between a second and third declension word.

	2 *masc*	1 *fem*	2 *neut*
nom sg	πολύς	πολλή	πολύ
gen sg	πολλοῦ	πολλῆς	πολλοῦ
dat sg	πολλῷ	πολλῇ	πολλῷ
acc sg	πολύν	πολλήν	πολύ
nom pl	πολλοί	πολλαί	πολλά
gen pl	πολλῶν	πολλῶν	πολλῶν
dat pl	πολλοῖς	πολλαῖς	πολλοῖς
acc pl	πολλούς	πολλάς	πολλά

---

6   All the rules are listed in *MBG*.

Summary

1. The demonstrative "this/these" is οὗτος and "that/those" is ἐκεῖνος. οὗτος always begins with either a rough breathing or tau. Neither uses a case ending in the nominative/accusative neuter singular.

2. When they function as a pronoun their case is determined by their function in the sentence, number and gender by their antecedent. You can supply a helping word if you wish, determined by natural gender.

3. When they function as an adjective, their case, number, and gender agree with the word they are modifying. They will always be in the predicate position although they are translated as attributive adjectives.

4. A demonstrative can weaken in force and be used as a personal pronoun.

5. The vocative is the case of direct address.

   ■ In the plural, it is identical to the nominative regardless of declension.

   ■ In the singular first declension, it is identical to the nominative.

   ■ In the singular second declension, it usually has the case ending epsilon.

   ■ In the singular third declension, it usually is the bare stem.

Vocabulary

γυνή, γυναικός, ἡ	woman, wife (215; *γυναικ)[7]
	γυνή is declined like σάρξ (n-3b[1]). The ικ is lost in the nominative singular.
δικαιοσύνη, -ης, ἡ	righteousness (92; *δικαιοσυνη)
δώδεκα	twelve (75). Indeclinable.[8]
ἑαυτοῦ, -ῆς, -οῦ	singular: himself/herself/itself plural: themselves (319; *ἑαυτο)
	ἑαυτοῦ is the reflexive pronoun. While it occurs predominantly in the third person, it can be used in the first and second person as well ("myself," "yourself").
	Because of the word's meaning, it can never occur in the nominative; so for this word the lexical form is the genitive singular. It follows the same inflectional pattern as αὐτός.
	ἑαυτοῦ in the plural can also be translated as first ("ourselves") or second ("yourselves") person, if the verb in the sentence calls for that.
ἐκεῖνος, -η, -ο	singular: that man/woman/thing plural: those men/women/things (265; 2-1-2; *ἐκεινο)

---

[7] *Gynecology* is the branch of medicine dealing with women's health and diseases.

[8] A *dodecagon* is a plane with twelve sides and twelve angles.

ἤ	or, than (343)
	Do not confuse this with the article ἡ, which always has a rough breathing.
κἀγώ	and I, but I (84).
	Indeclinable. κἀγώ is a crasis of καί and ἐγώ. The frequency includes the forms κἀμέ and κἀμοί.
μακάριος, -ία, -ιον	blessed, happy (50; 2-1-2; *μακαριο)[9]
μέγας, μεγάλη, μέγα[10]	large, great (243; 2-1-2; *μεγαλο)[11]
πόλις, -εως, ἡ	city (163; *πολς)[12]
πολύς, πολλή, πολύ	singular: much (416; 2-1-2; *πολλο)[13]
	plural: many
	adverb: often
πῶς	how? (103)[14]
σημεῖον, -ου, τό	sign, miracle (77; *σημειο)[15]

Total word count in the New Testament:	138,162
Number of words learned to date:	151
Number of word occurrences in this chapter:	2,445
Number of word occurrences to date:	88,624
Percent of total word count in the New Testament:	64.14%

Previous Words

οὗτος, αὕτη, τοῦτο	singular: this; he, she, it (1388; 2-1-2; *τουτο)
	plural: these

---

[9]   Metzger, *Lexical Aids*, suggests the cognate "macarism," which is a beatitude.

[10]   See the paradigm of this word in the Appendix (a-1a[2a]).

[11]   *Mega* is a common prefix meaning "large" or "great": *megaphone, megavolt, Megalosaurus*, which is a genus of extremely large dinosaurs (σαῦρος means "lizard").

[12]   *Metropolis* ("mother-city") is the parent city of a colony, especially an ancient Greek colony. The word came to be used of any capital or large city. *Neapolis* is the port city of Philippi (Acts 16:11).

[13]   *Poly* is a common combining form meaning "many": *polysyllabic, polyandry, polygamy, polyglot, polygon.*

[14]   There is another word πώς meaning "at all, somehow, in any way," occurring 15 times. The only difference between the two words is the accent.

[15]   In John's gospel especially, miracles are signs as to who Jesus truly is. *Semeio* is a combining form meaning "sign" or "symptom." *Semeiology* is sign language. *Semeiotic* means "pertaining to symptoms."

Chapter 14

Relative Pronoun

Exegetical Insight

One author refers to the author of the first of our four canonical Gospels as "meticulous Matthew." Matthew regularly displays intentional precision in his account of the Savior's earthly life and ministry in order to accentuate truths that are important for devotion and doctrine. This precision is quite evident in the genealogy Matthew uses to introduce Jesus the Christ at the beginning of his gospel. When he comes to the listing of Jesus he says, "... and Jacob the father of Joseph, the husband of Mary, *of whom* was born Jesus, who is called Christ" (Matt 1:16, NIV). To whom do the italicized words "of whom" refer? Joseph as father? Mary as mother? Both Joseph and Mary as parents? It is possible for the English words "of whom" to mean any of these.

However, behind the English words "of whom" stands the Greek relative pronoun ἧς. The feminine gender of the relative pronoun points specifically to Mary as the one from whom Jesus Christ was born. The genealogy regularly emphasizes the male who fathers a child, but here "meticulous Matthew" delivers a precise statement of the relationship of Jesus Christ to Joseph and Mary. While the genealogy establishes that Joseph is the legal father of Jesus, Matthew emphasizes that Mary is the biological parent "of whom" Jesus was born. Further, the passive voice of the verb ἐγεννήθη ("was born")—the only passive among the forty occurrences of γεννάω in the genealogy—prepares for Matthew's emphasis upon divine action in the conception and birth of Jesus (1:18-25).

In his comment on this verse, R. H. Gundry says, "the feminine gender of ἧς prepares for the virgin birth by shifting attention from Joseph to Mary." The Greek relative pronoun is a subtle signature of the relationship of one substantive to another. Here, by the use of the feminine form the author intentionally stresses that Mary is the mother of our Lord, and later he will clarify that the conception is miraculous, brought about by the Spirit of God coming upon her. Jesus Christ is indeed the son of David, the son of Abraham (1:1), but he is also the Son of God, Immanuel, "God with us" (1:23). This is no ordinary king in the line of David. This is our Savior and Lord, born of the virgin Mary.

Michael J. Wilkins

Overview

In this chapter you will learn:

- the relative pronouns "who," "that," and "which";

- that like any pronoun, their gender and number are determined by their antecedent, while their case is determined by their function in the relative clause;

- relative clauses are always dependent clauses, so they cannot contain the main subject and verb of the sentence.

English

14.1   The relative pronouns in English are "who," "whom," "that," "which," and "whose." Usage of these words today differs widely, and therefore the following examples merely reflect general usage.

- "Who" and "whom" are used to refer to humans (e.g., The teacher, whom the students love, won the teacher of the year award.).

- "Who" is used for masculine and feminine concepts and "which" for neuter.

- "That" can refer to either (e.g., The glass that broke was my favorite. I helped the boy that fell off his bike.).[1]

- "Whose" often refers to humans, but generally speaking it is accepted for non-humans as well (e.g., I sold the car whose color made me ill. I love the girl whose eyes sparkle in the moonlight.).

Notice that the relative pronouns can refer back to a singular ("the student who") or plural ("the students who") antecedent.

14.2   Relative pronouns do not introduce questions. They always refer to a noun or a noun phrase. For example, a relative pronoun is not used in a question like, "Whose eyes sparkled in the moon light?" The word "whose" in this example is an interrogative pronoun.

14.3   A relative pronoun introduces a clause that usually modifies a noun. In the examples just given,

- "whom" introduces the clause "the students loved" and modifies the noun "teacher";

- "that" introduces the clause "broke" and modifies the noun "glass."

Note how little the pronoun is inflected.

14.4   A **relative clause** is the relative pronoun and the clause it introduces. "The teacher *who has a halo around his head* teaches Greek."

---

[1]   "That" generally refers to impersonal objects and is used in restrictive clauses. "Which" is used for non-restrictive clauses.

14.5 Do not forget that clauses can perform many of the same functions as nouns and adjectives. A relative clause can be the

- subject (*"Whoever is with me* is not against me."),

- direct object ("I eat *what is placed before me.*"),

- or object of a preposition ("Give the Bible to *whoever asks for it.*").

This becomes important in our translation procedure because the relative clause must be viewed as a unit.

Greek

14.6 The relative pronoun in Greek functions basically the same way as the English except that it has case, number, and gender. They are ὅς, ἥ, and ὅ.

14.7 **The forms of the relative pronoun**

	2 masc	1 fem	2 neut	translation
nom sg	ὅς	ἥ	ὅ	who/which/that
gen sg	οὗ	ἧς	οὗ	of whom/which/whose
dat sg	ᾧ	ᾗ	ᾧ	to whom/which
acc sg	ὅν	ἥν	ὅ	whom/which/that
nom pl	οἵ	αἵ	ἅ	who/which/that
gen pl	ὧν	ὧν	ὧν	of whom/which/whose
dat pl	οἷς	αἷς	οἷς	to whom/which
acc pl	οὕς	ἅς	ἅ	whom/which/that

The accent helps distinguish the relative pronoun from the article in the nominative, which has no accent in the masculine and feminine (ὁ, ἡ; οἱ, αἱ).

Characteristics of Relative Pronouns

14.8 **Form.** Notice the similarities between the relative pronouns and the noun endings. They are almost identical. The neuter nominative and accusative singular do not have the nu but only the omicron, just like αὐτός and the demonstratives.

The relative pronouns are also similar to the article. The key for distinguishing the two is noting the breathings and accents. The relative pronouns always have a rough breathing mark and an accent. The article always has either a rough breathing mark or a tau, and may be unaccented. See the Appendix, page 347, for a comparison.

14.9 **Antecedent.** *The number and gender of a relative pronoun are the same as its antecedent,* just like αὐτός. You can see how looking for the antecedent will help check your translations and make them accurate.

Sometimes the antecedent will not be in the same verse as the relative pronoun; you will have to look at the preceding verse(s). Even then sometimes you will find no antecedent. How then do you determine what the relative pronoun is referring to? Context!

14.10 **Case of the relative pronoun.** *The case of the relative pronoun is determined by its function in the relative clause, not in the sentence.*

> ὃς οὐ λαμβάνει τὸν σταυρὸν αὐτοῦ καὶ ἀκολουθεῖ ὀπίσω μου, οὐκ ἔστιν μου ἄξιος *(Matt 10:38).*
>
> *Whoever* does not take his cross and follow me is not worthy of me.

> ἰδοὺ ὁ ἀστήρ, ὃν εἶδον ἐν τῇ ἀνατολῇ *(Matt 2:9)*
>
> Behold, the star *that* they had seen when it rose

Do not confuse the relative pronoun with the adjective, whose case is determined by the word it modifies.

> ὁ ἄνθρωπος ὃν γινώσκομεν διδάσκει ἡμᾶς.
>
> The man whom we know teaches us.

In this example you can see that even though the antecedent (ἄνθρωπος) is nominative, the relative pronoun (ὅν) is accusative because it is the direct object of the verb γινώσκομεν inside the relative clause.

14.11 **Translation**. A relative pronoun is translated various ways depending upon the function of the relative clause. This is an issue of English grammar and not Greek.

1. If the relative clause modifies a word, then the relative pronoun is translated with the simple "who," "which," or "that."

    The man who is sitting at the table is my pastor.

2. Relative clauses can also function as the subject, direct object, indirect object, object of a preposition, etc. In other words, they can perform almost any function that a noun can. In these cases, it may be necessary to add a pronoun to the clause to make better sounding English.

    For example, in the sentence *"Who will be first* will be last," the relative clause is the subject of the verb "will be." To make the translation smoother you could add a personal pronoun, *"He who will be first will be last."*

    > ὃς οὐ λαμβάνει τὸν σταυρὸν αὐτοῦ ... οὐκ ἔστιν μου ἄξιος *(Matt 10:38).*
    >
    > *He* who does not take his cross ... is not worthy of me.

    You can also add a demonstrative pronoun ("Give the good grade to *those* who deserve it.")

    Use your educated common sense to determine the appropriate pronoun.

Translation Procedure

14.12 As was the case with prepositional phrases, it is important to keep the relative clause together as a unit when you are dividing up the sentence.

> ὁ Ἰησοῦς / ἐλάλησεν / ὅ ἐστιν δίκαιον.
>
> Jesus spoke what is righteous.

14.13 Relative clauses are always dependent; they will never contain the main subject and verb of the sentence.

Summary

1. Relative pronouns introduce relative clauses, which are capable of performing many of the tasks of nouns and adjectives.

2. The relative pronouns are ὅς, ἥ, and ὅ. They follow the normal 2-1-2 declension patterns (like αὐτός) and always have a rough breathing and an accent.

3. Like other pronouns, the case of a relative pronoun is determined by its use in the relative clause, and its number and gender by its antecedent.

4. You can add a pronoun to your translation of a relative clause; use your educated common sense and context to determine the best pronoun.

5. Relative clauses are always dependent.

Vocabulary

ἀλήθεια, -ας, ἡ	truth (109; *ἀληθεια)[2]
εἰρήνη, -ης, ἡ	peace (92; *εἰρηνη)[3]
ἐνώπιον	gen: before (94)
ἐπαγγελία, -ας, ἡ	promise (52; *ἐπαγγελια)
ἑπτά	seven (88). Indeclinable.[4]
θρόνος, -ου, ὁ	throne (62; *θρονο)[5]
Ἰερουσαλήμ, ἡ	Jerusalem (77)
	Ἰερουσαλήμ is indeclinable. However, the article will be inflected.

---

[2] The girl's name *Alethea* means "truth." *Alethiology* is the science of the truth.

[3] *Irenic* (εἰρηνικός) means "peaceful."

[4] A *heptagon* has seven sides.

[5] *Throne.*

κατά (κατ᾽, καθ᾽)	gen: down from, against (473)[6] acc: according to, throughout, during When κατά is followed by a word beginning with a vowel and smooth breathing, the alpha elides (κατ᾽ ἐμοῦ). If the following word begins with a rough breathing, the alpha elides and the tau aspirates to a theta (καθ᾽ ὑμῶν).
κεφαλή, -ῆς, ἡ	head (75; *κεφαλη)[7]
ὁδός, -οῦ, ἡ	way, road, journey, conduct (101; *ὁδο) Notice that although this word appears to be masculine, it is really feminine. It is a second declension feminine noun. It looks like λόγος but is feminine. The article that modifies it will always be feminine.
ὅς, ἥ, ὅ	who (whom), which (1,407)
ὅτε	when (103)[8]
οὕτως	thus, so, in this manner (208)
πλοῖον, -ου, τό	ship, boat (68; *πλοιο)
ῥῆμα, -ατος, τό	word, saying (68; *ῥηματ)[9]
τε	and (so), so (215) τε is a postpositive and weaker in force than καί.
χείρ, χειρός, ἡ	hand, arm, finger (177; *χειρ)[10]
ψυχή, -ῆς, ἡ	soul, life, self (103; *ψυχη)[11]

Total word count in the New Testament:	138,162
Number of words learned to date:	169
Number of word occurrences in this chapter:	3,571
Number of word occurrences to date:	92,195
Percent of total word count in the New Testament:	66.73%

Previous Words

ἄν	When used in conjunction with a relative pronoun, ἄν makes the pronoun indefinite (e.g. "who" becomes "whoever").
ἐάν	if, when, -ever We have already learned this word in Chapter 9, but now you know to use "-ever" in your translation when it is associated with a relative pronoun.

---

[6]   *Cata* is a common combining form meaning "down." *Catabasis* is the declining stage of a disease. *Catalogue* (κατάλογος) is a counting down in the sense of creating a list. A *catastrophe* (καταστροφή) is a sudden disaster, a downturn.

[7]   *Hydrocephalus* (ὑδροκέφαλον) is the name given to the condition of an increase in the amount of water in the cranium with resulting brain damage.

[8]   Do not confuse this word with ὅτι.

[9]   *Rhetoric* (ῥητορική) is the art of using words effectively.

[10]   *Chirography* is writing. A *chiromancer* is a palmist, a palm reader.

[11]   *Psychology* is the study of a person's self.

Advanced Information

14.14 Attraction. Greek, as is the case with any language, does not always follow the basic rules. All spoken languages are in a constant state of flux, so nice, neat grammatical rules often break down.

This is the case with the relative pronoun. Its case is supposed to be determined by its function inside the relative clause, but in certain situations you will see that it is altered to be the same case as its antecedent, as if it were modifying it. This is called "attraction."

Attraction usually happens when the relative pronoun occurs in the immediate proximity to the antecedent, when the antecedent is dative or genitive, and when the relative pronoun normally would be accusative.

> ἤγγιζεν ὁ χρόνος τῆς ἐπαγγελίας ἧς ὡμολόγησεν ὁ θεὸς τῷ Ἀβραάμ *(Acts 7:17)*.
>
> The time of the promise *that* God promised to Abraham was drawing near.

The relative pronoun ἧς *should* have been the accusative ἥν because it is the direct object of ὡμολόγησεν, but it was attracted to the genitive case of its antecedent ἐπαγγελίας.

You aren't still referring to the books of the Bible by their English names, are you? Here are their names in Greek. There is too much here to learn all at once, but over time you should get them down.

Μαθθαῖον	Ῥωμαίους	Ἑβραίους
Μᾶρκον	Κορινθίους α΄	Ἰακώβου
Λουκᾶν	Κορινθίους β΄	Πέτρου α΄
Ἰωάννην	Γαλάτας	Πέτρου β΄
Πράξεις Ἀποστόλων	Ἐφεσίους	Ἰωάννου α΄
	Φιλιππησίους	Ἰωάννου β΄
	Κολοσσαεῖς	Ἰωάννου γ΄
	Θεσσαλονικεῖς α΄	Ἰούδα
	Θεσσαλονικεῖς β΄	Ἀποκάλυψις Ἰωάνναυ
	Τιμόθεον α΄	
	Τιμόθεον β΄	
	Τίτον	
	Φιλήμονα	

In your Greek Bible, the name of the Gospels are preeded by Κατά, which explains why they are in the accusative. Paul's letters and Hebrews are preceded by Πρός.

Overview 3

Chapters 15 – 20

It is now time to study verbs. There is much you have already learned.

- Verbs are formed with a stem and personal endings.

- Verbs are first, second, or third person, singular or plural.

- Verbs agree with their subject in person and number.

- Verbs do not require an expressed subject.

- You have also learned some of the forms of εἰμί.

Chapter 15

Just as I started nouns with an overview of English noun grammar (Chapter 5), so also Chapter 15 gives you an overview of English verbal grammar. There is not much new to learn, but this can be a central reference point.

Chapter 16

The present active indicative is the form of a verb used to describe an action that normally occurs in the present. You form it by combining the present tense stem with a connecting vowel and personal endings. I will give you a chart like the following for each part of the verb system; it is key to memorize.

> *Present tense stem + Connecting vowel +*
> *Primary active personal endings*
>
> λυ + ο + μεν ‣ λύομεν

Remember, a verb must agree with its subject in person and number. It does this by adding personal endings onto the end of the verb. Because there are three persons and two numbers, there are six personal endings for the present active. There are only four sets of these endings, or 24 forms. It is not that much to memorize.

After showing you the chart, I show you the paradigm of how the personal endings attach to the verb (see next page). I also introduce you to the Master Verb Chart. This is the other chart you must memorize; it shows you how the verb is put together in the different tenses. You can memorize this chart, or you can memorize hundreds and hundreds of verbal forms. I think this is easier. (You're welcome.)

	form	translation	connecting vowel	personal ending
1 sg	λύω	I am loosing	ο	–
2 sg	λύεις	You are loosing	ε	ς
3 sg	λύει	He/she/it is loosing	ε	ι
1 pl	λύομεν	We are loosing	ο	μεν
2 pl	λύετε	You are loosing	ε	τε
3 pl	λύουσι(ν)	They are loosing	ο	νσι

Master Verb Chart

Tense	Aug/ Redup	Tense stem	Tense form.	Conn. vowel	Personal endings	1st sing paradigm
Present act		pres		ο/ε	prim act	λύω

Chapter 17

Contract verbs are verbs whose root ends in a vowel, like ἀγαπάω. They use the same personal endings you learn in Chapter 16, but the ending contracts with the stem vowel. And so you have ἀγαπῶμεν (cf. λύομεν). The αο contracted to omega.

Chapter 18

In Chapters 16 and 17 you learned active verbs. This means that the subject of the sentence does the action of the verb. λύομεν means "we loose." If the verb is passive, it means the subject receives the action of the verb. Greek forms the passive by using a different set of six personal endings. λυόμεθα means "we are loosed."

Chapter 19

The future form of the Greek verb is formed by adding a tense formative to the end of the verb (a sigma), before adding the connecting vowel and personal ending. λύσομεν means "we will loose." If it is a contract verb, the final vowel lengthens before the tense formative. ἀγαπήσω means "I will love."

Chapter 20

This chapter may be a bit of a challenge, but its basic message is pretty easy. The most basic form of a word is its root. The root of ἀγαπάω is ἀγαπα. From this root is formed related noun and adjectival forms, and also different tense stems. In other words, the form of a verb in the future is *not* formed from the present tense form, but from the root.

In some words, this makes no difference. ἀγαπα goes to ἀγαπάω in the present and ἀγαπήσω in the future. You can see the root clearly in both the present and the future forms of the verb.

But there are other verbs in which the root is altered to form the present. The key is to realize that the other tenses are formed from the root, not from the present tense. So, for example, the root βαλ goes to βάλλω in the present (the lambda is doubled), but in all the other tenses there is only one lambda. The future is βαλῶ. (The sigma tense formative drops out for other reasons.)

Chapter 15

Introduction to Verbs

Exegetical Insight

In some translations of Matthew 18:18, it sounds like Jesus promised his disciples that whatever they bound on earth would be bound in heaven, and whatever they loosed on earth would be loosed in heaven. In other words, they had the power to bind and loose, and Heaven (i.e., God) would simply back up their decrees. But the matter is not quite so simple; the actions described in heaven are future perfect passives—which could be translated "will have already been bound in heaven … will have already been loosed in heaven." In other words, the heavenly decree confirming the earthly one is based on a prior verdict.

This is the language of the law court. Jewish legal issues were normally decided in Jesus' day by elders in the synagogue community (later by rabbis). Many Jewish people believed that the authority of Heaven stood behind the earthly judges when they decided cases based on a correct understanding of God's law. (This process came to be called "binding and loosing.") Jesus' contemporaries often envisioned God's justice in terms of a heavenly court; by obeying God's law, the earthly court simply ratified the decrees of the heavenly court. In Matthew 18:15-20, Christians who follow the careful procedures of verses 15-17 may be assured that they will act on the authority of God's court when they decide cases.

Just as we struggle to affirm absolutes in a relativist culture, Christians today sometimes wonder how to exercise discipline lovingly against a sinning member of the church. In this text, Jesus provides an answer: when the person refuses to turn from sin after repeated loving confrontation, the church by disciplining the person simply recognizes the spiritual reality that is already true in God's sight.

Craig S. Keener

Overview

In this chapter we will learn:

- the basic grammar relating to English verbs;

- the following terms: agreement, person, number, tense, time, voice, mood;

- the main components of the Greek verb (stem; connecting vowel; personal ending);

- the concept of "aspect" and its significance for a proper understanding of the Greek verb.

English Grammar

15.1 In Chapter 5, I covered the basic grammar relating to nouns. Now it is time to begin with verbs. However, you already know much of the verbal grammar from our discussion of εἰμί (Chapter 8). Most of the following will be a review.

15.2 **Verb.** A verb is a word that describes action or state of being.

> "I *am studying* Greek."
>
> "Greek *is* the heavenly language."

15.3 **Person.** There are three persons: first, second, and third.

- First person is the person speaking ("I," "we").

- Second person is the person being spoken to ("you").

- Third person is the person/thing being spoken about ("he," "she," "it," "they," all nouns and pronouns).

15.4 **Number** refers to whether a verb is **singular** (referring to one thing) or **plural** (referring to more than one thing).

- "I *am* the teacher."

- "They *are* the students."

15.5 **Agreement.** A verb must agree with its subject in person and number. This means that if a subject is singular, the verb must be singular. If the subject is third person, the verb must be third person.

For example, you would not say *"Bill say* to the class that there *are* no *test."* Since "Bill" and "test" are singular, you would say, *"Bill says* to the class that there *is* no *test."* The presence or absence of the "s" at the end of "says" is an example of agreement in English.

You also would not say, "I *were* here." "I" is singular but "were" is plural. You would say, "I *was* here."

15.6 **Time** refers to when the action of the verb takes place. In English the different "times" are past, present, and future.

15.7 **Tense** in English refers to both the *time* when the action of the verb takes place and the *form* of the word.

- If you study your Greek right now, then the verb is in the **present tense** ("I study").

  In the sentence, "I see the ball," the verb "see" is in the present tense and indicates an action occurring in the present time.

- If you are planning on doing it tomorrow, then the verb is in the **future tense** ("I will study").

  English forms the future with the helping verbs "will/shall."

- If you did it last night, then the verb is in the **past tense** ("I studied").

  English often forms the simple past tense by adding "-ed" to the verb ("study" to "studied").

While it is obvious, it bears emphasis that the time of the verb is from the standpoint of the speaker/writer, not the reader. What is present to the biblical writer may or may not be present to us.

15.8   **Aspect**. The concept of aspect is a contribution from the relatively new field of linguistics. Aspect is not the same as tense although it is related to it.[1]

What is the difference between saying "I studied last night" and "I was studying last night"?

■ "I studied last night" says that an event was completed last night. It does not give you a clue as to the precise nature of your study time other than that it was accomplished. It views the event as a completed whole. This is called the **completed** aspect. It is usually used of events in the past.

The completed aspect is formed in English by using the simple form of the verb ("I eat"; "I ate").

■ "I was studying last night" describes the studying as an ongoing action, a process, something that took place over a period of time. This is called the **continuous** aspect.[2]

The continuous aspect is formed with helping words ("I *am* eating; I *was* eating").

Aspect can be designated in the different times. Consider the following.

	present	*past*	*future*
completed	I study	I studied	I will study
continuous	I am studying	I was studying	I will be studying

15.9   **Completed and punctiliar**. The completed aspect is not the same as what is called *punctiliar*. The punctiliar describes an action as occurring in a single point of time.

It is like the difference between a movie (continuous) and a snapshot (punctiliar). While the completed aspect can describe an action that is in fact punctiliar, completed actions are not necessarily punctiliar. Only context (such as the meaning of the verb) can determine if the action is in fact punctiliar.

> καὶ φωνὴ ἐγένετο ἐκ τῶν οὐρανῶν· σὺ εἶ ὁ υἱός μου ὁ ἀγαπητός, ἐν σοὶ εὐδόκησα. (Mark 1:11).
>
> And a voice *came* from heaven, "You are my beloved Son; with you *I am well pleased*."

The aorist in ἐγένετο is clear: a voice simply came from heaven. But the aorist in εὐδόκησα is a real challenge. God, as it were, looks at the entire life of Jesus, from beginning to end (even though it has not yet happened) and says "I am well-pleased." That is a function of the aorist.

---

[1]   For an excellent introduction to this topic, see Constantine R. Campbell, *Basics of Verbal Aspect in Biblical Greek* (Zondervan, 2008).

[2]   "Completed" is also called "perfective," and "continuous" is also called "imperfective."

15.10 **Voice** refers to the relationship between the subject and the verb.

- If the subject *does* the action of the verb, then the verb is in the **active** voice. "Bill hit the ball. "Hit" is in the active voice because the subject, Bill, did the hitting.

- If the subject *receives* the action of the verb, the verb is in the **passive** voice. "Bill was hit by the ball." "Was hit" is the passive voice because the subject, Bill, was hit.

  The passive voice is formed in English by adding a helping verb ("was" in the example above) to the past participle.

15.11 **Mood** refers to the relationship between the verb and reality. A verb is in the **indicative** mood if it is describing something that *is,* as opposed to something that *may* or *might* be. This includes statements and questions. For example, "I am rich." "Are you rich?"

Every verb you encounter until Chapter 26 is in the indicative mood. When you learn the other moods, the precise meaning of the indicative will become clearer.

> I can't believe you've gotten this far in Greek and haven't learn to count in Greek. Shame on me! Here are the cardinals 1 through 10.
>
> 1. εἷς
> 2. δύο
> 3. τρεῖς
> 4. τέσσαρες
> 5. πέντε
> 6. ἕξ
> 7. ἑπτά
> 8. ὀκτώ
> 9. ἐννέα
> 10. δέκα
>
> There was variety in the spelling of these numbers depending on dialect. The cardinals 5 through 199 are indeclinable.

Greek Grammar

15.12 Do not try to learn the Greek forms you see in this chapter. They are given just to expose you to the concepts. You will start learning the actual forms in the next chapter.

15.13 **Agreement**. In Greek, the verb agrees with its subject. It accomplishes this by using **personal endings**, which are suffixes added to the end of the verb. For example, ω is a first person singular personal ending, and therefore λέγω means "I say." ουσι is a third person plural personal ending, and therefore λέγουσι means "they say."

The verbal stem *ἀκου means "to hear."

ἀκούω	I hear
ἀκούεις	You hear
ἀκούει	He/she/it hears
ἀκούομεν	We hear
ἀκούετε	You hear
ἀκούουσι	They hear

15.14 **Person.** As in English, there are three persons.

- First person is the person speaking (ἐγώ, ἡμεῖς): εἰμί, ἐσμέν, ἀκούω, ἀκούομεν.

- Second person is the person being spoken to (σύ, ὑμεῖς): εἶ, ἐστέ, ἀκούεις, ἀκούετε.

- Third person is the person/thing being spoken about (αὐτός, λόγοι): ἐστίν, εἰσίν, ἀκούει, ἀκούουσι.

A verb must agree with its subject in person. It does this by using the appropriate personal ending.

- εις is a normal ending for second person singular. Therefore, if the subject is "you" (σύ) the verb would end in εις. σὺ λέγεις means "You say."

- If the subject is "we" (ἡμεῖς) the verb would end in ομεν. ἡμεῖς λέγομεν means "We say."

Because the Greek verb always indicates person, the Greek sentence does not require an expressed subject. A verb by itself can be a complete sentence. Both ἐγὼ λέγω and λέγω mean "I say."

15.15 **Number**. As with nouns, verbs are either singular or plural. Different personal endings are used to differentiate number.

- If the subject is "I," then the personal ending will be a first person singular (ἀκούω).

- If the subject is "we," then the personal ending is a first person plural (ἀκούομεν).

- If the verb is referring to one individual, then the personal ending is third person singular (ἀκούει); but if there are many people, then the ending is third person plural (ἀκούουσι).

15.16 **Tense**. The term "tense" is used differently in Greek grammars from English; it is easy to become confused. It perhaps would be easiest at first simply to use "tense" and "time" interchangeably. But this would build a misconception into your basic thinking that will constantly get in the way of proper exegesis down the road. So, from the very beginning, I will use precise terminology.

The problem is that in Greek a tense carries two connotations: aspect and time. For example, the aorist tense describes an undefined action (aspect) that normally occurs in the past (time).

- I use the term "tense" to refer only to the *form* of the verb (e.g., present tense, future tense, aorist tense).

- I use the term "time" to describe "when" the action of that verb occurs.

Do not confuse "tense" and "time."

15.17 **Aspect**. This is perhaps the most difficult concept to grasp in Greek verbs, and yet it is the most important and most misunderstood. The basic genius of the Greek verb is not its ability to indicate *when* the action of the verb occurs (time), but *what type of action* it describes, or what we call "aspect." In Greek there are three aspects.

- The **continuous** aspect means that the action of the verb is thought of as an ongoing *process*. This is like the English continuous aspect. "I am eating." "They were studying."

- The **undefined** aspect means that the action of the verb is thought of as a *simple event*, without commenting on whether or not it is a process.[3] "I ate." "She left."

The continuous is like viewing a parade from the street. The undefined is like viewing a parade from a helicopter.[4]

An example that shows the importance of these distinctions is Jesus' words to his disciples: "If anyone wishes to come after me, let him deny himself and take up his cross and follow me" (Mark 8:34). "Deny" and "take up" are undefined while "follow" is continuous. The aspect of "deny" and "take up" does not tell us anything about the nature of those actions except that they are to occur. But the aspect of "follow" emphasizes that the commitment to discipleship involves a continual action, which in this context is a day to day action.[5]

Another example is Jesus' trial. In Mark 15:19 we read, "And they were striking his head with a reed and spitting on him and kneeling down in homage to him" (ESV). You get the sense from the English that they beat him over and over again, but you may not get that they spit on him repeatedly. ἐνέπτυον is explicitly continuous; they did it over and over again, which is expressed in the TNIV as, "Again and again they struck him on the head with a staff and spit on him." This is then countered by Jesus' words of forgiveness from the cross. "And Jesus said, 'Father, forgive them, for they know not what they do'" (ESV, Luke 23:34). What this translation obscures is that Jesus "said" it over and over; ἔλεγεν is explicitly continuous.

There is a third aspect in Greek, the "perfective," but you will not meet it until Chapter 25.

15.18 **Voice**. Greek uses a different set of personal endings to differentiate the **active** from the **passive**. ἐσθίω means "I eat," while ἐσθίομαι means "I am being eaten."

Greek has a third voice called the **middle**. Although it has several different nuances, for the time being equate the middle with the active. I will discuss the middle voice in Chapter 25.

The Main Components of the Greek Verb

15.19 **Chart**. For the time being, I will say that the Greek verb is comprised of three parts.

> *Stem + Connecting vowel + Personal endings*
>
> λυ + ο + μεν ▸ λύομεν

Here are the ordinals first through tenth.

1. πρῶτος
2. δεύτερος
3. τρίτος
4. τέταρτος
5. πέμπτος
6. ἕκτος
7. ἕβδομος
8. ὄγδοος
9. ἔνατος
10. δέκατος

---

[3] It is argued by some that "undefined" is not an aspect, and by "undefined" we simply mean the absence of aspect. This may or may not be technically correct, but it may be a helpful way of thinking for the time being. The "undefined aspect" is the absence of any specific aspect.

[4] Campbell's metaphor, see page 124, note 1.

[5] Another example would be, "How do you do?" versus "How are you doing?"

15.20 **Stem**. The stem of a verb is the part that carries its basic meaning. It is like the stem of a noun. The form λύομεν means "We destroy." The stem is *λυ.[6]

15.21 **Connecting vowel**. Often Greek adds a vowel after the stem. This is to aid in the pronunciation of the word because Greek will also add suffixes after the connecting vowel.

λέγετε means "You say." The stem is *λεγ. The connecting vowel is the second ε, and τε is the personal ending.

15.22 **Personal endings**. As you have seen, personal endings are suffixes that are added to the end of the verb and indicate person and number.

■ The stem *λεγ means "say" and the personal ending ω means "I," therefore λέγω means "I say."

■ λέγομεν means "we say," because the personal ending μεν means "we." ("o" is the connecting vowel.)

15.23 **Parse.** When you parse verbs, I suggest you do it as follows:[7] person, number, tense, voice, mood, lexical form, definition of inflected form.

For example, "λέγομεν is first person plural, present active indicative, of λέγω, meaning 'we say.' "

Because the only mood you will learn for quite a while is the indicative, just get used to saying "indicative" in your parsing.

15.24 **Lexical form.** The lexical form of verbs is the first person singular, present indicative. Always![8] *BBG* always lists words in the Vocabulary section in their lexical forms.

Conclusion

15.25 This chapter is not intended to teach you the specific forms of Greek verbs. The examples are intended merely to give you a general idea of the types of things you will be learning in the next several chapters.

Verbs are the most exciting part of the Greek language. Many times the theology of a passage, or a clearer insight into the nuance of the passage, is hidden in the aspect of the verb. But knowing verbs requires work, and without a good knowledge of verbs you will never enjoy the language. So hang in there, and keep on working.

---

[6]   While it is possible for the stem of a verb to undergo some changes, most of the changes are in the ending of the verb, just like the nouns. But there can also be changes at the beginning of the verb and sometimes in the stem itself (like the vowel shift from πατήρ to πατρός). I will discuss this in later chapters.

[7]   Teachers will differ on the parsing order, so this is only my suggestion.

[8]   Some of the older grammars list the infinitive form (λέγειν, "to say") as the lexical form, but lexicons are consistent now in listing verbs in the first person singular, present (λέγω, "I say").

Incidentally, it will be quite easy to mix nouns and verbs unintentionally. For example, verbs do not have case or gender; but in parsing verbs you might get confused and say that a verb is in the accusative. One of the main reasons why I taught you nouns first and then verbs is to help minimize this natural confusion.

Summary

1. A verb agrees with its subject in person (first; second; third) and number (singular; plural).

2. Agreement is accomplished through the use of personal endings.

3. The true significance of the Greek verb is its ability to describe aspect. A verb can be continuous, which means the process it describes is an ongoing action. Or a Greek verb can be undefined, which means that the author is not giving us a clue as to the true nature of the action other than to say that it occurred.

4. "Tense" describes the form of the verb.

5. "Time" describes when the action of the verb occurs.

6. Voice can be active (i.e., the subject does the action), passive (i.e., the subject receives the action of the verb), or middle (which we are equating with the active for the time being).

7. The indicative mood is the dominant mood, used to make a statement of fact or ask a question.

This third group is how the Greeks would write the numbers (e.g., "1").

1. α′
2. β′
3. γ′
4. δ′
5. ε′
6. ϛ′
7. η′
8. θ′
9. ι′
10. κ′

Notice that ζ was not used for "6" but rather ϛ, which is called a digamma (or stigma). It came between epsilon and eta. This is an old letter in the alphabet that dropped out of use many centuries before Koine, but it did show up periodically in counting. (For more information see 17.11.) You will discover that other letters had dropped out of the alphabet, most notably the consonantal iota (20.27).

Chapter 16

Present Active Indicative

Exegetical Insight

One of the elements of Greek grammar that you will meet in this lesson is that if a sentence does not contain a word in the nominative, the subject is included in the verb itself; you can tell what pronoun to use as the subject by the ending on the verb. But if the Greek sentence has a pronoun in the nominative, the author is placing emphasis on the subject of the verb.

Numerous times in John's gospel, beginning with John 6:35, Jesus uses the pronoun ἐγώ with the verb "to be" in the expression ἐγώ εἰμι ὁ ... ("*I am the ...*"; see also 6:41; 8:12; 9:5; 10:7,9,11,14; 11:25; 14:6; 15:1,5). In each case, he is emphasizing who *he* is. For example, when Jesus says ἐγώ εἰμι ὁ ἄρτος τῆς ζωῆς (6:35) he is, as it were, pointing a finger towards himself and saying, "If you want spiritual nourishment in your life, then look to me and me only, for *I am* the bread of life." The other ἐγώ εἰμι verses have a similar emphasis. Anything that we want in our spiritual lives we can find by looking to our blessed Savior Jesus Christ.

There is more. Jesus' use of ἐγώ εἰμι harks back to the Old Testament, to the story of Moses when he was approached by God at the burning bush (Exod 3). When Moses challenged the Lord to give his name, God replied by saying (in the Septuagint), ἐγώ εἰμι ὁ ὤν ("I am the one who is"). That is, Yahweh is the great "I AM" (Exod 3:14). Jesus taps into this famous title for God when he says to the Jews, "Before Abraham was, I am (ἐγώ εἰμι)" (John 8:58), ascribing to himself the very same name that Yahweh used in the Old Testament concerning himself. And this same name and expression underlie all of Jesus' ἐγώ εἰμι statements in John's Gospel.

Verlyn Verbrugge

Overview

In this chapter you will learn:

- that the present tense in the indicative describes an action that usually occurs in the present time;

- that the aspect of the present tense can be continuous or undefined;

- the three parts to a present active indicative verb: present tense stem, connecting vowel, personal ending;

- the primary active personal endings.

English

16.1 The present indicative describes an action occurring in the present. The active voice is used when the subject is performing the action of the verb. The indicative mood describes a fact or asks a question.

For example, "I see the tall man." "See" describes an action that is being performed by the subject of the sentence "I" at the present time.

Greek

16.2 The present active indicative verb in Greek is basically the same as in English. It describes an action that normally occurs in the present. It can be either a continuous ("I am studying") or undefined ("I study") action.[1]

Remember: the time of the verb is from the standpoint of the speaker/writer, not the reader. What is present to the biblical writer may or may not be present to us.

16.3 **Chart.** At the beginning of every chapter that introduces a new verbal form, I will include one of these summary charts.

The chart is one of the most important elements of each chapter, so be sure to learn it well. Of course, you first must read through the chapter for it to make sense.

In the present tense, a verb is composed of three parts: the present tense stem; the connecting vowel; a personal ending.

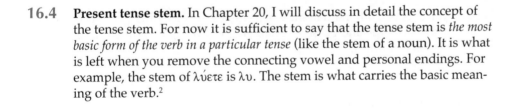

Present tense stem + Connecting vowel +
Primary active personal endings

λυ + ο + μεν ‣ λύομεν

Okay, you've learned 1 through 10, but that's not enough to do math or play football. Here are 11 through 20. For more numbers, check *MBG* (page 247).

11. ἕνδεκα
12. δώδεκα (or δεκαδύο)
13. δεκατρεῖς (or τρεισκαίδεκα)
14. δεκατέσσαρες
15. δεκαπέντε
16. ἑκκαίδεκα
17. ἑπτακαίδεκα
18. δεκαοκτώ (or ὀκτωκαίδεκα)
19. ἐννεακαίδεκα
20. εἴκοσι(ν)

16.4 **Present tense stem.** In Chapter 20, I will discuss in detail the concept of the tense stem. For now it is sufficient to say that the tense stem is *the most basic form of the verb in a particular tense* (like the stem of a noun). It is what is left when you remove the connecting vowel and personal endings. For example, the stem of λύετε is λυ. The stem is what carries the basic meaning of the verb.[2]

---

[1] Your teacher may have a preference as to which form to use by default. Ask.

[2] Often, the stem of a verb stays the same in all tenses. In a past tense, the stem of λύω is still *λυ. However, in many common verbs the stem changes in different tenses. For example, βάλλω is a present tense form and means "I throw." The present tense stem is *βαλλ. But in a past tense, the stem shifts to *βαλ (one lambda). This is why it is important to connect stems with tenses in your thinking. But more about this later.

16.5 **Connecting vowel.**[3] The connecting vowel is the vowel that connects the verbal stem to the personal ending. *In the indicative mood, if the personal ending begins with mu or nu, the connecting vowel is omicron; the connecting vowel in every other case is epsilon. If no personal ending is used, the connecting vowel can be either omicron or epsilon.*

$$\lambda \varepsilon \gamma + o + \mu \varepsilon \nu \quad \rightarrow \quad \lambda \acute{\varepsilon} \gamma o \mu \varepsilon \nu$$

$$\lambda \varepsilon \gamma + \varepsilon + \tau \varepsilon \quad \rightarrow \quad \lambda \acute{\varepsilon} \gamma \varepsilon \tau \varepsilon$$

$$\lambda \varepsilon \gamma + o + - \quad \rightarrow \quad \lambda \acute{\varepsilon} \gamma \omega$$

The connecting vowels are the same for all the tenses in the indicative mood. Their purpose is to help with pronunciation; it is easier to pronounce λέγομεν than λέγμεν.[4]

16.6 **Personal ending.** The personal ending is added to the connecting vowel in order to designate person and number. This is necessary because the verb must agree with its subject in person and number.

One of the advantages of a language using personal endings is that you can tell who is doing the action of the verb because the ending shows person and number. Even if the subject is not stated, you can discover it from the personal ending on the verb.

> Now have some fun. Perhaps you could do some simple math drills. Divide the class into teams and do some speed math on the board. You can use this formula:
>
> " ____ καί ____ είσιν ____ ."

Another advantage is that if the subject is expressed, you can confirm that it is the subject by checking the person and number of the verb against it. This double check should *always* be employed since you are really serious about learning the language.

For example, the verb λέγεις means "you say" (second person). If you have the two words σύ and ἄνθρωπος and both look like the subject, the verb tells you that the subject must be σύ because ἄνθρωπος is third person.

The disadvantage of using personal endings is that there is more to memorize, but this is really a small price to pay for the advantages you receive.

16.7 **Primary endings**. There are two sets of personal endings you need to learn. The **primary** personal endings are used in the present tense and in the tenses discussed through Chapter 20. I will discuss the **secondary** personal endings in Chapter 21 and the differences between primary and secondary endings.

16.8 **Voice.** Greek differentiates the present active voice (this chapter) from the present middle and passive (Chapter 18) by using two different sets of personal endings.

---

[3]   It is also called a "thematic" vowel.

[4]   Most grammars teach that the connecting vowel is a part of the personal ending, at least in the present tense. This is understandable: when the connecting vowel and true personal ending combine they are often altered. For example, a third person plural form is λέγουσι. It is formed from λεγ + ο + νσι ‣ λέγουσι. The nu drops out and the omicron lengthens to ου.

This teaching technique is fine for a while, but after you have learned a few tenses it becomes *extremely* important to see the difference between the connecting vowel and the personal ending. For this reason I will always list the true connecting vowel and true personal ending to the right of every paradigm. This way you can see the true similarities throughout the entire verbal paradigm as well as the different rules that govern the final form of the word.

Form of the Present Active Indicative

16.9   **Introduction.** The forms in our paradigms are listed first, second, and third person singular, and then first, second, and third person plural. From left to right I list the inflected forms, definition, the connecting vowel, and the personal ending. (The connecting vowels and personal endings are colored blue.) In some paradigms I include a similar paradigm for comparison in the far right column.

Pay special attention to the connecting vowel/personal ending combination and what is happening. This becomes important later on.

16.10   **Paradigm: Present active indicative.**[5] Be sure to read the footnotes to this paradigm.

	form	translation	connecting vowel	personal ending
1 sg	λύω	I am loosing	ο	–[6]
2 sg	λύεις	You are loosing	ε	ς[7]
3 sg	λύει	He/she/it is loosing	ε	ι[8]
1 pl	λύομεν	We are loosing	ο	μεν
2 pl	λύετε	You are loosing	ε	τε
3 pl	λύουσι(ν)	They are loosing	ο	νσι[9]

16.11   You will notice that the personal endings have sometimes been changed when they are actually affixed to the verbs. We are faced here with somewhat the same dilemma we were with nouns: you need to learn what the personal endings actually are, but at times they have been modified.[10]

> πόσα ἔτη ἔχεις; is "How old are you?" (Modern Greek is, πόσο χρόνων εἶσαι.) Go around and ask each other. Be sure to answer in Greek. ἔχω _____ ἔτη.

---

[5]   λύω has a wide and varied assortment of meanings. It is the word used for "breaking" the Sabbath, or for "destroying" the temple. It is commonly used in paradigms because it is short and regular. "Loose" is a general meaning that basically encompasses all its other meanings. If "loose" sounds strange to you, it may be easier to think in terms of "destroy."

[6]   No personal ending is used and the connecting vowel omicron lengthens to omega to compensate for the loss (*λυ + ο ‣ λύω).

[7]   The personal ending actually is σι. The sigma dropped out and was evidently added back on to the end (λυεσι ‣ λυει ‣ λύεις). This is the explanation in Smyth (#463b). It seems easier to think that the sigma and iota underwent metathesis, i.e., they switched places. Just remember that the ending is sigma and the connecting vowel changes.

[8]   The ending actually is τι, but the tau dropped out. The original form can be seen in ἐστί.

[9]   The third plural ending can take a movable nu.
   The nu in the original ending drops out because of the following sigma (just as it does in the accusative plural of second declension nouns), and the connecting vowel omicron lengthens to ου to compensate for the loss (λυονσι ‣ λυοσι ‣ λύουσι).
   It is important to remember that the ending actually is νσι because it will make other forms easier to remember.

[10]   For example, the genitive singular case ending for the second declension is omicron, but it contracts with the final stem vowel and we see λόγου (*λογο + ο ‣ λόγου). You memorized the ending as upsilon and remember that it actually is omicron.

With the primary active endings it is best to learn the endings as ω, εις, ει, ομεν, ετε, ουσι(ν), *but always be able to identify the connecting vowel and the true personal ending.*[11]

16.12 **Master Personal Ending Chart**. There are only two charts that you need to learn for verbs. The following is the first, and is called the Master Personal Ending Chart. (I will fill in the other three-fourths of this chart in later chapters.) The forms in the second column are the real personal endings; be sure to learn them as well.

In a sense, these two charts are like the one noun chart and eight noun rules. If you know them and a few rules, you can identify almost any verbal form in the New Testament.

	primary tenses		*secondary tenses*
active voice	1 λύω	–	
	2 λύεις	ς	
	3 λύει	ι	
	1 λύομεν	μεν	
	2 λύετε	τε	
	3 λύουσι(ν)	νσι	
middle/passive voice			

---

[11] You may be wondering why I asked you to learn what the true primary active endings are as well as the altered forms in the present active indicative. The answer is that on down the road it makes things easier if you know the true endings.

For example, the second person singular ending is ς, and the connecting vowel lengthens (ablaut) to ει (λυ + ε + ς ▸ λύεις). Why not learn the ending as ις? Because the second person singular ending in the secondary active is ς and there is no lengthening of the connecting vowel (ε + λυ + ε + ς ▸ ἔλυες). If you learn just ς as the primary ending, you already know the secondary.

You are just going to have to trust me on this one. If you really want to learn Greek well and not have to review paradigms for years to come, then learn the real endings.

Characteristics of the Present Active Indicative

16.13 **Aspect**. The present tense indicates either a continuous or undefined action. You can translate either "I am studying" or "I study." Choose the aspect that best fits the context. Aspect always takes precedence over time.

16.14 **Time**. The present tense form of a verb generally indicates an action occurring in the present time.[12]

Verbs and Personal Pronouns

16.15 **Personal pronouns in the nominative.** Because the personal ending indicates person, it is generally unnecessary to supply the personal pronoun as the subject of the sentence. Greek could say "I love Robin" by writing ἐγὼ ἀγαπῶ Ῥόβιν[13] or simply ἀγαπῶ Ῥόβιν. When a personal pronoun does occur, it is for *emphasis* or to clarify the *gender* of the subject.

■ *Emphasis*. ἐγὼ ἀγαπῶ Ῥόβιν would be saying "**I** love Robin." The combination of the personal pronoun and the "I" in the verb creates an emphatic expression. Often the emphasis is by way of contrast, as the examples below show.

> οὐχ ὡς ἐγὼ θέλω ἀλλ᾽ ὡς σύ (Matt 26:39).
>
> Not as *I* will but as *you* (will).

> Ἰησοῦς αὐτὸς οὐκ ἐβάπτιζεν ἀλλ᾽ οἱ μαθηταὶ αὐτοῦ (John 4:2).
>
> *Jesus* was not baptizing, but his disciples.

Some grammars ask you to translate the nominative form of the pronoun with an intensive pronoun: "I myself love Robin." "Jesus himself was not baptizing." Others permit you to avoid the awkward English and simply to recognize that the emphasis is there. Check with your teacher.

■ *Gender*. When you find αὐτός in the nominative, it tells you the gender of the subject—something the personal ending cannot. One note of caution: αὐτός can be used when the verb is first or second person. In this case αὐτός is translated first or second person ("I/we" or "you") and not third person ("he").

For example, αὐτὴ λέγεις (second person singular "you speak") ἀνθρώποις might seem to mean, "She speaks to men." This is incorrect. The αὐτή is merely adding emphasis to the subject, which is "You." It should be translated "You (yourself) speak to men."

Now for the really important stuff. You need to play (American) football. Use the numbers to draw the other team offsides: εἷς, ὀκτώ, δεκαπέντε. But what can we use for "hike." δίδωμι means "to give" (Chapter 34). The imperative (Chapter 35) is δός.

ἕξ, ἑπτακαίδεκα, ἑπτά, δός, δός.

---

[12] This is true only in the indicative mood. When you move into the other moods, you will see that the present tense has no time significance, or that the time significance is incidental.

[13] Ῥόβιν is not a real Greek word.

Summary

1. The present active indicative describes an action that usually occurs in the present time.

2. The present tense verb is composed of three parts: present verbal stem, connecting vowel, and primary personal ending.

3. The tense stem is the basic form of the verb in a particular tense.

4. In the indicative mood, if the personal ending begins with mu or nu, the connecting vowel is omicron; otherwise the connecting vowel is epsilon. If there is no personal ending, the connecting vowel can be either omicron or epsilon.

5. A verb agrees with its subject in person and number.

6. The present active tense uses the primary active endings: ω, εις, ει, ομεν, ετε, ουσι(ν). The real personal endings are -, ς, ι, μεν, τε, νσι.

7. A movable nu can be added to the third person plural personal ending.

16.16 **Master Verb Chart**. At the end of each chapter on verbs, I include my "Master Verb Chart." It lists the different parts of each verbal form. As you learn new verbal forms, the chart will grow. It is the second chart you must learn for verbs, and is in fact the key to the entire verbal system; learn it well. The full chart is in the Appendix.

There is a column for "Aug/Redup" and another for "Tense form." You will not learn what these mean until later chapters, so ignore them for now. The column entitled "1st sing paradigm" is the form of the paradigm verb in the first person singular.

Master Verb Chart

Tense	Aug/ Redup	Tense stem	Tense form.	Conn. vowel	Personal endings	1st sing paradigm
Present act		pres		o/ε	prim act	λύω

Vocabulary

Following the frequency of each verb, I list the word's present tense stem preceded with an asterisk. At first you should pronounce each verb with each of its six possible personal endings.

The line below the definition contains forms of the verb you do not yet know. If you are making your own flash cards, write these forms down on the definition side of the card. I will explain what the forms mean in later chapters.

ἀκούω	I hear, learn, obey, understand (428; *ακου)[14]
	(ἤκουον), ἀκούσω, ἤκουσα, ἀκήκοα, -, ἠκούσθην
	ἀκούω can take a direct object in either the genitive or accusative.
βλέπω	I see, look at (132; *βλεπ)
	(ἔβλεπον), βλέψω, ἔβλεψα, -, -, -
ἔχω	I have, hold (708; *σεχ)
	(εἶχον), ἕξω, ἔσχον, ἔσχηκα, -, -
	In the present tense, the sigma in the root is replaced with a rough breathing, which in turn is lost because of the chi. It will reappear in the future when the chi changes. See *MBG* if you want more information, page 260.
λύω	I loose, untie, destroy (42; *λυ)[15]
	(ἔλυον), λύσω, ἔλυσα, -, λέλυμαι, ἐλύθην
νόμος, -ου, ὁ	law, principle (194; *νομο)[16]
ὅπου	where (82)
πιστεύω	I believe, have faith (in), trust (241; *πιστευ)
	(ἐπίστευον), πιστεύσω, ἐπίστευσα, πεπίστευκα, πεπίστευμαι, ἐπιστεύθην
	πιστεύω can take a direct object in either the dative or accusative. It is the cognate verb of the noun πίστις and adjective πιστός.
πρόσωπον, -ου, τό	face, appearance (76; *προσωπο)[17]
τότε	then, thereafter (160)
τυφλός, -ή, -όν	blind (50; *τυφλο)[18]
χαρά, -ᾶς, ἡ	joy, delight (59; *χαρα)

Total word count in the New Testament:	138,162
Number of words learned to date:	180
Number of word occurrences in this chapter:	2,172
Number of word occurrences to date:	94,367
Percent of total word count in the New Testament:	68.30%

---

[14] *Acoustics* (ἀκουστικός) is the science of sound.

[15] λύω occurs less than fifty times, but because it is our paradigm verb you will have learned it anyway.

[16] An *autonomous* (αὐτόνομος) person is self-governed.

[17] *Prosopography* refers to describing a person's face.

[18] *Typhlosis* is the technical term for blindness.

Exegesis

The technical name for each use of the tense is in blue. These are the terms you will see in advanced grammars and commentaries. As you can see by the multiple entries, grammarians have not settled on any one name for many of the uses.

1. Sometimes a Greek present describes an action that happens immediately. In other words, it has no real continuous nature (instantaneous, aoristic, punctiliar).

> τέκνον, ἀφίενταί σου αἱ ἁμαρτίαι *(Mark 2:5).*
>
> My son, your sins *are forgiven.*

2. The Greek present can describe an ongoing action, even though in real time the action does not last very long (progressive, descriptive).

> ἐὰν γὰρ προσεύχωμαι γλώσσῃ, τὸ πνεῦμά μου προσεύχεται *(1 Cor 14:14).*
>
> For if I pray in a tongue, my spirit *is praying.*

3. Some actions occur repeatedly (iterative).

> ολλάκις γὰρ πίπτει εἰς τὸ πῦρ *(Matt 17:15).*
>
> For often *he falls* into the fire.

Or how about agreeing on a number, say εἴκοσι, and as soon as your numbers add up to εἴκοσι you hike the ball and run for a touchdown.

ἐννέα, πέντε, δύο, τέσσαρες, and run like mad!

4. Actions occur regularly but not necessarily at the same time (customary, habitual, general).

> νηστεύω δὶς τοῦ σαββάτου *(Luke 18:12).*
>
> I *fast* twice a week.

5. Sometimes the Greek present tense will be used to express a timeless fact (gnomic).

> ἱλαρὸν δότην ἀγαπᾷ ὁ θεός *(2 Cor 9:7).*
>
> God *loves* a cheerful giver.

6. Finally, because the Greek verb system views time as secondary to aspect, it is possible for the Greek present tense to refer to an action that occurs in the past. The idea is to make the telling of the past event more vivid by using the present tense (historical, dramatic). We have the same construction in English, but the Greeks used it much more than we do, so this usage is often translated with the past tense.

> βλέπει τὸν Ἰησοῦν ἐρχόμενον πρὸς αὐτόν *(John 1:29).*
>
> The next day *he saw* Jesus coming toward him.

7. A present tense verb can also be used to describe a future event (futuristic).

> ναί, ἔρχομαι ταχύ *(Rev 22:20).*
>
> Yes, I *am coming* quickly.

Chapter 17

Contract Verbs

(Present Active Indicative)

Exegetical Insight

The present active indicative often has an imperfective force; that is, it conveys the idea of ongoing or continuous action. When the Apostle Paul wrote his first letter to the Thessalonian Christians, he wanted to reassure these new believers that they were not forgotten—that he and his companions still cared deeply for them. He tells them, "We always thank God for all of you, mentioning you in our prayers" (1 Thess 1:2, NIV).

Paul expresses his constant practice of giving thanks to God by using the present active indicative verb εὐχαριστοῦμεν. The verb could also, of course, be interpreted as "simple" or "undefined" action with no overtones of continuous prayer. The adverb "always" (πάντοτε), however, reinforces our impression that Paul is stressing that he prays regularly for the Thessalonians. It is also likely that in using the plural "we," Paul is implying that he met often with Silas and Timothy to pray for these dear people. Certainly Paul also remembered the Thessalonians in his private times of prayer.

Far from being victimized by a group of itinerant moral preachers who sought their money and food, the Thessalonians were evangelized by a trio of men who proclaimed to them the living and true God. These were men whose lives had been touched deeply by the risen Christ and they poured themselves out to the Thessalonians in a loving and caring way. Their abrupt departure did not indicate a lack of concern; on the contrary, they were forced to leave, and now they prayed together constantly to the living God for these fledgling and vulnerable believers!

Clinton E. Arnold

Overview

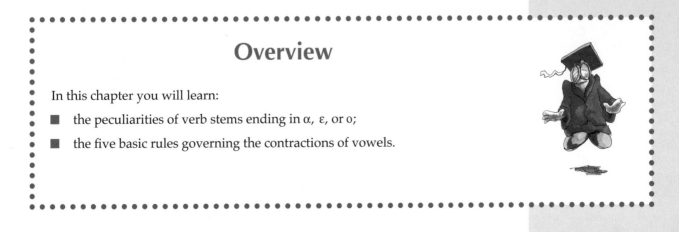

In this chapter you will learn:

- the peculiarities of verb stems ending in α, ε, or ο;
- the five basic rules governing the contractions of vowels.

Introduction

17.1 Contract verbs are verbs whose stems end in alpha, epsilon, or omicron.[1] That final vowel is called the "contract vowel." For example, the verb ἀγαπάω has a stem ending in alpha (*ἀγαπα).

Contract verbs follow the standard rules for verbs, but there is one additional point to learn. When the final stem vowel comes into contact with the connecting vowel, the two vowels **contract**.[2] The two vowels will join and often form a different vowel or a diphthong (e.g., *ποιε + ομεν ‣ ποιοῦμεν).

17.2 Contract verbs are categorized according to their final stem vowel. What is encouraging about contract verbs is that all alpha contracts behave similarly, as do all epsilon and all omicron contracts. In other words, all contract verbs with stems ending in alpha form their different inflected endings the same way. Once you learn the forms of ἀγαπάω, you know the inflection pattern of all other alpha contracts.

Contractions

17.3 Contract verbs are common, and you need to be able to "figure out" what vowels led to a certain contraction. If you cannot, you will not be able to discover the lexical form of the verb and thus its meaning.

For example, if you find the form ποιεῖτε, the ει is going to cause problems unless you recognize that ει can be the result of the contraction of two epsilons. Then you can see that ποιεῖτε is second person plural of an epsilon contract verb (ποιεῖτε ‣ ποιε + ετε).

Often you will discover that several vowel combinations could have given rise to the same contracted form. For example, ου is formed from the contractions of εο, οε, and οο. If you see ποιοῦμεν, the connecting vowel and personal ending are ομεν, but is its lexical form ποιέω or ποιόω?

You meet contractions only in two tenses, the present and the imperfect (Chapter 21). In the other tenses the contract vowel lengthens and there is no contraction, but more about this later.

17.4 Having said this, I do not want to overstate the significance of understanding contractions. While knowing what vowels formed the contraction is important for discovering the lexical form of the word, in most cases it is not significant for parsing. For example, can you parse the following forms (person and number) even if you do not know what vowels formed the contraction?

---

[1] The usual definition for contract verbs is that they have stems ending in a vowel. While this is true it is also confusing. ἀκούω has a stem ending in what appears to be a vowel, but it is not a contract verb.

Actually, the final upsilon in ἀκούω reflects an old letter called "digamma" that has long since dropped out of the Greek alphabet. It was replaced in most cases by an upsilon, but because it was a digamma the upsilon does not contract. Cf. 17.12.

[2] This is the same phenomena that you saw with case endings. The genitive singular case ending, second declension, is actually omicron. It contracts with the omicron of the noun stem to form ου (*λογο + ο ‣ λόγου).

	person	*number*
ποιοῦμεν		
πληροῦτε		
ἀγαπᾷς		
ποιῶ		
ἀγαπῶσι		

17.5 **Rules on contraction.**[3] Following are the rules showing what contractions are caused by what vowel combinations. There are a few other possibilities, but you will be shown them as we come across them. Rules 1 and 2 are the most common.

Rule 7 governs contractions of diphthongs, and illustrations of contracting diphthongs are listed throughout the rules.

You may also notice that the vowels listed as contracting in rules 1 through 6 are not the real personal endings but are the altered personal endings you have learned for λύω (ω, εις, ει, etc.).[4] Rule 8 explains this.

1. ου is formed from εο, οε, and οο.

ου	‹	εο	ποιοῦμεν	‹	ποιεομεν
ου	‹	οε	πληροῦτε	‹	πληροετε
ου	‹	οο	πληροῦμεν	‹	πληροομεν

2. ει is formed from εε.

ει	‹	εε	ποιεῖτε	‹	ποιεετε

3. ω is formed from almost any combination of omicron or omega with any other vowel, except for rule 1.

ω	‹	αο	ἀγαπῶμεν	‹	ἀγαπαομεν

We have a special situation in the lexical form of contract verbs. The alpha, epsilon, or omicron of the stem is listed in the lexical form because you need to know what that vowel is (e.g., ἀγαπάω).

Teachers differ on this point, but some would encourage you to start taking your Greek Bible to church. You will be amazed at how much you can follow as the English is read.

---

[3] I teach the rules governing contractions a little differently. Usually the rules move from the uncontracted form to the contracted. For example, "When epsilon and epsilon contract, they form ει." If you want to learn the rules this way, they are given in Advanced Information.

This approach, however, seems backwards. When you are reading the text, you start with the contracted form and need to know what formed the contraction. Also, the two most common rules, as they are usually presented, are exceptions (see rules 2 and 4 in Advanced Information).

Therefore, I teach the rules of contraction moving from the contracted form to the uncontracted.

[4] E.g., ποιοῦσιν contracts from *ποιε + ουσι (ποιουυσι ‣ ποιοῦσι), not *ποιε + νσι.

However, when the word occurs in the text in the first person singular, it will have contracted to the forms in the paradigm (ἀγαπῶ).[5]

4. α is formed from αε.

α	‹	αε	ἀγαπᾶτε	‹ ἀγαπαετε
ᾳ	‹	αει	ἀγαπᾷ	‹ ἀγαπαει

5. η is formed from εα.

ῃ	‹	εαι	ποιῇ ‹ ποιηι ‹ ποιεαι[6] ‹ ποιεσαι[7]

The relationship between αε and εα is easy to remember. "The first one wins." If the alpha is first (αε), they form a long alpha. If the epsilon is first (εα), they form an eta (which you can think of as being a long epsilon).

6. Miscellaneous

οι	‹	οει[8]	πληροῖς	‹ πληροεις
			πληροῖ	‹ πληροει

7. The contraction of diphthongs. What happens with a diphthong depends upon whether the contract vowel and the first vowel of the diphthong are the same or different vowels.

a. If the contract vowel and the first vowel of the diphthong are the *same*, they simplify (i.e., one of the double letters drops off).

ει	‹	εει	ποιεῖς	‹ ποιεεις
ου	‹	οου	πληροῦσι	‹ πληροουσι

b. If the contract vowel and the first vowel of the diphthong are *different*, they contract.[9] If the second vowel of the diphthong is an iota, it subscripts if possible; if it is an upsilon, it drops off.

ᾳ	‹	αει	ἀγαπᾷ	‹ ἀγαπαει
ου	‹	εου	ποιοῦσιν	‹ ποιεουσι

8. Contract verbs contract as if the true personal endings are those visible in the present active indicative.

1 sg	αω	▸	ἀγαπῶ
2 sg	αεις	▸	ἀγαπᾷς
3 sg	αει	▸	ἀγαπᾷ

---

[5] The following is advanced information, so you may want to ignore it. In the first person singular of epsilon and omicron contracts, there is one extra step in the contraction process. No personal ending is used, so the connecting vowel lengthens to compensate, and the ensuing contraction is between the contract vowel and the lengthened connecting vowel.

ποιεο ▸ ποιεω ▸ ποιῶ.

πληροο ▸ πληρωω ▸ πληρῶ.

If the contraction were with the contract vowel and the unlengthened connecting vowel, rule 1 would change the form of the first person singular of contract verbs.

ποιεο ▸ ποιούω.

πληροο ▸ πληρούω.

[6] The sigma drops out because it is between two vowels.

[7] You will meet this form in Chapter 18.

[8] This combination occurs in the second and third person singular of an omicron contract verb.

[9] You have seen no examples of this to this point.

1 pl	αομεν ▸	ἀγαπῶμεν
2 pl	αετε ▸	ἀγαπᾶτε
3 pl	αουσι ▸	ἀγαπῶσι(ν)

Be sure to learn these rules exactly. You will be meeting other contracted forms, and if you know the rules you will be able to figure them out.

Halftime Review

Of the seven rules, the first five are the most important.

1. ου is formed from εο, οε, and οο.

2. ει is formed from εε.

3. ω is formed from almost any combination of omicron or omega with any other vowel, except for rule 1.

4. α is formed from αε.

5. η is formed from εα.

Contract Verbs

17.6   Paradigm: Present active indicative (contract verbs)

ἀγαπάω means "I love," ποιέω means "I do," and πληρόω means "I fill." The contracting vowels are listed in parentheses. Work through the paradigm, explaining all the contractions. Pay special attention to any that may cause you difficulty.

am loving
I love̶
you love
He, she, it love
is loving

-άω		-έω		-όω	
ἀγαπῶ	(αω)	ποιῶ	(εω)	πληρῶ	(οω)
ἀγαπᾷς	(αεις)	ποιεῖς	(εεις)	πληροῖς	(οεις)
ἀγαπᾷ	(αει)	ποιεῖ	(εει)	πληροῖ	(οει)
ἀγαπῶμεν	(αομεν)	ποιοῦμεν	(εομεν)	πληροῦμεν	(οομεν)
ἀγαπᾶτε	(αετε)	ποιεῖτε	(εετε)	πληροῦτε	(οετε)
ἀγαπῶσι(ν)	(αουσι)	ποιοῦσι(ν)	(εουσι)	πληροῦσι(ν)	(οουσι)

17.7   Characteristics of contract verbs

There will almost always be a circumflex over the contracted vowels in the present indicative.

Notice that the endings are nearly the same even when a contraction has not taken place. The omega is the first person singular ending. The sigma is still present for the second person singular ending. The plural endings are virtually the same. Concentrate on the similarities.

17.8 **Hint**. Be sure to remember the rules for the connecting vowel. If you see ἀγαπᾶτε, you may recognize that the personal ending is τε, but is the verb ἀγαπάω, ἀγαπέω, or ἀγαπόω?

- Since the personal ending begins with tau (ἀγαπᾶτε), the connecting vowel must be an epsilon.

- Since ει is formed by εε, you know the verb cannot be an epsilon contract.

- Since ου is formed by οε, you know the verb cannot be an omicron contract.

- Therefore, the stem must be an alpha contract: ἀγαπάω.

17.9 In the Appendix (pages 343-44), there is a chart of all possible contractions of single vowels, and another chart for single vowels and diphthongs.

Summary

1. Contract verbs have stems ending in α, ε, or ο.

2. The Big Five

The Big Five

1. ου is formed from εο, οε, and οο.
2. ει is formed from εε.
3. ω is formed from almost any combination of omicron or omega with any other vowel, except for rule 1.
4. α is formed from αε.
5. η is formed from εα.

---

2. οι is formed from οει.

3. If the contract vowel and the first vowel of the diphthong are the same, they simplify.

   If the contract vowel and the first vowel of the diphthong are different, they contract. If the second vowel of the diphthong is an iota, it subscripts if possible; if it is an upsilon, it drops off.

4. Contract verbs contract as if the personal endings are those visible in the present active indicative.

5. The lexical form shows the contract vowel (ἀγαπάω), but if that form actually occurs in the text, the contract vowel and omicron will have contracted (ἀγαπῶ, ποιῶ, πληρῶ).

6. In the first person singular, no personal ending is used so the connecting vowel lengthens to omega.

Vocabulary

ἀγαπάω   I love, cherish (143; *ἀγαπα)[10]

(ἠγάπων), ἀγαπήσω, ἠγάπησα, ἠγάπηκα, ἠγάπημαι, ἠγαπήθην

δαιμόνιον, -ου, τό   demon (63; *δαιμονιο)[11]

ζητέω   I seek, desire, try to obtain (117; *ζητε)

(ἐζήτουν), ζητήσω, ἐζήτησα, -, -, ἐζητήθην

καλέω   I call, name, invite (148; *καλεϝ)[12]

(ἐκάλουν), καλέσω, ἐκάλεσα, κέκληκα, κέκλημαι, ἐκλήθην

On the root see 17.12. The digamma (ϝ) helps to explain apparent irregularities in other tenses, as you will see.

λαλέω   I speak, say (296; *λαλε)[13]

(ἐλάλουν), λαλήσω, ἐλάλησα, λελάληκα, λελάλημαι, ἐλαλήθην

οἶδα   I know, understand (318; *οιδα)

εἰδήσω, ᾔδειν, -, -, -

οἶδα is a different type of word. It actually is another tense (Perfect, Chapter 25), but it functions as if it were a present. Its paradigm is as follows.

1 sg	οἶδα	1 pl	οἴδαμεν
2 sg	οἶδας	2 pl	οἴδατε
3 sg	οἶδε(ν)	3 pl	οἴδασιν

ὅταν   whenever (123)

A crasis of ὅτε and ἄν. Introduces a dependent clause.

πλείων, πλεῖον   larger, more (55; *πλειο)[14]

πλείων is masculine and feminine, πλεῖον is neuter. It is a 3-3 adjective. The genitive of both is πλείονος. Notice the ablaut in the final stem vowel. See the Appendix for its paradigm (page 350). If you are following Track Two, just memorize this word for now; its forms will be explained in Chapter 10. Because of the word's meaning, it will often be followed by a word in the genitive. You can use the key word "than" with the word in the genitive. Accordance tags 11 of these occurrences as comparative adverbs.

πληρόω   I fill, complete, fulfill (86; *πληρο)

(ἐπλήρουν), πληρώσω, ἐπλήρωσα, πεπλήρωκα, πεπλήρωμαι, ἐπληρώθην

---

[10] Cognate verb of ἀγάπη and ἀγαπητός.

[11] *Demon* (δαίμων).

[12] The *Paraclete*, the Holy Spirit, is a Christian's counselor, advocate, one who is called (κλητός, "called") alongside (παρά) to aid.

[13] This word is onomatopoetic. Its meaning corresponds to the sound of the word ("lala").

[14] A *pleonasm* is a redundancy, using superfluous words.

> If you haven't felt the need to pray yet, you will soon enough. Here is a prayer a friend of mine uses in class. You should be able to figure out what most of it says. Why don't you memorize it and use it before every class? I will print the text a little larger so it is really clear. See page 147 for explanations.

> Πάτερ ἡμῶν, ὁ ἐν τοῖς οὐρανοῖς,
> ἴσθι μεθ᾽ ἡμῶν ἐν ταύτῃ τῇ ὥρᾳ·
> βοήθει ἡμῖν μανθάνουσιν τὴν Ἑλληνικὴν γλῶσσαν·
> δίδασκε ἡμῖν τὸν λόγον σου·
> ἐν τῷ ὀνόματι τοῦ Ἰησοῦ Χριστοῦ προσευχόμεθα,
> ἀμήν.

ποιέω   I do, make (568; *ποιε)[15]

(ἐποίουν), ποιήσω, ἐποίησα, πεποίηκα, πεποίημαι, –
The translation of this word can sometimes be quite idiomatic. It has a wide range of meaning.

τηρέω   I keep, guard, observe (70; *τηρε)

(ἐτήρουν), τηρήσω, ἐτήρησα, τετήρηκα, τετήρημαι, ἐτηρήθην

Total word count in the New Testament:	138,162
Number of words learned to date:	191
Number of word occurrences in this chapter:	1,987
Number of word occurrences to date:	96,354
Percent of total word count in the New Testament:	69.74%

Of contract verbs occurring fifty times or more in the New Testament, there is only one omicron contract (πληρόω), four alpha contracts (ἀγαπάω, γεννάω, ἐρωτάω, ἐπερωτάω), but many epsilon contracts.

Advanced Information

Here are the rules for contraction as they are normally listed.

17.10 **Rules for the contraction for single vowels** (i.e., total of two vowels).

The full form of the rules is given, but only those illustrations that apply to contract verbs are listed.[16] Exceptions 2 and 4 are by far the most frequent.

1. Two like vowels form their common long vowel.

  αα ▸ α

2. Exception: When ε and ε contract they form ει, and when ο and ο contract they form ου.

  εε ▸ ει ποιε + ε + τε ▸ ποιεῖτε

  οο ▸ ου πληρο + ο + μεν ▸ πληροῦμεν

3. An ο or ω will overcome an α, ε, or η regardless of their order, and form ω.

  οα ▸ ω

  αο ▸ ω ἀγαπα + ο + μεν ▸ ἀγαπῶμεν

4. Exception: When an ε and ο contract they form ου, regardless of their order.

  εο ▸ ου ποιε + ο + μεν ▸ ποιοῦμεν

  οε ▸ ου πληρο + ε + τε ▸ πληροῦτε

---

[15] A poem (ποίημα) literally means "something done." A poet (ποιητής) is "one who makes."

[16] It is difficult to know who deserves the credit for these rules since they are repeated in so many grammars. I learned them initially from J. Gresham Machen's grammar (143), and he cites White's *Beginner's Greek Book* (1895), pages 75-76.

5. If an α comes before an ε or an η, they will contract to an α.
If an ε or an η comes before an α, they will contract to an η.[17]

$$αε \rightarrow α \qquad \qquad ἀγαπα + ε + τε \rightarrow ἀγαπᾶτε$$

17.11 Rules for the contraction of a single vowel and a diphthong

Diphthongs follow the same rules as single vowels described above. However, because there are three and not two vowels involved, a few extra rules come into play. The only time this takes place in the present active indicative is the third person plural.

1. When a single vowel is followed by a diphthong that begins with the *same vowel* as the single, the two similar vowels simplify[18] and the second vowel remains the same.

$$οου \rightarrow ου \qquad \qquad πληρο + ουσι \rightarrow πληροῦσι$$
$$αα \rightarrow ᾳ$$
$$ααι \rightarrow αι \rightarrow ᾳ$$

2. When a single vowel is followed by a diphthong that begins with a *different vowel* than the single, the single vowel and the first vowel of the diphthong contract according to the regular rules. If the third vowel is an upsilon it will drop off. If it is an iota it will subscript.

$$αου \rightarrow ωυ \rightarrow ω \qquad ἀγαπα + ουσι \rightarrow ἀγαπῶσι$$
$$εου \rightarrow ουυ \rightarrow ου \qquad ποιε + ουσι \rightarrow ποιοῦσι$$

Exceptions

$$εοι \rightarrow οι$$
$$αει \rightarrow αι \rightarrow ᾳ \qquad ἀγαπα + ειν \rightarrow ἀγαπᾶν^{19}$$
$$οει \rightarrow οι \qquad \qquad πληρο + ει \rightarrow πληροῖ$$
$$οη \rightarrow οι$$

> Most of the forms in the prayer on page 145 you don't recognize (or can't figure out from the lexicon) are imperatives.
> - ἴσθι is the imperative of εἰμί.
> - βοήθει means "help."
> - δίδασκε means "teach."
> - μανθάνουσιν is a participle meaning, "who are learning."
>
> βοήθει is a good word to learn under any circumstances.

17.12 Digamma.

The digamma was a letter in the Greek alphabet that dropped out of use before the Koine period. In most cases it was replaced by the upsilon. It is written in today's grammars as ϝ or ͷ (uppercase F or ϝ). It was pronounced "w" and originally came between ε and ζ in the alphabet. It is classified as a "semiconsonant."

The fact that it used to be part of the language explains some of what appears to be irregularities in the language. For example, the root of ἀκούω is actually *ἀκοϝ. When the digamma dropped out of use, it was replaced by the upsilon, but the fact that it used to be a diagamma explains why there is no contraction with the omega.

I discuss the digamma in more detail in MBG, #27 (pages 45-47).

---

[17] There is no example of this rule in the present active, but there is in the present passive.
λυ + ε + σαι ▸ λυεαι ▸ λυηι ▸ λύῃ.

[18] One drops out. This is not an actual contraction, technically speaking.

[19] This word is an infinitive, and you will not meet these words until Chapter 32.

Chapter 18

Present Middle/Passive Indicative

Exegetical Insight

ἀρχηγός as a title for Jesus appears only four times in the New Testament, twice each in Acts (3:15; 5:31) and Hebrews (2:10; 12:2). It is notoriously difficult to translate. A survey of the Greek translation of the Old Testament (LXX) and nonbiblical uses of the term suggests a threefold connotation: (a) path-breaker (pioneer) who opens the way for others, hence, "guide," "hero;" (b) the source or founder, hence, "author," "initiator," "beginning;" (c) the leader-ruler, hence, "captain," "prince," "king."

These ideas are not necessarily exclusive of each other. In fact they probably all combine to speak of someone who explores new territory, opens a trail, and leads others to it. There he builds a city or fortress for those who follow and leads them in defense against attackers. When the peace has been won, he remains as their ruler and the city or community bears his name. He is thereafter honored as the founding hero.

The Old Testament speaks of several individuals who held such a position. For at least one our word is actually used. In Judges 11:6 ff., we learn that Jepthah was asked to become "head" over the inhabitants of Gilead in order to deliver them from the Ammonites

(v. 6); one version of the Greek translation uses the word ἀρχηγός here. Jepthah agreed on condition that the position would be made permanent. The elders consented and he was made κεφαλὴ καὶ ἀρχηγός even before the battle (vv. 8-11). At the conclusion of his struggles, "Jepthah judged Israel six years" (Judges 12:7).

In Acts 3:15 Peter accuses the Jews of killing the "ἀρχηγός of life," suggesting that Jesus is not only the origin of biological life, but also of "new life" and the guide-protector-provider-ruler-namesake of those identified with him. Later Peter speaks of Jesus as the "ἀρχηγόν and Savior, to give repentance to Israel" (5:31). The word "Savior" was associated with the judges of old. Jesus is the one who meets the emergency situation caused by the sin of God's people. He comes to bring not only deliverance but also the continuing service of ἀρχηγός. The writer to the Hebrews speaks of the suffering "ἀρχηγός of salvation" (2:10) and the "ἀρχηγός and Perfecter of our faith" (12:2). In each case Jesus as ἀρχηγός not only initiates and provides the new life for his people, but remains with them through it; they bear his name. He is their hero.

J. Julius Scott, Jr.

Overview

In this chapter you will learn:

- the passive voice in which the subject receives the action of the verb;

- that the present middle/passive is formed by joining the present tense stem, connecting vowel, and primary middle/passive endings;

- that in the present tense, the middle and passive are identical in form;

- about deponent verbs that are middle or passive in form but active in meaning.

English

18.1 When a verb is active, the subject is performing the action of the verb. When a verb is passive, the subject is receiving the action.

Active. "I *hit* the ball." "I" is the subject of the sentence and is the one performing the action of the verb "hit."

Passive. "I *am hit* by the ball." "I" is the subject of this sentence, but "I" is not doing the action of the verb "hit." The action of the verb is being performed by "ball," and it is being done to the subject, "I."

18.2 English forms the present passive by adding the helping verb "am/is/are" for the undefined and "am/are being" for the continuous, plus the past participle.

	continuous	*undefined*
present active	I am hitting	I hit
	They are hitting	They hit
present passive	I am being hit	I am hit
	They are being hit	They are hit

18.3 You can often identify a passive verb by placing "by" after the verb and seeing if it makes sense. "I was hit." "I was hit by what?" "I was hit by the ball." "Was hit" is a passive verb. Sometimes there will be a prepositional phrase specifying who or what is doing the action of the verb (e.g., "by the ball").

18.4 A full chart of the English tenses is given in the Appendix, page 351. If you are unsure of your English you may want to spend some time studying the chart.

18.5 When you use a helping verb to form the passive voice, the time of the verbal construction is determined by the helping verb, not the main verb.

For example, the active construction "I remember" shifts to "I am remembered" in the passive. Because "am" is present, the construction "am remembered" is present, even though "remembered" is a past participle.

Greek: Present Passive Indicative

18.6 **Chart: Present passive indicative**

> *Present tense stem + Connecting vowel +*
> *Primary passive personal endings*
>
> λυ + ο + μαι ‣ λύομαι

18.7 **Paradigm: Present passive indicative**. The present passive indicative verb functions basically the same in Greek as in English. To form the present passive indicative, Greek adds the primary passive endings to the verbal stem. Be sure to read the footnote to the second singular form.

	form	translation	conn. vow.	ending	pres. act.
1 sg	λύομαι	I am being loosed	ο	μαι	λύω
2 sg	λύῃ[1]	You are being loosed	ε	σαι	λύεις
3 sg	λύεται	He, she, it is being loosed	ε	ται	λύει
1 pl	λυόμεθα	We are being loosed	ο	μεθα	λύομεν
2 pl	λύεσθε	You are being loosed	ε	σθε	λύετε
3 pl	λύονται	They are being loosed	ο	νται	λύουσι(ν)

As you can see, the connecting vowels are more visible in the passive than they are in the active.

18.8 **Master Personal Ending Chart**. You can now learn another part of the Master Personal Ending Chart. You are halfway home. (The label reads "middle/passive." You will see what "middle" means below.)

---

[1] The second person singular ending is quite troublesome. Because the sigma occurs between vowels in the non-stem part of the word (λυ + ε + σαι), it will often drop out and the vowels will contract. In this case, they contracted to eta as per the rules, and the iota subscripted (λυ + ε + σαι ‣ λυεαι ‣ λυηι ‣ λύῃ). Be sure to remember that the true ending is σαι; this will become important later.

	primary tenses		secondary tenses
active voice	λύω	–	
	λύεις	ς	
	λύει	ι	
	λύομεν	μεν	
	λύετε	τε	
	λύουσι(ν)	νσι	
middle/passive voice	λύομαι	μαι	
	λύῃ	-σαι *Drops*	
	λύεται	ται	
	λυόμεθα	μεθα	
	λύεσθε	σθε	
	λύονται	νται	

[handwritten notes:]
Present Stem: λυ
+ Connecting Vowel: o/ε → μ,ν
+ Primary Personal Ending:

pres. stem + + Prim/mid/pass

1st p. s. μαι

18.9 **Person, number, tense, time, and aspect.** There is no difference between the active and passive on these points.

18.10 **"By."** It is common to find the equivalent of "by" in a Greek sentence after a passive verb. It will either be ὑπό followed by a noun in the genitive indicating a personal agent (e.g., ὑπὸ τοῦ θεοῦ), or the simple dative indicating an impersonal instrument (τῷ λόγῳ τοῦ θεοῦ).

> πάντα μοι παρεδόθη ὑπὸ τοῦ πατρός μου *(Matt 11:27).*
> All things were handed over to me *by* my Father.

Halftime Review

- The subject does the action of an active verb, and it receives the action of a passive verb.

- English forms the passive through the use of helping verbs, and the time of the verbal construction is determined by the helping verb and not the main verb.

- The Greek present passive is formed by using the primary tense stem, connecting vowel, and the primary passive personal endings: ομαι, ῃ, εται, ομεθα, εσθε, ονται.

- The true personal endings are μαι, σαι, ται, μεθα, σθε, νται.

- Passive verbs are often followed by some "by" construction that indicates who or what does the action of the verb.

Ἐρχομαι

Deponent Verbs

middle/Passive

← NEVER primary

18.11 Deponent Verb. This is a verb that is *middle or passive in form but active in meaning*. Its form is always middle or passive, but its meaning is always active. It can never have a passive meaning. I will discuss the middle voice below.

You can tell if a verb is deponent by its lexical form. Deponent verbs are always listed in the vocabulary sections with passive endings. In other words, if the lexical form ends in an omega, it is not deponent (e.g., ἀγαπάω). If the lexical form ends in -ομαι, the verb is deponent (e.g., ἔρχομαι). *You will have to remember that the word is a deponent.*

There is some interesting research currently happening that questions whether there actually is such a thing as deponency. For example, many deponent verbs are intransitive (36.10) and therefore cannot be passive. See the class website for an ongoing discussion.

> οὐκ οἴδατε ποίᾳ ἡμέρᾳ ὁ κύριος ὑμῶν ἔρχεται (Matt 24:42).
> You do not know on what day your Lord *is coming.*

18.12 Parsing. When parsing a deponent verb, instead of saying "active" or "passive" I recommend that you say "deponent." Be sure to translate the inflected form as active. For example, ἔρχεται is third person singular, present deponent indicative, of ἔρχομαι, meaning "he/she/it is coming."

18.13 In a single tense a verb will be either regular or deponent. It cannot be both. ἔρχομαι is always deponent in the present. It will never be ἔρχω.

However, a verb can be deponent in one tense and not deponent in another. ἔρχομαι is not deponent in the aorist past tense (Chapter 22).

Present Middle Indicative

18.14 While English has only two voices, Greek has three: active, middle, and passive. In the present tense the middle and passive are identical in form.

18.15 Chart: Present middle indicative

> *Present tense stem + Connecting vowel +*
> *Primary passive personal endings*
>
> ερχ + ο + μαι ‣ ἔρχομαι

18.16 Paradigm: Present middle indicative

	form	translation	conn. vow.	ending	pres. act.
1 sg	ἔρχομαι	I come	ο	μαι	λύω
2 sg	ἔρχῃ[2]	You come	ε	σαι	λύεις
3 sg	ἔρχεται	He, she, it comes	ε	ται	λύει

---

[2] For an explanation see page 150 note 1.

1 pl	ἐρχόμεθα	We come	ο	μεθα	λύομεν
2 pl	ἔρχεσθε	You come	ε	σθε	λύετε
3 pl	ἔρχονται	They come	ο	νται	λύουσι(ν)

18.17 Meaning. The meaning of a verb in the middle voice can be difficult to define, partly because it is often an issue of nuance. But let's make it easy for you now. In the next several chapters, the only middle verbs you will see are deponent, so they will always have an active meaning. Actually, the vast majority of middle forms in the New Testament, approximately 75%, are deponent. You will learn the true use of middles in a later chapter.

In the present tense, the middle and passive are identical in form. There is no way for you to know whether ἔρχομαι is middle or passive. But since all the middles I will show you for several chapters are deponent, you will translate all the present middle and passive deponents the same way, as actives.

Present Middle/Passive Forms of Contracts

18.18 Paradigm: Present middle/passive indicative (contract verbs). Contract verbs follow the same rules in the middle/passive as they do in the active.

	-άω	-έω	-όω
1 sg	ἀγαπῶμαι	ποιοῦμαι	πληροῦμαι
2 sg	ἀγαπᾷ[3]	ποιῇ[4]	πληροῖ[5]
3 sg	ἀγαπᾶται	ποιεῖται	πληροῦται
1 pl	ἀγαπώμεθα	ποιούμεθα	πληρούμεθα
2 pl	ἀγαπᾶσθε	ποιεῖσθε	πληροῦσθε
3 pl	ἀγαπῶνται	ποιοῦνται	πληροῦνται

Notice the many similarities between the regular present passive endings and their contracted forms. Concentrate on the similarities. You should be able to look at these contracted forms and discover what the original vowels were that formed this particular contraction.

In the middle/passive, you see the true personal endings (except second person singular). You do not have to deal with the issues raised by the eighth rule of contraction as you did in the active.

What is today? You don't know? You've been studying too much Greek! Here are the Greek names of the days. They are all feminine because they intrinsically modify ἡμέρα. Can you figure out what they mean?

- κυριακή (ἐν τῇ κυριακῇ ἡμέρᾳ; Rev 1:10)
- δευτέρα
- τρίτη
- τετάρτη
- πέμπτη (Didache 8:1)
- παρασκευή (John 19:42; Martyrdom of Polycarp 7:1)
- τὸ σάββατον

---

[3] αεσαι › ασαι › ααι › αι › ᾳ. Do not confuse this with the identical form that is a third person singular active. Context will tell you the difference.

[4] εεσαι › εσαι › εαι › ηι › ῃ.

[5] οεσαι › οεαι › οει › οι (irregular).

Summary

1. If a verb is in the passive voice, the subject is receiving the action of the verb.

2. To form the English passive you add a helping verb. The time of an English verb that has helping verbs is determined by the time of the helping verb.

3. The present middle/passive in Greek is formed by joining the present tense stem with the connecting vowel and the primary middle/passive endings. The primary middle/passive personal endings are μαι, σαι (which changes to η when joined with the connecting vowel), ται, μεθα, σθε, νται.

4. Deponent verbs are middle or passive in form but active in meaning. Their lexical form is always middle or passive but their meaning is always active. You can tell if a verb is deponent by its lexical form.

5. In the present tense, the middle and passive are identical in form. Most middles are deponent and therefore active in meaning.

Master Verb Chart

Tense	Aug/ Redup	Tense stem	Tense form.	Conn. vowel	Personal endings	1st sing paradigm
Present act		pres		o/ε	prim act	λύω
Present mid/pas		pres		o/ε	prim mid/pas	λύομαι

Vocabulary

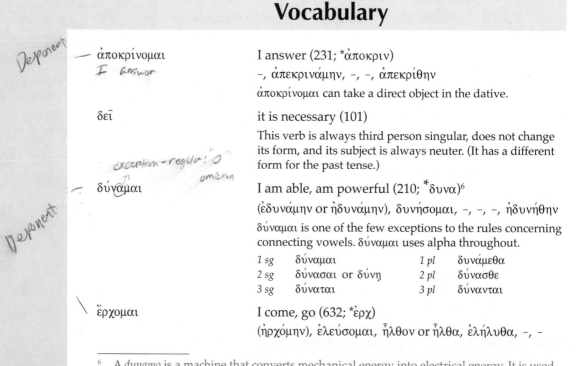

Deponent

— ἀποκρίνομαι
  I answer

δεῖ

exception – regular: o
  omicron
— δύναμαι

Deponent

\ ἔρχομαι

I answer (231; *ἀποκριν)
-, ἀπεκρινάμην, -, -, ἀπεκρίθην
ἀποκρίνομαι can take a direct object in the dative.

it is necessary (101)
This verb is always third person singular, does not change its form, and its subject is always neuter. (It has a different form for the past tense.)

I am able, am powerful (210; *δυνα)[6]
(ἐδυνάμην or ἠδυνάμην), δυνήσομαι, -, -, -, ἠδυνήθην
δύναμαι is one of the few exceptions to the rules concerning connecting vowels. δύναμαι uses alpha throughout.

1 sg	δύναμαι	1 pl	δυνάμεθα
2 sg	δύνασαι or δύνῃ	2 pl	δύνασθε
3 sg	δύναται	3 pl	δύνανται

I come, go (632; *ερχ)
(ἠρχόμην), ἐλεύσομαι, ἦλθον or ἦλθα, ἐλήλυθα, -, -

---

[6] A *dynamo* is a machine that converts mechanical energy into electrical energy. It is used metaphorically of a person with a lot of energy.

νύξ, νυκτός, ἡ	night (61; *νυκτ)[7]

If you are following Track Two, just memorize this word for now; its forms will be explained in Chapter 10.

ὅστις, ἥτις, ὅτι	whoever, whichever, whatever (153; *ὅ +*τιν)

This word is the combination of the relative and the indefinite pronouns (ὅς + τις). As such, both halves decline. See the Appendix for the full paradigm (page 349). If you are following Track Two, just memorize this word for now; its forms will be explained in Chapter 10.

Because ὅστις is formed with the relative pronoun, it will only introduce a dependent clause; the ὅστις clause cannot contain the main subject and verb.

In Koine Greek, this relative indefinite pronoun was starting to shift so that it could also be used as the relative pronoun. In other words, its indefinite significance can be lost and ὅστις can be translated the same as ὅς if required by the context.

The neuter singular ὅτι never occurs in our texts, but ὅ τι (two words) does occur nine times.

πορεύομαι *Deponent*	I go, proceed, live (153; *πορευ)
	(ἐπορευόμην), πορεύσομαι, -, -, πεπόρευμαι, ἐπορεύθην

συνάγω	I gather together, invite (59; *συναγ)[8]
	συνάξω, συνήγαγον, -, συνῆγμαι, συνήχθην

τόπος, -ου, ὁ	place, location (94; *τοπο)[9]
ὡς	as, like, when, that, how, about (504)[10]

Total word count in the New Testament:	138,162
Number of words learned to date:	201
Number of word occurrences in this chapter:	2,198
Number of word occurrences to date:	98,552
Percent of total word count in the New Testament:	71.33%

WORKBOOK SUMMARY

---

[7] *Nocturnal*, "pertaining to night," looks related to the Greek νύξ but according to Klein is actually from the Latin "nocturnus."

[8] In Chapter 21 you will learn the cognate noun, συναγωγή, which is a meeting place where people gather together.

[9] *Topology* is the science of describing a place. A *toponym* is the name of a place.

[10] "About" in the sense of "approximately."

Chapter 19

Future Active/Middle Indicative

Exegetical Insight

In English we think of the future tense as the tense of simple prediction. Greek often uses the future that way, too, but in many biblical passages it carries a different sense. Particularly when quoting the Old Testament (under the influence of a parallel Hebrew construction), the future is used to give a command. "Thou shalt not kill, thou shalt not commit adultery," and so on, are not predictions about the behavior of God's people, or we would have repeatedly proven God wrong! Rather they are commands, what grammarians often call the imperatival or volitive use of the future tense. We do this in English occasionally, particularly in casual speech. For example, the student insistently says to her friends about an upcoming party, "You *will* be there!" This is not a prediction but a demand!

An excellent New Testament example appears when both Jesus and Paul quote Genesis 2:24: "For this reason a man will leave his father and mother and be united to his wife, and they will become one flesh." In the context of the story of Adam and Eve, it is natural to take this as God's prediction about how married life will proceed among the offspring of these first two human beings, and there may be a partially predictive element intended here. But when Jesus cites this passage to refute the Pharisees' generally more lenient views on divorce (Matt 19:5), he knows full well that many of God's people have violated and will continue to violate this

creation ordinance. The same is true of Paul when he establishes the principles of a Christian marriage in the midst of the highly promiscuous pagan culture of Ephesus (Eph 5:31). Rather, both Jesus and Paul are using the future tense verbs of the Genesis text primarily in their imperatival sense—telling believers that God commands them to be faithful to their spouses for life.

That command remains crucial today, when Christians divorce for so many flimsy reasons that the Bible never condones. As the pastor who married my wife and me told us during premarital counseling, "There may be extreme instances in which divorce is biblically legitimate. But if you go into marriage looking for a way out, you will almost surely find it. Far better to commit to each other that you will never divorce, even if those extreme circumstances were to occur. Then you will have to turn to God, to Christian friends, and to each other to see you through the difficult times. And God will prove faithful." We have heeded this advice for thirty years now, and will continue to heed it for as long as we live. And in that period of time, while there have been struggles, there certainly has been nothing emerge to seriously threaten our marriage. God does remain faithful when we commit to his *commands*. And some of them come "disguised" in the future tense.

Craig L. Blomberg

Overview

In this chapter you will learn that:

■ the future tense indicates an action occurring in the future;

■ the future is formed by adding a sigma to the end of the future tense stem (λύσω);

■ contract verbs lengthen their contract vowel before the sigma (ἀγαπήσω);

■ knowing the Square of Stops is especially useful in identifying the future tense.

English

19.1 The future describes an action that will occur in the future. To form the future you add a helping verb ("will"/"shall") to the present tense stem of the verb.

The basic rule in older English for the future tense is that "shall" is used for the first person and "will" for the second and third. "I shall work hard." "You will work hard." "He will slack off." That distinction has generally fallen into disuse today, and "will" is used everywhere.

19.2 English verbs are centered on three different forms, and all the variations of the verb are formed from them.[1]

■ **Present.** The present tense is also used to form the future tense. "I eat." "I will eat."

■ **Past.** The past tense of "eat" is "ate."

■ **Past perfect.** The past perfect tense of "eat" is "eaten."

Usually the past tense of verbs is formed by adding "-ed": "kick, kicked, kicked." Other times you change the stem: "swim, swam, swum." Sometimes the past and past perfect are identical: "study, studied, studied." In the Appendix there is a chart showing all the basic forms of the English verb (page 351).

Future Active Indicative

19.3 **Meaning.** The future tense in Greek has the same meaning as in English. It describes an action that will occur in the future. As is true of the other tenses, the time reference of the verb is from the point of view of the writer, not the reader.

---

[1] English grammar seems to be in a constant state of change, and it is therefore difficult to say, "In English ...." But in teaching Greek I must simplify the issues somewhat. So much for disclaimers on English tenses.

19.4 Koine Greek has five tenses.[2] You have already learned the present tense, and now are learning the future. The imperfect, aorist, and perfect are yet to come.

However, because of how Greek forms its tense and voice combinations, there are seven distinct forms of a Greek verb. Although you do not know the other tenses, here is an example.

Greek	tense/voice	translation
ἀγαπάω	present	I love
ἠγάπων	imperfect	I was loving
ἀγαπήσω	future active	I will love
ἠγάπησα	aorist active	I loved
ἠγάπηκα	perfect active	I have loved
ἠγάπημαι	perfect passive	I have been loved
ἠγαπήθην	aorist passive	I was loved

The overly inquisitive will want to know why the Greek verb is changing its form—like why does the alpha change to eta, and what are those letters between the verb and the ending. Be patient; today's own trouble is sufficient. But I want you to see the overall structure of the verb system.

19.5 Lexicon listing. If you look up a verb in a lexicon, you will see something like the following.[3]

λύω, λύσω, ἔλυσα, λέλυκα, λέλυμαι, ἐλύθην

Compare this to the chart above. You will see that the lexicon is listing the first person singular form of the verb in the present (λύω), future active (λύσω), aorist active (ἔλυσα), perfect active (λέλυκα), perfect middle/passive (λέλυμαι), and aorist passive (ἐλύθην) tenses.

Therefore, if you want to see the future form of a verb, look at the second form in the lexicon. λύσω is the future active form of λύω.

In *BBG*, if there is a dash instead of a tense stem, it means that particular tense stem does not occur in the New Testament.

δοκέω, –, ἔδοξα, –, –, –

19.6 Tense stem. The basic form of the verb in each of these tense/voice combinations is called the "tense stem."

Can you see how ἀγαπάω forms its future tense stem? Its future tense stem is the same as its present tense stem (ἀγαπα). For some reason (which you are about to learn), the alpha lengthens to eta, a sigma is added, and the person ending is attached to the end (*ἀγαπα + σ + ω ▸ ἀγαπήσω).

> The imperfect is built on the present tense form of the verb. That is why there are six and not seven distinct forms of a Greek verb.

> These six different forms are almost universally called the "principal parts." I have not found this terminology helpful. Some English grammarians use the term "principal parts" to describe what others call "parts of speech": nouns, adjectives, verbs, etc. Others speak of the three principal parts of the verb: present ("eat"), past ("ate"), past perfect ("have eaten"). I call the six different forms of the verbs, "tense forms."

---

[2] There actually were two more, but they were dropping out of use, the pluperfect and future perfect.

[3] I list words like this but with one variation. In *BBG* you find something like this: λύω, (ἔλυον), λύσω, ἔλυσα, λέλυκα, λέλυμαι, ἐλύθην. The form in parentheses is the imperfect tense, and I will explain why I list verbs this way when you get to Chapter 21.

The point to learn is this:

- ἀγαπα is the *present* tense stem, meaning that all forms of ἀγαπάω in the present are formed from ἀγαπα.

- ἀγαπα is also the *future* active tense stem, meaning that all forms of ἀγαπάω in the future active are formed from ἀγαπα.

Pattern 1

19.7 There are four ways Greek verbs form their future tense stem. In this chapter we will look at Pattern 1.

19.8 Chart: Future active indicative

> *Future active tense stem + tense formative (σ) +*
>
> *Connecting vowel + Primary active personal endings*
>
> λυ + σ + ο + μεν ▸ λύσομεν

19.9 Future active tense stem. Verbs in Pattern 1 use the same tense stem in the future active as in the present.[4] *λυ is used in both the present (λύω) and the future (λύσω).

19.10 Tense formative. The future is formed by inserting a sigma between the future tense stem and the connecting vowel. This sigma is called the "tense formative" because it helps form the future tense.

> λύσω

19.11 Connecting vowel. The connecting vowel is the same as in the present.

> λύσομεν
> λύσετε

19.12 Personal endings. The future active indicative uses the same primary active endings as the present active. They contract with the connecting vowels as they do in the present, forming ω, εις, ει, ομεν, ετε, ουσι.

19.13 Paradigm: Future active indicative

	form	translation	conn. vow.	ending	pres. act.
1 sg	λύσω	I will loose	ο	–	λύω
2 sg	λύσεις	You will loose	ε	ς	λύεις
3 sg	λύσει	He/she/it will loose	ε	ι	λύει
1 pl	λύσομεν	We will loose	ο	μεν	λύομεν
2 pl	λύσετε	You will loose	ε	τε	λύετε
3 pl	λύσουσι(ν)	They will loose	ο	νσι	λύουσι(ν)

---

[4] Technically, this tense stem is the future active/middle tense stem, since as you will see the active and middle are both built on the same stem, like in the present. Some grammars call these the "regular" verbs, but most Greek verbs are quite regular.

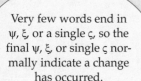

Halftime Review

- The future describes an action occurring in the future. Aspect is secondary to time.

- There are six basic forms of a Greek verb. The tense stem is the basic form of the verb in a tense.

- The present tense stem is used to form the present (active and middle/passive). The future tense stem is used to form the future active.

- The future active is formed from the future active tense stem + the tense formative (σ) + connecting vowel + primary active personal endings.

Characteristics of Future Active Indicative

19.14 **Translation**. To translate a future verb you add the word "will" or "shall." As a general rule, translate the future with the undefined aspect ("I will eat") rather than the continuous ("I will be eating").

> ἀγαπήσεις τὸν πλησίον σου ὡς σεαυτόν *(Matt 19:19)*.
> *You will love* your neighbor as yourself.

Of all the Greek tenses, the future has the strongest emphasis on time, describing an action occurring in the future. It is the one Greek tense in which aspect is secondary to time.

19.15 **Contract verbs**. So far you have learned what happens when the contract vowel comes into contact with the connecting vowel: they contract. But what happens if the contract vowel does not come into contact with another vowel?

Such is the case in the future tense, where the contract vowel is immediately followed by the tense formative. In this case, *the contract vowel lengthens before a tense formative*. Alpha and epsilon both lengthen to eta while omicron lengthens to omega.

*ἀγαπα	+	σ	+	ω	▸	ἀγαπήσω
*ποιε	+	σ	+	ω	▸	ποιήσω
*πληρο	+	σ	+	ω	▸	πληρώσω

As you will see, this lengthening before a tense formative occurs whenever there is a tense formative; it is not restricted to just the future tense. Notice that the accent is always over the lengthened contract vowel.

> Very few words end in ψ, ξ, or a single ς, so the final ψ, ξ, or single ς normally indicate a change has occurred.

19.16 **Square of stops**. If the stem of a verb ends in a stop, when the sigma is added to form the future you see the same types of changes that you saw in third declension nouns ending in a stop (e.g., *σαρκ + σ ▸ σάρξ). Whenever you see a psi or xi before the personal ending (e.g., βλέψω, διώξω), it is relatively safe to assume there is a sigma in there.

The following chart shows the Square of Stops, with a fourth column showing what consonant results from joining the stop with a sigma.

Labial	π	β	φ	▸	ψ
Velar	κ	γ	χ	▸	ξ
Dental	τ	δ	θ	▸	σ

Labial	πσ	▸	ψ		βλεπ	+	σω	▸	βλέψω
	βσ	▸	ψ						
	φσ	▸	ψ		γραφ	+	σω	▸	γράψω
Velar	κσ	▸	ξ		διωκ	+	σω	▸	διώξω
	γσ	▸	ξ		αγ	+	σω	▸	ἄξω
	χσ	▸	ξ		ἐλεγχ	+	σω	▸	ἐλέγξω
Dental	τσ	▸	σ						
	δσ	▸	σ		βαπτιδ	+	σω	▸	βαπτίσω
	θσ	▸	σ		πειθ	+	σω	▸	πείσω

> Have you noticed how inflected languages use less words than a language like English? However, when you try to move Greek into English poetry or songs, the words are normally too long. I have been trying to learn how to sing the children's son, "Head and Shoulders, Knees and Toes" in Greek, but the words are just too long. If you can figure it out, please let me know. The plural forms are in parentheses.

Pattern 1

19.17 As I said earlier, verbs follow four patterns in the formation of their future tense stem. These patterns carry over to the other tenses, so they are important to learn. In this chapter you have learned Pattern 1; the other patterns are in the next chapter.

> Head: κεφαλή
> Shoulder: ὦμος (ὦμοι)
> Knee: γόνυ (γόνατα)
> Toe: δάκτυλος (δάκτυλοι)

19.18 **Pattern 1 verbs use the same stem of the verb in both the present and the future active**. In other words, the present and future tense stems are identical to the root. The final form of the verb will be changed by the tense formative and other forces, but it is still the same stem. Many verbs fall into this pattern; these are the easy ones to learn.

19.19 There are three categories in this pattern. You already know them.

a. Roots ending in an iota or upsilon

*ἀκου ▸ ἀκούω
*ἀκου ▸ ἀκούσω

b. Contract verbs

*ποιε ▸ ποιέω
*ποιε ▸ ποιήσω

c. Roots ending in a stop

*βλεπ ▸ βλέπω
*βλεπ ▸ βλέψω

> Eye: ὀφθαλμός (ὀφθαλμοί)
> Ear: ὦτιον (ὦτα)
> Mouth: στόμα
> Nose: ῥίς

As you get further into Greek, knowing these patterns becomes important. You will be looking at a verb, wondering what tense it is, and once you realize that it is a Pattern 1 verb you can see that it is regular in its formation of its tense stems and you will be able to parse the form. So remember these three categories of verbs.

Future Middle Indicative

19.20 In the present tense, the middle and passive are the same form. In the future, the form of the middle is distinct from both the active and the passive. (You will learn the future passive in Chapter 24.) The future middle is formed from the future active tense stem but uses primary passive endings (e.g., πορεύσομαι).

As I said before, there is more to the middle than simply being equivalent to the active; but all the middles that you have seen so far, and will for some time, are deponent and therefore active in meaning. That is why the definitions in the following paradigm are active.

Because λύω does not have a deponent future middle, I will use πορεύομαι.

19.21 Chart: Future middle indicative

> *Future active tense stem + Tense formative (σ) +*
>
> *Connecting vowel + Primary passive personal endings*
>
> πορευ + σ + ο + μαι ▸ πορεύσομαι

19.22 Paradigm: Future middle indicative

	form	translation	conn. vow.	ending	pres. mid.
1 sg	πορεύσομαι	I will go	ο	μαι	λύομαι
2 sg	πορεύσῃ	You will go	ε	σαι	λύῃ
3 sg	πορεύσεται	He/she/it will go	ε	ται	λύεται
1 pl	πορευσόμεθα	We will go	ο	μεθα	λυόμεθα
2 pl	πορεύσεσθε	You will go	ε	σθε	λύεσθε
3 pl	πορεύσονται	They will go	ο	νται	λύονται

19.23 Deponent. A verb is not deponent in the future (or any other tense) merely because it is deponent in the present. So how do you know if a verb is deponent in the future?

As far as Pattern 1 verbs are concerned, they will use the same stem in the present and the future active; if the present is deponent then most likely the future is deponent, and vice versa.

> ἐγὼ ἀπὸ τοῦ νῦν εἰς τὰ ἔθνη <u>πορεύσομαι</u> (*Acts 18:6*).
>
> From now on I *will go* to the Gentiles.

But what if you want to confirm that a certain form is not an exception? You can look up the verb in a lexicon, and if the second tense form ends in -ομαι, then it is deponent in the future.

> γινώσκω, γνώσομαι, ἔγνων, ἔγνωκα, ἔγνωσμαι, ἐγνώσθην
>
> ἀκούω, ἀκούσω, ἤκουσα, ἀκήκοα, -, ἠκούσθην

You may have noticed that the stem of γνώσομαι is not the same as the stem of γινώσκω. This is because γινώσκω belongs to one of the other patterns that you will learn in the next chapter. It is active in the present and deponent in the future.

19.24 **Future of εἰμί.** The future of εἰμί is middle deponent. Its root is *εσ. Memorize this paradigm.

	form	translation	future middle
1 sg	ἔσομαι	I will be	πορεύσομαι
2 sg	ἔσῃ	You will be	πορεύσῃ
3 sg	ἔσται[5]	He/she/it will be	πορεύσεται
1 pl	ἐσόμεθα	We will be	πορευσόμεθα
2 pl	ἔσεσθε	You will be	πορεύσεσθε
3 pl	ἔσονται	They will be	πορεύσονται

Summary

1. The future tense indicates an action that will occur in the future. It usually carries the undefined aspect.

2. The future tense uses the tense formative sigma. The active uses the primary active endings while the middle uses primary passive. All future middle forms you have seen so far are deponent and therefore active in meaning.

3. Contract verbs lengthen their contract vowel before a tense formative.

4. Knowing the Square of Stops is especially useful in the future tense. When joined with a σ, labials go to ψ, velars go to ξ, and dentals drop out.

5. Many verbs use the same stem in forming both the present and the future tenses, including roots ending in iota or upsilon, contract verbs, and roots ending in a stop.

6. Verbs that are deponent in one tense are not necessarily deponent in another.

7. You should memorize the future of εἰμί.

---

[5] Notice that no connecting vowel is visible.

Master Verb Chart

Tense	Aug/ Redup	Tense stem	Tense form.	Conn. vowel	Personal endings	1st sing paradigm
Present act		pres		o/ε	prim act	λύω
Present mid/pas		pres		o/ε	prim mid/pas	λύομαι
Future act		fut act	σ	o/ε	prim act	λύσω
Future mid		fut act	σ	o/ε	prim mid/pas	πορεύσομαι

Vocabulary

It is important that from the very beginning you do not simply memorize these different tense stems. Learn to apply the rules and concentrate on recognition. Look at the different tense forms and ask yourself, would I recognize this form if I saw it? Do I understand how the different forms are related?

In the Appendix there is a list entitled, *Tense Forms of Verbs Occurring Fifty Times or More* (pages 370-80). It lists all the verbs you will learn in *BBG* with all their different forms in the different tenses. I have underlined those forms you may need to commit to memory. Refer to it regularly.

Remember those words I have been listing under the definition of a verb? Now you can start to see what I am doing. These words are the forms of the verb in the different tenses. The first form (not in parentheses) is the future tense form.

Ignore the future forms of λέγω, οἶδα, and ἔρχομαι until the next chapter.

βασιλεύς, -έως, ὁ	king (115; *βασιλεϝ)[6]
γεννάω	I beget, give birth to, produce (97; *γεννα)[7]
	γεννήσω, ἐγέννησα, γεγέννηκα, γεγέννημαι, ἐγεννήθην
ζάω	I live (140; *ζα)[8]
	(ἔζων), ζήσω, ἔζησα, -, -, -
Ἰουδαία, -ας, ἡ	Judea (44; * Ἰουδαια)[9]
Ἰουδαῖος, -αία, -αῖον	adjective: Jewish (194; * Ἰουδαιο)[10]
	noun: Jew
Ἰσραήλ, ὁ	Israel (68; * Ἰσραηλ)
	No genitive form is given because Ἰσραήλ is indeclinable.

---

[6]   A cognate noun of βασιλεία. The ευς suffix is often used to describe the person related to the thing described by the noun (e.g., ἁλιεύς, "fisherman"; γραμματεύς, "scribe"; ἱερεύς, "priest"). On ϝ see 17.12.

[7]   *Gen* is a combining form meaning, "something produced." Hydro*gen* produces water (ὕδωρ) as the result of burning.

[8]   *Zoology* is the study of life. Klein argues that this is from the modern Greek ζῳολογία, which in turn is based on ζῷον + λογία.

[9]   Although this word occurs less than fifty times, I felt you should learn it since it is so similar to its cognate adjective Ἰουδαῖος.

[10]   Ἰουδαῖος occurs nine times as an adjective, 186 times as a noun.

164   *Basics of Biblical Greek*

καρπός, –οῦ, ὁ	fruit, crop, result (66; *καρπο)[11]
μείζων, –ον	greater (48; *μειζον)

μείζων occurs only 48 times in the New Testament. I have included it here because it is the comparative form of the adjective μέγας that occurs more frequently. The neuter accusative singular (μεῖζον) can be used adverbially. Be sure to see its full paradigm in the Appendix (a-4b[1], page 350).

It is often followed by a word in the genitive, just like πλείων. You can use the key word "than."

ὅλος, –η, –ον	adjective: whole, complete (109; *ὁλο)
	adverb: entirely

ὅλος often occurs in the predicate position when it is functioning adjectivally.

προσκυνέω	I worship (60; *προσκυνε)[12]

(προσεκύνουν), προσκυνήσω, προσεκύνησα, –, –, –

Total word count in the New Testament:	138,162
Number of words learned to date:	211
Number of word occurrences in this chapter:	941
Number of word occurrences to date:	99,493
Percent of total word count in the New Testament:	72.01%

Previous Words

As you meet new tenses, I will list the new tense forms for words you already know in the Previous Words section. Be sure to review these words.

present	*future*

Regular verbs

ἀκούω	ἀκούσω
ἀποκρίνομαι	– [13]
δύναμαι	δυνήσομαι[14]
λύω	λύσω
πιστεύω	πιστεύσω
πορεύομαι	πορεύσομαι

Stems ending in a stop

βλέπω	βλέψω
ἔχω	ἕξω[15]
συνάγω	συνάξω

---

[11] *Carpology* is the study of fruit.

[12] προσκυνέω takes a direct object in either the dative or accusative.

[13] There is no future active or middle form of this word in the New Testament. When this is the case I put a dash in place of a future form.

[14] The alpha has lengthened to an eta just like a contract verb.

[15] Notice that the future has a rough breathing. See *MBG* for an explanation.

Contract stems

ἀγαπάω	ἀγαπήσω
ζητέω	ζητήσω
καλέω	καλέσω[16]
λαλέω	λαλήσω
πληρόω	πληρώσω
ποιέω	ποιήσω
τηρέω	τηρήσω

Exegesis

1. The basic use of the future is to describe something that will happen in the future (predictive).

> ὁ ἐναρξάμενος ἐν ὑμῖν ἔργον ἀγαθὸν ἐπιτελέσει *(Phil 1:6)*.
>
> He who began a good work in you *will bring it to completion.*

2. As in English, the Greek future can express a command (imperatival).

> ἀγαπήσεις κύριον τὸν θεόν σου *(Matt 22:37)*.
>
> *You shall love* the Lord your God.

3. The future can also state that a generic event will occur. It does not say that a particular occurrence is in mind, but that such events do occur (gnomic).

> οὐκ ἐπ᾽ ἄρτῳ μόνῳ ζήσεται ὁ ἄνθρωπος *(Matt 4:4)*.
>
> Man *shall* not *live* on bread alone.

In Modern Greek, we use θα to indicate the future. It functions like the English "will." θά είναι εκεί means, "He will be there."

---

[16] καλέω is one of the few contracts that does not lengthen its contract vowel. If you really want to know why, there used to be another letter after the epsilon, a digamma (ϝ), which has long since dropped off (καλεϝ; see 17.12). But because it was there, the verb does not lengthen the epsilon.

Chapter 20

Verbal Roots, and Other Forms of the Future

Exegetical Insight

Tucked into the first chapter of Hebrews is an Old Testament quotation, Ps. 102:25-27, and this quotation contains a number of interesting verbal forms addressed in the current chapter. Rabbis of the first century would string passages together to build up overwhelming evidence for an argument, and the quotation from Psalm 102, found in Hebrews 1:10-12, is one of several the author strings together to present powerful evidence that Jesus is superior to angels and worthy of our complete allegiance. This psalm, particularly, proclaims that Jesus is superior based on his role as the Creator and Terminator of the heavens and the earth. The idea here is that whereas angels are created, the Son of God, powerful beyond imagination, rules over the universe as the Creator of all things and, therefore, will wrap up all of the created order in the end! He will be the ultimate Terminator!

Notice especially the part of the psalm beginning in Hebrews 1:11, which deals with the wrapping up of the created order at the end of the age. The uses of the future here are "predictive" in that they tell what will happen at the end of the world. The psalm states of the heavens and the earth, "They *will perish*." Further, the psalm says of Jesus' lordship over the created order, the heavens and earth *"will grow old* like an article of clothing, and like a cloak you *will roll them up,* and like a piece of clothing they will be changed." Even though Jesus made his creation stable, with sturdy foundations, he never intended the creation to last forever. In fact, the heavens and the earth, like an article of clothing, one day will wear out to the point that they have to be rolled up and packed away because they no longer are useful (think of that old sweatshirt in your closet that is falling apart!). Jesus is so awesome in his power that he is the one who will do that. Unlike the creation, he is "the same," and his years *will not end.* As the eternal Lord of the universe, one who has the power to create all things and to wrap them up in the end, Jesus, the Son of God, is worthy of our worship and the full commitment of our lives!

George H. Guthrie

Overview

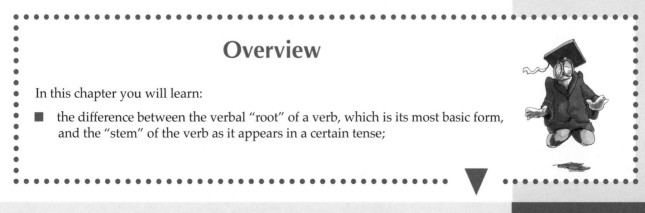

In this chapter you will learn:

■ the difference between the verbal "root" of a verb, which is its most basic form, and the "stem" of the verb as it appears in a certain tense;

- that sometimes the verbal root is the same as the present tense stem, and other times it is modified in the formation of the present tense;

- that tense stems are not formed from the present tense stem but from the root;

- liquid futures.

Verbal Roots and Tense Stems

20.1 **Pattern 1.** In the previous chapter you learned how to form the future when a verb has the same stem in the present and the future (ἀκούω ‣ ἀκ-ούσω). This includes stems ending in a stop (βλέπω ‣ βλέψω) and contract verbs (ἀγαπάω ‣ ἀγαπήσω).

Patterns 2-4. In this chapter you will learn about verbs whose present and future tense stems are different (βάλλω ‣ βαλῶ).

20.2 **Roots and Stems.** But before doing so, it is important to pause and discuss the difference between a verbal *stem* and its *root*. This may feel somewhat technical at first, but if you can grasp the concept now it will make a tremendous amount of difference later on. What you are learning here applies not only to the future tense but to all the other tenses as well. This is my last detailed discussion of morphology in *BBG*.

20.3 **Definitions**

a. *The **root** of a verb is its most basic form.*

For example, the root of ἀγαπάω is *ἀγαπα. (I preface the verbal root with an asterisk). This root shows itself in the verb ἀγαπάω as well as the cognate noun ἀγάπη and cognate adjective ἀγαπητός.

All verbs are listed in the vocabulary section with their verbal root. Be sure to memorize the root along with the lexical form.

λύω	I loose	(42; *λυ)
βάλλω	I throw	(122; *βαλ)

b. *The **stem** of a verb is the basic form of that verb in a particular tense.*

The stem is derived from the root. The verbal root *λυ forms its present tense as λύω and its future as λύσω. In the case of this Pattern 1 verb, the same stem is used in both tenses.

present: λυ ‣ λύω

future: λυ ‣ λύσω

But in the case of βάλλω ("I throw," *βαλ), which is a Pattern 4 verb, the present and future stems are different.

present: βαλλ ‣ βάλλω

future: βαλ ‣ βαλῶ

So remember, a root is the basic form of the verb. A stem is the basic form of a verb in a certain tense. The stem does not include the augment or tense formative.

20.4 **Relationship of the verbal root and the present tense stem.** The verbal root and the present tense stem can be the same, or the root can be altered when forming the present tense stem.

a. *In Pattern 1 verbs, the verbal root is the same as the present tense stem.*

The verbal root was not modified in forming its present tense stem. For example, the root *ἀγαπα comes unmodified into the present tense stem as ἀγαπα, which forms ἀγαπάω in the first person singular.

b. *In Pattern 2-4 verbs, the verbal root is modified when forming the present tense stem.*

For example, the root *βαλ is altered in the present tense stem to βαλλ, which forms βάλλω in the first person singular.

20.5 **Tense stem formed from verbal root.** If you assume that the present tense stem is the base form of the verb and all other tenses are derived from it, you will become confused and potentially discouraged since this approach forces you to memorize hundreds of "irregular" forms. However, if you will learn that the *different tense stems are formed from the verbal root and not the present tense stem*, memorization and frustration can be kept to a minimum.

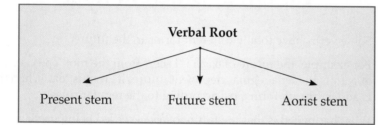

For example, the verbal root *βαλ is modified to form its present tense stem by doubling the lambda: βάλλω. However, when you arrive at the future, you will see only one lambda: βαλῶ. (This is a special future that does not use the sigma as a tense formative, but more about that later.) When you learn the aorist tense (Chapter 22), you will see that it as well has only one lambda: ἔβαλον. The point of the illustration is that if you learn the present tense as the base form, βαλῶ and ἔβαλον appear irregular. But if you learn the root as *βαλ, βαλῶ and ἔβαλον are perfectly regular, and these are two less forms to memorize. It is the present tense stem that is irregular.[1]

This may not sound significant right now, but it is. *You must realize that the present tense stem is the most "irregular" tense stem of all.* The verbal root is altered to form the present tense stem more than in all the other tenses combined. What adds confusion to this is that you memorize the potentially irregular present tense form, which may suggest the present is the verb's base form.

The present tense stem is built on the verbal root, which may or may not be modified when forming the present tense stem.

---

[1] Most grammars describe these changes by saying that the future and aorist tense stems have "lost" a lambda. Although this may be easier at first, it builds a significant error into your way of thinking that will come back to haunt you. The present tense stem is never altered to form another tense stem! The present tense stem is often a modified form of the verbal root.

So let's learn the rest of the patterns. In the Appendix there is a list of all verbs occurring fifty times or more in the New Testament with all their different tense forms (pages 370-80). The forms that you probably need to memorize are underlined. As you work through the following chapters, regularly refer to this chart. On the website there is also a spreadheet of these verbs, and you can mark it up to your heart's content.

Pattern 1: Root Not Modified

20.6   Verbs that follow this pattern do not modify their root in the formation of their present tense stem. Many verbs fall into this "regular"[2] category and were learned in Chapter 19. They include stems ending in an iota or upsilon, contract verbs, and roots ending in a stop.

$$^*ἀκου \;▸\; ἀκούω \;▸\; ἀκούσω$$
$$^*ποιε \;▸\; ποιέω \;▸\; ποιήσω$$
$$^*βλεπ \;▸\; βλέπω \;▸\; βλέψω$$

Pattern 2: Different Roots

20.7   Some verbs have totally different forms in the future.

For example, the future of ὁράω ("I see," from the root *ὁρα) is ὄψομαι. ὄψομαι is in fact a regular deponent future. Its root is *ὀπ. When the sigma is added, the πσ form a psi according to the regular rules.

What happened is that the future of ὁράω ceased being used, as did the present of ὄψομαι. The two forms "got together" and function as if they were the same word.[3] There are only nine verbs in the New Testament that do this (cf. v-8 in *MBG*). The first three are listed below; six more to go. By the way, most of these words are extremely common.

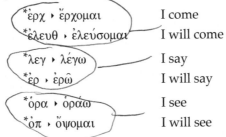

*ἐρχ ▸ ἔρχομαι	I come
*ἐλευθ ▸ ἐλεύσομαι	I will come
*λεγ ▸ λέγω	I say
*ἐρ ▸ ἐρῶ	I will say
*ὁρα ▸ ὁράω	I see
*ὀπ ▸ ὄψομαι	I will see

These words are easy to parse because you must simply memorize both roots. You may want to create a separate vocabulary card for each root.

---

[2]   I hesitate to use the words "regular" and "irregular" at all when discussing the formation of tenses. Part of the beauty of the Greek language is that it is so regular, *if you know the rules*. Even the verbs that appear to be extremely irregular are actually quite regular. If you want to see all the rules, check *MBG*. Just look up the verb in the index and go to its proper category.

    Another danger of discussing "irregular" futures is that you will not learn the regular rules as well as you should. It is easy to let the "irregular" formations govern your thinking, convincing you that futures are difficult to learn and you will simply have to memorize every single form. Resist this temptation. The basic rules govern the vast majority of futures.

[3]   This is a rather simplistic definition but sufficient for now.

Most of the time when a future tense is deponent and the present is not (or vice versa), the verb uses different roots to form the present and the future, like *ὁρα and *ὀπ.

Pattern 3: Liquid Futures

20.8 Technically, liquid futures are part of Pattern 4. However, all Greek teachers want their students to learn how liquid futures are formed, and some teachers may not feel the same way about Pattern 4, so I decided to keep them separate.

20.9 Liquid verbs for the most part are formed regularly. However,

- they use a slightly different tense formative,

- and the present and future tense stems are usually slightly different.

20.10 The consonants λ, μ, ν, and ρ are called "liquids" because the air flows around the tongue (λ, ρ) or the sound goes through the nose (μ, ν) when pronouncing the letter.[4] If the last letter of the verbal root is a liquid, that verb is called a "liquid verb."[5]

20.11 Chart: Future active indicative (liquid)

> *Future active tense stem + tense formative (εσ) +*
>
> *Connecting vowel + Primary active person endings*
>
> μεν + εσ + ο + μεν ‣ μενοῦμεν

Instead of adding a sigma as the tense formative, a liquid future adds εσ before the connecting vowel. However, this sigma does not like to stand between two vowels so it tends to drop out,[6] and the epsilon and connecting vowel contract.

> μεν + εσ + ο + μεν ‣ μενεομεν ‣ μενοῦμεν

This different way of forming the future does not effect the verb's meaning, only its form.

---

[4] Technically, only lambda and rho are liquids. Mu and nu are called "nasals." But because liquids and nasals often behave in the same manner, they are usually grouped together under the one heading of "liquid."

[5] Not all verbs whose present tense stem ends in a liquid are classified as a liquid. It depends upon whether or not that liquid consonant is actually part of the stem. (Some verbs add a liquid consonant to the root to form the present stem. This type of verb cannot have a liquid future since the future stem does not end in a liquid.) The only way really to know whether a verb will take a liquid future is to look it up in the lexicon and memorize it.

[6] This is called an "intervocalic sigma." Not all intervocalic sigmas drop out.

20.12 Paradigm: Future active indicative (liquid)

	liquid	definition	present contract	present liquid
1 sg	μενῶ	I will remain	ποιῶ	μένω
2 sg	μενεῖς	You will remain	ποιεῖς	μένεις
3 sg	μενεῖ	He/she/it will remain	ποιεῖ	μένει
1 pl	μενοῦμεν	We will remain	ποιοῦμεν	μένομεν
2 pl	μενεῖτε	You will remain	ποιεῖτε	μένετε
3 pl	μενοῦσι(ν)	They will remain	ποιοῦσι(ν)	μένουσι(ν)

20.13 Chart: Future middle indicative (liquid)

> *Future active tense stem + tense formative (εσ) +*
>
> *Connecting vowel + Primary passive person endings*
>
> μεν + εσ + ο + μεθα ▸ μενούμεθα

20.14 Paradigm: Future middle indicative (liquid)

	liquid	definition	present contract	present liquid
1 sg	μενοῦμαι	I will remain	ποιοῦμαι	μένομαι
2 sg	μενῇ	You will remain	ποιῇ	μένῃ
3 sg	μενεῖται	He/she/it will remain	ποιεῖται	μένεται
1 pl	μενούμεθα	We will remain	ποιούμεθα	μενόμεθα
2 pl	μενεῖσθε	You will remain	ποιεῖσθε	μένεσθε
3 pl	μενοῦνται	They will remain	ποιοῦνται	μένονται

20.15 **Present epsilon contracts**. The future of a liquid verb looks just like the present tense epsilon contract verb, including the accent. How will you tell them apart? For example, let's say you see μενεῖς. Is it a present epsilon contract or a liquid future?

■ You will have memorized the lexical form as μένω. There is no such word as μενέω.

■ You will notice that the final stem consonant is a liquid, and therefore μενεῖς is a liquid future.

20.16 **Accents.** The accent can also be helpful in identifying a liquid verb (but not in distinguishing it from an epsilon contract). A liquid future always has a circumflex over the contracted vowels except in the first person plural middle (μενούμεθα).

20.17 **Present and future liquids**. When comparing the present and future forms of a liquid, notice the differences. (See the two columns in 20.16 and 20.18.)

■ The accents are different (μένω ▸ μενῶ; μένομαι ▸ μενοῦμαι)

- There is no contraction in the present tense (μένομεν ‣ μενοῦμεν; μενόμεθα ‣ μενούμεθα).

20.18 Stem changes. Along with the different tense formative, the future tense stem of a liquid verb usually is different from its present tense stem (for various reasons). Here are all the examples up through the vocabulary in this chapter. Notice what is happening.

Addition of double consonant:	ἀποστέλλω	‣ ἀποστελῶ
	βάλλω	‣ βαλῶ
	ἐκβάλλω	‣ ἐκβαλῶ
Addition of iota:	αἴρω	‣ ἀρῶ
	ἀποκτείνω	‣ ἀποκτενῶ
	ἐγείρω	‣ ἐγερῶ
Different roots:	λέγω	‣ ἐρῶ

Only two liquid verbs you know so far show no change in their future tense stems.[7]

	κρίνω	‣ κρινῶ
	μένω	‣ μενῶ

20.19 Hint. It is often said that "consonants carry the meaning of a word, not the vowels." If you can think of a verb primarily in terms of its consonants, then the vocalic changes will not be a major problem.

For example, γινώσκω, from the root *γνω, becomes γνώσομαι in the future. If you recognize that the basic consonants carry the word (γν), you can still see them in γνώσομαι. (γινώσκω is a vocabulary word in this chapter.)

Halftime Review

You have covered a lot of ground so far. Let's stop for a moment and see how you are doing. Remember: a little extra work up front helps reduce memory work and increases understanding in the long run.

- The *root* of a verb is its most basic form. The *stem* of a verb is the basic form of that verb in a particular tense.

- All verbs form their tense stems from their root, not their present tense stem. The present tense is the most irregular of all tenses.

- In Pattern 1 verbs, the root is not modified in the formation of its present tense stem. The present and future tense stems will normally be identical.

- In Pattern 2 verbs, different roots are used to form the different tense stems.

- In Pattern 3 verbs (liquid verbs), their stems end in a liquid (λ, μ, ν, ρ) and they use εσ as the future tense formative. The sigma drops out before the connecting vowel, and the vowels contract, looking as if the verb were a present tense epsilon contract. Sometimes the stem vowel changes in the future.

---

[7] Of course, there have been changes with the tense formative dropping out and the vowels contracting. It is just that the stem does not appear to have changed.

Pattern 4: Root Modified Regularly

20.20 Roots in this category are modified in regular ways in the formation of their present tense stem. In most of the cases, knowing the pattern is sufficient for recognizing an inflected form. However, in a few of the cases it may be easier to memorize a certain form. These roots fall into three basic subpatterns.

I am getting into an area that some students have struggled with. You have two options, and your teacher will have made a decision here for you. You can either memorize the patterns, or you can memorize all the tense forms of all the verbs that fall into this category. Even if you choose the latter, please be sure to see the patterns. They will help you in your memorization.

A. Roots in a stop

20.21 Roots that follow this pattern end in a stop, but unlike the roots in Pattern 1, these roots are modified in the formation of their present tense stem.

- **ιζω/αζω verbs.** The present tense stems of verbs that end in ιζω or αζω are generally formed from roots that actually end in a **dental**.

  For example, βαπτίζω ("I baptize") is from the root *βαπτιδ. The final letter of the verbal root was changed to zeta to form the present tense stem.[8] It forms the future as βαπτίσω (*βαπτιδ + σω ‣ βαπτίσω), which is totally regular. Remember, dentals drop out before a sigma according to the Square of Stops.

- **ασσω verbs.** The present tense stem of verbs that end in ασσω are generally formed from roots that actually end in a **velar**.

  For example, ταράσσω ("I trouble") is from the root *ταραχ. The final letter of the verbal root was changed to σσ to form the present tense stem.[8] It forms the future regularly as ταράξω (*ταραχ + σω ‣ ταράξω). Remember, velars and a sigma form xi according to the Square of Stops.

B. Double consonants

20.22 Present tense stems that end in a double consonant are often from roots with a single consonant (excluding –ασσω verbs).

For example, βάλλω is from the root *βαλ. The double lambda only appears in the present tense stem; a single lambda is found in the other tenses (e.g., βαλῶ).

---

[8]   See the Advanced Information section for an explanation.

C. Letters added

20.23 Some roots add a letter (or letters) to form the present tense stem. The added letter(s) will not appear in the other tenses.

In the examples below, notice how the root is visible in the future.

- **Iota.** Some roots add an iota to form the present tense stem.

*αρ + ι	▸	αἴρω[9]	(present)
*αρ	▸	ἀρῶ	(future liquid)

- **(ι)σκ.** Some roots add σκ (or ισκ if the stem ends in a consonant) to form the present tense stem.

*ἀποθαν	▸	ἀποθνήσκω[10]	(present)
*ἀποθαν	▸	ἀποθανοῦμαι[11]	(future)
*γνω[12] + σκ	▸	γινώσκω	(present)
*γνω	▸	γνώσομαι	(future)

20.24 **Ablaut.** You have already seen in some nouns that their vowels change their length or even drop out (πατήρ ▸ πάτερ ▸ πατρός). The same can happen with verbs.

For example, the root *ἀποθαν loses its stem alpha in the formation of the present tense stem (and adds an η and ισκ after the modified stem).

*ἀποθαν ▸ ἀποθν + η + ισκ ▸ ἀποθνήσκω.

It is retained in the future: ἀποθανοῦμαι.

20.25 So what's the point of all this? There are two ways to learn all the tense forms. You can either memorize every tense form of every Pattern 4 verb, or you can learn roots and patterns that allow you to identify most of the tense stems and then memorize the few that are especially difficult.

Compound Verbs

20.26 A **compound verb** is a verb that is made up of two parts, a preposition and a verb. For example, ἐκβάλλω ("I throw out") is a compound of the preposition ἐκ ("out") and the verb βάλλω ("I throw").

Compound verbs form their tense stems the same way as the simple verb. For example, the future of βάλλω is βαλῶ, and the future of ἐκβάλλω is ἐκβαλῶ.

---

[9] The ρι switched order to ιρ ("metathesis").

[10] The alpha of the root has dropped out in the present tense stem, and the iota has subscripted.

[11] Liquid future.

[12] Advanced trivia: to form the present tense, the initial gamma doubles, is separated by an iota, and the original gamma drops off. σκ is then added. *γνω ▸ γιγνω ▸ γινω + σκ + ω ▸ γινώσκω.

Summary

1. The root of a verb is its most basic form. The stem of a verb is the basic form of that verb in a particular tense.

2. All tense stems are formed from the verbal root; the present tense stem is not the basis for the other tenses.

3. There are four patterns of how the verbal root forms the present tense stem.

   ■ Pattern 1. Verbal root and present tense stem are the same. This includes roots ending in iota or upsilon, contract verbs, and roots ending in a stop.

   ■ Pattern 2. The verb uses different roots.

   ■ Pattern 3. Liquid roots (λ, μ, ν, ρ) are generally used without modification (except for ablaut) in the present and future active stems. They use εσ as the tense formative in the future. The sigma drops out and the epsilon contracts with the connecting vowel. They look just like present tense epsilon contract verbs.

   ■ Pattern 4. Verbal root is regularly modified to form the present tense stem. This includes verbal roots ending in a stop (ιζω, αζω, σσω), stems ending in a double consonant, and roots that add one or more letter(s) (ισκ).

5. A compound verb is made up of a preposition and a verb. The compound verb always follows the tense forms of the simple verb.

Master Verb Chart

Tense	Aug/ Redup	Tense stem	Tense form.	Conn. vowel	Personal endings	1st sing paradigm
Present act		pres		o/ε	prim act	λύω
Present mid/pas		pres		o/ε	prim mid/pas	λύομαι
Future act		fut act	σ	o/ε	prim act	λύσω
Liquid fut act		fut act	εσ	o/ε	prim act	μενῶ
Future mid		fut act	σ	o/ε	prim mid/pas	πορεύσομαι
Liquid fut mid		fut act	εσ	o/ε	prim mid/pas	μενοῦμαι

Check It Out!

Here are the verbs that you have learned so far. Work through each one and identify its category. (οἶδα is omitted.)

root	present	future
*ἀγαπα	ἀγαπάω	ἀγαπήσω
*ἀκου	ἀκούω	ἀκούσω
*βαπτιδ	βαπτίζω	βαπτίσω
*βλεπ	βλέπω	βλέψω
*γεννα	γεννάω	γεννήσω
*γνω	γινώσκω	γνώσομαι
*δυνα	δύναμαι	δυνήσομαι
*ἐρχ, *ἐλευθ	ἔρχομαι	ἐλεύσομαι
*σεχ	ἔχω	ἕξω
*ζα	ζάω	ζήσω
*ζητε	ζητέω	ζητήσω
*καλε	καλέω	καλέσω
*λαλε	λαλέω	λαλήσω
*λεγ, *ἐρ	λέγω	ἐρῶ
*λυ	λύω	λύσω
*ὁρα, *ὀπ	ὁράω	ὄψομαι
*πιστευ	πιστεύω	πιστεύσω
*πληρο	πληρόω	πληρώσω
*ποιε	ποιέω	ποιήσω
*πορευ	πορεύομαι	πορεύσομαι
*προσκυνε	προσκυνέω	προσκυνήσω
*συναγ	συνάγω	συνάξω
*σωδ	σῴζω	σώσω
*τηρε	τηρέω	τηρήσω

When my children came home from their first day of Spanish class, a flood of Spanish poured out of their mouths. After a while I figured out the teacher had taught them the Spanish for "My hair is ___" and then taught them all the colors. They were having fun describing their make-believe punk hair colors.

How would you say, "My hair is …"?

αἱ τρίχες μου εἰσίν …

Let's do one better. How would you say, "Your hair is …"?

αἱ τρίχες σου εἰσίν …

Vocabulary

Be sure to check the verbal roots to see which verbs have altered the root in the formation of the present tense stem. If the verb uses more than one root, I will show you the different roots.

αἴρω
: I raise, take up, take away (101; *ἀρ)
: ἀρῶ, ἦρα, ἦρκα, ἦρμαι, ἤρθην
: See the explanation in 20.22 for the changes to the tense stem. αἴρω can take a direct object in the genitive.

ἀποκτείνω
: I kill (74; *ἀποκτεν)
: ἀποκτενῶ, ἀπέκτεινα, -, -, ἀπεκτάνθην

Here are some of
the colors:

Red: ἐρυθρός

Yellow: ξανθός

Black: μέλας

White: λευκός

Green: χλωρός

Blue: ὑάκινθος

Purple: πορφυρός

Golden: χρυσός

Go find someone to
insult!

ἀποστέλλω	I send (away) (132; *ἀποστελ)[13]
	ἀποστελῶ, ἀπέστειλα, ἀπέσταλκα, ἀπέσταλμαι, ἀπεστάλην
βαπτίζω	I baptize, dip, immerse (77; *βαπτιδ)[14]
	(ἐβάπτιζον), βαπτίσω, ἐβάπτισα, –, βεβάπτισμαι, ἐβαπτίσθην
γινώσκω	I know, come to know, realize, learn (222; *γνω)[15]
	(ἐγίνωσκον), γνώσομαι, ἔγνων, ἔγνωκα, ἔγνωσμαι, ἐγνώσθην
	On the root see 20.27.
γλῶσσα, -ης, ἡ	tongue, language (50; *γλωσσα)[16]
ἐγείρω	I raise up, wake (144; *ἐγερ)
	ἐγερῶ, ἤγειρα, –, ἐγήγερμαι, ἠγέρθην
ἐκβάλλω	I cast out, send out (81; ἐκ + *βαλ)[17]
	(ἐξέβαλλον), ἐκβαλῶ, ἐξέβαλον, –, –, ἐξεβλήθην
ἐκεῖ	there, in that place (105)
κρίνω	I judge, decide, prefer (114; *κριν)[18]
	(ἐκρινόμην), κρινῶ, ἔκρινα, κέκρικα, κέκριμαι, ἐκρίθην
λαός, -οῦ, ὁ	people, crowd (142; *λαο)[19]
μένω	I remain, live (118; *μεν)
	(ἔμενον), μενῶ, ἔμεινα, μεμένηκα, –, –
ὁράω	I see, notice, experience (454;*ὁρα; *ὀπ; *ἰδ)
	ὄψομαι, εἶδον, ἑώρακα, –, ὤφθην
	*ὁρα is used to form ὁράω and ἑώρακα. *ὀπ is used to form ὄψομαι and ὤφθην.*ἰδ is used to form εἶδον.
σοφία, -ας, ἡ	wisdom (51; *σοφια)[20]
στόμα, -ατος, τό	mouth (78; *στοματ)[21]

---

[13]   The cognate verb of ἀπόστολος.

[14]   *Baptism* is from the cognate noun βάπτισμα. The μα suffix is often used in Greek to specify the result of the action described by the root (cf. *Bl-D* #109[2]).

[15]   *Gnostics* were those who claimed to possess certain knowledge.

[16]   *Glossolalia* is the spiritual gift of speaking in other tongues, or languages. *Glossology* is the science of language.

[17]   ἐκβάλλω retains the meaning of its two parts. This cannot always be assumed in a Greek word.

[18]   A *critic* (κριτικός) is one who is able to judge.

[19]   *Laity* is actually from "lay" and the suffix "ity." "Lay" is from λαϊκός, which has the same meaning as λαός. The laity are a group of people distinct from the clergy, or any group of people separate from those belonging to a specific profession.

[20]   *Philosophy* is the love of wisdom.

[21]   *Stomatology* is the the study of the diseases of the mouth. *Stomach* (στόμαχος) is also derived from στόμα.

σῴζω[22] I save, deliver, rescue (106; *σωδ)[23]
(ἔσῳζον), σώσω, ἔσωσα, σέσωκα, σέσῳσμαι, ἐσώθην

Total word count in the New Testament: 138,162
Number of words learned to date: 227
Number of word occurrences in this chapter: 2,049
Number of word occurrences to date: 101,542
Percent of total word count in the New Testament: 73.49%

Previous Words

ἔρχομαι   ἐλεύσομαι (*ἐρχ; *ἐλευθ; class 8)

λέγω   ἐρῶ (*λεγ; *ἐρ; class 8)

οἶδα   εἰδήσω[24]

Advanced Information

20.27 **Consonantal iota.** One of the more important elements in this entire discussion is a letter in the Greek alphabet called the "consonantal iota" (ι). You have already met this letter in third declension stems such as in πίστεως.

Much of the change in verbal tense stems is also due to the consonantal iota.

■ The consonantal iota was added to roots ending in a stop to form their present tense stem, and the stop + ι became ιζω (*βαπτιδ + ι ‣ βαπτίζω) or σσω (*ταραχ + ι ‣ ταράσσω).

■ The consonantal iota was added to some roots ending in a consonant to form their present tense stem, and the consonant + ι became a double consonant (*βαλ + ι ‣ βάλλω).

■ The consonantal iota was added to some roots to form their present tense stem, and the ι became an iota and often moved to another place in the word (*ἀρ + ι ‣ ἀρι ‣ αἴρω). This is called "metathesis."

20.28 In *MBG* I have provided a thorough categorization of these types of changes. What you met in this chapter is a simplification of the material presented there.

---

[22] The iota subscript shows that this is actually an ιζω verb.

[23] *Soteriology* is the the study of salvation.

[24] The future active of οἶδα occurs only once in the New Testament (Heb 8:11). It may not be worth memorizing; ask your teacher.

Overview 4

Chapters 21 – 25

In this section you will learn the rest of the tenses and complete your knowledge of the indicative verbal system. If you are doing well so far in the text, these chapters will be easy. Just some new forms and a little new grammar.

Chapter 21

The essence of the Greek verb is not its ability to tell you when an action occurs. In the indicative time does play a role, but the primary significance of the Grek verb is its ability to describe *aspect,* or *type* of action.

You saw that in the present tense a verb can be either continuous ("I am studying") or undefined ("I study."). It's up to context to let you know which is intended in any one passage.

However, Greek uses two different tenses to describe past action. The imperfect (this chapter) describes a continuous action normally occuring in past time.

Greek forms the imperfect by augmenting the tense stem. The augment is a lengthening of the beginning of the verb.

- ■ If the verb begins with a consonant, an epsilon is added. *λυ goes to ἔλυον and means "I was loosing."

- ■ If the verb begins with a vowel, the vowel is lengthened. *ἀγαπα goes to ἠγάπων and means "I was loving."

The imperfect also uses a different set of endings ("secondary"). In this chapter you will learn both the active and the passive imperfect, and with them the last two sets of personal endings. You are now done with personal endings.

Chapter 22

The aorist describes an undefined action normally occuring in the past. The aorist is formed with an augment and secondary endings (just like the imperfect).

There are two ways to form an aorist. There is no difference in meaning, just form. In this chapter you will learn the second aorist. A verb forms its aorist either as a first or a second, not both (with a few exceptions, as you might have guessed by now).

The second aorist is formed with an augment, aorist tense stem, connecting vowel, and secondary personal endings. The root *λαβ goes to ἔλαβον.

Words that have second aorists are normally words that alter their root in the formation of their present tense stem. Otherwise, you could not tell the difference between a second aorist and an imperfect. *λαβ goes to the present as λαμβάνω. The mu and αν are added. Here is its paradigm.

	form	translation	conn. vow.	ending	imperfect
1 sg	ἔλαβον	I took	ο	ν	ἔλυον
2 sg	ἔλαβες	You took	ε	ς	ἔλυες
3 sg	ἔλαβε(ν)	He/she/it took	ε	– (ν)	ἔλυε(ν)
1 pl	ἐλάβομεν	We took	ο	μεν	ἐλύομεν
2 pl	ἐλάβετε	You took	ε	τε	ἐλύετε
3 pl	ἔλαβον	They took	ο	ν	ἔλυον

The Master Verb Chart is growing. Be sure to memorize it carefully.

Chapter 23

If a verb forms its aorist with a first aorist stem, then it has an augment, aorist tense stem, tense formative (σα), and secondary active endings. If a verb has a first aorist, most likely the root, present tense stem, and aorist tense stem will all be the same.

	first aorist	translation	ending	imperfect	second aorist
1 sg	ἔλυσα	I loosed	–	ἔλυον	ἔλαβον
2 sg	ἔλυσας	You loosed	ς	ἔλυες	ἔλαβες
3 sg	ἔλυσε(ν)	He/she/it loosed	– (ν)	ἔλυε(ν)	ἔλαβε(ν)
1 pl	ἐλύσαμεν	We loosed	μεν	ἐλύομεν	ἐλάβομεν
2 pl	ἐλύσατε	You loosed	τε	ἐλύετε	ἐλάβετε
3 pl	ἔλυσαν	They loosed	ν	ἔλυον	ἔλαβον

Chapter 24

The first aorist passive uses a tense formative (θησ) and active endings. *λυ goes to ἐλύθην ("I was loosed"). The second aorist passive uses eta as a tense formative. *γραφ goes to ἐγράφην ("I was written").

The future passive is formed from the same aorist tense stem (without the augment) but with primary middle/passive endings. *λυ goes to λυθήσομαι ("I will be written").

Chapter 25

We now come to the last tense, the perfect. The perfect indicates a completed action whose effects are felt in the present (of the speaker). We generally connect "have/has" with the perfect.

The perfect is formed with reduplication and the tense formative κα.

- If the verb begins with a consonant, the consonant is doubled and separated with an epsilon. *λυ goes to λέλυκα and means "I have loosed."

- If the verb begins with a vowel, the vowel is lengthened. *ἀγαπα goes to ἠγάπηκα and means "I have loved."

Lexicons list six verbal forms for each verb (assuming each occurs in the New Testament). They are present (λύω), future active (λύσω), aorist active (ἔλυσα), perfect active (λέλυκα), perfect middle/passive (λέλυμαι), and aorist passive (ἐλύθην).

Chapter 21

Imperfect Indicative

Exegetical Insight

The Greek imperfect tense is both limited and versatile in its usage. It is limited in that it only occurs in the indicative mood, but in that mood it has some interesting nuances of meaning. Basically, the imperfect expresses linear action in past time. That action may be repetitive, prolonged or just beginning. Sometimes, however, the imperfect expresses repeated *attempts*.

This is true in Galatians 1:13 where Paul says, "For you have heard of my previous way of life in Judaism, how I violently persecuted the church of God and tried to destroy it." Both verbs in the second clause of this verse are imperfects. The first one (ἐδίωκον) simply expresses repeated action in the past. Paul is saying that he often persecuted the church. The second one (ἐπόρθουν) is "tendential," i.e., it expresses attempted action. (This is why the *NIV* adds the word "tried," which does not occur in the Greek.) Paul repeatedly persecuted the church, but his violent acts did not, indeed could not, destroy it. His actions were only attempts, and feeble ones at that. Jesus' promise about his church was true then, as it is now: "The gates of Hades will not overcome it."

Walter W. Wessel

Overview

In this chapter you will learn:

- that the imperfect indicates a continuous action that usually occurs in the past;

- that the imperfect is formed with an augment, the present tense stem, a connecting vowel, and secondary personal endings;

- that an augment is a prefix indicating past time. If the verb begins with a consonant, the augment is an epsilon (λύω ‣ ἔλυον); if the verb begins with a vowel, the augment is the lengthened vowel (ἀγαπάω ‣ ἠγάπων);

- secondary active and passive endings, the final two sets of personal endings.

English

21.1 In English there is only one simple past tense. However, its aspect can be either completed or continuous. For example, "Bob *studied* (completed) last night, but I *was studying* (continuous) until the early hours of the morning."

The past continuous active is formed by using the past tense of the helping verb "was" (for the singular) or "were" (for the plural) and the present participial form of the verb (i.e., the "ing" form of the verb). "I *was studying*."

The passive uses the same helping verb but adds the present participle "being" and the past participle of the main verb. "I *was being studied*."

Greek

21.2 **Two past tenses**. Greek also can describe an action occurring in the past, but the difference is that it uses different tenses for different aspects. The **imperfect** tense describes a continuous action usually occurring in the past, while the **aorist** (Chapter 22) describes an undefined action usually occurring in the past. ἠγάπων is imperfect (continuous), meaning "I was loving." ἠγάπησα is aorist (undefined), meaning "I loved."[1]

21.3 **Augment**. The Greek verb indicates past time by adding a prefix, which is called an "augment." I will discuss this in more detail later, but the epsilon added to the beginning of λύω in the paradigm in 21.7 is the augment (λύω ▸ ἔλυον). It is roughly equivalent to "-ed" in English: "kick" ▸ "kicked."

21.4 **Primary and secondary endings**. As you saw in Chapter 16, there are two sets of paradigms to learn. *The **primary** tenses are defined as those that do not use the augment, and the **secondary** tenses are those that do use the augment.*

Four Sets of Personal Endings	
Primary active	Secondary active
Primary passive	Secondary passive

Primary tenses use primary personal endings, and secondary tenses use secondary personal endings. You learned the primary in association with the present tense. In this lesson you will learn the secondary endings and the imperfect tense. These four sets of endings correspond to the four areas of the Master Personal Ending Chart (21.14).

Present active	Imperfect active
Present passive	Imperfect passive

---

[1] The name "imperfect" comes from its basic significance. Because it describes a past continuous action, it does not tell us whether that action was ever completed or not. So it is imperfect, i.e., not completed, not perfected.

These four sets of endings are all the personal endings you need to know for the Greek verb. All other tenses draw from these endings, or some variation. You already know two of the four. Once you have learned the following two paradigms, you will know all the basic personal endings for verbs. Congratulations.

21.5 One advantage of learning about primary and secondary endings is that when you see a secondary ending you can assume the verb is augmented. This is a significant aid in parsing and should become a regular part of your parsing arsenal. Whenever you see a secondary ending, confirm that the verb is augmented.

Imperfect Active

21.6 Chart: Imperfect active indicative

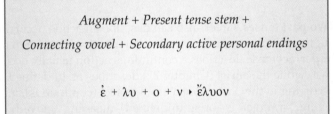

Augment + Present tense stem +

Connecting vowel + Secondary active personal endings

ἐ + λυ + ο + ν ‣ ἔλυον

21.7 Paradigm: Imperfect active indicative

List all the similarities you see between the primary and secondary endings.

	form	translation	conn. vow.	ending	present
1 sg	ἔλυον	I was loosing	ο	ν	λύω
2 sg	ἔλυες	You were loosing	ε	ς	λύεις
3 sg	ἔλυε(ν)	He/she/it was loosing	ε	– (ν)[2]	λύει
1 pl	ἐλύομεν	We were loosing	ο	μεν	λύομεν
2 pl	ἐλύετε	You were loosing	ε	τε	λύετε
3 pl	ἔλυον	They were loosing	ο	ν	λύουσι(ν)

Nu is the personal ending for both the first person singular and the third person plural active. The context will help you decide whether a particular form is first singular or third plural.

---

[2] No personal ending is used, so the connecting vowel stands alone, with the movable nu. This is somewhat the same as you saw in the first person singular active of the primary endings (see 16.10).

Imperfect Middle/Passive

21.8 **Chart: Imperfect middle/passive indicative**

> *Augment + Present tense stem +*
>
> *Connecting vowel + Secondary passive personal endings*
>
> ἐ + λυ + ο + μην ▸ ἐλυόμην

21.9 **Paradigm: Imperfect middle/passive indicative.** The translation is for the passive.

	form	translation	conn. vow.	ending	pres. pas.
1 sg	ἐλυόμην	I was being loosed	ο	μην	λύομαι
2 sg	ἐλύου	You were being loosed	ε	σο[3]	λύῃ
3 sg	ἐλύετο	He/she/it was being loosed	ε	το	λύεται
1 pl	ἐλυόμεθα	We were being loosed	ο	μεθα	λυόμεθα
2 pl	ἐλύεσθε	You were being loosed	ε	σθε	λύεσθε
3 pl	ἐλύοντο	They were being loosed	ο	ντο	λύονται

These secondary endings are not that different from the primary endings. This is why I asked you to learn what is really happening in the Greek verb. Otherwise you would not see the similarities as clearly. The connecting vowel is visible in almost every form.

Characteristics of Imperfect Verbs

21.10 **Augment.** The augment indicates past time. There are two different ways a word will augment, depending upon whether the stem of the verb begins with a consonant or a vowel.

a. If the verb *begins with a consonant*, the augment is an epsilon, always with smooth breathing.[4] For example, λύω is augmented as ἔλυον.

b. If a word *begins with a single vowel*, the augment is formed by lengthening that vowel.[5] For example, ἀγαπάω is augmented as ἠγάπων. The lengthening follows the standard pattern learned in the chapter on

---

[3] This is the only secondary personal ending that has changed significantly. The ending is actually σο. Because a sigma in an inflected ending normally cannot stand between two vowels, it drops out in this form and the connecting vowel and omicron contract to ου.

[4] This is called a "syllabic" augment since the augment adds another syllable to the word.

[5] This is called a "temporal" augment because it takes longer to say the word with the long vowel. Of course, "long" is a relative term; the time difference between saying an omega and an omicron is not that noticeable, but it is present.

contract verbs, except that an initial alpha lengthens to an eta and not an alpha.

augment		original		augment		original
η	‹	α		ι	‹	ι
η	‹	ε		υ	‹	υ
ω	‹	ο		ω	‹	ω
η	‹	η				

c. If a verb *begins with a diphthong*, either the first letter of the diphthong lengthens (ηὐχαρίστουν ‹ εὐχαριστέω), or the diphthong is not changed (εὕρισκον ‹ εὑρίσκω). Verbs beginning with ευ often do not show the augment. If the second vowel of the diphthong is an iota, it will subscript under the lengthened vowel.

augment		original		augment		original
ῃ	‹	αι		ηυ	‹	αυ
ῃ	‹	ει		ηυ	‹	ευ
ῳ	‹	οι				

21.11 Present tense stem. The present tense stem is used to form the imperfect tense.

The imperfect form is not usually listed with the other tense forms in lexicons because it is built on the present tense stem. However, if a verb occurs in the imperfect in the New Testament, I have included the imperfect in the listings but have put it in parentheses. This way you will always know what the augmented form looks like.

ἔρχομαι, (ἠρχόμην), ἐλεύσομαι, ἦλθον or ἦλθα, ἐλήλυθα, -, -

21.12 Connecting vowels. The imperfect is formed with the same connecting vowels as the present.

21.13 Secondary personal endings. The imperfect uses the secondary personal endings: ν, ς, -, μεν, τε, ν; μην, σο, το, μεθα, σθε, ντο.

Halftime Review

■ The imperfect descibes a continuous action normally occurring in the past.

■ The Master Personal Ending Chart is made up of the primary and secondary endings, active and middle/passive. Secondary tenses augment; primary do not.

■ The imperfect active is formed with the augment + present tense stem + connecting vowel + secondary active personal endings (e.g., ἔλυον).

■ The imperfect middle/passive is formed with the augment + present tense stem + connecting vowel + secondary passive personal endings (e.g., ἐλυόμην).

■ The augment is a prefix to the verb indicating past time. If the stem begins with a consonant, the augment is an epsilon. If the stem begins with a single vowel, the vowel lengthens. If the stem begins with a diphthong, either the first vowel of the diphthong lengthens or the diphthong is not changed.

Master Personal Ending Chart

21.14 You now know the four sets of personal endings. All other tenses use these endings, or some variation.

		primary tenses		*secondary tenses*	
active voice	λύω	–	ἔλυον	ν
	λύεις	ς	ἔλυες	ς
	λύει	ι	ἔλυε(ν)	–
	λύομεν	μεν	ἐλύομεν	μεν
	λύετε	τε	ἐλύετε	τε
	λύουσι(ν)	νσι	ἔλυον	ν
middle/passive voice	λύομαι	μαι	ἐλυόμην	μην
	λύῃ	σαι	ἐλύου	σο
	λύεται	ται	ἐλύετο	το
	λυόμεθα	μεθα	ἐλυόμεθα	μεθα
	λύεσθε	σθε	ἐλύεσθε	σθε
	λύονται	νται	ἐλύοντο	ντο

21.15 Recognition. Even though the personal endings for the imperfect are somewhat different from the present and future tenses, there are still many similarities.

Active

2 sg	λύεις	ἔλυες	Both end in a sigma. This is the only personal ending to do so. Therefore, whenever you see a verb whose personal ending ends in sigma, you know what it is, automatically.
1 pl	λύομεν	ἐλύομεν	Identical.
2 pl	λύετε	ἐλύετε	Identical.
3 pl	λύουσι	ἔλυον	The primary ending actually is νσι while the secondary is simply ν.

Passive

1 sg	λύομαι	ἐλυόμην	Both are three letters long beginning with mu.
2 sg	λύῃ	ἐλύου	Both have a sigma that drops out, which results in significantly different contractions. This ending is always the most troublesome.
3 sg	λύεται	ἐλύετο	ται in the primary and το in the secondary.
1 pl	λυόμεθα	ἐλυόμεθα	Endings are identical, just like the active.
2 pl	λύεσθε	ἐλύεσθε	Endings are identical, just like the active. While the tau is associated with the active (τε), the theta is characteristic of the passive (σθε); compare also the theta in the first person plural (μεθα).
3 pl	λύονται	ἐλύοντο	νται for the primary and ντο for the secondary.

21.16 Deponent verbs. If a verb is deponent in the present, it will also be deponent in the imperfect since both are using the same stem.

21.17 Parsing hint. When you see a verbal form, I recommend that the first question you ask is, *"Is this a present tense verb or something else?"* By doing this, you are really asking, "What is the tense stem of the inflected form I am looking at?" "Is it the same as the present tense stem or not?"

If the stem is the same as the present tense stem, and if there is no tense formative, then the verb is probably a present (or an imperfect if it is augmented). If the stem is different, then it is another tense that may have altered the root. The idea is to teach yourself that the verbal root, and whether it has been modified or not, is an important clue in the identification of verbal forms.[6]

21.18 Translating an imperfect. Almost everything in the imperfect tense (person, number, voice, mood) behaves the same as it does in the present tense. The only difference is the aspect and usually the time. In general, the imperfect tense is translated as a past continuous (e.g., "was studying").

> οἱ Φαρισαῖοι ἔλεγον τοῖς μαθηταῖς αὐτοῦ· διὰ τί μετὰ τῶν τελωνῶν καὶ ἁμαρτωλῶν ἐσθίει ὁ διδάσκαλος ὑμῶν; *(Matt 9:11)*
>
> The Pharisees *were saying* to his disciples, "Why does your teacher eat with tax collectors and sinners?"

> καὶ ἐβαπτίζοντο ἐν τῷ Ἰορδάνῃ ποταμῷ ὑπ᾽ αὐτοῦ *(Matt 3:6)*.
>
> And they were being baptized by him in the Jordan River.

Compound Verbs

21.19 In a compound verb, the augment comes after the preposition and before the stem of the verb. In other words, you augment the verbal part and not the preposition. The imperfect of καταβαίνω is κατέβαινον.

---

[6] If you are following Track Two, you have not yet seen an altered stem.

It makes sense to augment the verbal part of the compound. The augment indicates past time, and a preposition cannot indicate time; so the verbal part of the compound verb must receive the augment.

21.20 You will notice in the form κατέβαινον that the final alpha of κατά did not contract with the augment, otherwise it would be κατάβαινον (αε ‣ α).

- When the preposition ends in a vowel, that final vowel will usually drop out before the augment, as in κατέβαινον.

- In a few cases (such as compounds with περί), the final vowel of the preposition stays but it will not contract with the augment (e.g., περιπατέω ‣ περιεπάτουν).

21.21 When you augment a compound verb beginning with ἐκ, the kappa changes to a xi (ἐκβάλλω ‣ ἐξέβαλλον).[7]

Contract Verbs and εἰμί

21.22 **Paradigm: Imperfect active (contract).** You should be able to look at the following contracted forms and discover for yourself what vowels were involved in the contractions and why they contracted as they did. If you cannot, you may want to go back to Chapter 17 and review the rules.

	ἀγαπάω	ποιέω	πληρόω
	active		
1 sg	ἠγάπων	ἐποίουν	ἐπλήρουν
2 sg	ἠγάπας	ἐποίεις	ἐπλήρους
3 sg	ἠγάπα	ἐποίει[8]	ἐπλήρου[9]
1 pl	ἠγαπῶμεν	ἐποιοῦμεν	ἐπληροῦμεν
2 pl	ἠγαπᾶτε	ἐποιεῖτε	ἐπληροῦτε
3 pl	ἠγάπων	ἐποίουν	ἐπλήρουν
	middle/passive		
1 sg	ἠγαπώμην	ἐποιούμην	ἐπληρούμην
2 sg	ἠγαπῶ	ἐποιοῦ	ἐπληροῦ
3 sg	ἠγαπᾶτο	ἐποιεῖτο	ἐπληροῦτο
1 pl	ἠγαπώμεθα	ἐποιούμεθα	ἐπληρούμεθα
2 pl	ἠγαπᾶσθε	ἐποιεῖσθε	ἐπληροῦσθε
3 pl	ἠγαπῶντο	ἐποιοῦντο	ἐπληροῦντο

---

[7] If you really want to know why, the true form of the preposition is ἐξ. The sigma that is part of the xi is lost when the next letter is a consonant ("interconsonantal sigma"). When the augment is inserted, the sigma is no longer interconsonantal so it does not go away.

[8] Although there is no personal ending, the stem vowel (ε) is still contracting with the connecting vowel (ε).

[9] Although there is no personal ending, the stem vowel (o) is still contracting with the connecting vowel (ε).

21.23 Memorize the imperfect of εἰμί. You now know all the forms of εἰμί in the indicative mood.[10]

	form	translation
1 sg	ἤμην	I was
2 sg	ἦς[11]	You were
3 sg	ἦν	He/she/it was
1 pl	ἦμεν / ἤμεθα[12]	We were
2 pl	ἦτε	You were
3 pl	ἦσαν	They were

Summary

1. The imperfect indicates a continuous action usually in the past.

2. The imperfect is formed with an augment + present tense stem + connecting vowel + secondary endings. The imperfect is a secondary tense because it employs an augment.

3. The augment is a prefix to the verb indicating past time.

   ■ If the stem begins with a consonant, the augment is an epsilon.

   ■ If the stem begins with a single vowel, the vowel lengthens.

   ■ If the stem begins with a diphthong, either the first vowel of the diphthong lengthens or the diphthong is not changed.

   ■ If it is a compound verb, the augment is placed before the verbal part of the compound. If the preposition ends in a vowel it will either drop off or not contract with the augment.

4. The secondary personal endings are similar to the primary.

   ■ Active: ν, ς, –, μεν, τε, ν.

   ■ Passive: μην, σο, το, μεθα, σθε, ντο.

5. A verb that is deponent in the present will also be deponent in the imperfect.

6. Contract verbs follow the regular rules.

---

10 If you are following Track Two, you still have the future to learn.

11 There is an alternate form ἦσθα that occurs only twice (Matt 26:69; Mark 14:67).

12 ἦμεν occurs eight times in the New Testament. The alternate ἤμεθα occurs five times.

Master Verb Chart

Tense	Aug/ Redup	Tense stem	Tense form.	Conn. vowel	Personal endings	1st sing paradigm
Present act		pres		o/ε	prim act	λύω
Present mid/pas		pres		o/ε	prim mid/pas	λύομαι
Imperfect act	ε	pres		o/ε	sec act	ἔλυον
Imperfect mid/pas	ε	pres		o/ε	sec mid/pas	ἐλυόμην
Future act		fut act	σ	o/ε	prim act	λύσω
Liquid fut act		fut act	εσ	o/ε	prim act	μενῶ
Future mid		fut act	σ	o/ε	prim mid/pas	πορεύσομαι
Liquid fut mid		fut act	εσ	o/ε	prim mid/pas	μενοῦμαι

Vocabulary

ἀκολουθέω	I follow, accompany (90; *ἀκολουθε)[13] (ἠκολούθουν), ἀκολουθήσω, ἠκολούθησα, ἠκολούθηκα, -, -
	ἀκολουθέω normally takes a direct object in the dative.
διδάσκω	I teach (97; *δακ)[14] (ἐδίδασκον), διδάξω, ἐδίδαξα, -, -, ἐδιδάχθην[15]
ἐπερωτάω	I ask (for), question, demand of (56; *ἐπερωτα) (ἐπηρώτων), ἐπερωτήσω, ἐπηρώτησα, -, -, ἐπηρωτήθην
ἐρωτάω	I ask, request, entreat (63; *ἐρωτα) (ἠρώτων), ἐρωτήσω, ἠρώτησα, -, -, ἠρωτήθην
	ἐρωτάω takes a double accusative, which means the person asked and the thing asked for will both be in the accusative.
θέλω	I will, wish, desire, enjoy (208; *εθελε)[16] (ἤθελον), -, ἠθέλησα, -, -, -
	θέλω drops its initial epsilon in the present, and its final epsilon in the present and imperfect.
περιπατέω	I walk (around), live (95; *περιπατε)[17] (περιεπάτουν), περιπατήσω, περιεπάτησα, -, -, -
συναγωγή, -ῆς, ἡ	synagogue, meeting (56; *συναγωγη)[18]

---

[13] *Anacoluthon* is a construction in which the grammar does not follow, i.e., it is not correct. An *acolyte* (ἀκόλουθος) is an attendant or a follower, especially an altar attendant.

[14] The cognate verb of the noun διδάσκαλος. On the root see *MBG*, v-5a, page 312.

[15] Notice that the sigma of the stem is also absorbed by the xi.

[16] Metzger (*Lexical Aids*) reminds us of the *monothelite* heresy that said Christ had only one will, the divine.

[17] A *peripatetic* (περιπατητικός) philosopher walked around from place to place, teaching his followers as he traveled.

[18] The *synagogue* is where people gathered together for a meeting.

Φαρισαῖος, -ου, ὁ   Pharisee (98; *Φαρισαιο)[19]

χρόνος, -ου, ὁ   time (54; *χρονο)[20]

Total word count in the New Testament:	138,162
Number of words learned to date:	236
Number of word occurrences in this chapter:	817
Number of word occurrences to date:	102,359
Percent of total word count in the New Testament:	74.08%

Previous Words

There are two verbs you have already learned whose augment is unexpected.

δύναμαι   (ἐδυνάμην or ἠδυνάμην), δυνήσομαι, -, -, -, ἠδυνήθην

ἔχω   (εἶχον), ἕξω,[21] ἔσχον, ἔσχηκα, -, -

Advanced Information

21.24 **Irregular augments.** Some verbs appear to have irregular augments. Actually, they are not irregular, but it is one of those things where the rules governing the augment can become quite complicated. I will explain most apparent "irregularities" in the footnotes, but in some cases it might be simpler for you just to memorize them. Of course, if you can remember the rules, that is much better because the rules that are affecting any one particular augment are probably affecting other verbs as well.

For example, let's look at ἔχω. The imperfect of ἔχω is εἶχον. The verbal root is *σεχ. In the present the sigma is replaced by the rough breathing. But because the Greeks did not like the two aspirate sounds of the rough breathing and the chi in a row, the rough breathing deaspirates to a smooth breathing (*σεχ ‣ ἑχ ‣ ἐχ ‣ ἔχω).

In forming the imperfect, because the verbal root actually begins with a consonant, the augment is the epsilon. But then because the sigma here is between two vowels, it drops out, and the two epsilons contract to ει (ε + *σεχ ‣ εεχ ‣ εἶχον).

The future has a rough breathing (ἕξω). The tense formative sigma joins with the chi to form xi, but since there are not two aspirates in a row, the rough breathing can remain (*σεχ + σ + ω ‣ ἑχσω ‣ ἕξω).

Now, all this may sound complicated and unnecessary, and maybe at this point it is. But it is important you realize that Greek verbs are formed with rhyme and reason, that they do follow specific rules, and that eventually knowing these rules reduces the amount of memorization. As a result, a continuing use of Greek becomes a much greater possibility. And that is, after all, why you are learning this great language: to use it for the rest of our lives to understand and proclaim God's revelation as effectively as possible.

---

[19] Pharisee.

[20] A *chronograph* measures time. *Chronology* is the science of measuring time.

[21] On the rough breathing see 21.24 below.

21.25 Preparatory use of "there." So far, the only unusual aspect of εἰμί is that it takes a predicate nominative rather than a direct object. There is one other important aspect to the verb. It is permissible to add "There" before εἰμί to make a sensible English translation. Context will show you whether this is necessary or not, but normally εἰμί will be at the beginning of the clause when it carries this meaning.

For example, ἐστὶν οἶκος παρὰ τὴν θάλασσαν can mean, "There is a house by the sea." But it can also be, "A house is by the sea."

Exegesis

1. Generally, the imperfect describes an ongoing action that happened in the past (progressive, durative).

   > ἐδίδασκεν τοὺς μαθητὰς αὐτοῦ *(Mark 9:31)*.
   > *He was teaching* his disciples.

2. It can also place emphasis on the beginning of the action (ingressive, inceptive). Translators may add the word "began" to bring out this significance.

   > ἄγγελοι προσῆλθον καὶ διηκόνουν αὐτῷ *(Matt 4:11)*.
   > Angels came and *began to minister* to Him.

3. Some continuous actions do not occur constantly but rather repetitively (iterative). The translator can add a phrase like "kept on" to bring this out.

   > ἤρχετο πρὸς αὐτὸν *(Luke 18:3)*.
   > The widow *kept coming* to the judge.

   > ἤρχοντο πρὸς αὐτὸν καὶ ἔλεγον· χαῖρε *(John 19:3)*.
   > They … *went up* to him *again and again, saying,* "Hail" (NIV).

4. Other actions occur regularly, such as expressed by the English "used to" (customary).

   > Κατὰ δὲ ἑορτὴν ἀπέλυεν αὐτοῖς ἕνα δέσμιον *(Mark 15:6)*.
   > Now at the feast *he used to release* for them any one prisoner.

5. The imperfect can also describe what a person wishes to do (voluntative), tries to do (conative), or almost does (tendential). Often it is difficult to tell the difference between these three, and, as always, context is the guide.

   > ηὐχόμην γὰρ ἀνάθεμα εἶναι αὐτὸς ἐγώ *(Rom 9:3)*.
   > For *I could wish* that I myself were accursed.

   > ἐδίωκον τὴν ἐκκλησίαν τοῦ θεοῦ καὶ ἐπόρθουν αὐτήν *(Gal 1:13)*.
   > I *used to persecute* the church of God and *tried to destroy* it.

   > ὁ δὲ Ἰωάννης διεκώλυεν αὐτόν *(Matt 3:14)*.
   > John *would have prevented* him.

Chapter 22

Second Aorist Active/Middle Indicative

Exegetical Insight

The aorist (ἀόριστος) is the indefinite tense that states only the fact of the action without specifying its duration. When the aorist describes an action as a unit event it may accentuate one of three possibilities, as, imagine, a ball that has been thrown: 1) *let fly* (inceptive or ingressive); 2) *flew* (constative or durative); 3) *hit* (culminative or telic).

These aspects of the indefinite aorist may shed some light on a perplexing saying of Jesus in his Olivet discourse (Mark 13:30 and parallels). "I tell you the truth, this generation will certainly not pass away until all these things γένηται." The difficulty lies in the fact that Jesus has already described the end of the world in vv. 24f. in vivid terms of the sun and moon not giving their light, the stars falling from the sky, and the heavenly bodies being shaken. Unless the expression "this generation" (ἡ γενεὰ αὕτη) is stretched to include the entire age from Jesus' first to his second coming (a less likely option), the aorist γένηται must provide the clue. If we

view the verb as an ingressive aorist and translate it from the perspective of initiated action, the saying may be rendered, "I tell you the truth, this generation will certainly not pass away until all these things *begin* to come to pass."

This nuance of the same aorist form may also be seen in the angel Gabriel's words to Zechariah (Luke 1:20): "And now you will be silent and not able to speak until the day γένηται ταῦτα." Not only the birth but the adult ministry of John the Baptist is prophesied by Gabriel in vv. 13-17, yet Zechariah recovers his speech as soon as he writes the name of his infant son John on a tablet (vv. 62-64). Accordingly, v. 20 should be translated, "And now you will be silent and not able to speak until the day these things *begin* to happen."

The student is well advised, then, to pay careful attention to the contextual meaning of the larger sense unit and interpret the aorist as the pericope or paragraph would suggest.

Royce Gordon Gruenler

Overview

In this chapter you will learn that:

■ the aorist indicates an undefined action usually occurring in the past. For now, it should be translated with the simple past tense in English ("I *ate*," not "I *was eating*");

- Greek has two ways to form the aorist. The first aorist uses the unmodified verbal root for its aorist tense stem, which will always be different from the present tense stem;

- the second aorist is formed by using an augment, second aorist active tense stem, connecting vowel, and secondary endings.

English

22.1 The past tense of an English verb is formed one of two ways. A **regular**[1] verb forms its past tense by adding "-ed." "I *study* all the time." "I *studied* all last night." An **irregular**[2] verb forms its past tense by altering its actual stem. Usually the vowel is changed. "I *eat* breakfast every morning." "I *ate* last night as well."

As far as the meaning of the verb is concerned, it makes no difference which pattern is followed. "Swimmed" and "swam" would have the same meaning, if the former were a real word.

Greek

22.2 **Meaning**. In the last chapter, you studied one of the past tenses in Greek. The imperfect describes a continuous action that usually occurs in the past. The second past tense in Greek is the aorist. *The aorist tense describes an undefined action that normally occurs in the past.*[3]

22.3 **Translation**. As the imperfect is always continuous, the aorist is always undefined. It tells you that the action happened, but nothing more about the aspect of the action.

This means you will normally translate the aorist with the simple form of the English past tense: "I studied"; not, "I was studying."[4]

> καὶ ἦλθον πρὸς τὸν Ἰωάννην *(John 3:26)*.
> And *they came* to John.

22.4 **Two formations**. Greek has two different ways of forming the aorist tense, somewhat as English has two ways of forming the past tense. The Greek tense parallel to the English "regular" formation is called the **first aorist** (Chapter 23), and the Greek tense parallel to the English "irregular"

"Aorist" comes from ἀόριστος, which means "unmarked." This is the essence of its significance.

(To negate a word in Greek you add α to the front, much like we use "un" in English.)

---

[1] Also called a "weak" verb.

[2] Also called a "strong" verb.

[3] The word "aorist" means "undefined," "indefinite."

[4] Some teachers allow for the use of "have." "I have studied all night." This may be a valid translation of the aorist; however, the last tense you will learn is the perfect, and for didactic reasons it seems better to reserve the use of "have" for the perfect. Once you become used to the verbal system, you can be allowed the luxury of using "have" for the aorist as well. However, your teacher may prefer a different didactic method. Be sure to ask.

formation is called the **second aorist**. I will start with the second aorist because it is almost identical to the imperfect.

A Greek verb will be either first or second aorist, not both. For example, in Greek, "swim" would become "swam" or "swimmed" but never both.[5]

Second Aorist Active

22.5   **Chart: Second aorist active indicative**

> *Augment + Aorist active tense stem + Connecting vowel +*
> *Secondary active personal endings*
>
> ἐ + λαβ + ο + μεν ‣ ἐλάβομεν

λύω has a first aorist active form, so the paradigm in this chapter uses the second aorist of the verb λαμβάνω (*λαβ), which means "I take." Notice that the endings are identical to those used in the imperfect.

> ἔλαβεν οὖν τοὺς ἄρτους ὁ Ἰησοῦς *(John 6:11)*.
> Jesus then *took* the bread.

22.6   **Paradigm: Second aorist active indicative**

	form	translation	conn. vow.	ending	imperfect
1 sg	ἔλαβον	I took	ο	ν	ἔλυον
2 sg	ἔλαβες	You took	ε	ς	ἔλυες
3 sg	ἔλαβε(ν)	He/she/it took	ε	– (ν)	ἔλυε(ν)
1 pl	ἐλάβομεν	We took	ο	μεν	ἐλύομεν
2 pl	ἐλάβετε	You took	ε	τε	ἐλύετε
3 pl	ἔλαβον	They took	ο	ν	ἔλυον

22.7   **Augment**. Augmentation for the aorist follows the same rules as it did for the imperfect.

22.8   **Tense form**. The aorist active tense form is listed as the third form of the verb in the lexicon (e.g., ἔλαβον).

> λαμβάνω, (ἐλάμβανον), λήμψομαι, ἔλαβον, εἴληφα, εἴλημμαι, ἐλήμφθην

In the active voice, *a second aorist will always have a different stem from the present because the root will always have been modified to form the present tense stem.* Otherwise you could never distinguish an imperfect from a second aorist.

This sometimes involves a drastic change, such as when the verb uses different roots to form its tense stems (e.g., λέγω [*λεγ] becomes εἶπον [*ϝιπ]

---

5   There are a few exceptions to this rule, but only a few.

in the aorist). But most of the time the stem change is minor, and involves either the simplification of a double consonant (e.g., *βαλ ▸ βάλλω ▸ ἔβαλον) or a vowel changing (e.g., *λειπ ▸ λείπω ▸ ἔλιπον).

Almost always the second aorist tense stem is identical to its verbal root.

Memorize exactly. Because these changes often involve only one letter, it is important to memorize the verbal root and lexical form *exactly*. ἔβαλλον (imperfect) and ἔβαλον (second aorist) are distinguished by only one letter.

Translation hint. When you translate an inflected verbal form ask yourself, *"Am I looking at the present tense stem or not?"* If it is the present tense stem, then you may be looking at a present or imperfect. If the stem is different, you may be looking at a second aorist.

For example, if you see ἔλιπον, you know this cannot be a present or imperfect because the present tense stem is *λειπ, with an epsilon.

22.9 **Tense formative**. The second aorist active has no tense formative.

22.10 **Connecting vowels**. The second aorist active uses the same connecting vowels as the present (cf. 16.5).

22.11 **Personal endings**. Because the second aorist is an augmented tense, it uses secondary personal endings. In the active, the endings are identical to the imperfect active endings you have already learned. It will be easy to confuse these two tenses. The only difference between the imperfect and second aorist active is the tense stem (e.g., ἔβαλλον vs ἔβαλον).

Although the first person singular and the third person plural are identical in form (ἔβαλον), context usually clarifies which one is intended.

22.12 **Vocabulary listing.** In the Appendix (pages 382-83), I have listed all the verbs occurring fifty times or more that have second aorists. It may be helpful to make a separate vocabulary card for each second aorist.

22.13 **"Irregular" second aorists**. What I said about "irregular" future forms applies to the aorist as well. Some aorist forms may appear to be irregular but they actually are not. As you are memorizing your vocabulary and find difficult second aorist forms, you should decide whether you will recognize the second aorist based on the verbal root or whether you should just memorize it.

> You memorized 1 John 4:8 a while back. Now you can memorize the most famous verse of the Bible.
>
> οὕτως γὰρ ἠγάπησεν ὁ θεὸς τὸν κόσμον,
>
> ὥστε τὸν υἱὸν τὸν μονο-γενῆ ἔδωκεν,
>
> ἵνα πᾶς ὁ πιστεύων εἰς αὐτὸν
>
> μὴ ἀπόληται ἀλλ᾽ ἔχῃ ζωὴν αἰώνιον.
>
> That will really impress your folks and/or spouse, and show them why they are paying the big bucks to help you get a college or graduate degree!

Second Aorist Middle

22.14 **Chart: Second aorist middle indicative**

> *Augment + Aorist active tense stem[6] + Connecting vowel +*
> *Secondary middle/passive personal endings*
>
> ἐ + γεν + ο + μην ▸ ἐγενόμην

---

[6]   Technically, it is the aorist active/middle tense stem; but as I said earlier with the present middle/passive, I am simplifying this issue.

22.15 Paradigm: Second aorist middle indicative. Because λαμβάνω does not have an aorist middle deponent stem, this paradigm uses the aorist of γίνομαι.

	form	translation	conn. vow.	ending	imperfect
1 sg	ἐγενόμην	I became	ο	μην	ἐλυόμην
2 sg	ἐγένου	You became	ε	σο[7]	ἐλύου
3 sg	ἐγένετο	He/she/it became	ε	το	ἐλύετο
1 pl	ἐγενόμεθα	We became	ο	μεθα	ἐλυόμεθα
2 pl	ἐγένεσθε	You became	ε	σθε	ἐλύεσθε
3 pl	ἐγένοντο	They became	ο	ντο	ἐλύοντο

There is nothing surprising here. The aorist looks just like the imperfect except for the stem.

22.16 Middle deponent. If the third form of a verb in the lexicon ends in ομην, you know it is an aorist middle deponent.

γίνομαι, (ἐγινόμην), γενήσομαι, <u>ἐγενόμην</u>, γέγονα, γεγένημαι, ἐγενήθην

γίνομαι has a second aorist middle deponent: ἐγενόμην.

22.17 In the aorist, as in the future, the middle and passive are distinctly different forms. In the paradigm above, the definitions are active because the only aorist middle forms you have seen so far are deponent.

> The aorist is the default past tense. It may have no special meaning. Therefore, when the imperfect is used, there probably is some special meaning you should notice.

Summary

1. The aorist indicates an undefined action usually occurring in the past. For now it should be translated with the simple past tense in English.

2. Greek has two ways to form the aorist. There is no difference in meaning between the two, only their form.

3. The second aorist tense stem will usually have a vowel change to differentiate it from the present, although sometimes it will be a consonantal change. It is usually the unmodified verbal root.

4. The second aorist active is formed by using an augment, second aorist active tense stem, connecting vowel, and secondary active endings.

5. The second aorist middle is formed by using an augment, second aorist active tense stem, connecting vowel, and secondary middle/passive endings.

6. The second aorist looks like the imperfect except that it uses the second aorist tense stem.

---

[7] The sigma drops out because it is intervocalic (i.e., between two vowels), and the vowels contract to ου.

Master Verb Chart

Tense	Aug/ Redup	Tense stem	Tense form.	Conn. vowel	Personal endings	1st sing paradigm
Present act		pres		ο/ε	prim act	λύω
Present mid/pas		pres		ο/ε	prim mid/pas	λύομαι
Imperfect act	ε	pres		ο/ε	sec act	ἔλυον
Imperfect mid/pas	ε	pres		ο/ε	sec mid/pas	ἐλυόμην
Future act		fut act	σ	ο/ε	prim act	λύσω
Liquid fut act		fut act	εσ	ο/ε	prim act	μενῶ
Future mid		fut act	σ	ο/ε	prim mid/pas	πορεύσομαι
Liquid fut mid		fut act	εσ	ο/ε	prim mid/pas	μενοῦμαι
2nd aorist act	ε	aor act		ο/ε	sec act	ἔλαβον
2nd aorist mid	ε	aor act		ο/ε	sec mid/pas	ἐγενόμην

Vocabulary

Be sure to learn these second aorists well; they are common. You will learn the aorist form of προσεύχομαι and a few other verbs you already know in the next chapter.

ἀποθνῄσκω	I die, am about to die, am freed from (111; *ἀποθαν) (ἀπέθνῃσκον), ἀποθανοῦμαι, ἀπέθανον, -, -, -
ἄρτος, -ου, ὁ	bread, loaf, food (97; *ἀρτο)
βάλλω	I throw (122; *βαλ) (ἔβαλλον), βαλῶ, ἔβαλον, βέβληκα, βέβλημαι, ἐβλήθην
γῆ, γῆς, ἡ	earth, land, region, humanity (250; *γη)[8]
γίνομαι	I become, am, exist, happen, take place, am born, am created (669; *γεν)[9] (ἐγινόμην), γενήσομαι, ἐγενόμην, γέγονα, γεγένημαι, ἐγενήθην
	γίνομαι takes a predicate nominative, like εἰμί. γίνομαι has a wide range of meaning. I have found it helpful to think in two categories, "to be," or "to come into being." Most uses fall into one of these two groups. The root is clearly visible outside of the present tense stem.
εἰσέρχομαι	I come in(to), go in(to), enter (194; εἰσ + *ερχ; εἰσ + *ελευθ) εἰσελεύσομαι, εἰσῆλθον,[10] εἰσελήλυθα, -, -

---

[8]   *Geo* is used as a combining form meaning "earth": *geocentric, geology, geodesy.*

[9]   γίνομαι meaning "happen" gives us English cognates like *genesis* and *generate.*

[10]   The root undergoes ablaut, dropping out ευ.

ἐξέρχομαι	I go out (218; ἐξ + *ερχ; ἐξ + *ελευθ) (ἐξηρχόμην), ἐξελεύσομαι, ἐξῆλθον,[11] ἐξελήλυθα, -, -
ἔτι	still, yet, even (93)
εὑρίσκω	I find (176; *εὑρ)[12] (εὕρισκον or ηὕρισκον), εὑρήσω,[13] εὗρον, εὕρηκα, -, εὑρέθην
λαμβάνω	I take, receive (258; *λαβ) (ἐλάμβανον), λήμψομαι,[14] ἔλαβον, εἴληφα, -, ἐλήμφθην
οὔτε	and not, neither, nor (87, adverb)
προσέρχομαι	I come/go to (86; πρός + *ερχ / *ελευθ) (προσηρχόμην), -, προσῆλθον,[15] προσελήλυθα, -, -
προσεύχομαι	I pray (85; *προσευχ) (προσηυχόμην), προσεύξομαι, προσηυξάμην, -, -, -
πῦρ, πυρός, τό	fire (71; *πυρ)[16]

Total word count in the New Testament:	138,162
Number of words learned to date:	250
Number of word occurrences in this chapter:	2,517
Number of word occurrences to date:	104,876
Percent of total word count in the New Testament:	75.91%

Congratulations! You now know three out of every four word occurrences in the New Testament.

Previous Words

Please read the two footnotes for this list.

present	aorist
γινώσκω	ἔγνων
ἐκβάλλω	ἐξέβαλον
ἔρχομαι	ἦλθον
ἔχω	ἔσχον
λέγω	εἶπον[17]

---

[11] The root undergoes ablaut, dropping out ευ.

[12] *Heuristic* is an adjective that describes a person who learns by discovery. *Eureka*, meaning "I found it," is an interjection used by Archimedes when he discovered how to measure the purity of the king's gold crown.

[13] An eta is inserted after the tense stem, just as in γίνομαι.

[14] The future middle deponent is not that irregular. The alpha lengthens to eta (ablaut), the mu is inserted before the beta as it is in the present, and the beta turns to a psi because of the sigma in the tense formative. *λαβ ‣ ληβ ‣ λημβ + σομαι ‣ λήμψομαι.

[15] The root undergoes ablaut, dropping out ευ.

[16] A *pyromaniac* is a person who has a compulsive desire to start destructive fires.

[17] ϝ, the digamma, is another letter that, like the consonantal iota, dropped out of the Greek alphabet long before Koine Greek. That it was once present still affects the forms of words. In this case, because the root of εἶπον is *ϝιπ, the iota did not lengthen but rather an epsilon was added as its augment and the digamma dropped out (ε + ϝιπ ‣ εἶπον). See 17.12.

ὁράω   εἶδον[18]
συνάγω   συνήγαγον

The paradigm for ἔγνων is as follows.

1 sg	ἔγνων	1 pl	ἔγνωμεν
2 sg	ἔγνως	2 pl	ἔγνωτε
3 sg	ἔγνω	3 pl	ἔγνωσαν

You might expect the third plural to be ἔγνων, but this form never occurs in the New Testament. ἔγνωσαν is used in every instance (17 times).

22.18 You already know that οἶδα is actually a perfect with a present meaning. ἤδειν functions as the imperfect and aorist of οἶδα but actually is a pluperfect (Chapter 25), which explains why its forms are different.

1 sg	ἤδειν	1 pl	ἤδειμεν
2 sg	ἤδεις	2 pl	ἤδειτε
3 sg	ἤδει	3 pl	ἤδεισαν

WORKBOOK SUMMARY

Advanced Information

22.19 **Undefined vs. Punctiliar.** One of the primary areas of confusion in Greek exegesis comes when people confuse the Greek undefined with the English punctiliar aspect. The English punctiliar describes an action as occurring in a single point of time. "The tidal wave *hit* the boat."[19] The Greek undefined is not punctiliar. It tells you nothing about the action of the verb except that it happened.

It is interesting that Luke's version of Jesus' statement I mentioned in 15.17 is a little different from Mark's. He says, "If anyone wishes to come after me, let him deny himself and take up his cross *daily*, and follow me" (Luke 9:23). He includes "daily" to emphasize that the action of "taking up" occurs every day. Does this contradict the Markan account that simply says, "take up"? No. Both Mark and Luke use the same undefined aspect when saying "take up." The verb does not specify the nature of the action; it merely says that it should occur. But Luke includes the adverb "daily" to clarify that this action is a daily action. He could just have easily used the continuous aspect ("taking up") and arrived at the same meaning.[20]

---

[18] εἶδον is a second aorist without a present tense form. All the other words meaning "see" have their own aorist stems, and yet most grammars associate the word with ὁράω. ὁράω does have its own first aorist middle deponent form, ὠψάμην (aorist subjunctive), but it is quite rare, occurring in the New Testament only in Luke 13:28. I will list εἶδον as the aorist of ὁράω as do most grammars. I have listed its root as *ιδ. It technically is *ϝιδ, with an initial digamma (see 17.12). The digamma was a "w" sound, and from *ϝιδ we get *video*.

[19] The *continuous* version of this sentence would be, "The tidal wave *was hitting* the boat."

[20] If you want to get very specific, the Greek undefined aspect does not describe what actually happened. It describes how the writer chooses to tell you about the action. You could describe a waterfall with a continuous verb, emphasizing the continual flow of water. You could also use the undefined aspect to describe the waterfall. This would not mean that you did not know whether the water was continually falling or not. It means that you did not care to emphasize its continual flowing. You just wanted to say that the water started at the top and ended at the bottom.

Part of the misconception surrounding the Greek undefined aspect is due to the fact that it can be used to describe a punctiliar action. However, such a verb is not punctiliar because of its aspect but because of the context and the meaning of the word. You cannot use the continuous aspect to describe a punctiliar action, so by default you would use the undefined.

Exegesis

1. Generally, the aorist looks at an action as a whole and does not tell us anything about the precise nature of the action (constative).

   <u>ἐνέβη</u> εἰς τὸ πλοῖον καὶ <u>ἦλθεν</u> εἰς τὰ ὅρια Μαγαδάν *(Matt 15:39).*
   He got into the boat and *went* to the region of Magadan.

   This does not mean that the action was not a process; the writer simply does not tell us. This fact has been widely misunderstood in popular discussions; a person will say that because the verb is an aorist, then it must describe something that happened immediately, or once for all. This simply is not true.

   <u>ἐβασίλευσαν</u> μετὰ τοῦ Χριστοῦ χίλια ἔτη *(Rev 20:4).*
   They reigned with Christ for a thousand years.

   In this example, "reigned" is obviously continuous because of the meaning of the word, but for some reason it was not important for John to make this point grammatically explicit. I imagine John felt the meaning of the word made it sufficiently clear.

2. Other times the aorist places emphasis on the beginning of an action (ingressive). The translator may use a word like "became" to bring out the significance.

   ὁ δὲ βασιλεὺς <u>ὠργίσθη</u> *(Matt 22:7).*
   And the king *became furious.*

3. The aorist can be used to describe a timeless truth (gnomic). Here the time significance of the aorist completely falls away. These are often translated into English with the present tense.

   <u>ἐξηράνθη</u> ὁ χόρτος, καὶ τὸ ἄνθος <u>ἐξέπεσεν</u> *(1 Pet 1:24).*
   The grass *withers* and the flowers *falls.*

4. Because time is secondary to aspect, the Greek speaker can even use the aorist to describe an action that will occur in the future (proleptic). This stresses the certainty that the event will occur.

   οὓς <u>ἐδικαίωσεν</u>, τούτους καὶ <u>ἐδόξασεν</u> *(Rom 8:30).*
   Those whom he justified *he* also *glorified.*

Chapter 23

First Aorist Active/Middle Indicative

Exegetical Insight

The aorist tense has often been mishandled by both scholars and preachers. Aorist verbs too frequently are said to denote once-for-all action when the text has no such intention. Bill Mounce makes this abundantly clear in his lucid discussion below. Having been warned of this error, we should not go to the other extreme and fail to see that in some contexts the aorist does denote once-for-all action, not merely because the verb is an aorist but because of the context. Rom 6:10 says of Jesus, ὃ γὰρ ἀπέθανεν, τῇ ἁμαρτίᾳ ἀπέθανεν ἐφάπαξ ("for the death that he died, he died to sin once for all"). The aorist ἀπέθανεν ("he died") clearly refers to the once-for-all death of Jesus, for the verb is modified by the adverb ἐφάπαξ ("once for all"). Paul's purpose is to teach that by virtue of his death Jesus has conquered the power of sin and death once-for-all.

Jesus' victory over sin and death is not of mere historical interest, for Romans 6 teaches that those who belong to Jesus share his victory over sin. Verse 2 says, οἵτινες ἀπεθάνομεν τῇ ἁμαρτίᾳ, πῶς ἔτι ζήσομεν ἐν αὐτῇ ("we who have died to sin, how shall we still live in it?"). The subsequent verses (vv. 3–6) clarify that we died to sin by being baptized into Christ, for when we were baptized into him we were crucified together with Christ. The aorist ἀπεθάνομεν ("we died") in verse 2, therefore, denotes our once-for-all death to sin at our conversion. When we died with Christ the power of sin was broken decisively for us. This does not mean that we cannot sin any longer. Otherwise, the exhortation not to let sin reign in our lives would be superfluous (vv. 12–14). It does mean that the mastery, dominion, and lordship of sin has been broken in a decisive way for believers. Since Christ conquered sin at his death, and since we died with Christ, we now share in his victory over sin. "Therefore do not let sin reign in your mortal body, so that you obey its desires" (v. 12).

Thomas R. Schreiner

Overview

In this chapter you will learn that:

- first aorists are formed "regularly" by adding an augment, tense formative (σα), and secondary endings to the aorist tense stem (e.g., ἔλυσα);

- most first aorist tense stems are identical to their present tense stems;

- when the sigma of the tense formative is added to a stem ending in a stop, the same changes you saw in the future also occur in the first aorist (e.g., βλέπω ‣ ἔβλεψα);

- contract verbs lengthen their final stem vowel before the tense formative, just as they do in the future (e.g., γεννάω ‣ ἐγέννησα);

- liquid stems use α as a tense formative and not σα.

English

23.1 As I discussed in the previous chapter, English forms its past tense in two different ways. An "irregular" verb alters its stem. "*I am eating* my lunch now." "*I ate* my dinner last night." A "regular" verb adds "-ed" to the stem. "*I clean* my desk every day." "*I cleaned* mine last year."

Greek

23.2 As I also discussed in the previous chapter, Greek has two ways of forming the aorist tense. The second aorist is the Greek equivalent of the English "irregular" formulation in that it does not use a tense formative.

The first aorist is the Greek equivalent of the English "regular" formulation. In the first aorist,

- the tense stem is normally identical to the present tense stem and the verbal root,

- and the tense uses a tense formative (σα).

The majority of Greek verbs follow this pattern.

23.3 **Translation**. The aorist active is normally translated with the simple English past indicating undefined action. "I studied." Whether a verb is a first or second aorist has no connection to its meaning, just its form.

Remember that aspect is primary, and all the aorist tells you is that an event occurred; it tells you nothing more about the aspect of the event. And the aorist is not necessarily punctiliar; it is "undefined."

Characteristics of the First Aorist Active

23.4 **Chart: First aorist active indicative**

> *Augment + Aorist active tense stem +*
> *Tense formative (σα) + Secondary active personal endings*
>
> ἐ + λυ + σα + μεν ‣ ἐλύσαμεν

23.5 Paradigm: First aorist active indicative

	first aorist	translation	ending	imperfect	second aorist
1 sg	ἔλυσα[1]	I loosed	–	ἔλυον	ἔλαβον
2 sg	ἔλυσας	You loosed	ς	ἔλυες	ἔλαβες
3 sg	ἔλυσε(ν)[2]	He/she/it loosed	– (ν)	ἔλυε(ν)	ἔλαβε(ν)
1 pl	ἐλύσαμεν	We loosed	μεν	ἐλύομεν	ἐλάβομεν
2 pl	ἐλύσατε	You loosed	τε	ἐλύετε	ἐλάβετε
3 pl	ἔλυσαν	They loosed	ν	ἔλυον	ἔλαβον

23.6
Augment. The first aorist is augmented just as the second aorist and imperfect.

23.7
Tense form. The first aorist active is formed from the first aorist tense stem, which is generally the same form as the present tense stem and the verbal root. If the aorist stem of a verb is different from the present, the verb will usually have a second aorist.

23.8
Tense formative. Greek adds a tense formative between the stem and the personal endings to form the first aorist in the same way that it adds sigma to form the future. The first aorist active tense formative is σα.[3]

Because the tense formative ends with a vowel, there is no need for a connecting vowel; the personal endings are added directly to the tense formative.

The tense formative for the active is easy to spot. The only time it alters its form is the third person singular, where instead of the σα it is σε.

23.9
Personal endings. The first aorist active uses secondary personal endings because the aorist tense is augmented. This means it has the same personal endings as the imperfect and second aorist except in the first person singular.

If you have been memorizing the personal endings as a combination of connecting vowel and personal ending (e.g., ομεν), then you may not see the similarity between the endings in the first aorist and the imperfect as clearly. But if you have been keeping the connecting vowel and personal ending distinct (e.g., ο + μεν), then you already know the endings used in the first aorist.

23.10
Contract verbs. As was the case in the future, contract verbs lengthen their contract vowel before the tense formative. ἀγαπάω becomes ἠγάπησα.

> You know how to say things like:
> - "He is my …."
> - "She is your …."
> - They are our …."
>
> And you know some of the words for your family members. Put them together and have some fun.
> - Father: πατήρ
> - Mother: μητήρ
> - Brother: ἀδελφός
> - Sister: ἀδελφή
> - Uncle: θεῖος
> - Aunt: θεία

---

[1] No ending is used, so the tense formative stands by itself.

[2] No ending is used, but in this case (as opposed to the first person singular) the alpha of the tense formative is changed to an epsilon.

[3] Some argue that the tense formative is sigma, and the alpha is a connecting vowel. But see Smyth, #455–456.

23.11 Stems ending in a stop. You have already seen how the stops change when followed by a sigma, in both third declension nouns and verbs in the future. What is true in the future is also true in the first aorist active. First aorist stems ending in a labial form a psi when joined to the tense formative. Stems ending in a velar (including ασσω verbs) form a xi. Stems ending in a dental (including ιζω and αζω verbs) lose the dental.

πσ	▸	ψ		βλέπ	+	σα	▸	ἔβλεψα
βσ	▸	ψ		τρίβ	+	σα	▸	ἔτριψα
φσ	▸	ψ		γράφ	+	σα	▸	ἔγραψα
κσ	▸	ξ		πλέκ	+	σα	▸	ἔπλεξα
γσ	▸	ξ		πνίγ	+	σα	▸	ἔπνιξα
χσ	▸	ξ		βρέχ	+	σα	▸	ἔβρεξα
τσ[4]	▸	σ						
δσ	▸	σ		σπεύδ	+	σα	▸	ἔσπευσα
θσ	▸	σ		πείθ	+	σα	▸	ἔπεισα

23.12 Second aorist stems with first aorist endings. Occasionally you will find certain second aorist forms with an alpha instead of an omicron as the connecting vowel.

- Instead of εἶπον you will find εἶπαν (95x in New Testament),

- instead of ἦλθον you will find ἦλθαν (5x),

- instead of εἶδον you will find εἶδαν (5x),

- and instead of ἤνεγκον you will always find ἤνεγκαν (3x).

There is no difference in meaning, just in form.[5]

Halftime Review

- A first aorist is formed from an augment, the first aorist tense stem (usually the same as the present tense stem and the verbal root), a tense formative (σα), and secondary active personal endings.

- Contract verbs lengthen their final stem vowel before the tense formative.

- First and second aorist forms are translated the same (undefined, usually happening in the past).

- The final consonant of stems ending in a stop join with the sigma of the tense formative to form a psi (labials), xi (velars), or drop off (dentals).

- You will find some first aorist endings on secodn aorist forms.

---

[4] There is no example of this combination in aorist verbs in the New Testament.

[5] Here is the reason if you want to know. Greek, like any language, was always in a state of change. One type of formation overrides another, things are added, things are removed. One evidence of this state of flux can be seen in certain second aorist forms. Koine Greek was in the process of phasing out its second aorist endings while retaining the second aorist stems. As a result, you will occasionally run across second aorist stems with first aorist endings, such as εἶπαν and ἦλθαν.

Liquid Aorist Active

23.13 **Chart: First aorist active indicative (liquid)**

> *Augment + Aorist active tense stem +*
> *Tense formative (α) + Secondary active personal endings*
>
>
> ἐ + μειν + α + μεν ▸ ἐμείναμεν

Instead of adding σα as the tense formative, liquid verbs add only alpha and then sometimes modify the tense stem. The paradigmatic verb used here is μένω.

The phenomena of the liquids affect only the future and aorist tenses. They will not come into consideration in any of our remaining chapters.

23.14 **Paradigm: First aorist active indicative (liquid)**

	aorist liquid	*translation*	*first aorist*
1 sg	ἔμεινα	I remained	ἔλυσα
2 sg	ἔμεινας	You remained	ἔλυσας
3 sg	ἔμεινε(ν)	He/she/it remained	ἔλυσε(ν)
1 pl	ἐμείναμεν	We remained	ἐλύσαμεν
2 pl	ἐμείνατε	You remained	ἐλύσατε
3 pl	ἔμειναν	They remained	ἔλυσαν

As you can see, μένω has altered its stem in the aorist tense: the epsilon has changed to ει. All verbs that occur fifty times or more and have a liquid aorist are listed in the Appendix, page 381.

23.15 **Forms**. The keys to recognizing a liquid aorist are two:

■ the final stem consonant is a liquid;

■ the tense formative is α, not σα.

Aorist Middle Indicative

23.16 Like the future, the aorist uses distinct forms for the middle and the passive. (You will learn aorist passives in the next chapter.) Like the future middle, the aorist middle is identical to the aorist active except that it uses middle/passive personal endings.

23.17 Chart: First aorist middle indicative

> *Augment + Aorist active tense stem +*
>
> *Tense formative (σα) +*
>
> *Secondary middle/passive personal endings*
>
> ἐ + λυ + σα + μην ‣ ἐλυσάμην

23.18 Paradigm: First aorist middle indicative. The translations are still in the active because all the middles you will see in this chapter are deponent and therefore active in meaning.

	first aorist	translation	ending	second aorist
1 sg	ἐλυσάμην	I loosed	μην	ἐγενόμην
2 sg	ἐλύσω⁶	You loosed	σο	ἐγένου
3 sg	ἐλύσατο	He/she/it loosed	το	ἐγένετο
1 pl	ἐλυσάμεθα	We loosed	μεθα	ἐγενόμεθα
2 pl	ἐλύσασθε	You loosed	σθε	ἐγένεσθε
3 pl	ἐλύσαντο	They loosed	ντο	ἐγένοντο

23.19 As in the second aorist, you know that a verb is middle deponent in the aorist if the third tense form of the verb listed in the lexicon ends in "μην."

> ἀρνέομαι   I deny (33, v-1d[2a])
> (ἠρνούμην), ἀρνήσομαι, ἠρνησάμην, –, ἤρνημαι, –

23.20 Liquid future middles are formed as you might expect; see the Appendix (page 362) for the paradigm.

Summary

1. A verb that has a first aorist stem forms its aorist active by adding an augment, tense formative (σα), and secondary personal endings to the aorist tense stem, which is usually the same as the present tense stem and its verbal root.

2. The aorist middle is a distinct form from the passive, and is formed in the same way as is the active except that it uses middle/passive personal endings.

3. Like the second aorist, the first aorist describes an undefined action usually occurring in past time.

---

⁶ Remember that the actual personal ending is σο. When combined with the tense formative, the second sigma drops out because it is intervocalic (i.e., "between vowels") and the vowels contract to omega (*σα + σο ‣ σαο ‣ σω).

4. Contract verbs lengthen their final stem vowel before the tense formative.

5. Verbs with stems ending in a stop behave in the aorist as they do in the future in reference to the sigma of the tense formative.

6. Liquid aorists use α and not σα as their tense formative, and sometimes modify their tense stem.

Master Verb Chart

Tense	Aug/ Redup	Tense stem	Tense form.	Conn. vowel	Personal endings	1st sing paradigm
Present act		pres		o/ε	prim act	λύω
Present mid/pas		pres		o/ε	prim mid/pas	λύομαι
Imperfect act	ε	pres		o/ε	sec act	ἔλυον
Imperfect mid/pas	ε	pres		o/ε	sec mid/pas	ἐλυόμην
Future act		fut act	σ	o/ε	prim act	λύσω
Liquid fut act		fut act	εσ	o/ε	prim act	μενῶ
Future mid		fut act	σ	o/ε	prim mid/pas	πορεύσομαι
Liquid fut mid		fut act	εσ	o/ε	prim mid/pas	μενοῦμαι
1st aorist act	ε	aor act	σα		sec act	ἔλυσα
Liquid aorist act	ε	aor act	α		sec act	ἔμεινα
2nd aorist act	ε	aor act		o/ε	sec act	ἔλαβον
1st aorist mid	ε	aor act	σα		sec mid/pas	ἐλυσάμην
2nd aorist mid	ε	aor act		o/ε	sec mid/pas	ἐγενόμην

Vocabulary

ἀπέρχομαι   I depart (117; ἀπ + *ἐρχ / *ἐλευθ)
ἀπελεύσομαι, ἀπῆλθον, ἀπελήλυθα, -, -

ἄρχομαι   I begin (86; *ἀρχ)
ἄρξομαι, ἠρξάμην, -, -, -

ἄρχομαι is an unusual word. 84 times in the New Testament is functions as a middle deponent meaning "begin." However, two times it functions as a non-deponent (ἄρχω) and means "I rule" (Mark 10:42; Romans 15:12).

γράφω   I write (191; *γραφ)[7]
(ἔγραφον), γράψω, ἔγραψα, γέγραφα, γέγραπμαι or γέγραμμαι, ἐγράφην

διό   therefore, for this reason (53)

---

[7] *Graphic* (γραφικός) means, "pertaining to writing."

δοξάζω	I praise, honor, glorify (61; *δοξαδ)[8]
	(ἐδόξαζον), δοξάσω, ἐδόξασα, -, δεδόξασμαι, ἐδοξάσθην
δύναμις, -εως, ἡ	power, miracle (119; *δυναμι)[9]
κηρύσσω	I proclaim, preach (61; *κηρυγ)[10]
	(ἐκήρυσσον), -, ἐκήρυξα, -, -, ἐκηρύχθην
πίνω	I drink (73; *πι)[11]
	(ἔπινον), πίομαι, ἔπιον, πέπωκα, -, ἐπόθην

Total word count in the New Testament:	138,162
Number of words learned to date:	258
Number of word occurrences in this chapter:	761
Number of word occurrences to date:	105,637
Percent of total word count in the New Testament:	76.46%

Previous Words

Present	Aorist
Pattern 1a Verbs	
ἀκούω	ἤκουσα
δύναμαι	–
θέλω	ἠθέλησα[12]
λύω	ἔλυσα
πιστεύω	ἐπίστευσα
πορεύομαι	–
Pattern 1b Verbs (Contract Stems)	
ἀγαπάω	ἠγάπησα
ἀκολουθέω	ἠκολούθησα
γεννάω	ἐγέννησα
ἐπερωτάω	ἐπερώτησα
ζάω	ἔζησα
ζητέω	ἐζήτησα
καλέω	ἐκάλεσα[13]

---

[8] Verbal cognate of δόξα.

[9] This is the cognate noun of the verb δύναμαι. *Dynamite* comes from δύναμις, but you cannot define the latter by the former because English was not a language until hundreds of years later. See D. A. Carson, *Exegetical Fallacies*, pages 32–33.

[10] The *kerygma* is a term used by C. H. Dodd to describe the essential nature of the gospel message in the early church. See R. H. Mounce, *The Essential Nature of New Testament Preaching* (Eerdmans). *Kerygma* is from the cognate noun κηρύγμα.

[11] πίνω is from the root *πι to which was added a nu in the formation of the present tense stem (class v-3; see 20.24).
   A *potion* is something you drink (from *πι through the French, *potion*).

[12] Remember, the root of θέλω is *εθελε, which loses its initial and final epsilons in the present.

[13] As in the future, καλέω does not lengthen its final stem vowel before the tense formative.

λαλέω	ἐλάλησα
περιπατέω	περιεπάτησα
πληρόω	ἐπλήρωσα
ποιέω	ἐποίησα
προσκυνέω	προσεκύνησα[14]
τηρέω	ἐτήρησα

Pattern 1c Verbs (Stems Ending in a Stop)

βαπτίζω	ἐβάπτισα
βλέπω	ἔβλεψα
διδάσκω	ἐδίδαξα
προσεύχομαι	προσηυξάμην
σῴζω	ἔσωσα

Pattern 3 Verbs (Liquid Stems)

αἴρω	ἦρα
ἀποκρίνομαι	ἀπεκρινάμην
ἀποκτείνω	ἀπέκτεινα
ἀποστέλλω	ἀπέστειλα
ἐγείρω	ἤγειρα
κρίνω	ἔκρινα
μένω	ἔμεινα[15]

Are you feeling overwhelmed with the amount of Greek there is to learn? This is common. At first there was not much to learn, but you were learning how to learn.

Now things are starting to change. You have learned how to learn Greek, but now you are starting to be weighed down by the sheer volume of data to remember. Perhaps you need to call out like Nehemiah did when he had time only for a short prayer, as suggested by this verse.

προσηυξάμην πρὸς τὸν θεὸν τοῦ οὐρανοῦ.

Perhaps all he had time to say was, βοήθει.

---

[14] Notice that προσκυνέω is a compound verb (even though κυνέω does not occur in the New Testament) and augments as such.

[15] ε changes to ει (ablaut).

Chapter 24

Aorist and Future Passive Indicative

Exegetical Insight

The biblical writers are so open and direct in speaking of God's actions for us and for our salvation, that it may come as a surprise to students of New Testament Greek that sometimes God's sovereign grace is hidden in grammatical expressions that do not contain the name of God at all. This is the case with the construction Max Zerwick has called the "theological passive." Jewish reticence about speaking of God directly shows up quite often in Jesus' use of the future passive indicative—perhaps as a kind of understatement for rhetorical effect.

There are four classic examples in the Beatitudes, where Jesus says of those he pronounces "Blessed" that "they will be comforted" (Matt 5:4), "they will be filled" (5:6), "they will be shown mercy" (5:7), and "they will be called children of God" (5:9). The meaning is that *God* will comfort them, fill them, show them mercy, and call them

his children. In a promise of answered prayer, Jesus says, "Ask and it will be given you ... knock and it will be opened" (Luke 11:9). Clearly, *God* is the One who gives and who opens the door.

The aorist passive is used less often in this way, yet Peter speaks of the prophets to whom "it was revealed" (that is, to whom *God* revealed) that their prophecies were for us (1 Peter 1:12). God's sovereignty embraces even the terrible judgments in Revelation, where four horsemen were "given" (ἐδόθη) power to kill by sword, famine, and disease (Rev 6:8), and John himself was "given" (ἐδόθη) a reed to measure the temple court for judgment (11:1). Here too God is the unexpressed Giver.

In English the passive voice is often considered a sign of weak style, but in Greek it can be a clear signal that God is at work.

J. Ramsey Michaels

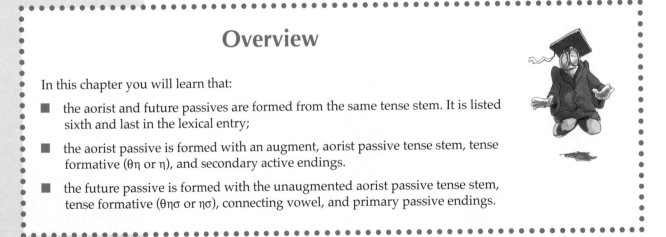

Overview

In this chapter you will learn that:

- the aorist and future passives are formed from the same tense stem. It is listed sixth and last in the lexical entry;

- the aorist passive is formed with an augment, aorist passive tense stem, tense formative (θη or η), and secondary active endings.

- the future passive is formed with the unaugmented aorist passive tense stem, tense formative (θησ or ησ), connecting vowel, and primary passive endings.

English

24.1 In English, the **past passive** is formed by using the helping verb "was"/"were" and the past participle form of the verb. "*I was flunked* by the Hebrew teacher."

The **future passive** is formed by using the helping verbs "will be" and the past participle form of the English verb. "*I will be flunked* if I do not study."[1]

A chart of all the English tenses is given in the Appendix on page 351.

Greek

24.2 You have already learned the aorist and future active and middle. In this chapter you will look at the aorist and future passive. Both these tenses are formed from the same tense stem, so it is natural to discuss them at the same time.

There are only four or five points to be learned in this chapter. The grammar is easy. You are also almost done with the Master Verb Chart.

First Aorist Passive

24.3 **Translation**. The aorist passive is translated with the helping verb "was"/"were" and designates an event of undefined aspect, normally in past time. "I was tested." "They were flunked."

> τότε ἐπληρώθη τὸ ῥηθὲν διὰ Ἰερεμίου τοῦ προφήτου (*Matt 2:17*).
> Then *was fulfilled* what was spoken by the prophet Jeremiah.

24.4 **Chart: First aorist passive indicative**

> *Augment + Aorist passive tense stem +*
> *Tense formative (θη) + Secondary active personal endings*
>
> ἐ + λυ + θη + ν ▸ ἐλύθην

Because the tense formative θη[2] ends in a vowel, the connecting vowels are unnecessary. Notice also that the aorist passive uses active endings.

---

[1] The future continuous passive is formed in the same way except that "being" is inserted. "I will be being flunked," which obviously is not a common tense in English.

[2] Advanced information for the curious: the tense formative actually is θε, which has lengthened to θη. You will see the shortened form in other situations.

24.5 Paradigm: First aorist passive indicative

	first aorist passive	translation	ending	imperfect act.
1 sg	ἐλύθην	I was loosed	ν	ἔλυον
2 sg	ἐλύθης	You were loosed	ς	ἔλυες
3 sg	ἐλύθη	He/she/it was loosed	–	ἔλυε
1 pl	ἐλύθημεν	We were loosed	μεν	ἐλύομεν
2 pl	ἐλύθητε	You were loosed	τε	ἐλύετε
3 pl	ἐλύθησαν[3]	They were loosed	σαν	ἔλυον

24.6
Augment. The aorist passive stem uses the augment, which normally indicates past time.

24.7
Tense form. The first aorist passive tense stem is generally the same as the present tense stem and the verbal root. If it is different, the verb will usually have a second aorist passive.

The aorist passive tense form of the verb is listed as the sixth form in the lexical entry: ἤχθην.

> ἄγω I lead (67; *ἀγ)
> (ἦγον), ἄξω, ἤγαγον, –, –, ἤχθην

24.8
Tense formative. The tense formative is θη and easy to spot because it never varies. Almost every time you see the θη you can assume the verb is an aorist passive.[4]

24.9
Secondary active endings. The aorist passive uses active endings. This use of active endings for the aorist passive will resurface several more times.

24.10
Stems ending in a stop. Stops change when immediately followed by a theta, according to the following pattern.[5]

πθ	▸	φθ		*βλεπ	+	θη	▸	ἐβλέφθην
βθ	▸	φθ		*ἐλημβ	+	θη	▸	ἐλήμφθην
κθ	▸	χθ		*διωκ	+	θη	▸	ἐδιώχθην
γθ	▸	χθ		*ἀγ	+	θη	▸	ἤχθην

---

[3] This form uses the alternative ending σαν instead of the nu used in the imperfect and second aorist. You have already seen this ending on the aorist active, third person plural of γινώσκω: ἔγνωσαν.

[4] The only exception to this is an epsilon contract verb like ἀκολουθέω, which, when used with a tense formative, has the θη combination because of the lengthened contract vowel (e.g., ἠκολούθησα, which is aorist active, or ἀκολουθήσω, which is future active).

[5] For you grammarian experts, this is called "aspiration." In one sense, in English it is what turns "t" to "th," or "p" to "ph," or "c" to "ch." It is like adding the "h" sound (which is an "aspirate"). The same holds true for Greek. Theta is like an aspirated tau.
  To put it another way, if you look at the Square of Stops, you can see the pattern.

π	β	φ	▸	φ
κ	γ	χ	▸	χ
τ	δ	θ	▸	σ

τθ	▸	σθ[6]		
δθ	▸	σθ	*βαπτιδ + θη	▸ ἐβαπτίσθην
θθ	▸	σθ	*πειθ + θη	▸ ἐπείσθην

Second Aorist Passive

24.11 Chart: Second aorist passive indicative

> Augment + Aorist passive tense stem +
>
> Tense formative (η) +
>
> Secondary active personal endings
>
> ἐ + γραφ + η + μεν ▸ ἐγράφημεν

The paradigm for the second aorist passive uses γράφω. In the case of this particular verb, the second aorist stem is not different from the present (γράφω ▸ ἐγράφην). This serves to emphasize how important it is to know your personal endings exactly, otherwise you might mistakenly think that one of these forms is an imperfect. The New Testament has only 32 words that occur in the second aorist passive (see *MBG*).

24.12 Paradigm: Second aorist passive indicative

	second aorist passive	translation	endings	first aorist passive
1 sg	ἐγράφην	I was written	ν	ἐλύθην
2 sg	ἐγράφης	You were written	ς	ἐλύθης
3 sg	ἐγράφη	He/she/it was written	–	ἐλύθη
1 pl	ἐγράφημεν	We were written	μεν	ἐλύθημεν
2 pl	ἐγράφητε	You were written	τε	ἐλύθητε
3 pl	ἐγράφησαν	They were written	σαν[7]	ἐλύθησαν

In the passive, sometimes the stem will be the same as in the present, sometimes the same as in the aorist active, and sometimes it will be different from both. It is therefore important to recognize the tense formative and personal endings used in the aorist passive.

---

[6] There is no example of this combination in aorist verbs in the New Testament.

[7] Same alternate ending as in the first aorist.

First Future Passive

24.13 **Translation**. The future passive is translated with the simple English ("undefined"), almost always referring to a future event: "I will be passed."

24.14 **Chart: future passive indicative**. The future passive is formed from the aorist passive tense stem. There is no augment. Whereas the aorist passive uses active endings, the future passive uses middle/passive endings.

> *Aorist passive tense stem (no augment) +*
>
> *Tense formative (θησ) + Connecting vowel +*
>
> *Primary middle/passive personal endings*
>
> λυ + θησ + ο + μαι ▸ λυθήσομαι

In summary, here are the relevent formations for this chapter.

tense	formative	endings
future active	σ	primary active
future middle	σ	primary middle/passive
aorist passive	θη	secondary active
future passive	θησ	primary middle/passive

24.15 **Paradigm: First future passive indicative**

	first fut. pas.	translation	conn. vowel	ending	future middle
1 sg	λυθήσομαι	I will be loosed	ο	μαι	πορεύσομαι
2 sg	λυθήσῃ	You will be loosed	ε	σαι[8]	πορεύσῃ
3 sg	λυθήσεται	He/she/it will be loosed	ε	ται	πορεύσεται
1 pl	λυθησόμεθα	We will be loosed	ο	μεθα	πορευσόμεθα
2 pl	λυθήσεσθε	You will be loosed	ε	σθε	πορεύσεσθε
3 pl	λυθήσονται	They will be loosed	ο	νται	πορεύσονται

24.16 **Differences between the future and aorist passive**

- In the future passive there is no augment. It should be obvious why.[9]

- The tense formative is θησ, not θη. If it helps, you could think of the θη as part of the aorist passive stem and the sigma making the necessary alterations to form the future passive (like the sigma in the future active and middle).

---

[8]   The sigma in the personal ending drops out because it is between two vowels, and the vowels contract normally.

[9]   The augment indicates past time, and this is the future.

■ The third person plural passive form -θησαν is aorist and not future. This is the only time in the first aorist passive that you have a sigma after the θη. All other times θησ indicates the future passive.

24.17 Deponent futures. The only way to form a future passive is to use the aorist passive tense stem. However, there are two kinds of future deponents: middle deponents built on the future active tense stem (e.g., γενήσομαι); and passive deponents built on the aorist passive tense stem (e.g., φοβηθήσομαι).

Second Future Passive

24.18 Chart. The second future passive is formed just like the first future passive except that the tense formative is ησ.

> *Aorist passive tense stem (no augment) +*
> *Tense formative (ησ) + Connecting vowel +*
> *Primary middle/passive personal endings*
>
> ἀποσταλ + ησ + ο + μαι ▸ ἀποσταλήσομαι

24.19 Paradigm: Second future passive indicative

	second fut. passive	translation	conn. vowel	endings
1 sg	ἀποσταλήσομαι	I will be sent	ο	μαι
2 sg	ἀποσταλήσῃ	You will be sent	ε	σαι[10]
3 sg	ἀποσταλήσεται	He/she/it will be sent	ε	ται
1 pl	ἀποσταλησόμεθα	We will be sent	ο	μεθα
2 pl	ἀποσταλήσεσθε	You will be sent	ε	σθε
3 pl	ἀποσταλήσονται	They will be sent	ο	νται

Summary

1. The aorist and future passives are formed from the same tense stem. It is listed sixth and last in the lexical entry.

2. The aorist passive is formed from the aorist passive tense stem (no augment), tense formative (θη or η), and secondary active endings.

3. The future passive is formed with the aorist passive tense stem (no augment), tense formative (θησ or ησ), connecting vowel, and primary passive endings.

---

[10] The sigma in the personal ending drops out because it is between two vowels, and the vowels contract normally.

Master Verb Chart

Tense	Aug/ Redup	Tense stem	Tense form.	Conn. vowel	Personal endings	1st sing paradigm
Present act		pres		o/ε	prim act	λύω
Present mid/pas		pres		o/ε	prim mid/pas	λύομαι
Imperfect act	ε	pres		o/ε	sec act	ἔλυον
Imperfect mid/pas	ε	pres		o/ε	sec mid/pas	ἐλυόμην
Future act		fut act	σ	o/ε	prim act	λύσω
Liquid fut act		fut act	εσ	o/ε	prim act	μενῶ
Future mid		fut act	σ	o/ε	prim mid/pas	πορεύσομαι
Liquid fut mid		fut act	εσ	o/ε	prim mid/pas	μενοῦμαι
1st future pas		aor pas	θησ	o/ε	prim mid/pas	λυθήσομαι
2nd future pas		aor pas	ησ	o/ε	prim mid/pas	ἀποσταλήσομαι
1st aorist act	ε	aor act	σα		sec act	ἔλυσα
Liquid aorist act	ε	aor act	α		sec act	ἔμεινα
2nd aorist act	ε	aor act		o/ε	sec act	ἔλαβον
1st aorist mid	ε	aor act	σα		sec mid/pas	ἐλυσάμην
2nd aorist mid	ε	aor act		o/ε	sec mid/pas	ἐγενόμην
1st aorist pas	ε	aor pas	θη		sec act	ἐλύθην
2nd aorist pas	ε	aor pas	η		sec act	ἐγράφην

There is only one more tense to learn!

Vocabulary

In Chapter 25 you will learn the last tense, the perfect. When grammars list a verb's tense forms, they place the perfect active and perfect middle/passive between the aorist active and aorist passive.

ἄγω	I lead, bring, arrest (67; *ἀγ)[11] (ἦγον), ἄξω, ἤγαγον,[12] –, –, ἤχθην[13]
αἷμα, -ατος, τό	blood (97, *αἱματ)[14]
ἕκαστος, -η, -ον	each, every (82; *ἑκαστο)
ἱμάτιον, -ου, τό	garment, cloak (60; *ἱματιο)[15]

---

[11] This is the verbal part of the compound συνάγω.

[12] ἄγω undergoes what is called "Attic reduplication." This means that the word both reduplicates and then augments the reduplicated alpha (αγ ‣ αγαγ ‣ ἤγαγον). This is a second aorist.

[13] The gamma has changed to a chi because of the following theta, in compliance with the rules (24.10).

[14] *Hematology* is the study of blood.

[15] The *himation* is a Greek garment worn over the tunic.

ὄρος, ὄρους, τό	mountain, hill (63; * ὀρο)[16]
ὑπάγω	I depart (79; ὑπ + *αγ) (ὑπῆγον), –, –, –, –, –
φοβέομαι	I fear (95; *φοβε)[17] (ἐφοβούμην), –, –, –, –, ἐφοβήθην Some do not list φοβέομαι as a deponent, and yet the meaning is always active. In the passive it can mean "I am seized with fear," "I am caused to be fearful." ἐφοβήθην is an aorist passive deponent.
χαίρω	I rejoice (74; *χαρ)[18] (ἔχαιρον), –, –, –, –, ἐχάρην[19] ἐχάρην is an aorist passive deponent.

Total word count in the New Testament:	138,162
Number of words learned to date:	266
Number of word occurrences in this chapter:	617
Number of word occurrences to date:	106,254
Percent of total word count in the New Testament:	76.9%

Previous Words

In the following chart, I list the aorist and future passive if they occur in the New Testament; otherwise, there is a dash. There are further discussions of the stems in the Appendix, pages 370-80.

present active	aorist passive	future passive
Pattern 1a verbs		
ἀκούω	ἠκούσθην[20]	ἀκουσθήσομαι
ἄρχομαι	–	–
δύναμαι	ἠδυνήθην	–
διδάσκω	ἐδιδάχθην[21]	–
ἔχω	–	–
λύω	ἐλύθην	λυθήσομαι
πιστεύω	ἐπιστεύθην	–
πορεύομαι	ἐπορεύθην	

---

[16] *Orology* and *orography* both mean the study of mountains.

[17] The English *phobia* derives from this root and is commonly used as a combining form.

[18] χαίρειν (an infinitive, Chapter 32) was the common greeting in Koine Greek (cf. Acts 15:23; James 1:1).

[19] ἐχάρην is quite regular. The stem diphthong αι has shifted to alpha (ablaut), and it is a second aorist.

[20] Several verbs insert a sigma after the tense stem and before the tense formative.

[21] The sigma has dropped out, and the kappa has changed to chi in accordance with the rules (24.10).

present active	aorist passive	future passive

Pattern 1b Verb (Contract Stems)

present active	aorist passive	future passive
ἀγαπάω	–	ἀγαπηθήσομαι
ἀκολουθέω	–	–
γεννάω	ἐγεννήθην	–
ἐπερωτάω	ἐπηρωτήθην	
ἐρωτάω	–	–
ζάω	–	–
ζητέω	–	ζητηθήσομαι
καλέω	ἐκλήθην	κληθήσομαι
λαλέω	ἐλαλήθην	λαληθήσομαι
ὁράω	ὤφθην[22]	ὀφθήσομαι
περιπατέω	–	–
πληρόω	ἐπληρώθην	πληρωθήσομαι
ποιέω	–	–
προσκυνέω	–	–
τηρέω	ἐτηρήθην	–

Pattern 1c Verbs (Stems Ending in a Stop)

present active	aorist passive	future passive
βαπτίζω	ἐβαπτίσθην	βαπτισθήσομαι
βλέπω	–	–
γράφω	ἐγράφην	–
δοξάζω	ἐδοξάσθην	–
κηρύσσω	ἐκηρύχθην	κηρυχθήσομαι
λαμβάνω	ἐλήμφθην[23]	–
προσέρχομαι	–	–
προσεύχομαι	–	–
συνάγω	συνήχθην	συναχθήσομαι
σῴζω	ἐσώθην	σωθήσομαι

Pattern 3 Verb (Liquid Stems)

present active	aorist passive	future passive
αἴρω	ἤρθην	ἀρθήσομαι
ἀποκρίνομαι	ἀπεκρίθην	ἀποκριθήσομαι
ἀποκτείνω	ἀπεκτάνθην	–
ἀποστέλλω	ἀπεστάλην	–
ἐγείρω	ἠγέρθην	ἐγερθήσομαι
ἐκβάλλω	ἐξεβλήθην	ἐκβληθήσομαι
θέλω	–	–
κρίνω	ἐκρίθην	κριθήσομαι

---

[22] The aorist passive of ὁράω is formed from a different root: *οπ. The omicron is augmented, and the pi is altered (i.e., "aspirated") to a phi because of the following theta (cf. 24.10). The same root is used in the formation of the future middle deponent: ὄψομαι.

[23] The same changes that occur in the future middle deponent occur in the aorist passive as well, along with the change of the final beta to a phi, in accordance with the rules (24.10).

present active	aorist passive	future passive
μένω	–	–
χαίρω	ἐχάρην	–

Pattern 4 Verbs (Ablaut and Stem Change)

present active	aorist passive	future passive
ἀπέρχομαι	–	–
ἀποθνῄσκω	–	–
βάλλω	ἐβλήθην	βληθήσομαι
γίνομαι	ἐγενήθην	–
γινώσκω	ἐγνώσθην	γνωσθήσομαι
ἔρχομαι	–	–
εὑρίσκω	εὑρέθην	εὑρεθήσομαι
λέγω	ἐρρέθην[24]	–
πίνω	ἐπόθην	–
προσέρχομαι	–	–

This photo is of a cursive New Testament manuscript, copied in the twelfth century. It contains Matthew 15:13-27a. Photo provided by the Center of the Study of New Testament Manuscripts (Dr. Damiel Wallace, director) and used by permission of Institut für neutestamentliche Textforschung.

---

[24] The aorist passive of λέγω is formed from a different root: *ερ. The same root is used in the formation of the future active: ἐρῶ.

Chapter 25

Perfect Indicative

Exegetical Insight

It is often the very first and the very last thing we say that is the most important, or the statement that is the most memorable. First impressions and last impressions are the lasting impressions. The same is true for Jesus. The first statement we hear him say is that he should be in his Father's house (Luke 2:49). Even at the age of twelve, he was aware of his divine lineage.

And as he hung on the cross, having lived a sinless life, having paid the penalty for your sins and mine, Jesus uttered his last words before dying. Τετέλεσται. "It is finished" (John 19:30). This one word summary of Jesus' life and death is perhaps the single most important statement in all of Scripture. The word means "to complete," "to bring to perfection." Jesus had fully done the work God the Father sent him to do. Paul spends Romans 5 discussing this very fact, that our salvation is sure because Christ's death totally defeated the effects of Adam's sin, completely.

But the tense of the verb, the "perfect" tense, brings out even more of what Jesus was saying. The perfect describes an action that was fully completed and has consequences at the time of speaking. Jesus could have used the aorist, ἐτελέσθη, and simply said, "The work is done." But there is more, there is hope for you and for me. Because Jesus fully completed his task, the ongoing effects are that you and I are offered the free gift of salvation so that we can be with him forever. Praise the Lord. Τετέλεσται.

William D. Mounce

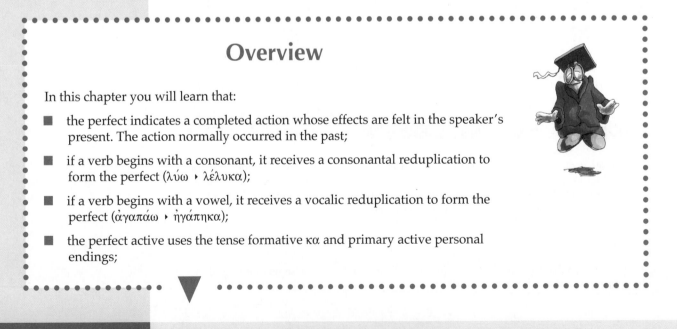

Overview

In this chapter you will learn that:

- the perfect indicates a completed action whose effects are felt in the speaker's present. The action normally occurred in the past;

- if a verb begins with a consonant, it receives a consonantal reduplication to form the perfect (λύω ‣ λέλυκα);

- if a verb begins with a vowel, it receives a vocalic reduplication to form the perfect (ἀγαπάω ‣ ἠγάπηκα);

- the perfect active uses the tense formative κα and primary active personal endings;

■ the perfect middle passive uses primary middle/passive personal endings;

■ the classical rule of the middle voice is that the subject does the action of the verb in some way that affects itself.

English

25.1   English has no exact counterpart to the Greek perfect tense.

■ The English past tense indicates that something happened in the past, whether it was continuous or undefined. "I wrote" means I did something previously, but it does not say whether I completed my writing.

■ When you use the helping verbs "have" or "has," the action described was done in the (recent) past and the statement is accurate up to now ("I have written").

■ The English present can describe an action with current consequences ("It is written"). This is close to the Greek perfect.

Greek

25.2   **Meaning**. The Greek perfect is one of the more interesting tenses and is often used to express great theological truths. The Greek perfect *describes an action that was brought to completion and whose effects are felt in the present.*[1] Because it describes a completed action, by implication the action described by the perfect verb normally occurred in the past.

For example, "Jesus died" is a simple statement of an event that happened in the past. In Greek this would be in the aorist. But if I used the Greek perfect to say, "Jesus has died," then you might expect the verse to continue by spelling out the present significance of that past action. "Jesus has died for my sins."

Another example is the verb "to write." When the Bible says, "It is written," this is usually in the perfect tense. Scripture was written in the past but is applicable in the present. That is why some translations choose the present "It is written," instead of "It has been written." This emphasizes its abiding significance. The translation "It stands written" would express this nuance even clearer.

> I am not sure how ancient Greeks told time, but based on Modern Greek here is how it might have worked.
> τί ὥρα φεύγει;
> is, "What time is it?"

25.3   **Translation**. It can become somewhat complicated to translate the perfect tense because of the absence of any exact English parallel. Choose between the two possibilities below, depending upon the needs of the context.

---

[1]   Remember: the time of the verb is from the standpoint of the speaker/writer, not the reader. What is present to the biblical writer may or may not be present to us.

To answer, "It is ten o'clock" you would say, ἐστὶν δέκα ἡ ὥρα. The ἡ ὥρα is optional. How would you say it is two o'clock?

■ Use the helping verbs "have/has" and the past participle form of the verb (e.g., "has written"). Be sure to remember the true significance of the Greek perfect. This will help you differentiate between the aorist ("I wrote") and the perfect ("I have written").

> θυγάτηρ, ἡ πίστις σου <u>σέσωκέν</u> σε· ὕπαγε εἰς εἰρήνην (*Mark 5:34*).
>
> Daughter, your faith *has saved* you. Go in peace.

■ Use the English present tense when the current implications of the action of the verb are emphasized by the context ("It is written").

> μετανοεῖτε· <u>ἤγγικεν</u> γὰρ ἡ βασιλεία τῶν οὐρανῶν (*Matt 3:2*).
>
> Repent, for the kingdom of heaven *is near.*

This is the last tense that you will learn (but see Advanced Information for the pluperfect). There are a few more variations, but this is the last actual tense. Once again, congratulations!

Perfect

25.4 Chart: Perfect active indicative

> *Reduplication + Perfect active tense stem +*
>
> *Tense formative (κα) + Primary active personal endings*
>
> λ + ε + λυ + κα + μεν ▸ λελύκαμεν

The perfect active is a primary tense and uses primary endings. However, because of the alpha in the tense formative it appears to be similar to the first aorist.

25.5 Paradigm: Perfect active indicative

	perfect active	translation	ending	aorist active
1 sg	λέλυκα	I have loosed	–	ἔλυσα
2 sg	λέλυκας	You have loosed	ς	ἔλυσας
3 sg	λέλυκε(ν)²	He/she/it has loosed	– (ν)	ἔλυσε(ν)
1 pl	λελύκαμεν	We have loosed	μεν	ἐλύσαμεν
2 pl	λελύκατε	You have loosed	τε	ἐλύσατε
3 pl	λελύκασι(ν)³	They have loosed	σι(ν)	ἔλυσαν

---

² The tense formative changes from κα to κε, much like the change in the first aorist from σα to σε.

³ The ending is actually νσι(ν), but the nu has dropped out because of the sigma. The third plural can also be λέλυκαν, which resembles the first aorist. There are thirty-one perfect active, third person plural, forms in the New Testament; this "alternate" form occurs nine times.

25.6 Chart: Perfect middle/passive indicative

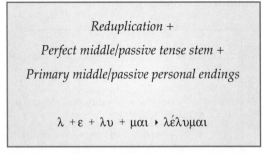

> *Reduplication +*
>
> *Perfect middle/passive tense stem +*
>
> *Primary middle/passive personal endings*
>
> λ + ε + λυ + μαι ‣ λέλυμαι

Note that there is no tense formative and no connecting vowel. The middle and passive are identical in the perfect, as they are in the present.

25.7 Paradigm: Perfect middle/passive indicative. The paradigm gives the translation of the passive.

	perfect mid./pas.	translation	ending	present mid./pas.
1 sg	λέλυμαι	I have been loosed	μαι	λύομαι
2 sg	λέλυσαι	You have been loosed	σαι⁴	λύῃ
3 sg	λέλυται	He/she/it has been loosed	ται	λύεται
1 pl	λελύμεθα	We have been loosed	μεθα	λυόμεθα
2 pl	λέλυσθε	You have been loosed	σθε	λύεσθε
3 pl	λέλυνται⁵	They have been loosed	νται	λύονται

25.8 Reduplication. The most notable difference in form between the perfect and other tenses is the reduplication of the initial letter. The fact that it is so obvious makes identification of the perfect relatively easy. There are several variations to the rules governing reduplication, but here are the basic guidelines.

1. **Consonantal reduplication**. *If a verb begins with a single consonant,[6] that consonant is reduplicated and the two consonants are separated by an epsilon.*

    λυ ‣ λελυ ‣ λέλυκα

    If the consonant that was reduplicated is φ, χ, or θ, the reduplicated consonant will change to π, κ, or τ, respectively. This makes the word easier to pronounce.

φανερόω	‣	φεφανερο	‣	πεφανέρωκα
χαρίζομαι	‣	χεχαριζ	‣	κεχάρισμαι
θεραπεύω	‣	θεθεραπευ	‣	τεθεράπευμαι

> If you want to include the number of minutes after the hour, just add καί and the number. What time is it if I say,
>
> ἐστὶν ὀκτὼ καὶ πέντε?

---

⁴ This is the only place where the true second person singular, primary passive ending appears without contraction obscuring its form. Elsewhere it is preceded by a vowel, the sigma drops out, and the vowels contract.

⁵ The third person plural perfect passive occurs only nine times in the New Testament, six of those being the form ἀφέωνται (from ἀφίημι). See Advanced Information.

⁶ "Single consonant" means that there is not another consonant immediately after it.

As you can see from looking at the Square of Stops, the stop in the right column ("aspirates") is shifting to its corresponding stop in the left column ("voiceless").[7]

voiceless	voiced	aspirates
π	β	φ
κ	γ	χ
τ	δ	θ

2. **Vocalic reduplication**. *If a verb begins with a vowel or diphthong, the vowel is lengthened.* Vocalic reduplication is identical in form to the augment in the imperfect and aorist.[8]

   ἀγαπάω   ▸   ἠγάπηκα
   αἰτέω   ▸   ἤτηκα

   It is common for a diphthong not to reduplicate. For example, the perfect form of εὑρίσκω is εὕρηκα.

   Now, when you see an initial augment / vocalic reduplication, the verb can be one of three tenses: imperfect; aorist; perfect.

   If the verb begins with *two consonants*,[9] the verb will usually undergo vocalic and not consonantal reduplication.[10]

   *γνω (γινώσκω) ▸ ἔγνωκα

3. **Compound verb**. *A compound verb reduplicates the verbal part of a compound verb,* just like the imperfect and aorist augment the verbal part of a compound.

   ἐκβάλλω   ▸   ἐκβέβληκα[11]

To say the number of minutes before the hour, use παρά. What time is it if I say,

ἐστὶν δώδεκὰ παρὰ ἐννέα ἡ ὥρα?

25.9 **Tense form.** The perfect active is the fourth tense form listed in the lexical entry, while the perfect middle / passive is the fifth.

ἀγαπάω, ἀγαπήσω, ἠγάπησα, <u>ἠγάπηκα</u>, <u>ἠγάπημαι</u>, ἠγαπήθην

Sometimes a perfect tense stem is identical to the present tense stem, while at other times it has undergone a change (such as a change in the stem vowel).

25.10 **Tense formative.** The tense formative for the perfect active is κα (λέλυκα). The perfect passive has no tense formative (λέλυμαι).

25.11 **Connecting vowel.** The perfect does not use a connecting vowel. In the active, the tense formative ends in a vowel so no connecting vowel is required. In the passive, the endings are attached directly to the stem.

---

[7] This is just the opposite of what happens to a stop followed by θη; see 24.10.

[8] However, the functions of vocalic reduplication and the augment are significantly different. Reduplication indicates the completion of an action. The augment indicates past time.

[9] This is called a "consonant cluster."

[10] If the second consonant is a lambda or rho, then the verb will usually reduplicate (γράφω ▸ γέγραφα).

[11] βέβληκα is the perfect active of βάλλω.

A good clue for recognizing the perfect middle/passive is the absence of both a tense formative and connecting vowels. This situation occurs only in the perfect middle/passive.

25.12 **Personal endings**. Because the perfect is not an augmented tense, it uses the primary personal endings. However, because of the alpha in the tense formative, the perfect active looks similar to the first aorist, which is a secondary tense.

In the middle/passive there is no connecting vowel. The final consonant of the stem and the initial consonant of the personal ending come into direct contact, and as a result the final stem consonant is often changed (e.g., γράφω ‣ γέγραμμαι). In the Advanced Information section of this chapter I have spelled out those changes. If this is too confusing, remember that in the perfect passive, the consonant immediately preceding the personal ending may be altered.

25.13 **Contract verbs**. Contract verbs lengthen their contract vowel in both the active and middle/passive, even though there is no tense formative in the middle/passive.

> ἀγαπάω ‣ ἠγάπηκα
> ἀγαπάω ‣ ἠγάπημαι

25.14 **Second perfects**. There are only a few second perfect actives in the New Testament, so they do not warrant a major discussion here. They are identical to the first perfect except that they use the tense formative α and not κα in the active. You know five verbs (along with their compound forms) that have second perfects.[12]

> ἀκούω ‣ ἀκήκοα   γράφω ‣ γέγραφα
> γίνομαι ‣ γέγονα   ἔρχομαι ‣ ἐλήλυθα
> λαμβάνω ‣ εἴληφα

There is no such thing as a second perfect in the middle/passive since there is no tense formative.

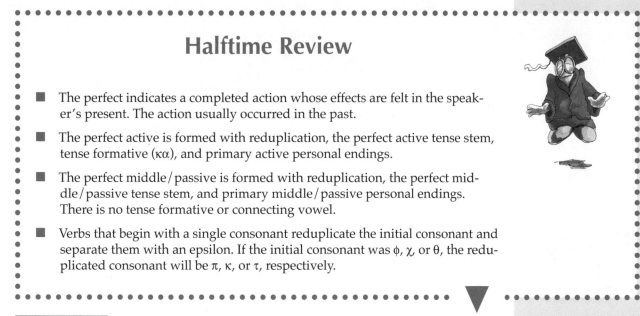

Halftime Review

- The perfect indicates a completed action whose effects are felt in the speaker's present. The action usually occurred in the past.

- The perfect active is formed with reduplication, the perfect active tense stem, tense formative (κα), and primary active personal endings.

- The perfect middle/passive is formed with reduplication, the perfect middle/passive tense stem, and primary middle/passive personal endings. There is no tense formative or connecting vowel.

- Verbs that begin with a single consonant reduplicate the initial consonant and separate them with an epsilon. If the initial consonant was φ, χ, or θ, the reduplicated consonant will be π, κ, or τ, respectively.

---

12 οἶδα actually is a second perfect.

- Verbs beginning with a consonant cluster or a vowel usually undergo a vocalic reduplication (lengthening). Although this looks like an augment, it is essentially different in function. Initial diphthongs usually do not reduplicate.

- Compound verbs reduplicate the verbal part of the word.

- Contract verbs lengthen their contract vowel in both active and middle/passive.

Middle Voice

25.15 It is time to learn the rest of the grammar pertaining to the middle voice.

- If a verb is in the *active*, then the subject does the action of the verb.

- If the verb is in the *passive*, then the subject receives the action of the verb.

- The general definition of the *middle* voice is that *the action of a verb in the middle voice in some way affects the subject*. I call this the "self-interest" nuance of the middle.

25.16 Indirect Middle is the technical name for this use of the middle. The subject does the action of the verb to the direct object, but the participation of the subject is emphasized.

> ὁ Πιλᾶτος … λαβὼν ὕδωρ ἀπενίψατο τὰς χεῖρας (*Matt 27:24*).
> Pilate took water and *washed* his hands.[13]

> δέξασθε τὸν ἔμφυτον λόγον τὸν δυνάμενον σῶσαι τὰς ψυχὰς ὑμῶν (*Jam 1:21*).
> *Receive* the implanted word, which is able to save your souls.[14]

This self-interest idea is one of the less likely options for the translation of the middle.[15] Context will show whether the self-interest nuance is present.

αἰτέω[16]	*active:*	I ask
	middle:	I ask (for myself)
βαπτίζω	*active:*	I baptize
	middle:	I dip myself
εὑρίσκω	*active:*	I find
	middle:	I obtain (for myself)

Most middle paradigms translate the middle as "I loose *for myself*," "They loose *for themselves*." The problem with learning the middle this way is that the actual force of the middle in the Koine is not normally reflexive, or else the force of the middle is so subtle that it is scarcely discernible.

---

[13] Wallace says the middle "puts a special focus on Pilate, as though this act could absolve him" (p421).

[14] This shows how difficult the middle voice is. Wallace again comments, "Although δέχομαι never occurs as an active, it should not be treated as a deponent verb. The lexical notion of receiving, welcoming connotes a special interest on the part of the subject" (421).

[15] Cf. Moule, *Idiom Book*, 24.

[16] *BDAG* does not say that αἰτέω has the self-interest sense in the New Testament, but see the exercises.

Just because a verb is in the middle does not mean the self-interest nuance is present.[17] It is possible that other verbs will have the self-interest nuance in specific contexts. As always, context must be the ultimate decider, .

In addition, some words we tend to learn as deponent (because they do not occur in an active form) are actually not deponent but are indirect middles.[18]

> If you want to say it is half past the hour, use καὶ ἥμισυς.
>
> If it is a quarter, use τέταρτος.

25.17 **Reflexive (Direct) Middle**. is the name for the reflexive use of the middle. In this case, the subject does the action of the verb and also receives the action.

> Ἰούδας ... ἀπελθὼν ἀπήγξατο *(Matt 27:5)*
>
> Judas went out and *hung himself.*

This was a common use of the middle in Classical Greek. If the subject of the verb performs an action to itself, Koine Greek usually required the reflexive pronoun (ἑαυτοῦ). This is called the **redundant middle**.[19]

> οὕτως καὶ ὑμεῖς λογίζεσθε ἑαυτοὺς [εἶναι] νεκροὺς μὲν τῇ ἁμαρτίᾳ ζῶντας δὲ τῷ θεῷ ἐν Χριστῷ Ἰησοῦ. *(Rom 6:11).*
>
> So you also must consider yourselves dead to sin and alive to God in Christ Jesus.

25.18 **Deponent Middle**. As a reminder, let me emphasize that in the majority of cases, the middle has the same meaning as the active. Either the verb is deponent (ἀποκρίνομαι, γίνομαι, δύναμαι, ἔρχομαι, πορεύομαι, etc.), or its middle meaning is active to the English mind.

25.19 Only a few verbs have both a middle deponent and a passive deponent form. For example, in the aorist γίνομαι has both a middle deponent (ἐγενόμην) and a passive deponent (ἐγενήθην) aorist form.

25.20 **Parsing**. How you parse a middle form is a bit arbitrary; but you need to be consistent, so here are my suggestions. Your teacher may prefer another system.

- ■ If you can clearly tell it is a middle (future; aorist), then say it is a middle.

---

[17] A good example of the problems caused by assuming that the Classical use of the middle is always present is found in 1 Corinthians 13:8, where Paul says that the gifts of tongues "will cease" (παύσονται). It is argued by some that because παύσονται is middle, Paul is saying the gift of tongues will cease in and of itself.

Regardless of one's views on the topic of spiritual gifts, I feel this is an incorrect interpretation of the middle. It assumes that the middle here has the Classical usage, even though *BDAG* lists no self-interest meaning for the middle of παύω. And when you look at the other eight occurrences of the verb, it is seen that the verb is a middle deponent and not reflexive. The best example is in Luke 8:24, where Jesus calms the sea. "Jesus awoke and rebuked the wind and the raging of the water and *they ceased,* and a calm took place." (ὁ δὲ διεγερθεὶς ἐπετίμησεν τῷ ἀνέμῳ καὶ τῷ κλύδωνι τοῦ ὕδατος καὶ ἐπαύσαντο καὶ ἐγένετο γαλήνη). The wind and water certainly did not cease "in and of themselves." The middle of this verb does not designate self-interest; it is deponent.

[18] If all this interests you, please read Wallace carefully (414-430).

[19] Many grammars say the middle is "reflexive," but I am uncomfortable with the term. The "direct reflexive" was common in Classical Greek but not in Koine. The only one in the New Testament is at Matt 27:5, but Moule (*Idiom Book*, 24) disputes even this one. There are a few verbs that are reflexive in the middle, but that has more to do with the meaning of the verb than the function of the middle voice.

However, if the middle is deponent, you should say "deponent" and not "middle" (or perhaps, "middle deponent"). The only way to know if a verb is deponent in the middle is to memorize it.

■ If you cannot tell it is middle (present; imperfect; perfect), for now assume it is passive or deponent. If it does not make sense in context, perhaps it is middle.

Congratulations

25.21 You now know all the tenses in the indicative. It is important that you spend some time going through the chart entitled *Tense Forms of Verbs Occurring Fifty Times or More in the New Testament* in the Appendix (pages 370-80). You need to see which forms you know and which ones you need to work on. If you can master this chart, verbs will be much easier for you.

In the website class there is also a spreadsheet of this chart, which makes it easy for you to rearrange and color-code to your heart's delight.

In the Appendix there is a summary chart of λύω in all the tenses and voices (page 357). There are also a series of charts covering all the indicative (pages 360-69). This would be a good time to review them, making sure you can recognize every form.[20]

25.22 **Master Verb Chart**. The *Master Verb Chart* is now complete for the indicative. To indicate reduplication I have simply entered λε as if you were reduplicating λύω. But remember that the perfect can also undergo vocalic reduplication to form the perfect.

Master Verb Chart

Tense	Aug/ Redup	Tense stem	Tense form.	Conn. vowel	Personal endings	1st sing paradigm
Present act		pres		o/ε	prim act	λύω
Present mid/pas		pres		o/ε	prim mid/pas	λύομαι
Imperfect act	ε	pres		o/ε	sec act	ἔλυον
Imperfect mid/pas	ε	pres		o/ε	sec mid/pas	ἐλυόμην
Future act		fut act	σ	o/ε	prim act	λύσω
Liquid fut act		fut act	εσ	o/ε	prim act	μενῶ
Future mid		fut act	σ	o/ε	prim mid/pas	πορεύσομαι
Liquid fut mid		fut act	εσ	o/ε	prim mid/pas	μενοῦμαι
1st future pas		aor pas	θησ	o/ε	prim mid/pas	λυθήσομαι
2nd future pas		aor pas	ησ	o/ε	prim mid/pas	ἀποσταλήσομαι
1st aorist act	ε	aor act	σα		sec act	ἔλυσα
Liquid aorist act	ε	aor act	α		sec act	ἔμεινα
2nd aorist act	ε	aor act		o/ε	sec act	ἔλαβον

---

[20] There is a class of verbs you will not meet until Chapter 34 whose lexical forms end in μι and not ω. This is the "athematic conjugation." Ignore these words in the charts until Chapter 34.

1st aorist mid	ε	aor act	σα		sec mid/pas		ἐλυσάμην
2nd aorist mid	ε	aor act		ο/ε	sec mid/pas		ἐγενόμην
1st aorist pas	ε	aor pas	θη		sec act		ἐλύθην
2nd aorist pas	ε	aor pas	η		sec act		ἐγράφην
1st perfect act	λε	perf act	κα		prim act		λέλυκα
2nd perfect act	λε	perf act	α		prim act		γέγονα
Perfect mid/pas	λε	perf m/p			prim mid/pas		λέλυμαι

Summary

1. The perfect indicates a completed action whose effects are felt in the speaker's present. The action usually occurred in the past.

2. The perfect active is formed with reduplication, the perfect active tense stem, tense formative (κα), and primary active personal endings.

3. The perfect middle/passive is formed with reduplication, the perfect middle/passive tense stem, and primary middle/passive personal endings. There is no tense formative or connecting vowel.

4. Verbs that begin with a single consonant reduplicate the initial consonant and separate them with an epsilon. If the initial consonant was φ, χ, or θ, the reduplicated consonant will be π, κ, or τ, respectively.

5. Verbs beginning with a consonant cluster or a vowel usually undergo a vocalic reduplication (lengthening). Although this looks like an augment, it is essentially different in function. Initial diphthongs usually do not reduplicate.

6. The perfect active uses κα for its tense formative and primary active endings. The perfect middle/passive has neither tense formative nor connecting vowels. The middle and passive forms are identical.

7. Compound verbs reduplicate the verbal part of the word.

8. Contract verbs lengthen their contract vowel in both the perfect active and perfect middle/passive.

9. The classical rule of the middle voice is that the subject does the action of the verb in some way that affects itself. Only context and the use of the word elsewhere can determine if this nuance is present in a specific verse. It cannot be automatically assumed.

   In most cases, a middle has the same meaning as the active. Either the middle is a true middle with an active meaning, or it is a deponent.

10. When parsing middles, if you can clearly tell that it is a middle, say so. If it is a middle deponent, say so. If you cannot tell whether a form is middle or passive, assume it is passive

Vocabulary

αἰτέω   I ask, demand (70; *αἰτε)
(ἤτουν), αἰτήσω, ἤτησα, ἤτηκα, -, -

αἰτέω is followed by a double accusative; both the person asked and the thing asked for are in the accusative.

μᾶλλον   more, rather (81)

When μᾶλλον is used with ἤ, ἤ is usually translated "than," not "or."

μαρτυρέω   I bear witness, testify (76; *μαρτυρε)[21]
(ἐμαρτύρουν), μαρτυρήσω, ἐμαρτύρησα, μεμαρτύρηκα, μεμαρτύρημαι, ἐμαρτυρήθην

Total word count in the New Testament:	138,162
Number of words learned to date:	269
Number of word occurrences in this chapter:	227
Number of word occurrences to date:	106,481
Percent of total word count in the New Testament:	77.07%

Previous Words

present	perfect active	perfect middle/passive
Pattern 1a verbs		
ἀκούω	ἀκήκοα	–
ἄρχομαι	–	–
δύναμαι	–	–
διδάσκω	–	–
ἔχω	ἔσχηκα	–
θέλω	–	–
λύω	–	λέλυμαι
πιστεύω	πεπίστευκα	πεπίστευμαι
πορεύομαι	–	πεπόρευμαι
Pattern 1b Verbs (Contract Stems)		
ἀγαπάω	ἠγάπηκα	ἠγάπημαι
ἀκολουθέω	ἠκολούθηκα	–
γεννάω	γεγέννηκα	γεγέννημαι
ζάω	–	–
ζητέω	–	–
καλέω[22]	κέκληκα	κέκλημαι

---

[21] The cognate noun μάρτυς means *witness*. A *martyr* is one who witnesses to the faith by dying.

[22] The same basic change has occurred to both perfect forms (see βάλλω below). The root of καλέω is *καλεό. The stem vowel (ablaut) and digamma have dropped out, and the final epsilon has lengthened to eta.

λαλέω	λελάληκα	λελάλημαι
ὁράω	ἑώρακα	–
πληρόω	πεπλήρωκα	πεπλήρωμαι
ποιέω	πεποίηκα	πεποίημαι
προσκυνέω	–	–
τηρέω	τετήρηκα	τετήρημαι

Pattern 1c Verbs (Stems Ending in a Stop)

ἄγω	–	–
βαπτίζω	–	βεβάπτισμαι
βλέπω	–	–
γράφω	γέγραφα	γέγραμμαι
δοξάζω	–	δεδόξασμαι
κηρύσσω	–	–
λαμβάνω	εἴληφα	–
προσέρχομαι	προσελήλυθα	–
προσεύχομαι	–	–
συνάγω	–	σύνηγμαι,

present	*perfect active*	*perfect middle/passive*
σῴζω	σέσωκα	σέσωσμαι[23]
ὑπάγω	–	–

Patern 3 Verbs (Liquid Stems)

αἴρω	ἦρκα	ἦρμαι
ἀποκτείνω	–	–
ἀποστέλλω	ἀπέσταλκα	ἀπέσταλμαι
ἐγείρω	–	ἐγήγερμαι
κρίνω	κέκρικα	κέκριμαι
μένω	μεμένηκα[24]	–
χαίρω	–	–

Pattern 4 Verbs (Ablaut and Stem Change)

ἀπέρχομαι	ἀπελήλυθα	–
ἀποθνῄσκω	–	–
βάλλω[25]	βέβληκα	βέβλημαι
γίνομαι	γέγονα	γεγένημαι
γινώσκω	ἔγνωκα	ἔγνωσμαι
ἐκβάλλω	–	–
ἔρχομαι	ἐλήλυθα	–

---

[23] σῴζω occurs in the New Testament once in the perfect passive indicative, and the sigma is not inserted before the μαι (σέσωται, Acts 4:9). It occurs twice as a participle, with the sigma inserted (σεσῳσμένοι, Eph 2:5, 8).

[24] The perfect of μένω does not occur in the New Testament, but the pluperfect does once, and the pluperfect is formed from the perfect tense stem.

[25] The same basic change has occurred to both perfect forms (see καλέω above). The root of βάλλω is *βαλ. The stem vowel has dropped out (ablaut), and the eta has been inserted after the stem.

εὑρίσκω	εὕρηκα	–
λέγω	εἴρηκα	εἴρημαι[26]
πίνω	πέπωκα	–

Advanced Information

25.23 **Stems ending in a stop**. Verbal roots that end in a stop undergo significant change in the perfect middle/passive because they are placed immediately next to the consonant of the personal ending. Here is the full paradigm of changes (cf. Smyth, #409).

	labial (π β φ)	*velar (κ γ χ)*	*dental (τ δ θ)*
	γράφω	διώκω	πείθω
μαι	γέγραμμαι	δεδίωγμαι	πέπεισμαι
σαι	γέγραψαι	δεδίωξαι	πέπεισαι
ται	γέγραπται	δεδίωκται	πέπεισται
μεθα	γεγράμμεθα	δεδιώγμεθα	πεπείσμεθα
σθε	γέγραφθε	δεδίωχθε	πέπεισθε
νται	εἰσὶ γεγραμμένοι	εἰσὶ δεδιωγμένοι	εἰσὶ πεπεισμένοι

In the second personal plural, in the labials the expected psi has become a phi (γέγραφσθε ‣ γεγραψθε ‣ γέγραφθε), and in the velars the expected xi has become a chi (δεδιωκσθε ‣ δεδιωξθε ‣ δεδίωχθε), contrary to the normal rules.

As you can see, Greek forms the third person plural differently. This is called a "periphrastic" construction, using a form of εἰμί and a participle. I will discuss this in Chapter 30.

25.24 **Pluperfect**. There is one more tense that I should mention, which is called the "pluperfect." It does not occur frequently, so some teachers may prefer not to discuss it now. There are 28 verbs in the New Testament that appear as a pluperfect a total of 86 times.[27]

The pluperfect is used to describe an action that was completed and whose effects are felt at a time after the completion but before the time of the speaker.

The pluperfect is formed from the perfect tense stem. Preceding the reduplication can be an augment, although this is not necessary, so I have placed the augment in parentheses. The first pluperfect is formed with the tense formative (κ) but the second pluperfect has none. Following the tense formative are the connecting vowels ει and secondary endings.[28]

---

[26] The perfect tense stem is built from the root *ερ, as is the aorist passive.

[27] οἶδα occurs 33 times as a pluperfect, but its pluperfect functions as an imperfect or aorist (cf. 22.18).

[28] The pluperfect active occurs 79 times, the middle/passive only 7.

active

	1 pluperfect	*2 pluperfect*
1 sg	(ἐ)λελύκειν	(ἐ)γεγράφειν
2 sg	(ἐ)λελύκεις	(ἐ)γεγράφεις
3 sg	(ἐ)λελύκει(ν)	(ἐ)γεγράφει(ν)
1 pl	(ἐ)λελύκειμεν	(ἐ)γεγράφειμεν
2 pl	(ἐ)λελύκειτε	(ἐ)γεγράφειτε
3 pl	(ἐ)λελύκεισαν	(ἐ)γεγράφεισαν

middle/passive

The middle/passive of the pluperfect follows the same pattern as the active except that it is formed from the perfect middle/passive tense form, and does not use a tense formative or connecting vowel.

	1 pluperfect
1 sg	(ἐ)λελύμην
2 sg	(ἐ)λέλυσο
3 sg	(ἐ)λέλυτο
1 pl	(ἐ)λελύμεθα
2 pl	(ἐ)λέλυσθε
3 pl	(ἐ)λέλυντο

25.25 **Future perfect**. The future perfect appears six times in the New Testament, every time in a periphrastic construction (see Chapter 30; Matt 16:19; 18:18; John 20:23). There is a question as to their precise meaning; see the survey by D. A. Carson[29] and the *Exegetical Insight* for Chapter 15.

Exegesis

1. Sometimes the emphasis of the perfect tense verb is on the fact that the action was completed (consummative, extensive).

> τὸν καλὸν ἀγῶνα ἠγώνισμαι, τὸν δρόμον τετέλεκα *(2 Tim 4:7).*
> I *have fought* the good fight, I *have finished* the race.

> ἡ ἀγάπη τοῦ θεοῦ ἐκκέχυται ἐν ταῖς καρδίαις ἡμῶν *(Rom 5:5).*
> God's love *has been poured* into our hearts.

2. Other times the emphasis is on the resulting state of the action (intensive) and is generally translated with the English present.

> ἄνθρωπε, ἀφέωνταί σοι αἱ ἁμαρτίαι σου *(Luke 5:20).*
> Man, your sins *are forgiven* you.

---

[29] D. A. Carson, "Matthew," *The Expositor's Bible Commentary* (Grand Rapids: Zondervan, 1995) 8:370–72.

Overview 5

Chapters 26 – 30

In this section you will be learning the Greek participle. Participles are verbal adjectives; once you can grasp that fact, the rest is pretty easy. You already know all the case endings they use. Their most basic translation is to append "-ing" to the verb.

Chapter 26

This chapter is an overview of all the participial grammar you will need to know. Participles are formed on verbs, to which is added the participial morpheme and case endings. A "morpheme" is the smallest unit of meaning. The participial morphemes below are in blue.

- λυ + ο + ντ + ες ▸ λύοντες ("loosing")

- πιστευ + σα + ντ + ες ▸ πιστεύσαντες ("believing")

- πεποιη + κ + οτ + ες ▸ πεποιηκότες ("having believed")

There are two basic types of participles.

- An adverbial participle modifies the meaning of the verb, just like an adverb.

- An adjectival participle modifies a noun or pronoun, just like an adjective. It can also function as a noun, just like an adjective.

There is no absolute time outside of the indicative system. A verbal form built on the non-indicative present tense stem does not necessaily describe an action occuring in the present. The only significance of verbs outside the indicative is aspect.

- Forms built on the present tense stem indicate a continuous action.

- Forms built on the aorist tense stem indicate an undefined action.

- Forms built on the perfect tense stem indicate a completed action.

This is true for all verbal forms outside the indicative.

Chapter 27

When participles can function as adverbs, the force of their meaning is directed toward the verb; they will agree in case, number, and gender with a word, normally the subject. Adverbial participles are always anarthrous, i.e., they are not preceeded by an article.

ὁ ἄνθρωπος ἀπέθανε διδάσκων τὴν κοινήν.

The man died *while teaching* Koine.

While participles do not designate absolute time, they do designate relative time; the time of the participle is relative to the time of the main verb. The present participle indicates an action occuring at the same time as the main verb.

To help you earn the forms of the participle, you will be asked to memorize six forms for each tense/voice combination. For example, here are the memory forms for the present active.

	masc	*fem*	*neut*
nom sg	ων	ουσα	ον
gen sg	οντος	ουσης	οντος

Here is the full paradigm.

	3 *masc*	1 *fem*	3 *neut*
nom sg	λύων	λύουσα	λῦον
gen sg	λύοντος	λυούσης	λύοντος
dat sg	λύοντι	λυούσῃ	λύοντι
acc sg	λύοντα	λύουσαν	λῦον
nom pl	λύοντες	λύουσαι	λύοντα
gen pl	λυόντων	λυουσῶν	λυόντων
dat pl	λύουσι(ν)	λυούσαις	λύουσι(ν)
acc pl	λύοντας	λυούσας	λύοντα

Chapter 28

Participles built on the aorist tense stem indicate an undefined action. Because there is no absolute time, the augment does not occur.

> *Unaugmented first aorist tense stem + Tense formative +*
> *Participle morpheme + Case endings*
>
> *active:*   λυ + σα + ντ + ες ‣ λύσαντες
> *middle:*   λυ + σα + μενο + ι ‣ λυσάμενοι
> *passive:* λυ + θε + ντ + ες ‣ λυθέντες

The aorist participle indicates an action occurring prior to the time of the main verb.

Chapter 29

When participles function adjectivally, their form is the same as adverbial participles except that they tend to be preceded by the article and are often translated as a relative clause.

> ὁ διδάσκαλός μου ὁ <u>λέγων τῷ ὀχλῷ</u> ἐστιν ἄγγελος.
> My teacher, *who is speaking to the crowd*, is an angel.

Chapter 30

Finally, participles build on the perfect tense stem indicate a completed action with ongoing results. <u>πεποιηκότες</u> could be translated, "having believed."

Chapter 26

Introduction to Participles

Overview

In this chapter you will learn that:

- a participle is an "-ing" word like "eating," sleeping," "procrastinating";

- a participle is a verbal adjective, sharing characteristics of both a verb and an adjective;

- as a verb, a participle has tense (present, aorist, perfect) and voice (active, middle, passive);

- as an adjective, a participle agrees with the noun it modifies in case, number, and gender.

English

26.1 Participles are formed by adding "-ing" to a verb.[1]

> "The man, *eating* by the window, is my Greek teacher."
> "After *eating*, I will go to bed."

26.2 *Participles are verbal adjectives.* A participle has verbal characteristics.

> "*While eating*, my Greek teacher gave us the final."

In this example, *eating* is a participle that tells us something about the verb *gave*. The teacher gave us the final while he was still eating. (*While* specifies when the action of the participle occurred.)

A participle also has adjectival aspects. "The woman, *sitting by the window*, is my Greek teacher." In this example, *sitting* is a participle telling us something about the noun "woman."

26.3 When a participle has modifiers such as a direct object or an adverb, the participle and modifiers form a **participial phrase**. In translation it is

---

[1] More accurately stated, "-ing" is added to form the active participle. "-ed" is added to form the passive participle. "Moved by the sermon, they all began to cry."

important to identify the beginning and the end of the participial phrase, much like you do with a relative clause.

26.4 In a sentence like, "While *eating*, he saw her." English requires that "he" is the one who is eating, not "her," since "he" is closer in word order to the participle. If the sentence were, "He saw her while eating," then "she" is doing the eating. Word order is often critical in English.

Greek

26.5 Almost everything said above about the English participle applies to the Greek as well. It is important to realize this. The Greek participle can be somewhat frustrating to learn if you do not see its many similarities with English.

Also realize that it is essential to learn the Greek participle if you are to translate the New Testament with any proficiency. Participles are common and important.

Chapters 26 through 30 deal with the participle. Although the chapters may seem lengthy, there is not that much new to learn in each one. Most of the grammar of participles is in this chapter, and the majority of the other four chapters deals with the form of the participle. And participles follow the normal first, second, and third declension inflection patterns, so there are no new case endings to learn.

Do not memorize the Greek forms in this chapter. They are just illustrations. Concentrate on learning the grammar. Here are the essentials of participial grammar.

26.6 **Adverbial and adjectival**. Because a participle is a verbal adjective, it shares the characteristics of both verbs and adjectives.

■ As a *verb* participles have tense (present, aorist, perfect) and voice (active, middle, passive).

■ As an *adjective* they agree with the word they are modifying in case, number, and gender.

It may sound strange at first to think that a word can have both tense and case, but the Greek participle does.

26.7 **Formation**. A participle can be built on any verb.

■ The participle λύοντες is built on λύω.

■ The participle πιστεύσαντες is built on πιστεύω.

■ The participle πεποιηκότες is built on ποιέω.

26.8 To form a participle, you start with the verb, sometimes add a connecting vowel, then add the **participle morpheme** and case endings.

> λυ + ο + ντ + ες ‣ λύοντες
>
> πιστευ + σα + ντ + ες ‣ πιστεύσαντες
>
> πεποιη + κ + οτ + ες ‣ πεποιηκότες

A "morpheme" is the smallest unit of meaning in the formation of a word. The participle morphemes above are ντ and οτ.

English has both *participles* and *gerunds*. When the -ing form is functioning adjectivally or adverbially, it is considered a participle. If it is functioning as a noun, it is considered a gerund. The two are identical in form.

Greek has no gerund, so we use the term *participle* to describe what in English are gerunds and participles. Actually, Greek uses an infinitive (Chapter 32) when English uses a gerund. For example, the sentence "Seeing is believing" in Greek would be "To see is to believe."

26.9 **Aspect**. The key to understanding the meaning of participles is to recognize that their significance is primarily one of aspect, i.e., type of action. This is the genius, the essence, of participles. They do not necessarily indicate when an action occurs ("time": past, present). Becausee there are three aspects, there are three participles.

- The *present* participle describes a *continuous* action and is formed from the present stem of a verb.

- The *aorist* participle describes an action without commenting on the nature of the action (*undefined*) and is formed from the aorist stem of a verb.

- The *perfect* participle describes a *completed action with present effects* and is formed from the perfect stem of a verb.

	aspect	tense stem
present	continuous	present
aorist	undefined	aorist
perfect	completed	perfect

26.10 **Two basic uses of the participle**. Because a participle is a verbal adjective, it performs one of two basic functions depending on whether its verbal or its adjectival aspect is emphasized.

- If it is an **adverbial participle**, the action described by the participle is primarily directed toward the verb. This kind of participle is usually translated with an adverbial phrase.

  "While studying for his Greek final, Ian fell asleep."

- If it is an **adjectival participle**, the action described by the participle primarily modifies a noun or pronoun. This kind of participle is usually translated as an adjectival phrase.

  "The book *lying on the window sill* belongs to Kathy."

Context determines whether a participle is adverbial or adjectival. Its form does not vary.

Verbal Side of the Participle

26.11 **Tense**. Participles can be built on the present, aorist, or perfect tense stems.[2] Memorize the morphemes.[3] They are in blue.

- The **present** participle λύοντες is built on the present tense stem of λύω (λυ + ο + ντ + ες).

- The **aorist** participle λύσαντες is built on the aorist tense stem of λύω (λυ + σα + ντ + ες). Notice that there is no augment.

- The **perfect** participle λελυκότες is built on the perfect tense stem of λύω (λε + λυ + κ + οτ + ες).

---

[2]   There also is a participle that is built on the future tense stem, but it occurs only twelve times in the New Testament. See Advanced Information in Chapter 28.

[3]   I use the nominative plural forms since they show the unmodified participle morpheme.

26.12 **Voice**. A participle can be active, middle, passive, or deponent. If the verb is deponent, its corresponding participle will be deponent. Greek uses different participle morphemes for the different voices.

- ■ ἀκούοντες is active, which means the word it is modifying is doing the action of the participle.

- ■ ἀκουόμενοι is passive, which means the word it is modifying is receiving the action of the participle.

- ■ ἐρχόμενοι is deponent, because ἔρχομαι, the verb on which it is built, is deponent.

Adjectival Side of the Participle

26.13 As an adjective, the participle agrees with the noun it modifies in case, number, and gender.

> The man, eating the chocolate, is my brother.

If this were in Greek, "eating" would be nominative singular masculine because it is modifying "man" (ἄνθρωπος), which is nominative singular masculine.

> ἔβλεψε τὸν ἄνθρωπον τὸν διδάσκοντα τὴν κοινήν.
>
> He saw the man *who was teaching* the Koine.

Because the participle διδάσκοντα is modifying ἄνθρωπον, and because ἄνθρωπον is accusative singular masculine, διδάσκοντα is also accusative singular masculine. This is how an adjective behaves, so the grammar is not new.

26.14 **Subject**. A participle technically does not have a subject. However, because a participle must agree in case, number, and gender with the word it is modifying, it is a relatively easy task to discover who or what is doing the action of the participle.

For example, if you were to say in Greek, "He saw her, while studying," the participle "studying" would be either nominative masculine (if he was studying) or accusative feminine (if she was studying). Greek does not use word order as does English in this situation.

In the example ἔβλεψε τὸν ἄνθρωπον τὸν διδάσκοντα τὴν κοινήν, you can tell that it was not the "He" (ἔβλεψε) who was teaching but the "man" (ἄνθρωπον), since the participle (διδάσκοντα) is accusative. If "He" were teaching, the participle would be διδάσκων (nominative).

Other Elements of the Participle

26.15 **Modifiers, etc.** A participle has other characteristics that it shares with verbs.

It can have a direct object in the accusative. "After studying *her Greek*, the student thought she had died and gone to heaven." "Greek" is the direct object of the participle "studying" and would be in the accusative.

A participle can also have modifiers such as prepositional phrases, adverbs, etc. "After studying *quietly for a long time*, I finally understood the paradigm." "Quietly" is an adverb, and "for a long time" is a prepositional phrase, both modifying the participle "studying."

26.16 **Negation**. The negation οὐ is normally used in the indicative. Since the participle is not an indicative form, participles are usually negated by μή. It has the same meaning as οὐ.

26.17 **No personal endings**. You will notice that the participle does not use personal verb endings. It is not a finite verbal form and therefore is not limited by a subject.

26.18 **Parsing**. Because the participle is a verbal adjective, there are eight things to remember. I suggest you start with its verbal characteristics and then move on to its adjectival. (Teachers will differ on their preferences, so be sure to ask.)

Tense, voice, "participle"[4] — case, number, gender — lexical form, meaning of inflected form.

ἀκούοντος: present active participle, genitive singular masculine, from ἀκούω, meaning "hearing."

The Following Chapters

26.19 To make the participle easier to learn, I have separated its basic uses into different chapters.

- Chapter 27 deals with present adverbial participles.
- Chapter 28 discusses aorist adverbial participles.
- Chapter 29 covers the adjectival use of participles.
- Chapter 30 introduces the perfect participle.

You have now learned the majority of the grammar of participles. It remains only to learn their forms, and you already know all their case endings from your study of adjectives.

---

[4]   A participle is not technically a "mood" like the indicative, but for simplicity's sake say it is a participle where you normally place the mood.

Summary

1. A participle is a verbal adjective, sharing characteristics of both a verb and an adjective.

2. As a verb, it has tense (present, aorist, perfect) and voice (active, middle, passive). If the verb is deponent, its corresponding participle will be deponent.

3. As an adjective, it agrees with the noun it modifies in case, number, and gender.

The Apostles' Creed

Πιστεύω εἰς Θεὸν Πατέρα,

    παντοκράτορα, ποιητὴν οὐρανοῦ καὶ γῆς.

Καὶ εἰς Ἰησοῦν Χρίστον, υἱὸν αὐτοῦ τὸν μονογενῆ, τὸν κύριον ἡμῶν,

    τὸν συλληφθέντα ἐκ πνεύματος ἁγίου,

    γεννηθέντα ἐκ Μαρίας τῆς παρθένου,

    παθόντα ἐπὶ Ποντίου Πιλάτου,

    σταυρωθέντα, θανόντα, καὶ ταφέντα,

    τῇ τρίτῃ ἡμέρᾳ ἀναστάντα ἀπὸ τῶν νεκρῶν,

    ἀνελθόντα εἰς τοὺς οὐρανούς,

    καθεζόμενον ἐν δεξιᾷ θεοῦ πατρὸς παντοδυνάμου,

    ἐκεῖθεν ἐρχόμενον κρῖναι ζῶντας καὶ νεκρούς.

Πιστεύω εἰς τὸ Πνεῦμα τὸ Ἅγιον,

ἁγίαν καθολικὴν ἐκκλησίαν,

ἁγίων κοινωνίαν,

ἄφεσιν ἁμαρτιῶν,

σαρκὸς ἀνάστασιν,

ζωὴν αἰώνιον.

Ἀμήν.

Chapter 27

Present (Continuous) Adverbial Participles

Exegetical Insight

At the heart of the Christian experience is a radical transformation from what we were by nature into what God intends us to become by grace. Nowhere is that transformation stated with greater clarity than in 2 Corinthians 3:18. And at the heart of this verse is a present middle participle that reveals the secret of Christian growth and maturity.

What this verse tells us is that a wonderful change is taking place in the life of the believer. Although a veil remains over the mind of the unbeliever (v. 15), that veil is lifted for those who are in Christ (vv. 14, 16). They are being changed into the image of Christ from one degree of glory to the next.

The secret of divine transformation lies in the participle κατοπτριζόμενοι. It comes from a verb which, in the middle, originally meant "to look into a mirror." Then it came to mean "to gaze upon" or "to contemplate." Taking the participle in the instrumental sense we read, "We all are being changed into the image of Christ *by beholding* the glory of the Lord."

Transformation into the likeness of Christ is the inevitable result of gazing upon his glory. We become like that which dominates our thoughts and affections. Like Nathaniel Hawthorne's "great stone face," which shaped the life of the one who spent his days looking at that craggy representation of all that was held to be good and pure, so also does the believer gradually take on a family resemblance to his or her Lord as he spends his time contemplating the glory of God.

Note that the participle is present tense. It is a continual contemplation that effects the transformation. As the participle is present tense, so also is the finite verb "are being changed" (μετα-μορφούμεθα). The transformation keeps pace with the contemplation. They are inextricably bound together. By continuing to behold the glory of the Lord we are continually being transformed into his image.

Robert H. Mounce

Overview

In this chapter you will learn that:

■ there is no time significance to a participle;

■ the present participle is built on the present tense stem of the verb and indicates a continuous action;

■ the present participle is formed with the present tense stem + connecting vowel + participle morpheme + case ending;

■ to translate you must first discover the participle's aspect, voice, and meaning. You can usually translate it with the "-ing" form of the verb, sometimes with the key words "while" or "because."

Greek

27.1 **Summary of the present adverbial participle.**

   a. The present participle is built on the *present tense stem* of the verb.

   b. It describes a *continuous* action.

      It will often be difficult to carry this nuance into your translation, but this must be the foremost consideration in your mind. Everything else pales in light of the aspect of the participle.

   c. In this chapter you are learning the adverbial participle, which means that *the action described by the participle is related to the verb*.

      The adverbial participle is usually translated as an adverbial clause. Use the -ing form of the participle in translation and, if appropriate, preface the translation of the participle with the adverb *while* or *because*.[1]

        ὁ ἄνθρωπος ἀπέθανε διδάσκων τὴν κοινήν.

        The man died *while teaching* Koine.

      He was currently teaching the language when he died. He died happy!

   d. Even though the participle is adverbial, it still *agrees with a noun or pronoun in case, number, and gender*.[2] For example, if the noun is ἄνθρωπος, the participle would be διδάσκων (nominative singular masculine).

   e. If the participle is *active*, the word it modifies does the action of the participle. If the participle is *passive,* the word it modifies receives the action of the participle.

   f. The adverbial participle is always *anarthrous* (i.e., not preceded by the article).

---

[1] As you advance in your understanding of the language, you will find that there are other ways to translate this participle, but at your present stage this practice is recommended. For you grammarians, it should be noted that if you do use "because," then in English you end up with an adverbial clause, not a participial clause.

[2] Usually the pronoun is implied in the verb as its subject.

27.2 Most grammars use the term "present" participle because this participle is built on the present tense stem of the verb. This nomenclature is helpful in learning the form of the participle. However, it tends to do a serious disservice because the student may infer that the present participle describes an action occurring in the present time, which it may not. It describes a continuous action. Because the participle is not in the indicative, there is no time significance to the participle.[3] I suggest adopting the terminology "continuous participle" because it rightly emphasizes the true significance of the participle that is built on the present tense stem: its aspect.

27.3   **Summary chart: present (continuous) participle**

> *Present tense stem + Connecting vowel +*
>
> *Participle morpheme + Case endings*
>
> πιστευ + ο + ντ + ες ▸ πιστεύοντες

To form a participle you add the participle morpheme to the end of the tense stem (with connecting vowel), and add the case ending to the participle morpheme.

Participles are formed from only four morphemes (which undergo some variation in the different tenses and genders). They must be memorized.

■ ντ is the usual active morpheme. It appears as ντ in the masculine and neuter, and is third declension.

　　λύοντες, λύοντα

■ ουσα is the active morpheme in the present feminine.[4] In the active participles, the feminine participle morpheme is always different from the masculine and neuter. The feminine participle is first declension in all tenses.

　　λύουσαι

■ μενο/η is the middle/passive morpheme.[5]

　　λυόμενος, λυομένη, λυόμενον

---

[3]   There is an implied time relationship between the time of the participle and the time of the main verb, but it is secondary to the true significance of the participle. See Advanced Information.

[4]   ουσα and ντ are morphologically related. If you want to learn why the changes are so drastic, see *MBG*, 91.

[5]   The slash means it sometimes is μενο (masculine and neuter) and other times μενη (feminine).

　　Advanced information: the actual morpheme is μεν; but in order to function as a first and second declension form it had to end with a vowel, so the usual declension vowels were added.

27.4 Participle Morpheme Chart[6]

	masc	*fem*	*neut*
act	ντ	ουσα	ντ
mid/pas	μενο	μενη	μενο

There are about 13 million native Greek speakers worldwide. Over 10 million live in Greece, with 5 million of those in Athens. Ελληνικά is the modern name of the language "Greek." "Modern Greek" uses the word of "new": Νέα ᾿Ελληνικα.

Learn to view the participle morpheme as an important indicator, much like the tense formatives.

- When you see a "οντ + case ending," you can be quite sure the word is an active participle.

- When you see a "ομενο/η + case ending," it is probably a middle/passive participle.

Present (Continuous) Participle: Active

27.5 Chart

Modern Greek was updated in 1982 with the removal of breathing marks and all accents except for the stress mark. The simplified system is called μονοτονικό.

> *Present tense stem + Connecting vowel +*
>
> *Active participle morpheme + Case endings*
>
> πιστευ + ο + ντ + ες ‣ πιστεύοντες

27.6 Paradigm: Present active participle.
The active participle morpheme in the masculine and neuter is ντ, which, when joined with the connecting vowel, looks like οντ. In the feminine the οντ has been replaced by ουσα.

	3	*1*	*3*
	masc	*fem*	*neut*
nom sg	λύων[7]	λύουσα	λῦον[8]
gen sg	λύοντος	λυούσης[9]	λύοντος
dat sg	λύοντι	λυούσῃ	λύοντι
acc sg	λύοντα	λύουσαν	λῦον

---

[6] οτ is the active morpheme used with the perfect. You will meet it in Chapter 30.

[7] No case ending is used, the tau drops off because it cannot stand at the end of a word (Noun Rule 8), and the omicron lengthens to omega to compensate for the loss (*λυ + οντ + – ‣ λυον ‣ λύων).

[8] As with the nominative singular masculine, no case ending is used, the tau drops out (Noun Rule 8), but in the neuter the connecting vowel does not lengthen.

[9] As you will remember, if the letter before the final stem vowel is epsilon, iota, or rho, then the genitive stays ας. Otherwise, it shifts to ης (7.14).

nom pl	λύοντες	λύουσαι	λύοντα
gen pl	λυόντων	λυουσῶν	λυόντων
dat pl	λύουσι(ν)[10]	λυούσαις	λύουσι(ν)[10]
acc pl	λύοντας	λυούσας	λύοντα

Notice how similar the endings are to those of πᾶς.

27.7 **Six forms**. One of the keys to learning the participle is to memorize the main six forms of each participle as listed below (nominative and genitive singular, all three genders, with the connecting vowel and case endings). Once you see the changes between nominative and genitive forms, it is easy to recognize the other forms. You may want to list the dative plural under the genitive singular forms as well, especially for third declension forms.

What would you think the passive of εἰμί would be? How would you translate it? Not possible, is it? There can be no passive form of εἰμί.

	masc	*fem*	*neut*
nom sg	ων	ουσα	ον
gen sg	οντος	ουσης	οντος

27.8 **Contract verbs**. Contract verbs are regular in their participial forms. The contract vowel contracts with the connecting vowel, as it does in the indicative.

ἀγαπα + οντος ▸ ἀγαπῶντος

27.9 **εἰμί**. The active forms of εἰμί look like the participle morpheme with case endings. They always have a smooth breathing. Translate them with the English participle "being."

27.10 **Paradigm: Present active participle of εἰμί**

	3 *masc*	*1* *fem*	*3* *neut*
nom sg	ὤν	οὖσα	ὄν
gen sg	ὄντος	οὔσης	ὄντος
dat sg	ὄντι	οὔσῃ	ὄντι
acc sg	ὄντα	οὖσαν	ὄν
nom pl	ὄντες	οὖσαι	ὄντα
gen pl	ὄντων	οὐσῶν	ὄντων
dat pl	οὖσι(ν)	οὔσαις	οὖσι(ν)
acc pl	ὄντας	οὔσας	ὄντα

---

[10] The ντ drops out because of the sigma, and the omicron lengthens to ου in order to compensate for the loss (οντσι ▸ οσι ▸ ουσι). Be sure not to confuse this form with the third person plural indicative (λύουσι, "they loose").

Present Participle: Middle/Passive

27.11 Chart

> *Present tense stem + Connecting vowel +*
>
> *Middle/passive participle morpheme + Case endings*
>
> λυ + ο + μενο + ι ‣ λυόμενοι

27.12 Paradigm: Present middle/passive participle. The middle/passive participle morpheme is **μενο/η**, which, when joined with the connecting vowel, looks like ομενο/η.

	2 masc	1 fem	2 neut
nom sg	λυόμενος	λυομένη	λυόμενον
gen sg	λυομένου	λυομένης	λυομένου
dat sg	λυομένῳ	λυομένη	λυομένῳ
acc sg	λυόμενον	λυομένην	λυόμενον
nom pl	λυόμενοι	λυόμεναι	λυόμενα
gen pl	λυομένων	λυομένων	λυομένων
dat pl	λυομένοις	λυομέναις	λυομένοις
acc pl	λυομένους	λυομένας	λυόμενα

	masc	fem	neut
nom sg	ομενος	ομενη	ομενον
gen sg	ομενου	ομενης	ομενου

Halftime Review

- Be sure you understand 27.1 well.

- The present (continuous) active participle is built from the present tense stem and the active participle morphemes. The memory forms are ων, ουσα, ον, οντος, ουσης, οντος.

- Participles from contract verbs and εἰμί are straight forward.

- The present (continuous) middle/passive participle is built from the present tense stem and the middle/passive participle morpheme. The memory forms are ομενος, ομενη, ομενον, ομενου, ομενης, ομενου.

Translation Procedure

27.13 **Initial questions.** You should ask the following three questions of any participle before attempting a translation.

Here are some cities in modern Greece you will recognize.

Ἀθήνα

Θεσσαλονίκη

Κόρινθος

Φίλιπποι

Βέροια

1. **Aspect?** If the participle is formed on the present tense stem, then it is a present participle. This means that your translation should be continuous if possible. (All the participles you will meet in this chapter and the next are continuous.)

2. **Voice?** The voice of a participle will be either active, middle, or passive, depending on the verb's stem and participle morpheme. (Do not forget about deponent verbs.)

3. **Meaning?** What does the lexical form of the verb mean? This includes finding the participle's case, number, and gender so you can see which word it is modifying.

27.14 **Translation.** Once you have the answers to all three questions, you can understand what the participle is saying. There are different ways to translate an adverbial participle, but the following three are common. Context will show you which one to use.

■ It is easiest to translate with the -ing form of the English verb.

> παραγίνεται Ἰωάννης ὁ βαπτιστὴς <u>κηρύσσων</u> ἐν τῇ ἐρήμῳ *(Matt 3:1)*.

> John the Baptist came, *preaching* in the desert.

If the participle is passive, use "being" and the English past participle.

> τί ἐξήλθατε εἰς τὴν ἔρημον θεάσασθαι; κάλαμον ὑπὸ ἀνέμου <u>σαλευόμενον</u>; *(Matt 11:7)*

> What did you go out into the wilderness to see? A reed *being shaken* by the wind?

If you are struggling to translate a participle, be satisfied with using "ing." Finish translating the verse, and then come back and see if you want to refine your translation with the options below.

■ Some adverbial participles require using the key word "while" before the -ing form. This is called the **temporal** use of the participle.

> <u>παράγων</u> εἶδεν Λευὶν τὸν τοῦ Ἀλφαίου *(Mark 2:14)*.

> *While passing by,* he saw Levi the son of Alphaeus.

■ Adverbial participles can give the *cause* or *reason* for something, and the key word "because" may be used. This is called the **causal** use of the participle.

> Ἰωσὴφ ... δίκαιος <u>ὢν</u> ... ἐβουλήθη λάθρα ἀπολῦσαι αὐτήν *(Matt 1:19)*.

> Joseph, *because he was* righteous, decided to divorce her quietly.

As you will see later, there are other uses of the participle and other ways to translate it, but these are sufficient for the time being.

It will often be impossible to convey the full force of the participle's aspect in your English translation, but you can in your preaching and teaching.

27.15 Participle Morpheme Chart. Memorize this chart carefully. One more row will be added in Chapter 30.

morpheme	tense/voice	case endings
ντ	active; aorist passive	3-1-3
μενο/η	middle; middle/passive	2-1-2

ντ is used in all active forms (except perfect, Chapter 30) and in the aorist passive. μεν is used in all middle forms and in all middle/passive forms.

27.16 Master Participle Chart. Just as there was with indicative verbs, so now you have a master chart for participles, showing how each form is put together. Memorize this with the same care that you did the Master Verb Chart.

tense & voice	redup	stem	t.f. c.v.	morpheme	nom. plural	six memory forms
present active		present	ο	ντ / ουσα	λέγοντες	ων, ουσα, ον οντος, ουσης, οντος
present mid/pas		present	ο	μενο/η	λεγόμενοι	ομενος, ομενη, ομενον ομενου, ομενης, ομενου

Summary

1. The present (continuous) participle is built on the present tense stem of the verb and indicates a continuous action. There is no time significance to a participle.

2. An adverbial participle describes an action that is related to the verb. Its form is determined by the word it modifies.

3. The adverbial participle is anarthrous.

4. The Participle Morpheme Chart and the Master Participle Chart (above).

5. The participle of εἰμί looks like the participle morpheme with a case ending, always with smooth breathing.

6. To translate you must first discover a participle's aspect, voice, and meaning. You can usually translate a present participle with the "-ing" form of the verb, sometimes with the key words "while" or "because."

Vocabulary

ἀναβαίνω	I go up, come up (82; ἀνά + *βα) (ἀνέβαινον), ἀναβήσομαι, ἀνέβην, ἀναβέβηκα, -, -
ἀρχιερεύς, -έως, ὁ	chief priest, high priest (122; *ἀρχιερεϝ)[11]
δεξιός, -ά, -όν	right (54; *δεξιο)[12]

You will usually have to add a word to your translation of this word. Context will tell you what it should be. Normally it will be "hand" or "side."

δύο	two (135)[13]

δύο is declined as follows.

nom pl	δύο
gen pl	δύο
dat pl	δυσί(ν)
acc pl	δύο

ἕτερος, -α, -ον	other, another, different (98; * ἑτερο)[14]
εὐαγγελίζω	I bring good news, preach (54; *εὐαγγελιδ)[15] (εὐηγγέλιζον), -, εὐηγγέλισα, -, εὐηγγέλισμαι, εὐηγγελίσθην

εὐαγγελίζω usually occurs in the middle (εὐαγγελίζομαι) with no difference in meaning from the active.

θεωρέω	I look at, behold (58; *θεωρε) (ἐθεώρουν), θεωρήσω, ἐθεώρησα, -, -, -
Ἱεροσόλυμα, τά	Jerusalem (62; *Ἱεροσόλυμα).

Ἱεροσόλυμα is normally neuter plural (61 times in the New Testament). One time it is feminine singular (Matt 2:3).

κάθημαι	I sit (down), live (91; *καθη)[16] (ἐκαθήμην), καθήσομαι, -, -, -, -
καταβαίνω	I go down, come down (81; κατά + *βα) (κατέβαινον), καταβήσομαι, κατέβην, καταβέβηκα, -, -
οὗ	where (24; adverb)

Do not confuse this word with the negation (οὐ) or the genitive masculine/neuter relative pronoun (οὗ). Although οὗ occurs only 27 times in the New Testament, it is so easily confused that I included it here.

---

[11] The two parts to this compound noun were switched in the word ἱεράρχης meaning "hierarch" (*sacred* [ἱερός] + *ruler* [ἀρχός]).

[12] δεξιός is related to the Latin word "dextra" that gave rise to the English adjective *dextral*, which means "right-handed."

[13] A *dyarchy* (also *diarchy*) is a dual government system. A *dyad* (δυάς) is two units viewed as one.

[14] *Heterodoxy* (ἑτερόδοξος) is unorthodoxy, holding a position different from the right one.

[15] The preacher *evangelizes* the audience with the good news of the gospel.

[16] When the pope speaks "ex cathedra" (which is actually from the Latin but with obvious links to the Greek), he is speaking with the full authority of the pope, as one who is sitting on the seat of authority.

παρακαλέω	I call, urge, exhort, comfort
	(109; παρά + *καλεϝ)[17]
	(παρεκάλουν), -, παρεκάλεσα, -, παρακέκλημαι,
	παρεκλήθην
πείθω	I persuade (52; *πειθ)
	(ἔπειθον), πείσω, ἔπεισα, πέποιθα, πέπεισμαι, ἐπείσθην
τρεῖς, τρία	three (69; *τρες)[18]

Total word count in the New Testament:	138,162
Number of words learned to date:	283
Number of word occurrences in this chapter:	1,091
Number of word occurrences to date:	107,572
Percent of total word count in the New Testament:	77.86%

Advanced Information

27.17 Most grammars view the following material as an essential part of the participle, and certainly in the long run it is necessary. But because there is already so much to learn about the participle, I thought it best to include the discussion of a participle's relative time here. If you can learn it, as well as everything else in this chapter, then by all means do so. If you are struggling, ignore it for the time being. But eventually, you should come back and learn it.

If you want to use this advanced information in translating the exercises, do your exercises first before reading this section. Then come back, read this discussion, and redo your exercises.

27.18 **Relative Time**. There is an important distinction between absolute and relative time. An indicative verb indicates **absolute** time. For example, if an indicative verb is present tense, then it usually indicates an action occurring in the present. If the Greek participle indicated absolute time, then the present participle would indicate an action occurring in the present.

However, the Greek participle does not indicate absolute time. It indicates **relative** time. This means that the time of the participle is relative to the time of the main verb. *The present participle describes an action occurring at the same time as the main verb.*[19]

27.19 In order to indicate relative time, you must change the way you translate the participle by using a helping verb ("studying" becomes "was studying.")

■ If the main verb is *aorist*, then the present participle is translated as *past* continuous (e.g., "was praying").

Περιπατῶν δὲ παρὰ τὴν θάλασσαν τῆς Γαλιλαίας εἶδεν δύο ἀδελφούς *(Matt 4:18)*.

And as he *was walking* by the Sea of Galilee, he *saw* two brothers.

---

[17] Jesus used the cognate noun παράκλητος, "Paraclete," for the Holy Spirit, one who is called (κλήτος) alongside (παρά) to encourage and help Christians (John 14:26).

[18] A *triad* (τριάς) is a group of three things. A *tricycle* has three wheels.

[19] The aorist participle, which is formed from the aorist tense stem, often indicates an action occurring *before* the time of the main verb. This will be discussed in 28.17.

■ If the main verb is a *present,* then the present participle is translated as *present* continuous (e.g., "is praying").

> πᾶν δένδρον μὴ <u>ποιοῦν</u> καρπὸν καλὸν <u>ἐκκόπτεται</u> καὶ εἰς πῦρ <u>βάλλεται</u> *(Matt 7:19).*
>
> Every tree *not bearing* good fruit *is cut down* and *thrown* into the fire.

You may want to add the appropriate pronoun (e.g., "he was studying"). Which pronoun you use is determined by the word the participle is modifying. Which helping verb you use is determined by the time of the main verb.

> Καὶ <u>παράγων</u> ὁ Ἰησοῦς ἐκεῖθεν <u>εἶδεν</u> ἄνθρωπον *(Matt 9:9).*
>
> And Jesus, as *he was passing* passed on from there, *saw* a man.

This is what is meant by "relative time." The time of the participle is relative to the time of the main verb.

27.20 When this distinction of relative time is taken into consideration in the translation of the participle, it must never overrule the significance of the aspect in your translation. *Aspect is always primary to time. When English allows your translation to indicate clearly only aspect or time, choose aspect.*

27.21 **"Subject" of the participle**. Technically speaking, the participle does not have a subject. However, because the participle agrees with the word it is modifying, you can almost always identify who or what is doing the action of the participle. Indicating the "subject" of the participle will help in exegesis. (This "subject" is the pronoun I suggested adding in 27.19.)

A way to indicate both the aspect and the "subject" is to include the appropriate pronoun and verb form.

■ *"While he was studying,* the teacher (διδάσκαλος) told the students (μαθητάς) about the exam."

■ *"While they were studying,* the teacher (διδάσκαλος) told the students (μαθητάς) about the exam."

Choose the pronoun that makes the identification most clear as to who or what is doing the action in the participle. Be sure to use the continuous form of the finite verb if possible. What you will discover is that it is often difficult, if not impossible, to translate this way word for word. You must ask yourself, "Now that I know what all the parts mean in Greek, how can I say the same thing in English?" Allow yourself a little freedom in your translation.

27.22 **How are you doing?** If you are struggling with the translation of the participle, then do not pay attention right now to this advanced discussion. Work with the basics of the participle until you are comfortable with them, and then start adding the pronoun and relative time.

Exegesis

The following uses of the adverbial participle apply to both the continuous and the undefined (see next chapter) participle.

1. The aorist participle can describe an action occurring before the time of the finite verb, while the present participle can describe something happening at the same time as the action of the main verb (temporal). "After" and "when/while" are often added to this type of participle.

   <u>νηστεύσας</u> ... ὕστερον ἐπείνασεν *(Matt 4:2).*
   After fasting ... he was hungry.

   <u>συναλιζόμενος</u> παρήγγειλεν αὐτοῖς *(Acts 1:4).*
   While staying with them he charged them.

2. The participle can indicate the manner in which the action of the finite verb occurs (manner).

   ἀκούσας δὲ ὁ νεανίσκος τὸν λόγον ἀπῆλθεν <u>λυπούμενος</u> *(Matt 19:22).*
   When the young man heard this, he went away *sad.*

3. The participle can indicate the means by which the action of the finite verb occurs (means).

   κοπιῶμεν <u>ἐργαζόμενοι</u> ταῖς ἰδίαις χερσίν *(1 Cor 4:12).*
   We toil *by working* with our own hands.

4. The participle can indicate the cause or reason or ground of the action of the finite verb (cause).

   ἠγαλλιάσατο πανοικεὶ <u>πεπιστευκὼς</u> τῷ θεῷ *(Acts 16:34).*
   He was filled with joy, along with his entire household, *because he had come to believe* in God.

5. The participle can indicate a condition that must be fulfilled if the action of the finite verb is to be accomplished (conditional).

   πάντα ὅσα ἂν αἰτήσητε ... <u>πιστεύοντες</u> λήμψεσθε *(Matt 21:22).*
   And whatever you ask in prayer, you will receive, *if you have faith.*

6. The participle can indicate that the action of the finite verb is true despite the action of the participle (concessive).

   Καὶ ὑμᾶς <u>ὄντας</u> νεκροὺς τοῖς παραπτώμασιν *(Eph 2:1)*
   And *although you were* dead in your transgressions

7. The participle can indicate the purpose of the finite verb (purpose). These are often translated as infinitives.

   ἄφες ἴδωμεν εἰ ἔρχεται Ἡλίας <u>σώσων</u> αὐτόν *(Matt 27:49).*
   Wait! Let's see if Elijah comes *to save* him.

8. The participle can indicate the result of the finite verb (result). This is close to the participle of purpose; the difference is whether the force of the participle is on the intention or the result.

> ἵνα τοὺς δύο κτίσῃ ἐν αὐτῷ εἰς ἕνα καινὸν ἄνθρωπον ποιῶν εἰρήνην *(Eph 2:15)*.
>
> In order to create in himself one new man out of the two, *thus making* peace.

9. Often participles are translated as indicative verbs. This may create a problem for exegesis, because you can't distinguish between the main verb—which is normally indicative and normally contains the main thought—and the dependent participle, which normally contains a modifying thought. Translators do this for several reasons.

10. When Greek sentences get too long for English translations, it is often easiest to treat a long participial phrase as an independent sentence. Ephesians 1:3-14 is one long sentence. V. 5 begins with a participial phrase, and many translations start a new English sentence by turning the participle into a finite verb, supply a subject, and hence turn a participial phrase into an independent sentence. The NET adds, "He did this," and the NRSV adds "He."

> προορίσας ἡμᾶς εἰς υἱοθεσίαν διὰ Ἰησοῦ Χριστοῦ *(Eph 1:5)*.
>
> NET: *He did this by predestining* us to adoption as his sons through Jesus Christ.
>
> NRSV: *He destined* us for adoption as his children through Jesus Christ.

11. Greek likes to have an aorist participle before the main verb, but in English we use two finite verbs.

> εὐθὺς ἀφέντες τὰ δίκτυα ἠκολούθησαν αὐτῷ *(Mark 1:18)*.
>
> Immediately *they left* their nets and followed Him.

The Doxology is harder to translate. Dr. J. I. Packer helped write it for me. We sat at dinner during an ESV translation meeting and he got the biggest kick out of helping. ὦ is the Greek way of saying "hmm" in poetry (i.e., taking up a beat). You can also see that final short vowels can be dropped for the sake of the poetry.

τὸν θεὸν ὦ δοξάζετε,
εὐδοκήσαντα δωρεάν,
τὰ κτίσματ᾽ ἃ πεποίηκεν,
πατέρα, υἱόν, καὶ πνεῦμα.
Ἀμήν.

Chapter 28

Aorist (Undefined) Adverbial Participles

Exegetical Insight

When the aorist participle is used adverbially, it is one of the flexible syntactical constructions in Koine Greek. It can be used to indicate almost any type of adverbial clause and is therefore one of the most common grammatical constructions in the New Testament. But its flexibility also creates some real problems for translators and biblical exegetes (as well as beginning students of Koine Greek). Since the meaning of the aorist adverbial participle is always determined by its relationship to the main verb in context, some of the most heated arguments in the interpretation of the New Testament center around the meaning of an aorist participle.

There is probably no better example of such an argument than the ongoing debate about the correct understanding of the aorist participle πιστεύσαντες in Acts 19:2. The meaning of this participle determines the meaning of Paul's question: Εἰ πνεῦμα ἅγιον ἐλάβετε πιστεύσαντες; The King James Version translated this question: "Have ye received the Holy Ghost since ye believed?" One of the common uses of the aorist participle is to indicate an action that occurs before the action of the main verb. The King James translation understands the aorist participle in this way and indicates that the believing would have occurred before the receiving of the Holy Spirit. Pentecostals have used this translation to support their claim that receiving the

Holy Spirit is an event distinct from and subsequent to believing in Christ. But traditional Protestant exegetes have argued that this interpretation is based on a misunderstanding of the use of the aorist participle. Koine Greek frequently uses the aorist participle to express action that is part of the action of an aorist finite verb, and this is clearly the case in Paul's question. Believing and receiving the Holy Spirit are both part of one experience. Most recent translations agree with this understanding of πιστεύσαντες and follow the Revised Standard Version's translation: "Did you receive the Holy Spirit when you believed?"

So which interpretation is right? It is essential to recognize that both are based on legitimate understandings of the use of the aorist adverbial participle in Koine Greek. Even in context, it is virtually impossible to prefer one over the other, and theological concerns usually determine which interpretation is chosen. So both interpretations can be considered correct understandings of Paul's question in Acts 19:2. The moral of this little exegetical note is that when dealing with the aorist adverbial participle, flexibility and a willingness to consider the validity of interpretations that differ from one's own are just as important as a knowledge of the complexities of Greek grammar.

J. M. Everts

In this chapter you will learn:

■ that the aorist participle is formed from the unaugmented aorist tense stem;

■ that the aorist participle indicates an undefined action;

■ that the aorist participle uses the participle morpheme ντ in the active and passive, and μεν in the middle;

■ that you should use "after" in your translation for the time being.

Introduction

28.1 In this chapter you will learn the aorist adverbial participle. The basic grammar of the aorist participle is the same as the present adverbial; the only two differences are the participle's form and aspect. This chapter may look long, but there is not that much new information to learn. It is mostly paradigms, and you already know most of the forms.

Greek

28.2 **Summary**. The aorist participle is formed on the aorist stem and indicates an undefined action.

Most grammars use the term "aorist" participle because this participle is built on the aorist tense stem of the verb. This nomenclature is helpful in learning the form of the participle. However, it tends to do a serious disservice because the student may infer that the aorist participle describes an action occurring in the past, which it does not. It describes an undefined action. Because the participle is not in the indicative, there is no time significance to the participle.[1] I suggest adopting the terminology "undefined participle" because it rightly emphasizes the true significance of the participle that is built on the aorist tense stem, its aspect.

28.3 **Translation**. The most important thing to remember about the aorist participle is its aspect. It indicates an undefined action. It tells you nothing about the aspect of the action other than it occurred.

> ἀκούσας δὲ ὁ βασιλεὺς Ἡρῴδης ἐταράχθη *(Matt 2:3)*.
> But when king Herod *heard* this, he was troubled.

It is difficult, if not impossible, to carry the aspect of the aorist participle over into English using the -ing form of the verb. But even if you are unable to indicate the true aspect of the aorist participle in your translation, you can always explain it in your teaching and preaching. In other words, it is your responsibility always to remember the true significance

---

[1] The relative time significance of the aorist participle is covered in the Advanced Information section.

of the aorist participle, and if an accurate translation is not possible without butchering the English language, you must at least explain the concept in words your audience can understand.

Never forget: the participle formed on the aorist tense stem indicates an undefined action.

28.4 **"After."** Just as you can use "while" in translating the present participle, you may use "after" with the aorist participle. I will discuss this in more detail below.

> οἱ δὲ <u>ἀκούσαντες</u> τοῦ βασιλέως ἐπορεύθησαν *(Matt 2:9).*
> And *after hearing* the king, they went on their way.

First Aorist (Undefined) Participle

28.5 **Chart**. If a verb has a first aorist indicative, it will use that unaugmented first aorist stem in the formation of the aorist participle.

> *Unaugmented first aorist tense stem +*
>
> *Tense formative (σα)+*
>
> *Participle morpheme + Case endings*
>
> *active:* λυ + σα + ντ + ες ‣ λύσαντες
> *middle:* λυ + σα + μενο + ι ‣ λυσάμενοι
> *passive:* λυ + θε + ντ + ες ‣ λυθέντες

28.6 **Augment**. An augment is used in the indicative mood to indicate past time. To be more specific, it indicates absolute past time. However, since the participle does not indicate absolute time, the aorist participle cannot have an augment. Therefore, the aorist participle is formed from the *unaugmented* aorist tense stem.

This process of unaugmenting is easy to spot if the augment is a simple epsilon. ἔλυσα unaugments to λυσα. However, if the augment is a lengthened initial vowel it can be a bit confusing. ἤγειρα unaugments to ἐγειρα, which can look like a present tense form except for the alpha.

> *ἐλθ ‣ ἠλθ ‣ ἠλθον ‣ ἐλθών

This whole process can get especially tricky in a compound verb like ἐκελύσας. You can spend a long time thumbing through a lexicon looking for some form like κελύω, perhaps assuming this form is an imperfect verb, all the while missing the fact that it is from the compound ἐκλύω. The moral of the story? Know your vocabulary! Know your verbal roots!

28.7 **Paradigm: First aorist active participle**. The active participle morpheme is **ντ**, which looks like **σαντ** with the tense formative. In the feminine the ντ has been replaced by **σα**.

	3 *masc*	1 *fem*	3 *neuter*
nom sg	λύσας[2]	λύσασα[3]	λῦσαν[4]
gen sg	λύσαντος	λυσάσης	λύσαντος
dat sg	λύσαντι	λυσάσῃ	λύσαντι
acc sg	λύσαντα	λύσασαν	λῦσαν
nom pl	λύσαντες	λύσασαι	λύσαντα
gen pl	λυσάντων	λυσασῶν	λυσάντων
dat pl	λύσασι(ν)	λυσάσαις	λύσασι(ν)
acc pl	λύσαντας	λυσάσας	λύσαντα

	masc	*fem*	*neut*
nom sg	σας	σασα	σαν
gen sg	σαντος	σασης	σαντος

28.8 **Tense formative**. Although the augment is dropped, you will still see the familiar σα tense formative.

28.9 **Paradigm: First aorist middle participle**. The middle participle morpheme is **μενο/η**, which looks like **σαμενο/η** with the tense formative.

	2 *masc*	1 *fem*	2 *neuter*
nom sg	λυσάμενος	λυσαμένη	λυσάμενον
gen sg	λυσαμένου	λυσαμένης	λυσαμένου
dat sg	λυσαμένῳ	λυσαμένῃ	λυσαμένῳ
acc sg	λυσάμενον	λυσαμένην	λυσάμενον
nom pl	λυσάμενοι	λυσάμεναι	λυσάμενα
gen pl	λυσαμένων	λυσαμένων	λυσαμένων
dat pl	λυσαμένοις	λυσαμέναις	λυσαμένοις
acc pl	λυσαμένους	λυσαμένας	λυσάμενα

	masc	*fem*	*neut*
nom sg	σαμενος	σαμενη	σαμενον
gen sg	σαμενου	σαμενης	σαμενου

[2] As is usual in the masculine third declension, the sigma case ending causes the preceding ντ to drop off.

[3] σα and ντ are morphologically related. If you want to learn why the changes are so drastic, see *MBG*, 91.

[4] As is usual in the neuter third declension, no case ending is used in the nominative/accusative, and therefore the final tau must drop off.

28.10 Paradigm: First aorist passive participle. The **passive** participle morpheme is **ντ**. The eta in the tense formative (θη) shortens to epsilon (θε), and the participle then looks like **θεντ**. In the feminine the ντ has been replaced by ισα.

	3 *masc*	1 *fem*	3 *neuter*
nom sg	λυθείς[5]	λυθεῖσα	λυθέν[6]
gen sg	λυθέντος	λυθείσης	λυθέντος
dat sg	λυθέντι	λυθείσῃ	λυθέντι
acc sg	λυθέντα	λυθεῖσαν	λυθέν
nom pl	λυθέντες	λυθεῖσαι	λυθέντα
gen pl	λυθέντων	λυθεισῶν	λυθέντων
dat pl	λυθεῖσι(ν)[7]	λυθείσαις	λυθεῖσι(ν)[7]
acc pl	λυθέντας	λυθείσας	λυθέντα

	masc	*fem*	*neut*
nom sg	θεις	θεισα	θεν
gen sg	θεντος	θεισης	θεντος

Halftime Review

- The first aorist (undefined) participle is formed from the unaugmented aorist tense stem + tense formative + participle morpheme + case endings.

- The undefined participle describes an undefined action; it does not describe a past event.

- You can use "after" in your translation of this participle.

- There are three sets of memory forms so far (σας, σασα, σαν, σαντος, σασης, σαντος, etc.).

---

[5] The case ending is sigma, the ντ drops out because of the sigma, and the epsilon lengthens to compensate for the loss (*θε + ντ + ς ‣ θες ‣ θεις).

[6] No case ending is used, and the tau drops off because it cannot end a word (Noun Rule 8).

[7] The ντ drops out because of the sigma, and the epsilon lengthens to ει in order to compensate for the loss.

Second Aorist (Undefined) Participle

28.11 If a verb has a second aorist form in the indicative, the aorist participle of that verb will use the second aorist stem.

> *Unaugmented second aorist tense stem +*
>
> *Connecting vowel +*
>
> *Participle morpheme + Case endings*
>
> | | |
> |---|---|
> | *active:* | βαλ + ο + ντ + ες ▸ βαλόντες |
> | *middle:* | γεν + ο + μενο + ι ▸ γενόμενοι |
> | *passive:* | γραφ + ε + ντ + ες ▸ γραφέντες |

There is one point that bears emphasis. The active and middle aorist participle formed from the second aorist stem will look just like the active and middle present participle except for the verbal stem and the accent.

	present participle	*second aorist participle*
active	βάλλων	βαλών
middle/passive	βαλλόμενος	βαλόμενος

This similarity is heightened by the fact that the stem of the aorist participle is unaugmented. For example, if you see the form βαλών, you could easily assume that it is a present participle from the verb βάλω. However, there is no such verb. βαλών is rather the aorist participle from βάλλω, which has a second aorist ἔβαλον. This illustrates why a good knowledge of Greek vocabulary and verbal roots is so important; otherwise, you would spend much of your time in the company of a lexicon.

For an explanation of the changes to the participle morphemes, see my discussion of the present participle.

Here are the question words in Greek. There is no reason for you to use English any longer (as long as you don't sound arrogant or pretentious). The words in parentheses are Modern Greek.

Who? τίς (ποιος)
What? ποῖος (τι)
When? πότε (πότε)
Where? πόθεν (πού)
Why? διὰ τί (γιατί)
How? πῶς (πώς)
How much or many? πόσος

28.12 Paradigm: Second aorist active participle. The active participle morpheme is **ντ**, which looks like **οντ** with the connecting vowel. In the feminine the οντ has been replaced by ουσα.

	3 *masc*	1 *fem*	3 *neuter*
nom sg	βαλών	βαλοῦσα	βαλόν
gen sg	βαλόντος	βαλούσης	βαλόντος
dat sg	βαλόντι	βαλούσῃ	βαλόντι
acc sg	βαλόντα	βαλοῦσαν	βαλόν
nom pl	βαλόντες	βαλοῦσαι	βαλόντα
gen pl	βαλόντων	βαλουσῶν	βαλόντων
dat pl	βαλοῦσι(ν)	βαλούσαις	βαλοῦσι(ν)
acc pl	βαλόντας	βαλούσας	βαλόντα

	masc	*fem*	*neut*
nom sg	ων	ουσα	ον
gen sg	οντος	ουσης	οντος

28.13 Paradigm: Second aorist middle participle. The middle participle morpheme is **μενο/η**, which looks like **ομενο/η** with the connecting vowel.

	2 *masc*	1 *fem*	2 *neuter*
nom sg	γενόμενος	γενομένη	γενόμενον
gen sg	γενομένου	γενομένης	γενομένου
dat sg	γενομένῳ	γενομένῃ	γενομένῳ
acc sg	γενόμενον	γενομένην	γενόμενον
nom pl	γενόμενοι	γενόμεναι	γενόμενα
gen pl	γενομένων	γενομένων	γενομένων
dat pl	γενομένοις	γενομέναις	γενομένοις
acc pl	γενομένους	γενομένας	γενόμενα

	masc	*fem*	*neut*
nom sg	ομενος	ομενη	ομενον
gen sg	ομενου	ομενης	ομενου

28.14 Paradigm: Second aorist passive participle. Of the verbs that occur fifty times or more in the New Testament, none have second aorist passive participles. But here is the paradigm for the sake of completeness. The passive participle morpheme is ντ. The tense formative (η) shortens to epsilon (ε), and the participle then looks like εντ. In the feminine the ντ has been replaced by ισα.

	3 masc	1 fem	3 neuter
nom sg	γραφείς[8]	γραφεῖσα	γραφέν[9]
gen sg	γραφέντος	γραφείσης	γραφέντος
dat sg	γραφέντι	γραφείσῃ	γραφέντι
acc sg	γραφέντα	γραφεῖσαν	γραφέν
nom pl	γραφέντες	γραφεῖσαι	γραφέντα
gen pl	γραφέντων	γραφεισῶν	γραφέντων
dat pl	γραφεῖσι(ν)	γραφείσαις	γραφεῖσι(ν)
acc pl	γραφέντας	γραφείσας	γραφέντα

	masc	fem	neut
nom sg	εις	εισα	εν
gen sg	εντος	εισης	εντος

There should be no confusion between present and second aorist passive participles since the middle and passive are distinct forms.

Odds 'n Ends

28.15 **By way of reminder**. The following rules hold true whether the participle is present or aorist.

■ The feminine participle always uses first declension endings (λύουσα, λυσαμένη).

■ When the masculine and neuter participles are active, they are third declension (λύων, λύον).

■ When the masculine and neuter participles are present middle or passive, or aorist middle, they are second declension (λυόμενος, λυόμενον; λυσάμενος, λυσάμενον), and when they are aorist passive they are third declension (λυθείς, λυθέν).

28.16 Here is a list of the verbs that could give you some trouble in their unaugmented aorist stems. Be sure to note the differences between γίνομαι (*γεν) and γινώσκω (*γνω).

present			aorist		
ἄγω	▸	ἄγων	ἤγαγον	▸	ἀγαγών
αἴρω	▸	αἴρων	ἦρα	▸	ἄρας
ὁράω	▸	ὁρῶν	εἶδον	▸	ἰδών
ἔρχομαι	▸	ἐρχόμενος	ἦλθον	▸	ἐλθών
εὑρίσκω	▸	εὑρίσκων	εὗρον	▸	εὑρών

---

[8] The case ending is sigma, the ντ drops out because of the sigma (rule 7), and the epsilon lengthens to compensate for the loss (rule 8; *ε + ντ + ς ▸ ες ▸ εις).

[9] No case ending is used, and the tau drops off because it cannot end a word (rule 8).

ἔχω	▸	ἔχων	ἔσχον	▸	(σχών)[10]
θέλω	▸	θέλων	ἠθέλησα	▸	θελήσας
λέγω	▸	λέγων	εἶπον	▸	εἰπών

Summary

1. The aorist participle is formed from the unaugmented aorist tense stem and indicates an undefined action. For the time being, use "after" in your translation if it fits the context.

2. Participle Morpheme Chart

morpheme	tense/voice	case endings
ντ	active; aorist passive	3-1-3
μενο / η	middle; middle / passive	2-1-2

3. Master Participle Chart

tense & voice	redup	stem	t.f. c.v.	morpheme	nom. plural	six memory forms
present active		present	ο	ντ / ουσα	λέγοντες	ων, ουσα, ον οντος, ουσης, οντος
present mid/pas		present	ο	μενο / η	λεγόμενοι	ομενος, ομενη, ομενον ομενου, ομενης, ομενου
1 aorist active		aorist active	σα	ντ / σα	λύσαντες	σας, σασα, σαν σαντος, σασης, σαντος
1 aorist middle		aorist active	σα	μενο / η	λυσάμενοι	σαμενος ...
1 aorist passive		aorist passive	θε	ντ	λυθέντες	θεις, θεισα, θεν θεντος, θεισης, θεντος
2 aorist active		aorist active	ο	ντ	βαλόντες	ων ...
2 aorist middle		aorist active	ο	μενο / η	γενόμενοι	ομενος ...
2 aorist passive		aorist passive	ε	ντ	γραφέντες	εις, εισα, εν εντος, εισης, εντος

Vocabulary

ἀσπάζομαι — I greet, salute (59; *ἀσπαδ)
(ἠσπαζόμην), –, ἠσπασάμην, –, –, –

γραμματεύς, –έως, ὁ — scribe (63; *γραμματεϝ)[11]

---

[10] The aorist participle of ἔχω does not occur in the New Testament.

[11] *Grammar* is from the Greek γραμματική, meaning characteristic of writing (γράμμα).

ἔφη	He / she / it was saying; he / she / it said
	Third person singular of φημί; it can be either imperfect active or second aorist active. This one form occurs forty-three times in the New Testament. I have included it as a vocabulary word because it is difficult for a first year student to recognize. It is not included in the vocabulary count.
ἱερόν, -οῦ, τό	temple (72; * ἱερο)[12]
κράζω	I cry out, call out (55; *κραγ)[13]
	(ἔκραζον), κράξω, ἔκραξα, κέκραγα, –, –
οὐχί	not (54, adverb)
παιδίον, -ου, τό	child, infant (52; *παιδιο)[14]
σπείρω	I sow (52, *σπερ)
	–, ἔσπειρα, –, ἔσπαρμαι, ἐσπάρην

Total word count in the New Testament:	138,162
Number of words learned to date:	290
Number of word occurrences in this chapter:	407
Number of word occurrences to date:	107,979
Percent of total word count in the New Testament:	78.18%

Advanced Information

28.17 **Relative time**. Whereas the present participle indicates an action occurring at the same time as the main verb, the aorist participle generally indicates an action occurring *before* the time of the main verb. There are, however, many exceptions to this general rule. (That is why it is only a *general* rule.) For example, many aorist participles indicate an action occurring at the same time as the main verb.

It is especially difficult to indicate relative time for the aorist participle using the -ing form of the verb. Using "after" instead of "while" when appropriate may help. It will also help to follow the advice in the Advanced Information section in the previous chapter.

28.18 The following chart shows the relationship among main verbs, present participles, and aorist participles. If you are confused with the names of the English tenses, the appropriate helping verbs are listed below their names. See the Appendix for a further discussion of English tenses (page 351).

main verb	present participle		aorist participle	
Future	"While" +	future continuous *will be eating*	"After" +	present *eating*

---

[12] *Hieroglyphics* is Egyptian writing, from the cognate ἱερός ("sacred," "holy") and γλύφω ("to carve, note down [on tablets]").

[13] This is one of the very few αζω verbs whose stem does not actually end in a dental; cf. v-2a(2) in *MBG*.

[14] A child is one who learns, who needs to be taught. *Paideutics* (παιδευτικός) and *pedagogy* are the art of teaching. The combining form *pedo* is also common, as in *pedobaptism*.

Present	"While" +	present continuous *is eating*	"After" +	simple past *eating*	
Imperfect	"While" +	past continuous *was eating*	"After" +	past perfect *had eaten*	
Aorist	"While" +	past continuous *was eating*	"After" +	past perfect *had eaten*	
Perfect	"While" +	perfect continuous *have been eating*	"After" +	past perfect *had eaten*	

28.19 Future participle. The future participle is used to describe what is "purposed, intended, or expected" in the future (Smyth, #2044). The future participle occurs twelve times in the New Testament. The forms are obvious, and I felt they did not require specific comment. Here they are.

Matt 27:49 οἱ δὲ λοιποὶ ἔλεγον, Ἄφες ἴδωμεν εἰ ἔρχεται Ἡλίας σώσων αὐτόν.

Luke 22:49 ἰδόντες δὲ οἱ περὶ αὐτὸν τὸ ἐσόμενον εἶπαν, Κύριε, εἰ πατάξομεν ἐν μαχαίρῃ;

John 6:64 ἀλλ᾽ εἰσὶν ἐξ ὑμῶν τινες οἳ οὐ πιστεύουσιν. ᾔδει γὰρ ἐξ ἀρχῆς ὁ Ἰησοῦς τίνες εἰσὶν οἱ μὴ πιστεύοντες καὶ τίς ἐστιν ὁ παραδώσων αὐτόν.

Acts 8:27 καὶ ἀναστὰς ἐπορεύθη· καὶ ἰδοὺ ἀνὴρ Αἰθίοψ εὐνοῦχος δυνάστης Κανδάκης βασιλίσσης Αἰθιόπων, ὃς ἦν ἐπὶ πάσης τῆς γάζης αὐτῆς, ὃς ἐληλύθει προσκυνήσων εἰς Ἰερουσαλήμ,

Acts 20:22 καὶ νῦν ἰδοὺ δεδεμένος ἐγὼ τῷ πνεύματι πορεύομαι εἰς Ἰερουσαλήμ, τὰ ἐν αὐτῇ συναντήσοντά μοι μὴ εἰδώς.

Acts 22:5 ὡς καὶ ὁ ἀρχιερεὺς μαρτυρεῖ μοι καὶ πᾶν τὸ πρεσβυτέριον· παρ᾽ ὧν καὶ ἐπιστολὰς δεξάμενος πρὸς τοὺς ἀδελφοὺς εἰς Δαμασκὸν ἐπορευόμην ἄξων καὶ τοὺς ἐκεῖσε ὄντας δεδεμένους εἰς Ἰερουσαλὴμ ἵνα τιμωρηθῶσιν.

Acts 24:11 δυναμένου σου ἐπιγνῶναι ὅτι οὐ πλείους εἰσίν μοι ἡμέραι δώδεκα ἀφ᾽ ἧς ἀνέβην προσκυνήσων εἰς Ἰερουσαλήμ,

Acts 24:17 δι᾽ ἐτῶν δὲ πλειόνων ἐλεημοσύνας ποιήσων εἰς τὸ ἔθνος μου παρεγενόμην καὶ προσφοράς,

1 Cor 15:37 καὶ ὃ σπείρεις, οὐ τὸ σῶμα τὸ γενησόμενον σπείρεις ἀλλὰ γυμνὸν κόκκον εἰ τύχοι σίτου ἤ τινος τῶν λοιπῶν·

Heb 3:5 καὶ Μωϋσῆς μὲν πιστὸς ἐν ὅλῳ τῷ οἴκῳ αὐτοῦ ὡς θεράπων εἰς μαρτύριον τῶν λαληθησομένων,

Heb 13:17 Πείθεσθε τοῖς ἡγουμένοις ὑμῶν καὶ ὑπείκετε, αὐτοὶ γὰρ ἀγρυπνοῦσιν ὑπὲρ τῶν ψυχῶν ὑμῶν ὡς λόγον ἀποδώσοντες, ἵνα μετὰ χαρᾶς τοῦτο ποιῶσιν καὶ μὴ στενάζοντες, ἀλυσιτελὲς γὰρ ὑμῖν τοῦτο.

1 Pet 3:13 Καὶ τίς ὁ κακώσων ὑμᾶς ἐὰν τοῦ ἀγαθοῦ ζηλωταὶ γένησθε;

κατακρινῶν could possibly be a future participle in Rom 8:34

Rom 8:34 τίς ὁ κατακρινῶν; Χριστὸς [Ἰησοῦς] ὁ ἀποθανών,

Chapter 29

Adjectival Participles

Exegetical Insight

In Romans 1:3–4 it is imperative to see that the two attributive participles (τοῦ γενομένου, "who was," and τοῦ ὁρισθέντος, "who was appointed") modify the word "son" (υἱοῦ) that appears at the beginning of verse 3. The two participial phrases communicate two complementary truths about the Son. First, "he was of the seed of David according to the flesh" (τοῦ γενομένου ἐκ σπέρματος Δαυὶδ κατὰ σάρκα). Since Jesus was a descendant of David, he fulfilled the Old Testament prophecies that a ruler would come from David's line (2 Sam 7:12–16; Isa 11:1–5, 10; Jer 23:5–6; 33:14–17; Ezek 34:23–24).

In saying that Jesus was David's descendant "according to the flesh," no criticism of his Davidic origin is implied. Nonetheless, the second attributive participle introduces something greater than being the fleshly descendant of David. The Son "was appointed to be the Son of God in power according to the Spirit of holiness by the resurrection of the dead" (τοῦ ὁρισθέντος υἱοῦ θεοῦ ἐν δυνάμει κατὰ πνεῦμα ἁγιωσύνης ἐξ ἀναστάσεως νεκρῶν).

The two stages of salvation history are present here. During his earthly life Jesus was the Messiah and the Son of David, but upon his resurrection he was appointed as the ruling and reigning Messiah. The title "Son of God" in verse 4, then, refers to the messianic kingship of Jesus, not his deity. Paul is not suggesting that Jesus was adopted as God's Son upon his resurrection. Remember that the phrase introduced with the attributive participle τοῦ ὁρισθέντος in verse 4 modifies the word "Son" (υἱοῦ) in verse 3. The "Son" was appointed by God to be "the Son of God." In other words, Jesus was already the Son before he was appointed to be the Son of God! The first usage (v. 3) of the word "Son," then, refers to Jesus' preexistent divinity that he shared with the Father from all eternity. Jesus' appointment as "the Son of God" (v. 4) refers to his installment as the messianic King at his resurrection.

How great Jesus Christ is! He is the eternal Son of God who reigns with the Father from all eternity. But he also deserves our worship as the messianic King, the God-Man who was appointed as the Son of God in power when he was raised from the dead.

Thomas R. Schreiner

You don't know a language until you know how to ask for the bathroom (or whatever you call it in your culture.)

ποῦ ἐστιν λουτρών;

English

29.1 A participle is a verbal adjective. As such, it not only has verbal but also adjectival characteristics. In other words, a participle can do whatever an adjective can do. For example, it can modify a noun.

> The man eating by the window is my Greek teacher.

In this example, the participle *eating* tells us something about the *man*.

29.2 But a participle can do more than simply modify a noun. One of its most obvious other talents is to act like a noun. In other words, a participle can be used substantivally. "The living have hope." In this example, the participle *living* is serving as a noun, specifically as the subject of the sentence.

Greek

29.3 Almost everything you have learned about participles so far applies here as well. The formation of the participle, its aspect, agreement with the word it modifies—all these apply to all participles.

29.4 Because a participle is a verbal adjective, it can behave not only as an adverb (chapters 27-28) but also as an adjective. This is called the "adjectival" participle. Adjectival participles can be attributive or substantive.

29.5 **Review of adjectival grammar**. I need to start by reviewing adjectival grammar (Chapter 9). Participles in this chapter are functioning as adjectives, and you need to see that grammatically there is little new here.

- Adjectives function in one of three ways: as an attributive, substantive, or predicate.

- When an adjective functions *attributively*, it agrees with the word it modifies in case, number, and gender and is preceded by an article.

> ὁ ἀγαθὸς λόγος ἐστίν ...

Be sure to watch your signs carefully; one is ἀνδρῶν and the other is γυναικῶν.

These signs are on
the Acropolis

■ When an adjective functions *substantivally*, its case is determined by its function in the sentence. Its gender and number are determined by what it stands for.

> ὁ ἀγαθός ἐστιν ...

If an adjective is substantival, there will not be a noun for it to modify. You will often have to include additional words in your translation depending on natural gender.

> ἡ ἀγαθή
> "the good *woman*"

Adjectival Participle

29.6 The adjectival participle has two functions, *attributive* (if it functions as an adjective) and *substantival* (if it functions as a noun).

The key words "while," "after," and "because" apply only to adverbial participles. They are not used with adjectival participles.

29.7 **Attributive**. The attributive participle will modify some other noun or pronoun in the sentence, and will agree with that word in case, number, and gender, just like an adjective. For the time being, it can be translated simply with the "-ing" form.

> ὁ ἄνθρωπος ὁ λέγων τῷ ὄχλῳ ἐστὶν ὁ διδάσκαλός μου.
> The man *speaking* to the crowd is my teacher.

This is the normal article-noun-article-modifier construction. In this case, the modifier is the participle and its indirect object, τῷ ὄχλῳ.

29.8 **Substantival**. Since an adjective can also function as a noun, so also can a participle. Remember: a participle is a *verbal adjective*, and anything an adjective can do a participle can do, usually better.

> ὁ τῷ ὄχλῳ λέγων ἐστὶν ὁ διδάσκαλός μου.
> The *one who is speaking*[1] to the crowd is my teacher.

> προσεύχεσθε ὑπὲρ τῶν διωκόντων ὑμᾶς *(Matt 5:44)*.
> Pray for *those persecuting* you.

What determines the case, number, and gender of a participle used substantivally?

■ The case is determined by the function of the participle in the sentence (just like it does with a substantival adjective). In the example above, λέγων is nominative because the participle is the subject of the sentence. διωκόντων is genitive because it is the object of the preposition ὑπέρ.

■ Its number and gender are determined by who or what the participle is representing. In the case of λέγων, there is only one teacher (i.e., singular) and he is a man (i.e., masculine). διωκόντων refers to many people (i.e., plural masculine).

---

[1]   I will discuss why I added "one who is" in 29.9.

29.9 **Translation of the substantival participle**. As is the case with a substantival adjective, the translation of a substantival participle will often require the addition of extra words, such as the "one who is" in the previous example. Try translating without these words.

> ὁ <u>λέγων</u> τῷ ὀχλῷ ἐστιν ὁ διδάσκαλός μου.
> The *speaking* to the crowd is my teacher.

Does not make much sense does it? This gets back to a point I made several chapters back. The translation of the Greek participle is often idiomatic. You must look at what the Greek means, and then figure out how to say the same thing in English. Going word for word will usually not work.

Just as you do with substantival adjectives, use common sense in the words you add.

- If the participle is singular you could use "one," "he," "she," or perhaps "that" if it is neuter.

> τῷ <u>θέλοντί</u> σοι κριθῆναι καὶ τὸν χιτῶνά σου λαβεῖν, ἄφες αὐτῷ καὶ τὸ ἱμάτιον *(Matt 5:40)*.
> To the *one wishing* to sue you to take your tunic, let him have your cloak as well.

- If it is plural you could use "they" or perhaps "those."

> μακάριοι οἱ <u>πενθοῦντες</u>, ὅτι αὐτοὶ παρακληθήσονται *(Matt 5:4)*.
> Blessd are *they who mourn*, for they will the comforted.

> τεθνήκασιν γὰρ οἱ <u>ζητοῦντες</u> τὴν ψυχὴν τοῦ παιδίου *(Matt 2:20)*.
> For *those seeking* the life of the child have died.

- Instead of "who" you might use "which," especially if the concept described by the participle is neuter.

> ταῦτά ἐστιν τὰ <u>κοινοῦντα</u> τὸν ἄνθρωπον *(Matt 15:20)*.
> These are *the things which defile* a person.

There is quite a bit of flexibility possible here, and the best way to figure out what words to use is to figure it out first in Greek and then switch to English. Additional rules would just confuse you now.

What case, number, and gender would a participle be if the translation is as follows?

	case	number	gender
the ones who			
that which			
to those who			
of that which			

29.10 **Aspect of an adjectival participle**. While the basic aspectual difference between a continuous (present) and undefined (aorist) participle is still true, the significance of aspect is lessened in the attributive participle and is weaker still in the substantival participle. This means that in your translation you do not need to work as hard to bring the aspect into your translation.

How about a little slang?
τι γίνεται; What's happening?
τι νεα; What's new?

29.11 Attributive or substantive? Since a participle can function as an adjective or a noun, how can you tell which is which? Again the answer is *context*, just as it is with adjectives. It is often the presence or absence of a noun that distinguishes between the two.

Take the example, ὁ λέγων τῷ ὄχλῳ ἐστιν ὁ διδάσκαλός μου. How can you tell whether ὁ λέγων is adjectival or substantival? Simple. Try translating it as adjectival. You cannot because there is nothing for it to modify. Therefore it must be substantival.

Adjectival or Adverbial

29.12 Adverbial or adjectival? There is no difference in form between the adverbial and adjectival participle. ἀκούοντες could be adjectival or adverbial. How then do you know whether the participle is adjectival or adverbial?

There are two clues to the answer to this question.

■ The first is whether or not the participle is preceded by the **article**. As a general rule, *the adverbial participle is always anarthrous while the adjectival participle is usually articular*. To state it in reverse, if the participle is articular, it cannot be adverbial. If it is anarthrous, it probably is adverbial.

The article will always agree with the participle in case, number, and gender.[2]

ὁ ἄνθρωπος ὁ λέγων τῷ ὄχλῳ ἐστιν ὁ διδάσκαλός μου.

■ **Context**. If there is no article present, the other clue is context. Which makes more sense? Adverbial or adjectival? Trying to translate the participle one way, and then the other, will usually answer the question. Remember: if there is an article, the participle *cannot* be adverbial. If there is *not* an article, it probably is adverbial.

Summary

Four different terms are important to know.

1. **Adverbial**. An adverbial participle agrees with a noun or pronoun in the sentence, but the action described by the participle is directed toward the verb. It often uses the key words *while* or *after*, depending upon whether it is present or aorist.

2. **Adjectival**. An adjectival participle modifies a noun or pronoun, or functions like a noun.

   a. **Attributive**. If an adjectival participle is attributing something to a noun or pronoun, it is called an attributive participle. For the time being, the simple

▼

---

[2] You should expect this, since this is also true of an adjective. Sometimes a word or phrase will be inserted between the article and participle, as is the case with adjectives (e.g., ὁ τῷ ὄχλῳ λέγων).

"-ing" form of the English verb is sufficient for translation. The participle will agree in case, number, and gender with the word it is modifying.

    b.   **Substantival**. If an adjectival participle is functioning as a noun, it is called a substantival participle. You will usually insert extra words into your translation to make sense of this construction. Use those words that enable you to repeat in English the true significance of the participle in Greek. Its case is determined by its function, its gender and number by the word it is replacing.

3.   The following chart illustrates the process of translating participles.

7 Questions to Ask of Any Participle You Meet

1.   What is the case, number, and gender of the participle, and why (i.e., what word is it modifying)?

2.   Is the action (or state of being) in the participle directed toward a verb (adverbial) or a noun (adjectival)?

3.   If it is adverbial, do you use "while" or "after"?

4.   If it is adjectival, is it attributive or substantival?

5.   What is the aspect of the participle? Continuous (present) or undefined (aorist)?

6.   What is the voice of the participle?

7.   What does the verb mean?

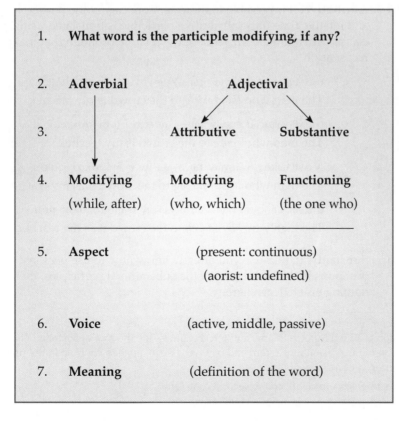

Vocabulary

δέχομαι	I take, receive (56; *δεχ) δέξομαι, ἐδεξάμην, –, δέδεγμαι, ἐδέχθην
δοκέω	I think, seem (62; *δοκ)[3] (ἐδόκουν), –, ἔδοξα, –, –, –
ἐσθίω	I eat (158; * ἐσθι; *φαγ)[4] (ἤσθιον), φάγομαι, ἔφαγον, –, –, –
πέμπω	I send (79, *πεμπ) πέμψω, ἔπεμψα, –, –, ἐπέμφθην
φέρω	I carry, bear, produce (66; *φερ; *οἰ; *ἐνεχ)[5] (ἔφερον), οἴσω, ἤνεγκα, ἐνήνοχα, –, ἠνέχθην

Total word count in the New Testament:	138,162
Number of words learned to date:	295
Number of word occurrences in this chapter:	421
Number of word occurrences to date:	108,400
Percent of total word count in the New Testament:	78.46%

Advanced Information

29.13 **Aspect and relative time**. The present and aorist participles have a relative time significance regardless of whether they are adverbial or adjectival. However, keeping this significance in the translation of the adjectival participle requires a few more steps.

29.14 **Attributive**. It is possible to indicate more clearly the participle's aspect and relative time if the attributive participle is translated using a relative clause with a finite verb. Choose the relative pronoun that makes the correct sense.

ὁ ἄνθρωπος ὁ λέγων τῷ ὄχλῳ ἐστὶν ὁ διδάσκαλός μου.
The man who *is speaking* to the crowd is my teacher.

ὁ ἄνθρωπος ὁ εἰπὼν τῷ ὄχλῳ ἐστὶν ὁ διδάσκαλός μου
The man who *spoke* to the crowd is my teacher.

ὁ ἄνθρωπος ὁ λέγων τῷ ὄχλῳ ἦν ὁ διδάσκαλός μου.
The man who *was speaking* to the crowd was my teacher.

ὁ ἄνθρωπος ὁ εἰπὼν τῷ ὄχλῳ ἦν ὁ διδάσκαλός μου.
The man who *had spoken* to the crowd was my teacher.

29.15 **Substantival**. Because you already know how to use personal and relative pronouns in the translation of the substantival participles, there is really nothing else to learn here.

---

[3] *Docetism* was an early Christian heresy that taught Jesus only appeared to be human. Epsilon is added to form the present tense stem. While the root of δοκέω is *δοκ, it adds an epsilon in the present tense stem and behaves like an epsilon contract in the present and imperfect. See *MBG*, v-1b(4).

[4] *Esophagus* is formed from the second root, *φαγ.

[5] *Christopher* (Χρίστοφερ) means *bearing Christ*.

Chapter 30

Perfect Participles and Genitive Absolutes

Exegetical Insight

The perfect tense is often used to teach important theological truths, and it is often not possible to translate its full significance. The phrase τῇ γὰρ χάριτί ἐστε σεσῳσμένοι διὰ πίστεως, translated in the NIV as, "For it is by grace you have been saved, through faith—" (Eph 2:8a), does not reveal the full meaning of ἐστε σεσῳσμένοι.

The perfect passive participle σεσῳσμένοι is used in tandem with ἐστε to form what is called a "periphrastic verb," a construction intended to place special emphasis on the continuing results. Paul is using this construction to emphasize that the effects of salvation are an ongoing part of a believer's life. What does this mean for contemporary Christian experience?

It means that the starting and the finishing lines are not the same. Salvation is indeed a process. Salvation has a beginning, a middle, and an end — justification, sanctification, and glorification. This experience is wholly dynamic, not incrementally static. At this point, the well-traveled "lifeboat analogy" is helpful. The unredeemed life is as if we were about to perish on a crippled ship threatening to sink as a result of sustaining irreparable damage in a menacing storm. Lifeboats arrive to rescue us and begin the perilous journey to the safety of the shore. Once in the saving vessel, however, the storm rages on. No one is quite sure when the storm may dissipate or when another

may erupt on the way to safety. While we may experience smooth sailing for a time, we very well could be smothered with peril again. Reaching the safe confines of the shore is the ultimate goal.

Making the exchange from a sinking to a saving vessel is the initiation of salvation, or justification; the voyage in the lifeboat is the working out of our salvation (see Phil 2:12), or sanctification; and reaching the shore is our final arrival in heaven. This is the consummation of salvation, or glorification. The aspect intended by ἐστε σεσῳσμένοι covers the entire journey. This understanding can yield a better translation and application, "For by grace you are being saved, through faith."

Additionally, the participle is in the passive voice, telling us that there is an external agent, the grace of God, at work in the process as well. While Paul is adamant one cannot work "for" salvation, he is just as convinced one must work "out" salvation. The Christian knows as well as Paul about the daily struggle involved in living the Christian life. Salvation is not totally automatic; serious effort is involved once it has begun. Struggling through the sanctification part of salvation, which is our post-conversion life, not only authenticates our relationship with Christ, it also drives us to grow deeper in our Christian experience.

Paul Jackson

Overview

In this chapter you will learn that:

■ the perfect participle is formed from one of the perfect tense stems (active and middle/passive) and indicates a completed action with results continuing into the present (of the speaker, not the reader);

■ a genitive absolute is a participial construction in which a participle and noun/pronoun in the genitive are not grammatically connected to any word in the rest of the sentence;

■ a periphrastic construction consists of a form of εἰμί and a participle, and is used in place of a finite verbal form;

■ there are other ways to translate adverbial participles.

Greek

30.1 **Summary**. This is the last participle you will learn. The perfect participle is formed on one of the perfect tense stems (active and middle/passive) and carries the same significance that the perfect does in the indicative. It indicates a completed action that has consequences in the present.

As is true in the indicative, so here the time is present from the standpoint of the speaker, not necessarily the reader. This error is made not infrequently.

30.2 **Translation**. My general suggestion is to use "(after) having ..." and the past perfect form of the verb (e.g., "after having eaten"). The use of "after" is optional, depending upon context.

30.3 **Reduplication**. The perfect participle is built on the perfect tense stem. The vocalic reduplication is retained, since it is not the same thing as the augment, indicating past time.

30.4 **Stem**. If a verb has a first perfect indicative, it will use that first perfect stem in the formation of the perfect participle. There are only a few second perfect participles, and they are discussed in the Advanced Information section.

Here are some one word answers.

Here: ὧδε   There: ἐκεί
Right: δεξιά   Left: ἀριστερά
Stop: στῆθι   Start: ξεκίνα
Entrance: εἴσοδος   Exit: ἔξοδος

What does the name of the second book in the Hebrew Testament mean?

First Perfect Participle

30.5   Chart: First perfect active participle

> *Reduplication + Perfect tense stem + Tense formative (κ) +*
>
> *Participle morpheme (οτ) + Case endings*
>
> λε + λυ + κ + οτ + ες ▸ λελυκότες

30.6   Paradigm: First perfect active participle. The active participle morpheme for the masculine and neuter is **οτ**, which looks like **κοτ** when joined with the tense formative. In the feminine, the οτ has been replaced by υια.[1]

	3 masc	1 fem	3 neut
nom sg	λελυκώς[2]	λελυκυῖα	λελυκός[3]
gen sg	λελυκότος	λελυκυίας	λελυκότος
dat sg	λελυκότι	λελυκυίᾳ	λελυκότι
acc sg	λελυκότα	λελυκυῖαν	λελυκός
nom pl	λελυκότες	λελυκυῖαι	λελυκότα
gen pl	λελυκότων	λελυκυιῶν	λελυκότων
dat pl	λελυκόσι(ν)	λελυκυίαις	λελυκόσι(ν)
acc pl	λελυκότας	λελυκυίας	λελυκότα

	masc	fem	neut
nom sg	κως	κυια	κος
gen sg	κοτος	κυιας	κοτος

30.7   Chart: First perfect middle/passive participle

> *Reduplication + Present tense stem +*
>
> *Participle morpheme (μεν) + Case endings*
>
> λε + λυ + μενο + ι ▸ λελυμένοι

---

[1] For details see *MBG*, 94.

[2] The case ending is a sigma. The tau drops out (Noun Rule 7) and the omicron lengthens to omega in order to compensate for the loss (Noun Rule 5). κοτς ▸ κος ▸ κως.

[3] The case ending is a sigma. The tau drops out (Noun Rule 7) but the omicron does not lengthen. κοτς ▸ κος.

30.8 **Paradigm: First perfect middle/passive participle**. The middle/passive participle morpheme is **μενο/η**.

	2 *masc*	1 *fem*	2 *neut*
nom sg	λελυμένος	λελυμένη	λελυμένον
gen sg	λελυμένου	λελυμένης	λελυμένου
dat sg	λελυμένῳ	λελυμένῃ	λελυμένῳ
acc sg	λελυμένον	λελυμένην	λελυμένον
nom pl	λελυμένοι	λελυμέναι	λελυμένα
gen pl	λελυμένων	λελυμένων	λελυμένων
dat pl	λελυμένοις	λελυμέναις	λελυμένοις
acc pl	λελυμένους	λελυμένας	λελυμένα

	masc	*fem*	*neut*
nom sg	μένος	μένη	μένον
gen sg	μένου	μένης	μένου

As in the indicative, there is no tense formative and no connecting vowel. This should make identification easier.[4]

Genitive Absolute

30.9 The grammatical definition of an "absolute" construction is a construction that has no grammatical relationship to the rest of the sentence.[5] The primary example of an absolute construction in Greek is the genitive absolute.

A genitive absolute is *a noun or pronoun and a participle in the genitive that are not grammatically connected to the rest of the sentence*.[6] In other words, there will be no word elsewhere in the sentence that the participial phrase modifies.

> καὶ εὐθὺς ἔτι αὐτοῦ λαλοῦντος παραγίνεται Ἰούδας (*Mark 14:43*).
> And immediately, *while he is still speaking*, Judas comes.

> ἐγένετο δὲ τοῦ δαιμονίου ἐξελθόντος ἐλάλησεν ὁ κωφός (*Luke 11:14*).
> And it happened that, *after the the demon had gone out*, the mute man spoke.

The participle is always anarthrous.

In rare cases there may be some grammatical connection. In these cases, the genitive absolute is probably reducing the complexity of the sentence.

---

[4] The accent will always be on the next to the last syllable, the "penult" (μέν).

[5] "Absolute" means "separated." It comes from the Latin "absolutus," which means "loosed." In English we have a similar construction called the "nominative absolute." It is a noun or pronoun with a participle that is not grammatically linked to the sentence. "*Weather permitting*, we will eat soon."

[6] It is possible not to have the noun or pronoun, but this is unusual (see *Bl-D* 423.6). If one is not present, you may assume it in your translation.

The majority of the genitive absolutes use a present participle, and many are some combination of αὐτοῦ and the participle of λαλέω or λέγω, or the participle of γίνομαι.

> ταῦτα αὐτοῦ λαλοῦντος πολλοὶ ἐπίστευσαν εἰς αὐτόν *(John 8:30).*
>
> *While he was saying these things,* many believed in him.

> ὀψίας δὲ γενομένης προσῆλθον αὐτῷ οἱ μαθηταί *(Matt 14:15).*
>
> Now *when it was evening,* the disciples came to him.

30.10 Helpful hints

- Notice how αὐτοῦ functions as the "subject" of the participle.[7] The genitive absolute is used when the noun or pronoun doing the action of the participle is different from the subject of the sentence.

- It is also possible for the participle to have modifiers, such as a direct object, adverb, etc., such as ἔτι in 30.9

- The genitive absolute tends to occur at the beginning of a sentence in narrative material.

30.11 Translation. The translation of the genitive absolute is idiomatic; you cannot translate word for word. See what it says in Greek, and then say the same basic thing in English, trying to emphasize the aspect of the participle. If you use an absolute construction in your translation, your English will actually be poor English, but for the time being this is okay.

30.12 These guidelines provide a starting point for translation.

1. Most genitive absolutes in the New Testament are temporal, and you will translate the genitive absolute as a *temporal clause.* Use "while" if the participle is present and "after" if the participle is aorist.

   > Ταῦτα αὐτοῦ λαλοῦντος αὐτοῖς, ἰδοὺ ἄρχων εἷς ἐλθὼν προσεκύνει αὐτῷ *(Matt 9:18).*
   >
   > *While he was saying these things to them,* behold, a ruler came in and knelt before him.

   > τοῦτο δὲ αὐτοῦ εἰπόντος ἐγένετο στάσις τῶν Φαρισαίων καὶ Σαδδουκαίων *(Acts 23:7).*
   >
   > *And when he had said this,* a dissension arose between the Pharisees and the Sadducees

2. If there is a "*subject*" in the genitive, use it and perhaps the finite form of the verb.

   > ἤδη δὲ αὐτοῦ καταβαίνοντος οἱ δοῦλοι αὐτοῦ ὑπήντησαν αὐτῷ *(John 4:51).*
   >
   > *As he was going down,* his servants met him.

30.13 In the following examples, differentiate among the regular participles and the genitive absolutes. Parse each participle.

> λέγοντες ταῦτα οἱ μαθηταὶ ἀπῆλθον ....
> λεγόντων προφήτων ταῦτα οἱ μαθηταὶ ἀπῆλθον ....

---

[7] I put "subject" in quotation marks because technically a participle cannot have a subject. But the word in the genitive functions as if it were the subject, and it is a helpful way to learn the construction.

εἰπόντες ταῦτα οἱ μαθηταὶ ἀπῆλθον ....

εἰπόντων προφήτων ταῦτα οἱ μαθηταὶ ἀπῆλθον ....

διδαχθέντες ὑπὸ τοῦ κυρίου ἐξῆλθον εἰς τὴν ἔρημον οἱ δοῦλοι.

διδαχθέντων προφήτων ὑπὸ τοῦ κυρίου ἐξῆλθον εἰς τὴν ἔρημον οἱ δοῦλοι.

Halftime Review

- The perfect participle is formed from one of the perfect tense stems (active and middle/passive) and indicates a completed action with results continuing into the present. The vocalic reduplication remains.

- The perfect active participle is formed from the perfect active tense stem (including reduplication) with οτ/υια.

- The perfect middle/passive participle is formed from the perfect middle/passive tense stem (including reduplication) with μενο/η.

- A genitive absolute is noun or pronoun and a participle in the genitive that are not grammatically connected to the rest of the sentence. The word in the genitive functions as a subject. It tends to occur at the beginning of a sentence in narrative material.

Periphrastic Constructions

30.14 One of the basic differences we have seen between English and Greek is that the different Greek tenses do not use helping verbs. English uses "will" to make a verb future and "be" to make it passive. Greek just uses different tense formatives, etc.

There is one situation, however, when Greek uses εἰμί and a participle together to state a single idea, and this is called a **periphrastic construction**.[8] Originally a periphrastic construction was used to emphasize the continuous force of the participle (which is why the aorist participle never occurs in this construction). However, by the time of Koine Greek, this emphasis is often lost. In fact, Koine Greek normally uses a periphrastic construction for the third person plural, perfect middle/passive.[9]

_____

[8] "Periphrastic" (περί + φράσις) means a "round about" way of saying something

[9] The third person plural perfect passive occurs only nine times in the New Testament, six of those being the form ἀφέωνται (from ἀφίημι). The third person plural middle perfect never occurs in the New Testament.

Here is the rule that governs whether a verb will form its third person plural, perfect middle/passive, periphrastically or not.

Verbs formed periphrastically:

- stems ending in a consonant (except nu; see below);
- stems adding a sigma to form the perfect passive tense stem.

Verbs not formed periphrastically:

- stems ending in nu drop the nu and are formed regularly;
- contract stems lengthen their final stem vowel.

Translate the periphrastic construction just as you would the regular formation of the tense; perhaps the continuous idea will be emphasized, but that is up to the context and not the verbal form (see Exegetical Insight).

30.15 Here are all the different forms a periphrastic construction can take. The form of εἰμί and the participle can be separated by several words.

periphrastic tense	construction		
Present	present of εἰμί	+	present participle
Imperfect	imperfect of εἰμί	+	present participle
Future	future of εἰμί	+	present participle
Perfect	present of εἰμί	+	perfect participle
Pluperfect	imperfect of εἰμί	+	perfect participle
Future perfect	future of εἰμί	+	perfect participle

Alternate Translations

30.16 So far you have learned a few ways to translate adverbial participles—present with "while" and "because," aorist with "after." This is a good place to start. But participles are used in other ways as well, and other ways of translating them will become necessary. Following are three more possibilities with their technical names.

■ **Instrumental participle**. Adverbial participles can indicate the *means* by which an action occurred. You may use the key word "by."

> κοπιῶμεν ἐργαζόμενοι ταῖς ἰδίαις χερσίν *(1 Cor 4:12)*.
> We toil *by working* with our hands.

See also the Exegetical Insight for Chapter 27.

■ **Concessive participle**. Some participles state a *concessive* idea and the key word is "though."

> ὀφθαλμοὺς ἔχοντες οὐ βλέπετε *(Mark 8:18)*.
> *Even though you have* eyes, you do not see.

■ As a **regular verb**. In certain constructions where a participle accompanies a verb, the participle is best translated as a finite verb.

> ὁ δὲ ἀποκριθεὶς εἶπεν· γέγραπται· οὐκ ἐπ᾽ ἄρτῳ μόνῳ ζήσεται ὁ ἄνθρωπος *(Matt 4:4)*.
> But he *answered* and said, "It is written, 'Man will not live on bread alone.'"

Some translations regularly omit the participle in this construction.

> Jesus answered, "It is written: 'Man does not live on bread alone'" (NIV).

Summary

1. The perfect participle indicates a completed action with results continuing into the present (of the writer). It is generally translated with "(after) having" and the past perfect form of the verb.

2. The perfect active participle is formed from the perfect active tense stem (including reduplication) with οτ/υια.

3. The perfect middle/passive participle is formed from the perfect middle/passive tense stem (including reduplication) with μενο/η.

4. A genitive absolute is a participial construction in which the participle in the genitive is unconnected to the main part of the sentence. It usually includes a noun or pronoun in the genitive that acts as the "subject" of the participle, and it can have modifiers. Translate the genitive absolute as a temporal clause using "while" and "after" unless the context does not allow it.

5. A periphrastic construction consists of a form of εἰμί and a participle that are used instead of a finite verbal form. It originally emphasized the continuous aspect of an action, but this cannot be assumed in Koine Greek. It is normally used in place of a third person plural perfect middle/passive.

6. An adverbial participle can indicate means or concession, and sometimes is best translated as a finite verb.

Summary of the Greek Participle

1. The participle is a verbal adjective. It can function adverbially or adjectivally (attributive; substantive).

2. If the participle is used adverbially, its form will agree with the noun or pronoun that is doing the action of the participle, normally the subject of the verb. It is *always* anarthrous.

3. Adverbial participles are often translated as a temporal clause ("while," "after"), but can also use the key words "because," "by," "though," or can be translated as a finite verb.

4. If the participle is used as an attributive adjective, then it will agree with the word it modifies in case, number, and gender, just like any adjective. It is *usually* articular.

5. If the participle is used as a substantive, then its case is determined by its function in the sentence. Its number and gender are determined by the word it refers to, just like a substantival adjective. You will most likely add words in your translation based on natural gender.

6. Because the participle does not indicate absolute time, the aorist participle is not unaugmented. The perfect participle does not lose its vocalic reduplication.

7. The **Participle Morpheme Chart** is now complete.

morpheme	tense/voice	case endings
ντ	all active (aorist passive)	3-1-3
οτ	perfect active	3-1-3
μενο / η	all middle/passive (all middle)	2-1-2

8. The **Master Participle Chart** is now complete.

tense & voice	redup	stem	t.f. c.v.	morpheme	nom. plural	six memory forms
present active		present	ο	ντ / ουσα	λέγοντες	ων, ουσα, ον οντος, ουσης, οντος
present mid/pas		present	ο	μενο / η	λεγόμενοι	ομενος, ομενη, ομενον ομενου, ομενης, ομενου
1 aorist active		aorist active	σα	ντ / σα	λύσαντες	σας, σασα, σαν σαντος, σασης, σαντος
1 aorist middle		aorist active	σα	μενο / η	λυσάμενοι	σαμενος ...
1 aorist passive		aorist passive	θε	ντ	λυθέντες	θεις, θεισα, θεν θεντος, θεισης, θεντος
2 aorist active		aorist active	ο	ντ	βαλόντες	ων ...
2 aorist middle		aorist active	ο	μενο / η	γενόμενοι	ομενος ...
2 aorist passive		aorist passive	ε	ντ	γραφέντες	εις, εισα, εν εντος, εισης, εντος
perfect active	λε	perfect active	κ	οτ	λελυκότες	κως, κυια, κος κοτος, κυιας, κοτος
perfect mid/pas	λε	perfect mid/pas		μενο / η	λελυμένοι	μενος ...

Vocabulary

μηδέ	but not, nor, not even (56)
πρεσβύτερος, -α, -ον	elder, older (66; *πρεσβυτερο)[10]

πρεσβύτερος can be used adjectivally to describe an older
person, or as a noun to describe an official in the church.

Total word count in the New Testament:	138,162
Number of words learned to date:	297
Number of word occurrences in this chapter:	122
Number of word occurrences to date:	108,522
Percent of total word count in the New Testament:	78.54%

Advanced Information

30.17 **Second perfect participles**. There are six verbs (excluding compound
forms) that have second perfects. Instead of memorizing paradigms, it is
easier to see the forms and know them well enough to recognize them.
They are all quite regular.

Their forms are identical to the first perfect except that the tense formative
is α and not κα. Since the middle/passive does not use a tense formative,
there can be no second perfect middle/passives.

If the form occurs only once, I will list the inflected form and reference. If a
form occurs more than once, I will list the nominative and genitive singular masculine forms, and the number of times all related forms occur.

lexical form	2 perfect active participle	reference or number of occurrences
ἀκούω	ἀκηκοότας	John 18:21
ἀνοίγω	ἀνεῳγότα	John 1:51
γίνομαι	γεγονώς, -ότος	14
ἔρχομαι	ἐληλυθώς, -ότος	4
λαμβάνω	εἰληφώς	Matt 25:24
πείθω	πεποιθώς, -ότος	9

30.18 εἰδώς is actually a perfect participle of οἶδα even though it carries a present meaning. It occurs 51 times in the New Testament, 23 times as εἰδώς
and 23 times as εἰδότες.

---

[10] A *presbyterian* church structure is rule by elders.

Overview 6
Chapters 31 – 36

Chapter 31

While the indicative mood describes what is—or at least how the speaker wants you to perceive reality—the subjunctive is used to express possibility, probability, exhortation, or an axiomatic concept. It is also used in statememts of purpose.

> ἐὰν γὰρ ἀγαπήσητε τοὺς ἀγαπῶντας ὑμᾶς, τίνα μισθὸν ἔχετε; *(Matt 5:46)*.
>
> For if *you love* those who love you, what reward do you have?

> Μὴ κρίνετε, ἵνα μὴ κριθῆτε *(Matt 7:1)*.
>
> Judge not, in order that *you be* not *judged*.

There are several keys to understanding a subjunctive verb.

■ The main sign is the lengthened connecting vowel (in blue below).

1 sg	λύω	1 pl	λύωμεν
2 sg	λύῃς	2 pl	λύητε
3 sg	λύῃ	3 pl	λύωσι(ν)

■ There are certain words that are followed by the subjunctive verb, and these words will become triggers in your thinking. They are ἵνα and ἐάν (and other words formed with ἄν).

■ Outside of the indicative system there is no absolute time, only aspect. A subjunctive formed on a present tense verb indicates a continuous action; a subjunctive formed from the aorist tense indicates an undefined action. There is no augment with the aorist, and there is no future or perfect subjunctive.

Chapter 32

The infinitive is a verbal noun and is generally translated with "to" and the verb.

> ἀπὸ τότε ἤρξατο ὁ Ἰησοῦς κηρύσσειν καὶ λέγειν· μετανοεῖτε *(Matt 4:17)*.
>
> From that time Jesus began *to preach* and *to say,* "Repent."

The forms just need to be memorized. Most end in -αι.

	present	1 aorist	2 aorist	perfect
active	λύειν·	λῦσαι	λαβεῖν	λελυκέναι
middle	λύεσθαι	λύσασθαι	λαβέσθαι	λελύσθαι
passive	λύεσθαι	λυθῆναι	γραφῆναι	λελύσθαι

Chapter 33

The imperative likewise just needs to be memorized. It has the same basic meaning in Greek as it does in English. Just remember that its primary significance is aspect, although this will often be difficult to bring into English.

> μετανοεῖτε, ἤγγικεν γὰρ ἡ βασιλεία τῶν οὐρανῶν *(Matt 3:2)*.
> *Repent,* for the kingdom of heaven is at hand.

> ποιήσατε οὖν καρπὸν ἄξιον τῆς μετανοίας *(Matt 3:8)*.
> Therefore, *produce* fruit worthy of repentance.

Chapter 34

In the last three chapters we meet a new type of verb. They are called μι verbs because they use μι instead of ω in the first person singular. At first they look a little strange, but the key to μι verbs is to learn their root and a few rules.

The most basic rules are that the μι verb reduplicates to form the present tense stem but uses an iota between the letters and not an epsilon as in the perfect. They also use a few alternative endings (μι, σι, ασι).

For example, the root *δο means "to give." Reduplicate it with an iota and add person endings, and there you have it: δίδωμι. But when you get to the future, look how regular it is: δώσω, δώσεις, δώσει, etc. The aorist uses κα and not σα as the tense formative.

	present	*aorist*	*perfect*
1 sg	δίδωμι	ἔδωκα	δέδωκα
2 sg	δίδως	ἔδωκας	δέδωκας
3 sg	δίδωσι(ν)	ἔδωκε(ν)	δέδωκε(ν)

Chapter 35

In the previous chapter we looked at just the non-indicative forms of δίδωμι. Now you will learn the non-indicative forms of δίδωμι. They are easy to recognize.

Chapter 36

Just like in contract verbs, so μι verbs are categoried by the last vowel in the stem. δίδωμι is from the root *δο and is an o-class μι verb; all μι verbs ending in omicron behave the same way.

There are also μι verbs with stems ending in alpha or epsilon. The nice thing is that they behave the same as δίδωμι except that the final stem vowel is different.

	*στα	*θε	*δο
1 sg	ἵστημι	τίθημι	δίδωμι
2 sg	ἵστης	τίθης	δίδως
3 sg	ἵστησι(ν)	τίθησι(ν)	δίδωσι(ν)

In the examples above, ἵστημι looses the reduplicated sigma: στα ‣ σιστα ‣ ἰστα ‣ ἵστημι. The reduplicated theta goes to tau in τίθημι: θε ‣ θιθε ‣ τιθε ‣ τίθημι.

As you can also see, the root vowel can also change its length from short to long (α ‣ η, ε ‣ η, ο ‣ ω).

Chapter 31

Subjunctive

Exegetical Insight

When we listen to someone we care about and respect deeply, we listen for more than the surface meaning. The content is important, but we are keen to catch also the attitude of the speaker, what his words imply about our relationship with him, what is most significant to him, what he emphasizes as he speaks, and so forth. When we study the New Testament we can look for such elements of meaning as well.

This chapter describes a fascinating combination used by the Greek language to show emphasis: it is the use of the two negatives οὐ μή with a subjunctive verb to indicate a strong negation about the future. The speaker uses the subjunctive verb to suggest a future possibility, but in the same phrase he emphatically denies (by means of the double negative) that such could ever happen. This linguistic combination occurs about eighty-five times in the New Testament, often in significant promises or reassurances about the future.

In Jesus' description of himself as the Good Shepherd in John 10, he gives one of the most treasured of these promises: "My sheep listen to my voice; I know them, and they follow me. I give them eternal life, and they shall never perish (οὐ μὴ ἀπόλωνται)" (10:27–28a NIV). It would have been enough to have οὐ with a future indicative verb here, but Jesus is more emphatic. The subjunctive combination strongly denies even the possibility that any of Jesus' sheep would perish: "they will certainly not perish," "they will by no means perish," is the sense of Jesus' assertion. This is reinforced by the addition of the phrase εἰς τὸν αἰῶνα, "forever." Jesus' emphatic promise is the bedrock of assurance and godly motivation for every one of his sheep!

Buist M. Fanning

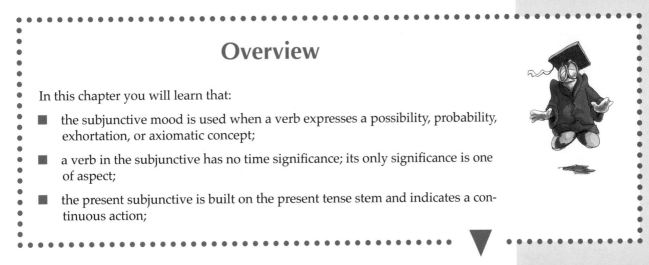

Overview

In this chapter you will learn that:

- the subjunctive mood is used when a verb expresses a possibility, probability, exhortation, or axiomatic concept;

- a verb in the subjunctive has no time significance; its only significance is one of aspect;

- the present subjunctive is built on the present tense stem and indicates a continuous action;

- the aorist subjunctive is built on the unaugmented aorist tense stem and indicates an undefined action;

- the sign of the subjunctive is the lengthened connecting vowel (e.g., λύωμεν). The endings are exactly the same in the aorist as in the present.

English

31.1 So far you have studied only the indicative mood.[1] If a verb is making a statement or asking a factual question, the verb is in the indicative.[2] As it is normally stated, the indicative is the mood of *reality*. It states what is.

> The book is red.
>
> I want to learn Greek.
>
> Why was Hebrew so hard?

31.2 The subjunctive does not describe what is, but what may (or might) be. In other words, it is the mood not of reality but of *possibility* (or *probability*). There may be a subtle distinction between "may" and "might," but for our purposes they can be viewed as identical.[3]

> I may learn Hebrew.
>
> I might have learned Greek if I had studied regularly.

31.3 A common use of the subjunctive in English is in an "if" clause.

> If I were a rich man, I would hire a Greek tutor.

If in fact the speaker were rich, he would not have used the subjunctive "were" but the indicative form: "I *am* rich and therefore I will hire a tutor." This would be a statement of fact, the mood being one of reality. However, if he were not rich, the speaker would use the subjunctive form "were": "If I were rich ...."[4]

31.4 Because the action described by a verb in the subjunctive is unfulfilled, it often refers to a future event.

Greek

31.5 The basic definition of the subjunctive and indicative moods in Greek is similar to English. There are, however, several significant differences.

---

[1] Remember, participles are technically not a mood.

[2] Technically, an indicative verb gives a person's *perception* of reality, or how he or she wants you to perceive reality. Otherwise, no one could lie or be mistaken.

[3] The technical distinction is that if the main verb is a present or future tense, you use "may;" if the main verb is a past tense, you use "might."

[4] "Were" is perhaps not the best example since it can be used both as an indicative and as a subjunctive, but it is the most common English subjunctive. "If I were rich" is correct English grammar, regardless of current usage.

31.6 **Aspect**. A Greek verb has absolute time significance only in the indicative. The only significance that a verb in the subjunctive has is one of aspect. This is the same as with the participle.

A verb in the present subjunctive indicates a continuous action; a verb in the aorist subjunctive indicates an undefined action. There is no concept of absolute past or present time in the subjunctive. Most grammars call the subjunctive formed from the present tense stem the "present subjunctive," and the subjunctive formed from the aorist tense stem the "aorist subjunctive." As is the case with participles, I urge you to adopt the terminology "continuous subjunctive" and "undefined subjunctive," because their true significance is aspect and not time.

> κύριε, ἐὰν θέλῃς δύνασαί με καθαρίσαι *(Matt 8:2)*.
>
> Lord, if *you are willing*, you are able to make me clean.

> ἐπὰν δὲ εὕρητε, ἀπαγγείλατέ μοι *(Matt 2:8)*.
>
> When you *have found* him, report to me.

It is difficult to bring out the aspect of the subjunctive verb in translation. One way is to use the key word "continue" with the present subjunctive. If you cannot translate this way, be sure to emphasize the aspect in your teaching and preaching.

> ὃς γὰρ ἐὰν θέλῃ τὴν ψυχὴν αὐτοῦ σῶσαι ἀπολέσει αὐτήν *(Mark 8:35)*.
>
> For whoever *continually wishes* to his life will lose it.

There are only two tenses that form the subjunctive, the present and aorist.[5] There is no future subjunctive. Because the aorist subjunctive is built on the unaugmented aorist tense stem, a first aorist subjunctive may look like a future (e.g., ἀγαπήσω). But remember, there is no future subjunctive.

31.7 **Form**. The good news is that the subjunctive uses the same endings as the indicative. All forms of the subjunctive use primary endings. The subjunctive merely lengthens the connecting vowel to indicate that the verb is in the subjunctive. Omicron lengthens to omega (e.g., λύωμεν) and epsilon lengthens to eta (e.g., λύητε).[6]

31.8 **Chart: Present (continuous) subjunctive**. The present subjunctive uses the present tense stem of the verb but lengthens the connecting vowel. λύομεν in the indicative becomes λύωμεν in the subjunctive.

> *Present tense stem +*
>
> *Lengthened connecting vowel (ω/η) +*
>
> *Primary personal endings*
>
> *active:* λυ + ω + μεν ‣ λύωμεν
>
> *middle/passive:* λυ + ω + μεθα ‣ λυώμεθα

> This is important. Outside the indicative mood there generally are only three tenses to communicate the three aspects. The aorist is the default. The fact that a subjunctive (or infinitive or imperative) is aorist may have no real meaning in terms of its aspect. Therefore, when you see a nonindicative present or perfect, pay special attention to its aspect.

---

5 There actually are a few examples of the perfect subjunctive; see Advanced Information.

6 ουσι(ν) goes to ωσι(ν) and ῃ stays as ῃ.

31.9 **Paradigm: Present subjunctive**. I have included the active subjunctive of εἰμί. It has no passive. For the forms of contract verbs in the subjunctive, see the Appendix (page 364).

	subjunctive	(εἰμί)	indicative

active

	subjunctive	(εἰμί)	indicative
1 sg	λύω	ὦ	λύω
2 sg	λύῃς	ᾖς	λύεις
3 sg	λύῃ	ᾖ[7]	λύει
1 pl	λύωμεν	ὦμεν	λύομεν
2 pl	λύητε	ἦτε	λύετε
3 pl	λύωσι(ν)	ὦσι(ν)	λύουσι(ν)

middle/passive

	subjunctive	indicative
1 sg	λύωμαι	λύομαι
2 sg	λύῃ	λύῃ
3 sg	λύηται	λύεται
1 pl	λυώμεθα	λυόμεθα
2 pl	λύησθε	λύεσθε
3 pl	λύωνται	λύονται

Notice that the endings are all regular, and that the present and aorist use the same endings. You do not have to memorize any new endings — just one rule. Notice also that the ending η occurs in third singular active and second singular middle/passive.

31.10 **Chart: Aorist (undefined) subjunctive**

> *Unaugmented aorist tense stem +*
>
> *(Tense formative +)*
>
> *Lengthened connecting vowel (ω/η) +*
>
> *Primary personal endings*
>
> *first aorist:*   λυ + σ + ω + μεν ‣ λύσωμεν
> *second aorist:* λαβ + ω + μεν ‣ λάβωμεν

Because the subjunctive does not indicate absolute past time, the augment must be removed, just as in the aorist participle.

The aorist subjunctive uses the aorist tense stem of the verb. If it is a first aorist stem, you will see the tense formative. If it is a second aorist stem, then it will be different from its present tense stem form. This is one of the main clues helping you to identify the subjunctive.

---

[7]   Do not confuse this form with similar words; see the Appendix.

Just as the aorist passive indicative uses active endings, so also the aorist passive subjunctive uses active endings. The aorist subjunctive uses exactly the same personal endings as the present subjunctive.

31.11 Paradigm: Aorist subjunctive

	subjunctive		indicative	
	1st aorist	2nd aorist	1st aorist	2nd aorist
active				
1 sg	λύσω	λάβω	ἔλυσα	ἔλαβον
2 sg	λύσῃς	λάβῃς	ἔλυσας	ἔλαβες
3 sg	λύσῃ	λάβῃ	ἔλυσε(ν)	ἔλαβε(ν)
1 pl	λύσωμεν	λάβωμεν	ἐλύσαμεν	ἐλάβομεν
2 pl	λύσητε	λάβητε	ἐλύσατε	ἐλάβετε
3 pl	λύσωσι(ν)	λάβωσι(ν)	ἔλυσαν	ἔλαβον
middle				
1 sg	λύσωμαι	γένωμαι	ἐλυσάμην	ἐγενόμην
2 sg	λύσῃ	γένῃ	ἐλύσω	ἐγένου
3 sg	λύσηται	γένηται	ἐλύσατο	ἐγένετο
1 pl	λυσώμεθα	γενώμεθα	ἐλυσάμεθα	ἐγενόμεθα
2 pl	λύσησθε	γένησθε	ἐλύσασθε	ἐγένεσθε
3 pl	λύσωνται	γένωνται	ἐλύσαντο	ἐγένοντο
passive				
1 sg	λυθῶ	γραφῶ	ἐλύθην	ἐγράφην
2 sg	λυθῇς	γραφῇς	ἐλύθης	ἐγράφης
3 sg	λυθῇ	γραφῇ	ἐλύθη	ἐγράφη
1 pl	λυθῶμεν	γραφῶμεν	ἐλύθημεν	ἐγράφημεν
2 pl	λυθῆτε	γραφῆτε	ἐλύθητε	ἐγράφητε
3 pl	λυθῶσι(ν)	γραφῶσι(ν)	ἐλύθησαν	ἐγράφησαν

Remember: there is no future subjunctive. It is easy to see an aorist subjunctive and think it is a future indicative or subjunctive. Also, do not confuse the lengthened connecting vowel of the subjunctive with the lengthened contract vowel in the indicative.

Don't forget, in modern Greek you say παρακαλώ for both "please" and "you're welcome." You say ευχαριστώ for "thank you," or ευχαριστώ πολύ for "thank you very much."

31.12 **Contract verbs**. The subjunctive of contract verbs are regular, but they are different enough that you should look through the paradigms. They do not all have the characteristic eta or omega due to the contractions.

	-άω	-έω	-όω
present active			
1 sg	γεννῶ	ποιῶ	φανερῶ
2 sg	γεννᾷς	ποιῇς	φανεροῖς
3 sg	γεννᾷ	ποιῇ	φανεροῖ
1 pl	γεννῶμεν	ποιῶμεν	φανερῶμεν
2 pl	γεννᾶτε	ποιῆτε	φανερῶτε
3 pl	γεννῶσι(ν)	ποιῶσι(ν)	φανερῶσι(ν)
present middle/passive			
1 sg	γεννῶμαι	ποιῶμαι	φανερῶμαι
2 sg	γεννᾷ	ποιῇ	φανεροῖ
3 sg	γεννᾶται	ποιῆται	φανερῶται
1 pl	γεννώμεθα	ποιώμεθα	φανερώμεθα
2 pl	γεννᾶσθε	ποιῆσθε	φανερῶσθε
3 pl	γεννῶνται	ποιῶνται	φανερῶνται

Halftime Review

- While the indicative is the mood of reality, the subjunctive is the mood of possibility or probability.

- The subjunctive formed from a present tense stem indicates a continuous action. The subjunctive formed from an aorist tense stem indicates an undefined action. There is no absolute time in the subjunctive.

- There is no future subjunctive.

- The continuous and undefined subjunctive use the same primary endings.

- The sign of the subjunctive is the lengthened connecting vowel.

Uses of the Subjunctive

31.13 **Different uses**. The subjunctive has a wider variety of uses in Greek than in English. The idea of "probability" is only one. The first two uses occur in dependent clauses, the second two in independent clauses.

Notice how rarely I use "may" or "might" in the translations. Use of these key words is only to help you get comfortable with the subjunctive and are not always required.

Dependent Clauses

31.14 **1. ἵνα and the subjunctive**. ἵνα is almost always followed by the subjunctive and can indicate purpose.

> τίς σοι ἔδωκεν τὴν ἐξουσίαν ταύτην ἵνα ταῦτα <u>ποιῇς</u>; *(Mark 11:28)*
> Who gave you this authority that *you do* these things?

> ἐπηρώτησαν αὐτὸν … ἵνα <u>κατηγορήσωσιν</u> αὐτοῦ *(Matt 12:10)*.
> They asked him … so that *they could accuse* him.

The phrases ἵνα μή can be translated "lest" or some equivalent. It is an idiomatic phrase.

> οἱ πατέρες, μὴ ἐρεθίζετε τὰ τέκνα ὑμῶν, <u>ἵνα μὴ ἀθυμῶσιν</u> *(Col 3:21)*.
> Fathers, do not provoke your children, *lest they become discouraged.*

Remember that the ἵνα clause can also give the content of the preceding verb.

> ἐκήρυξαν ἵνα <u>μετανοῶσιν</u> *(Mark 6:12)*.
> They preached that *they should repent.*

31.15 **2. ἐάν and the subjunctive**. This combination occurs in a **conditional statement**. A conditional statement is an "If … then …" sentence. "If I am smart, I will take Hebrew." The "if" clause is called the "protasis" and the "then" clause is called the "apodosis."

There is no conditional element in the apodosis. If the protasis is true, the the writer is saying the "then" clause is most certainly true.

> ἐὰν ὁμολογῶμεν τὰς ἁμαρτίας ἡμῶν, πιστός ἐστιν καὶ δίκαιος, ἵνα ἀφῇ ἡμῖν τὰς ἁμαρτίας καὶ καθαρίσῃ ἡμᾶς ἀπὸ πάσης ἀδικίας
> *(1 John 1:9)*.
> *If* we confess our sins, he *is* faithful and just to forgive us our sins and to cleanse us from all unrighteousness.

The conditional element applies only to the protasis; will you or will you not confess your sins? However, if you do confess your sins, then there can be no doubt that Jesus will forgive your sins and cleanse you.

Conditional sentences are classified by their form and are given the titles "first class," "second class," "third class," and "fourth class." Third class conditional sentences always have a protasis introduced by ἐάν and a verb in the subjunctive. The verb in the apodosis can be any tense or mood. There are two subdivisions of third class conditions.

Future more probable. A future condition says that if something might happen, then something else will definitely happen. The speaker is thinking of a specific event in the future.

> ταῦτά σοι πάντα δώσω, ἐὰν πεσὼν <u>προσκυνήσῃς</u> μοι *(Matt 4:9)*.
> All these I will give you, if you will fall down and *worship* me.

> ἐὰν γὰρ <u>ἀγαπήσητε</u> τοὺς ἀγαπῶντας ὑμᾶς, τίνα μισθὸν ἔχετε; *(Matt 5:46)*.
> For if *you love* those who love you, what reward do you have?

The issue of how to categorize and translate conditional sentences is debated. At this early time in your training, I cannot go into the debate in detail. In the exercises for this chapter there are two types of conditional sentences, and I will discuss those here. In Chapter 35 there is a summary of conditional sentences.

Exegesis raises the important question as to whether the speaker thinks the protasis is *likely* to occur, or whether it will only *possibly* occur. The Bible has examples of future more probable conditions in which the protasis is likely to be true and others in which the protasis is hypothetical. As always, context is the key.

Present general. A general condition is identical in form to the future more probable condition except that the verb in the apodosis must be in the present tense.

Its meaning is slightly different from the future more probable. Instead of saying something about a specific event that might happen, it is stating a general truth, an axiomatic truth. The subjunctive is appropriate because the truth of the statement is timeless.

> ἐάν τις περιπατῇ ἐν τῇ ἡμέρᾳ, οὐ προσκόπτει *(John 11:9)*.
> If anyone *walks* in the day, he does not stumble.

> ἐὰν θέλῃς δύνασαί με καθαρίσαι *(Matt 8:2)*.
> Lord, if *you are willing*, you can make me clean.

Apart from the tense of the verb in the apodosis, only context can tell you if the speaker is making a specific statement or stating a general truth.

Independent Clauses

31.16 **3. Hortatory subjunctive**. The first person subjunctive, either singular or plural, can be used as an exhortation. It will usually be plural and occur at the beginning of the sentence. Use "Let me" or "Let us" in your translation.

> προσευχώμεθα.
> *Let us pray.*

> ἐκβάλω τὸ κάρφος ἐκ τοῦ ὀφθαλμοῦ σοῦ *(Matt 7:4)*.
> *Let me take* the speck out of your eye.

> διέλθωμεν εἰς τὸ πέραν *(Mark 4:35)*.
> *Let us go across* to the other side.

Just because a verb is first person subjunctive does not mean it is necessarily hortatory. Context will decide.

31.17 **4. Deliberative subjunctive.** When a person asks a question and the answer is uncertain, the verb in the question is put in the subjunctive.

> μὴ οὖν μεριμνήσητε λέγοντες, τί φάγωμεν; ἤ· τί πίωμεν; ἤ· τί περιβαλώμεθα; *(Matt 6:31)*[8]
> Therefore do not worry saying, "What *should we eat*?" or, "What *should we drink*?" or, "What *should we wear*?"

Review of the Clues

31.18 What, then, are the clues that a word is in the subjunctive?

■ If you see ἵνα or ἐάν, the following verb will probably be in the subjunctive. The same holds true for the following words, mostly forms combined with ἄν.

- ὅταν (ὅτε + ἄν) whenever
- ἐάν (εἰ + ἄν) if
- ὃς ἄν whoever

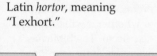

"Hortatory" comes from the Latin *hortor*, meaning "I exhort."

The Greek manuscripts of Rom 5:1 have an interesting difference. Some read ἔχωμεν and others read ἔχομεν. Say the two forms outloud to hear how easily they could be confused. What is the difference in meaning, especially as you look at the overall argument of Romans?

---

[8] You may have noticed that μὴ μεριμνήσητε states a prohibition. This is another use of the subjunctive and will be discussed in 33.17.

- ὅπου ἄν   wherever
- ἕως   until
- ἕως ἄν   until

When the word ἄν (by itself or in combination with another word) makes a statement more general, the verb will be in the subjunctive.

> ὃ ἂν βλασφημήσῃ εἰς τὸ πνεῦμα τὸ ἅγιον οὐκ ἔχει ἄφεσιν εἰς τὸν αἰῶνα (Mark 3:29).
>
> Whoever *blasphemes* against the Holy Spirit will never be forgiven.

■ Lengthened connecting vowel (ω/η)

■ No augment in the aorist.

Odds 'n Ends

31.19 Negation. The basic rule is that οὐ is used to negate a verb in the indicative while μή is used to negate everything else, including the subjunctive.

There is one specific construction using the subjunctive that needs to be stressed. The construction οὐ μή followed by the aorist subjunctive is a strong negation of a future situation, stronger than simply saying οὐ. The two negatives do not negate each other; they strengthen the construction to say "No!" more emphatically. See the *Exegetical Insight* for an example.

31.20 Questions. There are three ways to ask a question.

■ No indication is given as to the answer expected by the speaker.

> σὺ εἶ ὁ βασιλεὺς τῶν Ἰουδαίων; *(Matt 27:11)*
> Are you the king of the Jews?

■ If the question begins with οὐ, the speaker expects an affirmative answer.[9]

> Διδάσκαλε, οὐ μέλει σοι ὅτι ἀπολλύμεθα; *(Mark 4:38)*
> Teacher, do you not care that we are perishing?

The disciples were expecting Jesus to answer, "Yes, it is a concern."

■ If the question begins with μή, the speaker expects a negative answer.

> μὴ πάντες ἀπόστολοι; *(1 Cor 12:29)*
> Are all apostles?

Ask your teacher how you are to translate the latter two. Most translations do not indicate the expected answer. English can do the same thing the Greek is doing, even if it is a little burdensome sounding.

> Teacher, it is a concern to you that we are perishing, isn't it?
> All are not apostles, are they?

To emphasize to his disciples that they would see the truth of his definition of discipleship in the kingdom of God, Jesus says: Ἀμὴν λέγω ὑμῖν ὅτι εἰσίν τινες ὧδε τῶν ἑστηκότων οἵτινες οὐ μὴ γεύσωνται θανάτου ἕως ἂν ἴδωσιν τὴν βασιλείαν τοῦ θεοῦ ἐληλυθυῖαν ἐν δυνάμει. "Truly I say to you that there are some standing here who *will most assuredly not taste death* (οὐ μὴ γεύσωνται) until they see that the kingdom of God has come in power" (Mark 9:1).

---

9   Just because a question has an οὐ does not mean it expects an affirmative answer. καὶ ἔρχονται καὶ λέγουσιν αὐτῷ, διὰ τί οἱ μαθηταὶ Ἰωάννου καὶ οἱ μαθηταὶ τῶν Φαρισαίων νηστεύουσιν, οἱ δὲ σοὶ μαθηταὶ οὐ νηστεύουσιν; (Mark 2:18). "And they come and say to him, 'Why do the disciples of John and the disciples of the Pharisees fast, but your disciples do not fast?'" Here the οὐ immediately precedes the verb and negates it. But when οὐ is indicating the expected answer, that answer is "Yes." In most cases, it stands at the beginning of the question.

Master Nonindicative Verb Chart

31.21 As you did in the indicative, concentrate on learning this chart and how Greek puts the different forms together.

Master Nonindicative Verb Chart

Subjunctive

Tense	Aug/ Redup	Tense stem	Tense form.	Conn. vowel	Personal endings	1st sing paradigm
Present act		pres		ω/η	prim act	λύω
Present mid/pas		pres		ω/η	prim mid/pas	λύωμαι
1st aorist act		aor act	σ(α)	ω/η	prim act	λύσω
1st aorist mid		aor act	σ(α)	ω/η	prim mid/pas	λύσωμαι
1st aorist pas		aor pas	θ(η)	ω/η	prim act	λυθῶ
2nd aorist act		aor act		ω/η	prim act	λάβω
2nd aorist mid		aor act		ω/η	prim mid/pas	γένωμαι
2nd aorist pas		aor pas		ω/η	prim act	γράφω

Summary

1. The subjunctive mood is used when a verb expresses a possibility, probability, exhortation, or axiomatic concept.

2. A verb in the subjunctive has no time significance. Its only significance is one of aspect. The subjunctive built on the present tense stem indicates a continuous action. The subjunctive built on the unaugmented aorist tense stem indicates an undefined action.

3. The primary sign of the subjunctive is the lengthened connecting vowel. The endings are exactly the same in the aorist as in the present (primary endings).

4. The subjunctive is also used in a hortatory comment (to which you add the helping phrase "Let us") and in deliberative questions.

Signs of the Subjunctive

1. Following ἵνα, ἐάν, and other words formed with ἄν
2. Lengthened connecting vowel (ω/η)
3. No augment in the aorist

Vocabulary

λίθος, –ου, ὁ   stone (59; *λιθο)[10]

τοιοῦτος, –αύτη, –οῦτον   such, of such a kind (57; *τοιουτο)

Total word count in the New Testament:	138,162
Number of words learned to date:	299
Number of word occurrences in this chapter:	116
Number of word occurrences to date:	108,638
Percent of total word count in the New Testament:	78.63%

Advanced Information

31.22 Perfect subjunctive. The perfect subjunctive occurs only ten times in the New Testament. All ten are forms of οἶδα. There are other examples of the perfect subjunctive but they are all periphrastic.[11] It denotes an action as completed with results up to the time of the speaker.

1 sg	εἰδῶ	1 Cor 13:2; 14:11
2 sg	εἰδῆς	1 Tim 3:15
3 sg	–	
1 pl	εἰδῶμεν	1 Cor 2:12
2 pl	εἰδῆτε	Mt 9:6; Mk 2:10; Lk 5:24; Eph 6:21; 1 Jn 2:29; 5:13
3 pl	–	

We know how to say hello and goodbye. Here are as few similar phrases that are perhaps more Modern Greek than Koine, but you can see what they mean.

Modern	*Koine*	
καλημέρα	καλὴ ἡμέρα	Good morning
χαίρετε	καλὸς δειλινός	Good afternoon
καλησπέρα	καλὴ ἑσπέρα	Good evening
καληνύκτα	καλὴ νύξ	Good night

---

[10] *Lithography* is a printing method that originally used a flat stone but now uses metal. *Lithomancy* is divination using stone.

[11] Cf. Fanning, 396-397.

Chapter 32

Infinitive

Exegetical Insight

Infinitives often complete important ideas. No more important idea exists than the one Paul makes in 1 Corinthians 15:25. Here he says, "For it is necessary that he (Jesus) be reigning (βασιλεύειν) until he (God) has put all things in subjection under his (Jesus') feet." Now a Greek infinitive contains tense, something that is not clear in English infinitives. The tense in the case of this verse is a present tense, which describes a continuous action. So this present infinitive explains what is necessary about what God is in the process of doing through Jesus. (Remember that tense highlights type of action.) So Paul stresses that Jesus is in the process of ruling until the job of subjecting everything under his feet is complete. The remark about subjection is an allusion to Psalm 110:1, one of the New Testament's favorite Old Testament passages.

This idea is important because some think only of Jesus' rule as one anticipated in the future. There will be a total manifestation of that authority one day as the rest of 1 Corinthians 15 makes clear, but the process has already started in the second Adam, the one who reverses the presence of sin in the world and does so in each one of us daily as an expression of his authority to redeem us from the curse of sin. May his rule be manifest in us!

Darrell L. Bock

Overview

In this chapter you will learn that:

- the Greek infinitive is a verbal noun. It is not declined;

- all infinitive morphemes end in αι, except for the present active and second aorist active;

- the infinitive has no time significance, only aspect: continuous; undefined; perfected;

- the infinitive does not have a subject, but there will often be a word in the accusative functioning as if it were the subject;

- there are five main ways in which an infinitive is used.

English

32.1 An infinitive is a verbal noun, much like the participle is a verbal adjective. It is most easily recognized as a verb preceded by the word "to."

- *"To study* is my highest aspiration." In this case, the infinitive *to study* is the subject of the sentence.

- "I started *to sweat* when I realized finals were three weeks away." In this sentence, the infinitive *to sweat* is the direct object of the verb.

Greek

32.2 The same is true of the infinitive in Greek, although here it is capable of somewhat wider use.

- The infinitive is a verbal noun.

- It is always indeclinable (which means it does not change its form), but is viewed as singular neuter.

- When it is preceded by a definite article, the article is always neuter singular and its case is determined by the function of the infinitive.

    For example, if the infinitive is the subject, the article will be in the nominative (τὸ βάλλειν). If the infinitive is the object of a preposition that takes the dative, the article will be in the dative (τῷ βάλλειν).

- An infinitive can have a direct object and adverbial modifiers. "To study *for a long time* brings one into a state of ecstasy." In this case, the prepositional phrase *for a long time* modifies the infinitive *to study*.

An infinitive also has tense and voice, but this will be discussed below. The infinitive has no person and no number!

32.3 **Summary**. Infinitives can occur in three tenses: present, aorist, perfect. As you might suspect, because the infinitive is outside the indicative mood, these forms do not differentiate time but only aspect. This nuance will usually be difficult to bring into English.

tense	aspect	translation
present	continuous	"to continually study"
aorist	undefined	"to study"
perfect	completed	"to have studied"

32.4 **Infinitive Morpheme Chart**

	present	1st aorist	2nd aorist	perfect
active	ειν	σαι	ειν	κεναι
middle	εσθαι	σασθαι	εσθαι	σθαι
passive	εσθαι	θηναι	ηναι	σθαι

32.5 Paradigm: Infinitive

	present	1 aorist	2 aorist	perfect
active	λύειν	λῦσαι	λαβεῖν	λελυκέναι
middle	λύεσθαι	λύσασθαι	λαβέσθαι	λελύσθαι
passive	λύεσθαι	λυθῆναι	γραφῆναι	λελύσθαι

- ■ The *present* (continuous) infinitive is built on the present tense stem.

- ■ The *aorist active/middle* (undefined) infinitive is built on the aorist active/middle tense stem (without the augment).

   The *aorist passive* infinitive is built on the aorist passive tense stem (without the augment).

- ■ The *perfect active* (completed) infinitive is formed on the perfect active tense stem.

   The *perfect middle/passive* infinitive is formed on the perfect middle/passive tense stem.

- ■ The present infinitive of εἰμί is εἶναι, "to be." It has no aorist form.

32.6 Hints.

- ■ All the infinitives, except the present and second aorist active, end in αι.

- ■ The aorist infinitive that is built on the second aorist stem looks just like the present except for the stem change (and the accent).

- ■ Do not forget about the irregular contractions that occur with contract verbs in the present active infinitive. Alpha contracts form -ᾶν instead of the expected -αν (νικαειν ▸ νικαιν ▸ νικᾶν), while omicron contract verbs form οῦν instead of οῖν (πληροειν ▸ πληρουν ▸ πληροῦν).[1]

32.7 Definitions. As you can see from the definitions below, it is difficult to bring the sense of the present infinitive into English. You can say something like, "to continue to loose," but that is not very good English.

	present	1 aorist	2 aorist	perfect
active	to loose	to loose	to receive	to have loosed
middle	to loose	to loose	to receive	to have loosed
passive	to be loosed	to be loosed	to be written	to have been loosed

If you want to differentiate the meaning of the middle from the active, you could say, "to loose for oneself."

---

[1]   This is because ειν is actually a contraction of εεν. When you contract αεεν and οεεν, you end with αν and ουν according to the usual rules.

Meaning of the Infinitive

32.8 **Aspect**. As is the case in the participle and subjunctive, the infinitive has no time significance. The only difference between the infinitives built on the different stems is their aspect.

- The infinitive built on the *present* stem indicates a *continuous* action.

    Οὐδεὶς δύναται δυσὶ κυρίοις <u>δουλεύειν</u> *(Matt 6:24)*.

    No one is able *to serve* two masters.

- The infinitive built on the *aorist* stem indicates an *undefined* action.

    μὴ φοβηθῇς <u>παραλαβεῖν</u> Μαρίαν τὴν γυναῖκά σου *(Matt 1:20)*.

    Do not be afraid *to take* Mary as your wife.

- The infinitive built on the *perfect* stem indicates a *completed* action with ongoing implications.

    ἤκουσαν τοῦτο αὐτὸν <u>πεποιηκέναι</u> τὸ σημεῖον *(John 12:18)*.

    They heard he *had done* this sign.

- Because of the limitations of English, it is usually impossible to carry these nuances into English. You will probably use the simple present form of the verb in your translation of all infinitives (e.g., "to see," "to eat").

To help enforce the significance of the aspect in your mind, you may at first want to use "continue" in your translation of the present infinitive. βλέπειν means "to continue to see," while βλέψαι means "to see." You certainly would not want to use this technique when producing a finished translation, but for now it may be a good idea. But most importantly, in your studies and teaching you can always bring out the true significance of aspect.

32.9 **Subject**. Because an infinitive is not a finite[2] verbal form, it technically cannot have a subject. However, there is often a noun *in the accusative* that acts as if it were the subject of the infinitive. A parallel to this is the genitive absolute, where the noun or pronoun in the genitive acts as if it were the subject of the participle.[3]

    οὐκ ἤφιεν λαλεῖν <u>τὰ δαιμόνια</u> *(Mark 1:34)*.

    He would not permit the demons to speak.

If the infinitive has a direct object, it can sometimes become interesting to determine which word in the accusative is the "subject" and which is the direct object. Usually context will make it clear. As a general rule, the first accusative will be the "subject" and the second the direct object. βλέπειν

---

[2] A "finite" verbal form is one that is limited, specifically by a subject. In the sentence "Tom reads books," the verb *reads* is finite, limited. It does not apply to everyone, just the subject *Tom*. Similarly, an "infinitive" (the "in-" negates the following element of the word) is not limited by a subject; it is infinite, an infinitive.

[3] Technically, this accusative is called an "accusative of reference." If you were to read βλέπειν αὐτόν, this would be translated "to see with reference to him." αὐτόν behaves as if it were the subject of the infinitive.

αὐτόν αὐτήν would usually mean, "he (αὐτόν) to see her (αὐτήν)." (βλέπειν is an infinitive.)

ἐν τῷ εἰσαγαγεῖν τοὺς γονεῖς τὸ παιδίον Ἰησοῦν *(Luke 2:27)*
When the *parents* brought in the *child* Jesus

Two exceptions to this are the verbs ἔξεστιν ("it is lawful") and παραγγέλλω ("I command"), which take a "subject" in the dative.[4] Verbs that take their direct object in the dative will take the "subject" of their infinitive in the dative as well.

Odds 'n Ends

32.10 **Negation**. Because the infinitive is not the indicative mood, it is negated by μή and not οὐ.

32.11 **Parsing**. The necessary elements for parsing the infinitive are tense, voice, "infinitive," lexical form, and inflected meaning.

βλέψαι. Aorist active infinitive, from βλέπω, meaning "to see."

32.12 **Deponent**. If a verb is deponent in a certain tense, it will be deponent whether it is in the indicative, infinitive, or any other mood. The present deponent infinitive of ἔρχομαι is ἔρχεσθαι, meaning "to come."

Halftime Review

- An infinitive is a verbal noun.

- It is indeclinable, but is viewed as neuter singular (which controls the form of the accompanying article).

- It has no time significance, only aspect. The present infinitive is continuous, the aorist infinitive is undefined, and the perfect infinitive is completed. The aspectual significance is difficult to bring into English.

- You will need to memorize the twelve forms.

- Sometimes a word in the accusative acts as the "subject" of the infinitive.

Translation

32.13 **1. Substantive**. Because the infinitive is a verbal noun, it can perform any function that a substantive can. When used as a substantive, it will usually, but not always, be preceded by the definite article. This is called an **articular infinitive**. Translate this construction using "to" and the verb. This is a common construction, and yet its translation can be quite idiomatic, so feel free not to go "word for word."

---

4   Technically, it is called a "dative of reference."

ἐμοὶ τὸ ζῆν Χριστὸς καὶ τὸ ἀποθανεῖν κέρδος *(Phil 1:21).*

For to me, *to live* is Christ and *to die* is gain.

τὸ ἀγαπᾶν τὸν πλησίον ὡς ἑαυτὸν *(Mark 12:33)*

to love one's neighbor as oneself

32.14 2. Complementary infinitive. A finite verb's meaning may be incomplete apart from some additional information. An infinitive is often used to complete that meaning. Translate the infinitive using "to" and the verb.

ἤρξαντο λαλεῖν ἑτέραις γλώσσαις *(Acts 2:4).*

They began *to speak* in other tongues.

For example, δεῖ ("it is necessary") requires an infinitive to complete its meaning: δεῖ ἐσθίειν ("It is necessary to eat."). When an infinitive is used this way, it is called a "complementary infinitive," because the meaning of the infinitive complements the meaning of the verb.

The following five verbs will always be followed by a complementary infinitive.

δεῖ αὐτὴν ἐσθίειν.
It is necessary for her *to eat.*

ἔξεστιν ἐσθίειν αὐτῷ.
It is lawful for him *to eat.*

μέλλω ἐσθίειν.
I am about *to eat.*

δύναμαι ἐσθίειν.
I am able *to eat.*

ἄρχομαι ἐσθίειν.
I am beginning *to eat.*

> Is it anyone's birthday? Let's celebrate the day!
> γενέσια καλὰ εἴη means "Happy Birthday!"
>
> Let's sing in modern Greek. You know the tune.
> τὰ γενέσια καλά
> τὰ γενέσια καλά
> τὰ γενέσια τῆς Μαργαρίτιδος
> τὰ γενέσια καλά

The complementary infinitive can be used with other verbs but less frequently (e.g., θέλω, "I wish"; κελεύω, "I command"; ὀφείλω, "I ought").

32.15 3. Articular infinitive and preposition. When the articular infinitive is preceded by a preposition, there are specific rules of translation. These should be learned well because the construction is common. The preposition will always precede the infinitive. The case of the definite article is determined by the preposition.

This is perhaps the most difficult use of the infinitive; it certainly is the most idiomatic. Any attempt to translate word for word must be abandoned. You must look at the phrase in Greek, see what it means in Greek, and then say the same thing in English. You should make a separate vocabulary card for each of the following possibilities.

Below are listed six common constructions, the two most common being εἰς and μετά. I have listed the preposition, the case of the article, and the key word/phrase that you should associate with that preposition.

Result/purpose

1. διά (accusative) meaning *because* (indicating reason)

    διὰ τὸ βλέπειν αὐτόν

    Because he sees

    ὁ Ἰησοῦς χαρήσεται <u>διὰ τὸ βλέπειν αὐτὸν</u> ὅτι ἡμεῖς ἀγαπῶμεν αὐτόν.

    Jesus will rejoice *because he sees* that we love him.

    αὐτὸς δὲ Ἰησοῦς οὐκ ἐπίστευεν αὐτὸν αὐτοῖς <u>διὰ τὸ αὐτὸν γινώσκειν</u> πάντας *(John 2:24)*.

    But Jesus on his part did not entrust himself to them, *because he knew* all people.

2. εἰς (accusative) meaning *in order that* (indicating purpose)

    εἰς τὸ βλέπειν αὐτόν

    In order that he sees

    καθίζω ἐν ἐκκλησίᾳ <u>εἰς τὸ ἀκούειν με</u> τὸν λόγον τοῦ θεοῦ.

    I sit in church *in order that I might hear* the word of God.

    παραδώσουσιν αὐτὸν τοῖς ἔθνεσιν <u>εἰς τὸ ἐμπαῖξαι</u> καὶ <u>μαστιγῶσαι</u> καὶ <u>σταυρῶσαι</u> *(Matt 20:19)*.

    They will deliver him over to the Gentiles *to be mocked* and *flogged* and *crucified*.

3. πρός (accusative) meaning *in order that* (indicating purpose)

    πρὸς τὸ βλέπειν αὐτόν

    In order that he sees

    κηρύσσομεν τὸν εὐαγγέλιον <u>πρὸς τὸ βλέψαι ὑμᾶς</u> τὴν ἀλήθειαν.

    We proclaim the gospel *so that you may see* the truth.

    πάντα δὲ τὰ ἔργα αὐτῶν ποιοῦσιν <u>πρὸς τὸ θεαθῆναι</u> τοῖς ἀνθρώποις *(Matt 23:5)*.

    They do all their deeds *to be seen* by others.

Temporal

4. πρό (genitive) meaning *before* (indicating time)

    πρὸ τοῦ βλέπειν αὐτόν

    Before he sees

    ὁ Ἰησοῦς ἠγάπησεν ἡμᾶς <u>πρὸ τοῦ γνῶναι ἡμᾶς</u> αὐτόν.

    Jesus loved us *before we knew* him.

    οἶδεν γὰρ ὁ πατὴρ ὑμῶν ὧν χρείαν ἔχετε <u>πρὸ τοῦ ὑμᾶς αἰτῆσαι</u> αὐτόν *(Matt 6:8)*.

    For your Father knows what you need *before you ask* him

5. ἐν (dative) meaning *when/while* (indicating time)

> ἐν τῷ βλέπειν αὐτόν
> When he sees

> ὁ κύριος κρινεῖ ἡμᾶς ἐν τῷ ἔρχεσθαι αὐτὸν πάλιν.
> The Lord will judge us when he comes again.

> ἐν τῷ σπείρειν αὐτὸν ἃ μὲν ἔπεσεν παρὰ τὴν ὁδόν *(Matt 13:4)*.
> *As he sowed*, some seeds fell along the path.

6. μετά (accusative) meaning *after* (indicating time)

> μετὰ τὸ βλέπειν αὐτόν
> After he sees

> μετὰ τὸ βλέψαι τὸν Ἰησοῦν τοὺς ἁμαρτωλούς, ἔκλαυσε.
> After Jesus saw the sinners, he wept.

> μετὰ δὲ τὸ ἐγερθῆναί με προάξω ὑμᾶς εἰς τὴν Γαλιλαίαν *(Matt 26:32)*.
> But *after I am raised up,* I will go before you to Galilee.

There are two tricks that will help you translate the articular infinitive.

■ The first is to remember the key words associated with each preposition when used with the articular infinitive.

■ The second is to use the phrase "the act of." For example, the key word associated with διά is *because*. What does διὰ τὸ βλέπειν αὐτόν mean? "Because of the act of seeing with reference to him." Sometimes it is necessary to translate in this stilted manner to see what it means; then put it into proper English: "Because he sees."

32.16 **4. Purpose**. Another function of the infinitive is to express purpose, "in order that."

1. Purpose can be expressed using the articular infinitive preceded by εἰς or πρός (see above).

2. The articular infinitive with the article in the genitive (no preposition) can also express purpose.

> Ἡρῴδης ζητεῖν τὸ παιδίον τοῦ ἀπολέσαι αὐτό *(Matt 2:13)*.
> Herod is searching for the child *to destroy* him.

3. The infinitive all by itself (without a preposition or the article) can express purpose.

> Μὴ νομίσητε ὅτι ἦλθον καταλῦσαι τὸν νόμον *(Matt 5:17)*.
> Do not think that I came *to abolish* the law.

32.17 **5. Result**. ὥστε can be followed by an infinitive as a way of indicating the result of some action. Because we do not have a similar use of the infinitive in English, you will translate this infinitive with a finite verb.

> ἔπλησαν ἀμφότερα τὰ πλοῖα ὥστε βυθίζεσθαι αὐτά *(Luke 5:7)*.
> They filled both boats so full *that* they *began to sink.*

It is often difficult to differentiate between "purpose" and "result," but you can bring this out in your teaching and preaching.

Summary

1. The Greek infinitive is a verbal noun. It is not declined, although it is considered singular neuter and any accompanying article will be declined.

2. Infinitive Morpheme Chart

	present	*1st aorist*	*2nd aorist*	*perfect*
active	ειν	σαι	ειν	κεναι
middle	εσθαι	σασθαι	εσθαι	σθαι
passive	εσθαι	θηναι	ηναι	σθαι

3. Master Nonindicative Verb Chart: Infinitive

	present	*1 aorist*	*2 aorist*	*perfect*
active	λύειν	λῦσαι	λαβεῖν	λελυκέναι
middle	λύεσθαι	λύσασθαι	λαβέσθαι	λελύσθαι
passive	λύεσθαι	λυθῆναι	γραφῆναι	λελύσθαι
active	to loose	to loose	to receive	to have loosed
middle	to loose	to loose	to receive	to have thrown
passive	to be loosed	to be loosed	to be written	to have been thrown

4. The infinitive has no time significance, only aspect. The present infinitive is built on the present tense stem and indicates a continuous action. The aorist infinitive is built on the unaugmented aorist tense stem and indicates an undefined action. The perfect infinitive is built on the perfect tense stem and indicates a completed action.

5. Technically an infinitive does not have a subject, but there will often be a word in the accusative functioning as if it were the subject.

6. There are five main ways in which an infinitive is used.

    1. Substantive

    2. Complementary infinitive

    3. Articular infinitive preceded by a preposition

        *   διά   because
        *   εἰς   in order that
        *   πρός   in order that
        *   πρό   before
        *   ἐν   when, while
        *   μετά   after

    4. Purpose
        *   εἰς / πρός with an infinitive
        *   Articular infinitive with the definite article in the genitive (τοῦ)
        *   Infinitive by itself

    5. Result, expressed by ὥστε with the infinitive. Translate the infinitive as a finite verb.

Vocabulary

δίκαιος, -αία, -αιον   right, just, righteous (79, *δικαιο)

μέλλω   I am about to (109, *μελλε)[5]
        (ἔμελλον or ἤμελλον), μελλήσω, –, –, –, –

Total word count in the New Testament:	138,162
Number of words learned to date:	301
Number of word occurrences in this chapter:	188
Number of word occurrences to date:	108,826
Percent of total word count in the New Testament:	78.76%

Advanced Information

32.18 **Indirect discourse**. *Direct discourse* is reporting what someone else said. Since it is your intention to report exactly what the other person said, you use quotation marks.

> "The teacher said, 'Hand in the tests!'"

If you intend to repeat the basic idea of what someone else said, while not claiming to use exactly the same words, you use *indirect discourse* (also called *indirect speech*). Instead of quotation marks, you use the connecting word *that*.

> "He said that he wanted to study some more."

In Greek, indirect discourse is usually expressed with ὅτι followed by a verb in the indicative. However, indirect discourse can also be expressed with an infinitive.

32.19 A rather peculiar thing happens to the tense of the English verb in indirect discourse, and most of us are probably not aware of it. All of the following pertains to English grammar. When I am done with the English grammar, you will then see that Greek behaves differently.

John says, "I *want* to eat." When you tell someone else what John said with indirect discourse, if the main verb of the sentence is present ("says"), then the verb in the indirect discourse retains the same tense as the original saying. "John says that he *wants* to eat." If John originally said, "I *wanted* to eat," you would say, "John says that he *wanted* to eat."

However, when the main verb of the sentence is a past tense (e.g., "said"), then we shift the tense of the verb in the indirect discourse back one step in time.

For example, if the tense of the original saying is present, in indirect speech it will be in the past.

> Original (present):   "I want to eat."
>
> Indirect speech: John said that he *wanted* to eat.

If it originally were past, then in indirect speech it will be past perfect.

> Original (past):   "I *wanted* to eat."
>
> Indirect speech: John said that he had wanted to eat.

---

[5]   The second epsilon is lost in the present and imperfect tenses but remains in the future.

If it originally were future, then you use the word "would."

> Original (future):   "I will want to eat."
>
> Indirect speech: John said that he *would want* to eat.

If the original were past perfect, then in indirect discourse it would remain the same since English has no tense farther back in time.

> Original (past perfect):   "I had wanted to eat."
>
> Indirect speech: John said that he *had wanted* to eat.

32.20 The point of all this is that *whereas English switches the tense of the verb in indirect speech, Greek does not.* The tense and mood of the verb in Greek indirect discourse will always be the same tense and mood as the verb in the original statement. Of course, to make a good translation you would switch the tense and mood of your English translation.

> οὐκ ἤδει ὅτι ἀληθές <u>ἐστιν</u> τὸ γινόμενον διὰ τοῦ ἀγγέλου· ἐδόκει δὲ ὅραμα <u>βλέπειν</u> *(Acts 12:9)*.
>
> He did not know that what was happening through the angel *was* really true, and he kept thinking that he *was seeing* a vision.

The direct discourse would have been, "Is what is happening through the angel really true?" and, "I am seeing a vision," and hence the Greek has the present ἐστιν and βλέπειν. English moves "is" back to "was," and "am seeing" back to "was seeing."

The Lord's Prayer

Πάτερ ἡμῶν ὁ ἐν τοῖς οὐρανοῖς·
ἁγιασθήτω τὸ ὄνομά σου·
ἐλθέτω ἡ βασιλεία σου·
γενηθήτω τὸ θέλημά σου,
     ὡς ἐν οὐρανῷ καὶ ἐπὶ γῆς·
τὸν ἄρτον ἡμῶν τὸν ἐπιούσιον δὸς ἡμῖν σήμερον·
καὶ ἄφες ἡμῖν τὰ ὀφειλήματα ἡμῶν,
     ὡς καὶ ἡμεῖς ἀφήκαμεν τοῖς ὀφειλέταις ἡμῶν·
καὶ μὴ εἰσενέγκῃς ἡμᾶς εἰς πειρασμόν,
     ἀλλὰ ῥῦσαι ἡμᾶς ἀπὸ τοῦ πονηροῦ.

Chapter 33

Imperative

Exegetical Insight

There is no more forceful way in the Greek language to tell someone to do something than a simple imperative—particularly the second person imperative. Especially when such a command is given regarding a specific situation, the one giving that command sees himself as an authority figure. He expects those addressed to do exactly as he has ordered.

On his third missionary journey, the apostle Paul expended much energy in attempting to get the churches he had organized to participate in the collection "for the poor among the saints in Jerusalem" (Rom 15:26). When he addressed this issue in 1 Corinthians 16:1-4, he simply told the Corinthians to get busy regularly collecting money for this cause, using the second person imperative ποιήσατε (v. 1), followed by a third person imperative τιθέτω (v. 2). He gives no other reason than that this is what he had also "told" (διέταξα) the churches in Galatia to do.

Paul returns to the same issue in 2 Corinthians 8 and 9. But there one is struck by the numerous ways he uses

in order to try to motivate the Corinthians to participate in the collection. Most surprising is the fact that in these thirty-nine verses, there is only *one* imperative (ἐπιτελέσατε, 2 Cor 8:11). The other places where the NIV inserts an imperative (8:7,24; 9:7) are substantially weaker forms of expressing an imperatival idea. Such a radical shift in Paul's approach strongly suggests that he had lost much of his authority in Corinth, mostly because of the influence of his opponents. Other elements in this letter bear out this same factor.

Undoubtedly one main reason why Paul was losing his influence in Corinth was because he was trying to run the church from a distance (i.e., from Ephesus). That simply cannot be done. Unless pastors consistently take the necessary time to nurture good, wholesome relationships with their parishioners, they risk losing their ability to motivate the church to pay attention to their preaching of God's Word and to live the Christian life.

Verlyn Verbrugge

It is probably a good thing that both Greek and English are written here. The Greek phrase literally reads, "Do not come near."

Overview

In this chapter you will learn that:

■ the imperative mood is used when making a command (e.g., "Eat!");

■ the imperative occurs in the present and aorist tenses, and its only significance is aspect;

■ there are several ways of stating prohibitions and negations.

English

33.1 A verb is in the imperative mood when it is making a command. In English, it is the second person form of the indicative with "you" as the understood subject — "Study!" means "You study!" Sometimes an exclamation mark is used as the sentence's punctuation.

The English imperative is usually not inflected. There are other words that you can add to the sentence to strengthen or further define the intent of the imperative. "Go quickly!"

Greek

33.2 The imperative is basically the same in Greek as it is in English. It is the mood of command. However, as is the case with participles and infinitives, the imperative has a greater range of meaning in Greek. It has second and third person, and the aspect is significant. It does not indicate time.

33.3 **Person**. Greek has both second and third person imperatives. Because there is no English equivalent to a third person imperative, your translation will be a little idiomatic.

■ βλέπε (second person singular) means "(You) look!"

■ βλεπέτω (third person singular) means "Let him look," "He must look," or even "Have him look." The key words "let" or "must" and a pronoun supplied from the person of the verb ("him") can be added to make sense of the construction.

33.4 **Aspect**. The imperative built on the present tense stem is called the *present* imperative and indicates a continuous action. The imperative built on the aorist tense stem (without augment) is called the *aorist* imperative and indicates an undefined action.[1]

There is no time significance with the imperative. The present imperative does not necessarily indicate a command in the present. Once again I

---

[1] There are only four perfect imperatives in the New Testament. See Advanced Information.

encourage the adoption of the terminology "continuous imperative" and "undefined imperative."

Sometimes, to get the significance of the aspect into English, you could use the key word "continually" in your translation of the present imperative, although this is somewhat stilted English: "keep eating."

Form

33.5 **Chart: Present and Aorist Imperative**. The second singular forms must be memorized; the remaining are regular. The translation is the same for both imperatives.

> *Present tense stem + Connecting vowel +*
>
> *Imperative morpheme*
>
> λυ + ε + τω ▸ λυέτω

> *Unaugmented aorist tense stem + Tense formative +*
>
> *Imperative morpheme*
>
> λυ + σα + τω ▸ λυσάτω

33.6 **Imperative Morpheme Chart**. The second person singular imperatives seem to be irregular.[2] They should just be memorized. The other forms are delightfully regular. Think of the σθ in the middle/passive (e.g., σθε) as replacing the tau in the active (τε).

	active and aorist passive	*middle/passive*
2 sg	?	?
3 sg	τω	σθω
2 pl	τε	σθε
3 pl	τωσαν	σθωσαν

33.7 The imperative morphemes in the present active and aorist active are identical, as they are in the present middle and aorist middle. The morphemes in the aorist passive are identical to the aorist active.

---

2   Of course, they are not; cf. *MBG*, #70.

33.8 Paradigm: Imperative

	present	first aorist	translation

active

	present	first aorist	translation
2 sg	λῦε	λῦσον	(You) Loose!
3 sg	λυέτω	λυσάτω	Let him loose!
2 pl	λύετε	λύσατε	(You) loose!
3 pl	λυέτωσαν	λυσάτωσαν	Let them loose!

middle

	present	first aorist	translation
2 sg	λύου	λῦσαι	(You) loose for yourself!
3 sg	λυέσθω	λυσάσθω	Let him loose for himself!
2 pl	λύεσθε	λύσασθε	(You) loose for yourself!
3 pl	λυέσθωσαν	λυσάσθωσαν	Let them loose for themselves!

passive

	present	first aorist	translation
2 sg	λύου	λύθητι	(You) be loosed!
3 sg	λυέσθω	λυθήτω	Let him be loosed!
2 pl	λύεσθε	λύθητε	(You) be loosed!
3 pl	λυέσθωσαν	λυθήτωσαν	Let them be loosed!

Be sure to memorize specifically the second person singular forms. The present uses the connecting vowel epsilon, and first aorist drops the augment but keeps the tense formatives σα and θη.

33.9 Confusing forms

■ Do not be fooled by the imperative second person plural (active and middle) endings (ετε, εσθε; σατε, σασθε). They are the same as the indicative. In the present, context will usually decide whether a particular form is a statement or a command. In the aorist, there will not be an augment.

For example, Jesus says to his disciples, ἔχετε πίστιν θεοῦ (Mark 11:22). Is ἔχετε an indicative in which case Jesus is making a statement, or is it an imperative in which case Jesus is telling them to have faith? Interestingly there is a textual variant here: some manuscripts add εἰ before ἔχετε πίστιν θεοῦ, "If you have faith in God...," making ἔχετε an indicative.[3]

■ The ending of λύου (second singular present middle/passive) looks just like the second person singular middle/passive ending of the imperfect indicative (without the augment, ἐλύου).

■ The ending of λῦσαι makes it look like it is the aorist active infinitive.

33.10 Second aorist.
The aorist imperative that is built on a second aorist stem uses the same endings as the present imperative. The only difference is the tense stem. The second aorist passive imperative looks just like the first aorist passive except for the absence of the theta.

---

[3] See also the difficult translation of John 14:1-2.

	active	middle	passive
2 sg	λάβε	γενοῦ	γράφητι
3 sg	λαβέτω	γενέσθω	γραφήτω
2 pl	λάβετε	γένεσθε	γράφητε
3 pl	λαβέτωσαν	γενέσθωσαν	γραφήτωσαν

33.11 Contract verbs. The contractions with the imperative are all regular. Of course, there will be contractions only in the present. The present active is as follows. See the Appendix for the middle/passive paradigm (page 365).

	α contract	ε contract	ο contract
2 sg	ἀγάπα	ποίει	πλήρου
3 sg	ἀγαπάτω	ποιείτω	πληρούτω
2 pl	ἀγαπᾶτε	ποιεῖτε	πληροῦτε
3 pl	ἀγαπάτωσαν	ποιείτωσαν	πληρούτωσαν

33.12 εἰμί. To form the imperative of εἰμί, normal morphemes are added to the root *εσ. εἰμί has no aorist imperative.

2 sg	ἴσθι
3 sg	ἔστω
2 pl	ἔστε
3 pl	ἔστωσαν

33.13 Deponent. If a verb is deponent in the indicative, so also will be its imperative. The present imperative second person singular of ἔρχομαι is ἔρχου, meaning "Come!"

33.14 Parsing. When parsing an imperative, I suggest you list the tense, voice, "imperative," person, number, lexical form, definition of inflected meaning.

ποιείτω. present active imperative, third person singular, from ποιέω, meaning "Let him do!"

Meaning

33.15 Aspect. As has been the case in all non-indicative moods, the only significance of the imperative is its aspect. It has no time significance. Because of the differences between Greek and English, it will often be impossible to carry this over into English. At first you may want to use "continue" or "keep on" in your translation of the present imperative. For example, βλέπε (present) means "Keep on looking!" while βλέψον (aorist) means "Look!"

You have already learned that βοήθει means "help." In Modern Greek the word for "stop" is στάματα. The word for "go away" is φύγε.

33.16 Command. The imperative mood is used when a verb expresses a command.

> ἀκολούθει μοι *(Mark 2:14)*.
>
> *Follow* me!
>
> δότε αὐτοῖς ὑμεῖς φαγεῖν *(Mark 6:37)*.
>
> *You give* them something to eat.

33.17 It is also used to encourage or request someone to do something. This is called the **Imperative of Entreaty**. You do not "command" God to do something; you "entreat" him, both in English and in Greek, e.g., "Give us this day our daily bread."

> κύριε, δίδαξον ἡμᾶς προσεύχεσθαι *(Luke 11:1)*.
>
> Lord, *teach* us to pray.
>
> ἐλθέτω ἡ βασιλεία σου, γενηθήτω τὸ θέλημά σου *(Matt 6:10)*.
>
> *May* your kingdom *come, may* your will *be done.*

Matt 6:10 gives what I think is an unfortunate example of compromised translation. I would guess that virually no one who prays the Lord's Prayer with the traditional "Your kingdom come" knows that they are using an imperative to call on God to send his kingdom. The NET ("may your kingdom come") and NLT ("May your Kingdom come soon") bravely make an attempt to convey the clear meaning of the Greek, placing clarity of translation above tradition.

Prohibition and Other Types of Negation

33.18 In Greek there are several different ways to say or command "No!" The beauty of the constructions is that each one has its own nuance, information available to those who understand Greek. Unfortunately these nuances are seldom carried over into the translations.

1. οὐ *with the future indicative.* This is the simple negation.

   > οὐ μοιχεύσεις, οὐ φονεύσεις, οὐ κλέψεις, οὐκ ἐπιθυμήσεις *(Rom 13:9)*.
   >
   > *You shall not commit adultery, You shall not murder, You shall not steal, You shall not covet.*

2. μή *plus the present imperative.* Because it is a present imperative, the speaker is prohibiting a continuous action.

   > μὴ μεριμνᾶτε τῇ ψυχῇ ὑμῶν *(Matt 6:25)*.
   >
   > *Do not worry* about your life.

3. μή *plus the aorist imperative.* Because it is an aorist imperative, the speaker is prohibiting an undefined action.

   > μὴ γνώτω ἡ ἀριστερά σου τί ποιεῖ ἡ δεξιά σου *(Matt 6:3)*
   >
   > *Do* not *let* your left hand *know* what your right hand is doing.

4. μή *plus the aorist subjunctive.* This construction says "No!" more strongly than 1 above.[4]

   > μὴ νομίσητε ὅτι ἦλθον καταλῦσαι τὸν νόμον ἢ τοὺς προφήτας *(Matt 5:17)*.
   >
   > *Do not think* that I have come to abolish the Law or the Prophets.

5. οὐ μή *plus the aorist subjunctive.* When Greek uses a double negative, one does not negate the other as in English. The οὐ and μή combine

---

[4] Some grammarians argue that 1 and 4 have the same force.

in a very firm, "This will certainly not occur!" This is stronger than 4 above and refers to a future situation.

> μὴ φοβηθῇς παραλαβεῖν Μαρίαν τὴν γυναῖκά σου *(Matt 1:20)*.
> *Do not be afraid* to take Mary home as your wife.

If the writer uses οὐ μή and the aorist subjunctive, the prohibition is exceptionally strong. Often the translator will add a word like "never" to make the prohibition more emphatic.

> οἱ λόγοι μου <u>οὐ μὴ παρέλθωσιν</u> *(Matt 24:35)*.
> My words *will never pass away*.

"Never" is really an over-translation, because the construction is only an emphatic negation; it is not a statement about "forever." But English does not have a construction equal to the strength of this strong negation, so perhaps this is as close as we can get to the Greek.

In the Advanced Information I will finetune your understanding of the significance of the present and aorist imperatives used in prohibitions.

Summary

1. The imperative is the form of the verb used for commands.

2. It occurs in the second person (like English) and the third (in which case you use the key word "Let" and supply a pronoun).

3. The imperative built on the present tense stem indicates a continuous action. The imperative built on the aorist tense stem (without augment) indicates an undefined action. There is no time significance with the imperative.

4. Imperative Morpheme Chart. You must memorize the second person singular forms.

	active and aorist passive	*middle/passive*
2 sg	?	?
3 sg	τω	σθω
2 pl	τε	σθε
3 pl	τωσαν	σθωσαν

5. Imperative

		active	middle/passive	passive
present	2 sg	λῦε	λύου	λύου
	3 sg	λυέτω	λυέσθω	λυέσθω
1st aorist	2 sg	λῦσον	λῦσαι	λύθητι
	3 sg	λυσάτω	λυσάσθω	λυθήτω
2nd aorist	2 sg	λάβε	γενοῦ	γράφητι
	3 sg	λαβέτω	γενέσθω	γραφήτω

6. The difference between aspect is difficult to carry over into English. You can use "continue" in the translation of the present.

7. There are five different kinds of prohibitions and negations using the indicative, imperative, and subjunctive.

   ■ οὐ with the future indicative.

   ■ μή plus the present imperative. Prohibits a continuous action.

   ■ μή plus the aorist imperative. Prohibits an undefined action.

   ■ μή plus the aorist subjunctive. "No!"

   ■ οὐ μή plus the aorist subjunctive. "This will certainly not occur!"

Vocabulary

ἀπόλλυμι[5]	active: I destroy, kill (90; ἀπ᾿ + *ὀλ)[6]
	middle: I perish, die
	(ἀπώλλυον), ἀπολέσω or ἀπολῶ, ἀπώλεσα, ἀπόλωλα, –, –
	Because ἀπόλλυμι is a compound verb the alpha does not augment, but the omicron does. In the present tense this verb follows the athematic conjugation (Chapter 34). In the other tenses it follows the thematic conjugation you have been learning so far. You can see this in how it forms its other tense forms.
ἀπολύω	I release (66; ἀπό + *λυ)
	(ἀπέλυον), ἀπολύσω, ἀπέλυσα, –, ἀπολέλυμαι, ἀπελύθην
εἴτε	if, whether (65; particle)

---

[5] The stem of this verb is *ολ. It belongs to a class of verbs that add νυ to the root to form the present tense stem, but the nu assimilates to a lambda (cf. *MBG*, #13 and page 309). *ολ + νυ ‣ ολλυ ‣ ὄλλυμι. This is why there is a single lambda in the other tenses.

[6] *Apollyon*, from Ἀπολλύων, is the destroying angel in Rev 9:11.

Total word count in the New Testament:	138,162
Number of words learned to date:	304
Number of word occurrences in this chapter:	221
Number of word occurrences to date:	109,047
Percent of total word count in the New Testament:	78.92%

Advanced Information

33.19 **Recent research on prohibitions**. For many years it has been argued that the force of the present imperative has the basic meaning, "Stop doing what you are presently doing!" while the force of the aorist imperative is "Don't start!" Moulton[7] recounts a discussion with Davidson who was learning modern Greek and thought he had discovered the difference between the continuous and the undefined imperative in a prohibition. His friend spoke modern Greek, and one day he was yelling at a dog to stop barking. He used the continuous imperative. "Stop barking!" Davidson went to Plato's *Apology* and reasoned that what is true in modern Greek was also true in Classial Greek. The present tense prohibition is used to prohibit an action already in process. This, he thought, had been carried over into Koine Greek.

However, it is currently being questioned whether this is accurate.[8] My position is that a prohibition with the present tense is prohibiting a continuous action while a prohibition with the aorist is prohibiting an undefined action. The neighbor was telling the dog to stop its continual barking.

Following Fanning, I also hold that the present tense prohibition tends to be used for "attitudes and conduct" ("general precept") while the aorist tends to be used for "specific cases" ("specific command").[9]

This has important ramifications for exegesis. For example, Paul tells Timothy to have nothing to do with silly myths, using a present imperative (παραιτοῦ; 1 Tim 4:7). If the present imperative commands cessation from an action currently under way, this means Timothy was participating in the myths. This creates a picture of Timothy that is irreconcilable with his mission at Ephesus and what we know of him elsewhere. But if a present imperative does not carry this meaning, then Paul is stating a command regarding a "general precept" that is continuous in nature—continually stay away from the myths—and is saying nothing about Timothy's current involvement, or noninvolvement, in the Ephesian myths.

33.20 **Perfect imperative**. There are four perfect imperatives in the New Testament.

■ πεφίμωσο (φιμόω, Mark 4:39)

■ ἔρρωσθε (ῥώννυμι, Acts 15:29)

■ ἴστε (οἶδα, Eph 5:5; James 1:19)

---

7   *A Grammar of New Testament Greek,* 3rd edition (London: T & T Clark, 1985) 1:122.

8   See the discussion in Fanning (325–88) and Wallace (485, 714–17).

9   Fanning, 327; citing *Bl-D*, 335. He adds, "The present pictures an occurrence from an internal perspective, focusing on the course or internal details of the occurrence but with no focus on the end-points, while the aorist views it from an external perspective, seeing the occurrence as a whole from beginning to end without focus on the internal details which may be involved" (page 388).

Chapter 34

Indicative of δίδωμι

Exegetical Insight

The cross, and by extension Christ's crucifixion, has always been of central importance to the Christian faith. This was especially the case for Paul. Outside of the Gospels Paul is the chief writer to speak of the cross (σταυρός). Similarly, except for the Gospels, the verbal form σταυρόω occurs most frequently in Paul's letters.

Galatians 6:14–15 is contained within the interpretive key of the letter (6:11–18), written with the authority of Paul's own hand (6:11). In verse 14 Paul uses both the noun and verbal form, indicating that the cross of our Lord Jesus Christ (ἐν τῷ σταυρῷ τοῦ κυρίου ἡμῶν Ἰησοῦ Χριστοῦ) is his only cause for boasting, and the instrument or means by which (δι᾽ οὗ) the world has been crucified (κόσμος ἐσταύρωται) with reference to him. He goes on to say, in essence, that the only thing that matters is new creation (compare similar statements in Gal. 5:6; 1 Cor. 7:19). For Paul the cross was the central point (or crux) in redemptive-history that brings about new creation (see 2 Cor. 5:17).

This emphasis on the importance of the cross was also expressed in early New Testament manuscripts. Sometime during the composition of the earliest manuscripts, scribes started to write the names for God, Jesus, Christ, and Lord in abbreviated forms with a supralinear stroke, now called *nomina sacra* (Latin for "sacred names"). Over time additional words were also written in this way. As early as 200 A.D. the words σταυρός and σταυρόω were also written as *nomina sacra*. In addition, a unique form was developed for these words where the T and P were combined to form ⳨. This staurogram, as it is now called, is one of the earliest visual representations of the cross and the crucifixion of Christ.

In our culture the cross is often treated as a casual fashion accessory, but for the Christian it is of supreme importance. It represents the point in history where the mercy and justice of God met. It is the means by which the false ideologies of the world are crucified to us, and the means by which we are created anew. "For the word of the cross is folly to those who are perishing, but to us who are being saved it is the power of God" (1 Cor. 1:18).

Rick D. Bennett, Jr.

Overview

In this chapter you will learn:

- a different category of verbs that, especially in the present, are formed differently;

- the five rules that govern their formation.

English

34.1 There is nothing remotely like μι verbs in English.

Greek

34.2 So far, the endings used by verbs have all been basically the same. Because of contractions and consonantal changes, these endings have sometimes looked a little different, but for the most part they have been the same. The first person singular active ends in omega, and most of the tenses use connecting vowels or have tense formatives ending in a vowel. All the forms you know belong to the *thematic conjugation* because of the use of the thematic vowel, or what I have called the "connecting vowel."

Actually, εἰμί is a μι verb, but it is so different from other μι verbs that the comparison is not always helpful.

34.3 Actually there is another conjugation that goes by several names. It is sometimes called the *athematic*[1] *conjugation* because it does not use a thematic vowel. At other times it is called the *μι conjugation*, or *μι verbs*, because the lexical form ends not in omega (λύω) but in μι (δίδωμι, "I give").

σιώπα is "Be quiet."
πεφίμωσο is "Calm down."

There is good news and bad news about these verbs. The bad news is that their forms change so drastically that they can become almost unrecognizable. The good news is that there are very few of them. The bad news is that these few μι verbs are common. The good news is that most of the changes occur only in the present tense.

Like declensions, the differences do not affect the meaning of the words, only their form. It does not matter whether δίδωμι was formed as a μι verb or as a thematic verb (δίδω, which is not a real word). It would still mean, "I give."

34.4 There are two ways to learn the forms of μι verbs. The first is to memorize all 330 forms, but this is nearly impossible because the forms are so varied and unusual. The second is a better approach. If you memorize the five basic rules below, you can figure out what the different inflected forms mean when you see them. Let's do the latter.

The only disadvantage of learning μι verbs this way is that you will not have the security of knowing the full paradigm. But even those people who use Greek regularly have trouble in reproducing the μι verb paradigms from rote memory. It simply is not necessary. It is much better to learn five rules and concentrate on recognition.

There is something else that helps us learn μι verbs. While μι verbs are common, they do not occur in many forms. If you memorized the complete paradigm, you would be learning hundreds of forms that never occur in the New Testament. So why memorize them?

---

[1] The English word "athematic" is a compound of the Greek alpha privative (much like the prefixes "un-" ["unlikely"] or "ir-" ["irregular"] in English) with the noun "thematic," which refers to the use of a thematic vowel. Hence, "athematic" means "without a thematic vowel."

34.5 **Four classes.** μι verbs are classified by their stem vowel. δίδωμι has an o-class vowel for its stem vowel (*δο), and all μι verbs with an o-class vowel follow the same pattern as δίδωμι. This is like contract verbs in which all alpha contracts follow the same pattern as ἀγαπάω. In this chapter you will learn the pattern of δίδωμι.

The other three classes are stems ending in alpha (*στα ‣ ἵστημι), epsilon (*θε ‣ τίθημι), and upsilon (*δεικνυ ‣ δείκνυμι). These three classes are discussed in the next chapter. What is nice about μι verbs is that if you know one pattern, you know them all. In other words, whatever δίδωμι does in the future, τίθημι will also do in the future, although the stem vowel will be an eta instead of omega.

The Rules

34.6 **Rule One:** μι verbs reduplicate their initial stem letter to form the present, and separate the reduplicated consonant with an iota.

The root of δίδωμι is *δο. To form the present tense stem the initial delta is reduplicated, separated with an iota, and the personal ending μι is added (see rule 3 below). In the present singular the omicron lengthens to omega (rule 4).

δο ‣ διδο ‣ διδω ‣ δίδωμι

It is therefore essential that you always memorize the root of a μι verb along with its lexical form. As always, they are listed in the vocabulary section. The only time you will see the reduplication with the iota is in the present and imperfect. In the other tenses, you will need to be able to identify the root.

For example, parse δώσω. If you are working from the present tense stem, you will not be able to. But if you recognize that the verb stem is *δο, then this is clearly the first person singular future and is regular (with a lengthened stem vowel; rule 4).

δο ‣ δω + σ + ω ‣ δώσω

If you reduplicate the verbal root to form the present tense stem, how can you tell the difference between the present and the perfect? Think about it. Right. The perfect will also have reduplication, but there the vowel separating the reduplicated consonant is an epsilon, just like in the thematic conjugation. *δο ‣ δεδο ‣ δέδωκα.

	present	*aorist*	*perfect*	*εἰμί*
1 sg	δίδωμι	ἔδωκα	δέδωκα	εἰμί
2 sg	δίδως	ἔδωκας	δέδωκας	εἶ
3 sg	δίδωσι(ν)	ἔδωκε(ν)	δέδωκε(ν)	ἐστί(ν)
1 pl	δίδομεν	ἐδώκαμεν	δεδώκαμεν	ἐσμέν
2 pl	δίδοτε	ἐδώκατε	δεδώκατε	ἐστέ
3 pl	διδόασι(ν)	ἔδωκαν	δέδωκαν	εἰσίν

34.7   **Rule Two:** μι verbs do not ordinarily use a connecting (i.e., "thematic") vowel in the present indicative. The personal ending is added directly to the stem.

δι + δο + μεν ▸ δίδομεν.

A connecting vowel is used in the imperfect singular and future. (See the chart at 34.11.)

34.8   **Rule Three:** μι verbs employ three different personal endings in the present active indicative. Compare the following chart of the present active indicative.

	μι verbs		thematic conjugation	
1 sg	δίδωμι	μι	λύω	–
2 sg	δίδως	ς	λύεις	ς
3 sg	δίδωσι(ν)	σι	λύει	ι
1 pl	δίδομεν	μεν	λύομεν	μεν
2 pl	δίδοτε	τε	λύετε	τε
3 pl	διδόασι(ν)	ασι	λύουσι(ν)	νσι

As you can see, μι verbs use the same endings as the thematic conjugation in three places, δίδως, δίδομεν, and δίδοτε. But in the other three places the endings are different: δίδωμι; δίδωσι(ν); διδόασι(ν). These must be memorized.

However, the present active is the only place that μι verbs use different endings. In all other tenses, they use the same endings as the thematic conjugation. This does not mean they will look absolutely identical (although in most places they do); it means that if you have been learning the true personal endings, there is nothing more to learn. For example, in the present middle/passive the paradigm is as follows.

	μι verbs		thematic conjugation	
1 sg	δίδομαι	μαι	λύομαι	μαι
2 sg	δίδοσαι	σαι	λύῃ	σαι
3 sg	δίδοται	ται	λύεται	ται
1 pl	διδόμεθα	μεθα	λυόμεθα	μεθα
2 pl	δίδοσθε	σθε	λύεσθε	σθε
3 pl	δίδονται	νται	λύονται	νται

Even though the second person singular (σαι) looks a little unusual from what you learned with λύω, as you saw in the perfect middle/passive (e.g., λέλυσαι), this is the real form of the personal ending. It has undergone contractions in most of the thematic forms because the sigma drops out.[2]

34.9   **Rule Four:** the stem vowel of μι verbs can lengthen, shorten, or drop out (ablaut). Although there are rules governing when the stem vowel is long or short, or has dropped out, all that you are concerned with is

_____

[2]   It does not drop out in the athematic conjugation because it is not preceded by a connecting vowel.

recognition; therefore these rules are just burdensome. You do not have to know when they shorten; you just have to recognize that they do.[3]

For example, in the present active paradigm the vowel is long in the singular (δίδωμι) but short in the plural (δίδομεν). In the middle/passive it is always short.

Take the form δώσω. It does not really matter whether you see the form δώσω or δόσω. Once you recognize that the verbal root is *δο, δώσω could only be one form: future.

See the paradigm in 34.11 if you are curious about the length of the stem vowel.

34.10 **Rule Five:** most of the μι verbs use κα as their tense formative in the aorist. These are called "kappa aorists." Compare the paradigm with that of the first aorist and perfect.

	μι verbs	thematic conjugation	
1 sg	ἔδωκα	ἔλυσα	λέλυκα
2 sg	ἔδωκας	ἔλυσας	λέλυκας
3 sg	ἔδωκε(ν)	ἔλυσε(ν)	λέλυκε(ν)
1 pl	ἐδώκαμεν	ἐλύσαμεν	λελύκαμεν
2 pl	ἐδώκατε	ἐλύσατε	λελύκατε
3 pl	ἔδωκαν	ἔλυσαν	λέλυκαν

How can you tell the difference between the aorist of a μι verb and the perfect of a verb in the thematic conjugation that also uses κα as its tense formative? Right. The perfect has reduplication (with an epsilon separating the reduplicated consonants): ἔδωκα vs. λέλυκα.

34.11 δίδωμι **in the indicative (active).**

	present	imperfect	future	aorist	perfect
1 sg	δίδωμι	ἐδίδουν	δώσω	ἔδωκα	δέδωκα
2 sg	δίδως	ἐδίδους	δώσεις	ἔδωκας	δέδωκας
3 sg	δίδωσι(ν)	ἐδίδου	δώσει	ἔδωκε(ν)	δέδωκε(ν)
1 pl	δίδομεν	ἐδίδομεν	δώσομεν	ἐδώκαμεν	δεδώκαμεν
2 pl	δίδοτε	ἐδίδοτε	δώσετε	ἐδώκατε	δεδώκατε
3 pl	διδόασι(ν)	ἐδίδουν	δώσουσι(ν)	ἔδωκαν	δέδωκαν

In the imperfect singular, the endings are formed with a connecting vowel. In the future they are identical to the forms in the thematic conjugation. You will see the non-indicative forms in the next chapter.

---

[3] Your teacher may have a different preference. Be sure to ask.

Let's Practice

Let's look at several inflected forms and see how easy it is to apply the rules.

δώσετε   You have the bare verbal root (*δο) without augment, reduplication, or κα. But is has a sigma. It can only be a future: second person plural.

ἐδίδους   The reduplication with an iota shows it is the present tense stem; the augment confirms that this is an imperfect. Second person singular.

ἔδωκα   The simple verbal root plus augment and tense formative κα means this must be aorist. First person singular.

δίδωσιν   The reduplicated stem with an iota and without an augment confirms this is a present. Third person singular.[4]

δέδωκε   The reduplication may suggest present, but notice that the intervening vowel is an epsilon. This must therefore be a perfect, third person singular.

Summary

1. μι verbs reduplicate their initial stem letter to form the present and separate the reduplicated consonant with an iota. It is essential that you memorize the root of a μι verb along with its lexical form.

2. μι verbs do not ordinarily use a connecting vowel in the present indicative ("athematic").

3. μι verbs employ three different personal endings in the present active indicative: δίδωμι; δίδωσι(ν); διδόασι(ν).

4. The stem vowel of μι verbs can lengthen, shorten, or drop out. It is not so important to know when this will happen, but merely to recognize that it does.

5. Most of the μι verbs use κα for the tense formative in the aorist.

Vocabulary

δίδωμι   I give (out), entrust, give back, put (415; *δο)[5]
(ἐδίδουν) δώσω, ἔδωκα, δέδωκα, δέδομαι, ἐδόθην

When δίδωμι is used outside the indicative mood, you can find second aorist forms such as δῶ (subjunctive), δός (imperative), δοῦναι (infinitive), and δούς (participle).

ἔθνος, -ους, τό   singular: nation (162, *ἔθνες)[6]
plural: the Gentiles

---

4   It could also be subjunctive, but that is discussed in the next chapter.

5   An *antidote* (ἀντί + δοτος) is something given to work against something else, such as poison.

6   *Ethnic.*

λοιπός, -ή, -όν	adjective: remaining (55; *λοιπο) noun: (the) rest adverb: for the rest, henceforth
Μωϋσῆς, -έως, ὁ	Moses (80) Μωϋσῆς has an irregular declension pattern: Μωϋσῆς, Μωϋσέως, Μωϋσεῖ, Μωϋσῆν.
παραδίδωμι	I entrust, hand over, betray (119; παρά + *δο) (παρεδίδουν), παραδώσω, παρέδωκα, παραδέδωκα, παραδέδομαι, παρεδόθην
πίπτω	I fall (90; *πετ)[7] (ἔπιπτον), πεσοῦμαι, ἔπεσον or ἔπεσα, πέπτωκα, –, – πίπτω both a second (ἔπεσον) and a first (ἔπεσα) aorist.
ὑπάρχω	I am, exist (60; *ὑπ᾽ + *ἀρχ) (ὑπῆρχον), –, –, –, –, – τά ὑπάρχοντα means "one's belongings." ὑπάρχω can take a predicate nominative, like εἰμί and γίνομαι.

Total word count in the New Testament:	138,162
Number of words learned to date:	311
Number of word occurrences in this chapter:	981
Number of word occurrences to date:	110,028
Percent of total word count in the New Testament:	79.63%

Here are some food phrases.
Modern Greek is in parentheses.

"I am hungry": πεινῶ (πεινάω)
"What is there to eat?": τί φαγεῖν; (τί θά φάμε;)
"When will we eat?": πότε φαγεῖν; (πότε θά φάμε;)
Breakfast: ἀρκετός (πρωινό)
Lunch: δεῖπνον is the main meal of the day (μεσημεριανό)
γεύμα is the generic meal in Modern Greek.
hors d'oeuvres (Modern): μεζέδακι

---

[7] The verbal root loses its stem vowel epsilon in the present and the stem is reduplicated, even though it is not a μι verb (*πετ ‣ πτ ‣ πιπτ + ω ‣ πίπτω). The tau drops out before the sigma in the future and aorist but remains in the perfect active.

Chapter 35

Nonindicative of δίδωμι; Conditional Sentences

Exegetical Insight

In the doxology at the end of Romans 11 (v. 36), Paul spells out three distinct theological concepts as he discusses the relationship between God and all things. His use of three different Greek prepositions (Chapter 8) shows his structure distinctly, and he is relying on the specific differences in meaning among the three prepositions to convey his message. This kind of precision and exactness can be lost in English translations.

ἐξ αὐτοῦ καὶ δι᾽ αὐτοῦ καὶ εἰς αὐτὸν τὰ πάντα· αὐτῷ ἡ δόξα εἰς τοὺς αἰῶνας, ἀμήν.

1. All things come *out of* (ἐξ) him in that he is the *source* or *origin* of all things. 2. All things come *through* (δι᾽) him in that he is the *agent* or *guide* of all things. 3. All things come *unto* or *to* (εἰς) him in that he is the ultimate *goal* of all things.

Glory be to God, our Creator, Sustainer, and Exalted Lord, the One who is the source, guide, and goal of all things!

Deborah Gill

Overview

In this chapter you will learn:

- the non-indicative forms of δίδωμι;
- first and second class conditional sentences.

Subjunctive of δίδωμι

35.1 Subjunctive. The nonindicative forms of μι verbs are even easier to identify than the indicative forms. In the subjunctive the reduplicated stem is the only difference between the present and the aorist.

Important: δίδωμι has first aorist forms in the indicative and second aorist forms elsewhere.

Here is the subjunctive of δίδωμι. The present subjunctive of δίδωμι does not occur in the New Testament,[1] but you need to see the forms as a basis for learning the other μι verbs (Chapter 36). The aorist active subjunctive of δίδωμι and compounds formed from δίδωμι occur 36 times, never in the middle, and only four times in the passive (δοθῇ, παραδοθῶ).

	present	second aorist
active		
1 sg	διδῶ	δῶ
2 sg	διδῷς	δῷς
3 sg	διδῷ	δῷ[2]
1 pl	διδῶμεν	δῶμεν
2 pl	διδῶτε	δῶτε
3 pl	διδῶσι(ν)	δῶσι(ν)
middle		
1 sg	διδῶμαι	δῶμαι
2 sg	διδῷ	δῷ
3 sg	διδῶται	δῶται
1 pl	διδώμεθα	δώμεθα
2 pl	διδῶσθε	δῶσθε
3 pl	διδῶνται	δῶνται
passive		
1 sg	διδῶμαι	δοθῶ
2 sg	διδῷ	δοθῇς
3 sg	διδῶται	δοθῇ
1 pl	διδώμεθα	δοθῶμεν
2 pl	διδῶσθε	δοθῆτε
3 pl	διδῶνται	δοθῶσι(ν)

Imperative of δίδωμι

35.2 **Imperative**. The imperatives are also easy to recognize. Remember that μι verbs do not use a thematic vowel, so the imperative morpheme is added directly to the verbal root.

Only the second person forms occur in the New Testament. δίδωμι (and compounds) do not occur in the middle or passive imperative, but I have incuded the forms so you can see how they are formed.

---

[1]   The compound παραδίδωμι occurs once in the present active subjunctive, as παραδιδῷ in 1 Cor 15:24. No compound formed from δίδωμι occurs in the present middle or passive in the New Testament.

[2]   In Mark 8:37 it is written as δοῖ.

	present	second aorist
active		
2 sg	δίδου	δός
3 sg	διδότω	δότω
2 pl	δίδοτε	δότε
3 pl	διδότωσαν	δότωσαν
middle		
2 sg	δίδοσο	δοῦ
3 sg	διδόσθω	δόσθω
2 pl	δίδοσθε	δόσθε
3 pl	διδόσθωσαν	δόσθωσαν
passive		
2 sg	δίδοσο	δόθητι
3 sg	διδόσθω	δοθήτω
2 pl	δίδοσθε	δόθητε
3 pl	διδόσθωσαν	δοθήτωσαν

You may have noticed in older English books the abbreviation κτλ. It means, "etc." and is from the Greek καὶ τὰ λοιπά ("and the remaining things").

Infinitive of δίδωμι

35.3 **Infinitive.** There are no surprises here.

	present	second aorist
active	διδόναι	δοῦναι
middle	δίδοσθαι	δόσθαι[3]
passive	δίδοσθαι[4]	δοθῆναι

Participle of δίδωμι

35.4 **Participle.** There are no surprises here either.

	present	second aorist
active	διδούς, διδοῦσα, διδόν	δούς, δοῦσα, δόν
	διδόντος, διδούσης, διδόντος	δόντος, δούσης, δόντος
middle	διδόμενος, η, ον	δόμενος, η, ον[5]
	διδομένου, ης, ου	δομένου, ης, ου
passive	διδόμενος, η, ον[6]	δοθείς, δοθεῖσα, δοθέν
	διδομένου, ης, ου	δοθέντος, δοθείσης, δοθέντος

---

[3] No examples in the New Testament.

[4] Only occurs as middle/passive twice, as παραδίδοσθαι (Matt 17:22; Luke 9:44).

[5] No examples in the New Testament.

[6] Occurs once as middle/passive, as διδόμενον (Luke 22:19).

Conditional Sentences

35.5 In Chapter 31 you learned the two versions of third class conditional sentence. Both have a protasis introduced with ἐάν and a verb in the subjunctive. Sometimes the protasis is hypothetical.

■ The **future more probable** describes a condition that might be true in the future.

■ The **present general** describes a condition that is generally true at all times. The verb in the apodosis is always in the present tense.

35.6 There are four types of conditional sentences. There is no complete example of the fourth class in the New Testament, so I will concentrate here on the first two. By way of review:

■ The "if" clause is the *protasis*; the "then" clause is the *apodosis*.

■ Conditional sentences are most easily classified by their structure, specifically, the word that introduces the protasis, the tense and mood of the verb in the protasis, and sometimes the tense of the verb in the apodosis.

■ Only the protasis is conditional. If the protasis is true, then the apodosis must be true (if the statement is in fact a factually correct statement).

■ Language is only a portrayal of reality. Whether the protasis is actually true or not, regardless of what the author says (see second class conditions), is decided by context and the reader.

■ Conditional sentences can overlap.

You should read Wallace's discussion on conditional sentences (*GGBB*, 679–712). It is excellent, and goes into much more detail.

35.7 **First class conditional sentences.** Also called "conditions of fact." These sentences are saying that if something is true, and let's assume for the sake of the argument that it is true, then such and such will occur.

The apodosis is introduced with εἰ and the verb is in the indicative.[7]

■ Most of the time you will translate εἰ as "if." The protasis is assumed true for the sake of the argument, but you are not sure whether the protasis is in fact accurate. Sometimes it clearly is not.

εἰ ἡ δεξιά σου χεὶρ σκανδαλίζει σε, ἔκκοψον αὐτήν *(Matt 5:30).*
If your right hand causes you to sin, cut it off.

εἰ δὲ ἀνάστασις νεκρῶν οὐκ ἔστιν, οὐδὲ Χριστὸς ἐγήγερται *(1 Cor 15:13).*
But if there is no resurrection of the dead, then not even Christ has been raised.

---

[7]   Wallace counts about 300 examples of first class conditions in the New Testament (*GGBB*, 690).

- Sometimes the apodosis is true, and you may want to translate εἰ as "since."[8]

> εἰ γὰρ πιστεύομεν ὅτι Ἰησοῦς ἀπέθανεν καὶ ἀνέστη, οὕτως καὶ ὁ θεὸς τοὺς κοιμηθέντας διὰ τοῦ Ἰησοῦ ἄξει σὺν αὐτῷ *(1 Thess 4:14)*.
>
> *For since we believe that Jesus died and rose again,* even so God, through Jesus, will bring with him those who have fallen asleep.

This may be over-translating a bit, saying more than what the sentence actually means, but there are times when using "if" adds an element of uncertainty that is not appropriate to the verse.

35.8 Second class conditional sentences. Also called "contrary to fact." This construction is saying that if something is true—even though it is not—then such and such would occur. The falseness of the protasis is assumed in the argument.

The apodosis is introduced with εἰ and an indicative verb; the apodosis will normally have ἄν and a verb in a secondary tense in the indicative.[9]

> εἰ γὰρ ἔγνωσαν, οὐκ ἂν τὸν κύριον τῆς δόξης ἐσταύρωσαν *(1 Cor 2:8)*.
>
> *For if they had known,* they would not have crucified the Lord of glory.

35.9 Summary

class	protasis	apodosis
First class	εἰ + indicative any tense; negated by οὐ	any mood; any tense
Second class	εἰ + indicative past tense; negated by μή	ἄν + indicative same tense as in the protasis
Third class	ἐάν + subjunctive negated by μή	any mood; any tense
Fourth class	εἰ + optative	ἄν + optative

Summary

We are halfway through this lesson, so let's stop and review what we have learned.

- The nonindicative of δίδωμι is pretty straight forward. Just pay close attention to its root.

- First class conditional sentences say that if something is true (and sometimes from context it clearly will be true), then such and such will occur. The apodosis is introduced with εἰ and its verb is in the indicative.

---

[8] Wallace says about 37% of the first class conditional statements in the New Testament fall into this category (*GGBB*, 690). He warns that using "since" is over-translating.

[9] Wallace counts about 50 examples of this construction in the New Testament (*GGBB*, 694). The imperfect is used in both clauses to describe present time.

■ Second class conditional sentence say that if something were true (and from context it will not be true), then such and such would happen. The apodosis is introduced with εἰ and an indicative verb, and the apodosis will normally have ἄν and a verb in a secondary tense in the indicative.

Vocabulary

There is no new vocabulary in this chapter. You may want to take the time to start reviewing all your vocabulary. My guess is there is a final exam on the horizon. However, here are some important words you can learn.

ἁγιάζω	I consecrate, sanctify (28, v-2a[1]) –, ἡγίασα, –, ἡγίασμαι, ἡγιάσθην
ἁμαρτάνω	I sin (43, v-3a[2a]) ἁμαρτήσω, ἥμαρτον or ἡμάρτησα, ἡμάρτηκα, –, –
ἁμαρτωλός, -όν	sinful; noun: sinner (47, a-3a)
ἀνάστασις, -εως, ἡ	resurrection (42, n-3e[5b])
ἀπαγγέλλω	I report, tell (45, cv-2d[1]) (ἀπήγγελλον), ἀπαγγελῶ, ἀπήγγειλα, –, –, ἀπηγγέλην
διακονέω	I serve (37, v-1d[2a]) (διηκόνουν), διακονήσω, διηκόνησα, –, –, διηκονήθην
διακονία, -ας, ἡ	service (34, n-1a)
δικαιόω	I justify, vindicate (39, v-1d[3]) δικαιώσω, ἐδικαίωσα, –, δεδικαίωμαι, ἐδικαιώθην
θλῖψις, -εως, ἡ	affliction, tribulation (45, n-3e[5b])
ἱλαστήριον, -ου, τό	propitiation, expiation, place of propitiation (2, n-2c)
σταυρόω	I crucify (46, v-1d[3]) σταυρώσω, ἐσταύρωσα, –, ἐσταύρωμαι, ἐσταυρώθην
σωτήρ, -ῆρος, ὁ	savior, deliverer (24, n-3f[2a])
σωτηρία, -ας, ἡ	salvation, deliverance (46, n-1a)
φανερόω	I reveal, make known (49, v-1d[3]) φανερώσω, ἐφανέρωσα, –, πεφανέρωμαι, ἐφανερώθην
φόβος, -ου, ὁ	fear, reverence (47, n-2a)

Advanced Information

35.10 **Optative**. There is one more mood in Koine Greek, the optative. Whereas the subjunctive is the mood of probability or possibility, the optative is the mood of "wish." Whereas the subjunctive is one step removed from reality, the optative is two.

There are sixty-eight examples of the optative in the New Testament. It is found only in the present (continuous aspect; twenty-three times) and aorist (undefined aspect; forty-five times). It occurs twenty-eight times in Luke-Acts and thirty-one times in Paul. εἴη occurs twelve times and γένοιτο seventeen times, fifteen of which are the Pauline phrase μὴ γένοιτο, "God forbid!"

- Because the optative can have no real time significance, it can have no augment.

- The connecting vowel is omicron.

- The tense formative for the aorist active/middle is σα, which contracts with the mood formative so that all forms have σαι.

  The tense formative for the aorist passive is θε, and the mood formative is ιη, which result in θειη in all forms.

- Its mood formative in the thematic conjugation is ι (except in the aorist passive where it is ιη), and in the athematic conjugation it is ιη. All forms of the present optative will have οι.

- The optative uses secondary personal endings except in the first person singular active, where it uses μι.

To see fuller paradigms, see *MBG*.

	present	*future*	*first aorist*	*second aorist*
active				
1 sg	λύοιμι	λύσοιμι	λύσαιμι	βάλοιμι
2 sg	λύοις	λύσοις	λύσαις	βάλοις
3 sg	λύοι	λύσοι	λύσαι	βάλοι
1 pl	λύοιμεν	λύσοιμεν	λύσαιμεν	βάλοιμεν
2 pl	λύοιτε	λύσοιτε	λύσαιτε	βάλοιτε
3 pl	λύοιεν	λύσοιεν	λύσαιεν	βάλοιεν
middle				
1 sg	λυοίμην	λυσοίμην	λυσαίμην	βαλοίμην
2 sg	λύοιο	λύσοιο	λύσαιο	βάλοιο
3 sg	λύοιτο	λύσοιτο	λύσαιτο	βάλοιτο
1 pl	λυοίμεθα	λυσοίμεθα	λυσαίμεθα	βαλοίμεθα
2 pl	λύοισθε	λύσοισθε	λύσαισθε	βάλοισθε
3 pl	λύοιντο	λύσοιντο	λύσαιντο	βάλοιντο
passive				
1 sg	λυοίμην	λυθησοίμην	λυθείην	γραφείην
2 sg	λύοιο	λυθήσοιο	λυθείης	γραφείης
3 sg	λύοιτο	λυθήσοιτο	λυθείη	γραφείη
1 pl	λυοίμεθα	λυθησοίμεθα	λυθείημεν	γραφείημεν
2 pl	λύοισθε	λυθήσοισθε	λυθείητε	γραφείητε
3 pl	λύοιντο	λυθήσοιντο	λυθείησαν	γραφείησαν

Chapter 36

ἵστημι, τίθημι, δείκνυμι;
Odds 'n Ends

Exegetical Insight

The μι verbs are the last thing that you learn in *Basics of Biblical Greek*, and there is a tendency to think that because they are last and because there are not many of them, they are not all that important. Stop right here! These verbs are some of the most theologically rich verbs in the entire Greek New Testament, and you should learn them thoroughly. Some of the most blessed concepts in the Bible, words that comfort and cheer our hearts, are expressed through the common μι verbs and through verbs derived from them. Here are a few of these verses.

δίδωμι — "For God so loved the world that he *gave* his one and only Son" (John 3:16).

παραδίδωμι — "He who did not spare his own Son, but *gave* him *up* for us all" (Rom 8:32); "For what I received I *passed on* to you as of first importance" (1 Cor 15:3).

ἵστημι — "It is by faith you *stand firm*" (2 Cor 1:24).

παρίστημι — "*Offer* your bodies as living sacrifices, holy and pleasing to God" (Rom 12:1).

ἀνίστημι — "God has *raised* this Jesus to life, and we are all witnesses of the fact" (Acts 2:32).

τίθημι — "God did not *appoint* us to suffer wrath but to receive salvation" (1 Thess 5:9).

προστίθημι — The Lord *added* to their number those who were being saved" (Acts 4:7).

δείκνυμι — "After he said this, he *showed* them his hands and his side" (John 20:20).

ἀφίημι — "God is faithful and just and will *forgive* us our sins" (1 John 1:9); "*Forgive* us our debts, as we also *have forgiven* our debtors" (Matt 6:12).

These verses are only a small beginning of those that could be cited. A lot of theology, a lot of Christian comfort, and a lot of exhortation to Christian living are riding on the μι verbs. You would do well to study them thoroughly and to learn them by heart.

Verlyn Verbrugge

Overview

In this chapter you will learn:

- that what was true of δίδωμι is also true of the other μι verbs;

- that the secret is to watch what happens to the verbal root of δίδωμι, and see that the same types of changes occur to the roots of the other μι verbs.

- that when ὁ is present, it is emphasizing the identity of the word/phrase it modifies;

- that when ὁ is not present, it is the quality of the substantive that is being emphasized. ὁ can also function as a grammatical marker;

- the difference between transitive and intransitive verbs;

- "normal" word order.

Other μι Verbs

36.1 In the previous chapter you learned the essentials of μι verbs and how the rules apply to μι verbs with a stem vowel of omicron (δίδωμι) in the active indicative. All that remains is to see that what is true of δίδωμι is also true of the other μι verbs whose stem vowel is alpha (ἵστημι), epsilon (τίθημι), or upsilon (δείκνυμι).

36.2 In the following chart of the present active indicative you can see the similarity among the different μι verbs.

- They use the same endings.

- They reduplicate to form the present tense stem (although that reduplication is hidden in ἵστημι and absent in δείκνυμι).

- What happens to the stem vowel in δίδωμι also happens to the other stem vowels even though they are different vowels (except for δείκνυμι, which stays the same). Both alpha and epsilon lengthen to eta.

	*στα	*θε	*δο	*δεικνυ
1 sg	ἵστημι	τίθημι	δίδωμι	δείκνυμι
2 sg	ἵστης	τίθης	δίδως	δεικνύεις
3 sg	ἵστησι(ν)	τίθησι(ν)	δίδωσι(ν)	δείκνυσι(ν)
1 pl	ἵσταμεν	τίθεμεν	δίδομεν	δείκνυμεν
2 pl	ἵστατε	τίθετε	δίδοτε	δείκνυτε
3 pl	ἱστᾶσι(ν)	τιθέασι(ν)	διδόασι(ν)	δεικνύασι(ν)

The stem of ἵστημι is *στα. When it reduplicates, the reduplicated sigma drops out and is replaced by a rough breathing.

> στα ‣ σιστα ‣ ἵστημι

The stem of τίθημι is *θε. When it reduplicates, the reduplicated theta changes to a tau.

> θε ‣ θιθε ‣ τίθημι

Except for its personal endings, δείκνυμι behaves more like a thematic verb.

36.3   The most effective thing to do at this point is to look through the μι verb paradigms in the Appendix. You can see all the forms of δίδωμι and the other μι verbs. Look at the patterns. See how the rules are put into effect. Concentrate on recognition. I will not reproduce the paradigms here.

36.4   In Koine Greek, μι verbs were slowly being replaced by the thematic conjugation. As a result, μι verbs sometimes occur in the athematic and at other times as a "regular" thematic form with no difference in meaning. For example, both ἵστημι and ἱστάνω occur.[1]

He also explains the second person singular form δεικνύεις instead of the expected δεικνύες.

Definite Article

36.5   As we come to the end of learning the building blocks of Greek, there are a few odds 'n ends that I need to cover.

So far you have been translating the article if it is present (except with proper names and abstract nouns), and not including it if it is absent (except in prepositional phrases). Let's fine-tune the grammar a little. Wallace has an excellent (and detailed) discussion on the article, and you will want to read it (*GGBB*, 206–290). I am following the structure of his discussion.[2]

36.6   The primary function of the article is *not* to make a word definite. For example, proper names are definite without the article. This is also why the Jehovah Witnesses' understanding of John 1:1 is wrong. θεὸς ἦν ὁ λόγος means, "the Word was God," not "a god," even though the article does not occur before θεός.[3]

Discussions of the meaning of the article are divided based on the presence or absence of the article.

36.7   When the article is present, it is emphasizing *identity*.

■   ὁ can function as the English definite article.

> οἱ μαθηταὶ Ἰωάννου νηστεύουσιν πυκνά *(Luke 5:33).*
> *The* disciples of John often fast.

■   The anaphoric article refers you back to the previous reference.

> κήρυξον τὸν λόγον *(2 Tim 4:2).*
> Preach *the* word (referring back to the discussion in 2 Timothy 3).

---

[1]   Nu was added to the verbal root in order to form the present tense stem; class 3 verbs. Cf. *MBG*, v-3 (pages 304–305).

[2]   Wallace begins his discussion of the article with a level of fondness found only among grammarians. "One of the greatest gifts bequeathed by the Greeks to Western civilization was the article. European intellectual life was profoundly impacted by this gift of clarity.... In short, there is no more important aspect of Greek grammar than the article to help shape our understanding of the thought and theology of the NT writers."

[3]   See Wallace's Exegetical Insight in Chapter 6 and also GGBB (page 266–69).

- The deictic article points out someone/thing present and is often best translated as a demonstrative.

    προσῆλθον αὐτῷ οἱ μαθηταὶ λέγοντες· ἔρημός ἐστιν ὁ τόπος (*Matt 14:15*).

    The disciples came to him and said, "*This* place is desolate."

- The article par excellence identifies a substantive as "in a class by itself."

    ὁ προφήτης εἶ σύ; καὶ ἀπεκρίθη· οὔ. (*John 1:21*).

    Are you *the* Prophet?" And he answered, "No."

- The monadic article identifies a substantive as unique, one-of-a-kind.

    ἴδε ὁ ἀμνὸς τοῦ θεοῦ ὁ αἴρων τὴν ἁμαρτίαν τοῦ κόσμου (*John 1:29*).

    Behold, *the* Lamb of God, who takes away the sin of the world.

- Sometimes ὁ functions with a participle or an adjective to make it into a noun.

    Πᾶς ὁ γεγεννημένος ἐκ τοῦ θεοῦ ἁμαρτίαν οὐ ποιεῖ (*1 John 3:9*)
    Everyone *who has been born* of God does not sin.

- ὁ can function as a personal, possessive, or relative pronoun.

    Οἱ δὲ εἶπαν πρὸς αὐτόν (*Luke 5:33*)
    And *they* said to him

    Οἱ ἄνδρες, ἀγαπᾶτε τὰς γυναῖκας (*Eph 5:25*).
    Husbands, love *your* wives.

    ὅμοιοί εἰσιν παιδίοις τοῖς ἐν ἀγορᾷ καθημένοις καὶ προσφωνοῦσιν ἀλλήλοις (*Luke 7:32*).
    They are like children *who* sit in the marketplace and call to one another.

36.8 When the article is not present, it is generally emphasizing the *quality* of the substantive. This is a difficult concept to grasp and it will probably take you a while.

    ὁ θεὸς ἀγάπη ἐστίν (*1 John 4:8*).

    God is *love*. (It is not so much that God loves, but that he is in very essence love.)

However, other times the article is not used simply because a word is not specific.

    ἔρχεται γυνὴ ἐκ τῆς Σαμαρείας ἀντλῆσαι ὕδωρ (*John 4:7*).

    A woman of Samaria came to draw water. (At this point in the story she was simply a woman, not any one in particular.)

36.9 ὁ can also function simply as a grammatical marker, for example showing that the following word modifies the previous. We have seen this repeatedly since Chapter 9.

    μετὰ τῶν ἀγγέλων τῶν ἁγίων (*Mark 8:38*)
    with the holy angels

Verb

36.10 Verbs are transitive or intransitive.

■ A **transitive** verb is one that carries the force of its action over to an object. In other words, transitive verbs require a direct object.

φέρετέ μοι αὐτὸν ὧδε *(Matt 17:17)*.

Bring him here to me.

■ An **intransitive** verb is one that does not carry its action over to an object. There may be other modifiers present, but there will not be a direct object.

λέγει αὐτῷ· ἀκολούθει μοι. καὶ ἀναστὰς ἠκολούθησεν αὐτῷ *(Matt 9:9)*.

He said to him, "Follow me." And he *rose* and followed him.

Sentence Structure

36.11 While you have experienced the fact that Greek sentences can be structured many different ways, there actually is a "normal" order: verb, subject, object.

When the speaker wants to emphasize a word, that word is moved out of its "normal" position. In most cases, this means the most important word(s) come first. The difference is largely one of nuance and not basic meaning.

τῇ γὰρ χάριτί ἐστε σεσῳσμένοι διὰ πίστεως *(Eph 2:8)*.

For *by grace* you have been saved through faith.

Summary

■ μι verbs with stem vowels in alpha (ἵστημι) and epsilon (τίθημι) behave just like μι verbs with stem vowels in omicron (δίδωμι). δείκνυμι, however, is somewhat different and in many ways more like the thematic conjugation.

■ The athematic conjugation was in the process of being lost in Koine Greek, and consequently some μι verbs have thematic forms.

■ When ὁ is present, it emphasizes the identity of the word/phrase it modifies.

■ When ὁ is not present, it emphasizes the quality of the substantive.

■ ὁ can also function as a grammatical marker;

■ Transitive verbs require an object, intransitive do not.

■ "Normal" word order is verb, subject, object.

Vocabulary

In Chapter 33 you learned ἀπόλλυμι, and in 34 you learned δίδωμι and παραδίδωμι, three of the nine μι verbs that occur fifty times or more in the New Testament. The other six such μι verbs are listed in this vocabulary. These six are not all used in the exercises for this chapter, but you should learn them.

ἀνίστημι   intransitive: I rise, get up (108; ἀνά + *στα)
transitive: I raise
ἀναστήσω, ἀνέστησα, –, –, –

ἀνοίγω   I open (77; ἀν + * οιγ)
ἀνοίξω, ἠνέῳξα or ἀνέῳξα, ἀνέῳγα, ἀνέῳγμαι or ἠνέῳγμαι, ἠνεῴχθην or ἠνοίχθην or ἀνεῴχθην or ἠνοίγην (2 aorist)

ἀνοίγω was originally a compound verb, and at times it is augmented as if it still were compound, and at other times as if it were a simple verb. You can even find forms with two augments.

ἀφίημι   I let go, leave, permit; forgive (143; ἀφ + *σε)[4]
(ἤφιον), ἀφήσω, ἀφῆκα, –, ἀφέωμαι, ἀφέθην

The root of this verb is *σε. Like ἵστημι, the reduplicated sigma dropped off and was replaced with a rough breathing. The initial sigma was also dropped because it was intervocalic. σε ‣ σισε ‣ ἱσε ‣ ἵημι.

It is a compound with ἀπό and the pi has aspirated to a phi because of the rough breathing that actually is there, although unseen. ἵημι occurs in the New Testament only as a compound.

δείκνυμι   I show, explain (30; *δεικνυ)[5]
δείξω, ἔδειξα, δέδειχα, –, ἐδείχθην

Even though δείκνυμι occurs less than fifty times, it has been included so the paradigms can be complete. Outside of the present and imperfect tenses, it forms its tense stems from the root *δεικ and is not a μι verb.

ἴδιος, -α, -ον   one's own (114; * ἰδιο)[6]

ἴδιος can be used in the sense of one's own "people" or "land." It can also be used adverbially to mean "individually."

ἵστημι   intransitive: I stand (154; *στα)
transitive: I cause to stand
(ἵστην), στήσω, ἔστησα or ἔστην, ἕστηκα, –, ἐστάθην

ἵστημι is transitive in the present, future, and first aorist. It is intransitive in the second aorist and perfect. This is the one μι verb that does not use a kappa aorist. It has a second aorist, ἔστην. Notice the shift to the rough breathing in the perfect active.

---

[4]   *Aphesis* is the gradual loss of an initial unaccented vowel, such as in the English *esquire* to *squire* (cf. *MBG*, #7.10).

[5]   In grammar, a *deictic* word is one that is demonstrative, one that points out, such as the demonstrative pronoun.

[6]   *Idiosyncrasy* (συγκρᾶσις, "a mixing together") is a temperament or behavior peculiar to one person or group.

μέσος, –η, –ον	middle, in the midst (58; *μεσο)[7]
τίθημι	I put, place (100; *θε)[8]
	(ἐτίθην), θήσω, ἔθηκα, τέθεικα, τέθειμαι, ἐτέθην
φημί	I say, affirm (66; *φε)
	(ἔφη), –, ἔφη, –, –, –

ἔφη can be either imperfect or aorist, and is third singular. You learned this as a vocabulary word earlier.

Total word count in the New Testament:	138,162
Number of words learned to date:	320
Number of word occurrences in this chapter:	850
Number of word occurrences to date:	110,878
Percent of total word count in the New Testament:	80.25%

Congratulations! You know all 320 words that occur most frequently in the New Testament, and four out of five word occurrences in the New Testament.

If you learned the extra vocabulary in chapter 35, then here are your statistics.

Total word count in the New Testament:	138,162
Number of words learned to date:	335
Number of word occurrences in this chapter:	574
Number of word occurrences to date:	111,452
Percent of total word count in the New Testament:	80.67%

---

[7]   *Meso* is a combining form that when added to another word carries the meaning of "middle," such as "mesomorphic" (the state between liquid and crystalline), "mesoplast" (the nucleus of a cell), and "Mesozoic" (the age between the Paleozoic and Cenozoic ages).

[8]   The cognate θέσις is a "placing," a "proposition." In logic a "thesis" is an unprovable statement, a proposition, assumed to be true.

Postscript

Where Do We Go from Here?

Congratulations. You have finished learning the building blocks of biblical Greek; now the real fun begins. But what should you do next?

1. There is no substitute at this point for reading the biblical text, reading as much as you can. You need to be exposed to large sections of the New Testament to have fun (if for no other reason).

2. There are two additional chapters in the workbook. One covers 2 John and the other Mark 2:1-3:6. There is nothing new to learn in these chapters; they are just there to have fun and be encouraged.

3. I wrote a third volume in this series, *A Graded Reader of Biblical Greek*. It starts with easy passages and slowly works into more difficult Greek. I start with Mark and John because you are so familiar with them; most of our exercises came from the early chapters of Mark. Pay close attention to the footnotes in this text. They will help carry you into the next stage by exposing you to intermediate Greek grammar inductively.

4. The *Graded Reader* includes a forty-page summary of Daniel Wallace's intermediate Greek grammar (see below). It is well worth reading.

5. The *Graded Reader* is tied into Daniel B. Wallace's *Greek Grammar Beyond the Basics: An Exegetical Syntax of the New Testament* (volume four in this series). His grammar is cross-indexed in my *Graded Reader*. It is essential at some time that you sit down and read through a complete grammar. However, the further you are into the *Graded Reader*, the easier it will be to remember his grammatical discussions. You may also want to check out his abridgment, *The Basics of New Testament Syntax*.

6. *The Morphology of Biblical Greek* (volume five in this series) is designed to show you what is really happening to the forms of the Greek words you meet. Read the introductory discussion so you can see how to use the book; and as you come across forms that you do not understand, look up the word in the index and from there go to its relevant discussion. But do not become bogged down in this process right away. It is much better to have some fun and read lots of Greek.

7. My *The Analytical Lexicon to the Greek New Testament* can help you with those difficult parsings. Be sure to read the introductory discussion "How to Use the Analytical" for warnings about the misuse of the book.

8. Do not forget to review. This is essential. You will lose all pleasure in the language if you have to look up every other verb in order to parse it, or every other word in the lexicon to discover its meaning. Purchase Warren Trenchard's *Complete Vocabulary Guide to the Greek New Testament* or Bruce Metzger's *Lexical Aids for Students of New Testament Greek*. They will help you review your vocabulary, fill out the definitions, and make it easier to

memorize more vocabulary if you wish. You should memorize at least all words occurring twenty times or more, and most second-year Greek teachers take you down to ten occurrences.

9.   But most importantly, do not forget why you have learned the language of God's Word. It is a tool for ministry, helping you to get closer to what God has said through his writers. It is a tool that allows you to use other tools, such as good commentaries.

I once heard a story, perhaps apocryphal, about a sailor who was in love with a woman from another country. He wanted to be married and so he tried to familiarize himself with her native country. He studied its customs, history, etc. But finally he realized that if he really wanted to understand her, he would have to learn her native language. I believe that learning Greek is nothing more than a natural extension of our loving relationship with Jesus Christ. Although many translations are good, they are one step further removed from what Jesus said. Ultimately, you want to know him and his message as well as possible. A knowledge of the Greek language is essential to achieve this goal.

May your days be filled with blessing and your ministry fruitful as you seek to share your love and knowledge of Jesus Christ with those around you.

Bill Mounce

Appendix

Detailed Table of Contents

General

Introduction

In the Appendixes I have collected all the charts you need to read Greek. The listing is not exhaustive; if you want to see every chart, see *MBG*.

Remember, the charts are not for you to memorize. You should memorize the eight rules and master charts. Then use the rest of these charts to test yourself, to see if you really know the rules.

Crasis in the New Testament

καὶ ἐγώ	▸	κἀγώ
καὶ ἐμοί	▸	κἀμοί
καὶ ἐκεῖ	▸	κἀκεῖ
καὶ ἐκεῖθεν	▸	κἀκεῖθεν
καὶ ἐκεῖνος	▸	κἀκεῖνος
καὶ ἐάν or ἄν	▸	κἄν

When Accents and Breathings Are Especially Important

1. τις, τι; τίς, τί
2. ἡ, ἤ, ἥ, ᾗ, ᾔ
3. οἱ, αἱ; οἵ, αἵ
4. ὁ, ὅ; ὅν, ὄν
5. ὤν, ὦν
6. ἧς, ἧς; ἦν, ἤν
7. ὤ (interjection), ὦ (subj. of εἰμί), ᾧ (rel. pronoun)
8. αὐτή, αὕτη
9. αὐταί, αὗται
10. οὐ, οὗ
11. ἔξω, ἔξω
12. ἐν, ἔν
13. Liquid futures
14. ἀλλά, ἄλλα
15. εἰ, εἶ
16. εἰς, εἷς
17. ποτέ, πότε
18. ἄρα, ἆρα

Square of Stops

Labial	π	β	φ
Velar	κ	γ	χ
Dental	τ	δ	θ

Spatial Representation of Prepositions

General Guidelines for the Cases

Genitive: Indicates motion away from ("separation"; ἀπό)

Dative: Indicates rest (ἐν)

Accusative: Indicates motion (εἰς)

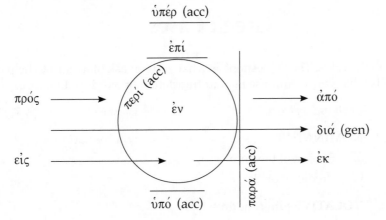

Other Prepositions that are not Spatially Diagrammed

ἀντί gen: instead of, for
      dat: beside, in the presence of

διά acc: on account of

ἐπί gen: on, over, when
      dat: on the basis of, at

κατά gen: against
      acc: according to

μετά gen: with
      acc: after

παρά gen: from

περί gen: concerning, about

ὑπέρ gen: in behalf of

ὑπό gen: by

Contractions of Single Vowels

Following is a chart of all possible contractions of single vowels. The four most common (and troublesome) are in blue.

	α	ε	η	ι	υ	ο	ω
α	α	α	α	αι	αυ	ω	ω
ε	η	ει	η	ει	ευ	ου	ω
η	η	η	η	ῃ	ηυ	ω	ω
ο	ω	ου	ω	οι	ου	ου	ω
ω	ω	ω	ω	ῳ	ωυ	ω	ω

Contraction of Vowels and Diphthongs

	α / αι	ει[1]	ει[2]	η	οι	ου[3]	ω
α	ᾳ	ᾳ	α	ᾳ	ῳ	ω	ῳ
ε	η	ει	ει	η	οι	ου	ω
η	ῃ	ῃ	η	ῃ	ῳ		ῳ
ο	ῳ	οι	ου	οι	οι	ου	ῳ

Greek Cases

This is a summary of all the cases. The "Question" is what you can ask of a word to help determine its case. The "Key word" is what you should use in your translation of words in that case.

English cases	Greek cases and uses	Question	Key word
1. Subjective (he)	1. **NOMINATIVE**	who? what?	
	a. Subject of the verb		
	b. Predicate of "is"		
	VOCATIVE (direct address)		"O"
2. Possessive (his)	2. **GENITIVE**	whose?	
	a. Possessive		"of"
	b. Object of Preposition		
	c. Direct object of certain verbs		
	d. Ablative (separation)		"from"
3. Objective (him)	3. **DATIVE**		
	a. Indirect object	to whom? to what?	"to" / "for"
	b. Object of Preposition		
	c. Direct object of certain verbs		
	d. Instrumental (means)	by what?	"by" / "with"
	e. Locative (place)	where?	"in"
4. Objective (him)	4. **ACCUSATIVE**		
	a. Direct object of most verbs	whom? what?	
	b. Object of preposition		

The word has the ____ case ending, so I know that it functions as the _____ in the sentence; therefore I translate it with the key word _____ .

Always precede a word in a certain case with a "key word" for that case, if there is one.

---

[1] "Genuine" diphthong (not formed by a contraction)

[2] "Spurious" diphthong (formed by a contraction)

[3] Spurious

Noun System

Master Case Ending Chart & The Eight Noun Rules

A dash means that no case ending is used. An underline means that the final stem vowel changes to the one listed in the chart (rule 5). The case endings for the masc/fem in the third declension are repeated for the sake of clarity, even though in several cases they are the same as in the first and second declensions.

	first/second declension			*third declension*	
	masc	*fem*	*neut*	*masc/fem*	*neut*
nom sg	ς	–	ν	ς	_ᵃ
gen sg	υᵇ	ς	υ	ος	ος
dat sg	ιᶜ	ι	ι	ιᵈ	ι
acc sg	ν	ν	ν	α/νᵉ	–
nom pl	ι	ι	<u>α</u>	ες	αᶠ
gen pl	<u>ω</u>ν	<u>ω</u>ν	<u>ω</u>ν	ων	ων
dat pl	ις	ις	ις	σι(ν)ᵍ	σι(ν)
acc pl	υςʰ	ς	<u>α</u>	αςⁱ	α

ᵃ Be prepared for the final stem letter to undergo changes (Rule 8).

ᵇ The ending is actually omicron, which contracts with the final stem vowel and forms ου (Rule 5).

ᶜ The vowel lengthens (Rule 5) and the iota subscripts (Rule 4).

ᵈ Because third declension stems end in a consonant, the iota cannot subscript as it does in the first and second declensions; so it remains on the line.

ᵉ On some words the case ending alternates between alpha and nu; see 11.12.

ᶠ As opposed to the first and second declensions, this alpha is an actual case ending and not a changed stem vowel. This is also true in the accusative plural.

ᵍ The nu is a movable nu. Notice that the ending σι is a flipped version of ις found in the first and second declensions.

ʰ The actual case ending for the first and second declension is νς, but the nu drops out because of the following sigma. In the first declension the alpha simply joins with the sigma (*ωρα + νς ▸ ὥρας), but in the second declension the final stem omicron lengthens to ου (Rule 5; λογονς ▸ λογος ▸ λόγους).

ⁱ As opposed to the first declension (e.g., ὥρα), the alpha here is part of the case ending.

The following chart shows what the endings look like when attached to the final stem vowel.

	masc	fem		neut	masc/fem	neut
nom sg	ος	α	η	ον	ς	–
gen sg	ου	ας	ης	ου	ος	ος
dat sg	ῳ	ᾳ	ῃ	ῳ	ι	ι
acc sg	ον	αν	ην	ον	α / ν	–

	masc	fem	neut	masc/fem	neut
nom pl	οι	αι	α	ες	α
gen pl	ων	ων	ων	ων	ων
dat pl	οις	αις	οις	σι(ν)	σι(ν)
acc pl	ους	ας	α	ας	α

The Eight Noun Rules

1. **Stems ending in alpha or eta are in the first declension, stems ending in omicron are in the second, and consonantal stems are in the third.**

2. **Every neuter word has the same form in the nominative and accusative.**

3. **Almost all neuter words end in alpha in the nominative and accusative plural.**
   - In the second declension, the alpha is the changed stem vowel; in the third it is the case ending.

4. **In the dative singular, the iota subscripts if possible.**
   - Because an iota can subscript only under a long vowel, it subscripts only in the first and second declensions.

5. **Vowels often change their length ("ablaut").**
   - "Contraction" occurs when two vowels meet and form a different vowel or diphthong.
     λογο + ι ▸ λόγῳ. λογο + ο ▸ λόγου. γραφη + ων ▸ γραφῶν[1]
   - "Compensatory lengthening" occurs when a vowel is lengthened to compensate for the loss of another letter.
     λογο + νς ▸ λόγος ▸ λόγους

6. **In the genitive and dative, the masculine and neuter will always be identical.**

7. **The Square of Stops**
   - Labials + sigma form psi; velars plus sigma form xi; dentals plus sigma form sigma.
   - The ντ combination drops out when followed by sigma (παντ + ς ▸ πᾶς).
   - Whatever happens in the nominative singular third declension also happens in the dative plural. σαρκ + σ ▸ σάρξ. σαρκ + σι ▸ σαρξί.

8. **A tau cannot stand at the end of a word and will drop off.**
   - When no case ending is used in stems ending in -ματ, the tau drops out. ὀνοματ + – ▸ ὀνοματ ▸ ὄνομα.

---

[1] The omega of the genitive plural will absorb any preceding vowel.

Nouns, Adjectives, and Pronouns

First Declension Nouns

	n-1a	n-1b	n-1c	n-1d	Article		
nom sg	ὥρα	γραφή	δόξα	νεανίας	ὁ	ἡ	τό
gen sg	ὥρας	γραφῆς	δόξης	νεανίου	τοῦ	τῆς	τοῦ
dat sg	ὥρᾳ	γραφῇ	δόξῃ	νεανίᾳ	τῷ	τῇ	τῷ
acc sg	ὥραν	γραφήν	δόξαν	νεανίαν	τόν	τήν	τό
voc sg	ὥρα	γραφή	δόξα	νεανία			
n/v pl	ὧραι	γραφαί	δόξαι	νεανίαι	οἱ	αἱ	τά
gen pl	ὡρῶν	γραφῶν	δοξῶν	νεανιῶν	τῶν	τῶν	τῶν
dat pl	ὥραις	γραφαῖς	δόξαις	νεανίαις	τοῖς	ταῖς	τοῖς
acc pl	ὥρας	γραφάς	δόξας	νεανίας	τούς	τάς	τά

	n-1e	n-1f	n-1g	n-1h	Relative pronoun		
nom sg	σατανᾶς	προφήτης	Μανασσῆς	μνᾶ	ὅς	ἥ	ὅ
gen sg	σατανᾶ	προφήτου	Μανασσῆ	μνᾶς	οὗ	ἧς	οὗ
dat sg	σατανᾷ	προφήτῃ	–	μνᾷ	ᾧ	ᾗ	ᾧ
acc sg	σατανᾶν	προφήτην	Μανασσῆ	μνᾶν	ὅν	ἥν	ὅ
voc sg	σατανᾶ	προφῆτα	–	μνᾶ			
n/v pl	–	προφῆται	–	μναῖ	οἵ	αἵ	ἅ
gen pl	–	προφητῶν	–	μνῶν	ὧν	ὧν	ὧν
dat pl	–	προφήταις	–	μναῖς	οἷς	αἷς	οἷς
acc pl	–	προφήτας	–	μνᾶς	οὕς	ἅς	ἅ

Second Declension Nouns

	n-2a	n-2b	n-2c	n-2d(1)	n-2d(2)	n-2e
nom sg	λόγος	ὁδός	ἔργον	χειμάρρους	ὀστοῦν	κῶς
gen sg	λόγου	ὁδοῦ	ἔργου	χειμάρρου	ὀστοῦ	κῶ
dat sg	λόγῳ	ὁδῷ	ἔργῳ	χειμάρρῳ	ὀστῷ	κῷ
acc sg	λόγον	ὁδόν	ἔργον	χειμάρρουν	ὀστοῦν	–
voc sg	λόγε	ὁδέ	ἔργον	χειμάρρους	ὀστοῦν	κῶς
n/v pl	λόγοι	ὁδοί	ἔργα	χειμαρροι	ὀστᾶ	–
gen pl	λόγων	ὁδῶν	ἔργων	χειμάρρων	ὀστῶν	–
dat pl	λόγοις	ὁδοῖς	ἔργοις	χειμάρροις	ὀστοῖς	–
acc pl	λόγους	ὁδούς	ἔργα	χειμάρρους	ὀστᾶ	–

Third Declension Nouns

	n-3b(1)	n-3b(1)	n-3b(3)	n-3c(1)	n-3c(2)	n-3c(4)
nom sg	σάρξ	γυνή	θρίξ[1]	χάρις	ἐλπίς	ὄνομα
gen sg	σαρκός	γυναικός	τριχός	χάριτος	ἐλπίδος	ὀνόματος
dat sg	σαρκί	γυναικί	τριχί	χάριτι	ἐλπίδι	ὀνόματι
acc sg	σάρκα	γυναῖκα	τρίχα	χάριν	ἐλπίδα	ὄνομα
voc sg	σάρξ	γύναι	θρίξ	–	–	–
n/v pl	σάρκες	γυναῖκες	τρίχες	χάριτες	ἐλπίδες	ὀνόματα
gen pl	σαρκῶν	γυναικῶν	τριχῶν	χαρίτων	ἐλπίδων	ὀνομάτων
dat pl	σαρξί(ν)	γυναιξί(ν)	θριξί(ν)	χάρισι(ν)	ἐλπίσι(ν)	ὀνόμασι(ν)
acc pl	σάρκας	γυναῖκας	τρίχας	χάριτας	ἐλπίδας	ὀνόματα

	n-3c(5b)	n-3c(6a)	n-3c(6b)	n-3c(6c)	n-3d(2a)	n-3d(2b)
n/v sg	ἄρχων	τέρας	ὕδωρ	φῶς	σωσθένης	γένος
gen sg	ἄρχοντος	τέρατος	ὕδατος	φωτός	σωσθένους	γένους
dat sg	ἄρχοντι	τέρατι	ὕδατι	φωτί	–	γένει
acc sg	ἄρχοντα	τέρας	ὕδωρ	φῶς	σωσθένην	γένος
n/v pl	ἄρχοντες	τέρατα	ὕδατα	φῶτα	–	γένη
gen pl	ἀρχόντων	τεράτων	ὑδάτων	φώτων	–	γενῶν
dat pl	ἄρχουσι(ν)	τέρασι(ν)	ὕδασι(ν)	–	–	γένεσι(ν)
acc pl	ἄρχοντας	τέρατα	ὕδατα	φῶτα	–	γένη

	n-3e(1)	n-3e(3)	n-3e(4)	n-3e(5b)	n-3f(1a)	n-3f(1b)
nom sg	ἰχθύς	βασιλεύς	νοῦς	πόλις	αἰών	ἡγεμών
gen sg	ἰχθύος	βασιλέως	νοός	πόλεως	αἰῶνος	ἡγεμόνος
dat sg	ἰχθύι	βασιλεῖ	νοΐ	πόλει	αἰῶνι	ἡγεμόνι
acc sg	ἰχθύν	βασιλέα	νοῦν	πόλιν	αἰῶνα	ἡγεμόνα
voc sg	ἰχθύ	βασιλεῦ	νοῦ	πόλι	αἰών	ἡγεμών
n/v pl	ἰχθύες	βασιλεῖς	νόες	πόλεις	αἰῶνες	ἡγεμόνες
gen pl	ἰχθύων	βασιλέων	νοῶν	πόλεων	αἰώνων	ἡγεμόνων
dat pl	ἰχθύσι(ν)	βασιλεῦσι(ν)	νουσί(ν)	πόλεσι(ν)	αἰῶσι(ν)	ἡγεμόσι(ν)
acc pl	ἰχθύας	βασιλεῖς	νόας	πόλεις	αἰῶνας	ἡγεμόνας

	n-3f(2a)	n-3f(2b)	n-3f(2c)	n-3f(2c)	n-3f(2c)	n-3f(2c)
nom sg	σωτήρ	ῥήτωρ	ἀνήρ	θυγάτηρ	πατήρ	μήτηρ
gen sg	σωτῆρος	ῥήτορος	ἀνδρός	θυγατρός	πατρός	μητρός
dat sg	σωτῆρι	ῥήτορι	ἀνδρί	θυγατρί	πατρί	μητρί
acc sg	σωτῆρα	ῥήτορα	ἄνδρα	θυγατέρα	πατέρα	μητέρα
voc sg	–	ῥῆτορ	ἄνερ	θυγάτερ	πάτερ	μῆτερ
n/v pl	σωτῆρες	ῥήτορες	ἄνδρες	θυγατέρες	πατέρες	–
gen pl	σωτήρων	ῥητόρων	ἀνδρῶν	θυγατέρων	πατέρων	–
dat pl	σωτῆρσι(ν)	ῥήτορσι(ν)	ἀνδράσι(ν)	–	πατράσι(ν)	–
acc pl	σωτῆρας	ῥήτορας	ἄνδρας	θυγατέρας	πατέρας	μητέρας

---

[1] With this particular word, the initial letter varies between theta and tau depending upon whether the final consonant is a xi or a chi in the nominative singular and dative plural. See *MBG* for an explanation.

Adjectives

a-1a (2-1-2)

	masc	fem	neut	masc	fem	neut
nom sg	ἅγιος	ἁγία	ἅγιον	ἀγαθός	ἀγαθή	ἀγαθόν
gen sg	ἁγίου	ἁγίας	ἁγίου	ἀγαθοῦ	ἀγαθῆς	ἀγαθοῦ
dat sg	ἁγίῳ	ἁγίᾳ	ἁγίῳ	ἀγαθῷ	ἀγαθῇ	ἀγαθῷ
acc sg	ἅγιον	ἁγίαν	ἅγιον	ἀγαθόν	ἀγαθήν	ἀγαθόν
voc sg	ἅγιε	ἁγία	ἅγιον	ἀγαθέ	ἀγαθή	ἀγαθόν
nom pl	ἅγιοι	ἅγιαι	ἅγια	ἀγαθοί	ἀγαθαί	ἀγαθά
gen pl	ἁγίων	ἁγίων	ἁγίων	ἀγαθῶν	ἀγαθῶν	ἀγαθῶν
dat pl	ἁγίοις	ἁγίαις	ἁγίοις	ἀγαθοῖς	ἀγαθαῖς	ἀγαθοῖς
acc pl	ἁγίους	ἁγίας	ἅγια	ἀγαθούς	ἀγαθάς	ἀγαθά

a-1a(2b) (2-1-2)

	masc	fem	neut	masc	fem	neut
nom sg	οὗτος	αὕτη	τοῦτο	μέγας	μεγάλη	μέγα
gen sg	τούτου	ταύτης	τούτου	μεγάλου	μεγάλης	μεγάλου
dat sg	τούτῳ	ταύτῃ	τούτῳ	μεγάλῳ	μεγάλη	μεγάλῳ
acc sg	τοῦτον	ταύτην	τοῦτο	μέγαν	μεγάλην	μέγα
nom pl	οὗτοι	αὗται	ταῦτα	μεγάλοι	μεγάλαι	μεγάλα
gen pl	τούτων	τούτων	τούτων	μεγάλων	μεγάλων	μεγάλων
dat pl	τούτοις	ταύταις	τούτοις	μεγάλοις	μεγάλαις	μεγάλοις
acc pl	τούτους	ταύτας	ταῦτα	μεγάλους	μεγάλας	μεγάλα

a-1a(2a) (2-1-2)   a-1a(2b) (3-3-3)

	masc	fem	neut	masc	fem	neut
nom sg	πολύς	πολλή	πολύ	ὅστις	ἥτις	ὅτι
gen sg	πολλοῦ	πολλῆς	πολλοῦ	οὗτινος	ἧστινος	οὗτινος
dat sg	πολλῷ	πολλῇ	πολλῷ	ᾧτινι	ᾗτινι	ᾧτινι
acc sg	πολύν	πολλήν	πολύ	ὅντινα	ἥντινα	ὅτι
nom pl	πολλοί	πολλαί	πολλά	οἵτινες	αἵτινες	ἅτινα
gen pl	πολλῶν	πολλῶν	πολλῶν	ὧντινων	ὧντινων	ὧντινων
dat pl	πολλοῖς	πολλαῖς	πολλοῖς	οἷστισι(ν)	αἷστισι(ν)	οἷστισι(ν)
acc pl	πολλούς	πολλάς	πολλά	οὕστινας	ἅστινας	ἅτινα

a-2a (3-1-3)   a-2b (3-1-3)

	masc	fem	neut	masc	fem	neut
nom sg	πᾶς	πᾶσα	πᾶν	ταχύς	ταχεῖα	ταχύ
gen sg	παντός	πάσης	παντός	ταχέως	ταχείας	ταχέως
dat sg	παντί	πάσῃ	παντί	ταχεῖ	ταχείᾳ	ταχεῖ
acc sg	πάντα	πᾶσαν	πᾶν	ταχύν	ταχεῖαν	ταχύ
nom pl	πάντες	πᾶσαι	πάντα	ταχεῖς	ταχεῖαι	ταχέα
gen pl	πάντων	πασῶν	πάντων	ταχέων	ταχειῶν	ταχέων
dat pl	πᾶσι	πάσαις	πᾶσι	ταχέσι	ταχείαις	ταχέσι
acc pl	πάντας	πάσας	πάντα	ταχεῖς	ταχείας	ταχέα

Adjectives/Pronouns

	masc & fem	neut		masc & fem	neut			
a-3a (2-2)	**a-4a (3-3)**					**a-1a(2b) (2-1-2)**		
nom sg	ἁμαρτωλός	ἁμαρτωλόν	ἀληθής	ἀληθές	αὐτός	αὐτή	αὐτό
gen sg	ἁμαρτωλοῦ	ἁμαρτωλοῦ	ἀληθοῦς	ἀληθοῦς	αὐτοῦ	αὐτῆς	αὐτοῦ
dat sg	ἁμαρτωλῷ	ἁμαρτωλῷ	ἀληθεῖ	ἀληθεῖ	αὐτῷ	αὐτῇ	αὐτῷ
acc sg	ἁμαρτωλόν	ἁμαρτωλόν	ἀληθῆ	ἀληθές	αὐτόν	αὐτήν	αὐτό
voc sg	ἁμαρτωλέ	ἁμαρτωλόν	-	–	-	-	–
nom pl	ἁμαρτωλοί	ἁμαρτωλά	ἀληθεῖς	ἀληθῆ	αὐτοί	αὐταί	αὐτά
gen pl	ἁμαρτωλῶν	ἁμαρτωλῶν	ἀληθῶν	ἀληθῶν	αὐτῶν	αὐτῶν	αὐτῶν
dat pl	ἁμαρτωλοῖς	ἁμαρτωλοῖς	ἀληθέσι(ν)	ἀληθέσι(ν)	αὐτοῖς	αὐταῖς	αὐτοῖς
acc pl	ἁμαρτωλούς	ἁμαρτωλά	ἀληθεῖς	ἀληθῆ	αὐτούς	αὐτάς	αὐτά

a-4b(1) (3-3)

	masc & fem	neut	masc & fem	neut
nom sg	πλείων	πλεῖον	μείζων	μεῖζον
gen sg	πλείονος	πλείονος	μείζονος	μείζονος
dat sg	πλείονι	πλείονι	μείζονι	μείζονι
acc sg	πλείονα	πλεῖον	μείζονα	μεῖζον
nom pl	πλείονες	πλείονα	μείζονες	μείζονα
gen pl	πλειόνων	πλειόνων	μειζόνων	μειζόνων
dat pl	πλείοσι(ν)	πλείοσι(ν)	μείζοσι(ν)	μείζοσι(ν)
acc pl	πλείονας	πλείονα	μείζονας	μείζονα

a-4b(2) (3-3; interrogative, indefinite)   **a-4b(2) (3-1-3)**

	masc & fem	neut	masc & fem	neut			
nom sg	τίς	τί	τις	τι	εἷς	μία	ἕν
gen sg	τίνος	τίνος	τινός	τινός	ἑνός	μιᾶς	ἑνός
dat sg	τίνι	τίνι	τινί	τινί	ἑνί	μιᾷ	ἑνί
acc sg	τίνα	τί	τινά	τι	ἕνα	μίαν	ἕν
nom pl	τίνες	τίνα	τινές	τινά			
gen pl	τίνων	τίνων	τινῶν	τινῶν			
dat pl	τίσι(ν)	τίσι(ν)	τισί(ν)	τισί(ν)			
acc pl	τίνας	τίνα	τινάς	τινά			

a-5

	1st person		*2nd person*			*1st person*	*2nd person*
nom sg	ἐγώ		σύ		*nom pl*	ἡμεῖς	ὑμεῖς
gen sg	ἐμοῦ	(μου)	σοῦ	(σου)	*gen pl*	ἡμῶν	ὑμῶν
dat sg	ἐμοί	(μοι)	σοί	(σοι)	*dat pl*	ἡμῖν	ὑμῖν
acc sg	ἐμέ	(με)	σέ	(σε)	*acc pl*	ἡμᾶς	ὑμᾶς

Verb System

English Verb Tenses

This is the basic verb chart and terminology followed in BBG. It is possible to be more complex; but for the basic task of learning a foreign language, this is sufficient. All forms are listed in the active and then in the passive, starting first with a regular verb (e.g., "study") and then an irregular (e.g., "eat").

	Past simple	Past progressive	Past perfect
reg act	I studied	I was studying	I had studied
irreg act	I ate	I was eating	I had eaten
reg pas	I was studied	I was being studied	I had been studied
irreg pas	I was eaten	I was being eaten	I had been eaten

	Present simple	Present progressive	Present perfect
reg act	I study	I am studying	I have studied
irreg act	I eat	I am eating	I have eaten
reg pas	I am studied	I am being studied	I have been studied
irreg pas	I am eaten	I am being eaten	I have been eaten

	Future simple	Future progressive	Future perfect
reg act	I will study	I will be studying	I will have studied
irreg act	I will eat	I will be eating	I will have eaten
reg pas	I will be studied	I will be being studied	I will have been studied
irreg pas	I will be eaten	I will be being eaten	I will have been eaten

Verbal Rules

1. Primary and Secondary endings

	primary				secondary		
	regular		alternate[1]		regular		alternate

active

1 sg	λύω	ο	–[2]	μι	ἔλυον	ο	ν	
2 sg	λύεις	ε	ς		ἔλυες	ε	ς	
3 sg	λύει	ε	ι	σι(ν)	ἔλυε(ν)	ε	–	
1 pl	λύομεν	ο	μεν		ἐλύομεν	ο	μεν	
2 pl	λύετε	ε	τε		ἐλύετε	ε	τε	
3 pl	λύουσι(ν)	ο	νσι(ν)[3]	ασι(ν)	ἔλυον	ο	ν	σαν

middle/passive

1 sg	λύομαι	ο	μαι		ἐλυόμην	ο	μην	
2 sg	λύῃ	ε	σαι[4]		ἐλύου	ε	σο[5]	
3 sg	λύεται	ε	ται		ἐλύετο	ε	το	
1 pl	λυόμεθα	ο	μεθα		ἐλυόμεθα	ο	μεθα	
2 pl	λύεσθε	ε	σθε		ἐλύεσθε	ε	σθε	
3 pl	λύονται	ο	νται		ἐλύοντο	ο	ντο	

Primary Endings are used on the unaugmented tenses. In the indicative these are the present, future, and perfect. In the subjunctive it is all tenses.

Secondary Endings are used on the augmented tenses. In the indicative these are the imperfect, aorist, and pluperfect. In the optative it is all tenses (even though the optative is not augmented).

The μι conjugation uses the alternate endings.

---

[1] Alternate endings are used for μι verbs and a few thematic forms.

[2] No ending is used. The omega that stands at the end of the first person singular of verbs in the thematic conjugation is really the lengthened connecting vowel omicron.

[3] In every case the nu will drop out because of the following sigma. What happens to the preceeding vowel varies.

[4] In almost every case (except perfect passive), the sigma drops out and the vowels contract. This is why this ending varies from tense to tense.

[5] In almost every case, the sigma drops out because it is intervocalic and the vowels contract. This is why this ending varies from tense to tense.

2. Augments occur in the imperfect, aorist, and pluperfect.
    *   It is removed in the non-indicative moods.

3. Reduplication occurs in the perfect and present.
    *   Consonantal reduplication reduplicates the initial consonant; vocalic reduplication lengthens the initial vowel.
    *   Reduplication with an epsilon always signals a perfect.
    *   Reduplication with an iota signals the present of a μι verb.

4. Verbal roots
    *   Altered verbal stems show some patterns, but others should be memorized. See *Verbal Stems of Words Occurring More than Fifty Times*, page 370.

5. Differences among tense stems
    *   Double consonants simplify to single consonants (v-1).
    *   Verbs containing an iota lose the iota (v-2).
    *   Verbs containing a nu lose the nu (v-3).
    *   Verbs containing a tau lose the tau (v-4).
    *   Verbs ending in ισκ lose the ισκ (v-5).
    *   μι verbs (v-6)
    *   Vowels lengthen, shorten, or drop out altogether (v-7).
    *   Some verbs use different roots to form their different tense stems (v-8).

6. Tense Formatives often use an ε in the third person singular.
    *   σα ‣ σε   First aorist active/middle
    *   α ‣ ε   Liquid aorists
    *   κα ‣ κε   Perfect (third plural varies between καν and κασι(ν))

7. Vowels
    *   Connecting vowels (o/ε) are used in the present, imperfect, future, second aorist, and participles.
    *   Contract vowels contract in the present and imperfect. Elsewhere they lengthen before the tense formative or personal ending.
    *   Contractions also occur in liquid futures.

8. Second singular passive.
    *   The sigma usually drops out.

9. Miscellaneous
    *   ξ/ψ   When these occur at the end of a verbal stem, they are usually the result of a stop plus a sigma.
    *   φ/χ   When these occur before a theta (as in the aorist passive), they are probably an aspirated labial or velar.

Master Verb Charts

Master Verb Chart

Tense	Aug/ Redup	Tense stem	Tense form.	Conn. vowel	Personal endings	1st sing paradigm
Present act		pres		o/ε	prim act	λύω
Present mid/pas		pres		o/ε	prim mid/pas	λύομαι
Imperfect act	ε	pres		o/ε	sec act	ἔλυον
Imperfect mid/pas	ε	pres		o/ε	sec mid/pas	ἐλυόμην
Future act		fut act	σ	o/ε	prim act	λύσω
Liquid fut act		fut act	εσ	o/ε	prim act	μενῶ
Future mid		fut act	σ	o/ε	prim mid/pas	πορεύσομαι
Liquid fut mid		fut act	εσ	o/ε	prim mid/pas	μενοῦμαι
1st future pas		aor pas	θησ	o/ε	prim mid/pas	λυθήσομαι
2nd future pas		aor pas	ησ	o/ε	prim mid/pas	ἀποσταλήσομαι
1st aorist act	ε	aor act	σα		sec act	ἔλυσα
Liquid aorist act	ε	aor act	α		sec act	ἔμεινα
2nd aorist act	ε	aor act		o/ε	sec act	ἔλαβον
1st aorist mid	ε	aor act	σα		sec mid/pas	ἐλυσάμην
2nd aorist mid	ε	aor act		o/ε	sec mid/pas	ἐγενόμην
1st aorist pas	ε	aor pas	θη		sec act	ἐλύθην
2nd aorist pas	ε	aor pas	η		sec act	ἐγράφην
1st perfect act	λε	perf act	κα		prim act	λέλυκα
2nd perfect act	λε	perf act	α		prim act	γέγονα
Perfect mid/pas	λε	perf pas			prim mid/pas	λέλυμαι

Participle Morpheme Chart

morpheme	tense/voice	case endings
ντ	active; aorist passive	3-1-3
οτ	perfect active	3-1-3
μενο / η	aorist middle; middle/passive	2-1-2

Master Participle Chart

tense & voice	redup	stem	t.f. or c.v.	morpheme	nom. plural	six memory forms
present active		present	ο	ντ / ουσα	λέγοντες	ων, ουσα, ον οντος, ουσης, οντος
present mid/pas		present	ο	μενο / η	λεγόμενοι	ομενος, ομενη, ομενον ομενου, ομενης, ομενου
1 aorist active		aorist active	σα	ντ / σα	λύσαντες	σας, σασα, σαν σαντος, σασης, σαντος
1 aorist middle		aorist active	σα	μενο / η	λυσάμενοι	σαμενος ...
1 aorist passive		aorist passive	θε	ντ	λυθέντες	θεις, θεισα, θεν θεντος, θεισης, θεντος
2 aorist active		aorist active	ο	ντ	βαλόντες	ων ...
2 aorist middle		aorist active	ο	μενο / η	γενόμενοι	ομενος ...
2 aorist passive		aorist passive	ε	ντ	γραφέντες	εις, εισα, εν εντος, εισης, εντος
perfect active	λε	perfect active	κ	οτ	λελυκότες	κως, κυια, κος κοτος, κυιας, κοτος
perfect mid/pas	λε	perfect mid / pas		μενο / η	λελυμένοι	μενος ...

Master Nonindicative Verb Chart

Subjunctive

Tense	Tense stem	Tense form.	Conn. vowel	Personal endings	1st sing paradigm
Present act	pres		ω / η	prim act	λύω
Present mid/pas	pres		ω / η	prim mid / pas	λύωμαι
1st aorist act	aor act	σ(α)	ω / η	prim act	λύσω
1st aorist mid	aor act	σ(α)	ω / η	prim mid / pas	λύσωμαι
1st aorist pas	aor pas	θ(η)	ω / η	prim act	λυθῶ
2nd aorist act	aor act		ω / η	prim act	λάβω
2nd aorist mid	aor act		ω / η	prim mid / pas	γένωμαι
2nd aorist pas	aor pas		ω / η	prim act	γραφῶ

Infinitive

	present	1st aorist	2nd aorist	perfect
active	ειν	σαι	ειν	κεναι
middle	εσθαι	σασθαι	εσθαι	σθαι
passive	εσθαι	θηναι	ηναι	σθαι

	present	1st aorist	2nd aorist	perfect
active	λύειν	λῦσαι	λαβεῖν	λελυκέναι
middle	λύεσθαι	λύσασθαι	λαβέσθαι	λελύσθαι
passive	λύεσθαι	λυθῆναι	γραφῆναι	λελύσθαι

Imperative

	active	middle/passive
2 sg	?	?
3 sg	τω	σθω
2 pl	τε	σθε
3 pl	τωσαν	σθωσαν

		active	middle/passive	passive
present	2 sg	λῦε	λύου	λύου
	3 sg	λυέτω	λυέσθω	λυέσθω
1st aorist	2 sg	λῦσον	λῦσαι	λύθητι
	3 sg	λυσάτω	λυσάσθω	λυθήτω
2nd aorist	2 sg	λάβε	γενοῦ	γράφητι
	3 sg	λαβέτω	γενέσθω	γραφήτω

Basics of Biblical Greek

Verb Paradigms

Overview of Indicative

	present	imperfect	future	1st aorist	2nd aorist	perfect
active indicative						
1 sg	λύω	ἔλυον	λύσω	ἔλυσα	ἔλαβον	λέλυκα
2 sg	λύεις	ἔλυες	λύσεις	ἔλυσας	ἔλαβες	λέλυκας
3 sg	λύει	ἔλυε(ν)	λύσει	ἔλυσε(ν)	ἔλαβε(ν)	λέλυκε(ν)
1 pl	λύομεν	ἐλύομεν	λύσομεν	ἐλύσαμεν	ἐλάβομεν	λελύκαμεν
2 pl	λύετε	ἐλύετε	λύσετε	ἐλύσατε	ἐλάβετε	λελύκατε
3 pl	λύουσι(ν)	ἔλυον	λύσουσι(ν)	ἔλυσαν	ἔλαβον	λελύκασι(ν)
middle indicative						
1 sg	λύομαι	ἐλυόμην	λύσομαι	ἐλυσάμην	ἐγενόμην	λέλυμαι
2 sg	λύῃ	ἐλύου	λύσῃ	ἐλύσω	ἐγένου	λέλυσαι
3 sg	λύεται	ἐλύετο	λύσεται	ἐλύσατο	ἐγένετο	λέλυται
1 pl	λυόμεθα	ἐλυόμεθα	λυσόμεθα	ἐλυσάμεθα	ἐγενόμεθα	λελύμεθα
2 pl	λύεσθε	ἐλύεσθε	λύσεσθε	ἐλύσασθε	ἐγένεσθε	λέλυσθε
3 pl	λύονται	ἐλύοντο	λύσονται	ἐλύσαντο	ἐγένοντο	λέλυνται
passive indicative						
1 sg	λύομαι	ἐλυόμην	λυθήσομαι	ἐλύθην	ἐγράφην	λέλυμαι
2 sg	λύῃ	ἐλύου	λυθήσῃ	ἐλύθης	ἐγράφης	λέλυσαι
3 sg	λύεται	ἐλύετο	λυθήσεται	ἐλύθη	ἐγράφη	λέλυται
1 pl	λυόμεθα	ἐλυόμεθα	λυθησόμεθα	ἐλύθημεν	ἐγράφημεν	λελύμεθα
2 pl	λύεσθε	ἐλύεσθε	λυθήσεσθε	ἐλύθητε	ἐγράφητε	λέλυσθε
3 pl	λύονται	ἐλύοντο	λυθήσονται	ἐλύθησαν	ἐγράφησαν	λέλυνται

Overview of Subjunctive

	present	first aorist	second aorist

active subjunctive

	present	first aorist	second aorist
1 sg	λύω	λύσω	λάβω
2 sg	λύῃς	λύσῃς	λάβῃς
3 sg	λύῃ	λύσῃ	λάβῃ
1 pl	λύωμεν	λύσωμεν	λάβωμεν
2 pl	λύητε	λύσητε	λάβητε
3 pl	λύωσι(ν)	λύσωσι(ν)	λάβωσι(ν)

middle subjunctive

	present	first aorist	second aorist
1 sg	λύωμαι	λύσωμαι	γένωμαι
2 sg	λύῃ	λύσῃ	γένῃ
3 sg	λύηται	λύσηται	γένηται
1 pl	λυώμεθα	λυσώμεθα	γενώμεθα
2 pl	λύησθε	λύσησθε	γένησθε
3 pl	λύωνται	λύσωνται	γένωνται

passive subjunctive

	present	first aorist	second aorist
1 sg	λύωμαι	λυθῶ	γραφῶ
2 sg	λύῃ	λυθῇς	γραφῇς
3 sg	λύηται	λυθῇ	γραφῇ
1 pl	λυώμεθα	λυθῶμεν	γραφῶμεν
2 pl	λύησθε	λυθῆτε	γραφῆτε
3 pl	λύωνται	λυθῶσι(ν)	γραφῶσι(ν)

Overview of Infinitive

	present	first aorist	second aorist	perfect
active	λύειν	λῦσαι	λαβεῖν	λελυκέναι
middle	λύεσθαι	λύσασθαι	λαβέσθαι	λέλυσθαι
passive	λύεσθαι	λυθῆναι	γραφῆναι	λέλυσθαι

Overview of Imperative

	present	first aorist	second aorist

active imperative

	present	first aorist	second aorist
2 sg	λῦε	λῦσον	λάβε
3 sg	λυέτω	λυσάτω	λαβέτω
2 pl	λύετε	λύσατε	λάβετε
3 pl	λυέτωσαν	λυσάτωσαν	λαβέτωσαν

middle imperative

2 sg	λύου	λῦσαι	γένου
3 sg	λυέσθω	λυσάσθω	γενέσθω
2 pl	λύεσθε	λύσασθε	γένεσθε
3 pl	λυέσθωσαν	λυσάσθωσαν	γενέσθωσαν

passive imperative

2 sg	λύου	λύθητι	γράφητι
3 sg	λυέσθω	λυθήτω	γραφήτω
2 pl	λύεσθε	λύθητε	γράφητε
3 pl	λυέσθωσαν	λυθήτωσαν	γραφήτωσαν

εἰμί

indicative

	present	imperfect	future
1 sg	εἰμί	ἤμην	ἔσομαι
2 sg	εἶ	ἦς	ἔσῃ
3 sg	ἐστί(ν)	ἦν	ἔσται
1 pl	ἐσμέν	ἦμεν, ἤμεθα	ἐσόμεθα
2 pl	ἐστέ	ἦτε	ἔσεσθε
3 pl	εἰσί(ν)	ἦσαν	ἔσονται

non-indicative

	subjunctive	imperative	active infinitive
1 sg	ὦ		εἶναι
2 sg	ᾖς	ἴσθι	
3 sg	ᾖ	ἔστω	
1 pl	ὦμεν		
2 pl	ἦτε	ἔστε	
3 pl	ὦσι(ν)	ἔστωσαν	

participle

	masc	fem	neut		masc	fem	neut
nom sg	ὤν	οὖσα	ὄν	*nom pl*	ὄντες	οὖσαι	ὄντα
gen sg	ὄντος	οὔσης	ὄντος	*gen pl*	ὄντων	οὐσῶν	ὄντων
dat sg	ὄντι	οὔσῃ	ὄντι	*dat pl*	οὖσι(ν)	οὔσαις	οὖσι(ν)
acc sg	ὄντα	οὖσαν	ὄν	*acc pl*	ὄντας	οὔσας	ὄντα

Indicative (#40)

Present Indicative (#41)

Thematic Uncontracted   ### Thematic Contracted

active

		-άω	-έω	-όω
1 sg	λύω	γεννῶ	ποιῶ	φανερῶ
2 sg	λύεις	γεννᾷς	ποιεῖς	φανεροῖς
3 sg	λύει	γεννᾷ	ποιεῖ	φανεροῖ
1 pl	λύομεν	γεννῶμεν	ποιοῦμεν	φανεροῦμεν
2 pl	λύετε	γεννᾶτε	ποιεῖτε	φανεροῦτε
3 pl	λύουσι(ν)	γεννῶσι(ν)	ποιοῦσι(ν)	φανεροῦσι(ν)

middle/passive

1 sg	λύομαι	γεννῶμαι	ποιοῦμαι	φανεροῦμαι
2 sg	λύῃ	γεννᾷ	ποιῇ	φανεροῖ
3 sg	λύεται	γεννᾶται	ποιεῖται	φανεροῦται
1 pl	λυόμεθα	γεννώμεθα	ποιούμεθα	φανερούμεθα
2 pl	λύεσθε	γεννᾶσθε	ποιεῖσθε	φανεροῦσθε
3 pl	λύονται	γεννῶνται	ποιοῦνται	φανεροῦντα

Athematic

active

1 sg	ἵστημι	τίθημι	δίδωμι	δείκνυμι
2 sg	ἵστης	τίθης	δίδως	δεικνύεις
3 sg	ἵστησι(ν)	τίθησι(ν)	δίδωσι(ν)	δείκνυσι(ν)
1 pl	ἵσταμεν	τίθεμεν	δίδομεν	δείκνυμεν
2 pl	ἵστατε	τίθετε	δίδοτε	δείκνυτε
3 pl	ἱστᾶσι(ν)	τιθέασι(ν)	διδόασι(ν)	δεικνύασι(ν)

middle/passive

1 sg	ἵσταμαι	τίθεμαι	δίδομαι	δείκνυμαι
2 sg	ἵστασαι	τίθεσαι	δίδοσαι	δείκνυσαι
3 sg	ἵσταται	τίθεται	δίδοται	δείκνυται
1 pl	ἱστάμεθα	τιθέμεθα	διδόμεθα	δεικνύμεθα
2 pl	ἵστασθε	τίθεσθε	δίδοσθε	δείκνυσθε
3 pl	ἵστανται	τίθενται	δίδονται	δείκνυνται

Imperfect Indicative (#42)

Thematic Uncontracted

Thematic Contracted

active

1 sg	ἔλυον	ἐγέννων	ἐποίουν	ἐφανέρουν
2 sg	ἔλυες	ἐγέννας	ἐποίεις	ἐφανέρους
3 sg	ἔλυε(ν)	ἐγέννα	ἐποίει	ἐφανέρου
1 pl	ἐλύομεν	ἐγεννῶμεν	ἐποιοῦμεν	ἐφανεροῦμεν
2 pl	ἐλύετε	ἐγεννᾶτε	ἐποιεῖτε	ἐφανεροῦτε
3 pl	ἔλυον	ἐγέννων	ἐποίουν	ἐφανέρουν

middle/passive

1 sg	ἐλυόμην	ἐγεννώμην	ἐποιούμην	ἐφανερούμην
2 sg	ἐλύου	ἐγεννῶ	ἐποιοῦ	ἐφανεροῦ
3 sg	ἐλύετο	ἐγεννᾶτο	ἐποιεῖτο	ἐφανεροῦτο
1 pl	ἐλυόμεθα	ἐγεννώμεθα	ἐποιούμεθα	ἐφανερούμεθα
2 pl	ἐλύεσθε	ἐγεννᾶσθε	ἐποιεῖσθε	ἐφανεροῦσθε
3 pl	ἐλύοντο	ἐγεννῶντο	ἐποιοῦντο	ἐφανεροῦντο

Athematic

active

1 sg	ἵστην	ἐτίθην	ἐδίδουν	ἐδείκνυν
2 sg	ἵστης	ἐτίθεις	ἐδίδους	ἐδείκνυς
3 sg	ἵστη	ἐτίθει	ἐδίδου	ἐδείκνυ
1 pl	ἵσταμεν	ἐτίθεμεν	ἐδίδομεν	ἐδείκνυμεν
2 pl	ἵστατε	ἐτίθετε	ἐδίδοτε	ἐδείκνυτε
3 pl	ἵστασαν	ἐτίθεσαν	ἐδίδοσαν	ἐδείκνυσαν

middle/passive

1 sg	ἱστάμην	ἐτιθέμην	ἐδιδόμην	ἐδεικνύμην
2 sg	ἵστασο	ἐτίθεσο	ἐδίδοσο	ἐδείκνυσο
3 sg	ἵστατο	ἐτίθετο	ἐδίδοτο	ἐδείκνυτο
1 pl	ἱστάμεθα	ἐτιθέμεθα	ἐδιδόμεθα	ἐδεικνύμεθα
2 pl	ἵστασθε	ἐτίθεσθε	ἐδίδοσθε	ἐδείκνυσθε
3 pl	ἵσταντο	ἐτίθεντο	ἐδίδοντο	ἐδείκνυντο

Future Indicative (#43)

	Thematic Uncontracted	Liquid	Athematic		
active					
1 sg	λύσω	μενῶ	στήσω	θήσω	δώσω
2 sg	λύσεις	μενεῖς	στήσεις	θήσεις	δώσεις
3 sg	λύσει	μενεῖ	στήσει	θήσει	δώσει
1 pl	λύσομεν	μενοῦμεν	στήσομεν	θήσομεν	δώσομεν
2 pl	λύσετε	μενεῖτε	στήσετε	θήσετε	δώσετε
3 pl	λύσουσι(ν)	μενοῦσι(ν)	στήσουσι(ν)	θήσουσιν(ν)	δώσουσι(ν)
middle					
1 sg	πορεύσομαι	μενοῦμαι	στήσομαι	θήσομαι	δώσομαι
2 sg	πορεύσῃ	μενῇ	στήσῃ	θήσῃ	δώσῃ
3 sg	πορεύσεται	μενεῖται	στήσεται	θήσεται	δώσεται
1 pl	πορευσόμεθα	μενούμεθα	στησόμεθα	θησόμεθα	δωσόμεθα
2 pl	πορεύσεσθε	μενεῖσθε	στήσεσθε	θήσεσθε	δώσεσθε
3 pl	πορεύσονται	μενοῦνται	στήσονται	θήσονται	δώσονται

Aorist Active/Middle Indicative (#44)

Thematic Aorist Active and Middle

	first aorist	liquid aorist	second aorist	first aorist athematic		
active						
1 sg	ἔλυσα	ἔμεινα	ἔβαλον	ἔστησα	ἔθηκα	ἔδωκα
2 sg	ἔλυσας	ἔμεινας	ἔβαλες	ἔστησας	ἔθηκας	ἔδωκας
3 sg	ἔλυσε	ἔμεινε	ἔβαλε(ν)	ἔστησε(ν)	ἔθηκε(ν)	ἔδωκε(ν)
1 pl	ἐλύσαμεν	ἐμείναμεν	ἐβάλομεν	ἐστήσαμεν	ἐθήκαμεν	ἐδώκαμεν
2 pl	ἐλύσατε	ἐμείνατε	ἐβάλετε	ἐστήσατε	ἐθήκατε	ἐδώκατε
3 pl	ἔλυσαν	ἔμειναν	ἔβαλον	ἔστησεν	ἔθηκαν	ἔδωκαν
middle						
1 sg	ἐλυσάμην	ἐμεινάμην	ἐγενόμην	—		
2 sg	ἐλύσω	ἐμείνω	ἐγένου	ἔθου		
3 sg	ἐλύσατο	ἐμείνατο	ἐγένετο	ἔθετο		
1 pl	ἐλυσάμεθα	ἐμεινάμεθα	ἐγενόμεθα	—		
2 pl	ἐλύσασθε	ἐμείνασθε	ἐγένεσθε	ἔθεσθε		
3 pl	ἐλύσαντο	ἐμείναντο	ἐγένοντο	ἔθεντο		

Athematic Second Aorist

active

				middle		
1 sg	ἔστην	ἔθην	ἔδων	ἐστάμην	ἐθέμην	ἐδόμην
2 sg	ἔστης	ἔθης	ἔδως	ἔστω	ἔθου	ἔδου
3 sg	ἔστη	ἔθη	ἔδω	ἔστατο	ἔθετο	ἔδοτο
1 pl	ἔστημεν	ἔθεμεν	ἔδομεν	ἐστάμεθα	ἐθέμεθα	ἐδόμεθα
2 pl	ἔστητε	ἔθετε	ἔδοτε	ἔστασθε	ἔθεσθε	ἔδοσθε
3 pl	ἔστησαν	ἔθεσαν	ἔδοσαν	ἔσταντο	ἔθεντο	ἔδοντο

Perfect Indicative (#45 – #46)

	first perfect	second perfect	athematic	first perfect	athematic	
active				**middle/passive**		
1 sg	λέλυκα	γέγονα	ἕστηκα	λέλυμαι	τέθειμαι	δέδομαι
2 sg	λέλυκας	γέγονας	ἕστηκας	λέλυσαι	τέθεισαι	δέδοσαι
3 sg	λέλυκε(ν)	γέγονε(ν)	ἕστηκε(ν)	λέλυται	τέθειται	δέδοται
1 pl	λελύκαμεν	γεγόναμεν	ἕσταμεν	λελύμεθα	τεθείμεθα	δεδόμεθα
2 pl	λελύκατε	γεγόνατε	ἕστατε	λέλυσθε	τέθεισθε	δέδοσθε
3 pl	λελύκασι(ν)	γεγόνασι(ν)	ἑστᾶσι(ν)	λέλυνται	τέθεινται	δέδονται

Aorist/Future Passive Indicative (#47)

	first aorist	second aorist		first future	second future	

Thematic Aorist Active / **Thematic Future Passive**

1 sg	ἐλύθην	ἐγράφην		λυθήσομαι	γραφήσομαι	
2 sg	ἐλύθης	ἐγράφης		λυθήσῃ	γραφήσῃ	
3 sg	ἐλύθη	ἐγράφη		λυθήσεται	γραφήσεται	
1 pl	ἐλύθημεν	ἐγράφημεν		λυθησόμεθα	γραφησόμεθα	
2 pl	ἐλύθητε	ἐγράφητε		λυθήσεσθε	γραφήσεσθε	
3 pl	ἐλύθησαν	ἐγράφησαν		λυθήσονται	γραφήσονται	

Athematic Aorist Passive / **Athematic Future Passive**

1 sg	ἐστάθην	ἐτέθην	ἐδόθην	σταθήσομαι	τεθήσομαι	δοθήσομαι
2 sg	ἐστάθης	ἐτέθης	ἐδόθης	σταθήσῃ	τεθήσῃ	δοθήσῃ
3 sg	ἐστάθην	ἐτέθη	ἐδόθη	σταθήσεται	τεθήσεται	δοθήσεται
1 pl	ἐστάθημεν	ἐτέθημεν	ἐδόθημεν	σταθησόμεθα	τεθησόμεθα	δοθησόμεθα
2 pl	ἐστάθητε	ἐτέθητε	ἐδόθητε	σταθήσεσθε	τεθήσεσθε	δοθήσεσθε
3 pl	ἐστάθησαν	ἐτέθησαν	ἐδόθησαν	σταθήσονται	τεθήσονται	δοθήσονται

Subjunctive (#50)

Thematic Uncontracted

	present	aorist		perfect
active				
1 sg	λύω	λύσω		λελύκω
2 sg	λύῃς	λύσῃς		λελύκῃς
3 sg	λύῃ	λύσῃ		λελύκῃ
1 pl	λύωμεν	λύσωμεν		λελύκωμεν
2 pl	λύητε	λύσητε		λελύκητε
3 pl	λύωσι(ν)	λύσωσι(ν)		λελύκωσι(ν)
middle (passive)				
1 sg	λύωμαι	λύσωμαι	λυθῶ	λελυμένος ὦ
2 sg	λύῃ	λύσῃ	λυθῇς	λελυμένος ᾖς
3 sg	λύηται	λύσηται	λυθῇ	λελυμένος ᾖ
1 pl	λυώμεθα	λυσώμεθα	λυθῶμεν	λελυμένοι ὦμεν
2 pl	λύησθε	λύσησθε	λυθῆτε	λελυμένοι ἦτε
3 pl	λύωνται	λύσωνται	λυθῶσι(ν)	λελυμένοι ὦσι

Thematic Contracted

	-άω	-έω	-όω
present active			
1 sg	γεννῶ	ποιῶ	φανερῶ
2 sg	γεννᾷς	ποιῇς	φανεροῖς
3 sg	γεννᾷ	ποιῇ	φανεροῖ
1 pl	γεννῶμεν	ποιῶμεν	φανερῶμεν
2 pl	γεννᾶτε	ποιῆτε	φανερῶτε
3 pl	γεννῶσι(ν)	ποιῶσι(ν)	φανερῶσι(ν)
present middle/passive			
1 sg	γεννῶμαι	ποιῶμαι	φανερῶμαι
2 sg	γεννᾷ	ποιῇ	φανεροῖ
3 sg	γεννᾶται	ποιῆται	φανερῶται
1 pl	γεννώμεθα	ποιώμεθα	φανερώμεθα
2 pl	γεννᾶσθε	ποιῆσθε	φανερῶσθε
3 pl	γεννῶνται	ποιῶνται	φανερῶνται

Athematic

	present active		
1 sg	ἱστῶ	τιθῶ	διδῶ
2 sg	ἱστῇς	τιθῇς	διδῶς
3 sg	ἱστῇ	τιθῇ	διδῷ
1 pl	ἱστῶμεν	τιθῶμεν	διδῶμεν
2 pl	ἱστῆτε	τιθῆτε	διδῶτε
3 pl	ἱστῶσι(ν)	τιθῶσι(ν)	διδῶσι(ν)

	present middle/passive		
1 sg	ἱστῶμαι	τιθῶμαι	διδῶμαι
2 sg	ἱστῇ	τιθῇ	διδῷ
3 sg	ἱστῆται	τιθῆται	διδῶται
1 pl	ἱστώμεθα	τιθώμεθα	διδώμεθα
2 pl	ἱστῆσθε	τιθῆσθε	διδῶσθε
3 pl	ἱστῶνται	τιθῶνται	διδῶνται

	second aorist active		
1 sg	στῶ	θῶ	δῶ
2 sg	στῇς	θῇς	δῷς
3 sg	στῇ	θῇ	δῷ
1 pl	στῶμεν	θῶμεν	δῶμεν
2 pl	στῆτε	θῆτε	δῶτε
3 pl	στῶσι(ν)	θῶσι(ν)	δῶσι(ν)

	second aorist middle		
1 sg	στῶμαι	θῶμαι	δῶμαι
2 sg	στῇ	θῇ	δῷ
3 sg	στῆται	θῆται	δῶται
1 pl	στώμεθα	θώμεθα	δώμεθα
2 pl	στῆσθε	θῆσθε	δῶσθε
3 pl	στῶνται	θῶνται	δῶνται

Imperative (#70)

Thematic: Uncontracted

active

	present	1 aorist	2 aorist	perfect
2 sg	λῦε	λῦσον	βάλε	λέλυκε
3 sg	λυέτω	λυσάτω	βαλέτω	λελυκέτω
2 pl	λύετε	λύσατε	βάλετε	λελύκετε
3 pl	λυέτωσαν	λυσάτωσαν	βαλέτωσαν	λελυκέτωσαν

middle/passive

	present	1 aorist	2 aorist	perfect
2 sg	λύου	λῦσαι	γενοῦ	λέλυσο
3 sg	λυέσθω	λυσάσθω	γενέσθω	λελύσθω
2 pl	λύεσθε	λύσασθε	γένεσθε	λέλυσθε
3 pl	λυέσθωσαν	λυσάσθωσαν	γενέσθωσαν	λελύσθωσαν

first aorist passive

2 sg	λύθητι
3 sg	λυθήτω
2 pl	λύθητε
3 pl	λυθήτωσαν

Thematic: Contracted

present active

	-άω	-έω	-όω
2 sg	γέννα	ποίει	φανέρου
3 sg	γεννάτω	ποιείτω	φανερούτω
2 pl	γεννᾶτε	ποιεῖτε	φανεροῦτε
3 pl	γεννάτωσαν	ποιείτωσαν	φανερούτωσαν

(middle/passive)

	-άω	-έω	-όω
2 sg	γεννῶ	ποιοῦ	φανεροῦ
3 sg	γεννάσθω	ποιείσθω	φανερούσθω
2 pl	γεννᾶσθε	ποιεῖσθε	φανεροῦσθε
3 pl	γεννάσθωσαν	ποιείσθωσαν	φανερούσθωσαν

(first aorist passive)

	-άω	-έω	-όω
2 sg	γεννήθητι	ποιήθητι	φανερώθητι
3 sg	γεννηθήτω	ποιηθήτω	φανερωθήτω
2 pl	γεννήθητε	ποιήθητε	φανερώθητε
3 pl	γεννηθήτωσαν	ποιηθήτωσαν	φανερωθήτωσαν

Athematic

present active

2 sg	ἵστη	τίθει	δίδου	δείκνυ
3 sg	ἱστάτω	τιθέτω	διδότω	δεικνύτω
2 pl	ἵστατε	τίθετε	δίδοτε	δείκνυτε
3 pl	ἱστάτωσαν	τιθέτωσαν	διδότωσαν	δεικνύτωσαν

aorist active

2 sg	στῆθι	θές	δός
3 sg	στήτω	θέτω	δότω
2 pl	στῆτε	θέτε	δότε
3 pl	στήτωσαν	θέτωσαν	δότωσαν

present middle/passive

2 sg	ἵστασο	τίθεσο	δίδοσο	δείκνυσο
3 sg	ἱστάσθω	τιθέσθω	διδόσθω	δεικνύσθω
2 pl	ἵστασθε	τίθεσθε	δίδοσθε	δείκνυσθε
3 pl	ἱστάσθωσαν	τιθέσθωσαν	διδόσθωσαν	δεικνύσθωσαν

aorist middle

2 sg	στῶ	θοῦ	δοῦ
3 sg	στάσθω	θέσθω	δόσθω
2 pl	στάσθε	θέσθε	δόσθε
3 pl	στάσθωσαν	θέσθωσαν	δόσθωσαν

Infinitive (#80)

	present	future	1st aorist	2nd aorist	1st perfect	2nd perfect
Active						
thematic	λύειν	λύσειν	λῦσαι	βαλεῖν	λελυκέναι	γεγονέναι
contract	γεννᾶν	γεννήσειν	γεννῆσαι		γεγεννηκέναι	
	ποιεῖν	ποιήσειν	ποιῆσαι		πεποιηκέναι	
	φανεροῦν	φανερώσειν	φανερῶσαι		πεφανερωκέναι	
μι	ἱστάναι	στήσειν	στῆσαι	στῆναι	ἑστηκέναι	
	τιθέναι	θήσειν		θεῖναι	τεθεικέναι	
	διδόναι	δώσειν		δοῦναι	δεδωκέναι	
	δεικνύναι					
	εἶναι					
liquid	μένειν	μενεῖν	μεῖναι			

Middle and Middle/Passive

	present	future	1st aorist	2nd aorist	1st perfect	2nd perfect
thematic	λύεσθαι	πορεύσεσθαι	λύσασθαι		λελύσθαι	
contract	γεννᾶσθαι	γεννήσεσθαι	γεννήσασθαι		γεγεννῆσθαι	
	ποιεῖσθαι	ποιήσεσθαι	ποιήσασθαι		πεποιῆσθαι	
	φανεροῦσθαι	φανερώσεσθαι	φανερώσασθαι		πεφανερῶσθαι	
μι	ἵστασθαι	στήσεσθαι	στήσασθαι	στάσθαι	ἑστάναι	
	τίθεσθαι	θήσεσθαι		θέσθαι		
	δίδοσθαι	δώσεσθαι		δόσθαι		
		δείκνυσθαι				
		ἔσεσθαι				
liquid	μένεσθαι	μενεῖσθαι	μείνασθαι			

Passive

	present	future	1st aorist	2nd aorist	1st perfect	2nd perfect
thematic	λύεσθαι	λυθήσεσθαι	λυθῆναι	γραφῆναι		
contract	γεννᾶσθαι	γεννηθήσεσθαι	γεννηθῆναι			
	ποιεῖσθαι	ποιηθήσεσθαι	ποιηθῆναι			
	φανεροῦσθαι	φανερωθήσεσθαι	φανερωθῆναι			

Infinitive Morpheme Chart

	present	1st aorist	2nd aorist	perfect
active	ειν	σαι	ειν	κεναι
middle	εσθαι	σασθαι	εσθαι	σθαι
passive	εσθαι	θηναι	ηναι	σθαι

Participle (#90)

Thematic: Uncontracted

present active

nom sg	λύων	λύουσα	λῦον
gen sg	λύοντος	λυούσης	λύοντος
dat sg	λύοντι	λυούσῃ	λύοντι
acc sg	λύοντα	λύουσαν	λῦον
nom pl	λύοντες	λύουσαι	λύοντα
gen pl	λυόντων	λυουσῶν	λυόντων
dat pl	λύουσι(ν)	λυούσαις	λύουσι(ν)
acc pl	λύοντας	λυούσας	λύοντα

present middle/passive

nom sg	λυόμενος	λυομένη	λυόμενον
gen sg	λυομένου	λυομένης	λυομένου
dat sg	λυομένῳ	λυομένῃ	λυομένῳ
acc sg	λυόμενον	λυομένην	λυόμενον
nom pl	λυόμενοι	λυόμεναι	λυόμενα
gen pl	λυομένων	λυομένων	λυομένων
dat pl	λυομένοις	λυομέναις	λυομένοις
acc pl	λυομένους	λυομένας	λυόμενα

first aorist active

nom sg	λύσας	λύσασα	λῦσαν
gen sg	λύσαντος	λυσάσης	λύσαντος
dat sg	λύσαντι	λυσάσῃ	λύσαντι
acc sg	λύσαντα	λύσασαν	λῦσαν
nom pl	λύσαντες	λύσασαι	λύσαντα
gen pl	λυσάντων	λυσασῶν	λυσάντων
dat pl	λύσασι(ν)	λυσάσαις	λύσασι(ν)
acc pl	λύσαντας	λυσάσας	λύσαντα

second aorist active

nom sg	βαλών	βαλοῦσα	βαλόν
gen sg	βαλόντος	βαλούσης	βαλόντος
dat sg	βαλόντι	βαλούσῃ	βαλόντι
acc sg	βαλόντα	βαλοῦσαν	βαλόν
nom pl	βαλόντες	βαλοῦσαι	βαλόντα
gen pl	βαλόντων	βαλουσῶν	βαλόντων
dat pl	βαλοῦσι(ν)	βαλούσαις	βαλοῦσι(ν)
acc pl	βαλόντας	βαλούσας	βαλόντα

first aorist middle

nom sg	λυσάμενος	λυσαμένη	λυσάμενον
gen sg	λυσαμένου	λυσαμένης	λυσαμένου
dat sg	λυσαμένῳ	λυσαμένῃ	λυσαμένῳ
acc sg	λυσάμενον	λυσαμένην	λυσάμενον
nom pl	λυσάμενοι	λυσάμεναι	λυσάμενα
gen pl	λυσαμένων	λυσαμένων	λυσαμένων
dat pl	λυσαμένοις	λυσαμέναις	λυσαμένοις
acc pl	λυσαμένους	λυσαμένας	λυσάμενα

second aorist middle

nom sg	βαλόμενος	βαλομένη	βαλόμενον
gen sg	βαλομένου	βαλομένης	βαλομένου
dat sg	βαλομένῳ	βαλομένῃ	βαλομένῳ
acc sg	βαλόμενον	βαλομένην	βαλόμενον
nom pl	βαλόμενοι	βαλόμεναι	βαλόμενα
gen pl	βαλομένων	βαλομένων	βαλομένων
dat pl	βαλομένοις	βαλομέναις	βαλομένοις
acc pl	βαλομένους	βαλομένας	βαλόμενα

first aorist passive

nom sg	λυθείς	λυθεῖσα	λυθέν
gen sg	λυθέντος	λυθείσης	λυθέντος
dat sg	λυθέντι	λυθείσῃ	λυθέντι
acc sg	λυθέντα	λυθεῖσαν	λυθέν
nom pl	λυθέντες	λυθεῖσαι	λυθέντα
gen pl	λυθέντων	λυθεισῶν	λυθέντων
dat pl	λυθεῖσι(ν)	λυθείσαις	λυθεῖσι(ν)
acc pl	λυθέντας	λυθείσας	λυθέντα

second aorist passive

γραφείς	γραφεῖσα	γραφέν
γραφέντος	γραφείσης	γραφέντος
γραφέντι	γραφείσῃ	γραφέντι
γραφέντα	γραφεῖσαν	γραφέν
γραφέντες	γραφεῖσαι	γραφέντα
γραφέντων	γραφεισῶν	γραφέντων
γραφεῖσι(ν)	γραφείσαις	γραφεῖσι(ν)
γραφέντας	γραφείσας	γραφέντα

perfect active

nom sg	λελυκώς	λελυκυῖα	λελυκός
gen sg	λελυκότος	λελυκυίας	λελυκότος
dat sg	λελυκότι	λελυκυίᾳ	λελυκότι
acc sg	λελυκότα	λελυκυῖαν	λελυκός
nom pl	λελυκότες	λελυκυῖαι	λελυκότα
gen pl	λελυκότων	λελυκυιῶν	λελυκότων
dat pl	λελυκόσι(ν)	λελυκυίαις	λελυκόσι(ν)
acc pl	λελυκότας	λελυκυίας	λελυκότα

perfect middle/passive

nom sg	λελυμένος	λελυμένη	λελυμένον
gen sg	λελυμένου	λελυμένης	λελυμένου

Athematic

present active

nom sg	ἱστάς	ἱστᾶσα	ἱστάν
gen sg	ἱστάντος	ἱστάσης	ἱστάντος
nom sg	τιθείς	τιθεῖσα	τιθέν
gen sg	τιθέντος	τιθείσης	τιθέντος
nom sg	διδούς	διδοῦσα	διδόν
gen sg	διδόντος	διδούσης	διδόντος
nom sg	δεικνύς	δεικνῦσα	δεικνύν
gen sg	δεικνύντος	δεικνύσης	δεικνύντος

present middle/passive

nom sg	ἱστάμενος	ἱσταμένη	ἱστάμενον
gen sg	ἱσταμένου	ἱσταμένης	ἱσταμένου
nom sg	τιθέμενος	τιθεμένη	τιθέμενον
gen sg	τιθεμένου	τιθεμένης	τιθεμένου
nom sg	διδόμενος	διδομένη	διδόμενον
gen sg	διδομένου	διδομένης	διδομένου
nom sg	δεικνύμενος	δεικνυμένη	δεικνύμενον
gen sg	δεικνυμένου	δεικνυμένης	δεικνυμένου

first aorist active

nom sg	στήσας	στήσασα	στῆσαν
gen sg	στήσαντος	στησάσης	στήσαντος
nom sg	θήκας	θήκασα	θήκαν
gen sg	θήκαντος	θηκάσης	θήκαντος
nom sg			
gen sg			

second aorist active

στάς	στᾶσα	στάν
στάντος	στάσης	στάντος
θείς	θεῖσα	θέν
θέντος	θείσης	θέντος
δούς	δοῦσα	δόν
δόντος	δούσης	δόντος

first aorist middle

nom sg	στησάμενος	στησαμένη	στησάμενον
gen sg	στησαμένου	στησαμένης	στησαμένου
nom sg	θηκάμενος	θηκαμένη	θηκάμενον
gen sg	θηκαμένου	θηκαμένης	θηκαμένου
nom sg			
gen sg			

second aorist middle

στάμενος	σταμένη	στάμενον
σταμένου	σταμένης	σταμένου
θέμενος	θεμένη	θέμενον
θεμένου	θεμένης	θεμένου
δόμενος	δομένη	δόμενον
δομένου	δομένης	δομένου

first aorist passive

nom sg	σταθείς	σταθεῖσα	σταθέν
gen sg	σταθέντος	σταθείσης	σταθέντος
nom sg	τεθείς	τεθεῖσα	τεθέν
gen sg	τεθέντος	τεθείσης	τεθέντος
nom sg	δοθείς	δοθεῖσα	δοθέν
gen sg	δοθέντος	δοθείσης	δοθέντος

perfect active

nom sg	ἑστηκώς
gen sg	ἑστηκότος
nom sg	τεθεικώς
gen sg	τεθεικότος
nom sg	δεδωκώς
gen sg	δεδωκότος

second perfect active

ἑστώς	ἑστῶσα	ἑστός
ἑστότος	ἑστώσης	ἑστότος

perfect middle/passive

nom sg	ἑστημένος	ἑστημένη	ἑστήμενον
gen sg	ἑστημένου	ἑστημένης	ἑστημένου
nom sg	τεθειμένος	τεθειμένη	τεθείμενον
gen sg	τεθειμένου	τεθειμένης	τεθειμένου
nom sg	δεδομένος	δεδομένη	δεδομεηνον
gen sg	δεδομένου	δεδομένης	δεδομένου

Tense Forms of Verbs Occurring Fifty Times or More in the New Testament

The chart on the following pages lists the verbs occurring fifty times or more in the New Testament, including their different basic tense forms that specifically occur in the New Testament. The words are available in spreadsheet format on the class website.

Three Verb Categories

As far as memorization is concerned, there are three different classes of verbs.

- *Regular verbs.* You should not memorize the tense forms of these verbs. There is no reason to.

- *Verbs that undergo regular changes.* As you worked through *BBG*, you saw patterns in the formation of the different tense stems. If you know the rules governing these changes, there is no reason to memorize these verbs either. The rules that you need to know are listed below, and the changes are explained in the footnotes to the tense forms.

- *Verbal forms that you need to memorize.* Some tense forms are so difficult that it is easiest simply to memorize them. These forms are in blue in the following chart. Resist the temptation to memorize forms that are not underlined. Learn the rules and memorize as few forms as possible.

  If a compound verb has a tense stem that should be memorized, only the simple form of that verb is underlined. For example, the aorist passive of βάλλω (ἐβλήθην) is underlined, but the aorist passive of ἐκβάλλω (ἐξεβλήθην) is not underlined. If you know the first, you should know the second.

Rules Governing the Chart

1. Do not memorize the entire chart. If you rely on rote memory, then you probably will not be able to continue using Greek throughout your ministry.

2. The tense stems follow the usual order: present, future active/middle, aorist active/middle, perfect active, perfect middle/passive, aorist/future passive.

3. If the verb—in simple or compound form—does not occur in a specific tense in the Greek Testament, it is not listed. There is a dash in its place.

4. Changes to a compound verb are explained in the listing of the simple verb. For example, εἰσέρχομαι is explained under ἔρχομαι.

   If the simple verb is not included in this chart, one of the compound verbs has the explanations and the other compounds with the same simple verb reference that compound. For example, the root *βαίνω does not occur. I have described the changes of the root *βαίνω under ἀναβαίνω, and καταβαίνω refers you to ἀναβαίνω.

5. These 91 verbs are the most important to memorize. The basic rule is that the more a word is used, the more "irregular" or modified it becomes. Therefore, as you learn verbs that occur less than fifty times, there is an increased chance that they will be fully regular.

6. "Regular" and "irregular" are unfortunate choices of terms, because Greek verbs are regular. It is just that in some cases the rules governing the changes are so esoteric that it is simplest to memorize the verbal form and not the rules.

7. All explanations of changes assume you know the verbal root(s) of the verb. Roots are listed in the footnote to the present tense stem, preceded by an asterisk (e.g., *ἀγαπα).

   It also assumes you know the Master Verb Chart.

8. If something is not explained in the footnotes for a tense, look first to the footnote on the present tense form. If it is not explained there, then one of the basic rules listed below governs the change.

Rules Governing the Morphological Changes in These Stems

If you learn the following rules, the only verb tenses that you need to memorize are those that are underlined in the following chart. As I said above, resist the temptation to memorize forms that are not so marked. Learn the rules and keep the memory work to a minimum. This will increase the chances you will use Greek in the years to come.

1. The present tense is by far the most "irregular" because the verbal root has often undergone some change in the formation of the present tense stem.
   - Single lambda becomes double lambda (*βαλ ‣ βάλλω ‣ ἔβαλον).
   - Iota is added to form the present tense stem (*ἀρ ‣ αρι ‣ αιρ ‣ αἴρω ‣ ἦρα).

2. Verbs ending in αζω and ιζω have roots ending in a dental. Once you recognize that, the other tense stems are usually regular.

   *βαπτιδ, βαπτίζω, βαπτίσω, ἐβάπτισα, –, βεβάπτισμαι, ἐβαπτίσθην.

3. When a verb undergoes ablaut, it is seldom necessary to know what stem vowel will be used in a certain tense.

   It is most important to use this clue to tell you whether a verbal form is in the present or not. If there has been ablaut, then you know it is not in the present tense, and you can find other clues as to its proper parsing (ἀποστέλλω ‣ ἀπέστειλα ‣ ἀπέσταλκα).

   If a verb undergoes ablaut throughout the tenses, it is usually noted in the footnote to the present tense form.

4. It is common for a verb to insert an eta (καλέω ‣ ἐκλήθην) or a sigma (ἀκούω ‣ ἠκούσθην) before the tense formative in the aorist passive and sometimes before the ending in the perfect middle/passive (βάλλω ‣ βέβλημαι; δοξάζω ‣ δεδόξασμαι).

   This is especially common in ιζω and αζω type verbs (βαπτίζω ‣ ἐβαπτίσθην).

5. The consonant before the tense formative in the perfect middle/passive and aorist passive is often changed, especially if the stem ends in a stop (ἄγω ‣ ἤχθην). It is usually not important to be able to predict what the new consonant will be; just get used to seeing an unusual consonant there and look elsewhere for clues as to the verb's parsing.

6. Square of stops plus sigma.

labials (π β φ)	+ σ ‣ ψ	βλεπ + σω ‣ βλέψω
velars (κ γ χ)	+ σ ‣ ξ	κηρυγ + σω ‣ κηρύξω
dentals (τ δ θ)	+ σ ‣ σ	βαπτιδ + σω ‣ βαπτίσω

ἀγαπάω[1]	ἀγαπήσω	ἠγάπησα	ἠγάπηκα	ἠγάπημαι	ἠγαπήθην
ἄγω[2]	ἄξω	ἤγαγον[3]	–	ἦγμαι	ἤχθην[4]
αἴρω[5]	ἀρῶ	ἦρα	ἦρκα	ἦρμαι	ἤρθην
αἰτέω[6]	αἰτήσω	ᾔτησα	ᾔτηκα	ᾔτημαι	–
ἀκολουθέω[7]	ἀκολουθήσω	ἠκολούθησα	ἠκολούθηκα	–	–
ἀκούω[8]	ἀκούσω	ἤκουσα	ἀκήκοα[9]	–	ἠκούσθην[10]
ἀναβαίνω[11]	ἀναβήσομαι[12]	ἀνέβην[13]	ἀναβέβηκα	–	–
ἀνίστημι[14]	ἀναστήσω	ἀνέστησα	ἀνέστηκα	ἀνέστημαι	ἀνεστάθην
ἀνοίγω[15]	–	ἀνέῳξα[16]	–	–	ἀνεῴχθην[17]
ἀπέρχομαι[18]	ἀπελεύσομαι	ἀπῆλθον	ἀπελήλυθα	–	–
ἀποθνῄσκω[19]	ἀποθανοῦμαι[20]	ἀπέθανον[21]	–	–	–

---

[1] *αγαπα

[2] *αγ

[3] *αγ. An unusual second aorist. There actually is a reduplication and an augment. The stem reduplicates (*αγ ‣ αγαγ) and then the reduplicated vowel lengthens (αγαγ ‣ ηγαγ ‣ ἤγαγον).

[4] The final gamma of the stem has been changed to a chi because of the theta.

[5] *αρ. The iota is added to the root to form the present tense stem and it consequently does not occur in the other tenses. αἴρω is a liquid verb and uses εσ and alpha as the tense formatives in the future and aorist active tenses.

[6] *αἰτε

[7] *ακολουθε. It is easy to mistake the θη in the other tense forms as the aorist passive tense formative. This is the only commonly used Greek verb that ends in θε, so this is not a frequent mistake.

[8] *ακου

[9] An unusual perfect. Because it is a second perfect, the tense formative is alpha, not κα.

[10] Inserts a sigma before the theta of the tense formative.

[11] *αναβα. A compound of ἀνα and *βαίνω. The stem of βαίνω is *βα, to which is added ιν to form the present tense stem; therefore ιν does not occur in the other tenses. In the other tense stems, the alpha lengthens to an eta.

[12] Deponent future middle.

[13] Second aorist.

[14] *ανιστα. Compound verb formed by ἀνα plus *στα. See ἵστημι.

[15] *ανοιγ. This is a strange word, one of the most troublesome when it comes to augments. It used to be a compound verb (ἀν[α] + οἴγω), but in Koine it is beginning to "forget" it was a compound, and the augment is sometimes placed at the beginning of the preposition or sometimes at both places.

[16] Shows a double augment with the iota subscripting (ανοιγ + σα ‣ ἀνεοιξα ‣ ἀνεωιξα ‣ ἀνέῳξα). Can also be ἠνέῳξα, which adds a third augment by lengthening the first vowel.

[17] Shows the same augmentation pattern as in the aorist active. Here the final stem gamma has changed to a chi because of the theta in the tense formative. Can also be ἠνεῴχθην.

[18] *αποερχ. A compound verb formed with ἀπό plus *ερχ. See ἔρχομαι.

[19] *αποθαν. ἀποθνῄσκω is a compound verb, ἀπό plus *θαν, as you can see by the augment in the aorist active (ἀπέθανον). If you recognize that the root is *ἀποθαν, knowing how it was altered in the present tense is not essential. But in case you want to know: in the formation of the present tense, the alpha dropped out (ablaut), eta and ισκ were added, and the iota subscripts. αποθαν ‣ αποθν ‣ αποθνη ‣ αποθνισκ ‣ ἀποθνῄσκω.

[20] Future middle deponent

[21] Second aorist

ἀποκρίνομαι[1]	–	ἀπεκρινάμην[2]	–	–	ἀπεκρίθην[3]
ἀποκτείνω[4]	ἀποκτενῶ[5]	ἀπέκτεινα[6]	–	–	ἀπεκτάνθην[7]
ἀπόλλυμι[8]	ἀπολέσω	ἀπώλεσα	ἀπόλωλα[9]	–	–
ἀπολύω[10]	ἀπολύσω	ἀπέλυσα	–	ἀπολέλυμαι	ἀπελύθην
ἀποστέλλω[11]	ἀποστελῶ[12]	ἀπέστειλα[13]	ἀπέσταλκα[14]	ἀπέσταλμαι[15]	ἀπεστάλην[16]
ἄρχομαι[17]	ἄρξομαι[18]	ἠρξάμην[19]	–	–	–
ἀσπάζομαι[20]	–	ἠσπασάμην[21]	–	–	–
ἀφίημι[22]	ἀφήσω	ἀφῆκα[23]	–	ἀφέωμαι[24]	ἀφέθην[25]

---

[1] *αποκριν. All forms of this liquid word are deponent.

[2] Liquid aorist (απεκριν + α + μην › ἀπεκρινάμην).

[3] Aorist passive deponent. Loses its stem nu before the theta; this is not normal.

[4] *αποκτεν. A liquid verb. Notice the ablaut of the final stem vowel/diphthong.

[5] Liquid future (αποκτεν + εσ + ω › ἀποκτενῶ)

[6] Due to ablaut, the stem vowel has shift from epsilon to ει. Because it is a liquid aorist, the tense formative is alpha.

[7] Due to ablaut, the stem vowel has changed from ε to α.

[8] *απολε. This is a compound verb, as you can tell from the augment in the aorist active (ἀπώλεσα). I put the present in blue because it is difficult to remember how the root is altered in the formation of the present.

[9] Second perfect

[10] *απολυ

[11] *αποστελ. The lambda was doubled for the present tense stem. There is therefore a single lambda throughout the other tenses. It is a liquid verb, so it uses εσ and alpha for its tense formatives in the future and aorist active tenses. Notice also the ablaut in the final stem vowel/diphthong. These changes are all normal, so you should not have to memorize the tense forms.

[12] Liquid future

[13] Liquid aorist. The stem vowel has changed due to ablaut.

[14] The stem vowel has changed due to ablaut.

[15] The stem vowel has changed due to ablaut.

[16] Second aorist. The stem vowel has changed due to ablaut.

[17] *αρχ

[18] Future middle deponent

[19] Aorist middle deponent

[20] *ασπαδ

[21] Middle deponent

[22] This is a compound verb formed from ἀφ (ἀπό) and ἵημι. The root of ἵημι is *σε. The sigma reduplicates and then the reduplicated sigma is replaced by a rough breathing and the stem sigma drops off; the iota is the vowel between the replicated sigma. σε › σισε › ἱσε ‹ ἵημι.

[23] κα aorist

[24] Inserts an ω before the personal ending.

[25] The stem vowel shortens from η to ε due to ablaut.

βάλλω[1]	βαλῶ[2]	ἔβαλον[3]	βέβληκα[4]	βέβλημαι[5]	ἐβλήθην[6]
βαπτίζω[7]	βαπτίσω	ἐβάπτισα	–	βεβάπτισμαι[8]	ἐβαπτίσθην
βλέπω[9]	βλέψω	ἔβλεψα	–	–	–
γεννάω[10]	γεννήσω	ἐγέννησα	γεγέννηκα	γεγέννημαι	ἐγεννήθην
γίνομαι[11]	γενήσομαι[12]	ἐγενόμην[13]	γέγονα[14]	γεγέννημαι[15]	ἐγενήθην[16]
γινώσκω[17]	γνώσομαι[18]	ἔγνων[19]	ἔγνωκα	ἔγνωσμαι[20]	ἐγνώσθην[21]
γράφω[22]	γράψω	ἔγραψα	γέγραφα[23]	γέγραμμαι[24]	ἐγράφην[25]
δεῖ[26]	–	–	–	–	–

---

[1] *βαλ. The lambda doubles in the formation of the present tense stem. It is a liquid verb.

[2] Liquid future (*βαλ + εσ + ω ‣ βαλῶ)

[3] Usually liquid aorists are first aorist and use the alpha as the tense formative. βάλλω follows the pattern of a normal second aorist.

[4] Due to ablaut, the stem vowel has dropped out and an eta has been inserted before the tense formative. This form follows the normal rules, but many students still have trouble with it so you may want to memorize it.

[5] See the explanation for the perfect active tense form.

[6] See the explanation for the perfect active tense form.

[7] *βαπτιδ

[8] The dental + μ combination forms σμ.

[9] *βλεπ

[10] *γεννα

[11] The root of γίνομαι is *γεν. This is important to note in keeping it separate from γεννάω (*γεννα) and γινώσκω (*γνο). Here are some hints for keeping these three words separate.
- γίνομαι will always have a vowel between the gamma and nu. Usually it will be an epsilon.
- γεννάω always has the double nu and is fully regular.
- γινώσκω, except in the present tense, does not have a vowel between the gamma and nu.

[12] Future middle deponent

[13] Second aorist middle deponent

[14] The stem vowel has shifted from epsilon to omicron due to ablaut. It is a second perfect and therefore uses the tense formative alpha.

[15] Inserts the eta before the personal ending.

[16] Inserts the eta before the personal ending.

[17] *γνω. See the discussion of γίνομαι above. The stem is *γνω, to which was added ισκ to form the present tense stem. Actually, the iota in the present tense stem is the result of reduplication, after which the original gamma dropped off and the stem vowel lengthened: γνω ‣ γιγνω ‣ γινω + σκω ‣ γινώσκω.

[18] Future middle deponent

[19] Second aorist

[20] Inserts a sigma before the tense formative.

[21] Inserts a sigma before the tense formative.

[22] *γραφ

[23] Second perfect

[24] The φμ combination forms μμ.

[25] Second aorist

[26] This is an impersonal, third person singular, form that never changes.

δέχομαι[1]	δέξομαι[2]	ἐδεξάμην[3]	–	δέδεγμαι[4]	ἐδέχθην
διδάσκω[5]	διδάξω	ἐδίδαξα	–	–	ἐδιδάχθην[6]
δίδωμι[7]	δώσω	ἔδωκα	δέδωκα	δέδομαι	ἐδόθην
δοκέω[8]	–	ἔδοξα	–	–	–
δοξάζω[9]	δοξάσω	ἐδόξασα	–	δεδόξασμαι[10]	ἐδοξάσθην[11]
δύναμαι[12]	δυνήσομαι[13]	–	–	–	ἠδυνήθην[14]
ἐγείρω[15]	ἐγερῶ	ἤγειρα[16]	–	ἐγήγερμαι[17]	ἠγέρθην
εἰμί[18]	ἔσομαι	ἤμην[19]	–	–	–
εἰσέρχομαι[20]	εἰσελεύσομαι	εἰσῆλθον	εἰσελήλυθα	–	–
ἐκβάλλω[21]	ἐκβαλῶ	ἐξέβαλον	ἐκβέβληκα	ἐκβέβλημαι	ἐξεβλήθην
ἐξέρχομαι[22]	ἐξελεύσομαι	ἐξῆλθον	ἐξελήλυθα		
ἐπερωτάω[23]	ἐπερωτήσω	ἐπηρώτησα	–	–	ἐπηρωτήθην
ἔρχομαι[24]	ἐλεύσομαι[25]	ἦλθον[26]	ἐλήλυθα[27]	–	–

---

[1] *δεχ

[2] Future middle deponent

[3] Aorist middle deponent

[4] The χμ combination forms γμ.

[5] *δακ. An unusual root that adds σκ to form the present tense stem (the κ of the root drops out). Evidently it reduplicates to διδακ throughout all the tense forms. See *MBG*, v-5a, p. 312.

[6] The σ is lost altogether when the κθ combination forms χθ.

[7] *δο. δίδωμι is regular if you know the rules for the formation of μι verbs.

[8] *δοκ. Adds ε to the root to form the present tense stem.

[9] *δοξαδ

[10] The δμ combination forms σμ.

[11] The δθ combination forms σθ.

[12] *δυν. Uses an alpha as the connecting vowel in the present.

[13] Future middle deponent

[14] The verb augments in the aorist passive as if the root began with a vowel.

[15] *εγερ. An iota is added in the formation of the present tense stem. It is a liquid verb. Notice the ablaut throughout the different tense stems.

[16] Stem change due to ablaut.

[17] Reduplicates and undergoes vocalic reduplication: εγερ ‣ εγεγερ ‣ εγηγερ ‣ ἐγήγερμαι.

[18] Just memorize this verb.

[19] Actually an imperfect, but I have no column here for the imperfect.

[20] See ἔρχομαι.

[21] See βάλλω.

[22] See ἔρχομαι.

[23] See ἐρωτάω.

[24] *ερχ. The different tense stems of this verb are actually quite regular. They look so different because they are based on different verbal roots. Most find it easiest to memorize them.

[25] *ελευθ. Future middle deponent.

[26] *ελευθ, just like the future. The ευ has dropped out due to ablaut (*ελευθ ‣ ελθ ‣ ἦλθον). Second aorist.

[27] *ελευθ, just like the future. The form has both reduplicated and then undergone vocalic reduplication, and the ε has dropped out. It is a second perfect. *ελευθ ‣ ελελευθ ‣ εληλυθ ‣ ἐλήλυθα.

ἐρωτάω[1]	ἐρωτήσω	ἠρώτησα	–	–	ἠρωτήθην
ἐσθίω[2]	φάγομαι[3]	ἔφαγον[4]	–	–	–
εὐαγγελίζω[5]	–	εὐηγγέλισα	–	εὐηγγέλισμαι[6]	εὐηγγελίσθην[7]
εὑρίσκω[8]	εὑρήσω[9]	εὗρον[10]	εὕρηκα[11]	–	εὑρέθην[12]
ἔχω[13]	ἕξω	ἔσχον	ἔσχηκα	–	–
ζάω[14]	ζήσω[15]	ἔζησα	–	–	–
ζητέω[16]	ζητήσω	ἐζήτησα	–	–	ἐζητήθην
θέλω[17]	–	ἠθέλησα	–	–	–
θεωρέω[18]	θεωρήσω	ἐθεώρησα	–	–	–
ἵστημι[19]	στήσω	ἔστησα[20]	ἕστηκα[21]	–	ἐστάθην

---

[1] *ερωτα

[2] Formed from two different stems, *εσθι (used in the present) and *φαγ (used in the future and aorist).

[3] *φαγ. Future middle deponent

[4] *φαγ. Second aorist

[5] *ευαγγελιδ. A compound verb as seen by the augment.

[6] The δμ combination forms σμ.

[7] The δθ combination forms σθ.

[8] The stem is *εὑρ. ισκ was added to form the present tense stem.

[9] An eta was added before the tense formative.

[10] Second aorist. Does not augment.

[11] An eta was added before the tense formative.

[12] An epsilon was added before the tense formative.

[13] What happens to ἔχω is quite fascinating, but perhaps at first you might just want to memorize the tense stems. If you are really interested in what is happening, here it is.

The root is *σεχ. In the present tense the sigma is replaced by the rough breathing so you just have ἔχω. But because the Greeks did not like the two "aspirate" sounds of the rough breathing and the chi in a row, the rough breathing "deaspirates" to a smooth breathing (σεχ ‣ ἑχ ‣ ἐχ ‣ ἐχω).

Therefore, in forming the imperfect, because the verbal root actually begins with a consonant, the augment is the epsilon. But then the sigma is between two vowels, so it drops out and εε contract to ει (ε + σεχ ‣ εεχ ‣ εῖχον).

In the future the tense formative sigma joins with the chi to form xi, but then there are not two aspirates in a row, so the rough breathing can remain.

In the aorist and perfect active, the ε between the sigma and chi drops out. In the perfect, an eta is added before the tense formative.

[14] *ζα

[15] Some list as a deponent: ζήσομαι.

[16] *ζητε

[17] The stem of θέλω originally was *εθελε. This explains the augment in the aorist active. If the aorist passive occurred in the New Testament, it would be ἠθελήθην.

[18] *θεωρε

[19] *στα. When the initial sigma was reduplicated in the formation of the present tense stem, the sigma was dropped in accordance with the rules and was replaced with a rough breathing. The same phenomena occurs in the perfect active.

[20] Also has a second aorist form, ἔστην.

[21] For a discussion of the rough breathing see the footnote to the present tense stem.

κάθημαι[1]	καθήσομαι	–	–	–	–
καλέω[2]	καλέσω	ἐκάλεσα	κέκληκα	κέκλημαι	ἐκλήθην
καταβαίνω[3]	καταβήσομαι	κατέβην	–	–	–
κηρύσσω[4]	–	ἐκήρυξα	–	κεκήρυγμαι	ἐκηρύχθην[5]
κράζω[6]	κράξω	ἔκραξα	κέκραγα[7]	–	–
κρατέω[8]	κρατήσω	ἐκράτησα	κεκράτηκα	κεκράτημαι	–
κρίνω[9]	κρινῶ	ἔκρινα	κέκρικα	κέκριμαι	ἐκρίθην
λαλέω[10]	λαλήσω	ἐλάλησα	λελάληκα	λελάλημαι	ἐλαλήθην
λαμβάνω[11]	λήμψομαι[12]	ἔλαβον[13]	εἴληφα[14]	εἴλημμαι[15]	ἐλήμφθην[16]
λέγω[17]	ἐρῶ[18]	εἶπον[19]	εἴρηκα[20]	εἴρημαι[21]	ἐρρέθην[22]

---

[1] κατα + *εμ. Formed from the present tense stem *καθη.

[2] The stem of this word used to have a digamma (ϝ, see 17.12) after the epsilon (καλεϝ), and therefore the epsilon does not always lengthen as you might expect. In the final three tense stems, the alpha drops out (ablaut) and the epsilon lengthens. You might find it easier to memorize these forms.

[3] See ἀναβαίνω.

[4] *κηρυγ

[5] The γθ combination changes to χθ.

[6] *κραγ

[7] Second perfect

[8] *κρατε

[9] *κριν. A liquid verb. The ν is lost in the final three tenses.

[10] *λαλε

[11] *λαβ. Actually, the same root is used to form all the tense stems. We give explanations for the different tense stems, and they are quite straightforward, but you may want to memorize the different forms. The key to remember with these different tenses is that the root is *λαβ, and these three letters are always present in some form. The alpha undergoes ablaut, and the beta is changed by the letter that follows it, but the three letters are always present. A mu is inserted in the present, future, and aorist passive stems.

[12] *λαβ. The alpha lengthens to eta, a mu is inserted, and the beta joins with the sigma of the tense formative to form psi. It is a future middle deponent. *λαβ ‣ ληβ ‣ λημβ + σομαι ‣ λήμψομαι.

[13] *λαβ. Second aorist.

[14] *λαβ. The vocalic reduplication is ει instead of the usual epsilon (see MBG for an explanation), the stem vowel alpha lengthens to eta (ablaut), and the beta is aspirated to a phi. It is a second perfect, so the tense formative is alpha and not κα. *λαβ ‣ ειλαβ ‣ ειληβ ‣ ειληφ ‣ εἴληφα.

[15] The same changes present in the perfect active are present here as well. The beta has changed to mu because of the following mu.

[16] The same changes present in the perfect active are present here as well, except that the augment is the simple epsilon. The beta has changed to phi because of the following theta.

[17] Three different roots are used to form this verb: *λεγ (present), *ερ (future, perfect, aorist passive), and *ιπ (aorist active). Memorize the forms.

[18] *ϝερ. Liquid future. The digamma (ϝ) has dropped out.

[19] *ϝιπ. Second aorist. It receives a syllabic augment, the digamma (ϝ) drops out because it is between vowels, and they contract. ε + ϝιπ + ο + ν ‣ εἶπον.

[20] *ϝερ. It received the syllabic augment and the digamma (ϝ) dropped out. It inserts an eta before the tense formative. ε + ϝερ + η + κα ‣ εερηκα ‣ εἴρηκα.

[21] Follows the same pattern of change as in the perfect active.

[22] *ϝερ. When the digamma (ϝ) was lost, evidently the rho doubled. An epsilon was inserted before the tense formative, much like an eta can be inserted.

μαρτυρέω[1]	μαρτυρήσω	ἐμαρτύρησα	μεμαρτύρηκα	μεμαρτύρημαι	ἐμαρτυρήθην
μέλλω[2]	μελλήσω[3]	–	–	–	–
μένω[4]	μενῶ[5]	ἔμεινα[6]	μεμένηκα[7]	–	–
οἶδα[8]	εἰδήσω	ᾔδειν	–	–	–
ὁράω[9]	ὄψομαι[10]	εἶδον[11]	ἑώρακα[12]	–	ὤφθην[13]
ὀφείλω[14]	–	–	–	–	–
παραδίδωμι[15]	παραδώσω	παρέδωκα	παραδέδωκα	παραδέδομαι	παρεδόθην
παρακαλέω[16]	παρακαλέσω	παρεκάλεσα	παρακέκληκα	παρακέκλημαι	παρεκλήθην
πείθω[17]	πείσω	ἔπεισα	πέποιθα[18]	πέπεισμαι[19]	ἐπείσθην[20]
πέμπω[21]	πέμψω	ἔπεμψα	–	–	ἐπέμφθην
περιπατέω[22]	περιπατήσω	περιεπάτησα	–	–	–
πίνω[23]	πίομαι[24]	ἔπιον[25]	πέπωκα[26]	–	ἐπόθην[27]

---

[1] *μαρτυρε

[2] *μελλ

[3] There used to be an epsilon in the root after the second lambda (*μελλε). This is visible only in the future.

[4] *μεν. A liquid, and the stem vowels change due to ablaut.

[5] Liquid future

[6] Liquid aorist, with a stem vowel change (ablaut)

[7] An eta is inserted before the tense formative.

[8] A strange verb. οἶδα actually is a second perfect form functioning as a present, and ᾔδειν is actually a pluperfect functioning as an aorist. Just memorize the forms. If you want an explanation, see *MBG*.

[9] The stem *ορα is used to form the present and perfect active. In the aorist the root is *ϝιδ. The other tense stems use the stem *οπ, which is altered according to the regular rules.

[10] *οπ. Future middle deponent.

[11] There is the second aorist middle deponent form ὠψάμην that is formed from the same root as the future active and aorist passive: *οπ. It only occurs at Luke 13:28. Most view εἶδον (*ιδ) as the aorist of ὁράω.

[12] There is both a lengthening and an augment: ορα › ωρα › εωρα › ἑώρακα.

[13] *οπ. The πθ combination forms φθ.

[14] *οφειλ

[15] παρα + *δο. See δίδωμι.

[16] παρα + *καλεϝ. See καλέω.

[17] *πειθ

[18] The stem vowels change from ει to οι due to ablaut. Second perfect.

[19] The θμ combination forms σμ.

[20] The dental + theta combination usually forms σθ.

[21] *πεμπ

[22] *περιπατε. A compound verb, but the simple πατέω does not occur. Notice that contrary to most compound verbs, περί does not lose its iota (elision) when the augment is added.

[23] *πι. The nu is added to the root to form the present tense stem.

[24] Future middle deponent

[25] Second aorist

[26] The stem vowel iota has shifted to omega due to ablaut.

[27] The stem vowel iota has shifted to omicron due to ablaut.

πίπτω[1]	πεσοῦμαι[2]	ἔπεσον[3]	πέπτωκα[4]	–	–
πιστεύω[5]	πιστεύσω	ἐπίστευσα	πεπίστευκα	πεπίστευμαι	ἐπιστεύθην
πληρόω[6]	πληρώσω	ἐπλήρωσα	πεπλήρωκα	πεπλήρωμαι	ἐπληρώθην
ποιέω[7]	ποιήσω	ἐποίησα	πεποίηκα	πεποίημαι	ἐποιήθην
πορεύομαι[8]	πορεύσομαι[9]	–	–	πεπόρευμαι	ἐπορεύθην[10]
προσέρχομαι[11]	προσελεύσομαι	προσῆλθον	προσελήλυθα	–	–
προσεύχομαι[12]	προσεύξομαι[13]	προσηυξάμην[14]	–	–	–
προσκυνέω[15]	προσκυνήσω	προσεκύνησα	–	–	–
συνάγω[16]	συνάξω	συνήγαγον	–	συνῆγμαι	συνήχθην
σῴζω[17]	σώσω[18]	ἔσωσα[19]	σέσωκα[20]	σέσωσμαι[21]	ἐσώθην[22]
τηρέω[23]	τηρήσω	ἐτήρησα	τετήρηκα	τετήρημαι	ἐτηρήθην

---

[1] Memorize the different forms. The stem is actually *πετ. The pi reduplicated and the epsilon dropped out in the formation of the present tense: *πετ ‣ πτ ‣ πιπτ ‣ πίπτω.

[2] The tau has dropped out because of the sigma tense formative, and for some reason there is a contraction. *πετ + σ + ο + μαι ‣ πεσομαι ‣ πεσοῦμαι.

[3] Second aorist. The tau has dropped out because of the sigma, which implies that πίπτω would have a first aorist. But actually it is a second aorist.

[4] The epsilon has dropped out and an omega has been inserted before the tense formative.

[5] *πιστευ

[6] *πληρο

[7] *ποιε

[8] *πορευ

[9] Future middle deponent

[10] Aorist passive deponent

[11] *προσερχ. See ἔρχομαι.

[12] *προσευχ

[13] Future middle deponent

[14] Aorist middle deponent

[15] *προσκυνε

[16] *συναγ. See ἄγω.

[17] *σωδ. Lexicons vary as to whether the iota subscript should be included.

[18] Dentals drop out before a sigma.

[19] Dentals drop out before a sigma.

[20] The delta has dropped out.

[21] The δμ combination forms σμ. σῴζω occurs in the New Testament once in the indicative, and the sigma is not inserted (σέσωται, Acts 4:9). It occurs twice as a participle, with the sigma inserted (σεσωσμένοι, Eph 2:5, 8).

[22] The δθ combination usually produces σθ, although here the sigma has dropped out. It is not unusual for the final sigma to drop out of a word in the aorist passive.

[23] *τηρε

τίθημι[1]	θήσω	ἔθηκα[2]	τέθεικα[3]	τέθειμαι[4]	ἐτέθην[5]
ὑπάγω[6]	ὑπάξω	ὑπήγαγον	–	ὑπῆγμαι	ὑπήχθην
ὑπάρχω[7]	ὑπάρξομαι[8]	ὑπηρξάμην[9]	–	–	–
φέρω[10]	οἴσω	ἤνεγκα	ἐνήνοχα[11]	–	ἠνέχθην
φημί[12]	–	ἔφη	–	–	–
φοβέομαι[13]	–	–	–	–	ἐφοβήθην[14]
χαίρω[15]	–	–	–	–	ἐχάρην[16]

---

[1] *θε. τίθημι forms its stems as a regular μι verb, except for the ablaut in the perfect and for the deaspiration in the aorist passive (θ › τ).

[2] μι verbs use κα for their tense formative in the aorist active.

[3] The stem vowel has shifted to ει due to ablaut.

[4] The stem vowel has shifted to ει due to ablaut.

[5] Believe it or not, this form is regular. When the θη is added for the aorist passive, there is the θεθ combination. The Greeks tried to avoid two aspirates (theta is an aspirate) in successive vowels, so they deaspirated the first one, i.e., shifted it to a tau. ε + *θε + θη + ν › εθεθην › ἐτέθην.

[6] *ὑπαγ. See ἄγω.

[7] *ὑπαρχ

[8] Future middle deponent

[9] Aorist middle deponent

[10] Just memorize the different forms. There are three different stems present here. See *MBG* for an explanation.

[11] Second perfect.

[12] *φη. See *MBG* for an explanation.

[13] *φοβε

[14] Aorist passive deponent

[15] *χαρ. The iota was added to form the present tense stem and is therefore not present in the other tense stems.

[16] Second aorist passive

Liquid Verbs

(Occurring Fifty Times and More in the New Testament)

αἴρω
I take up, take away
ἀρῶ, ἦρα, ἦρκα, ἦρμαι, ἤρθην

ἀποθνήσκω
I die
(ἀπέθνησκον), ἀποθανοῦμαι, ἀπέθανον, –, –, –

ἀποκρίνομαι
I answer
–, ἀπεκρινάμην, –, –, ἀπεκρίθην

ἀποκτείνω
I kill
ἀποκτενῶ, ἀπέκτεινα, –, –, ἀπεκτάνθην

ἀποστέλλω
I send
ἀποστελῶ, ἀπέστειλα, ἀπέσταλκα, ἀπέσταλμαι, ἀπεστάλην

βάλλω
I throw, put
(ἔβαλλον), βαλῶ, ἔβαλον, βέβληκα, βέβλημαι, ἐβλήθην

ἐγείρω
I raise up
ἐγερῶ, ἤγειρα, –, ἐγήγερμαι, ἠγέρθην

εἰμί
I am
(ἤμην), ἔσομαι, –, –, –, –

ἐκβάλλω
I cast out
(ἐξέβαλλον), ἐκβαλῶ, ἐξέβαλον, ἐκβέβληκα, ἐκβέβλημαι, ἐξεβλήθην

κρίνω
I judge, decide
(ἔκρινον), κρινῶ, ἔκρινα, κέκρικα, κέκριμαι, ἐκρίθην

λέγω
I say, speak
(ἔλεγον), ἐρῶ, εἶπον, εἴρηκα, εἴρημαι, ἐρρέθην

μέλλω
I am about to
(ἔμελλον or ἤμελλον), μελλήσω, –, –, –, –,

μένω
I remain
(ἔμενον), μενῶ, ἔμεινα, μεμένηκα, –, –,

πίνω
I drink
(ἔπινον), πίομαι, ἔπιον, πέπωκα, –, ἐπόθην

φέρω
I carry
(ἔφερον), οἴσω, ἤνεγκα, ἐνήνοχα, –, ἠνέχθην

χαίρω
I rejoice
(ἔχαιρον), –, –, –, –, ἐχάρην

ἄγω
I lead
(ἦγον), ἄξω, ἤγαγον, –, ἦγμαι, ἤχθην

ἀναβαίνω
I go up
(ἀνέβαινον), ἀναβήσομαι, ἀνέβην, –, –, –

Second Aorists

(Of Verbs Occurring Fifty Times and More in the New Testament)

ἀπέρχομαι
: I depart
ἀπελεύσομαι, ἀπῆλθον, ἀπελήλυθα, –, –

ἀποθνῄσκω
: I die
(ἀπέθνῃσκον), ἀποθανοῦμαι, ἀπέθανον, –, –, –

ἀποστέλλω
: I send (away)
ἀποστελῶ, ἀπέστειλα,[1] ἀπέσταλκα, ἀπέσταλμαι, ἀπεστάλην

βάλλω
: I throw
(ἔβαλλον), βαλῶ, ἔβαλον, βέβληκα, βέβλημαι, ἐβλήθην

γίνομαι
: I become
(ἐγινόμην), γενήσομαι, ἐγενόμην, γέγονα, γεγένημαι, ἐγενήθην

γινώσκω
: I know
(ἐγίνωσκον), γνώσομαι, ἔγνων, ἔγνωκα, ἔγνωσμαι, ἐγνώσθην

γράφω
: I write
(ἔγραφον), γράψω, ἔγραψα,[2] γέγραφα, γέγραμμαι or γέγραμμαι, ἐγράφην

εἰσέρχομαι
: I go into
εἰσελεύσομαι, εἰσῆλθον, εἰσελήλυθα, –, –

ἐκβάλλω
: I cast out
(ἐξέβαλλον), ἐκβαλῶ, ἐξέβαλον, ἐκβέβληκα, ἐκβέβλημαι, ἐξεβλήθην

ἐξέρχομαι
: I go out
(ἐξηρχόμην), ἐξελεύσομαι, ἐξῆλθον, ἐξελήλυθα, –, –

ἔρχομαι
: I come
(ἠρχόμην), ἐλεύσομαι, ἦλθον, ἐλήλυθα, –, –

ἐσθίω
: I eat
(ἤσθιον), φάγομαι, ἔφαγον, –, –, –

εὑρίσκω
: I find
(εὕρισκον or ηὕρισκον), εὑρήσω, εὗρον, εὕρηκα, –, εὑρέθην

ἔχω
: I have
(εἶχον), ἕξω, ἔσχον, ἔσχηκα, –, –

καταβαίνω
: I go down
(κατέβαινον), καταβήσομαι, κατέβην, –, –, –

λαμβάνω
: I take
(ἐλάμβανον), λήμψομαι, ἔλαβον, εἴληφα, εἴλημμαι, ἐλήμφθην

λέγω
: I say
(ἔλεγον), ἐρῶ, εἶπον, εἴρηκα, εἴρημαι, ἐρρέθην

---

[1]   The active is first aorist (liquid) but the passive is second aorist.

[2]   The active is first aorist but the passive is second aorist.

ὁράω   I see
                      ὄψομαι, εἶδον, ἑώρακα, –, ὤφθην

πίνω   I drink
                      (ἔπινον), πίομαι, ἔπιον, πέπωκα, –, ἐπόθην

πίπτω   I fall
                      (ἔπιπτον), πεσοῦμαι, ἔπεσον, πέπτωκα, –, –

προσέρχομαι   I come to
                      (προσηρχόμην), προσελεύσομαι, προσῆλθον, προσελήλυθα, –, –

συνάγω   I gather together
                      συνάξω, συνήγαγον, –, συνῆγμαι, συνήχθην

φημί   I say, affirm
                      (ἔφη), –, ἔφη, –, –, –

χαίρω   I rejoice
                      (ἔχαιρον), –, –, –, –, ἐχάρην

Words Occurring Fifty Times and More in the New Testament (by frequency)

When you are done with this grammar, this list will be helpful for your vocabulary review. Start with the most frequently used words and work down. "Chpt" refers to the chapter in BBG where you learn the word. The words are available in spreadsheet format on the class website.

Freq	Chpt	Word	Definition
19,867	6	ὁ, ἡ, τό	the
9,018	4	καί	and, even, also, namely
5,597	6	αὐτός, -ή, -ό	personal: he, she, it (him, her); they (them) reflexive: him/her/itself identical: same
2,792	6	δέ (δ᾽)	but, and
2,752	6	ἐν	dat: in, on, among
2,460	8	εἰμί	I am, exist, live, am present (ἤμην), ἔσομαι, –, –, –, –
2,353	8	λέγω	I say, speak (ἔλεγον), ἐρῶ, εἶπον, εἴρηκα, εἴρημαι, ἐρρέθην
1,840	11	ὑμεῖς	you (plural)
1,767	7	εἰς	acc: into, in, among
1,718	4	ἐγώ	I
1,623	6	οὐ (οὐκ, οὐχ)	not
1,387	7	οὗτος, αὕτη, τοῦτο	singular: this; he, her, it plural: these
1,365	14	ὅς, ἥ, ὅ	who, whom
1,317	4	θεός -οῦ, ὁ	God, god
1,296	6	ὅτι	that, since, because
1,244	10	πᾶς, πᾶσα, πᾶν	singular: each, every plural: all
1,067	7	σύ	you
1,042	7	μή	not, lest
1,041	7	γάρ	for, then
917	7	Ἰησοῦς, -οῦ, ὁ	Jesus, Joshua
914	8	ἐκ (ἐξ)	gen: from, out of
890	11	ἐπί (ἐπ᾽, ἐφ᾽)	gen: on, over, when dat: on the basis of, at acc: on, to, against
864	11	ἡμεῖς	we
717	7	κύριος -ου, ὁ	Lord, lord, master, sir
708	16	ἔχω	I have, hold (εἶχον), ἕξω, ἔσχον, ἔσχηκα, –, –
700	8	πρός	acc: to, towards, with

Freq	Chpt	Word	Definition
669	22	γίνομαι	I become, am, exist, happen, am born, am created (ἐγινόμην), γενήσομαι, ἐγενόμην, γέγονα, γεγένημαι, ἐγενήθην
667	8	διά (δι᾽)	gen: through acc: on account of
663	8	ἵνα	in order that, that
646	8	ἀπό (ἀπ᾽, ἀφ᾽)	gen: (away) from
638	8	ἀλλά (ἀλλ᾽)	but, yet, except
632	18	ἔρχομαι	I come, go (ἠρχόμην), ἐλεύσομαι, ἦλθον or ἦλθα, ἐλήλυθα, –, –
568	17	ποιέω	I do, make (ἐποίουν), ποιήσω, ἐποίησα, πεποίηκα, πεποίημαι, –
555	10	τίς, τί	who? what? which? why?
550	4	ἄνθρωπος, -ου, ὁ	man, mankind, person, people, humankind, human being
529	4	Χριστός, -οῦ, ὁ	Christ, Messiah, Anointed One
525	10	τις, τι	someone/thing, certain one/thing, anyone/thing
504	18	ὡς	as, like, when, that, how, about
503	10	εἰ	if
499	12	οὖν	therefore, then, accordingly
473	14	κατά (κατ᾽, καθ᾽)	gen: down from, against acc: according to, throughout, during
469	8	μετά (μετ᾽, μεθ᾽)	gen: with acc: after
454	20	ὁράω	I see, notice, experience ὄψομαι, εἶδον, ἑώρακα, –, ὤφθην
428	16	ἀκούω	I hear, learn, obey, understand (ἤκουον), ἀκούσω, ἤκουσα, ἀκήκοα, –, ἠκούσθην
416	13	πολύς, πολλή, πολύ	singular: much plural: many adverb: often
415	34	δίδωμι	I give (out), entrust, give back, put (ἐδίδουν), δώσω, ἔδωκα, δέδωκα, δέδομαι, ἐδόθην
413	11	πατήρ, πατρός, ὁ	father
389	8	ἡμέρα, -ας, ἡ	day
379	4	πνεῦμα, -ατος, τό	spirit, Spirit, wind, breath, inner life
377	7	υἱός, -οῦ, ὁ	son, descendant
351	9	ἐάν	if, when
344	10	εἷς, μία, ἕν	one
343	11	ἀδελφός, -οῦ, ὁ	brother
343	13	ἤ	or, than
333	10	περί	gen: concerning, about acc: around
330	4	λόγος, -ου, ὁ	word, Word, statement, message
319	13	ἑαυτοῦ, -ῆς, -οῦ	singular: himself/herself/itself plural: themselves
318	17	οἶδα	I know, understand εἰδήσω, ᾔδειν, –, –, –

Freq	Chpt	Word	Definition
296	17	λαλέω	I speak, say (ἐλάλουν), λαλήσω, ἐλάλησα, λελάληκα, λελάλημαι, ἐλαλήθην
273	7	οὐρανός, -οῦ, ὁ	heaven, sky
265	13	ἐκεῖνος, -η, -ο	singular: that (man/woman/thing) plural: those (men/women, things)
261	12	μαθητής, -οῦ, ὁ	disciple
258	22	λαμβάνω	I take, receive (ἐλάμβανον), λήμψομαι, ἔλαβον, εἴληφα, –, ἐλήμφθην
250	22	γῆ, γῆς, ἡ	earth, land, region, humanity
243	13	μέγας, μεγάλη, μέγα	large, great
243	11	πίστις, -εως, ἡ	faith, belief
241	16	πιστεύω	I believe, I have faith (in), trust (ἐπίστευον), πιστεύσω, ἐπίστευσα, πεπίστευκα, πεπίστευμαι, ἐπιστεύθην
234	10	οὐδείς, οὐδεμία, οὐδέν	no one, none, nothing
233	10	ἅγιος, -ία, -ιον	adjective: holy plural noun: saints
231	18	ἀποκρίνομαι	I answer –, ἀπεκρινάμην, –, –, ἀπεκρίθην
231	10	ὄνομα, -ατος, τό	name, reputation
222	20	γινώσκω	I know, come to know, realize, learn (ἐγίνωσκον), γνώσομαι, ἔγνων, ἔγνωκα, ἔγνωσμαι, ἐγνώσθην
220	8	ὑπό (ὑπ', ὑφ')	gen: by (preposition) acc: under
218	22	ἐξέρχομαι	I go out (ἐξηρχόμην), ἐξελεύσομαι, ἐξῆλθον, ἐξελήλυθα, –, –
216	11	ἀνήρ, ἀνδρός, ὁ	man, male, husband
215	13	γυνή, γυναικός, ἡ	woman, wife
215	14	τε	and (so), so
210	18	δύναμαι	I am able, am powerful (ἐδυνάμην or ἠδυνάμην), δυνήσομαι, –, –, –, ἠδυνήθην
208	21	θέλω	I will, wish, desire, enjoy (ἤθελον), –, ἠθέλησα, –, –, –
208	14	οὕτως	thus, so, in this manner
200	11	ἰδού	See! Behold!
195	19	Ἰουδαῖος, -αία, -αῖον	adjective: Jewish noun: Jew
194	22	εἰσέρχομαι	I come in(to), go in(to), enter εἰσελεύσομαι, εἰσῆλθον, εἰσελήλυθα, –, –
194	16	νόμος, -ου, ὁ	law, principle
194	8	παρά (παρ')	gen: from dat: beside, in the presence of acc: alongside of
191	23	γράφω	I write (ἔγραφον), γράψω, ἔγραψα, γέγραφα, γέγραπμαι or γέγραμμαι, ἐγράφην
186	4	κόσμος, ου, ὁ	world, universe, humankind
182	9	καθώς	as, even as

Freq	Chpt	Word	Definition
179	12	μέν	on the one hand, indeed
177	14	χείρ, χειρός, ἡ	hand, arm, finger
176	22	εὑρίσκω	I find (εὕρισκον or ηὕρισκον), εὑρήσω, εὗρον, εὕρηκα, –, εὑρέθην
175	4	ἄγγελος, -ου, ὁ	angel, messenger
175	8	ὄχλος, -ου, ὁ	crowd, multitude
173	7	ἁμαρτία, -ας, ἡ	sin
169	6	ἔργον, -ου, τό	work, deed, action
167	11	ἄν	an untranslatable, uninflected word, used to make a definite statement contingent upon something
166	4	δόξα, -ης, ἡ	glory, majesty, fame
162	6	βασιλεία, -ας, ἡ	kingdom
162	34	ἔθνος, -ους, τό	singular: nation plural: Gentiles
162	13	πόλις, -εως, ἡ	city
160	16	τότε	then, thereafter
158	29	ἐσθίω	I eat (ἤσθιον), φάγομαι, ἔφαγον, –, –, –
158	4	Παῦλος, -ου, ὁ	Paul
156	4	καρδία, -ας, ἡ	heart, inner self
156	4	Πέτρος, -ου, ὁ	Peter
156	9	πρῶτος, -η, -ον	first, earlier
155	6	ἄλλος, -η, -ο	other, another
155	11	χάρις, -ιτος, ἡ	grace, favor, kindness
154	36	ἵστημι	intransitive: I stand transitive: I cause to stand (ἵστην), στήσω, ἔστησα or ἔστην, ἔστηκα, –, ἐστάθην
153	18	πορεύομαι	I go, proceed, live (ἐπορευόμην), πορεύσομαι, –, –, πεπόρευμαι, ἐπορεύθην
150	12	ὑπέρ	gen: in behalf of acc: above
148	17	καλέω	I call, name, invite (ἐκάλουν), καλέσω, ἐκάλεσα, κέκληκα, κέκλημαι, ἐκλήθην
147	6	νῦν	now, the present
147	10	σάρξ, σαρκός, ἡ	flesh, body
146	12	ἕως	conj: until prep (gen): as far as
144	20	ἐγείρω	I raise up, wake ἐγερῶ, ἤγειρα, –, ἐγήγερμαι, ἠγέρθην
144	18	ὅστις, ἥτις, ὅτι	whoever, whichever, whatever
144	4	προφήτης, -ου, ὁ	prophet
143	17	ἀγαπάω	I love, cherish (ἠγάπων), ἀγαπήσω, ἠγάπησα, ἠγάπηκα, ἠγάπημαι, ἠγαπήθην
143	36	ἀφίημι	I let go, leave, permit (ἤφιον), ἀφήσω, ἀφῆκα, –, ἀφέωμαι, ἀφέθην
143	11	οὐδέ	and not, not even, neither, nor
142	20	λαός, -οῦ, ὁ	people, crowd

Freq	Chpt	Word	Definition
142	10	σῶμα, -ατος, τό	body
141	12	πάλιν	again
140	19	ζάω	I live
			(ἔζων), ζήσω, ἔζησα, –, –, –
139	4	φωνή, -ῆς, ἡ	sound, noise, voice
135	27	δύο	two
135	4	ζωή, -ῆς, ἡ	life
135	8	Ἰωάννης, -ου, ὁ	John
132	16	βλέπω	I see, look at
			(ἔβλεπον), βλέψω, ἔβλεψα, –, –, –
132	20	ἀποστέλλω	I send (away)
			ἀποστελῶ, ἀπέστειλα, ἀπέσταλκα, ἀπέσταλμαι, ἀπεστάλην
129	4	ἀμήν	verily, truly, amen, so let it be
128	9	νεκρός, -ά, -όν	adjective: dead
			noun: dead body, corpse
128	10	σύν	dat: with
124	9	δοῦλος, -ου, ὁ	slave, servant
123	17	ὅταν	whenever
122	12	αἰών, -ῶνος, ὁ	age, eternity
122	27	ἀρχιερεύς, -έως, ὁ	chief priest, high priest
122	22	βάλλω	I throw
			(ἔβαλλον), βαλῶ, ἔβαλον, βέβληκα, βέβλημαι, ἐβλήθην
120	8	θάνατος, -ου, ὁ	death
119	23	δύναμις, -εως, ἡ	power, miracle
119	34	παραδίδωμι	I entrust, hand over, betray
			(παρεδίδουν), παραδώσω, παρέδωκα or παρέδοσα, παραδέδωκα, παραδέδομαι, παρεδόθην
118	20	μένω	I remain, live
			(ἔμενον), μενῶ, ἔμεινα, μεμένηκα, –, –
117	23	ἀπέρχομαι	I depart
			ἀπελεύσομαι, ἀπῆλθον, ἀπελήλυθα, –, -
117	17	ζητέω	I seek, desire, try to obtain
			(ἐζήτουν), ζητήσω, ἐζήτησα, –, –, ἐζητήθην
116	6	ἀγάπη, -ης, ἡ	love
115	19	βασιλεύς, -έως, ὁ	king
114	11	ἐκκλησία, -ας, ἡ	a church, (the) Church, assembly, congregation
114	36	ἴδιος, -ία, -ιον	one's own (e.g., people, home)
114	20	κρίνω	I judge, decide, prefer
			(ἐκρινόμην), κρινῶ, ἔκρινα, κέκρικα, κέκριμαι, ἐκρίθην
114	12	μόνος, -η, -ον	alone, only
114	8	οἶκος, -ου, ὁ	house, home
111	22	ἀποθνήσκω	I die, am about to die, am freed from
			(ἀπέθνησκον), ἀποθανοῦμαι, ἀπέθανον, –, –, –
110	12	ὅσος, -η, -ον	as great as, as many as
109	14	ἀλήθεια, -ας, ἡ	truth

Freq	Chpt	Word	Definition
109	32	μέλλω	I am about to (ἔμελλον or ἤμελλον), μελλήσω, –, –, –, –
109	19	ὅλος, -η, -ον	adj: whole, complete adverb: entirely
109	27	παρακαλέω	I call, urge, exhort, comfort (παρεκάλουν), –, παρεκάλεσα, –, παρακέκλημαι, παρεκλήθην
108	36	ἀνίστημι	intransitive: I rise, get up transitive: I raise ἀναστήσω, ανέστησα, –, –, –
106	20	σῴζω	I save, deliver, rescue (ἔσῳζον), σώσω, ἔσωσα, σέσωκα, σέσωσμαι, ἐσώθην
106	6	ὥρα, -ας, ἡ	hour, occasion, moment
105	20	ἐκεῖ	there, in that place
103	14	ὅτε	when
103	13	πῶς	how?
103	14	ψυχή, -ῆς, ἡ	soul, life, self
102	9	ἀγαθός, -ή, -όν	good, useful
102	7	ἐξουσία, -ας, ἡ	authority, power
101	20	αἴρω	I raise, take up, take away ἀρῶ, ἦρα, ἦρκα, ἦρμαι, ἤρθην
101	18	δεῖ	it is necessary
101	14	ὁδός, -οῦ, ἡ	way, road, journey, conduct
100	9	ἀλλήλων	one another
100	12	ὀφθαλμός, -οῦ, ὁ	eye, sight
100	11	καλός, -ή, -όν	beautiful, good
100	36	τίθημι	I put, place (ἐτίθουν), θήσω, ἔθηκα, τέθεικα, τέθειμαι, ἐτέθην
99	27	ἕτερος, -α, -ον	other, another, different
99	10	τέκνον, -ου, τό	child, descendant
98	21	Φαρισαῖος, -ου, ὁ	Pharisee
97	24	αἷμα, -ατος, τό	blood
97	22	ἄρτος, -ου, ὁ	bread, loaf, food
97	19	γεννάω	I beget, give birth to, produce γεννήσω, ἐγέννησα, γεγέννηκα, γεγέννημαι, ἐγεννήθην
97	21	διδάσκω	I teach (ἐδίδασκον), διδάξω, ἐδίδαξα, –, –, ἐδιδάχθην
95	21	περιπατέω	I walk (around), live (περιεπάτουν), περιπατήσω, περιεπάτησα, –, –, –
95	24	φοβέομαι	I fear (ἐφοβούμην), –, –, –, –, ἐφοβήθην
94	14	ἐνώπιον	gen: before
94	18	τόπος, -ου, ὁ	place, location
93	22	ἔτι	still, yet, even
93	8	οἰκία, -ας, ἡ	house, home
93	12	πούς, ποδός, ὁ	foot
92	13	δικαιοσύνη, -ης, ἡ	righteousness
92	14	εἰρήνη, -ης, ἡ	peace

Freq	Chpt	Word	Definition
91	8	θάλασσα, -ης, ἡ	sea, lake
91	27	κάθημαι	I sit (down), live (ἐκαθήμην), καθήσομαι, –, –, –, –
90	21	ἀκολουθέω	I follow, accompany (ἠκολούθουν), ἀκολουθήσω, ἠκολούθησα, ἠκολούθηκα, –, –
90	33	ἀπόλλυμι	active: I destroy, kill middle: I perish, die (ἀπώλλυον), ἀπολέσω or ἀπολῶ, ἀπώλεσα, ἀπόλωλα, –, -
90	12	μηδείς, μηδεμία, μηδέν	no one/thing
90	34	πίπτω	I fall (ἔπιπτον), πεσοῦμαι, ἔπεσον or ἔπεσα, πέπτωκα, –, –
88	14	ἑπτά	seven
87	22	οὔτε	and not, neither, nor
86	23	ἄρχομαι	I begin ἄρξομαι, ἠρξάμην, –, –, –
86	17	πληρόω	I fill, complete, fulfill (ἐπλήρουν), πληρώσω, ἐπλήρωσα, πεπλήρωκα, πεπλήρωμαι, ἐπληρώθην
86	22	προσέρχομαι	I come/go to (προσηρχόμην), –, προσῆλθον, προσελήλυθα, –, –
85	6	καιρός, -οῦ, ὁ	(appointed) time, season
85	22	προσεύχομαι	I pray (προσηυχόμην), προσεύξομαι, προσηυξάμην, –, –, –
84	13	κἀγώ	and I, but I
83	11	μήτηρ, μητρός, ἡ	mother
83	7	ὥστε	therefore, so that
82	27	ἀναβαίνω	I go up, come up (ἀνέβαινον), ἀναβήσομαι, ἀνέβην, ἀναβέβηκα, –, –
82	24	ἕκαστος, -η, -ον	each, every
82	16	ὅπου	where
81	20	ἐκβάλλω	I cast out, send out (ἐξέβαλλον), –, ἐξέβαλον, –, –, ἐξεβλήθην
81	27	καταβαίνω	I go down, come down (κατέβαινον), καταβήσομαι, κατέβην, καταβέβηκα, –, –
81	25	μᾶλλον	more, rather
80	4	ἀπόστολος, -ου, ὁ	apostle, envoy, messenger
80	34	Μωϋσῆς, -έως, ὁ	Moses
79	32	δίκαιος, -ία, -ιον	right, just, righteous
79	29	πέμπω	I send πέμψω, ἔπεμψα, –, –, ἐπέμφθην
79	24	ὑπάγω	I depart (ὑπῆγον), –, –, –, –, –
78	9	πονηρός, -ά, -όν	evil, bad
78	20	στόμα, -ατος, τό	mouth
77	36	ἀνοίγω	I open ἀνοίξω, ἠνέῳξα or ἀνέῳξα, ἀνέῳγα, ἀγέῳγμαι or ἠνέῳγμαι, ἠνεῴχθην or ἠνοίχθην

Freq	Chpt	Word	Definition
77	20	βαπτίζω	I baptize, dip, immerse
			(ἐβάπτιζον), βαπτίσω, ἐβάπτισα, –, βεβάπτισμαι, ἐβαπτίσθην
77	14	Ἰερουσαλήμ, ἡ	Jerusalem
77	13	σημεῖον, -ου, τό	sign, miracle
76	9	ἐμός, ἐμή, ἐμόν	my, mine
76	7	εὐαγγέλιον, -ου, τό	good news, Gospel
76	25	μαρτυρέω	I bear witness, testify
			(ἐμαρτύρουν), μαρτυρήσω, ἐμαρτύρησα, μεμαρτύρηκα,
			μεμαρτύρημαι, ἐμαρτυρήθην
76	16	πρόσωπον, -ου, τό	face, appearance
76	11	ὕδωρ, ὕδατος, τό	water
75	13	δώδεκα	twelve
75	14	κεφαλή, -ῆς, ἡ	head
75	4	Σίμων, -ωνος, ὁ	Simon
74	20	ἀποκτείνω	I kill
			ἀποκτενῶ, ἀπέκτεινα, –, –, ἀπεκτάνθην
74	24	χαίρω	I rejoice
			(ἔχαιρον), –, –, –, –, ἐχάρην
73	4	Ἀβραάμ, ὁ	Abraham
73	23	πίνω	I drink
			(ἔπινον), πίομαι, ἔπιον, πέπωκα, –, ἐπόθην
73	22	πῦρ, πυρός, τό	fire
73	11	φῶς, φωτός, τό	light
71	9	αἰώνιος, -ον	eternal
71	28	ἱερόν, -οῦ, τό	temple
70	25	αἰτέω	I ask, demand
			(ᾔτουν), αἰτήσω, ᾔτησα, ᾔτηκα, –, –
70	17	τηρέω	I keep, guard, observe
			(ἐτήρουν), τηρήσω, ἐτήρησα, τετήρηκα, τετήρημαι, ἐτηρήθην
68	19	Ἰσραήλ, ὁ	Israel
68	14	πλοῖον, -ου, τό	ship, boat
68	14	ῥῆμα, -ατος, τό	word, saying
68	4	σάββατον, -ου, τό	Sabbath, week
68	27	τρεῖς, τρία	three
67	24	ἄγω	I lead, bring, arrest
			(ἦγον), ἄξω, ἤγαγον, –, –, ἤχθην
67	9	ἐντολή, -ῆς, ἡ	commandment
67	9	πιστός, -ή, -όν	faithful, believing
66	33	ἀπολύω	I release
			(ἀπέλυον), ἀπολύσω, ἀπέλυσα, –, ἀπολέλυμαι, ἀπελύθην
66	19	καρπός, -οῦ, ὁ	fruit, crop, result
66	30	πρεσβύτερος, -α, -ον	elder, older
66	29	φέρω	I carry, bear, produce
			(ἔφερον), οἴσω, ἤνεγκα, ἐνήνοχα, –, ἠνέχθην
66	36	φημί	I say, affirm
			(ἔφη), –, ἔφη, –, –, –
65	33	εἴτε	if, whether

Freq	Chpt	Word	Definition
63	28	γραμματεύς, -έως, ὁ	scribe
63	17	δαιμόνιον, -ου, τό	demon
63	21	ἐρωτάω	I ask, request, entreat (ἠρώτων), ἐρωτήσω, ἠρώτησα, –, –, ἠρωτήθην
63	11	ἔξω	adverb: without prep (gen): outside
63	24	ὄρος, ὄρους, τό	mountain, hill
62	29	δοκέω	I think, seem (ἐδόκουν), –, ἔδοξα, –, –, –
62	11	θέλημα, -ατος, τό	will, desire
62	14	θρόνος, -ου, ὁ	throne
62	27	Ἱεροσόλυμα, τά	Jerusalem
61	9	ἀγαπητός, -ή, -όν	beloved
61	4	Γαλιλαία, -ας, ἡ	Galilee
61	23	δοξάζω	I praise, honor, glorify (ἐδόξαζον), δοξάσω, ἐδόξασα, –, δεδόξασμαι, ἐδοξάσθην
61	10	ἤδη	now, already
61	23	κηρύσσω	I proclaim, preach (ἐκήρυσσον), –, ἐκήρυξα, –, –, ἐκηρύχθην
61	18	νύξ, νυκτός, ἡ	night
61	11	ὧδε	here
60	24	ἱμάτιον, -ου, τό	garment, cloak
60	19	προσκυνέω	I worship (προσεκύνουν), προσκυνήσω, προσεκύνησα, –, –, –
60	34	ὑπάρχω	I am, exist (ὑπῆρχον), –, –, –, –, – τά ὑπάρχοντα: one's belongings
59	28	ἀσπάζομαι	I greet, salute (ἠσπαζόμην), –, ἠσπασάμην, –, –, –
59	4	Δαυίδ, ὁ	David
59	12	διδάσκαλος, -ου, ὁ	teacher
59	31	λίθος, -ου, ὁ	stone
59	18	συνάγω	I gather together, invite συνάξω, συνήγαγον, –, συνῆγμαι, συνήχθην
59	16	χαρά, -ᾶς, ἡ	joy, delight
58	27	θεωρέω	I look at, behold θεωρήσω, ἐθεώρησα, –, –, –
58	36	μέσος, -η, -ον	middle, in the midst
57	31	τοιοῦτος, -αύτη, -οῦτον	such, of such a kind
56	29	δέχομαι	I take, receive δέξομαι, ἐδεξάμην, –, δέδεγμαι, ἐδέχθην
56	21	ἐπερωτάω	I ask (for), question, demand of (ἐπηρώτων), ἐπερωτήσω, ἐπηρώτησα, –, –, ἐπηρωτήθην
56	28	κράζω	I cry out, call out (ἔκραζον), κράξω, ἔκραξα, κέκραγα, –, –
56	30	μηδέ	but not, nor, not even
56	21	συναγωγή, -ῆς, ἡ	synagogue, meeting

Freq	Chpt	Word	Definition
56	9	τρίτος, -η, -ον	third
55	7	ἀρχή, -ῆς, ἡ	beginning, ruler
55	34	λοιπός, -ή, -όν	adjective: remaining noun: (the) rest adverb: for the rest, henceforth
55	4	Πιλᾶτος, -ου, ὁ	Pilate
55	17	πλείων, πλεῖον	larger, more
54	27	δεξιός, -ά, -όν	right
54	27	εὐαγγελίζω	I bring good news, preach (εὐηγγέλιζον), –, εὐηγγέλισα, –, εὐηγγέλισμαι, εὐηγγελίσθην
54	27	οὗ	where
54	28	οὐχί	not
54	21	χρόνος, -ου, ὁ	time
53	23	διό	therefore, for this reason
53	11	ἐλπίς, -ίδος, ἡ	hope, expectation
53	12	ὅπως	how, that, in order that
52	14	ἐπαγγελία, -ας, ἡ	promise
52	4	ἔσχατος, -η, -ον	last
52	28	παιδίον, -ου, τό	child, infant
52	27	πείθω	I persuade (ἔπειθον), πείσω, ἔπεισα, πέποιθα, πέπεισμαι, ἐπείσθην
52	28	σπείρω	I sow –, ἔσπειρα, –, ἔσπαρμαι, ἐσπάρην
51	12	εὐθύς	immediately
51	20	σοφία, -ας, ἡ	wisdom
50	20	γλῶσσα, -ης, ἡ	tongue, language
50	4	γραφή, -ῆς, ἡ	writing, Scripture
50	9	κακός, -ή, -όν	bad, evil
50	13	μακάριος, -ία, -ιον	blessed, happy
50	8	παραβολή, -ῆς, ἡ	parable
50	16	τυφλός, -ή, -όν	blind
48	19	μείζων, -ον	greater
43	19	Ἰουδαία, -ας, ἡ	Judea
42	16	λύω	I loose, untie, destroy (ἔλυον), λύσω, ἔλυσα, –, λέλυμαι, ἐλύθην
34	11	ἴδε	See! Behold!
30	36	δείκνυμι	I show, explain δείξω, ἔδειξα, δέδειχα, –, ἐδείχθην

Lexicon

The definitions in this lexicon are derived from Prof. Bruce Metzger's *Lexical Aids* and Warren Trenchard's *Complete Vocabulary Guide* (both used with permission). It includes all the words that occur ten times or more in the Greek Testament. Words learned in BBG are in blue. The definition is followed by its frequency in the New Testament, its chapter in BBG if applicable, and its category in *MBG*. Following is a quick summary of the MBG nomenclature.

"n-" means the word is a noun.

> n-1 is first declension.
>
> n-2 is second declension.
>
> n-3 is third declension.

"a-" means the word is an adjective.

> a-1 are adjectives with three endings where the masculine and neuter are second declension and the feminine is first declension (ἅγιος, -ία, -ιον).

> a-2 are adjectives with three endings where the masculine and neuter are third declension and the feminine is first declension (πᾶς, πᾶσα, πᾶν).

> a-3 are adjectives with two endings where the masculine and feminine are the same ending (second declension) and the neuter has a separate set of endings (second declension; ἁμαρτωλός, όν).

> a-4 are adjectives with two endings where the masculine and feminine are the same ending (third declension) and the neuter has a separate ending (third declension; ἀληθής, ές).

> a-5 are irregular adjectives.

"v-" means that the word is a verb.

The verbs in this list are broken down into v-1 through v-8. Since these categories are somewhat complicated, detailed comment is deferred to *MBG*. Following are a few simple categories.

> v-1 Apparently regular verbs (λύω, ἀγαπάω).

> v-2 Present tense has a consonantal iota that is not used in the other tenses (*βαπτιδ + ι ‣ βαπτίζω ‣ βαπτίσω).

> v-3 Present tense has a nu that is lost in the other tenses (*πι ‣ πίνω ‣ ἔπιον).

> v-4 Present tense has a tau that is lost in the other tenses (*κρυπ ‣ κρύπτω ‣ ἔκρυψα).

> v-5 Present tense has (ι)σκ that are lost in the other tenses (*αρε ‣ ἀρέσκω ‣ ἤρεσα).

The following three categories contain words that fall into the first five categories, but have also been included in these three categories.

> v-6 The μι verbs (δίδωμι).

> v-7 Verbs that undergo ablaut (ἀκούω ‣ ἀκήκοα).

> v-8 Verbs that use different verbal roots in the formation of their tense stems (λέγω, ἐρῶ, εἶπον).

"cv-" means the word is a compound verb. The tense forms for the verbs are given in traditional order: present, (imperfect), future active, aorist active, perfect active, perfect middle/passive, aorist passive. The imperfect is included (in parentheses) if it occurs in the New Testament. If a tense form does not occur in the New Testament, it is replaced with a dash.

ἄλφα

Ἀβραάμ, ὁ   Abraham (73, chpt 4, n-3g[2])

ἀγαθός, -ή, -όν   good, useful (102, chpt 9, a-1a[2a])

ἀγαλλιάω   I exult (11, v-1d[1b]) –, ἠγαλλίασα, –, –, ἠγαλλιάθην

ἀγαπάω   I love, cherish (143, chpt 17, v-1d[1a]) (ἠγάπων), ἀγαπήσω, ἠγάπησα, ἠγάπηκα, ἠγάπημαι, ἠγαπήθην

ἀγάπη, -ης, ἡ   love (116, chpt 6, n-1b)

ἀγαπητός, -ή, -όν   beloved (61, chpt 9, a-1a[2a])

ἄγγελος, -ου, ὁ   angel, messenger (175, chpt 4, n-2a)

ἁγιάζω   I consecrate, sanctify (28, v-2a[1]) –, ἡγίασα, –, ἡγίασμαι, ἡγιάσθην

ἁγιασμός, -οῦ, ὁ   holiness, consecration (10, n-2a)

ἅγιος, -ία, -ιον   holy; plural noun: saints (233, chpt 10, a-1a[1])

ἀγνοέω   I do not know (22, v-1d[2a]) (ἠγνόουν), –, ἠγνόησα, –, –, –

ἀγορά, -ᾶς, ἡ   marketplace (11, n-1a)

ἀγοράζω   I buy (30, v-2a[1]) (ἠγόραζον), –, ἠγόρασα, –, ἠγόρασμαι, ἠγοράσθην

Ἀγρίππας, -α, ὁ   Agrippa (11, n-1e)

ἀγρός, -οῦ, ὁ   field, land (36, n-2a)

ἄγω   I lead, bring, arrest (69, chpt 24, v-1b[2]) (ἦγον), ἄξω, ἤγαγον, –, –, ἤχθην

ἀδελφή, -ῆς, ἡ   sister (26, n-1b)

ἀδελφός, -οῦ, ὁ   brother (343, chpt 11, n-2a)

ᾅδης, -ου, ὁ   Hades (10, n-1f)

ἀδικέω   I do wrong, injure (28, v-1d[2a]) ἀδικήσω, ἠδίκησα, –, –, ἠδικήθην

ἀδικία, -ας, ἡ   unrighteousness (25, n-1a)

ἄδικος, -ον   unjust (12, a-3a)

ἀδύνατος, -ον   impossible (10, a-3a)

ἀθετέω   I nullify, reject (16, v-1d[2a]) ἀθετήσω, ἠθέτησα, –, –, –

Αἴγυπτος, -ου, ἡ   Egypt (25, n-2b)

αἷμα, -ατος, τό   blood (97, chpt 24, n-3c[4])

αἴρω   I raise, take up, take away (101, chpt 20, v-2d[2]) ἀρῶ, ἦρα, ἦρκα, ἦρμαι, ἤρθην

αἰτέω   I ask, demand (70, chpt 25, v-1d[2a]) (ᾔτουν), αἰτήσω, ᾔτησα, ᾔτηκα, –, –

αἰτία, -ας, ἡ   cause, charge, accusation (20, n-1a)

αἰών, -ῶνος, ὁ   age, eternity (122, chpt 12, n-3f[1a])

αἰώνιος, -ον   eternal (71, chpt 9, a-3b[1])

ἀκαθαρσία, -ας, ἡ   immorality (10, n-1a)

ἀκάθαρτος, -ον   unclean, impure (32, a-3a)

ἄκανθα, -ης, ἡ   thorn plant (14, n-1c)

ἀκοή, -ῆς, ἡ   hearing, report (24, n-1b)

ἀκολουθέω   I follow, accompany (90, chpt 21, v-1d[2a]) (ἠκολούθουν), ἀκολουθήσω, ἠκολούθησα, ἠκολούθηκα, –, –

ἀκούω   I hear, learn, obey, understand (428, chpt 16, v-1a[8]) (ἤκουον), ἀκούσω, ἤκουσα, ἀκήκοα, –, ἠκούσθην

ἀκροβυστία, -ας, ἡ   uncircumcision (20, n-1a)

ἀλέκτωρ, -ορος, ὁ   rooster (12, n-3f[2b])

ἀλήθεια, -ας, ἡ   truth (109, chpt 14, n-1a)

ἀληθής, -ές   true, truthful (26, a-4a)

ἀληθινός, -ή, -όν   true, genuine (28, a-1a[2a])

ἀληθῶς   truly (18, adverb)

ἀλλά (ἀλλ᾽)   but, yet, except (638, chpt 8, particle)

ἀλλήλων   one another (100, chpt 9, a-1a[2b])

ἄλλος, -η, -ο   other, another (155, chpt 6, a-1a[2b])

ἀλλότριος, -α, -ον   not one's own, strange (14, a-1a[1])

ἅλυσις, -εως, ἡ   chain (11, n-3e[5b])

ἅμα   at the same time; prep (dat): together with (10, adverb)

ἁμαρτάνω   I sin (43, v-3a[2a]) ἁμαρτήσω, ἥμαρτον or ἡμάρτησα, ἡμάρτηκα, –, –

ἁμαρτία, -ας, ἡ   sin (173, chpt 7, n-1a)

ἁμαρτωλός, -όν   sinful; noun: sinner (47, a-3a)

ἀμήν   verily, truly, amen, so let it be (129, chpt 4, particle)

ἀμπελών, -ῶνος, ὁ   vineyard (23, n-3f[1a])

ἀμφότεροι, -αι, -α   both (14, a-1a[1])

ἄν   an untranslatable, uninflected word, used to make a definite statement contingent upon something (166, chpt 11)

ἀνά   acc: among, between; with numerals: each (13, preposition)

ἀναβαίνω   I go up, come up (82, chpt 27, cv-2d[7]) (ἀνέβαινον), ἀναβήσομαι, ἀνέβην, ἀναβέβηκα, –, –

ἀναβλέπω   I look up, receive sight (25, cv-1b[1]) –, ἀνέβλεψα, –, –, –

ἀναγγέλλω   I proclaim, announce, report (14, cv-2d[1]) (ἀνήγγελλον), ἀναγγελῶ, ἀνήγγειλα, –, –, ἀνηγγέλην

ἀναγινώσκω   I read (32, cv-5a) (ἀνεγίνωσκον), –, ἀνέγνων, –, –, ἀνεγνώσθην

ἀνάγκη, -ης, ἡ   necessity, pressure, distress (17, n-1b)

ἀνάγω   I lead up; middle: I put out to sea (23, cv-1b[2]) –, ἀνήγαγον, –, –, ἀνήχθην

ἀναιρέω   I destroy, do away with (24, cv-1d[2a]) ἀνελῶ, ἀνεῖλα, –, –, ἀνηρέθην

ἀνάκειμαι   I recline (at meals) (14, cv-6b) (ἀνεκείμην), –, –, –, –, –

ἀνακρίνω   I question, examine (16, cv-2d[6]) –, ἀνέκρινα, –, –, ἀνεκρίθην

ἀναλαμβάνω   I take up (13, cv-3a[2b]) –, ἀνέλαβον, –, –, ἀνελήμφθην

Ἀνανίας, -ου, ὁ   Ananias (11, n-1d)

ἀναπαύω   I give rest, refresh; middle: I take a rest (12, cv-1a[5]) ἀναπαύσω, ἀνέπαυσα, –, ἀναπέπαυμαι, –

ἀναπίπτω   I lie down, recline (12, cv-1b[3]) –, ἀνέπεσα, –, –, –

ἀνάστασις, -εως, ἡ   resurrection (42, n-3e[5b])

ἀναστροφή, -ῆς, ἡ   way of life, conduct (13, n-1b)

ἀνατολή, -ῆς, ἡ   east (11, n-1b)

ἀναφέρω   I offer up, bring up (10, cv-1c[1]) (ἀνεφερόμην), –, ἀνήνεγκα or ἀνήνεκον, –, –, –

ἀναχωρέω   I withdraw (14, cv-1d[2a]) –, ἀνεχώρησα, –, –, –

Ἀνδρέας, -ου, ὁ   Andrew (13, n-1d)

ἄνεμος, -ου, ὁ   wind (31, n-2a)

ἀνέχομαι   I endure (15, cv-1b[2]) (ἀνηρχόμην), ἀνέξομαι, ἀνεσχόμην, –, –, –

ἀνήρ, ἀνδρός, ὁ   man, male, husband (216, chpt 11, n-3f[2c])

ἀνθίστημι   I oppose (14, cv-6a) (ἀνθιστόμην), –, ἀντέστην, ἀνθέστηκα, –, –

ἄνθρωπος, -ου, ὁ   man, mankind, person, people, humankind, human being (550, chpt 4, n-2a)

ἀνίστημι   intransitive: I rise, get up; transitive: I raise (108, chpt 36, cv-6a) ἀναστήσω, ἀνέστησα, –, –, –

ἀνοίγω   I open (77, chpt 36, v-1b[2]) ἀνοίξω, ἤνεῳξα or ἀνέῳξα, ἀνέῳγα, ἀγέῳγμαι or ἠνέῳγμαι, ἠνεῴχθην or ἠνοίχθην

ἀνομία, -ας, ἡ   lawlessness (15, n-1a)

ἀντί   gen: in behalf of, for, instead of (22, preposition)

Ἀντιόχεια, -ας, ἡ   Antioch (18, n-1a)

ἄνωθεν   from above, again (13, adverb)

ἄξιος, -α, -ον   worthy (41, a-1a[1])

ἀπαγγέλλω   I report, tell (45, cv-2d[1]) (ἀπήγγελλον), ἀπαγγελῶ, ἀπήγγειλα, –, –, ἀπηγγέλην

ἀπάγω   I lead away (15, cv-1b[2]) –, ἀπήγαγον, –, –, ἀπήχθην

ἅπαξ   once, once for all (14, adverb)

ἀπαρνέομαι   I deny (11, cv-1d[2a]) ἀπαρνήσομαι, ἀπήρνησα, –, –, ἀπαρνηθήσομαι

ἅπας, -ασα, -αν   all (34, a-2a)

ἀπειθέω   I disobey (14, v-1d[2a]) (ἠπείθουν), –, ἠπείθησα, –, –, –

ἀπέρχομαι   I depart (117, chpt 23, cv-1b[2]) ἀπελεύσομαι, ἀπῆλθον, ἀπελήλυθα, –, –

ἀπέχω   I receive in full, am distant; middle: I abstain (19, cv-1b[2]) (ἀπεῖχον), –, –, –, –, –

ἀπιστία, -ας, ἡ   unbelief (11, n-1a)

ἄπιστος, -ον   unbelieving (23, a-3a)

ἀπό   gen: (away) from (646, chpt 8, preposition)

ἀποδίδωμι   I pay, recompense; middle: I sell (48, cv-6a) (ἀπεδίδουν), ἀποδώσω, ἀπέδωκα, –, –, ἀπεδόθην

ἀποθνήσκω   I die, am about to die, am freed from (111, chpt 22, cv-5a) (ἀπέθνησκον), ἀποθανοῦμαι, ἀπέθανον, –, –, –

ἀποκαλύπτω   I reveal (26, cv-4) ἀποκαλύψω, ἀπεκάλυψα, –, –, ἀπεκαλύφθην

ἀποκάλυψις, -εως, ἡ   revelation (18, n-3e[5b])

ἀποκρίνομαι   I answer (231, chpt 18, cv-2d[6]) –, ἀπεκρινάμην, –, –, ἀπεκρίθην

ἀποκτείνω   I kill (74, chpt 20, cv-2d[5]) ἀποκτενῶ, ἀπέκτεινα, –, –, ἀπεκτάνθην

ἀπολαμβάνω   I receive (10, cv-3a[2b]) ἀπολήμψομαι, ἀπέλαβον, –, –, –

ἀπόλλυμι   I destroy, kill; middle: I perish, die (90, chpt 33, cv-3c[2]) (ἀπώλλυον), ἀπολέσω or ἀπολῶ, ἀπώλεσα, ἀπόλωλα, –, –

Ἀπολλῶς, -ῶ, ὁ   Apollos (10, n-2e)

ἀπολογέομαι   I defend myself (10, cv-1d[2a]) (ἀπελογούμην), ἀπολογήσω, ἀπελογησάμην, –, –, ἀπελογήθην

ἀπολύτρωσις, -εως, ἡ   redemption (10, n-3e[5b])

ἀπολύω   I release (66, chpt 33, cv-1a[4])
(ἀπέλυον), ἀπολύσω, ἀπέλυσα, –, ἀπολέλυμαι,
ἀπελύθην

ἀποστέλλω   I send (away) (132, chpt 20, cv-2d[1])
ἀποστελῶ, ἀπέστειλα, ἀπέσταλκα, ἀπέσταλμαι,
ἀπεστάλην

ἀπόστολος, -ου, ὁ   apostle, envoy,
messenger (80, chpt 4, n-2a)

ἅπτω   I kindle; middle: I touch, take hold of (39,
v-4) –, ἧψα, –, –, –

ἀπώλεια, -ας, ἡ   destruction (18, n-1a)

ἄρα   then, therefore (49, particle)

ἀργύριον, -ου, τό   silver, money (20, n-2c)

ἀρέσκω   I please (17, v-5a)
(ἤρεσκον), –, ἤρεσα, –, –, –

ἀριθμός, -οῦ, ὁ   number (18, n-2a)

ἀρνέομαι   I deny (33, v-1d[2a]) (ἠρνούμην),
ἀρνήσομαι, ἠρνησάμην, –, ἤρνημαι, –

ἀρνίον, -ου, τό   sheep, lamb (30, n-2c)

ἁρπάζω   I seize, snatch (14, v-2a[2])
ἁρπάσω, ἥρπασα, –, –, ἡρπάσθην or ἡρπάγην

ἄρτι   now (36, adverb)

ἄρτος, -ου, ὁ   bread, loaf, food (97, chpt 22,
n-2a)

ἀρχαῖος, -αία, -αῖον   ancient, old (11, a-1a[1])

ἀρχή, -ῆς, ἡ   beginning, ruler (55, chpt 7, n-1b)

ἀρχιερεύς, -έως, ὁ   chief priest, high priest (122,
chpt 27, n-3e[3])

ἄρχομαι   I begin (86, chpt 23, v-1b[2])
ἄρξομαι, ἠρξάμην, –, –, –

ἄρχων, -οντος, ὁ   ruler, official (37, n-3c[5b])

ἀσέλγεια, -ας, ἡ   licentiousness, debauchery,
sensuality (10, n-1a)

ἀσθένεια, -ας, ἡ   weakness, sickness (24, n-1a)

ἀσθενέω   I am sick, am weak (33, v-1d[2a])
(ἠσθενοῦν), –, ἠσθένησα, ἠσθένηκα, –, –

ἀσθενής, -ές   weak, sick (26, a-4a)

Ἀσία, -ας, ἡ   Asia (18, n-1a)

ἀσκός, -οῦ, ὁ   leather bottle, wineskin (12, n-2a)

ἀσπάζομαι   I greet, salute (59, chpt 28, v-2a[1])
(ἠσπαζόμην), –, ἠσπασάμην, –, –, –

ἀσπασμός, -οῦ, ὁ   greeting (10, n-2a)

ἀστήρ, -έρος, ὁ   star (24, n-3f[2b])

ἀτενίζω   I look intently at, stare at (14, v-2a[1])
–, ἠτένισα, –, –, –

αὐλή, -ῆς, ἡ   courtyard (12, n-1b)

αὐξάνω   I grow, increase (21, v-3a[1])
(ηὔξανον), αὐξήσω, ηὔξησα, –, –, ηὐξήθην

αὔριον   next day (14, adverb)

αὐτός, -ή, -ό   he, she, it; him/her/itself;
same (5,597, chpt 6, a-1a[2b])

ἀφαιρέω   I take away, cut off (10, cv-1d[2a])
ἀφελῶ, ἀφεῖλον, –, –, ἀφαιρεθήσομαι

ἄφεσις, -εως, ἡ   forgiveness, pardon (17,
n-3e[5b])

ἀφίημι   I let go, leave, permit; forgive (143, chpt
36, cv-6a) (ἤφιον), ἀφήσω, ἀφῆκα, –, ἀφέωμαι,
ἀφέθην

ἀφίστημι   I go away, withdraw (14, cv-6a)
(ἀφιστόμην), ἀποστήσομαι, ἀπέστησα, –, –, –

ἀφορίζω   I separate, set apart (10, cv-2a[1])
(ἀφώριζον), ἀφοριῶ or ἀφορίσω, ἀφώρισα, –,
ἀφώρισμαι, ἀπωρίσθην

ἄφρων, -ον   foolish, ignorant (11, a-4b[1])

Ἀχαΐα, -ας, ἡ   Achaia (10, n-1a)

ἄχρι, ἄχρις   gen: until, as far as; conj: until (49,
preposition)

βῆτα

Βαβυλών, -ῶνος, ἡ   Babylon (12, n-3f[1a])

βάλλω   I throw (122, chpt 22, v-2d[1]) (ἔβαλλον),
βαλῶ, ἔβαλον, βέβληκα, βέβλημαι, ἐβλήθην

βαπτίζω   I baptize (77, chpt 20, v-2a[1])
(ἐβάπτιζον), βαπτίσω, ἐβάπτισα, –, βεβάπτισμαι,
ἐβαπτίσθην

βάπτισμα, -ατος, τό   baptism (19, n-3c[4])

βαπτιστής, -οῦ, ὁ   Baptist, Baptizer (12, n-1f)

Βαραββᾶς, -ᾶ, ὁ   Barabbas (11, n-1e)

Βαρναβᾶς, -ᾶ, ὁ   Barnabas (28, n-1e)

βασανίζω   I torment (12, v-2a[1]) (ἐβασάνιζον), –,
ἐβασάνισα, –, –, βασανισθήσομαι

βασιλεία, -ας, ἡ   kingdom (162, chpt 6, n-1a)

βασιλεύς, -έως, ὁ   king (115, chpt 19, n-3e[3])

βασιλεύω   I reign, rule (21, v-1a[6])
βασιλεύσω, ἐβασίλευσα, –, –, –

βαστάζω   I bear, carry (27, v-2a[1])
(ἐβάσταζον), βαστάσω, ἐβάστασα, –, –, –

Βηθανία, -ας, ἡ   Bethany (12, n-1a)

βῆμα, -ατος, τό   tribunal, judgment seat (12,
n-3c[4])

βιβλίον, -ου, τό   scroll, book (34, n-2c)

βίβλος, -ου, ἡ   book (10, n-2b)

βίος, -ου, ὁ   life (10, n-2a)

βλασφημέω   I blaspheme, revile (34, v-1d[2a])
(ἐβλασφήμουν), –, ἐβλασφήμησα, –, –,
βλασφημηθήσομαι

βλασφημία, -ας, ἡ   blasphemy, slander (18, n-1a)

βλέπω   I see, look at (132, chpt 16, v-1b[1])
(ἔβλεπον), βλέψω, ἔβλεψα, –, –, –

βοάω   I cry out, shout (12, v-1d[1a])
–, ἐβόησα, –, –, –

βουλή, -ῆς, ἡ   plan, purpose (12, n-1b)

βούλομαι   I intend, plan (37, v-1d[2c])
(ἐβουλόμην), –, –, –, –, ἐβουλήθην

βροντή, -ῆς, ἡ   thunder (12, n-1b)

βρῶμα, -ατος, τό   food (17, n-3c[4])

βρῶσις, -εως, ἡ   eating, consuming (11, n-3e[5b])

γάμμα

Γαλιλαία, -ας, ἡ   Galilee (61, chpt 4, n-1a)

Γαλιλαῖος, -α, -ον   Galilean (11, a-1a[1])

γαμέω   I marry (28, v-1d[2a]) (ἐγάμουν), –, ἔγημα
or ἐγάμησα, γεγάμηκα, –, ἐγαμήθην

γάμος, -ου, ὁ   wedding (16, n-2a)

γάρ   for, then (1,041, chpt 7, conjunction)

γε   indeed, at least, even (26, particle)

γέεννα, -ης, ἡ   Gehenna, hell (12, n-1c)

γέμω   I am full (11, v-1c[2])

γενεά, -ᾶς, ἡ   generation (43, n-1a)

γεννάω   I beget, give birth to, produce (97, chpt
19, v-1d[1a]) γεννήσω, ἐγέννησα, γεγέννηκα,
γεγέννημαι, ἐγεννήθην

γένος, -ους, τό   race, people, descendant,
kind (20, n-3d[2b])

γεύομαι   I taste (15, v-1a[6])
γεύσομαι, ἐγευσάμην, –, –, –

γεωργός, -οῦ, ὁ   farmer (19, n-2a)

γῆ, γῆς, ἡ   earth, land, region, humanity (250,
chpt 22, n-1h)

γίνομαι   I become, am, exist, happen, take place,
am born, created (669, chpt 22, v-1c[2])
(ἐγινόμην), γενήσομαι, ἐγενόμην, γέγονα,
γεγένημαι, ἐγενήθην

γινώσκω   I know, come to know, realize,
learn (222, chpt 20, v-5a) (ἐγίνωσκον),
γνώσομαι, ἔγνων, ἔγνωκα, ἔγνωσμαι, ἐγνώσθην

γλῶσσα, -ης, ἡ   tongue, language (50, chpt 20,
n-1c)

γνωρίζω   I make known (25, v-2a[1])
γνωρίσω, ἐγνώρισα, –, –, ἐγνωρίσθην

γνῶσις, -εως, ἡ   knowledge (29, n-3e[5b])

γνωστός, -ή, -όν   known; noun:
acquaintance (15, a-1a[2a])

γονεύς, -έως, ὁ   parent (20, n-3e[3])

γόνυ, -ατος, τό   knee (12, n-3c[6d])

γράμμα, -ατος, τό   letter, document (14, n-3c[4])

γραμματεύς, -έως, ὁ   scribe (63, chpt 28, n-3e[3])

γραφή, -ῆς, ἡ   writing, Scripture (50, chpt 4,
n-1b)

γράφω   I write (191, chpt 23, v-1b[1])
(ἔγραφον), γράψω, ἔγραψα, γέγραφα, γέγραμμαι
or γέγραμμαι, ἐγράφην

γρηγορέω   I am alert, I am watchful (22, v-1d[2a])
–, ἐγρηγόρησα, –, –, –

γυμνός, -ή, -όν   naked (15, a-1a[2a])

γυνή, γυναικός, ἡ   woman, wife (215, chpt 13,
n-3b[1])

δέλτα

δαιμονίζομαι   I am demon possessed (13, v-2a[1])
–, –, –, –, ἐδαιμονίσθην

δαιμόνιον, -ου, τό   demon (63, chpt 17, n-2c)

δάκρυον, -ου, τό   tear; plural: weeping (10, n-2c)

Δαμασκός, -οῦ, ὁ   Damascus (15, n-2b)

Δαυίδ, ὁ   David (59, chpt 4, n-3g[2])

δέ (δ᾽)   but, and (2,792, chpt 6, particle)

δέησις, -εως, ἡ   prayer, entreaty (18, n-3e[5b])

δεῖ   it is necessary (101, chpt 18, v-1d[2c])

δείκνυμι   I show, explain (30, chapt 36, v-3c[2])
δείξω, ἔδειξα, δέδειχα, –, ἐδείχθην

δεῖπνον, -ου, τό   dinner (16, n-2c)

δέκα   ten (25, n-3g[2])

δένδρον, -ου, τό   tree (25, n-2c)

δεξιός, -ά, -όν   right (54, chpt 27, a-1a[1])

δέομαι   I ask, request (22, v-1d[2c])
(ἐδούμην), –, –, –, –, ἐδεήθην

δέρω   I beat, whip (15, v-1c[1])
–, ἔδειρα, –, –, δαρήσομαι

δέσμιος, -ου, ὁ   prisoner (16, n-2a)

δεσμός, -οῦ, ὁ   bond, fetter (18, n-2a)

δεσπότης, -ου, ὁ   master, lord (10, n-1f)

δεῦτε   Come! (12, adverb)

δεύτερος, -α, -ον   second (43, a-1a[1])

δέχομαι   I take, receive (56, chpt 29, v-1b[2])
δέξομαι, ἐδεξάμην, –, δέδεγμαι, ἐδέχθην

δέω   I bind (43, v-1d[2b])
–, ἔδησα, δέδεκα, δέδεμαι, ἐδέθην

δηνάριον, -ου, τό   denarius (16, n-2c)

διά   (gen: through; acc: on account of (667, chpt 8, preposition)

διάβολος, -ον   slanderous; noun: the devil (37, a-3a)

διαθήκη, -ης, ἡ   covenant (33, n-1b)

διακονέω   I serve (37, v-1d[2a]) (διηκόνουν), διακονήσω, διηκόνησα, –, –, διηκονήθην

διακονία, -ας, ἡ   service (34, n-1a)

διάκονος, -ου, ὁ, ἡ   assistant, servant, deacon (29, n-2a)

διακρίνω   I judge, differentiate; middle: I doubt, waver (19, cv-1c[2])
(διεκρινόμην), –, διεκρίνα, –, –, διεκρίθην

διαλέγομαι   I discuss, argue (13, cv-1b[2])
(διελεγόμην), –, διελεξάμην, –, –, διελέχθην

διαλογίζομαι   I consider, argue (16, cv-2a[1])
(διελογιζόμην), –, –, –, –, –

διαλογισμός, -οῦ, ὁ   reasoning, dispute (14, n-2a)

διαμαρτύρομαι   I testify, solemnly urge (15, cv-1c[1]) –, διεμαρτυράμην, –, –, –

διαμερίζω   I divide, distribute (11, cv-2a[1])
(διεμέριζον), –, διεμερισάμην, –, διαμεμέρισμαι, διεμερίσθην

διάνοια, -ας, ἡ   the mind, understanding (12, n-1a)

διατάσσω   I order, command (16, cv-2b)
διατάξομαι, διέταξα, διατέταχα, διατέταγμαι, διετάχθην

διαφέρω   I am worth more, I differ (13, cv-1c[1])
(διεφερόμην), –, διήνεγκα, –, –, –

διδασκαλία, -ας, ἡ   teaching (21, n-1a)

διδάσκαλος, -ου, ὁ   teacher (59, chpt 12, n-2a)

διδάσκω   I teach (97, chpt 21, v-5a)
(ἐδίδασκον), διδάξω, ἐδίδαξα, –, –, ἐδιδάχθην

διδαχή, -ῆς, ἡ   teaching (30, n-1b)

δίδωμι   I give (out), entrust, give back, put (415, chpt 34, v-6a) (ἐδίδουν), δώσω, ἔδωκα, δέδωκα, δέδομαι, ἐδόθην

διέρχομαι   I go through (43, cv-1b[2])
(διηρχόμην), διελεύσομαι, διῆλθον, διελήλυθα, –, –

δίκαιος, -αία, -αιον   right, just, righteous (79, chpt 32, a-1a[1])

δικαιοσύνη, -ης, ἡ   righteousness (92, chpt 13, n-1b)

δικαιόω   I justify, vindicate (39, v-1d[3])
δικαιώσω, ἐδικαίωσα, –, δεδικαίωμαι, ἐδικαιώθην

δικαίωμα, -ατος, τό   regulation, requirement, righteous deed (10, n-3c[4])

δίκτυον, -ου, τό   fishnet (12, n-2c)

διό   therefore, for this reason (53, chpt 23, conjunction)

διότι   for, because (23, conjunction)

διψάω   I am thirsty, I thirst (16, v-1d[1a])
διψήσω, ἐδίψησα, –, –, –

διωγμός, -οῦ, ὁ   persecution (10, n-2a)

διώκω   I persecute, pursue (45, v-1b[2])
(ἐδίωκον), διώξω, ἐδίωξα, –, δεδίωγμαι, διωχθήσομαι

δοκέω   I think, seem (62, chpt 29, v-1b[4])
(ἐδόκουν), –, ἔδοξα, –, –, –

δοκιμάζω   I test, approve (22, v-2a[1])
δοκιμάσω, ἐδοκίμασα, –, δεδοκίμασμαι, –

δόλος, -ου, ὁ   deceit, treachery (11, n-2a)

δόξα, -ης, ἡ   glory, majesty, fame (166, chpt 4, n-1c)

δοξάζω   I glorify, praise, honor (61, chpt 23, v-2a[1]) (ἐδόξαζον), δοξάσω, ἐδόξασα, –, δεδόξασμαι, ἐδοξάσθην

δουλεύω   I serve, obey, I am a slave (25, v-1a[6])
δουλεύσω, ἐδούλευσα, δεδούλευκα, –, –

δοῦλος, -ου, ὁ   slave, servant (126, chpt 9, a-1a[2a])

δράκων, -οντος, ὁ   dragon, serpent (13, n-3c[5b])

δύναμαι   I am powerful, am able (210, chpt 18, v-6b) (ἐδυνάμην or ἠδυνάμην), δυνήσομαι, –, –, –, ἠδυνήθην

δύναμις, -εως, ἡ   power, miracle (119, chpt 23, n-3e[5b])

δυνατός, -ή, -όν   able, capable, possible (32, a-1a[2a])

δύο   two (135, chpt 27, a-5)

δώδεκα   twelve (75, chpt 13, n-3g[2])

δωρεά, -ᾶς, ἡ   gift (11, n-1a)

δῶρον, -ου, τό   gift (19, n-2c)

ἐ ψιλόν

ἐάν if, when (334, chpt 9, conjunction)

ἑαυτοῦ, -ῆς, -οῦ singular: of himself/herself/itself; plural: of themselves (319, chpt 13, a-1a[2b])

ἐάω I permit, let go (11, v-1d[1b]) (εἴων), ἐάσω, εἴασα, –, –, –

ἐγγίζω I come near, approach (42, v-2a[1]) (ἤγγιζον), ἐγγιῶ, ἤγγισα, ἤγγικα, –, –

ἐγγύς near (31, adverb)

ἐγείρω I raise up, wake (144, chpt 20, v-2d[3]) ἐγερῶ, ἤγειρα, –, ἐγήγερμαι, ἠγέρθην

ἐγκαταλείπω I forsake, abandon (10, cv-1b[1]) ἐγκαταλείψω, ἐγκατέλιπον, –, –, ἐγκατελείφθην

ἐγώ I (1,718, chpt 4, a-5)

ἔθνος, -ους, τό nation; plural: Gentiles (162, chpt 34, n-3d[2b])

ἔθος, -ους, τό custom, habit (12, n-3d[2b])

εἰ if (502, chpt 10, particle)

εἴδωλον, -ου, τό image, idol (11, n-2c)

εἴκοσι twenty (11, n-3g[2])

εἰκών, -όνος, ἡ image, likeness (23, n-3f[1b])

εἰμί I am, exist, live, am present (2,462, chpt 8, v-6b) (ἤμην), ἔσομαι, –, –, –, –

εἶπεν he/she/it said (third person singular of λέγω; 613, chpt 7)

εἰρήνη, -ης, ἡ peace (92, chpt 14, n-1b)

εἰς acc: into, in, among (1,767, chpt 7, preposition)

εἷς, μία, ἕν one (345, chpt 10, a-4b[2])

εἰσάγω I lead in, bring in (11, cv-1b[2]) –, εἰσήγαγον, –, –, –

εἰσέρχομαι I come in(to), go in(to), enter (194, chpt 22, cv-1b[2]) εἰσελεύσομαι, εἰσῆλθον, εἰσελήλυθα, –, –

εἰσπορεύομαι I enter, go into (18, cv-1a[6]) (εἰσεπορευόμην), –, –, –, –, –

εἶτα then (15, adverb)

εἴτε if, whether (65, chpt 33, particle)

ἐκ (ἐξ) gen: from, out of (914, chpt 8, preposition)

ἕκαστος, -η, -ον each, every (82, chpt 24, a-1a[2a])

ἑκατόν one hundred (17, a-5b)

ἑκατοντάρχης, -ου, ὁ centurion (20, n-1f)

ἐκβάλλω I cast out, send out (81, chpt 20, cv-2d[1]) (ἐξέβαλλον), ἐκβαλῶ, ἐξέβαλον, –, –, ἐξεβλήθην

ἐκεῖ there, in that place (105, chpt 20, adverb)

ἐκεῖθεν from there (37, adverb)

ἐκεῖνος, -η, -ο singular: that (man/woman/thing); plural: those (men/women/things) (265, chpt 13, a-1a[2b])

ἐκκλησία, -ας, ἡ a church, (the) Church, assembly, congregation (114, chpt 11, n-1a)

ἐκκόπτω I cut off, cut down (10, cv-4) ἐκκόψω, –, –, –, ἐξεκόπην

ἐκλέγομαι I choose, select (22, cv-1b[2]) (ἐξελεγόμην), –, ἐξελεξάμην, –, ἐκλέλεγμαι, –

ἐκλεκτός, -ή, -όν chosen, elect (22, a-1a[2a])

ἐκπίπτω I fall, run aground (10, cv-1b[3]) –, ἐξέπεσα, ἐκπέπτωκα, –, –

ἐκπλήσσω I am amazed (13, cv-2b) (ἐξεπλησσόμην), –, –, –, –, ἐξεπλάγην

ἐκπορεύομαι I go out, come out (33, cv-1a[6]) (ἐξεπορευόμην), ἐκπορεύσομαι, –, –, –, –

ἐκτείνω I stretch forth (16, cv-2d[5]) ἐκτενῶ, ἐξέτεινα, –, –, –

ἕκτος, -η, -ον sixth (14, a-1a[2a])

ἐκχέω I pour out (16, cv-1a[7]) ἐκχεῶ, ἐξέχεα, –, –, –

ἐκχύννω I pour out (11, cv-3a[1]) (ἐξεχυννόμην), –, –, ἐκκέχυμαι, ἐξεχύθην

ἐλαία, -ας, ἡ olive tree (15, n-1a)

ἔλαιον, -ου, τό olive oil (11, n-2c)

ἐλάχιστος, -η, -ον least, smallest (14, a-1a[2a])

ἐλέγχω I convict, reprove, expose (17, v-1b[2]) ἐλέγξω, ἤλεγξα, –, –, ἠλέγχθην

ἐλεέω I have mercy (28, v-1d[2a]) ἐλεήσω, ἠλέησα, –, ἠλέημαι, ἠλεήθην

ἐλεημοσύνη, -ης, ἡ alms (13, n-1b)

ἔλεος, -ους, τό mercy, compassion (27, n-3d[2b])

ἐλευθερία, -ας, ἡ freedom, liberty (11, n-1a)

ἐλεύθερος, -α, -ον free (23, a-1a[1])

Ἕλλην, -ηνος, ὁ Greek (25, n-3f[1a])

ἐλπίζω I hope (31, v-2a[1]) (ἤλπιζον), ἐλπιῶ, ἤλπισα, ἤλπικα, –, –

ἐλπίς, -ίδος, ἡ hope, expectation (53, chpt 11, n-3c[2])

ἐμαυτοῦ, -ῆς of myself (37, a-1a[2a])

ἐμβαίνω I embark (16, cv-2d[7]) –, ἐνέβην, –, –, –

ἐμβλέπω   I look at, gaze upon (12, cv-1b[1])
(ἐνέβλεπον), –, ἐνέβλεψα, –, –, –

ἐμός, ἐμή, ἐμόν   my, mine (76, chpt 9, a-1a[2a])

ἐμπαίζω   I mock, ridicule (13, cv-2a[2])
(ἐνέπαιζον), ἐμπαίξω, ἐνέπαιξα, –, –, ἐνεπαίχθην

ἔμπροσθεν   gen: in front of, before (48, preposition; adverb)

ἐμφανίζω   I make known, make visible, bring charges (10, cv-2a[1])
ἐμφανίσω, ἐνεφάνισα, –, –, ἐνεφανίσθην

ἐν   dat: in, on, among (2,752, chpt 6, preposition)

ἔνατος, -η, -ον   ninth (10, a-1a[2a])

ἐνδείκνυμι   I show, demonstrate (11, cv-3c[2])
–, ἐνεδειξάμην, –, –, –

ἐνδύω   I put on, clothe (27, v-1a[4])
–, ἐνέδυσα, –, ἐνδέδυμαι, –

ἕνεκα or ἕνεκεν   gen: because of, on account of (19, preposition)

ἐνεργέω   I work, effect (21, cv-1d[2a])
(ἐνηργούμην), –, ἐνήργησα, –, –, –

ἐνιαυτός, -οῦ, ὁ   year (14, n-2a)

ἔνοχος, -ον   liable, guilty (10, a-3a)

ἐντέλλω   I command (15, cv-2d[1])
ἐντελοῦμαι, ἐνετειλάμην, –, ἐντέταλμαι, –

ἐντεῦθεν   from here (10, adverb)

ἐντολή, -ῆς, ἡ   commandment (67, chpt 9, n-1b)

ἐνώπιον   gen: before (94, chpt 14, preposition)

ἕξ   six (13, n-3g[2])

ἐξάγω   I lead out (12, cv-1b[2])
–, ἐξήγαγον, –, –, –

ἐξαποστέλλω   I send out (13, cv-2d[1])
ἐξαποστελῶ, ἐξαπέστειλα, –, –, ἐξαπεστάλην

ἐξέρχομαι   I go out (218, chpt 22, cv-1b[2])
(ἐξηρχόμην), ἐξελεύσομαι, ἐξῆλθον, ἐξελήλυθα, –, –

ἔξεστιν   it is lawful, it is right (31, cv-6b)

ἐξίστημι   I am amazed, I amaze (17, cv-6a)
(ἐξιστάμην), –, ἐξέστησα, ἐξέστακα, –, –

ἐξομολογέω   I confess, profess, praise (10, cv-1d[2a]) ἐξομολογήσομαι, ἐξωμολόγησα, –, –, –

ἐξουθενέω   I despise, disdain (11, v-1d[2a])
–, ἐξουθένησα, –, ἐξουθένημαι, ἐξουθενήθην

ἐξουσία, -ας, ἡ   authority, power (102, chpt 7, n-1a)

ἔξω   adverb: without; prep (gen): outside (63, chpt 11, adverb)

ἔξωθεν   gen: outside, from outside (13, adverb)

ἑορτή, -ῆς, ἡ   festival (25, n-1b)

ἐπαγγελία, -ας, ἡ   promise (52, chpt 14, n-1a)

ἐπαγγέλλομαι   I promise (15, cv-2d[1])
–, ἐπηγγειλάμην, –, ἐπήγγελμαι, –

ἔπαινος, -ου, ὁ   praise (11, n-2a)

ἐπαίρω   I lift up (19, cv-2d[2])
–, ἐπῆρα, –, –, ἐπήρθην

ἐπαισχύνομαι   I am ashamed (11, cv-1c[2])
–, –, –, –, ἐπαισχύνθην

ἐπάνω   above (19, adverb)
prep (gen): over

ἐπαύριον   on the next day (17, adverb)

ἐπεί   because, since (26, conjunction)

ἐπειδή   since, because (10, conjunction)

ἔπειτα   then (16, adverb)

ἐπερωτάω   I ask (for), question, demand of (56, chpt 21, cv-1d[1a]) (ἐπηρώτων), ἐπερωτήσω, ἐπηρώτησα, –, –, ἐπηρωτήθην

ἐπί (ἐπ’, ἐφ’)   gen: on, over, when; dat: on the basis of, at; acc: on, to, against (890, chpt 11, preposition)

ἐπιβάλλω   I lay upon (18, cv-2d[1])
(ἐπέβαλλον), ἐπιβαλῶ, ἐπέβαλον, –, –, –

ἐπιγινώσκω   I know (44, cv-5a)
(ἐπεγίνωσκον), ἐπιγινώσομαι, ἐπέγνων, ἐπέγνωκα, –, ἐπεγνώσθην

ἐπίγνωσις, -εως, ἡ   knowledge (20, n-3e[5b])

ἐπιζητέω   I wish for, want, seek after (13, cv-1d[2a]) (ἐπεζήτουν), –, ἐπεζήτησα, –, –, –

ἐπιθυμέω   I desire, long for (16, cv-1d[2a])
(ἐπεθύμουν), ἐπιθυμήσω, ἐπεθύμησα, –, –, –

ἐπιθυμία, -ας, ἡ   lust, desire (38, n-1a)

ἐπικαλέω   I name; middle: I call upon, appeal to (30, cv-1d[2b])
–, ἐπεκάλεσα, –, ἐπικέκλημαι, ἐπεκλήθην

ἐπιλαμβάνομαι   I take hold of (19, cv-3a[2b])
–, ἐπελαβόμην, –, –, –

ἐπιμένω   I remain, persist (16, cv-1c[2])
(ἐπέμενον), ἐπιμενῶ, ἐπέμεινα, –, –, –

ἐπιπίπτω   I fall upon (11, cv-1b[3])
–, ἐπέπεσον, ἐπιπέπτωκα, –, –

ἐπισκέπτομαι   I visit, look after (11, cv-4)
ἐπισκέψομαι, ἐπεσκεψάμην, –, –, –

ἐπίσταμαι   I understand (14, cv-6b)

ἐπιστολή, -ῆς, ἡ   letter, epistle (24, n-1b)

ἐπιστρέφω   I turn, return (36, cv-1b[1])
ἐπιστρέψω, ἐπέστρεψα, –, –, ἐπεστράφην

ἐπιτάσσω   I command, order (10, cv-2b)
    –, ἐπέταξα, –, –, –

ἐπιτελέω   I finish, complete (10, cv-1d[2])
    ἐπιτελέσω, ἐπετέλεσα, –, –, –

ἐπιτίθημι   I lay upon (39, cv-6a)
    (ἐπετίθουν), ἐπιθήσω, ἐπέθηκα, –, –, –

ἐπιτιμάω   I rebuke, warn (29, cv-1d[1a])
    (ἐπετίμων), –, ἐπετίμησα, –, –, –

ἐπιτρέπω   I permit, allow (18, cv-1b[1])
    –, ἐπέτρεψα, –, –, ἐπετράπην

ἐπουράνιος, -ον   heavenly; noun: heaven (19, a-3a)

ἑπτά   seven (88, chpt 14, n-3g[2])

ἐργάζομαι   I work, do (41, v-2a[1])
    (ἠργαζόμην), –, ἠργασάμην, –, εἴργασμαι, –

ἐργάτης, -ου, ὁ   worker (16, n-1f)

ἔργον, -ου, τό   work, deed, action (169, chpt 6, n-2c)

ἔρημος, -ον   adjective: deserted, desolate (a-3a); noun: desert, wilderness (n-2b) (48)

ἔρχομαι   I come, go (632, chpt 18, v-1b[2])
    (ἠρχόμην), ἐλεύσομαι, ἦλθον or ἦλθα, ἐλήλυθα, –, –

ἐρωτάω   I ask (for), request, entreat (63, chpt 21, v-1d[1a]) (ἠρώτων), ἐρωτήσω, ἠρώτησα, –, –, ἠρωτήθην

ἐσθίω   I eat (158, chpt 29, v-1b[3])
    (ἤσθιον), φάγομαι, ἔφαγον, –, –, –

ἔσχατος, -η, -ον   last (52, chpt 4, a-1a[2a])

ἔσωθεν   from within, within (12, adverb)

ἕτερος, -α, -ον   other, another, different (98, chpt 27, a-1a[1])

ἔτι   still, yet, even (93, chpt 22, adverb)

ἑτοιμάζω   I prepare (40, v-2a[1])
    –, ἡτοίμασα, ἡτοίμακα, ἡτοίμασμαι, ἡτοιμάσθην

ἕτοιμος, -η, -ον   ready (17, a-3b[2])

ἔτος, -ους, τό   year (49, n-3d[2b])

εὐαγγελίζω   I bring good news, preach (54, chpt 27, v-2a[1]) (εὐηγγέλιζον), –, εὐηγγέλισα, –, εὐηγγέλισμαι, εὐηγγελίσθην

εὐαγγέλιον, -ου, τό   good news, Gospel (76, chpt 7, n-2c)

εὐδοκέω   I am well pleased (21, v-1d[2a])
    –, εὐδόκησα, –, –, –

εὐθέως   immediately (36, adverb)

εὐθύς   immediately (59, chpt 12, adverb)

εὐλογέω   I bless (41, v-1d[2a]) εὐλογήσω, εὐλόγησα, εὐλόγηκα, εὐλόγημαι, –

εὐλογία, -ας, ἡ   blessing (16, n-1a)

εὑρίσκω   I find (176, chpt 22, v-5b) (εὕρισκον or ηὕρισκον), εὑρήσω, εὗρον, εὕρηκα, –, εὑρέθην

εὐσέβεια, -ας, ἡ   piety, godliness (15, n-1a)

εὐφραίνω   I rejoice (14, v-2d[4])
    (εὐφραινόμην), –, –, –, –, ηὐφράνθην

εὐχαριστέω   I give thanks (38, v-1d[2a]) –, εὐχαρίστησα or ηὐχαρίστησα, –, –, εὐχαριστήθην

εὐχαριστία, -ας, ἡ   thanksgiving (15, n-1a)

Ἔφεσος, -ου, ἡ   Ephesus (16, n-2b)

ἐφίστημι   I stand at, stand near (21, cv-6a)
    –, ἐπέστην, ἐφέστηκα, –, –

ἐχθρός, -ά, -όν   hostile; noun: enemy (32, a-1a[1])

ἔχω   I have, hold (708, chpt 16, v-1b[2])
    (εἶχον), ἕξω, ἔσχον, ἔσχηκα, –, –

ἕως   until; prep (gen): as far as (146, chpt 12, conjunction, preposition)

ζῆτα

Ζαχαρίας, -ου ὁ   Zechariah (11, n-1d)

ζάω   I live (140, chpt 19, v-1d[1a])
    (ἔζων), ζήσω, ἔζησα, –, –, –

Ζεβεδαῖος, -ου, ὁ   Zebedee (12, n-2a)

ζῆλος, -ου, ὁ   zeal, jealousy (16, n-2a)

ζηλόω   I strive, desire, envy (11, v-1d[3])
    –, ἐζήλωσα, –, –, –

ζητέω   I seek, desire, try to obtain (117, chpt 17, v-1d[2a])
    (ἐζήτουν), ζητήσω, ἐζήτησα, –, –, ἐζητήθην

ζύμη, -ης, ἡ   leaven (13, n-1b)

ζωή, -ῆς, ἡ   life (135, chpt 4, n-1b)

ζῷον, -ου, τό   living thing (23, n-2c)

ζωοποιέω   I make alive (11, cv-1d[2a])
    ζωοποιήσω, ζωοποίησα, –, –, ζωοποιήθην

ἦτα

ἤ   or, than (343, chpt 13, particle)

ἡγεμών, -όνος, ὁ   governor (20, n-3f[1b])

ἡγέομαι   I consider, think, lead (28, v-1d[2a])
    –, ἡγησάμην, –, ἥγημαι, –

ἤδη   now, already (61, chpt 10, adverb)

ἥκω   I have come (26, v-1b[2])
    ἥξω, ἧξα, ἧκα, –, –

Ἠλίας, -ου, ὁ   Elijah (29, n-1d)

ἥλιος, -ου, ὁ sun (32, n-2a)

ἡμεῖς we (864, chpt 11, a-5a)

ἡμέρα, -ας, ἡ day (389, chpt 8, n-1a)

Ἡρῴδης, -ου, ὁ Herod (43, n-1f)

Ἡσαΐας, -ου ὁ Isaiah (22, n-1d)

θῆτα

θάλασσα, -ης, ἡ sea, lake (91, chpt 8, n-1c)

θάνατος, -ου, ὁ death (120, chpt 8, n-2a)

θανατόω I put to death (11, v-1d[3])
θανατώσω, ἐθανάτωσα, –, –, ἐθανατώθην

θάπτω I bury (11, v-4) –, ἔθαψα, –, –, ἐτάφην

θαυμάζω I marvel, wonder at (43, v-2a[1])
(ἐθαύμαζον), –, ἐθαύμασα, –, –, ἐθαυμάσθην

θεάομαι I behold (22, v-1d[1b])
–, ἐθεασάμην, –, τεθέαμαι, ἐθεάθην

θέλημα, -ατος, τό will, desire (62, chpt 11, n-3c[4])

θέλω I will, wish, desire, enjoy (208, chpt 21, v-1d[2c]) (ἤθελον), –, ἠθέλησα, –, –, –

θεμέλιος, -ου, ὁ foundation (15, n-2a)

θεός, -οῦ, ὁ God, god (1,317, chpt 4, n-2a)

θεραπεύω I heal (43, v-1a[6])
(ἐθεράπευον), θεραπεύσω, ἐθεράπευσα, –, τεθεράπευμαι, ἐθεραπεύθην

θερίζω I reap (21, v-2a[1])
θερίσω, ἐθέρισα, –, –, ἐθερίσθην

θερισμός, -οῦ, ὁ harvest (13, n-2a)

θεωρέω I look at, behold (58, chpt 27, v-1d[2a])
(ἐθεώρουν), θεωρήσω, ἐθεώρησα, –, –, –

θηρίον, -ου, τό animal, beast (46, n-2c)

θησαυρός. -οῦ, ὁ treasure, repository (17, n-2a)

θλίβω I oppress, afflict (10, v-1b[1])
–, –, –, τέθλιμμαι, –

θλῖψις, -εως, ἡ affliction, tribulation (45, n-3e[5b])

θρίξ, τριχός, ἡ hair (15, n-3b[3])

θρόνος, -ου, ὁ throne (62, chpt 14, n-2a)

θυγάτηρ, -τρός, ἡ daughter (28, n-3f[2c])

θυμός, -οῦ, ὁ wrath, anger (18, n-2a)

θύρα, -ας, ἡ door (39, n-1a)

θυσία, -ας, ἡ sacrifice, offering (28, n-1a)

θυσιαστήριον, -ου, τό altar (23, n-2c)

θύω I sacrifice, kill (14, v-1a[4])
(ἔθυον), –, ἔθυσα, –, τέθυμαι, ἐτύθην

Θωμᾶς, -ᾶ, ἡ Thomas (11, n-1e)

ἰῶτα

Ἰακώβ, ὁ Jacob (27, n-3g[2])

Ἰάκωβος, -ου, ὁ James (42, n-2a)

ἰάομαι I heal (26, v-1d[1b])
(ἰώμην), ἰάσομαι, ἰασάμην, –, ἴαμαι, ἰάθην

ἴδε See! Behold! (29, chpt 11; particle)

ἴδιος, -ια, -ιον one's own (e.g., people, home; 114, chpt 36, a-1a[1])

ἰδού See! Behold! (200, chpt 11, particle)

ἱερεύς, -έως, ὁ priest (31, n-3e[3])

ἱερόν, -οῦ, τό temple (72, chpt 28, n-2c)

Ἱεροσόλυμα, τά Jerusalem (62, chpt 27, n-1a)

Ἱερουσαλήμ, ἡ Jerusalem (77, chpt 14, n-3g[2])

Ἰησοῦς, -οῦ, ὁ Jesus, Joshua (917, chpt 7, n-3g[1])

ἱκανός, -ή, -όν considerable, many, able (39, a-1a[2a])

ἱμάτιον, -ου, τό garment (60, chpt 24, n-2c)

ἵνα in order that, that (663, chpt 8, conjunction)

Ἰόππη, -ης, ἡ Joppa (10, n-1b)

Ἰορδάνης, -ου, ὁ Jordon (15, n-1f)

Ἰουδαία, -ας, ἡ Judea (43, chpt 19, n-1a)

Ἰουδαῖος, -αία, -αῖον Jewish; noun: a Jew (195, chpt 19, a-1a[1])

Ἰούδας, -α, ὁ Judas, Judah (44, n-1e)

ἵππος, -ου, ὁ horse (17, n-2a)

Ἰσαάκ, ὁ Isaac (20, n-3g[2])

Ἰσραήλ, ὁ Israel (68, chpt 19, n-3g[2])

ἵστημι intransitive: I stand; transitive: I cause to stand (155, chpt 36, v-6a) (ἵστην), στήσω, ἔστησα or ἔστην, ἕστηκα, –, ἐστάθην

ἰσχυρός, -ά, -όν strong (29, a-1a[1])

ἰσχύς, -ύος, ἡ strength, power (10, n-3e[1])

ἰσχύω I have power, I am able (28, v-1a[4])
(ἴσχυον), ἰσχύσω, ἴσχυσα, –, –, –

ἰχθύς, -ύος, ὁ fish (20, n-3e[1])

Ἰωάννης, -ου, ὁ John (135, chpt 8, n-1f)

Ἰωσήφ, ὁ Joseph (35, n-3g[2])

κάππα

κἀγώ and I, but I (84, chpt 13, a-5)

καθάπερ just as (13, adverb; conjunction)

καθαρίζω I cleanse, purify (31, v-2a[1]) καθαριῶ, ἐκαθάρισα, –, κεκαθάρισμαι, ἐκαθαρίσθην

καθαρός, -ά, -όν pure, clean (27, a-1a[1])

καθεύδω I sleep (22, v-1b[3]) (ἐκάθευδον), –, –, –, –, –

κάθημαι I sit (down), live (91, chpt 27, v-6b) (ἐκαθήμην), καθήσομαι, –, –, –, –

καθίζω I sit down, seat (46, v-2a[1]) καθίσω, ἐκάθισα, κεκάθικα, –, –

καθίστημι I appoint, authorize (21, cv-6a) καταστήσω, κατέστησα, –, –, κατεστάθην

καθώς as, even as (182, chpt 9, adverb)

καί and, even, also, namely (9,018, chpt 4, conjunction)

καινός, -ή, -όν new (42, a-1a[2a])

καιρός, -οῦ, ὁ (appointed) time, season (85, chpt 6, n-2a)

Καῖσαρ, -ος, ὁ Caesar (29, n-3f[2a])

Καισάρεια, -ας, ἡ Caesarea (17, n-1a)

καίω I burn, light (12, v-2c) καύσω, ἔκαυσα, –, κέκαυμαι, ἐκαύθην

κἀκεῖ and there (10, adverb)

κἀκεῖθεν and from there, and then (10, adverb)

κἀκεῖνος and that one (22, a-1a[2b])

κακία, -ας, ἡ malice, wickedness (11, n-1a)

κακός, -ή, -όν bad, evil (50, chpt 9, a-1a[2a])

κακῶς badly (16, adverb)

κάλαμος, -ου, ὁ reed (12, n-2a)

καλέω I call, name, invite (148, chpt 17, v-1d[2b]) (ἐκάλουν), καλέσω, ἐκάλεσα, κέκληκα, κέκλημαι, ἐκλήθην

καλός, -ή, -όν beautiful, good (100, chpt 11, a-1a[2a])

καλῶς well, commendably (37, adverb)

κἄν and if, even if (17, particle)

καπνός, -οῦ, ὁ smoke (13, n-2a)

καρδία, -ας, ἡ heart (156, chpt 4, n-1a)

καρπός, -οῦ, ὁ fruit, crop, result (67, chpt 19, n-2a)

κατά gen: down from, against; acc: according to, throughout, during (473, chpt 14, preposition)

καταβαίνω I go down, come down (81, chpt 27, cv-2d[7]) (κατέβαινον), καταβήσομαι, κατέβην, καταβέβηκα, –, –

καταβολή, -ῆς, ἡ foundation (11, n-1b)

καταγγέλλω I proclaim (18, cv-2d[1]) (κατήγγελλον), –, κατήγγειλα, –, –, κατηγγέλην

καταισχύνω I put to shame, disappoint (13, cv-1c[2]) (κατησχυνόμην), –, –, –, –, κατησχύνθην

κατακαίω I burn up, consume (12, cv-2c) (κατέκαινον), κατακαύσω, κατέκαυσα, –, –, κατεκάην

κατάκειμαι I lie down, recline (12, cv-6b) (κατεκείμην), –, –, –, –, –

κατακρίνω I condemn (18, cv-2d[6]) κατακρινῶ, κατέκρινα, –, κατακέκριμαι, κατεκρίθην

καταλαμβάνω I attain, grasp (15, cv-3a[2b]) –, κατέλαβον, κατείληφα, κατείλημαι, κατελήμφθην

καταλείπω I leave behind (24, cv-1b[1]) καταλείψω, κατέλειψα or κατέλιπον, –, καταλέλειμαι, κατελείφθην

καταλύω I destroy, put an end to (17, cv-1a[4]) καταλύσω, κατέλυσα, –, –, κατελύθην

κατανοέω I consider, notice (14, cv-1d[2a]) (κατενόουν), –, κατενόησα, –, –, –

κατανταω I arrive at (13, cv-1d[1a]) καταντήσω, κατήντησα, κατήντηκα, –, –

καταργέω I abolish, nullify (27, cv-1d[2a]) καταργήσω, κατήργησα, κατήργηκα, κατήργημαι, κατηργήθην

καταρτίζω I restore, prepare (13, cv-2a[1]) καταρτίσω, κατήρτισα, –, κατήρτισμαι, –

κατασκευάζω I prepare (11, cv-2a[1]) κατασκευάσω, κατεσκεύασα, –, κατεσκεύασμαι, κατεσκευάσθην

κατεργάζομαι I accomplish, produce (22, cv-2a[1]) –, κατειργασάμην, –, κατείργασμαι, κατειργάσθην

κατέρχομαι I come down (16, cv-1b[2]) –, κατῆλθον, –, –, –

κατεσθίω I consume, devour (14, cv-1b[3]) καταφάγομαι, κατέφαγον, –, –, –

κατέχω I restrain, hold fast (17, cv-1b[2]) (κατεῖχον), –, κατέσχον, –, –, –

κατηγορέω I accuse (23, v-1d[2a]) (κατηγόρουν), κατηγορήσω, κατηγόρησα, –, –, –

κατοικέω I inhabit, dwell (44, cv-1d[2a]) –, κατῴκησα, –, –, –

καυχάομαι I boast (37, v-1d[1a]) καυχήσομαι, ἐκαυχησάμην, –, κεκαύχημαι, –

καύχημα, -ατος, τό boast (11, n-3c[4])

καύχησις, -εως, ἡ boasting (11, n-3e[5b])

Καφαρναούμ, ἡ Capernaum (16, n-3g[2])

κεῖμαι I lie, am laid (24, v-6b) (ἐκειόμην), –, –, –, –, –

κελεύω   I command, order (25, v-1a[6])
(ἐκέλευον), –, ἐκέλευσα, –, –, –

κενός, -ή, -όν   empty, vain (18, a-1a[2a])

κέρας, -ατος, τό   horn (11, n-3c[6a])

κερδαίνω   I gain (17, v-2d[7])
κερδήσω, ἐκέρδησα, –, –, κερδηθήσομαι

κεφαλή, -ῆς, ἡ   head (75, chpt 14, n-1b)

κηρύσσω   I proclaim, preach (61, chpt 23, v-2b)
(ἐκήρυσσον), –, ἐκήρυξα, –, –, ἐκηρύχθην

κλάδος, -ου, ὁ   branch (11, n-2a)

κλαίω   I weep (40, v-2c)
(ἔκλαιον), κλαύσω, ἔκλαυσα, –, –, –

κλάω   I break (14, v-1d[1b]) –, ἔκλασα, –, –, –

κλείω   I shut (16, v-1a[3])
κλείσω, ἔκλεισα, –, κέκλεισμαι, ἐκλείσθην

κλέπτης, -ου, ὁ   thief (16, n-1f)

κλέπτω   I steal (13, v-4) κλέψω, ἔκλεψα, –, –, –

κληρονομέω   I acquire, inherit (18, v-1d[2a])
κληρονομήσω, ἐκληρονόμησα, κεκληρονόμηκα,
–, –

κληρονομία, -ας, ἡ   inheritance (14, n-1a)

κληρονόμος, -ου, ὁ   heir (15, n-2a)

κλῆρος, -ου, ὁ   lot, portion (11, n-2a)

κλῆσις, -εως, ἡ   call, calling (11, n-3e[5b])

κλητός, -ή, -όν   called (10, a-1a[2a])

κοιλία, -ας, ἡ   belly, womb (22, n-1a)

κοιμάω   I sleep, fall asleep (18, v-1d[1a])
–, –, –, κεκοίμημαι, ἐκοιμήθην

κοινός, -ή, -όν   common, ceremonially
unclean (14, a-1a[2a])

κοινόω   I make impure, defile (14, v-1d[3])
–, ἐκοίνωσα, κεκοίνωκα, κεκοίνωμαι, –

κοινωνία, -ας, ἡ   fellowship, participation (19,
n-1a)

κοινωνός, -οῦ, ὁ   partner, sharer (10, n-2a)

κολλάω   I join, cling to (12, v-1d[1a])
–, –, –, –, ἐκολλήθην

κομίζω   I bring; middle: I receive (10, v-2a[1])
κομίσομαι, ἐκομισάμην, –, –, –

κοπιάω   I toil, labor (23, v-1d[1b])
–, ἐκοπίασα, κεκοπίακα, –, –

κόπος, -ου, ὁ   labor, trouble (18, n-2a)

κοσμέω   I adorn, put in order (10, v-1d[2a])
(ἐκόσμουν), –, ἐκόσμησα, –, κεκόσμημαι, –

κόσμος, ου, ὁ   world, universe, humankind (186,
chpt 4, n-2a)

κράβαττος, -ου, ὁ   mattress, pallet, bed (of a
poor person) (11, n-2a)

κράζω   I cry out, call out (56, chpt 28, v-2a[2])
(ἔκραζον), κράξω, ἔκραξα, κέκραγα, –, –

κρατέω   I seize, hold (47, v-1d[2a]) (ἐκράτουν),
κρατήσω, ἐκράτησα, κεκράτηκα, κεκράτημαι, –

κράτος, -ους, τό   power, might (12, n-3d[2b])

κρείσσων,-ονος   better (19, a-4b[1]). Also spelled
κρείττων.

κρίμα, -ατος, τό   judgment (27, n-3c[4])

κρίνω   I judge, decide, prefer (114, chpt 20,
v-2d[6]) (ἐκρινόμην), κρινῶ, ἔκρινα, κέκρικα,
κέκριμαι, ἐκρίθην

κρίσις, -εως, ἡ   judgment (47, n-3e[5b])

κριτής, -οῦ, ὁ   judge (19, n-1f)

κρυπτός, -ή, -όν   hidden (17, a-1a[2a])

κρύπτω   I hide (18, v-4)
–, ἔκρυψα, –, κέκρυμμαι, ἐκρύβην

κτίζω   I create (15, v-2a[1])
–, ἔκτισα, –, ἔκτισμαι, ἐκτίσθην

κτίσις, -εως, ἡ   creation, creature (19, n-3e[5b])

κύριος, -ου, ὁ   Lord, lord, master, sir (717, chpt
7, n-2a)

κωλύω   I forbid, hinder (23, v-1a[4])
(ἐκώλυον), –, ἐκώλυσα, –, –, ἐκωλύθην

κώμη, -ης, ἡ   village (27, n-1b)

κωφός, -ή, -όν   mute, deaf (14, a-1a[2a])

λάμβδα

Λάζαρος, -ου, ὁ   Lazarus (15, n-2a)

λαλέω   I speak, say (296, chpt 17, v-1d[2a])
(ἐλάλουν), λαλήσω, ἐλάλησα, λελάληκα,
λελάλημαι, ἐλαλήθην

λαμβάνω   I take, receive (258, chpt 22, v-3a[2b])
(ἐλάμβανον), λήμψομαι, ἔλαβον, εἴληφα, –,
ἐλήμφθην

λαός, -οῦ, ὁ   people, crowd (142, chpt 20, n-2a)

λατρεύω   I serve, worship (21, v-1a[6])
λατρεύσω, ἐλάτρευσα, –, –, –

λέγω   I say, speak (2,353, chpt 8, v-1b[2])
(ἔλεγον), ἐρῶ, εἶπον, εἴρηκα, εἴρημαι, ἐρρέθην

λευκός, -ή, -όν   white (25, a-1a[2a])

λῃστής, -οῦ, ὁ   robber, revolutionary (15, n-1f)

λίαν   very much, exceedingly (12, adverb)

λίθος, -ου, ὁ   stone (59, chpt 31, n-2a)

λίμνη, -ης, ἡ   lake (11, n-1b)

λιμός, -οῦ, ὁ   hunger, famine (12, n-2a)

λογίζομαι   I reckon, think (40, v-2a[1])
(ἐλογιζόμην), –, ἐλογισάμην –, –, ἐλογίσθην

λόγος, -ου, ὁ   word, Word, statement, message (330, chpt 4, n-2a)

λοιπός, -ή, -όν   remaining; noun: (the) rest; adverb: for the rest, henceforth (55, chpt 34, a-1a[2a])

λυπέω   I grieve (26, v-1d[2a])
–, ἐλύπησα, λελύπηκα, –, ἐλυπήθην

λύπη, -ης, ἡ   grief, sorrow (16, n-1b)

λυχνία, -ας, ἡ   lampstand (12, n-1a)

λύχνος, -ου, ὁ   lamp (14, n-2a)

λύω   I loose (42, chpt 16, v-1a[4])
(ἔλυον), λύσω, ἔλυσα, –, λέλυμαι, ἐλύθην

μῦ

Μαγδαληνή, -ῆς, ἡ   Magdalene (12, n-1b)

μαθητής, -οῦ, ὁ   disciple (261, chpt 12, n-1f)

μακάριος, -ία, -ιον   blessed, happy (50, chpt 13, a-1a[1])

Μακεδονία, -ας, ἡ   Macedonia (22, n-1a)

μακράν   far away (10, adverb)

μακρόθεν   from a distance, from afar (14, adverb)

μακροθυμέω   I am patient (10, v-1d[2a])
–, ἐμακροθύμησα, –, –, –

μακροθυμία, -ας, ἡ   patience, forbearance, steadfastness (14, n-1a)

μάλιστα   most of all, especially (12, adverb)

μᾶλλον   more, rather (81, chpt 25, adverb)

μανθάνω   I learn (25, v-3a[2b])
–, ἔμαθον, μεμάθηκα, –, –

Μάρθα, -ας, ἡ   Martha (13, n-1a)

Μαρία, -ας, ἡ   Mary (27, n-1a)

Μαριάμ, ἡ   Mary (27, n-3g[2])

μαρτυρέω   I bear witness, testify (76, chpt 25, v-1d[2a]) (ἐμαρτύρουν), μαρτυρήσω, ἐμαρτύρησα, μεμαρτύρηκα, μεμαρτύρημαι, ἐμαρτυρήθην

μαρτυρία, -ας, ἡ   testimony (37, n-1a)

μαρτύριον, -ίου, τό   testimony, proof (19, n-2c)

μάρτυς, -υρος, ὁ   witness (35, n-3f[2a])

μάχαιρα, -ης, ἡ   sword (29, n-1c)

μέγας, μεγάλη, μέγα   large, great (243, chpt 13, a-1a[2a])

μείζων, ον   greater (48, chpt 19, a-4b[1])

μέλει   it is a concern (10, v-1d[2c])
(ἔμελεν), –, –, –, –, –

μέλλω   I am about to (109, chpt 32, v-1d[2c])
(ἔμελλον or ἤμελλον), μελλήσω, –, –, –, –

μέλος, -ους, τό   member, part (34, n-3d[2b])

μέν   on the one hand, indeed (179, chpt 12, particle)

μένω   I remain, live (118, chpt 20, v-1c[2])
(ἔμενον), μενῶ, ἔμεινα, μεμένηκα, –, –

μερίζω   I divide (14, v-2a[1])
–, ἐμέρισα, –, μεμέρισμαι, ἐμερίσθην

μεριμνάω   I am anxious, I care for (19, v-1d[1a])
μεριμνήσω, ἐμερίμνησα, –, –, –

μέρος, -ους, τό   part (42, n-3d[2b])

μέσος, -η, -ον   middle, in the midst (58, chpt 36, a-1a[2a])

μετά (μετ᾿, μεθ᾿)   gen: with; acc: after (469, chpt 8, preposition)

μεταβαίνω   I go over, pass over (12, cv-2d[6])
μεταβήσομαι, μετέβην, μεταβέβηκα, –, –

μετανοέω   I repent (34, cv-1d[2a])
μετανοήσω, μετενόησα, –, –, –

μετάνοια, -ας, ἡ   repentance (22, n-1a)

μετρέω   I measure, apportion (11, v-1d[2a])
–, ἐμέτρησα, –, –, ἐμετρήθην

μέτρον, -ου, τό   measure (14, n-2c)

μέχρι or μέχρις   gen: until, as far as (17, preposition; conjunction)

μή   not, lest (1,042, chpt 7, particle)

μηδέ   but not, nor, not even (56, chpt 30, particle)

μηδείς, μηδεμία, μηδέν   no one/thing (90, chpt 12, a-4b[2])

μηκέτι   no longer (22, adverb)

μήν, μηνός, ὁ   month (18, n-3f[1a])

μήποτε   lest (25, particle)

μήτε   and not, neither, nor (34, conjunction)

μήτηρ, μητρός, ἡ   mother (83, chpt 11, n-3f[2c])

μήτι   interrogative particle in questions expecting a negative answer (18, particle)

μικρός, -ά, -όν   small, little (46, a-1a[1])

μιμνῄσκομαι   I remember (23, v-5a)
–, –, –, μέμνημαι, ἐμνήσθην

μισέω   I hate (40, v-1d[2a]) (ἐμίσουν), μισήσω, ἐμίσησα, μεμίσηκα, μεμίσημαι, –

μισθός, -οῦ, ὁ   wages, reward (29, n-2a)

μνημεῖον, -ου, τό   grave, tomb (40, n-2c)

μνημονεύω I remember (21, v-1a[6])
  (ἐμνημόνευον), –, ἐμνημόνευσα, –, –, –

μοιχεύω I commit adultery (15, v-1a[6])
  μοιχεύσω, ἐμοίχευσα, –, –, ἐμοιχεύθην

μόνος, -η, -ον alone, only (114, chpt 12,
  a-1a[2a])

μύρον, -ου, τό ointment, perfume (14, n-2c)

μυστήριον, -ου, τό mystery, secret (28, n-2c)

μωρός, -ά, -όν foolish; noun: foolishness (12,
  a-1a[1])

Μωϋσῆς, -έως, ὁ Moses (80, chpt 34, n-3g[1])

νῦ

Ναζωραῖος, -ου, ὁ Nazarene (13, n-2a)

ναί yes, certainly (33, particle)

ναός, -οῦ, ὁ temple (45, n-2a)

νεανίσκος, -ου, ὁ youth, young man (11, n-2a)

νεκρός, -ά, -όν dead; noun: dead body,
  corpse (128, chpt 9, a-1a[1])

νέος, -α, -ον new, young (24, a-1a[1])

νεφέλη, -ης, ἡ cloud (25, n-1b)

νήπιος, -ίου, ὁ infant, child (15, a-1a[1])

νηστεύω I fast (20, v-1a[6])
  νηστεύσω, ἐνήστευσα, –, –, –

νικάω I conquer, overcome (28, v-1d[1a])
  νικήσω, ἐνίκησα, νενίκηκα, –, –

νίπτω I wash (17, v-4) –, ἔνιψα, –, –, –

νοέω I understand (14, v-1d[2a])
  νοήσω, ἐνόησα, νενόηκα, –, –

νομίζω I suppose, consider (15, v-2a[1])
  (ἐνόμιζον), –, ἐνόμισα, –, –, –

νόμος, -ου, ὁ law, principle (194, chpt 16, n-2a)

νόσος, -ου, ἡ disease (11, n-2b)

νοῦς, νοός, ὁ mind, understanding (24, n-3e[4])

νυμφίος, -ου, ὁ bridegroom (16, n-2a)

νῦν now; noun: (the) present (148, chpt 6,
  adverb)

νυνί now (20, adverb)

νύξ, νυκτός, ἡ night (61, chpt 18, n-3c[1])

ξῖ

ξενίζω I entertain, astonish (10, v-2a[1])
  –, ἐξένισα, –, –, ἐξενίσθην

ξένος, -η, -ον strange, foreign (14, a-1a[2a])

ξηραίνω I dry up (15, v-2d[4])
  –, ἐξήρανα, –, ἐξήραμμαι, ἐξηράνθην

ξύλον, -ου, τό tree, wood (20, n-2c)

ὀ μικρόν

ὁ, ἡ, τό the (19,867, chpt 6, a-1a[2b])

ὅδε, ἥδε, τόδε this (10, a-1a[2b])

ὁδός, -οῦ, ἡ way, road, journey, conduct (101,
  chpt 14, n-2b)

ὀδούς, -όντος, ὁ tooth (12, n-3c[5a])

ὅθεν from where, for which reason (15, adverb)

οἶδα I know, understand (318, chpt 17, v-1b[3])
  εἰδήσω, ᾔδειν, –, –, –

οἰκία, -ας, ἡ house, home (93, chpt 8, n-1a)

οἰκοδεσπότης, -ου, ὁ master of the house (12,
  n-1f)

οἰκοδομέω I build (40, v-1d[2a]) (ᾠκοδόμουν),
  οἰκοδομήσω, ᾠκοδόμησα, –, ᾠκοδόμημαι,
  οἰκοδομήθην

οἰκοδομή, -ῆς, ἡ building, edification (18, n-1b)

οἰκονόμος, -ου, ὁ steward, administrator (10,
  n-2a)

οἶκος, -ου, ὁ house, home (114, chpt 8, n-2a)

οἰκουμένη, -ης, ἡ the inhabited world (15, n-1b)

οἶνος, -ου, ὁ wine (34, n-2a)

οἷος, -α, -ον of what sort, such as (14, a-1a[1])

ὀλίγος, -η, -ον little, few (40, a-1a[2a])

ὅλος, -η, -ον whole, complete; adverb:
  entirely (109, chpt 19, a-1a[2a])

ὀμνύω or ὄμνυμι I swear, take an oath (26,
  v-3c[2]) –, ὤμοσα, –, –, –

ὁμοθυμαδόν with one mind (11, adverb)

ὅμοιος, -οία, -οιον like, similar (45, a-1a[1])

ὁμοιόω I make like, compare (15, v-1d[3])
  ὁμοιώσω, ὡμοίωσα, –, –, ὡμοιώθην

ὁμοίως likewise, in the same way (30, adverb)

ὁμολογέω I confess, profess (26, v-1d[2a])
  (ὡμολόγουν), ὁμολογήσω, ὡμολόγησα, –, –, –

ὄνομα, -ατος, τό name, reputation (231, chpt 10,
  n-3c[4])

ὀνομάζω I name (10, v-2a[1])
  –, ὠνόμασα, –, –, ὠνομάσθην

ὄντως really; adjective: real (10, adverb)

ὀπίσω gen: behind, after (35, preposition,
  adverb)

ὅπου where (82, chpt 16, particle)

ὅπως   how, that, in order that (53, chpt 12, conjunction; adverb)

ὅραμα, -ατος, τό   vision (12, n-3c[4])

ὁράω   I see, notice, experience (454, chpt 20, v-1d[1a]) ὄψομαι, εἶδον, ἑώρακα, –, ὤφθην

ὀργή, -ῆς, ἡ   wrath, anger (36, n-1b)

ὅριον, -ου, τό   boundary, region (12, n-2c)

ὅρκος, -ου, ὁ   oath (10, n-2a)

ὄρος, ὄρους, τό   mountain, hill (63, chpt 24, n-3d[2b])

ὅς, ἥ, ὅ   who, whom (1,365, chpt 14, a-1a[2b])

ὅσος, -η, -ον   as great as, as many as (110, chpt 12, a-1a[2a])

ὅστις, ἥτις, ὅτι   whoever, whichever, whatever (145, chpt 18, a-1a[2b])

ὅταν   whenever (123, chpt 17, particle)

ὅτε   when (103, chpt 14, particle)

ὅτι   that, since, because (1,296, chpt 6, conjunction)

οὗ   where (24, chpt 27, adverb)

οὐ, οὐκ, οὐχ   not (1,623, chpt 6, adverb)

οὐαί   Woe! Alas! (46, interjection)

οὐδέ   and not, not even, neither, nor (143, chpt 11, conjunction)

οὐδείς, οὐδεμία, οὐδέν   no one, none, nothing (234, chpt 10, a-2a)

οὐδέποτε   never (16, adverb)

οὐκέτι   no longer (47, adverb)

οὖν   therefore, then, accordingly (499, chpt 12, particle)

οὔπω   not yet (26, adverb)

οὐρανός, -οῦ, ὁ   heaven, sky (273, chpt 7, n-2a)

οὖς, ὠτός, τό   ear (36, n-3c[6c])

οὔτε   and not, neither, nor (87, chpt 22, adverb)

οὗτος, αὕτη, τοῦτο   singular: this; he, she, it; plural: these; they (1,387, chpt 7, a-1a[2b])

οὕτως   thus, so, in this manner (208, chpt 14, adverb)

οὐχί   not (54, chpt 28, adverb)

ὀφείλω   I owe, ought (35, v-2d[1]) (ὤφειλον), –, –, –, –, –

ὀφθαλμός, -οῦ, ὁ   eye, sight (100, chpt 12, n-2a)

ὄφις, -εως, ὁ   serpent (14, n-3e[5b])

ὄχλος, -ου, ὁ   crowd, multitude (175, chpt 8, n-2a)

ὄψιος, -α, -ον   evening (15, a-1a[1])

πῖ

πάθημα, -ατος, τό   suffering (16, n-3c[4])

παιδεύω   I discipline, train (13, v-1a[6]) (ἐπαίδευον), –, ἐπαίδευσα, –, πεπαίδευμαι, ἐπαιδεύθην

παιδίον, -ου, τό   child, infant (52, chpt 28, n-2c)

παιδίσκη, -ης, ἡ   maid servant (13, n-1b)

παῖς, παιδός, ὁ or ἡ   boy, son, servant; girl (24, n-3c[2])

παλαιός, -ά, -όν   old (19, a-1a[1])

πάλιν   again (141, chpt 12, adverb)

παντοκράτωρ, -ορος, ὁ   the Almighty (10, n-3f[2b])

πάντοτε   always (41, adverb)

παρά   gen: from; dat: beside, in the presence of; acc: alongside of (194, chpt 8, preposition)

παραβολή, -ῆς, ἡ   parable (50, chpt 8, n-1b)

παραγγέλλω   I command (32, cv-2d[1]) (παρήγγελλον), –, παρήγγειλα, –, παρήγγελμαι, –

παραγίνομαι   I come, arrive (37, cv-1c[2]) (παρεγινόμην), –, παρεγενόμην, –, –, –

παράγω   I pass by (10, cv-1b[2])

παραδίδωμι   I entrust, hand over, betray (119, chpt 34, cv-6a) (παρεδίδουν), παραδώσω, παρέδωκα, παραδέδωκα, παραδέδομαι, παρεδόθην

παράδοσις, -εως, ἡ   tradition (13, n-3e[5b])

παραιτέομαι   I reject, refuse (12, cv-1d[2a]) (παρῃτούμην), –, παρῃτησάμην, –, παρῄτημαι, –

παρακαλέω   I call, urge, exhort, comfort (109, chpt 27, cv-1d[2b]) (παρεκάλουν), –, παρεκάλεσα, –, παρακέκλημαι, παρεκλήθην

παράκλησις, -εως, ἡ   comfort, encouragement (29, n-3e[5b])

παραλαμβάνω   I take, take over (49, cv-3a[2b]) παραλήμψομαι, παρέλαβον, –, –, παραλημφθήσομαι

παραλυτικός, -ή, -όν   lame; noun: a paralytic (10, a-1a[2a])

παράπτωμα, -ατος, τό   wrongdoing, sin (19, n-3c[4])

παρατίθημι   I set before; middle: I entrust (19, cv-6a) παραθήσω, παρέθηκα, –, –, –

παραχρῆμα   immediately (18, adverb)

πάρειμι   I am present, have arrived (24, cv-6b) (παρήμην), παρέσομαι, –, –, –, –

παρεμβολή, -ῆς, ἡ   barracks, camp (10, n-1b)

παρέρχομαι   I pass away, pass by (29, cv-1b[2])
παρελεύσομαι, παρῆλθον, παρελήλυθα, –, –

παρέχω   I offer (16, cv-1b[2])
(παρεῖχον), παρέξω, παρέσχον, –, –, –

παρθένος, -ου, ἡ   virgin (15, n-2a)

παρίστημι   I present, I am present (41, cv-6a)
παραστήσω, παρέστησα, παρέστηκα, –,
παρεστάθην

παρουσία, -ας, ἡ   coming, presence (24, n-1a)

παρρησία, -ας, ἡ   boldness, openness (31, n-1a)

πᾶς, πᾶσα, πᾶν   singular: each, every; plural:
all (1,243, chpt 10, a-2a)

πάσχα, τό   Passover (29, n-3g[2])

πάσχω   I suffer (42, v-5a)
–, ἔπαθον, πέπονθα, –, –

πατάσσω   I strike (10, v-2b)
πατάξω, ἐπάταξα, –, –, –

πατήρ, πατρός, ὁ   father (413, chpt 11, n-3f[2c])

Παῦλος, -ου, ὁ   Paul (158, chpt 4, n-2a)

παύω   I stop, cease (15, v-1a[5]) (ἐπαυόμην),
παύσομαι, ἐπαυσάμην, –, πέπαυμαι, –

πείθω   I persuade (53, chpt 27, v-1b[3]) (ἔπειθον),
πείσω, ἔπεισα, πέποιθα, πέπεισμαι, ἐπείσθην

πεινάω   I hunger, I am hungry (23, v-1d[1b])
πεινάσω, ἐπείνασα, –, –, –

πειράζω   I test, tempt (38, v-2a[1]) (ἐπείραζον), –,
ἐπείρασα, –, πεπείρασμαι, ἐπειράσθην

πειρασμός, -οῦ, ὁ   temptation, test (21, n-2a)

πέμπω   I send (79, chpt 29, v-1b[1])
πέμψω, ἔπεμψα, –, –, ἐπέμφθην

πενθέω   I mourn (10, v-1d[2a])
πενθήσω, ἐπένθησα, –, –, –

πέντε   five (38, n-3g[2])

πέραν   on the other side (23, adverb, also as a
preposition with the genitive)

περί   gen: concerning, about; acc: around (333,
chpt 10, preposition)

περιβάλλω   I put on, clothe (23, cv-2d[1])
περιβαλῶ, περιέβαλον, –, περιβέβλημαι, –

περιπατέω   I walk (around), live (95, chpt
21, cv-1d[2a]) (περιεπάτουν), περιπατήσω,
περιεπάτησα, –, –, –

περισσεύω   I abound (39, v-1a[6]) (ἐπερίσσευον),
–, ἐπερίσσευσα, –, –, περισσευθήσομαι

περισσότερος, -τέρα, -ον   greater, more (16,
a-1a[1])

περισσοτέρως   greater, more (12, adverb)

περιστερά, -ᾶς, ἡ   dove (10, n-1a)

περιτέμνω   I circumcise (17, cv-3a[1])
–, περιέτεμον, –, περιτέτμημαι, περιετμήθην

περιτομή, -ῆς, ἡ   circumcision (36, n-1b)

πετεινόν, -οῦ, τό   bird (14, n-2c)

πέτρα, -ας, ἡ   rock (15, n-1a)

Πέτρος, -ου, ὁ   Peter (156, chpt 4, n-2a)

πηγή, -ῆς, ἡ   spring, fountain (11, n-1b)

πιάζω   I seize, take hold of (12, v-2a[1])
–, ἐπίασα, –, –, ἐπιάσθην

Πιλᾶτος, -ου, ὁ   Pilate (55, chpt 4, n-2a)

πίμπλημι   I fill, fulfill (24, v-6a)
–, ἔπλησα, –, –, ἐπλήσθην

πίνω   I drink (73, chpt 23, v-3a[1])
(ἔπινον), πίομαι, ἔπιον, πέπωκα, –, ἐπόθην

πίπτω   I fall (90, chpt 34, v-1b[3]) (ἔπιπτον),
πεσοῦμαι, ἔπεσον or ἔπεσα, πέπτωκα, –, –

πιστεύω   I believe, have faith (in), trust (241,
chpt 16, v-1a[6]) (ἐπίστευον), πιστεύσω,
ἐπίστευσα, πεπίστευκα, πεπίστευμαι, ἐπιστεύθην

πίστις, πίστεως, ἡ   faith, belief (243, chpt 11,
n-3e[5b])

πιστός, -ή, -όν   faithful, believing (67, chpt 9,
a-1a[2a])

πλανάω   I go astray, mislead (39, v-1d[1a])
πλανήσω, ἐπλάνησα, –, πεπλάνημαι, ἐπλανήθην

πλάνη, -ης, ἡ   error (10, n-1b)

πλείων, πλεῖον   larger, more (55, chpt 17, a-4b[1])

πλεονεξία, -ας, ἡ   greediness (10, n-1a)

πληγή, -ῆς, ἡ   plague, blow, wound (22, n-1b)

πλῆθος, -ους, τό   multitude (31, n-3d[2b])

πληθύνω   I multiply, increase (12, v-1c[2])
(ἐπληθυνόμην), πληθυνῶ, ἐπλήθυνα, –, –, –

πλήν   nevertheless, but; gen: except (31, adverb)

πλήρης, -ες   full (17, a-4a)

πληρόω   I fill, complete, fulfill (86, chpt 17,
v-1d[3]) (ἐπλήρουν), πληρώσω, ἐπλήρωσα,
πεπλήρωκα, πεπλήρωμαι, ἐπληρώθην

πλήρωμα, -ατος, τό   fullness (17, n-3c[4])

πλησίον   near; noun: neighbor (17, adverb)

πλοῖον, -ου, τό   ship, boat (68, chpt 14, n-2c)

πλούσιος, -α, -ον   rich (28, a-1a[1])

πλουτέω   I am rich (12, v-1d[2a])
–, ἐπλούτησα, πεπλούτηκα, –, –

πλοῦτος, -ου, ὁ   wealth (22, n-2a)

πνεῦμα, -ατος, τό   spirit, Spirit, wind, breath, inner life (379, chpt 4, n-3c[4])

πνευματικός, -ή, -όν   spiritual (26, a-1a[2a])

πόθεν   from where? from whom? (29, adverb)

ποιέω   I do, make (568, chpt 17, v-1d[2a]) (ἐποίουν), ποιήσω, ἐποίησα, πεποίηκα, πεποίημαι, –

ποικίλος, -η, -ον   diverse, manifold (10, a-1a[2a])

ποιμαίνω   I shepherd (11, v-2d[4]) ποιμανῶ, ἐποίμανα, –, –, –

ποιμήν, -ένος, ὁ   shepherd (18, n-3f[1b])

ποῖος, -α, -ον   of what kind? which? what? (33, a-1a[1])

πόλεμος, -ου, ὁ   war (18, n-2a)

πόλις, -εως, ἡ   city (162, chpt 13, n-3e[5b])

πολλάκις   often, frequently (18, adverb)

πολύς, πολλή, πολύ   singular: much; plural: many; adverb: often (416, chpt 13, a-1a[2a])

πονηρός, -ά, -όν   evil, bad (78, chpt 9, a-1a[1])

πορεύομαι   I go, proceed, live (153, chpt 18, v-1a[6]) (ἐπορευόμην), πορεύσομαι, –, –, πεπόρευμαι, ἐπορεύθην

πορνεία, -ας, ἡ   fornication (25, n-1a)

πόρνη, -ης, ἡ   prostitute (12, n-1b)

πόρνος, -ου, ὁ   fornicator (10, n-2a)

πόσος, -η, -ον   how great? how much? how many? (27, a-1a[2a])

ποταμός, -οῦ, ὁ   river (17, n-2a)

ποτέ   at some time (29, particle)

πότε   when? (19, adverb)

ποτήριον, -ου, τό   cup (31, n-2c)

ποτίζω   I give to drink (15, v-2a[1]) (ἐπότιζον), –, ἐπότισα, πεπότικα, –, ἐποτίσθην

ποῦ   where? (48, adverb)

πούς, ποδός, ὁ   foot (93, chpt 12, n-3c[2])

πρᾶγμα, -ατος, τό   deed, matter, thing (11, n-3c[4])

πράσσω   I do (39, v-2b) πράξω, ἔπραξα, πέπραχα, πέπραγμαι, –

πραΰτης, -ῆτος, ἡ   gentleness, humility (11, n-3c[1])

πρεσβύτερος, -α, -ον   elder (66, chpt 30, a-1a[1])

πρίν   before (13, conjunction; preposition)

πρό   gen: before (47, preposition)

προάγω   I go before (20, cv-1b[2]) (προῆγον), προάξω, προήγαγον, –, –, –

πρόβατον, -ου, τό   sheep (39, n-2c)

πρόθεσις, -εως, ἡ   plan, purpose (12, n-3e[5b])

προλέγω   I tell beforehand (15, cv-1b[2]) –, προεῖπον or προεῖπα, –, προείρηκα or προείρημαι, –

πρός   acc: to, towards, with (700, chpt 8, preposition)

προσδέχομαι   I receive, wait for (14, cv-1b[2]) (προσεδεχόμην), –, προσεδεξάμην, –, –, –

προσδοκάω   I wait for, expect (16, cv-1d[1a]) (προσεδόκων), –, –, –, –, –

προσέρχομαι   I come/go to (86, chpt 22, cv-1b[2]) (προσηρχόμην), –, προσῆλθον, προσελήλυθα, –, –

προσευχή, -ῆς, ἡ   prayer (36, n-1b)

προσεύχομαι   I pray (85, chpt 22, cv-1b[2]) (προσηυχόμην), προσεύξομαι, προσηυξάμην, –, –, –

προσέχω   I am concerned about, I give heed to (24, cv-1b[2]) (προσεῖχον), –, –, προσέσχηκα, –, –

προσκαλέω   I summon (29, cv-1d[2a]) –, προσεκαλεσάμην, –, προσκέκλημαι, –

προσκαρτερέω   I am devoted to, I am faithful (10, cv-1d[2a]) προσκαρτερήσω, –, –, –, –

προσκυνέω   I worship (60, chpt 19, cv-3b]) (προσεκύνουν), προσκυνήσω, προσεκύνησα, –, –, –

προσλαμβάνω   I receive (12, cv-3a[2b]) –, προσελαβόμην, –, –, –

προστίθημι   I add to (18, cv-6a) (προσετίθουν), –, προσέθηκα, –, –, προσετέθην

προσφέρω   I bring to, offer, present (47, cv-1c[1]) (προσέφερον), –, προσήνεγκον or προσήνεγκα, προσενήνοχα, –, προσηνέχθην

πρόσωπον, -ου, τό   face, appearance (76, chpt 16, n-2c)

πρότερος, -α, -ον   former, earlier (11, a-1a[1])

προφητεία, -ας, ἡ   prophecy (19, n-1a)

προφητεύω   I prophesy (28, v-1a[6]) (ἐπροφήτευον), προφητεύσω, ἐπροφήτευσα or προεφήτευσα, –, –, –

προφήτης, -ου, ὁ   prophet (144, chpt 4, n-1f)

πρωΐ   early (in the morning) (12, adverb)

πρῶτος, -η, -ον   first, earlier (155, chpt 9, a-1a[2a])

πτωχός, -ή, -όν   poor; noun: a poor person (34, a-1a[2a])

πύλη, -ης, ἡ   gate, door (10, n-1b)

πυλών, -ῶνος, ὁ   gateway, gate (18, n-3f[1a])

πυνθάνομαι   I inquire (12, v-3a[2b]) (ἐπυνθανόμην), –, ἐπυθόμην, –, –, –

πῦρ, πυρός, τό   fire (71, chpt 22, n-3f[2a])

πωλέω   I sell (22, v-1d[2a]) (ἐπώλουν), –, ἐπώλησα, –, –, –

πῶλος, -ου, ὁ   colt (12, n-2a)

πῶς   how? (103, chpt 13, particle)

πώς   somehow, perhaps (15, particle)

ῥῶ

ῥαββί, ὁ   rabbi, master (15, n-3g[2])

ῥάβδος, -ου, ἡ   staff, rod (12, n-2b)

ῥῆμα, -ατος, τό   word, saying (68, chpt 14, n-3c[4])

ῥίζα, -ης, ἡ   root (17, n-1c)

ῥύομαι   I rescue, deliver (17, v-1a[4]) ῥύσομαι, ἐρρυσάμην, –, –, ἐρρύσθην

Ῥωμαῖος, -α, -ον   Roman (12, a-1a[1])

σίγμα

σάββατον, -ου, τό   Sabbath, week (68, chpt 4, n-2c)

Σαδδουκαῖος, -ου, ὁ   Sadducee (14, n-2a)

σαλεύω   I shake (15, v-1a[6]) –, ἐσάλευσα, –, σεσάλευμαι, ἐσαλεύθην

σάλπιγξ, -ιγγος, ἡ   trumpet (11, n-3b[2])

σαλπίζω   I blow a trumpet (12, v-2a[1]) σαλπίσω, ἐσάλπισα, –, –, –

Σαμάρεια, -ας, ἡ   Samaria (11, n-1a)

σάρξ, σαρκός, ἡ   flesh, body (147, chpt 10, n-3b[1])

σατανᾶς, -ᾶ, ὁ   Satan (36, n-1e)

Σαῦλος, -ου, ὁ   Saul (15, n-2a)

σεαυτοῦ, -ῆς   of yourself (43, a-1a[2b])

σέβω   I worship (10, v-1b[1])

σεισμός, -οῦ, ὁ   earthquake (14, n-2a)

σημεῖον, -ου, τό   sign, miracle (77, chpt 13, n-2c)

σήμερον   today (41, adverb)

σιγάω   I keep silent, become silent (10, v-1d[1a]) –, ἐσίγησα, –, σεσίγημαι, –

Σίλας, -ᾶ, ὁ   Silas (12, n-1e)

Σίμων, -ωνος, ὁ   Simon (75, chpt 4, n-3f[1a])

σῖτος, -ου, ὁ   wheat (14, n-2a)

σιωπάω   I keep silent, become silent (10, v-1d[1a]) (ἐσιώπων), σιωπήσω, ἐσιώπησα, –, –, –

σκανδαλίζω   I cause to sin, stumble, take offense (29, v-2a[1]) (ἐσκανδαλιζόμην), –, ἐσκανδάλισα, –, –, ἐσκανδαλίσθην

σκάνδαλον, -ου, τό   temptation to sin, offense (15, n-2c)

σκεῦος, -ους, τό   instrument, vessel; plural: goods, things (23, n-3d[2b])

σκηνή, -ῆς, ἡ   tent, tabernacle (20, n-1b)

σκοτία, -ας, ἡ   darkness (16, n-1a)

σκότος, -ους, τό   darkness (31, n-3d[2b])

Σολομών, -ῶνος, ὁ   Solomon (12, n-3c[5b])

σός, σή, σόν   your, yours (singular) (25, a-1a[2a])

σοφία, -ας, ἡ   wisdom (51, chpt 20, n-1a)

σοφός, -ή, -όν   wise (20, a-1a[2a])

σπείρω   I sow (52, chpt 28, v-2d[3]) –, ἔσπειρα, –, ἔσπαρμαι, ἐσπάρην

σπέρμα, -ατος, τό   seed, descendants (43, n-3c[4])

σπλαγχνίζομαι   I have pity, feel sympathy (12, v-2a[1]) –, –, –, –, ἐσπλαγχνίσθην

σπλάγχνον, -ου, τό   heart, affection (11, n-2c)

σπουδάζω   I am eager, I am zealous, I hasten (11, v-2a[1]) σπουδάσω, ἐσπούδασα, –, –, –

σπουδή, -ῆς, ἡ   earnestness, diligence (12, n-1b)

σταυρός, -οῦ, ὁ   cross (27, n-2a)

σταυρόω   I crucify (46, v-1d[3]) σταυρώσω, ἐσταύρωσα, –, ἐσταύρωμαι, ἐσταυρώθην

στέφανος, -ου, ὁ   wreath, crown (18, n-1e)

στήκω   I stand firm (11, v-1b[2]) (ἔστηκεν), –, –, –, –, –

στηρίζω   I establish, strengthen (13, v-2a[2]) στηρίξω, ἐστήριξα or ἐστήρισα, –, ἐστήριγμαι, ἐστηρίχθην

στόμα, -ατος, τό   mouth (78, chpt 20, n-3c[4])

στρατηγός, -οῦ, ὁ   commander, magistrate (10, n-2a)

στρατιώτης, -οῦ, ὁ   soldier (26, n-1f)

στρέφω   I turn (21, v-1b[1]) –, ἔστρεψα, –, –, ἐστράφην

σύ   you (singular) (1,067, chpt 7, a-5a)

συγγενής, -ές   related; noun: a relative (11, a-4a)

συζητέω I dispute, discuss (10, cv-1d[2a]) (συνεζήτουν), –, –, –, –, –

συκῆ, -ῆς, ἡ fig tree (16, n-1h)

συλλαμβάνω I seize, conceive (16, cv-3a[2b]) συλλήμψομαι, συνέλαβον, συνείληφα, –, συνελήμφθην

συμφέρω I am useful; it is profitable (15, cv-1c[1]) –, συνήνεγκα, –, –, –

σύν dat: with (128, chpt 10, preposition)

συνάγω I gather together, invite (59, chpt 18, cv-1b[2]) συνάξω, συνήγαγον, –, συνῆγμαι, συνήχθην

συναγωγή, -ῆς, ἡ synagogue, meeting (56, chpt 21, n-1b)

σύνδουλος, -ου, ὁ fellow slave (10, n-2a)

συνέδριον, -ου, τό the Sanhedrin, a council (22, n-2c)

συνείδησις, -εως, ἡ conscience (30, n-3e(5b))

συνεργός, -οῦ, ὁ helping; noun: helper, fellow worker (13, n-2a)

συνέρχομαι I assemble, travel with (30, cv-1b[2]) (συνηρχόμην), –, συνῆλθον, συνελήλυθα, –, –

συνέχω I distress, oppress (12, cv-1b[2]) (συνειχόμην), συνέξω, συνέσχον, –, –, –

συνίημι I understand (26, cv-6a) συνήσω, συνῆκα, –, –, –

συνίστημι I commend, demonstrate (16, cv-6a) –, συνέστησα, συνέστηκα, –, –. Also formed as a thematic verb, συνιστάνω.

σφάζω I slaughter (10, v-2a[2]) σφάξω, ἔσφαξα, –, ἔσφαγμαι, ἐσφάγην

σφόδρα extremely, greatly (11, adverb)

σφραγίζω I seal, mark (15, v-2a[1]) –, ἐσφράγισα, –, ἐσφράγισμαι, ἐσφραγίσθην

σφραγίς, -ῖδος, ἡ seal (16, n-3c[2])

σχίζω I split, divide (11, v-2a[1]) σχίσω, ἔσχισα, –, –, ἐσχίσθην

σῴζω I save, deliver, rescue (106, chpt 20, v-2a[1]) (ἔσῳζον), σώσω, ἔσωσα, σέσωκα, σέσωσμαι, ἐσώθην

σῶμα, -ατος, τό body (142, chpt 10, n-3c[4])

σωτήρ, -ῆρος, ὁ savior, deliverer (24, n-3f[2a])

σωτηρία, -ας, ἡ salvation, deliverance (46, n-1a)

ταῦ

τάλαντον, -ου, τό talent (a Greek monetary unit) (14, n-2c)

ταπεινόω I humble (14, v-1d[3]) ταπεινώσω, ἐταπείνωσα, –, –, ἐταπεινώθην

ταράσσω I trouble, disturb (17, v-2b) –, ἐτάραξα, –, τετάραγμαι, ἐταράχθην

ταχέως quickly (15, adverb)

ταχύς, -εῖα, -ύ quick, swift; adverb: quickly (13, a-2b)

τε and (so), so (215, chpt 14, particle)

τέκνον, -ου, τό child, descendant (99, chpt 10, n-2c)

τέλειος, -α, -ον perfect, complete (19, a-1a[1])

τελειόω I perfect, complete, accomplish (23, v-1d[3]) –, ἐτελείωσα, τετελείωκα, τετελείωμαι, ἐτελειώθην

τελευτάω I die (11, v-1d[1a]) –, ἐτελεύτησα, τετελεύτηκα, –, –

τελέω I finish, fulfill (28, v-1d[2b]) τελέσω, ἐτέλεσα, τετέλεκα, τετέλεσμαι, ἐτελέσθην

τέλος, -ους, τό end, goal (40, n-3d[2b])

τελώνης, -ου, ὁ tax collector (21, n-1f)

τέρας, -ατος, τό wonder, omen (16, n-3c[6a])

τέσσαρες, -ων four (41, a-4b[2])

τεσσεράκοντα forty (22, n-3g[2], indeclinable)

τέταρτος, -η, -ον fourth (10, a-1a[2a])

τηρέω I keep, guard, observe (70, chpt 17, v-1d[2a]) (ἐτήρουν), τηρήσω, ἐτήρησα, τετήρηκα, τετήρημαι, ἐτηρήθην

τίθημι I put, place (100, chpt 36, v-6a) (ἐτίθην), θήσω, ἔθηκα, τέθεικα, τέθειμαι, ἐτέθην

τίκτω I give birth to (18, v-1b[2]) τέξομαι, ἔτεκον, –, –, ἐτέχθην

τιμάω I honor (21, v-1d[1a]) τιμήσω, ἐτίμησα, –, τετίμημαι, –

τιμή, -ῆς, ἡ honor, price (41, n-1b)

τίμιος, -α, -ον costly, precious (13, a-1a[1])

Τιμόθεος, -ου, ὁ Timothy (24, n-2a)

τις, τι someone, something, a certain one, a certain thing, anyone, anything (543, chpt 10, a-4b[2])

τίς, τί who? what? which? why? (546, chpt 10, a-4b[2])

Τίτος, -ου, ὁ Titus (13, n-2a)

τοιοῦτος, -αύτη, -οῦτον such, of such a kind (57, chpt 31, a-1a[2b])

τολμάω I dare, bring myself to (16, v-1d[1a]) (ἐτόλμων), τολμήσω, ἐτόλμησα, –, –, –

τόπος, -ου, ὁ place, location (94, chpt 18, n-2a)

τοσοῦτος, -αύτη, -οῦτον so great, so much, so many (20, a-1a[2b])

τότε then, thereafter (160, chpt 16, adverb)

τράπεζα, -ης, ἡ table (15, n-1c)

τρεῖς, τρία three (69, chpt 27, a-4a)

τρέχω I run (20, v-1b[2])
  (ἔτρεχον), –, ἔδραμον, –, –, –

τριάκοντα thirty (11, n-3g[2])

τρίς three times (12, adverb)

τρίτος, -η, -ον third (56, chpt 9, a-1a[2a])

τρόπος, -ου, ὁ manner, way (13, n-2a)

τροφή, -ῆς, ἡ food (16, n-1b)

τυγχάνω I attain; it happens, turn outs (12, v-3a[2b]) –, ἔτυχον, τέτευχα, –, –

τύπος, -ου, ὁ type, pattern (15, n-2a)

τύπτω I strike (13, v-4) (ἔτυπτον), –, –, –, –, –

Τύρος, -ου, ὁ Tyre (11, n-2b)

τυφλός, -ή, -όν blind (50, chpt 16, a-1a[2a])

ὖ ψιλόν

ὑγιαίνω I am healthy, I am sound (12, v-2d[4])

ὑγιής, -ές whole, healthy (11, a-4a)

ὕδωρ, ὕδατος, τό water (76, chpt 11, n-3c[6b])

υἱός, -οῦ, ὁ son, descendant (377, chpt 7, n-2a)

ὑμεῖς you (plural) (1,840, chpt 11, a-5a)

ὑμέτερος, -α, -ον your (plural) (11, a-1a[1])

ὑπάγω I depart (79, chpt 24, cv-1b[2])
  (ὑπῆγον), –, –, –, –, –

ὑπακοή, -ῆς, ἡ obedience (15, n-1b)

ὑπακούω I obey (21, cv-1a[8])
  (ὑπήκουον), –, ὑπήκουσα, –, –, –

ὑπαντάω I meet, go to meet (10, cv-1d[1a])
  ὑπαντήσω, ὑπήντησα, –, –, –

ὑπάρχω I am, exist; τὰ ὑπάρχοντα: one's belongings (60, chpt 34, cv-1b[2])
  (ὑπῆρχον), –, –, –, –, –

ὑπέρ gen: in behalf of; acc: above (150, chpt 12, preposition)

ὑπηρέτης, -ου, ὁ servant, assistant (20, n-1f)

ὑπό gen: by; acc: under (220, chpt 8, preposition)

ὑπόδημα, -ατος, τό sandal, shoe (10, n-3c[4])

ὑποκάτω gen: under, below (11, preposition)

ὑποκριτής, -οῦ, ὁ hypocrite (17, n-1f)

ὑπομένω I endure (17, cv-1c[2])
  –, ὑπέμεινα, ὑπομεμένηκα, –, –

ὑπομονή, -ῆς, ἡ endurance, perseverance (32, n-1b)

ὑποστρέφω I return, turn back (35, cv-1b[1])
  (ὑπέστρεφον), ὑποστρέψω, ὑπέστρεψα, –, –, -

ὑποτάσσω I subject, subordinate (38, cv-2b)
  –, ὑπέταξα, –, ὑποτέταγμαι, ὑπετάγην

ὑστερέω I lack (16, v-1d[2a])
  –, ὑστέρησα, ὑστέρηκα, –, ὑστερήθην

ὕστερος, -α, -ον later, then; adverb: finally (12, a-1a[1])

ὑψηλός, -ή, -όν high, exalted (11, a-1a[2a])

ὕψιστος, -η, -ον highest (13, a-1a[2a])

ὑψόω I exalt, lift up (20, v-1d[3])
  ὑψώσω, ὕψωσα, –, –, ὑψώθην

φῖ

φαίνω I shine; passive: I appear (31, v-2d[4])
  φανήσομαι, ἔφανα, –, –, ἐφάνην

φανερός, -ά, -όν visible, evident, known (18, a-1a[1])

φανερόω I reveal, make known (49, v-1d[3])
  φανερώσω, ἐφανέρωσα, –, πεφανέρωμαι, ἐφανερώθην

Φαρισαῖος, -ου, ὁ Pharisee (98, chpt 21, n-2a)

φείδομαι I spare (10, v-1b[3])
  φείσομαι, ἐφεισάμην, –, –, –

φέρω I carry, bear, produce (66, chpt 29, v-1c[1])
  (ἔφερον), οἴσω, ἤνεγκα, ἐνήνοχα, –, ἠνέχθην

φεύγω I flee (29, v-1b[2])
  φεύξομαι, ἔφυγον, πέφευγα, –, –

φημί I say, affirm (66, chpt 36, v-6b)
  (ἔφη), –, ἔφη, –, –, –

Φῆστος, -ου, ὁ Festus (13, n-2a)

φιάλη, -ης, ἡ bowl (12, n-1b)

φιλέω I love, like (25, v-1d[2a])
  (ἐφίλουν), –, ἐφίλησα, πεφίληκα, –, –

Φίλιππος, -ου, ὁ Philip (36, n-2a)

φίλος, -η, -ον beloved; noun: friend (29, a-1a[2a])

φοβέομαι I fear (95, chpt 24, v-1d[2a])
  (ἐφοβούμην), –, –, –, –, ἐφοβήθην

φόβος, -ου, ὁ fear, reverence (47, n-2a)

φονεύω I kill, murder (12, v-1a[6])
  φονεύσω, ἐφόνευσα, –, –, –

φρονέω   I think, regard   (26, v-1d[2a])
(ἐφρονούμην), φρονήσω, –, –, –, –

φρόνιμος, -ον   prudent, sensible   (14, a-3a)

φυλακή, -ῆς, ἡ   prison, watch   (47, n-1b)

φυλάσσω   I guard, observe   (31, v-2b)
φυλάξω, ἐφύλαξα, –, –, –

φυλή, -ῆς, ἡ   tribe, nation   (31, n-1b)

φύσις, -εως, ἡ   nature   (14, n-3e[5b])

φυτεύω   I plant   (11, v-1a[6]) (ἐφύτευον), –,
ἐφύτευσα, –, πεφύτευμαι, ἐφυτεύθην

φωνέω   I call out, summon   (43, v-1d[2a])
(ἐφώνουν), φωνήσω, ἐφώνησα, –, –, ἐφωνήθην

φωνή, -ῆς, ἡ   sound, noise, voice   (139, chpt 4,
n-1b)

φῶς, φωτός, τό   light   (73, chpt 11, n-3c[6c])

φωτίζω   I illuminate, enlighten   (11, v-2a[1])
φωτίσω, ἐφώτισα, –, πεφώτισμαι, ἐφωτίσθην

χῖ

χαίρω   I rejoice   (74, chpt 24, v-2d[2])
(ἔχαιρον), –, –, –, –, ἐχάρην

χαρά, -ᾶς, ἡ   joy, delight   (59, chpt 16, n-1a)

χαρίζομαι   I give freely, forgive   (23, v-2a[1])
χαρίσομαι, ἐχαρισάμην, –, κεχάρισμαι, ἐχαρίσθην

χάρις, -ιτος, ἡ   grace, favor, kindness   (155, chpt
11, n-3c[1])

χάρισμα, -ατος, τό   gift   (17, n-3c[4])

χείρ, χειρός, ἡ   hand, arm, finger   (177, chpt 14,
n-3f[2a])

χείρων, -ον   worse   (11, a-4b[1])

χήρα, -ας, ἡ   widow   (26, n-1a)

χιλίαρχος, -ου, ὁ   military tribune   (21, n-2a)

χιλιάς, -άδος, ἡ   thousand   (23, n-3c[2])

χίλιοι, -αι, -α   thousand   (10, a-1a[1])

χιτών, -ῶνος, ὁ   tunic   (11, n-3f[1a])

χοῖρος, -ου, ὁ   pig   (12, n-2a)

χορτάζω   I feed, fill, satisfy   (16, v-2a[1])
–, ἐχόρτασα, –, –, ἐχορτάσθην

χόρτος, -ου, ὁ   grass, hay   (15, n-2a)

χράομαι   I use, make use of   (11, v-1d[1a])
(ἐχρώμην), –, ἐχρησάμην, –, κέχρημαι, –

χρεία, -ας, ἡ   need   (49, n-1a)

χρηστότης, -ητος, ἡ   goodness, kindness   (10,
n-3c[1])

Χριστός, -οῦ, ὁ   Christ, Messiah, Anointed
One   (529, chpt 4, n-2a)

χρόνος, -ου, ὁ   time   (54, chpt 21, n-2a)

χρυσίον, -ου, τό   gold   (12, n-2c)

χρυσός, -οῦ, ὁ   gold   (10, n-2a)

χρυσοῦς, -ῆ, -οῦν   golden   (18, a-1b)

χωλός, -ή, -όν   lame   (14, a-1a[2a])

χώρα, -ας, ἡ   land, region   (28, n-1a)

χωρέω   I go out, reach   (10, v-1d[2a])
–, ἐχώρησα, –, –, –

χωρίζω   I separate   (13, v-2a[1])
χωρίσω, ἐχώρισα, –, κεχώρισμαι, ἐχωρίσθην

χωρίον, -ου, τό   place, land, field   (10, n-2c)

χωρίς   gen: without, apart from   (41, preposition)

ψῖ

ψεύδομαι   I lie   (12, v-1b[3])
–, ἐψευσάμην, –, –, –

ψευδοπροφήτης, -ου, ὁ   false prophet   (11, n-1f)

ψεῦδος, -ους, τό   lie   (10, n-3d[2b])

ψεύστης, -ου, ὁ   liar   (10, n-1f)

ψυχή, -ῆς, ἡ   soul, life, self   (103, chpt 14, n-1b)

ὦ μέγα

ὦ   O!   (20, n-3g[2])

ὧδε   here   (61, chpt 11, adverb)

ὥρα, -ας, ἡ   hour, occasion, moment   (106, chpt
6, n-1a)

ὡς   as, like, when, that, how, about   (504, chpt 18,
adverb)

ὡσαύτως   similarly, likewise   (17, adverb)

ὡσεί   as, like, about   (21, particle)

ὥσπερ   just as   (36, particle)

ὥστε   therefore, so that   (83, chpt 7, particle)

ὠφελέω   I help, benefit   (15, v-1d[2a])
ὠφελήσω, ὠφέλησα, –, –, ὠφελήθην

Index

D

dative case 21, 44–45, 53, 344

declension 24–25, 30
  first 35, 47, 48, 49, 347
  second 35, 47, 347
  third 35, 77–89, 94–96, 348

decline 101

definite article 68, 115, 299, 347

demonstrative pronoun/adjective 106–112, 116

dental 84, 174, 206, 346, 371

dependent clause 58, 117

dependent construction 76

deponent 152, 162, 188, 198, 217, 302, 313

diaeresis 13

digamma 147

diphthong 10, 14, 142, 147, 186, 344
  genuine 344
  spurious 344

direct discourse 307

direct object 20, 25, 29, 31, 34, 41, 115, 344

double consonant 15, 174

E

ἐάν 293

εἰδώς 284

eight noun rules 35, 47, 84, 346

εἰμί 58–60, 163, 189, 190, 234, 248, 313, 319, 359

English verb tenses 351

epsilon 10

eta 10

Everts, J. M. 257

F

Fanning, Buist M. xii, 287

feminine 29, 30, 33, 34, 46

first aorist 206
  active/middle 203–211
  liquid 207

flash card 4, 57

FlashWorks xxii

fog, the 38

future 123, 167–179
  active/middle 156–166
  continuous passive 213
  liquid 171–173, 172
  passive 213
  perfect 235

G

gamma nasal 9

gender 21, 24–25, 26, 29, 91, 101, 135

genitive absolute 278–280

genitive case 21, 43–44, 48, 49, 52, 344

Gill, Deborah 325

Graded Reader of Biblical Greek, A 339

Gramcord xi

Greek
  Attic 1
  Classical 1
  Koine 1

Gruenler, Royce Gordon 194

Guthrie, George H. 167

H

head noun 43

helping verb 124, 223

I

imperative 286, 309–317, 326, 359, 365
  continuous 311
  perfect 317
  undefined 311

imperfect indicative 182–193

ἵνα 293

indeclinable 30, 299

independent clause 294

indicative 125, 131, 357, 360–363

indirect discourse 307

indirect object 21, 43, 44, 53, 344

infinitive 285, 298–308, 327, 358, 366

inflection 23–25, 29, 30, 31

instrumental case 54, 344

intensive pronoun 103

intransitive verb 336

Basics of Biblical Greek Workbook

William D. Mounce

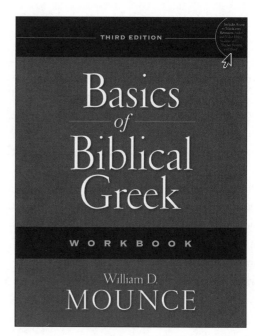

Accompanying the third edition of *Basics of Biblical Greek Grammar* is an updated edition of the *Basics of Biblical Greek Workbook* for learning biblical Greek. These two books correspond lesson for lesson. They are by far the best-selling and most widely accepted textbooks for learning New Testament Greek.

This workbook continues the excellence of the workbook of the second edition. Features include:

- Four distinct exercise sections to each lesson: parsing, warm-ups, ten verses from the New Testament to translate, and ten additional sentences to translate (made-up sentences, verses from the NT, LXX, or early Christian literature)
- Summary of grammatical concepts taught inductively in a workbook lesson
- Reference key to where the passages used in each lesson are derived from
- Two tracks in the workbook: track 1 allows you to go through the Grammar in the normal order; track 2 has totally different exercises that allow you to teach verbs earlier.
- Two optional chapters at the end that enable you to read, translate, and study an entire book of the New Testament (2 John) and a lengthy passage (Mark 2:1–3:6)
- Workbook has 3-hole, perforated pages

Softcover: 978-0-310-28767-4

Pick up a copy today at your favorite bookstore!

The Zondervan Vocabulary Builder Series
Basics of Biblical Greek Vocabulary Cards

William D. Mounce

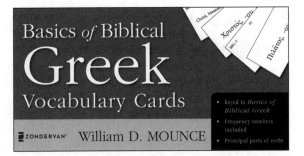

Features:
- Keyed to William D. Mounce's *Basics of Biblical Greek Grammar*
- Frequency numbers on every card
- Principal parts given for verbs
- Cards numbered for easy assignment
- First 320 cards based on order of *Basics of Biblical Greek Grammar*
- Cards 321–1,000 ordered according to frequency

Flashcards: 978-0-310-25987-9

Zondervan Get an A! Study Guides
Biblical Greek

William D. Mounce

In the fast-paced world of ministry students and pastors need critical information at their fingertips. The *Zondervan Get an A! Study Guide to Biblical Greek* is a handy, at-a-glance study aid ideal for last minute review, a quick overview of grammar and forms, or a study aid in translation or sermon preparation. It contains four information-packed sheets that are laminated and three-hole-punched, making it both durable and portable. The study guide is tied to *Basics of Biblical Greek Grammar*.

Laminated Sheet: 978-0-310-26294-7

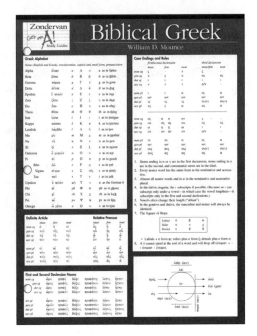

Pick up a copy today at your favorite bookstore!

ZONDERVAN®
.com

Basics of Biblical Greek Vocabulary

William D. Mounce

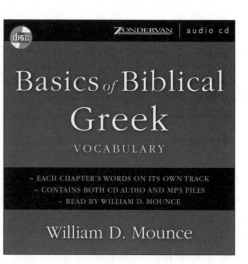

This audio CD contains all the Greek words found in the vocabulary sections of *Basics of Biblical Greek* by William D. Mounce, presented in the order of the lessons. Listen to and learn your vocabulary words while you're working in the house, driving, walking, and the like.

Audio CD: 978-0-310-27076-8

Biblical Greek Survival Kit

William D. Mounce

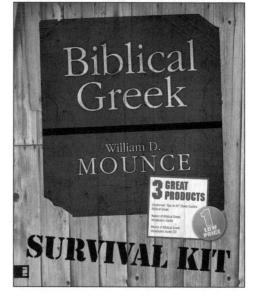

Be equipped for success in first year Greek and save money! *Biblical Greek Survival Kit* is an excellent supplemental "text" for biblical Greek courses. This value-priced kit ($8 less than items purchased separately) includes:

- *Basics of Biblical Greek Vocabulary Cards* — this set contains all words occurring in the Greek New Testament more than 15 times. The first 320 cards are in the order that these words occur in *Basics of Biblical Greek Grammar*.
- *Basics of Biblical Greek Vocabulary Audio CD* (also in mp3 format) — with all the words contained in *Basics of Biblical Greek*, in chapter order.
- *Zondervan Get an A! Study Guides: Biblical Greek* — all the noun and verb paradigms you need to know all in one handy place.

Mixed Media Set: 978-0-310-27582-4

Pick up a copy today at your favorite bookstore!

ZONDERVAN®
.com

Greek for the Rest of Us

Mastering Bible Study without Mastering Biblical Languages

William D. Mounce

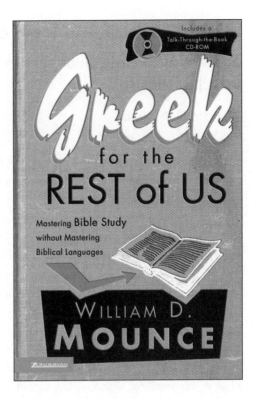

You don't have to be a Greek student to understand biblical Greek.

If you'd love to learn Greek so you can study your Bible better, but you can't spare two years for college or seminary courses, then *Greek for the Rest of Us* is for you. Developed by renowned Greek teacher William Mounce, this revolutionary crash-course on "baby Greek" will acquaint you with the essentials of the language and deepen your understanding of God's Word. You'll gain a sound knowledge of essential Greek, and you'll learn how to use tools that will add muscle to your Bible studies.

In six sections, *Greek for the Rest of Us* will help you:

· Recite the Greek alphabet
· Read and pronounce Greek words
· Learn the Greek noun and verbal system
· Conduct Greek word studies
· Decipher why translations are different
· Read better commentaries

Greek for the Rest of Us also includes an appendix on biblical Hebrew. The author's website (www.teknia.com) gives additional helps.

Softcover: 978-0-310-28289-1

Pick up a copy today at your favorite bookstore!

Interlinear for the Rest of Us

The Reverse Interlinear for New Testament Word Studies

William D. Mounce

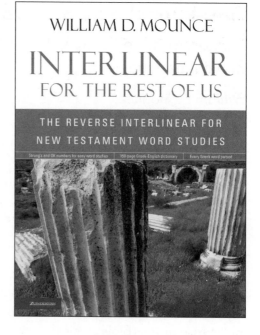

Most interlinear Bibles are superb resources for Greek students. But what about the rest of us who don't know Greek?

Here is the answer. While other interlinear Bibles assume that you know Greek, *Interlinear for the Rest of Us* assumes that you don't, or that you've forgotten much of what you once knew. Designed for busy pastors, Sunday school teachers, and anyone who wants a practical tool for studying the Scriptures, this interlinear makes reading easy by flip-flopping the usual order of appearance in an interlinear. It uses the English text as the main text rather than the Greek, so there is no confusion about the meaning of what you're reading. Discover the Greek words behind the English translation. Conduct your own word studies using Greek word study books—without knowing Greek.

Interlinear passages appear in a "staff" with four interrelated lines. From top to bottom, the lines are:

- English text in New International Version
- Corresponding Greek words
- Parsing information
- Goodrick-Kohlenberger numbers
- Greek text in normal Greek order is at the bottom of the page, underneath the interlinear section.

Included at the back of this volume is *Mounce's Greek-English Dictionary*, keyed to both Goodrick-Kohlenberger and Strong's numbering systems

Ideal for use with *Greek for the Rest of Us* and other Greek study tools

Hardcover, Printed: 978-0-310-26303-6

Pick up a copy today at your favorite bookstore!

ZONDERVAN®
.com

Sing and Learn New Testament Greek

The Easiest Way to Learn Greek Grammar

Kenneth Berding

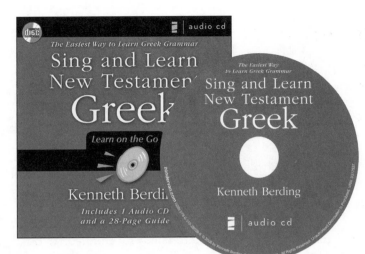

Sing and Learn New Testament Greek provides a way for learning (and remembering!) New Testament Greek grammar forms through simple songs.

The CD includes songs for the alphabet, indicative verb endings, participles, infinitives, imperatives, contract forms, and prepositions, among others. All but the last song can be sung in 15 seconds or less, and it has been designed to be used alongside of any introductory grammar. Includes: a CD (containing eleven songs and a PowerPoint with paradigm charts for classroom use), and a booklet with the same paradigm charts for students' personal use.

Audio CD: 978-0-310-28099-6

Basics of Verbal Aspect in Biblical Greek

Constantine R. Campbell

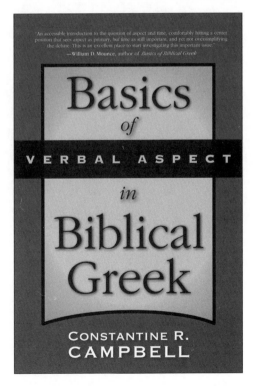

Verbal aspect in the Greek language has been a topic of significant debate in recent scholarship. The majority of scholars now believe that an understanding of verbal aspect is even more important than verb tense (past, present, etc.). Until now, however, there have been no accessible textbooks, both in terms of level and price.

In this book, Constantine Campbell investigates the function of verbal aspect within the New Testament Greek narrative. The book includes exercises, an answer key, glossary of key concepts, an appendix covering the topic of space and time in ancient Greek thinking, and an index to Scripture passages cited.

Softcover: 978-0-310-29083-4

We want to hear from you. Please send your comments about this book to us in care of zreview@zondervan.com. Thank you.

ZONDERVAN.com/
AUTHORTRACKER
follow your favorite authors

121594